PRACTICAL ESTATE PLANNING IN 2010

HOWARD M. ZARITSKY

Attorney
Rapidan, Virginia

THOMSON REUTERS

Dedication

This book, like all of my others, is dedicated to my wife, Martha Altschuller Zaritsky, who thought that this book was worth writing, and that I might be the only person willing to do it.

Acknowledgments

I would like to thank several people at Thomson Reuters who made this book possible including Kathy Silva, Director of WG&L Tax Treatises, who approved this project and convinced others to approve it, because she thought it was important; Bruce Furst, my editor, who worked tirelessly on this project because he thought it was important too, and because he does not know how to work any other way; Mark Canizio and Carol Andronofsky, my copy editors, who worked on this project with relentless dedication; and Dean Whang, my data manager, who did the same. Without all of these people, this book would still be another idea in a pile on my desk. My warmest thanks to all of you.

Preface

January 1, 2010 begins a most singular year in tax history. For the first time in over ninety-five years, there is no estate tax on estates of decedents dying this year. For the first time in thirty-five years, there is no generation-skipping transfer (GST) tax on generation-skipping transfers. In addition, the traditional estate tax value basis rules have been replaced with a modified carryover basis. All of these changes are the result of a little-known budget rule that virtually commanded that the Economic Growth and Tax Relief Reconciliation Act of 2001 (EGTRRA) terminate its estate, gift, and GST tax breaks at the end of calendar year 2010, and restore the taxes, applying all of their pre-2002 rules, on January 1, 2011.

Practitioners must quickly learn an entirely new set of rules by which to plan estates in 2010, and then on January 1, 2011, consign most of that knowledge to history and to audits of transactions that occurred in 2010. Many clients will simply reject making significant changes in their estate plan that will be effective for only one year, but some clients are of an age or health that does not give them that option. Other clients, will want to know, quite reasonably, whether these new rules contain serious planning opportunities that will not exist after December 31, 2010.

This book is designed to assist practitioners in handling these problems and answering these questions. This book consists of six chapters.

Chapter 1 provides an introduction to the new rules that apply in 2010, as well as to the rules that will be returning in 2011 unless Congress takes further action. On this point, we should have learned by now that the odds favor Congress doing little or nothing with respect to the estate, gift, and GST taxes. We may anticipate that a return to the pre-2002 law will not occur on January 1, 2011, but we should not count on it.

Chapter 1 also discusses the constitutional issues raised by a possible retroactive reinstatement of the estate and GST taxes. This has been discussed seriously on Capitol Hill, and it is a distinct possibility. The chance of a retroactive reimposition of these taxes seriously affects drafting and planning in 2010.

Chapter 2 discusses how the absence of an estate tax and the limited absence of the GST tax affect formula clauses in documents already drafted. Clients who die in 2010 are likely to leave wills, revocable trusts, and sometimes irrevocable trusts that are seriously ambiguous, generating substantial amounts of litigation. Practitioners should consider contacting their clients to urge that their documents be clarified to avoid this possible legal morass. Chapter 2 helps explain how best to clarify these ambiguities.

Chapter 3 discusses how practitioners should plan with the new modified carryover basis rules. This includes discussions of how best to allocate the new aggregate and spousal property basis increases, how to maximize their availability, and how to determine which assets are eligible for these allocations. It also discusses how to deal with negative basis assets, built-in losses, the $250,000 exclusion for gain recognized on the sale of a personal residence, passive losses, charitable remainder trusts, partnership interests, and the problems generated by the long-term holding period requirements. It also discusses the reporting requirements now imposed with respect to estates of decedents dying in 2010.

Chapter 4 discusses how best to plan generation-skipping transfers in 2010. This is one of the most difficult areas of estate planning in 2010 because actions taken in 2010 may generate significant GST taxes years after the estate and GST taxes have been restored, and because the application of EGTRRA's sunset rule is most perplexing with respect to the GST tax. Chapter 4 also discusses how the GST tax should be interpreted with respect to testamentary transfers in 2010, annual exclusion gifts made in 2010, inter vivos reverse QTIPs created in 2010, and the estate tax inclusion period on transfers before 2010.

Chapter 5 addresses a myriad of other problems raised by the termination of the estate and GST taxes in 2010, including the effects of the new 35% top gift tax rate and the incomplete gift rule of Section 2511(c) on lifetime transfers made in 2010, the effect of these rules on irrevocable life insurance trusts, and the problems affecting the administration of estates of decedents dying in 2010. It also discusses the administration of trusts in 2010 and international aspects of estate planning in 2010. Chapter 5 concludes with suggestions on communicating with clients in 2010, and provides a sample client letter explaining the new rules to them.

Chapter 6 is a checklist of what the practical estate planner should do in 2010.

This book also includes two appendices. Appendix A includes ten sample forms of wills and revocable trusts suggesting estate plans for common situations. These forms, like all forms, are a starting point in preparing your own clients' instruments. The ultimate responsibility for preparing suitable estate planning documents still lies with the attorney himself or herself.

Appendix B includes those portions of EGTRRA that are the topic of this book, including the estate, gift, and GST tax provisions, as well as the sunset rules. Sometimes, referring to the actual statutes is important.

I sincerely hope that this book will assist practitioners in adjusting quickly to these strange new rules, and in providing their clients the type of quick, efficient, and practical estate planning services that we all strive to deliver.

Howard M. Zaritsky

March 2010

Summary of Contents

1   The Law in 2010 and 2011: A Technical Analysis
2   Formula Bequests in Light of the Repeal of the Estate and GST Taxes and the Imposition of Carryover Basis
3   Planning for the Modified Carryover Basis Rules
4   Generation-Skipping Transfer Tax Planning In 2010
5   Other Problems In 2010 Estate Planning
6   A Checklist for Planning and Drafting in 2010 or What Do I Do Now?

APPENDIX A   SAMPLE FORMS
APPENDIX B   SELECT EGTRRA PROVISIONS

TABLE OF IRC SECTIONS
TABLE OF TREASURY REGULATIONS
TABLE OF REVENUE RULINGS, REVENUE PROCEDURES, AND OTHER IRS RELEASES
TABLE OF PUBLIC LAWS
TABLE OF CASES

INDEX

Table of Contents

1   The Law in 2010 and 2011: A Technical Analysis

¶ 1.01	Introduction			1-2
¶ 1.02	Repeal and Restoration of the Estate Tax			1-3
	[1]	General Repeal of Estate Tax		1-3
	[2]	Recapture Estate Taxes Preserved		1-4
	[3]	Estate Tax Preserved for Certain Qualified Domestic Trusts		1-5
¶ 1.03	Repeal of the GST Tax			1-6
¶ 1.04	Taxable Gifts			1-8
¶ 1.05	Carryover Basis for Property Received From a Decedent			1-11
	[1]	The Traditional Basis Rules		1-11
	[2]	The Modified Carryover Basis Rule		1-12
		[a]	Basis Adjustments	1-12
			[i] $1.3 million aggregate basis increase.	1-12
			[ii] Spousal property basis increase.	1-13
			[iii] Assets to which basis increases may be allocated.	1-18
			[iv] Assets to which basis increase may not be allocated.	1-22
		[b]	When Carryover Basis Is Worse Than Estate Tax	1-24
	[3]	Special Recognition and Nonrecognition Rules		1-25
		[a]	Gain on Liability in Excess of Basis	1-25
		[b]	$250,000 Exclusion of Gain on Sale of Principal Residence	1-27
		[c]	Limit on Gain Recognized on Pecuniary Bequests	1-28
		[d]	Bequests to Foreign Persons	1-29
	[4]	Reporting Requirements		1-29
¶ 1.06	Sunset of EGTRRA—What 2011 Might Look Like (And It Isn't Pretty)			1-31
	[1]	Technical Examination of the Sunset Rule		1-31
	[2]	Taxes, Rates, and Exemptions		1-33
	[3]	Other Undone EGTRRA Changes		1-34
		[a]	Restored State Death Tax Credit	1-34
		[b]	Tightened (Slightly) Conservation Easement Rules	1-35
		[c]	Tightened (Significantly) Rules for Allocating GST Exemption	1-35
			[i] Automatic allocation to certain lifetime transfers.	1-35
			[ii] Retroactive allocations would no longer be permitted.	1-36
			[iii] Elimination of the rules for qualified severance.	1-36

      [iv]   Clouding the determination of the value
of property on a timely allocation of
GST exemption. 1-37

      [v]   Reducing Treasury's power to extend
time to allocate GST exemption. 1-37

      [vi] Eliminate substantial compliance rule
for allocations. 1-38

  [d]   Reinstate the Qualified Family Owned
Business Interest Deduction 1-38

  [e]   Slight Tightening of the Deferred Payment of
Estate Taxes Attributable to Closely Held
Business Interests 1-39

  [f]   Reclouding the Waiver of Statute of
Limitations on Certain Farm Valuations 1-40

¶ 1.07   Possible Retroactive Reinstatement of the Estate and GST
Taxes 1-40

2   Formula Bequests in Light of the Repeal of the Estate and GST Taxes and the Imposition of Carryover Basis

¶ 2.01   Introduction 2-2

¶ 2.02   Marital/Nonmarital Formula Clauses During Estate Tax
Repeal 2-2

¶ 2.03   Document References to the Absence of an Estate or GST
Tax 2-3

¶ 2.04   Credit Shelter/Marital Deduction Formula Clauses in Light
of Estate Tax Repeal 2-5

  [1]   The Problem With Pre-2010 Formulas 2-5

  [2]   Alternate Marital/Nonmarital Formulas in 2010 2-9

      [a]   Preserving the Status Quo 2-10

      [b]   Basis Driven Divisions 2-10

          [i]   Smallest possible nonmarital share. 2-11

          [ii] Largest possible nonmarital share. 2-12

          [iii] "Fairly representative" division. 2-13

      [c]   Other Divisions 2-14

¶ 2.05   GST Formula Clauses and GST Tax Repeal 2-16

  [1]   The Problems With Present Formulas 2-16

  [2]   Alternate Generation-Skipping Transfer Tax Formulas
for 2010 2-20

      [a]   The Effective Date Problem 2-20

      [b]   The Formula Division of the Estate 2-23

      [c]   Granting a Power of Appointment Over a
GST-Exempt Trust 2-25

¶ 2.06   State Death Tax Formula Clauses in Light of Estate Tax
Repeal 2-29

  [1]   The Problems With Present Formulas 2-29

  [2]   Decoupling 2-29

      [a]   Determining Which State Taxes Apply to
Your Client 2-29

          [i]   Apportionment. 2-30

          [ii] Nondomiciliary taxation of tangible
property. 2-30

		[iii]	Multiple domiciles.	2-32
	[b]	Decoupled State Taxes		2-34
	[3]	State Death Tax Formulas		2-36
	[a]	The State-Only QTIP		2-36
	[b]	When There Is No State-Only QTIP		2-38
¶ 2.07		Best Formula Solutions for 2010		2-39
	[1]	One-Trust Arrangement		2-39
	[2]	QTIP Trust Plus Disclaimer		2-42
	[3]	Substantial Sprinkling Nonmarital Trust		2-44

3   Planning for the Modified Carryover Basis Rules

¶ 3.01		Introduction		3-2
¶ 3.02		The Carryover Basis Rules Apply After 2010		3-3
¶ 3.03		Allocating the Carryover Basis Increases		3-4
	[1]	The Tax Return Under Section 6018		3-4
	[a]	Small Estates		3-5
	[b]	The Meaning of "Cash"		3-6
	[c]	Estates of Nonresident Alien Individuals		3-6
	[d]	Identifying the Decedent's "Executor"		3-8
	[e]	Designing the Executor's Authority to Allocate Basis Increases		3-10
	[2]	Spousal Property Basis Increase		3-13
	[a]	Specific Gift		3-14
	[i]	Form of the spousal gift.		3-14
	[ii]	Amount of the gift.		3-16
	[b]	Granting the Executor Discretion to Select Assets to Absorb the Spousal Property Basis Increase		3-17
	[3]	Property Acquired From a Decedent		3-19
	[a]	Property Acquired by the Decedent's Estate From the Decedent		3-19
	[i]	Property appointed to the decedent's estate.		3-20
	[ii]	Contingent remainder in the decedent's estate.		3-20
	[b]	Property Transferred by the Decedent During Life		3-21
	[i]	Property in a qualified revocable trust.		3-21
	[ii]	Property subject to a reserved right to alter, amend, or terminate.		3-24
	[c]	Property Passing Without Consideration		3-26
	[4]	Property Owned by the Decedent		3-27
	[a]	Property in a Qualified Revocable Trust		3-28
	[b]	Property Subject to a Power of Appointment		3-28
	[c]	Property Owned Jointly With a Right of Survivorship		3-31
	[i]	Property owned jointly with a surviving spouse.		3-32
	[ii]	Property owned jointly with someone other than the surviving spouse.		3-32
	[iii]	Property acquired jointly by gift, bequest, etc.		3-33

	[d]	Community Property	3-33
	[e]	QTIP Assets	3-34
	[f]	Lifetime Transfers With Retained Beneficial Enjoyment	3-35
	[g]	Property Acquired by the Decedent Within Three Years of Death	3-35
	[h]	Assets Specifically Excluded From Basis Increases	3-36
¶ 3.04		Planning With Negative Basis Assets	3-37
¶ 3.05		The Basis Increase for Built-In Losses and Loss Carryovers	3-40
¶ 3.06		Planning With the $250,000 Personal Residence Exclusion	3-41
¶ 3.07		Gathering Basis Information	3-42
¶ 3.08		Drafting Survivorship Presumptions	3-42
¶ 3.09		Planning With the Holding Period Rules	3-43
¶ 3.10		Passive Losses Under the Carryover Basis Rules	3-45
¶ 3.11		Charitable Remainder Trusts and the Carryover Basis Rules	3-45
¶ 3.12		Carryover Basis and Partnership Interests	3-46
¶ 3.13		Harvesting Losses	3-47

4   Generation-Skipping Transfer Tax Planning In 2010

¶ 4.01		Introduction	4-2
¶ 4.02		Retroactive Reimposition of the GST Tax	4-2
¶ 4.03		Section 2664 and EGTRRA's Sunset Rule For the GST Tax	4-3
	[1]	The Scope of Section 2664	4-3
	[2]	The Scope of EGTRRA's Sunset Rule	4-9
	[a]	Section 2653(a) and the Generation Move-Down Rule for Post-2010 Distributions and Terminations for Trusts Created by 2010 Generation-Skipping Transfers	4-10
	[b]	Section 2654(a)(2) and Basis in 2010 Taxable Terminations	4-13
	[c]	Post-2010 Effect of Pre-2010 GST Exemption Allocations	4-13
	[d]	Post-2010 Effect of Pre-2010 Automatic Allocations	4-14
	[e]	Post-2010 Effect of Pre-2010 Qualified Severances	4-16
	[f]	Post-2010 Effect of Certain Pre-2010 Retroactive Allocations	4-17
¶ 4.04		The GST Exemption in 2010	4-18
¶ 4.05		Applying the GST Tax to 2010 Testamentary Transfers	4-20
¶ 4.06		2010 Gifts to Section 2642(c) Annual Exclusion Trusts	4-22
¶ 4.07		2010 Inter Vivos Reverse QTIPs	4-24
¶ 4.08		Estate Tax Inclusion Periods in 2010	4-26
¶ 4.09		GST Tax Planning Suggestions For 2010	4-26
	[1]	Prefer Outright Transfers Over Transfers in Trust	4-26

       [2]   Avoid Haste, But Consider the Opportunities of
             Prompt Action   4-27
       [3]   Formula Generation-Skipping Transfers   4-28
       [4]   Disclaimer-Based Planning   4-35

---

5   **Other Problems in 2010 Estate Planning**

¶ 5.01   Introduction   5-2
¶ 5.02   Lifetime Gifts   5-2
       [1]   Locking in the 35 Percent Gift Tax Rate   5-2
       [2]   Incomplete Gifts and Section 2511(c)   5-5
          [a]   Legislative History   5-6
          [b]   Incomplete Gift Trusts That Shift Income   5-7
          [c]   Section 2511(c) and Grantor Trusts   5-11
          [d]   Charitable Remainder Trusts and Section
              2511(c)   5-11
       [3]   Gift Tax Reporting Requirements   5-13
       [4]   Annual Exclusion Gifts in 2010   5-13
¶ 5.03   Irrevocable Life Insurance Trusts In 2010   5-15
¶ 5.04   Administration of Estates of Decedents Dying in 2010   5-16
       [1]   Return Requirements   5-16
       [2]   Negative Basis Assets   5-18
       [3]   Contesting Constitutionality of Retroactive
             Reinstatement of the Estate Tax   5-19
       [4]   Selling Estate Assets   5-19
¶ 5.05   Administration of Trusts in 2010   5-21
       [1]   Generation-Skipping Trusts   5-21
       [2]   Section 645 Election and Pecuniary Distributions . . .   5-23
¶ 5.06   International Aspects of Planning in 2010   5-23
       [1]   Lower Basis Increases   5-23
       [2]   Negative Basis Assets to Foreign Beneficiaries   5-26
       [3]   Section 684: Recognition of Gain on Certain
             Transfers to Foreign Persons   5-27
¶ 5.07   Client Communications   5-28

---

6   **A Checklist for Planning and Drafting in 2010 or What
          Do I Do Now?**

¶ 6.01   Phase 1: Get In Touch With Your Clients   6-2
¶ 6.02   Phase 2: Fix Formula Problems In Wills and Revocable
      Trusts   6-2
       [1]   Married Clients—Harmonious Family—With an
             Estate of $3.5 Million to $6 Million   6-2
       [2]   Married Client—Non-Harmonious Family—With an
             Estate of $3.5 Million to $6 Million   6-3
       [3]   Married Client—Harmonious Family—With an
             Estate of $6 Million to $10 Million   6-4
       [4]   Married Client—Non-Harmonious Family—With an
             Estate of $6 Million to $10 Million   6-5
       [5]   Married Client—Harmonious or Non-Harmonious
             Family—With an Estate Over $10 Million   6-6

[6]	Unmarried Surviving Spouse With an Estate of $3.5 Million to $5 Million	6-7
[7]	Unmarried Surviving Spouse With an Estate Over $5 Million	6-7

¶ 6.03   Phase 3: Find Other Formula/Tax Reference Problems   6-8

¶ 6.04   Phase 4: Fix Carryover Basis Problems   6-8

¶ 6.05   Phase 5: Fix Problems With Lifetime Gifts   6-9

¶ 6.06   Phase 6: Advise Trustee of Generation-Skipping Trust   6-10

¶ 6.07   Phase 7: Advise Executor of the Estate of a 2010 Decedent   6-11

¶ 6.08   Phase 8: Advise a Nonresident Alien   6-12

APPENDIX A   SAMPLE FORMS A-1

A.01   Form 1: Single Trust Will for Estate of $3.5 Million to $6 Million—QTIP Trust—Executor Divides Trust Into Nonmarital, State-Only QTIP, and Marital Deduction Shares if There is an Estate Tax—Executor Divides Into State-Only Marital and Marital Trusts if There is No Estate Tax—Trustee Can Distribute to Spouse Minimum Amount of Appreciated Assets Sufficient to Enable Spouse to Take Advantage of Aggregate Basis Increase at Surviving Spouse's Death—Remainder Passes Outright to Children and Descendants (No GST Tax Planning) A-3

A.02   Form 2: Single Trust Revocable Trust for Estate of $3.5 Million to $6 Million—QTIP Trust—Trustee Divides Trust Into Nonmarital, State-Only QTIP, and Marital Deduction Shares if There is an Estate Tax—Trustee Divides Into State-Only Marital and Marital Trusts if There is No Estate Tax—Trustee Can Distribute to Spouse Minimum Amount of Appreciated Assets Sufficient to Enable Spouse to Take Advantage of Aggregate Basis Increase at Surviving Spouse's Death—Remainder Passes Outright to Children and Descendants (No GST Tax Planning)—Same Planning as Form 1, But in a Revocable Trust A-19

A.03   Form 3: Will With Disclaimer Based Planning for Estate of $3.5 Million to $6 Million—All Left to QTIP Trust— Disclaimer of QTIP Trust Funds Nonmarital Trust for Spouse and Descendants—QTIP Trust Can Be Divided to Create State-Only QTIP Trust—Trustee Can Distribute to Spouse Minimum Amount of Appreciated Assets Sufficient to Enable Spouse to Take Advantage of Aggregate Basis Increase at Surviving Spouse's Death—Remainder Passes Outright to Children and Descendants (No GST Tax Planning) A-35

A.04   Form 4: Revocable Trust With Disclaimer Based Planning
        for Estate of $3.5 Million to $6 Million—All Left to QTIP
        Trust—Disclaimer of QTIP Trust Funds Nonmarital Trust
        for Spouse and Descendants—QTIP Trust Can Be Divided
        to Create State-Only QTIP Trust—Trustee Can Distribute to
        Spouse Minimum Amount of Appreciated Assets Sufficient
        to Enable Spouse to Take Advantage of Aggregate Basis
        Increase at Surviving Spouse's Death—Remainder Passes
        Outright to Children and Descendants (No GST Tax
        Planning)—Same Planning as Form 3, but in a Revocable
        Trust A-49

A.05   Form 5: Will for Estate of $6 Million to $10
        Million--Marital Deduction Tax Planning—GST Tax
        Planning With Lifetime Trust for Children and Reverse
        QTIP—Creates a 40% Nonmarital Share in 2010 to Absorb
        Aggregate Property Basis Increase—Trustee Can Distribute
        From QTIP Minimum Amount of Principal Sufficient to
        Give Spouse Enough Appreciation to Take Advantage of
        Aggregate Basis Increase at Surviving Spouse's Death—No
        State Estate Tax Planning Because Relevant State Death
        Taxes are Repealed or Provide Exemption Equal to Federal
        Applicable Exclusion Amount A-63

A.06   Form 6: Revocable Trust for Estate of $6 Million to $10
        Million—Marital Deduction Tax Planning—GST Tax
        Planning With Lifetime Trust for Children and Reverse
        QTIP—Creates a 40% Nonmarital Share in 2010 to Absorb
        Aggregate Property Basis Increase—Trustee Can Distribute
        From QTIP Minimum Amount of Principal Sufficient to
        Give Spouse Enough Appreciation to Take Advantage of
        Aggregate Basis Increase at Surviving Spouse's Death—No
        State Estate Tax Planning Because Relevant State Death
        Taxes are Repealed or Provide Exemption Equal to Federal
        Applicable Exclusion Amount—Same Planning as Form 5,
        but in a Revocable Trust A-83

A.07   Form 7: Will for Estate of $6 Million to $10 Million—
        Marital Deduction Tax Planning—GST Tax Planning With
        Lifetime Trust for Children and Reverse QTIP—Creates a
        Nonmarital Share Equal to State Estate Tax Exemption—
        Trustee Can Distribute From QTIP Minimum Amount of
        Principal Sufficient to Give Spouse Enough Appreciation to
        Take Advantage of Aggregate Basis Increase at Surviving
        Spouse's Death—Creates State-Only QTIP A-104

A.08   Form 8: Revocable Trust for Estate of $6 Million to $10
        Million—Marital Deduction Tax Planning—GST Tax
        Planning With Lifetime Trust for Children and Reverse
        QTIP—Creates a Nonmarital Share Equal to State Estate
        Tax Exemption—Trustee Can Distribute From QTIP
        Minimum Amount of Principal Sufficient to Give Spouse
        Enough Appreciation to Take Advantage of Aggregate Basis
        Increase at Surviving Spouse's Death—Creates State-Only
        QTIP—Same Planning as Form 7, but in a Revocable Trust   A-126

A.09   Form 9: Will for Estate over $10 Million—Marital
        Deduction and GST Tax Planning—Dynasty Trust for
        Children and Descendants—GST Exemption Used Even if
        it Generates Estate Tax at First Spouse's Death—No State
        QTIP in Order to Reduce State Estate Taxes at Surviving
        Spouse's Death—2010 Disposition of 40% of Estate to
        Nonmarital Share—Trustee Can Distribute From QTIP
        Minimum Amount of Principal Sufficient to Give Spouse
        Enough Appreciation to Take Advantage of Aggregate Basis
        Increase at Surviving Spouse's Death A-149
A.10   Form 10: Revocable Trust for Estate Over $10 Million—
        Marital Deduction and GST Tax Planning—Dynasty Trust
        for Children and Descendants—GST Exemption Used Even
        if it Generates Estate Tax at First Spouse's Death—No
        State QTIP in Order to Reduce State Estate Taxes at
        Surviving Spouse's Death—2010 Disposition of 40% of
        Estate to Nonmarital Share—Trustee Can Distribute From
        QTIP Minimum Amount of Principal Sufficient to Give
        Spouse Enough Appreciation to Take Advantage of
        Aggregate Basis Increase at Surviving Spouse's Death—
        Same Planning as Form 9, but in a Revocable Trust A-167

Appendix B   Select EGTRRA Provisions B-1
B.01   The Estate, Gift, and Generation-Skipping Transfer Tax
        Provisions of the Economic Growth and Tax Relief
        Reconciliation Act of 2001. . . . .   B-1
B.02   EGTRRA's Sunset Provision B-28
B.03   2002 Technical Changes to the Estate, Gift, and
        Generation-Skipping Transfer Tax Provisions of the
        Economic Growth and Tax Reform Reconciliation Act of
        2001. . . . .   B-29

Table of IRC Sections T-1
Table of Treasury Regulations T-5
Table of Revenue Rulings, Revenue Procedures, and Other
        IRS Releases T-7
Table of Public Laws T-9
Table of Cases T-11
Index I-1

CHAPTER 1

The Law in 2010 and 2011: A Technical Analysis

¶ 1.01	Introduction	1-2
¶ 1.02	Repeal and Restoration of the Estate Tax	1-3
	[1] General Repeal of Estate Tax	1-3
	[2] Recapture Estate Taxes Preserved	1-4
	[3] Estate Tax Preserved for Certain Qualified Domestic Trusts	1-5
¶ 1.03	Repeal of the GST Tax	1-6
¶ 1.04	Taxable Gifts	1-8
¶ 1.05	Carryover Basis for Property Received From a Decedent . . .	1-11
	[1] The Traditional Basis Rules	1-11
	[2] The Modified Carryover Basis Rule	1-12
	[a] Basis Adjustments	1-12
	[i] $1.3 million aggregate basis increase. . . .	1-12
	[ii] Spousal property basis increase.	1-13
	[iii] Assets to which basis increases may be allocated.	1-18
	[iv] Assets to which basis increase may not be allocated.	1-22
	[b] When Carryover Basis Is Worse Than Estate Tax	1-24
	[3] Special Recognition and Nonrecognition Rules	1-25
	[a] Gain on Liability in Excess of Basis	1-25
	[b] $250,000 Exclusion of Gain on Sale of Principal Residence	1-27
	[c] Limit on Gain Recognized on Pecuniary Bequests	1-28
	[d] Bequests to Foreign Persons	1-29
	[4] Reporting Requirements	1-29
¶ 1.06	Sunset of EGTRRA—What 2011 Might Look Like (And It Isn't Pretty)	1-31

[1]   Technical Examination of the Sunset Rule   1-31
[2]   Taxes, Rates, and Exemptions   1-33
[3]   Other Undone EGTRRA Changes   1-34
        [a]   Restored State Death Tax Credit   1-34
        [b]   Tightened (Slightly) Conservation Easement
                Rules   1-35
        [c]   Tightened (Significantly) Rules for Allocating
                GST Exemption   1-35
                [i]   Automatic allocation to certain lifetime
                        transfers.   1-35
                [ii]   Retroactive allocations would no longer
                        be permitted.   1-36
                [iii]   Elimination of the rules for qualified
                        severance.   1-36
                [iv]   Clouding the determination of the value
                        of property on a timely allocation of
                        GST exemption.   1-37
                [v]   Reducing Treasury's power to extend
                        time to allocate GST exemption.   1-37
                [vi]   Eliminate substantial compliance rule for
                        allocations.   1-38
        [d]   Reinstate the Qualified Family Owned
                Business Interest Deduction   1-38
        [e]   Slight Tightening of the Deferred Payment of
                Estate Taxes Attributable to Closely Held
                Business Interests   1-39
        [f]   Reclouding the Waiver of Statute of
                Limitations on Certain Farm Valuations   1-40
¶ 1.07   Possible Retroactive Reinstatement of the Estate and GST
         Taxes   1-40

¶ 1.01 INTRODUCTION

Practitioners face an entirely new set of rules in 2010, thanks to the Economic Growth and Tax Relief Reconciliation Act of 2001 (EGTRRA)[1] and eight years of congressional inability to reach a consensus about the future of the wealth transfer taxes. As promised by EGTRRA in 2001, the estate and generation-skipping transfer (GST) taxes are repealed for decedents dying in 2010 and for generation-skipping transfers occurring in 2010, while the gift tax remains in effect (but with a 35 percent top tax rate). In exchange for the elimination of two of the three wealth transfer taxes, the rules for determining the adjusted basis of property received from a decedent's estate change dramati-

---

[1] Pub. L. No. 107-16, 107th Cong., 1st Sess. (June 7, 2001), 115 Stat. 38.

cally—property takes a modified carryover basis if it is received from the estate of a decedent who died in 2010.

No one can predict accurately what Congress will do in 2010 regarding the estate and GST taxes. It might reinstate the estate and GST taxes retroactively.[2] It might reinstate the estate and GST taxes prospectively from the date of enactment or some earlier date, such as the date on which the bill to reinstate the taxes is introduced. It might remain deadlocked and allow the year to pass without any change in the current law. Anyone who claims to know what Congress will do should be considered a dangerously unreliable source of information.

Then, barring congressional action to change the current state of the law, in 2011, the estate, gift, and GST taxes return to their pre-EGTRRA form, with sometimes surprising results.

Accordingly, estate planners must now re-evaluate all estate plans they prepared that did not fully address both the absence of estate and GST taxes in 2010 and the full imposition of the carryover basis rules in 2010. They must also alter their practices regarding lifetime transfers, with respect to transactions occurring in 2010.

This chapter reviews the key provisions of the tax law in effect during 2010, and the changes that will occur when EGTRRA restores the estate and GST taxes in 2011. It also discusses the requirements of EGTRRA's sunset rules and the constitutional issues surrounding the possible retroactive reinstatement of the estate and GST taxes.

¶ 1.02 REPEAL AND RESTORATION OF THE ESTATE TAX

[1] General Repeal of Estate Tax

The most far-reaching and potentially important provision of EGTRRA was Section 501(a), which repealed the estate tax with respect to estates of decedents dying after December 31, 2009.[3] This was reached as a compromise between legislators who favored retaining the estate tax and those who favored its repeal.

> **EXAMPLE 1-1:** Dave dies on January 2, 2010, leaving an estate of $12 million. Dave's will leaves his entire estate to his two children, Adam and Beth, in equal shares. No estate tax is imposed with respect to Dave's es-

---

[2] On the constitutional issues raised by such reinstatement, see infra ¶ 1.07.

[3] IRC § 2210(a).

tate, and Adam and Beth are each be entitled to receive their $6 million inheritance without reduction for federal estate taxes.[4]

The repeal of the estate tax applies with respect to estates of decedents who die during 2010. The date and time of a decedent's death is determined based on the place in which the decedent was domiciled at the instant of his or her death, rather than where he or she was physically located at the time death occurred.[5]

> **EXAMPLE 1-2:** Adam and Brian are twin brothers. Each has an estate worth approximately $100 million. Adam lives in Manhattan and Brian lives in Los Angeles. The brothers decided to celebrate New Year's Eve 2010 together at Adam's apartment in Manhattan. At 1:00 a.m., January 1, 2010, the brothers are both killed in a traffic accident, going from their third to fourth parties of the night. Adam is deemed to have died on January 1, 2010, and his estate will owe no federal estate tax. Brian is deemed to have died on December 31, 2009, which was the time and date on which he died in Los Angeles, his domicile. Therefore, Brian's estate owes approximately $43,425,000 in federal estate taxes.

> **EXAMPLE 1-3:** Assume the same facts as in Example 1-2, except that Adam and Brian decided to celebrate New Year's Eve in Paris. They died at 1:00 a.m., January 1, 2010, in Paris. Both of them are deemed to have died in 2009, because the time differences between Paris and both Manhattan and Los Angeles will place the time of their death in 2009.

[2] Recapture Estate Taxes Preserved

The legislative history states that EGTRRA distinguishes between the imposition of the estate tax on a decedent dying after December 31, 2009, and the imposition of a special recapture tax after that date with respect to the estate of a decedent who dies before January 1, 2010. The legislative history further states that the post-2009 disposition of property for which the estate of a decedent who died before January 1, 2010, was allowed (1) the tax benefits of special use valuation (Section 2032A); (2) the deduction for interests in qualified family owned businesses (Section 2057); or (3) the deferral of estate taxes attributable to a business interest (Section 6166), will still result in the recapture of the previous estate tax benefits to the extent provided under pre-2010 law.[6]

---

[4] The shares passing to Adam and Beth will, of course, remain subject to state death taxes.

[5] Rev. Rul. 66-85, 1966-1 CB 213, as modified by Rev. Rul. 74-424, 1974-2 CB 294.

[6] See HR Conf. Rep. No. 84, 107th Cong., 1st Sess., 147 Cong. Rec. H2773–H2774 (May 25, 2001).

Accordingly, the repeal of the estate tax does not prevent the imposition of these recapture taxes.

> **EXAMPLE 1-4:** Dave died on January 2, 2005. Dave's estate valued an interest in real estate owned by Dave and used as part of Dave's farm under Section 2032A's special use valuation rules. Under Section 2032A if the property ceases to be used as a family farm or business within ten years after Dave's death, an additional estate tax will be imposed, to recapture the estate taxes saved by the special valuation election. Dave's family ceases to use the farm as a family farm in 2010, five years after Dave's death. The recapture tax is imposed with respect to Dave's estate even though the cessation of the use of the property as a family farm or business occurred in 2010, after the repeal of the estate tax.

[3] Estate Tax Preserved for Certain Qualified Domestic Trusts

In certain cases, the estate tax will continue to be imposed after 2009 with respect to qualified domestic trusts (QDOTs) created for the benefit of a noncitizen surviving spouse where the predeceasing spouse, whose will or trust created the QDOT, died before January 1, 2010.[7] The federal estate tax will be imposed with respect to an estate of a decedent dying after December 31, 2009, on any QDOT distribution before the date of the noncitizen surviving spouse's death if the distribution is made after December 31, 2009, but before January 1, 2021. The estate tax is not imposed on the value of the property remaining in a QDOT on the date of the noncitizen surviving spouse's death if such surviving spouse dies after December 31, 2009.

> **EXAMPLE 1-5:** Delilah dies in 2003, leaving $10 million of her estate in trust for her husband, Sam, who is not a U.S. citizen. The trust for Sam is a QDOT, and provides that all income will be paid to Sam not less often than annually, and that no principal may be paid to anyone other than Sam during his lifetime. The trust is required always to have at least one U.S. trustee, and the trust instrument also states that no distribution (other than a distribution of income) may be made from the trust unless a U.S. trustee has the right to withhold from such distribution the estate tax im-

---

[7] IRC § 2210(b). On the rules for QDOTs, generally, see Bittker & Lokken, Federal Taxation of Income, Estates and Gifts ¶ 129.2.5 (Thomson Reuters/WG&L, 2d ed. 1993); Henkel, Estate Planning and Wealth Preservation: Strategies and Solutions ¶ 52.11 (Thomson Reuters/WG&L 1997); Peschel & Spurgeon, Federal Taxation of Trusts, Grantors and Beneficiaries ¶ 7.10 (Thomson Reuters/WG&L, 3d ed. 1997); Stephens, Maxfield, Lind & Calfee, Federal Estate and Gift Taxation ¶ 5.08A (Thomson Reuters/WG&L, 8th ed. 2002); Streng, U.S. International Estate Planning ¶ 10.04 (Thomson Reuters/WG&L, 2d ed. 2001); Westfall & Mair, Estate Planning Law and Taxation ¶ 16.01 (Thomson Reuters/WG&L, 4th ed. 2001).

posed by Section 2056A. In 2010, the trustee distributes $1 million of principal to Sam. The trustee is required to withhold and pay over to the IRS an estate tax on the $1 million, calculated as directed in Section 2056A(b)(2).[8]

¶ 1.03 REPEAL OF THE GST TAX

Section 2664, added by EGTRRA, states that the GST tax rules do not apply to "generation-skipping transfers after December 31, 2009." The term "generation-skipping transfers" is a term of art, defined specifically to mean direct skip transfers, taxable terminations, and taxable distributions.[9] It does not, however, include transfers to a trust that is itself not a skip person but from which a taxable termination or distribution could later be made.

Therefore, direct skip transfers, taxable terminations and taxable distributions that occur in 2010 are not subject to the GST tax. Taxable terminations and distributions that occur after 2010 with respect to certain transfers in trust made in 2010, however, may be subject to the GST tax. It is distinctly possible that transfers made in trust in 2010 and exempt from tax in 2010, may still produce taxable distributions and taxable terminations after 2010 though the law is not entirely clear.[10]

---

[8] Under Section 2056A(b)(2), the amount of the estate tax paid by the trust on the distribution is the estate tax that would have been imposed on Deliliah's estate if her taxable estate had been increased by the sum of—

1. The $1 million amount distributed, plus
2. Any aggregate amount involved in previous taxable events with respect to the same trust, reduced by
3. The estate tax that would have been imposed on Deliliah's estate if her taxable estate had been increased by the amount involved in the previous taxable events.

[9] IRC § 2611(a). A "direct skip" is a transfer on which estate or gift tax is imposed, made to a skip person (someone assigned to a generation that is at least two generations below that of the transferor, such as a grandchild or great-grandchild). IRC § 2612(c). A "taxable distribution" is a trust distribution of income or principal to a skip person, other than one that also constitutes a taxable termination or a direct skip. IRC § 2612(b). A "taxable termination" is the termination (by death, lapse of time, release of power, or otherwise) of an interest in property held in a trust, unless a non-skip person has an interest in such property immediately after the termination and unless the trust cannot make a distribution to a skip person after the termination. IRC § 2612(a). See discussion in Harrington, Plaine & Zaritsky, Generation-Skipping Transfer Tax ¶ 2.05 (Thomson Reuters/ WG&L, 2d ed. 2001).

[10] See detailed discussion in Chapter 4.

EXAMPLE 1-6: Dave makes a January 2, 2010, gift of $1 million outright to his granddaughter, Gretchen. Gretchen is an adult and the property is held by her outright and free of trust. Dave pays a 35 percent gift tax on this gift, but he pays no GST tax.

EXAMPLE 1-7: Assume the same facts as in Example 1-6, except that Gretchen is a minor and Dave makes the gift to her in trust. The trustee is directed to distribute income and principal to Gretchen as appropriate for any purpose, and to turn the entire trust fund over to her when she reaches thirty-five years of age. If Gretchen dies before age 35, the trust passes under her will as part of her estate. The trust itself is a skip person because no non-skip person have beneficial interests in the trust. Therefore, the gift in trust is a direct skip transfer. No GST tax is imposed on the 2010 gift to the trust.

EXAMPLE 1-8: Assume the same facts as in Example 1-7. In 2011, the trustee distributes $100,000 to Gretchen. This may be a taxable distribution upon which GST tax is imposed. This distribution would not have been a taxable distribution had the trust been funded in 2009, because Section 2653(a) would have deemed Dave to belong to the first generation above Gretchen for purpose of future distributions. Section 2653(a) is, however, part of "this chapter" referred to in Section 2664, and so it arguably does not apply to a direct skip transfer made in 2010. Therefore, the distributions to Gretchen from this trust after December 31, 2010, including the $100,000 distribution made in 2011, may be subject to the GST tax. Furthermore, as the GST exemption in 2010 was $–0–, under Sections 2631(c) and 2010(c), Dave could not have avoided this tax by allocating GST exemption to the transfer. This result may be changed, however, by EGTRRA's sunset rule, discussed in detail in Chapter 4, which requires that after 2010, the GST tax law be interpreted as if EGTRRA had never been enacted.

EXAMPLE 1-9: In 2001, Donald created a trust for the benefit of his two children, Adam and Beth, and his several grandchildren. Donald allocated none of his GST exemption to the trust. The trust directs that the trustee distribute income and principal to and among all of the beneficiaries in such shares as the trustee deems appropriate and for any purpose. Adam died in 2004 and Beth died in 2010. Beth was the last non-skip person to hold a beneficial interest in the trust and, therefore, her death is a taxable termination. The trust assets are worth $10 million in 2010. No GST tax is imposed on the trust assets on account of Beth's death.

EXAMPLE 1-10: Assume the same facts as in Example 1-9, except that in 2011, after the GST tax has been restored according to EGTRRA, the trustee distributes $100,000 to the grandchildren from the trust assets. This is a taxable distribution on which the GST tax may be imposed. Normally, Section 2611(b) does not tax any transfer to the extent that the transferred property was already "subject to a prior tax imposed under this chapter" if the "transferee in the prior transfer was assigned to the same generation as (or a lower generation than) the generation assignment of the transferee in this transfer." This rule would prevent the subsequent distributions from the trust from being subject to another GST tax after a taxable termination has already occurred of the interest of the immediately higher generation. This rule should not apply to the distribution in 2011, however, because the property in the trust in 2011 was not subject to a prior tax under the GST tax rules. Therefore, it is probable that the distributions in 2011 would be subject to tax. This result may be changed, however, by EGTRRA's sunset rule, discussed in detail in Chapter 4, which requires that after 2010, the GST tax law be interpreted as if EGTRRA had never been enacted.

EXAMPLE 1-11: Assume the same facts as in Example 1-10, except that Beth is still alive in 2010. During that year, the trustee distributes $200,000 to the grandchildren. This is a taxable distribution that is exempt from the GST tax in 2010.

EXAMPLE 1-12: Donna creates a $10 million trust in 2010, and directs the trustee to hold and apply the income and principal for the benefit of Donna's children, grandchildren, and more remote descendants. Donna creates this trust under the law of a state that has no rule against perpetuities, and so it will continue indefinitely until the trust funds are fully expended or Donna's line of descendants ends. The GST exemption in 2010 is $–0–, under Sections 2631(c) and 2010(c), and Donna cannot allocate any exemption to this transfer. Therefore, this trust will be fully subject to the GST tax on any future taxable terminations or taxable distributions. It is possible, however, that when the GST exemption is restored in 2011, Donna may be able to make a late allocation of exemption to this transfer, as discussed in Chapter 4.

¶ 1.04 TAXABLE GIFTS

EGTRRA retains the gift tax after the repeal of the estate and GST taxes, but it lowers the top gift tax rate to 35 percent for transfers made in 2010. The legislative history indicates that Congress was concerned that the unlimited right to make gifts without gift tax would lead to the use of intrafamily gifts to shift income from family members in higher income tax brackets to those in lower income tax brackets.[11]

---

[11] The House version of the estate tax repeal, HR Rep. No. 8, 106th Cong., 1st Sess. (2001), repealed the gift tax along with the estate and GST taxes, but permitted the IRS to ignore any gift that was made in order to frustrate the income tax. The House bill also called for "a study of opportunities for avoidance of the income tax, if any, and potential increases [sic] in income tax revenues by reason of enactment of the bill." HR Rep. No.

EGTRRA also added Section 2511(c), which, as amended in 2002, states that, after the repeal of the estate and GST taxes

> Notwithstanding any other provision of this section and except as provided in regulations, a transfer in trust shall be treated as a transfer of property by gift, unless the trust is treated as wholly owned by the donor or the donor's spouse under subpart E of part I of subchapter J of Chapter 1.[12]

The Joint Committee on Taxation stated of Section 2511(c), when it was amended in 2002 to create the provision we now find

> The provision clarifies that the effect of section 511(e) of the Act (effective for gifts made after 2009) is to treat certain transfers in trust as transfers of property by gift. The result of the clarification is that the gift tax annual exclusion and the marital and charitable deductions may apply to such transfers. Under the provision as clarified, certain amounts transferred in trust will be treated as transfers of property by gift, despite the fact that such transfers would be regarded as incomplete gifts or would not be treated as transferred under the law applicable to gifts made prior to 2010.
>
> For example, if in 2010 an individual transfers property in trust to pay the income to one person for life, remainder to such persons and in such portions as the settlor may decide, then the entire value of the property will be treated as being transferred by gift under the provision, even though the transfer of the remainder interest in the trust would not be treated as a completed gift under current Treas. Reg. sec. 25.2511-2(c). Similarly, if in 2010 an individual transfers property in trust to pay the income to one person for life, and makes no transfer of a remainder interest, the entire value of the property will be treated as being transferred by gift under the provision.[13]

37, 107th Cong., 1st Sess. 31 (2001). The Senate reinstated the gift tax. See HR Rep. No. 84, 107th Cong., 1st Sess. 189, 191 (2001). Congress may also have been concerned that the absence of a gift tax would permit lifetime transfer of income-producing assets and wealth to nonresident alien family members who might not be subject to U.S. taxes.

[12] IRC § 2511(c), as amended by Pub. L. No. 107-358, § 2, 107th Cong., 2d Sess. (2002). For a detailed discussion of the grantor trust rules, see Bittker & Lokken, Federal Taxation of Income, Estates and Gifts ch. 80 (Thomson Reuters/WG&L, 3d ed. 2003); Peschel & Spurgeon, Federal Taxation of Trusts, Grantors and Beneficiaries chs. 4–5 (Thomson Reuters/WG&L, 3d ed. 1997); Westfall & Mair, Estate Planning Law and Taxation ¶ 17.02 (Thomson Reuters/WG&L, 4th ed. 2001); Danforth, Lane & Zaritsky, Federal Income Taxation of Estates and Trusts chs. 7–13 (Thomson Reuters/WG&L, 3d ed. 2001).

[13] Staff of Joint Comm. on Taxation, 107th Cong., 2d Sess., "General Explanation of Tax Legislation Enacted in the 107th Congress," 249–250 (2003).

Section 2511(c) appears, therefore, to have been intended only to eliminate the use of a specific type of trust the transfers to which were completed gifts for income tax purposes, but not completed gifts for gift tax purposes.[14] Such trusts were often used to shift the incidence of state income tax on investment income from a state that imposed a high tax to one that imposed a lower tax or none at all.

> **EXAMPLE 1-13:** In 2009, Dave creates a trust that allowed the trustee to distribute income and principal (including all or none) to and among a class of beneficiaries that included Dave, his wife, his children and more remote descendants, his siblings, and his parents. The trustee was to make distributions as directed by either the unanimous decision of the distribution committee or by the joint decision of Dave and one member of the committee. The initial distribution committee was Dave's brother, Dan, and Dave's father, Don. The trust instrument requires that the committee always must include two beneficiaries of the trust, other than Dave or his wife. Dave also reserved a testamentary special power to appoint the trust principal, including any accumulated and undistributed income, to anyone other than himself, his estate, his creditors, or the creditors of his estate. The trust is arguably not a grantor trust, because any distribution of income or principal to Dave or his wife can be made only with the consent of an adverse party. Furthermore, Dave's limited power of appointment gives him the power to change the trust beneficiaries, and causes any gifts to the trust to be incomplete for gift tax purposes. The distributions of income to beneficiaries other than Dave or his wife would be completed taxable gifts, but Dave's transfer of the underlying principal would not be deemed a completed taxable gift.[15]

> **EXAMPLE 1-14:** Assume the same facts as in Example 1-13, except that Dave creates the trust in 2010. The transfers to the trust are treated as completed taxable gifts because the trust is not a grantor trust.

---

[14] See, e.g., Priv. Ltr. Ruls. 200502014, 200612002, 200637025, 200647001, 200715005, 200729005 and 200731009. See also IRS Info. Rel. 2007-123 (July 9, 2007), stating that the IRS was considering withdrawing these rulings because of inconsistencies with Rev. Rul. 76-503, 1976-2 CB 275, and Rev. Rul. 77-158, 1977-1 CB 285. In Rev. Rul. 76-503, a trust was created by three siblings, each of whom named an adult child as one of the three trustees who, acting unanimously, had complete discretionary power over the assets of the trust and individually had the right to name a relative as successor. A trustee is replaced upon death or resignation by a successor trustee. The IRS stated that the surviving trustees are in no better position to exercise the power after a decedent-trustee's death than before the death, so the IRS concluded that the interests of the co-trustees are not adverse to exercise of the power in favor of the decedent-trustee. The IRS determined that one third of the trust fund was includible in a decedent-trustee's estate as property subject to a general power of appointment under Section 2041.

[15] See Staff of Joint Comm. on Taxation, "Technical Explanation of the Job Creation and Worker Assistance Act of 2002," 107th Cong., 1st Sess. 38 (2002) (Comm. Print).

¶ 1.05 CARRYOVER BASIS FOR PROPERTY RECEIVED FROM A DECEDENT

[1] The Traditional Basis Rules

A person who receives property from a decedent who dies in a year other than 2010, takes an adjusted income tax basis in that property equal to the fair market value of the property on the date of death or, if elected by the decedent's executor, the alternate valuation date, according to current law.[16] Thus, both appreciation and depreciation in the value of property received from a decedent, up to the value of the property on the date of death or alternate valuation date, is eliminated. Certain assets, such as items of income in respect of a decedent, do not, however, qualify for this basis adjustment.

A donee's basis in property received by lifetime gift is equal to the donor's basis in the asset at the time of the gift, increased by any gift tax paid on the net appreciation in the property's value at the time of the gift, for purposes of determining gain and loss on the subsequent disposition of the asset.[17] However, if the fair market value at the time of the gift is lower than the donor's adjusted basis, the donee's basis for determining loss on the subsequent disposition of the asset is the fair market value of asset on the date of the gift. A donee who sells such "built-in loss" property for more than the donor's adjusted basis, but for less than the property's fair market value at the time of the gift, realizes neither a gain nor a loss.[18]

---

[16] IRC § 1014. The alternate valuation date is generally the date six months after the date of death or, if earlier, the date on which the particular asset is sold, exchanged, or otherwise disposed of by the estate. IRC § 2032. See discussion of the alternate valuation date election in Henkel, Estate Planning and Wealth Preservation: Strategies and Solutions ¶ 50.07 (Thomson Reuters/WG&L 1997); Kasner, Strauss & Strauss, Post Mortem Tax Planning ¶ 7.01 (Thomson Reuters/WG&L, 3d ed. 1998); Stephens, Maxfield, Lind & Calfee, Federal Estate and Gift Taxation ¶ 4.03 (Thomson Reuters/WG&L, 8th ed. 2002).

[17] IRC § 1015(d)(6). If the fair market value of the property on the date of the gift is less than the donor's adjusted income tax basis, the donee's adjusted basis is reduced to the lower figure for purposes of computing the amount of any loss recognized by the donee on a later sale or other disposition of the property. IRC § 1015(c). This rule is intended to prevent the gift of deductible losses by lower-bracket donors to higher-bracket donees.

[18] IRC § 1015(d). A donee may not have all of the relevant facts from which to determine the donor's basis. The IRS, in such cases, will attempt to obtain such information from the donor, the last owner, or someone else who might know such facts. If that proves impossible, the donee's basis is the property's approximate fair market value on the date it was acquired by its last owner. Reg § 1.1015-1(a)(3).

[2] The Modified Carryover Basis Rule

EGTRRA gives a person who receives property from a decedent who dies after December 31, 2009, and before January 1, 2011, an adjusted basis in the property equal to the lesser of the fair market value of such property on the date of the decedent's death or the adjusted basis of the property in the hands of the decedent.[19] Thus, the step-down in basis under present law for loss assets received from a decedent is preserved, while the step-up in basis for appreciated assets is eliminated.

> **EXAMPLE 1-15:** Dave dies on January 2, 2010, leaving an estate that includes the following assets:

Asset	Dave's Basis	Value on Date of Death
Acme Co. stock	$ 100,000	$ 200,000
Beta Limited partnership interest	$ 300,000	$ 250,000

> Dave's will leaves his estate to his son, Adam. Adam takes Dave's $100,000 basis in the Acme stock, but he takes a $250,000 basis in the Beta partnership interest (the lesser of Dave's basis or its fair market value on the date of death).[20]

[a] Basis Adjustments

EGTRRA permits the executor of a decedent's estate to allocate additional basis to and among a decedent's assets. The two basis adjustments are the $1.3 million "aggregate basis increase" and the $3 million "spousal property basis increase."

[i] $1.3 million aggregate basis increase. EGTRRA permits the executor of a decedent's estate to allocate among the decedent's assets a $1.3 million "aggregate basis increase."[21] The allocation of the aggregate basis increase is made by the executor on an asset-by-asset basis, and cannot raise the basis of any asset above its fair market value on the date of the decedent's death.[22] Once made, the allocation can be changed only as permitted by the Secretary of the Treasury.[23]

---

[19] IRC §§ 1014(f), 1022(a).

[20] These figures do not take into account any additional basis that may be allocated by Dave's executor. See discussion infra ¶ 1.05[2][a].

[21] IRC § 1022(b)(2)(B).

[22] IRC § 1022(d)(2).

[23] IRC § 1022(b)(3)(B).

EXAMPLE 1-16: Dave dies on January 2, 2010, leaving his estate to his son, Adam. Dave's estate includes the following assets:

Asset	Dave's Basis	Value on Date of Death
Acme Co. stock	$ 300,000	$ 1,000,000
Beta partnership interest	$ 500,000	$ 750,000
Gamma stock	$ 500,000	$ 750,000
Residence	$ 400,000	$ 500,000
Total	$ 1,700,000	$ 3,000,000

The executor of Dave's estate can allocate the $1.3 million aggregate basis increase among these assets, increasing the basis of each asset to its fair market value. This will raise the total basis of Dave's assets from $1.7 million to $3 million. Dave's estate or Adam can now sell the assets for their fair market value on the date of Dave's death without realizing any taxable gain.

The $1.3 million limitation on the aggregate basis increase is increased by two types of otherwise-unused losses. First, the executor can add to the $1.3 million aggregate basis increase the sum of the amount of any capital loss carryover (under Section 1212(b)) and the amount of any net operating loss carryover (under Section 172) that could (but for the decedent's death) have been carried from the decedent's last taxable year to a later taxable year of the decedent. Second, the executor can add to the $1.3 million aggregate basis increase the sum of the amount of any losses that would have been allowable (under Section 165) had the property acquired from the decedent been sold at fair market value immediately before the decedent's death.[24]

Estates of nonresidents who are not U.S. citizens are allowed an aggregate basis increase of only $60,000, rather than $1.3 million.[25] The aggregate basis increase for estates of nonresident aliens is also determined without the two adjustments for losses and loss carryovers.[26]

The $1.3 million and $60,000 figures are indexed for inflation after 2010, if the estate tax is not reinstated. The $1.3 million figure will be increased in increments of $100,000, and the $60,000 figure in increments of $5,000.[27]

[ii] Spousal property basis increase. The executor of a decedent's estate may also increase the basis of property acquired from the decedent by the decedent's surviving spouse by up to $3 million, in addition to any adjustments made by the $1.3 million aggregate basis increase.[28] This is referred to as the

---

[24] IRC § 1022(b)(2)(C).

[25] IRC § 1022(b)(3).

[26] IRC § 1022(b)(3).

[27] IRC § 1022(d)(4).

[28] IRC § 1022(c).

"spousal property basis increase."[29] Again, the amount allocated to the property received from a decedent by the surviving spouse cannot increase its basis above the fair market value of the property on the date of the decedent's death.[30]

> **EXAMPLE 1-17:** Dave dies on January 2, 2010, leaving his $7 million estate to his son, Adam, and his wife, Wilma. Dave's estate consists of the following assets:

Asset	Dave's Basis	Value on Date of Death
Acme Co. stock	$ 300,000	$ 3,000,000
Beta partnership interest	$ 500,000	$ 1,000,000
Gamma stock	$ 500,000	$ 2,000,000
Residence	$ 300,000	$ 1,000,000
Total	$ 1,600,000	$ 7,000,000

> Dave's will leaves his Gamma stock to Adam and he leaves the rest of his estate to Wilma. The executor of Dave's estate can allocate $1.3 million of aggregate basis adjustment among Dave's assets, increasing the basis of each asset, but not beyond its fair market value. Dave's executor can also allocate up to $3 million of spousal property basis increase to the Acme stock, Beta partnership interest, and residence, all of which were left to Wilma, increasing the basis of these assets, but not above their fair market value.

> Dave's executor makes the following basis adjustments:

Asset	Carryover Basis	Allocated Basis	Total Basis Increase
Acme Co. stock	$ 300,000	$ 2,700,000 (spousal)	$ 3,000,000
Beta partnership interest	$ 500,000	$ 300,000 (spousal)	$ 800,000
Gamma stock	$ 500,000	$ 1,300,000 (aggregate)	$ 1,800,000
Residence	$ 300,000	$ 0	$ 300,000
Total	$ 1,600,000	$ 4,300,000	$ 5,900,000

> As a result of these allocations, the basis of the property received by Adam and Wilma has been increased by the entire $4.3 million of availa-

---

[29] The $3 million figure applies to estates of nonresident aliens and to surviving spouses who are not U.S. citizens, and no rules comparable to the QDOT rules are incorporated into the carryover basis rules. See discussion of QDOTs in Henkel, Estate Planning and Wealth Preservation: Strategies and Solutions ¶ 52.11; Kasner, Strauss & Strauss, Post Mortem Tax Planning ¶ 15.12 (Thomson Reuters/WG&L, 3d ed. 1998); Stephens, Maxfield, Lind & Calfee, Federal Estate and Gift Taxation ¶ 5.07 (Thomson Reuters/WG&L, 8th ed. 2002).

[30] IRC § 1022(d)(2).

ble basis adjustments, and $4.3 million of potential future taxable gains have been eliminated.[31]

The spousal property basis increase is allowed only for property passing to a surviving spouse outright or in a qualified terminable interest property (QTIP) trust.[32] No increase can be made to property passing outright to the surviving spouse if the property constitutes a terminable interest, under rules substantially identical to the present estate tax marital deduction rules regarding nondeductible terminable interests.[33] Therefore, property will not be treated as passing outright to a surviving spouse if

1. On the lapse of time, on the occurrence of an event or contingency, or on the failure of an event or contingency to occur, an interest passing to the surviving spouse will terminate or fail;[34]

2. An interest in such property passes or has passed (for less than an adequate and full consideration in money or money's worth) from the decedent to any person other than the surviving spouse (or the surviving spouse's estate);[35] and

3. The person to whom such other interest has passed (or that person's heirs or assigns) can possess or enjoy any part of the property after such termination or failure of the interest so passing to the surviving spouse.[36]

Additionally, an interest passing outright to a surviving spouse is a terminable interest if it is to be acquired for the surviving spouse, pursuant to the decedent's directions, by his executor or by the trustee of a trust.[37]

For this purpose, an interest is not treated as a terminable interest merely because it is a bond, note, or similar contractual obligation, the discharge of which would not have the effect of an annuity for life or for a term.[38] Such obligations do, in fact, expire after a stated term of years, and thus could arguably be terminable interests.

Furthermore, an interest conditioned upon the occurrence of an event or accomplishment of some achievement is usually a terminable interest, but an interest passing to the surviving spouse is not a terminable interest if the surviving spouse's death will cause a termination or failure of such interest only

---

[31] For a discussion of the factors to be considered in allocating basis increases, see ¶ 3.03.

[32] IRC § 1022(c).

[33] IRC §§ 1022(c)(4)(B), 1022(c)(4)(C).

[34] IRC § 1022(c)(4)(B).

[35] IRC § 1022(c)(4)(B)(i)(I).

[36] IRC § 1022(c)(4)(B)(i)(II).

[37] IRC § 1022(c)(4)(B)(ii).

[38] IRC § 1022(c)(4)(B) (flush portion).

if (1) it occurs within a period not exceeding six months after the decedent's death; (2) it occurs as a result of a common disaster resulting in the death of the decedent and the surviving spouse; or (3) it occurs in the case of either such event, provided that the spouse does in fact survive and the interest does not terminate.[39]

> **EXAMPLE 1-18:** Dave dies on January 2, 2010, leaving his $7 million estate to his wife, Wilma, if she survives him by one year. Dave's estate passes to Dave's children, in equal shares, if Wilma does not survive Dave by at least one year. A bequest to a surviving spouse is a terminable interest if its receipt is conditioned upon survivorship for a period of more than six months.[40] Therefore, even if Wilma survives Dave by a year, no spousal property basis increase will be available for the property passing from Dave to Wilma.

> **EXAMPLE 1-19:** Assume the same facts as in Example 1-18, except that instead of requiring that Wilma survive for one year, Dave's will requires that she survive until his estate is finally distributed. It is not possible to establish that Dave's estate will in all events be finally distributed within six months, so this gift also is a terminable interest.[41] Therefore, even if Wilma survives Dave and lives until his estate his distributed, no spousal property basis increase will be available for the property passing from Dave to Wilma.

A QTIP trust is defined for this purpose by adopting the same requirements imposed under current estate tax marital deduction rules, except that no election is required from the decedent's executor.[42] Thus, a trust is a QTIP trust for this purpose if

1. The property passes to the trust from the decedent;[43]
2. The surviving spouse is entitled to all the income from the property, payable at least annually, or has a life estate or usufruct interest for life in the property;[44] and

---

[39] IRC § 1022(c)(4)(C).

[40] Reg. § 20.2056(b)-3(b).

[41] Reg. § 20.2056(b)-3(d), Ex. 4.

[42] IRC § 1022(c)(5). See discussion of the nondeductible terminable interest rules at Stephens, Maxfield, Lind & Calfee, Federal Estate and Gift Taxation ¶ 5.06 (Thomson Reuters/WG&L, 8th ed. 2002); Westfall & Mair, Estate Planning Law and Taxation ch. 16 (Thomson Reuters/WG&L, 4th ed. 2001).

[43] IRC § 1022(c)(5)(A)(i). A "usufruct" is the civil law equivalent of a life estate for a surviving spouse, and usually entitles the spouse to the lifetime use and right to consume the property. Usufructs are created under the law of many foreign countries, and the law of Louisiana.

[44] IRC § 1022(c)(5)(B)(i).

3. No person (including the surviving spouse) has a power to appoint any part of the property to any person other than the surviving spouse.[45]

EXAMPLE 1-20: Dave dies on January 2, 2010, leaving his $7 million estate in a trust for the lifetime benefit of his wife, Wilma, and thereafter to be distributed to his two children. The trust requires that all income be paid to Wilma during her lifetime, not less often than quarter-annually. It also authorizes the trustee (an independent bank) to distribute to Wilma as much principal as the trustee deems appropriate for any reason. The trust does not authorize the trustee or anyone else to distribute principal or income to anyone other than Wilma during her lifetime. The trust is a QTIP trust for carryover basis purposes, and the executor of Dave's estate may increase the basis of assets passing to the trust by the $1.3 million aggregate basis increase, the $3 million spousal property basis increase, or both.

EXAMPLE 1-21: Assume the same facts as in Example 1-20, except that Wilma is given lifetime power to appoint the trust principal to and among Dave's children to the extent needed to meet emergency health needs. Wilma's power of appointment permits her to appoint trust assets to someone other than Wilma during her lifetime, and thus disqualifies the trust for QTIP treatment. Dave's executor, therefore, cannot allocate to the trust a spousal property basis increase. Dave's executor, however, may allocate to the trust any portion of Dave's $1.3 million aggregate basis increase.

Section 1022 states that an annuity shall be treated like an income interest in property (regardless of whether the property from which the annuity is payable can be separately identified) to the extent that the Treasury so provides in regulations.[46] It appears that an annuity will not qualify as qualified spousal property until such regulations are promulgated, despite the fact that regulations on the same subject have already been promulgated with respect to the estate tax marital deduction.[47]

---

[45] IRC § 1022(c)(5)(B)(ii). This limitation does not apply to a testamentary power of appointment held by the spouse or another person. IRC § 1022(c)(5)(B) (flush portion).

[46] IRC § 1022(c)(5)(B) (flush portion).

[47] See Reg. § 20.2056(b)-7(h), Exs. 11 and 12. These regulations, when issued, could cause a charitable remainder trust to qualify for the spousal property basis increase. See Berall, Harrison, Blattmachr & Detzel, "Planning for Carryover Basis That Can Be/Should Be/Must Be Done Now," 29 Est. Plan. 99, 100 (Mar. 2002).

This definition would cover a typical QTIP marital trust or usufruct,[48] but is not clear that it would cover a legal life estate in property.[49] It is clear that no spousal property basis increase can be allocated to

1. An estate trust that allows the trustee to accumulate income for ultimate distribution to the surviving spouse's estate;[50]
2. A power of appointment marital trust that gave the surviving spouse a lifetime power to appoint the trust assets to someone else; or
3. A charitable remainder trust in which the spouse is the sole lifetime beneficiary because the spouse is not entitled to all of the trust income.

The practical estate planner should, therefore, avoid using these marital trusts unless sufficient other assets are left to a surviving spouse to take full advantage of the spousal property basis increase.

The $3 million figure for the spousal property basis increase is indexed for inflation after 2010 if the estate tax is not reinstated. This increase is in increments of $250,000.[51]

[iii] Assets to which basis increases may be allocated. The aggregate basis increase and the spousal property basis increase can be allocated only to property acquired from the decedent, and then only to the extent the property was owned by the decedent on the date of death.[52] Property is deemed acquired from a decedent if it is

1. Acquired by devise, bequest, or inheritance;
2. Acquired by the decedent's estate from the decedent;
3. Acquired by or under the terms of a qualified revocable trust (under Section 645) to which the decedent transferred the property during his or her lifetime;
4. Acquired by or under the terms of a trust to which the decedent transferred the property during his or her lifetime, and over which the decedent retained any power to make any change in the beneficial enjoyment of such trust, or to alter, amend, or terminate such trust; or

---

[48] See IRC § 1022(c)(5)(B)(i).

[49] See Berall, Harrison, Blattmachr & Detzel, "Planning for Carryover Basis That Can Be/Should Be/Must Be Done Now," 29 Est. Plan. 99, 101 (Mar. 2002).

[50] See Reg. § 20.2056(e)-2(b).

[51] IRC § 1022(d)(4).

[52] On what constitutes property owned by a decedent on the date of death generally, see Stephens, Maxfield, Lind & Calfee, Federal Estate and Gift Taxation ¶ 4.05 (Thomson Reuters/WG&L, 8th ed. 2002).

5. Passing from the decedent by reason of the decedent's death to the extent passing without consideration.[53]

The extent of a decedent's ownership of an asset is, for this purpose, determined by the application of certain special rules.

First, the decedent is deemed to have owned a portion of the value of property owned jointly by the decedent and another person as joint tenants with a right of survivorship or as tenants by the entirety. The portion of such joint property that is deemed owned by the decedent is based on rules similar to those currently contained in Section 2040. The decedent is deemed to have owned 50 percent of any asset owned as joint tenants with right of survivorship solely with the decedent's surviving spouse, or as tenants by the entirety, without regard to which spouse contributed towards the acquisition cost or how the property was acquired.[54] By contrast, the decedent is deemed to have owned a proportionate share of the value of property owned jointly with a right of survivorship with someone other than the surviving spouse (whether or not the surviving spouse also owns an interest in the same property) determined in proportion to the part of the consideration furnished by the decedent in the acquisition of the property.[55] Property acquired by gift, bequest, devise, or inheritance by the decedent and any other person as joint tenants with right of survivorship in interests that are not otherwise specified or fixed by law is treated as if the decedent owned a fractional part determined by dividing the value of the property by the number of joint tenants.[56]

Second, a decedent is treated as owning any assets that are held by any revocable trust deemed owned by the decedent for income tax purposes under Section 676 because of a power retained by the decedent to reacquire the trust assets and revest them in himself or herself.[57]

---

[53] IRC § 1022(e). See current IRC §§ 1014(b)(2) and 1014(b)(3), for similar rules. See discussion of these rules in Bittker & Lokken, Federal Taxation of Income, Estates and Gifts ¶ 41.4 (Thomson Reuters/WG&L, 3d ed. 2000); Henkel, Estate Planning and Wealth Preservation: Strategies and Solutions ¶ 8.06 (Thomson Reuters/WG&L 1997); Kasner, Strauss & Strauss, Post Mortem Tax Planning ¶ 3.09 (Thomson Reuters/WG&L, 3d ed. 1998); Danforth, Lane & Zaritsky, Federal Income Taxation of Estates and Trusts ¶ 2.15 (Thomson Reuters/WG&L, 3d ed. 2001); Westfall & Mair, Estate Planning Law and Taxation ¶ 2.02 (Thomson Reuters/WG&L, 4th ed. 2001).

[54] IRC § 1022(d)(1)(B)(i)(I).

[55] IRC § 1022(d)(1)(B)(i)(II).

[56] IRC § 1022(d)(1)(B)(i)(II).

[57] IRC § 1022(d)(1)(B)(ii). The statute refers to a trust that is a "qualified revocable trust" as defined in Section 645(b)(1). On the rules for qualified revocable trusts, see Danforth, Lane & Zaritsky, Federal Income Taxation of Estates and Trusts ¶ 1.06 (Thomson Reuters/WG&L, 3d ed. 2001); Westfall & Mair, Estate Planning Law and Taxation ¶ 14.07[2] (Thomson Reuters/WG&L, 4th ed. 2001).

Third, a decedent is deemed not to own property merely because he or she holds a power of appointment over that property.[58] This provision appears to have been intended to prevent the use of the so-called "tax basis trust," under which one spouse would create a trust to hold appreciated assets and give the other spouse a general power of appointment over the trust, with the intent of obtaining a basis increase when the other spouse died.[59]

Fourth, the decedent is deemed to own the surviving spouse's one-half interest in property owned by the decedent and the surviving spouse as community property under the laws of any state, U.S. possession, or foreign country, if the decedent owns the other half.[60]

EXAMPLE 1-22: Dave dies on January 2, 2010, survived by his wife, Wilma, and his two children, Adam and Beth. Dave, at his death, owns the following assets and interests in assets:

Asset	Basis	Value
Residence	$ 300,000	$1,000,000
Stock of Acme Co.	$ 300,000	$2,000,000
Stock of Beta Co.	$2,000,000	$4,000,000
Money market fund	$1,000,000	$1,000,000

The residence is owned by Dave and Wilma as tenants by the entirety. The Acme stock is owned by Dave and his son, Adam, as joint tenants with a right of survivorship. The Acme stock was bought by Dave

---

[58] IRC § 1022(d)(1)(B)(iii).

[59] See Tech. Adv. Mem. 9308002 (Nov. 16, 1992); Priv. Ltr. Ruls. 200101021 (Oct. 2, 2000), 200403094 (Jan. 16, 2004), 200604028 (Jan. 27, 2006), and discussions in Henkel, Estate Planning and Wealth Preservation: Strategies and Solutions ¶ 4.07 (Thomson Reuters/WG&L 1997); Zaritsky, Tax Planning for Family Wealth Transfers: Analysis With Forms ¶ 8.07[6] (Thomson Reuters/WG&L, 4th ed. 2002); see also Fletcher, "Tax Basis Revocable Trusts," 63 Tax Notes 1183 (May 30, 1994); Fletcher, "Drafting Revocable Trusts to Facilitate a Stepped-Up Basis," 22 Est. Plan. 100 (Mar./Apr. 1995); Fletcher & Zaritsky, "Tax Basis Revocable Trusts: How They Work After Technical Advice Memorandum 9308002," 35 Tax Mgmt. Memo. 319 (1994); Mulligan, "Income, Estate and Gift Tax Effects of Spousal Joint Trusts," 22 Est. Plan. 195 (July/Aug. 1995); Nicholson, "Ruling on the Joint Spousal Trust Ignores Statutory Intent," 59 Tax Notes 121 (Apr. 5, 1993); O'Sullivan & Weaver, "Using Two Trusts With Reciprocal Spousal General Powers of Appointment," 30 Est. Plan. 283 (June 2003). For another use of the tax-basis trust to make a poorer spouse's unused unified credit transferable, see Bergner, "Waste Not Want Not—Creative Use of General Powers of Appointment to Fund Tax-Advantaged Trusts," 41 U. Miami Est. Plan. Inst. ch. 12 (2007); Cason, "IRS Ruling Approves 'Poorer Spouse Funding Technique,'" 31 Est. Plan. 234 (2004); Easton, "How to Fully Fund a Credit-Shelter Trust Without Transferring Assets or Using Retirement Plans," 105 J. Tax'n 349 (2006); Gans & Blattmachr, "Making Spousal Estate Tax Exemptions Transferable," 19 Prob. & Prop. 10 (Nov./Dec. 2005); Mulligan, "Is It Safe to Use a Power of Appointment In Predeceasing Spouse to Avoid Wasting Applicable Exclusion Amount?" 32 Tax Mgmt. Est., Gifts & Tr. J. 191 (July 12, 2007).

[60] IRC § 1022(d)(1)(B)(iv).

and Adam in 1990, and Dave contributed the entire purchase price. The Beta Co. shares are held by Dave's revocable trust. The money market fund is owned by Dave alone.

Dave's executor can allocate the $1.3 million aggregate basis increase and $3 million spousal property basis increase to and among Dave's 50 percent interest in the residence, all of the Acme stock, and all of the Beta stock. No allocation needs to be made to the money market fund, because it already has a basis equal to its fair market value.

EXAMPLE 1-23: Dave and his wife, Wilma, create a joint revocable trust to which they each contribute $3 million in appreciated assets. Each has the right to revoke the trust and withdraw the assets he or she contributed. The first spouse to die also has the right to appoint the entire trust fund, including the share contributed by the surviving spouse, either outright or in further trust, to and among the surviving spouse, the couple's descendants, and the creditors of the first deceased spouse's estate. Dave dies on January 2, 2010.

The executor of Dave's estate can allocate Dave's $1.3 million aggregate basis increase and $3 million spousal property basis increase only to the one half of the trust that is attributable to Dave's contribution, because only that portion of the trust is deemed a qualified revocable trust. The executor cannot allocate these basis increases to the one half of the trust fund that Wilma contributed, and over which Dave holds a general power of appointment.

It is important to note that there are several major differences between the property to which a basis allocation may be made and the property includible in a decedent's gross estate for federal estate tax purposes. First, qualifying terminable interest property, though includible in the gross estate of a surviving spouse for federal estate tax purposes,[61] is not property owned by a decedent and is not eligible to receive basis adjustments under the carryover basis rules, because it is not owned by the decedent at death.[62]

EXAMPLE 1-24: In 2005, Donna died leaving $5 million to a trust for her husband, Dick, directing that he be paid all of the income at least annually and that the independent trustee be empowered to distribute such principal to Dick as the trustee deems appropriate for any purpose. At Dick's death, the trust assets will be distributed to Donna and Dick's two children, outright and free of trust. Donna's executor elected to deduct this gift as qualifying terminable interest property under Section 2056(b)(7). The trust fund, in 2010, is worth $10 million. Dick dies in 2010. No portion of Dick's $1.3 million aggregate basis adjustment may

---

[61] IRC § 2044.

[62] IRC § 1022(d)(1)(A) (limiting the basis adjustments to property "owned by the decedent at the time of death").

be allocated to the funds in the QTIP, because Dick does not own those funds.

> **EXAMPLE 1-25:** Assume the same facts as in Example 1-24, except that on January 1, 2005, the trustee of the QTIP trust distributes outright to Dick $3 million of trust assets that have an adjusted basis of $1.7 million. The $7 million remaining in the QTIP trust fund is not eligible for the aggregate basis adjustment under the carryover basis rules, but the $3 million that the trustee distributed outright to Dick is eligible for the aggregate basis adjustment, because Dick owned them at his death.

Second, property that the decedent has transferred during life and over which he or she has retained beneficial enjoyment, while includible in the decedent's gross estate for federal estate tax purposes,[63] is not eligible to receive basis adjustments under the carryover basis rules, because it is not owned by the decedent at death.[64]

> **EXAMPLE 1-26:** In 2005, Donna gave a vacation home worth $1 million to her daughter, and reserved the lifetime right to reside there whenever Donna chose to do so. Donna died in 2010, when the vacation home was worth $2 million. The basis of the vacation home is $200,000—Donna's original purchase price. No portion of Donna's $1.3 million aggregate basis adjustment may be allocated to the vacation home, because Donna did not own it at her death.

[iv] Assets to which basis increase may not be allocated. The executor cannot allocate the aggregate basis increase or spousal property basis increase to the following types of assets:

1. Items of income in respect of a decedent (Section 691);[65]
2. Property acquired by the decedent by lifetime transfer, from someone other than the decedent's spouse, for less than adequate and full consideration in money or money's worth during the three-year period ending on the date of death; however, property acquired by the decedent from the decedent's spouse will not be eligible for the spousal basis adjustment or aggregate basis adjustment if the spouse acquired it by gift, in whole or in part, or by other lifetime transfer for less than full and adequate consideration in money or money's worth during the three-year period prior to the decedent's death;[66] or

---

[63] IRC § 2036(a)(1).

[64] IRC § 1022(d)(1)(A).

[65] IRC § 1022(f). On what constitutes income in respect of a decedent, see Danforth, Lane & Zaritsky, Federal Income Taxation of Estates and Trusts ¶ 15.05 (Thomson Reuters/WG&L, 3d ed. 2001).

[66] IRC § 1022(d)(1).

3. Stock of a foreign personal holding company, a domestic international sales corporation (DISC) or former DISC, or a foreign investment company or passive foreign investment company (unless the company is a qualified electing fund under Section 1295 with respect to the decedent).[67]

The exception to the three-year rule for gifts made to one's spouse is odd because it opens the door to deathbed transfers of appreciated assets between spouses in order to take full advantage of the spousal property basis adjustment.[68]

> **EXAMPLE 1-27:** Harry and Wanda are a married couple. Harry is terminally ill and has only a few months to live. Harry's separate assets include $1 million of cash and $2.5 million of appreciated securities with an adjusted basis of $1.2 million. Wanda's separate assets include $3.5 million of securities, with an adjusted basis of $500,000. If Wanda gives her securities to Harry, who then leaves them outright to Wanda, the spousal property basis adjustment can be applied to the securities, which will eliminate the potential $3 million taxable gain in the securities re-received by Wanda. Harry's other assets reflect only $1.3 million of appreciation, which can be offset by the aggregate basis increase. Without the pre-death transfer of securities to Harry, the spousal property basis adjustment would have been wasted.

The prohibition on the allocation of the aggregate basis increase or spousal property basis increase to items of income in respect of a decedent will pose a particular problem for individuals whose estates consist largely of interests in qualified retirement plan benefits, which are items of income in respect of a decedent.[69] Such items are treated far less favorably than is property that represents appreciation in the value of capital.

> **EXAMPLE 1-28:** Dave dies on January 2, 2010, survived by his wife, Wilma, and his two children, Adam and Beth. Dave, at his death, owns the following assets and interests in assets:
>
> | Asset | Basis | Value |
> |---|---|---|
> | Residence | $ 300,000 | $ 1,000,000 |
> | Individual retirement account | 0 | $ 2,000,000 |
> | Stock of Beta Co. | $ 1,000,000 | $ 3,000,000 |

---

[67] IRC § 1022(d)(1)(D).

[68] See Burke & McCouch, "Estate Tax Repeal: Through the Looking Glass," 22 Va. Tax Rev. 187, 209-210 (Fall 2002), noting that "[t]his exception represents an open invitation to spouses to engage in basis-laundering transactions that would be branded as abusive in any other context."

[69] See Danforth, Lane & Zaritsky, Federal Income Taxation of Estates and Trusts ¶ 15.05[1][b] (Thomson Reuters/WG&L, 3d ed. 2001).

Real estate	$ 100,000	$ 2,000,000
Total	$ 1,400,000	$ 8,000,000

The residence is owned by Dave and Wilma as tenants by the entirety. The individual retirement account is not a Roth IRA, and its balance is attributable largely to a roll-over from Dave's qualified retirement plan. The rental real estate was given to Dave by his father in 2009.

Dave's executor can allocate the $1.3 million aggregate basis increase and $3 million spousal property basis increase among Dave's 50 percent of the residence and his Beta Co. stock. Dave's executor cannot allocate any basis adjustment to Dave's retirement account, because it is income in respect of a decedent. Dave's executor cannot allocate any basis adjustment to the land, because it was given to Dave by his father within three years of Dave's death.

The severe treatment of items of income in respect of a decedent should be contrasted with the favorable treatment of life insurance proceeds. EGTRRA does not alter the present income tax exclusion for life insurance proceeds. The appreciation in the value of investments held within a life insurance policy, therefore, escapes income taxation under even the carryover basis rules, without any need to allocate any of the decedent's carryover basis adjustments to the proceeds.[70]

[b] When Carryover Basis Is Worse Than Estate Tax

Generally, carryover basis is more favorable to a decedent's heirs than the estate tax because (1) the capital gains tax rate (15 percent) is far lower than the estate tax rate (45 percent) and (2) the capital gains tax is imposed only on the net appreciation in the value of assets, while the estate tax is imposed on the full fair market value of the asset. The substitution of carryover basis for the estate tax can, however, substantially increase the total taxes imposed on a surviving spouse receiving an estate in which there is more than $4.3 million of net appreciation.

Currently, the unlimited estate tax marital deduction eliminates all estate taxes on most property received from a decedent by a surviving spouse who is a U.S. citizen. The present tax law also increases the adjusted basis of all assets includible in the gross estate to the value of such assets on the date of the decedent's death or the alternate valuation date. EGTRRA, in eliminating the

---

[70] See Burke & McCouch, "Estate Tax Repeal: Through the Looking Glass," 22 Va. Tax Rev. 187, 212 (Fall 2002), which states that

In effect, this amounts to forgiveness of tax on any mortality gain at death, entirely outside the scope of the carryover basis provisions. As a result, even in the absence of the estate tax, life insurance will retain its entrenched tax-privileged status under the new regime.

estate and GST taxes on such an estate in 2010, also eliminated the basis increase at death for appreciated assets included in the decedent's estate. Therefore, if there is more than $4.3 million of appreciation in the value of the assets owned by the decedent, the carryover basis rules will increase the potential income taxes on the surviving spouse's sale of the inherited appreciated property by more than the estate tax repeal eliminates the estate taxes payable on such property.

> **EXAMPLE 1-29:** Dave leaves his entire $20 million estate to Wilma. Dave's basis in the assets in his estate is $5 million. None of Dave's estate is income in respect of a decendent. Dave dies on December 30, 2009. The estate tax marital deduction eliminates any estate tax with respect to his estate and the basis rules give Wilma a $20 million basis in the assets she receives from Dave's estate. Therefore, Wilma receives the entire $20 million with neither an estate tax liability nor any potential income tax liability.
>
> Under EGTRRA, however, if Dave dies in 2010, Wilma owes no estate tax because the estate tax will have been repealed, but she will take Dave's adjusted basis in the assets, increased by the aggregate basis increase and spousal property basis increase. This gives Wilma a total basis of not more than $9.3 million in the assets received from Dave's estate. The sale of Dave's assets by Wilma will result in realization and recognition of a $10.7 million capital gain, on which there would be an income tax liability of at least approximately $1,605,000. Thus, EGTRRA will have increased the tax cost of passing Dave's estate to Wilma by $1,605,000.

[3] Special Recognition and Nonrecognition Rules

EGTRRA includes several special rules designed to prevent both attempts to frustrate the operation of the carryover basis rules and certain unintended adverse consequences of the carryover basis rules. The four key special rules are discussed below in ¶¶ 1.05[3][a]–[d].

[a] Gain on Liability in Excess of Basis

Generally, the amount realized on the transfer of property includes the amount of any debt to which the property is subject, and thus a transferor will recognize gain if the debt exceeds the transferor's basis.[71] EGTRRA attempts

---

[71] IRC § 1001; Reg. § 1.1001-2; see discussion in Bittker & Lokken, Federal Taxation of Income, Estates and Gifts ¶ 43.4 (Thomson Reuters/WG&L, 3d ed. 2000); Bittker & McMahon, Federal Income Taxation of Individuals ¶ 29.15 (Thomson Reuters/WG&L,

to avoid causing unexpected recognition of gain by providing that the amount of the gain recognized by a decedent on the distribution of encumbered property to his or her estate, or by the decedent's estate on the distribution of encumbered property to a beneficiary (other than a tax-exempt beneficiary), does not include the excess of the amount of the debt to which the property is subject over the decedent's basis in the property.[72]

> **EXAMPLE 1-30:** Dave's estate includes an office building worth $1 million. Dave's basis in the building was $250,000. The property is subject to a nonrecourse mortgage in the amount of $600,000. Dave's estate distributes the property to one of Dave's children. Neither the death of Dave nor the distribution of the property to the beneficiary requires recognition of gain to the extent of the $350,000 excess of this debt over Dave's basis in the building.[73]

This rule does not, however, protect the beneficiary from recognizing gain on a later disposition of the property received from a decedent if it is subject to a debt in excess of the beneficiary's basis.

> **EXAMPLE 1-31:** Assume the same facts as in Example 1-30, except that, after inheriting the building, Dave's son, Adam, sells it for $1 million. The buyer pays Adam $400,000 in cash, and assumes the $600,000 mortgage. Adam recognizes a $650,000 gain on the sale because Adam's adjusted basis was $350,000, and the amount realized includes both the $400,000 cash and $600,000 basis assumption.

These rules restrict the benefit of the spousal property basis adjustment to transfers benefitting the spouse, but a creative estate planner can shift the benefit of that basis increase to other family members, through the use of liabilities. Under the carryover basis rules, as discussed above, liabilities in excess of basis are generally disregarded in determining whether gain is recognized on a

---

3d ed. 2002); Zaritsky, Tax Planning for Family Wealth Transfers: Analysis With Forms ¶ 11.02 (Thomson Reuters/WG&L, 4th ed. 2002).

[72] IRC § 1022(g)(1). For this purpose, a "tax-exempt beneficiary" includes

(A) the United States, any State or political subdivision thereof, any possession of the United States, any Indian tribal government (within the meaning of section 7871), or any agency or instrumentality of any of the foregoing,

(B) an organization (other than a cooperative described in section 521) which is exempt from tax imposed by Chapter 1,

(C) any foreign person or entity (within the meaning of section 168(h)(2)), and

(D) to the extent provided in regulations, any person to whom property is transferred for the principal purpose of tax avoidance.

IRC § 1022(g)(2). It does not appear to include a charitable remainder trust.

[73] See HR Conf. Rep. No. 84, 107th Cong., 1st Sess. (2001), 147 Cong. Rec. H2774 (May 25, 2001).

disposition and in determining the basis of the recipient of the property.[74] This rule does not, however, prevent a basis increase for encumbered property passing to a surviving spouse even if the spouse ultimately bears the burden of the liabilities.

> **EXAMPLE 1-32:** Harry and Wanda are a married couple. Harry borrows $5 million secured by $5 million worth of real property with a $700,000 adjusted basis. Harry leaves the $5 million in cash to his daughter, Debbie, and leaves the real property to Wanda. Wanda's property receives a $1.3 million aggregate basis increase and a $3 million spousal property basis increase under the carryover basis rules, eliminating all of the potential gain. Wanda will ultimately be required to repay the $5 million liability because she has received property that is subject to the debt. This will produce a net benefit of zero for Wanda, while giving Debbie $5 million tax-free.[75]

[b] $250,000 Exclusion of Gain on Sale of Principal Residence

The carryover basis rules extend the exclusion of up to $250,000 of the gain on the sale of an individual's principal residence to sales by a decedent's estate or beneficiaries if the property was used by the decedent as a principal residence for two or more years during the five-year period prior to the sale.[76] The legislative history states that the decedent's period of ownership and occupancy will be added to any actual occupancy by the heir in determining whether the heir is entitled to the benefit of the $250,000 exclusion.[77] This rule allows estates and beneficiaries to preserve this valuable tax benefit despite the use of the decedent's basis in the residence under the carryover basis rules.

> **EXAMPLE 1-33:** Dave bought the house that he uses as his principal residence in 2006. Dave's basis in the house is $250,000 and its value at Dave's death on January 2, 2010, is $500,000. Dave's will leaves his house to his daughter, Beth. If the estate sells the house, Dave's estate

---

[74] IRC § 1022(g).

[75] Burke & McCouch, "Estate Tax Repeal: Through the Looking Glass," 22 Va. Tax Rev. 187, 209 (Fall 2002). See also discussion of the treatment of liabilities in Berall, Harrison, Blattmachr & Detzel, "Planning for Carryover Basis That Can Be/Should Be/ Must Be Done Now," 29 Est. Plan. 99, 103-104 (Mar. 2002).

[76] IRC § 121(d)(9).

[77] See HR Conf. Rep. No. 84, 107th Cong., 1st Sess. (2001), 147 Cong. Rec. H2774 (May 25, 2001). On Section 121 generally, see Frolik & Brown, Advising the Elderly or Disabled Client ¶ 16.02 (Thomson Reuters/WG&L, 2d ed. 2004); Frolik, Residence Options for Older or Disabled Clients ¶ 5.02 (Thomson Reuters/WG&L 1997); Henkel, Estate Planning and Wealth Preservation: Strategies and Solutions ¶ 40.10 (Thomson Reuters/WG&L 1997).

can take advantage of the $250,000 exclusion under Section 121 because Dave owned and used it as his primary residence for more than two of the five years prior to his death. Beth can take advantage of the exclusion if the estate distributes the house to Beth and she sells it, because she will be treated as having owned the house and used it as a principal residence during the years that Dave did.

[c] Limit on Gain Recognized on Pecuniary Bequests

Generally, gain is recognized on an estate's or trust's distribution of appreciated property in satisfaction of a required distribution of a pecuniary amount.[78] EGTRRA provides that gain on the transfer of property in satisfaction of a pecuniary bequest under a will (or similar disposition under a trust) after 2009 will be recognized only to the extent that the fair market value of the property at the time of the transfer exceeds its fair market value on the date of the decedent's death.[79] The basis of the distributed property in the hands of the distributee will be equal to its basis in the hands of the distributing fiduciary, increased by any gain recognized on the distribution.[80] This rule eliminates any gain that would otherwise be attributable to the appreciation in the value of assets distributed by an estate or trust in statisfaction of a pecuniary gift after December 31, 2009, merely because of the carryover of the decedent's basis in the asset to the estate.

> **EXAMPLE 1-34:** Dave died on January 2, 2010. Dave's will directs the executor to distribute $100,000 to Dave's daughter, Beth. Dave's executor distributes to Beth stock that Dave owned on the date of his death. The stock has a $20,000 basis in the hands of the executor, and it was worth $75,000 on the date of Dave's death. The stock is worth $100,000 on the date of distribution. Dave's estate recognizes a $25,000 gain on the distribution—the difference between the value of the stock on the date of the distribution and its value on the date of Dave's death ($100,000 − $75,000 = $25,000). Beth's adjusted basis in the stock is $50,000, includ-

---

[78] Reg. § 1.661(a)-2(f)(1); see also discussion in Danforth, Lane & Zaritsky, Federal Income Taxation of Estates and Trusts ¶ 4.11[1] (Thomson Reuters/WG&L, 3d ed. 2001).

[79] Distributions by trusts are eligible for the same treatment, to the extent provided in regulations. The regulations will extend this treatment to situations in which a person has a right to receive a distribution from a trust by reason of the decedent's death, and the trustee satisfies that right with a distribution in kind. IRC § 1040(b).

[80] IRC § 1040. On the recognition of gain on a trust's or estate's distribution of appreciated property in satisfaction of a pecuniary sum, see Peschel & Spurgeon, Federal Taxation of Trusts, Grantors and Beneficiaries ¶ 17.06 (Thomson Reuters/WG&L, 3d ed. 1997); Danforth, Lane & Zaritsky, Federal Income Taxation of Estates and Trusts ¶ 4.11 (Thomson Reuters/WG&L, 3d ed. 2001).

ing both Dave's basis ($25,000) and the gain recognized by the estate on the distribution ($25,000).

[d] Bequests to Foreign Persons

Section 684 currently requires that a donor treat as a sale or exchange the transfer of appreciated property to a foreign trust or estate. The amount of gain that must be recognized by the transferor is the excess of the fair market value of the property transferred over the transferor's adjusted basis in such property.[81] EGTRRA extends this rule to testamentary transfers made to foreign individuals after 2009.[82]

> **EXAMPLE 1-35:** Dave died on January 2, 2010. Dave's will directs his executor to distribute all of Dave's stock of Delta Corporation to Dave's niece, Nancy, who is a British subject living in England. The Delta shares are worth $250,000 on the date of Dave's death, and Dave's basis in those shares is $50,000. Dave's estate will be required to recognize a $200,000 gain on this distribution ($250,000 value − $50,000 basis) under the special extension of Section 684.

[4] Reporting Requirements

The Internal Revenue Code states that the aggregate basis adjustment and the spousal property adjustment are available only to the extent that the decedent's executor allocates them pursuant to Section 1022.[83] The Code also states that the allocation must be made on a tax return filed pursuant to Section 6018.[84]

Section 7701(a)(4) states that the term "executor" means "the executor or administrator of the decedent, or, if there is no executor or administrator appointed, qualified, and acting within the United States, then any person in actual or constructive possession of any property of the decedent." An estate that has no appointed executor or administrator may have multiple "executors" for purposes of allocating basis increases, and they may not always agree on the best allocation, as discussed at ¶ 3.03[1][d].

---

[81] See discussion of Section 684 in Bittker & Lokken, Federal Taxation of Income, Estates and Gifts ¶ 71.1 (Thomson Reuters/WG&L, 3d ed. 2001); Danforth, Lane & Zaritsky, Federal Income Taxation of Estates and Trusts ¶¶ 2.17, 6.03 (Thomson Reuters/WG&L, 3d ed. 2001).

[82] IRC § 684.

[83] IRC § 1022(b)(1)(A).

[84] IRC § 6018(b)(1).

EGTRRA substitutes a "basis return" under Section 6018 for the federal estate tax return, and adopts other reporting requirements deemed necessary to enforce the new carryover basis rules.[85] Section 6018 requires the executor of the estate of a decedent who dies after December 31, 2009, to file a return containing basis information if the fair market value of all property (other than cash) acquired from the decedent exceeds the dollar amount applicable" under Section 1022's aggregate basis increase.[86] The Code, therefore, does not actually provide a mechanism by which the executor of a more modest estate, say, one with a total fair market value of under $1.3 million (excluding cash), can allocate the two basis adjustments. Presumably, the IRS will provide guidance stating that such a return will be deemed filed automatically.

The executor who files a return under Section 6018 must report the basis and likely character of potential gain (capital or ordinary) of all property acquired from a decedent if the total fair market value of the property acquired from a decedent's estate (other than cash) exceeds the $1.3 million aggregate basis adjustment (determined without regard losses and loss carryovers that are otherwise added to the $1.3 million figure for purposes of allocating the aggregate basis increase).[87] The executor must also report on the return any appreciated property with a value of more than $25,000 that was acquired from a decedent, but that was ineligible for allocation of any portion of the aggregate basis increase because it was (1) acquired by the decedent in a transfer for less than adequate and full consideration within three years of the decedent's death and (2) required to be included on a gift tax return.[88]

The decedent's executor must include in this return

1. The name and taxpayer identification number (TIN) of the recipient of such property;
2. An accurate description of such property;
3. The adjusted basis of such property in the hands of the decedent and its fair market value at the time of death;
4. The decedent's holding period for such property;
5. Sufficient information to determine whether any gain on the sale of the property would be treated as ordinary income;
6. The amount of aggregate basis increase and any spousal basis increase for property acquired by a spouse allocated to each asset; and
7. Such other information as the IRS may by regulations prescribe.

---

[85] IRC §§ 6018, 6019, 6716.

[86] IRC § 6018(b)(1).

[87] IRC § 6018(b).

[88] These rules are modified for estates of nonresident alien individuals to take into account only tangible property situated within the United States and other property acquired from a U.S. decedent, and looking to the $60,000 limitation, rather than the $1.3 million limitation. IRC § 6018(b)(3).

These returns must be filed with the decedent's income tax return for the decedent's last taxable year. The executor must also report to the recipient of the property, the name, address, and telephone number of the executor, as well as the data provided to the IRS regarding the asset acquired by this recipient.

EGTRRA imposes a penalty of $10,000 for each failure to report to the IRS transfers at death of non-cash assets in excess of $1.3 million in value, and a penalty of $500 for each failure to report to the IRS the decedent's receipt of appreciated property valued in excess of $25,000 within three years of death. A $50 penalty is imposed for each failure to provide the required information to a beneficiary.[89]

No penalty is imposed with respect to any failure to report that is due to reasonable cause. A failure to file the required return with the IRS or a beneficiary due to intentional disregard of the rules is punishable by a penalty equal to 5 percent of the fair market value of the property for which reporting was required, determined at the date of the decedent's death (for property passing at death) or determined at the time of gift (for a lifetime gift).

¶ 1.06 SUNSET OF EGTRRA—WHAT 2011 MIGHT LOOK LIKE (AND IT ISN'T PRETTY)

[1] Technical Examination of the Sunset Rule

Section 901 of EGTRRA states, in applicable part, that

(a) IN GENERAL.—All provisions of, and amendments made by, this Act shall not apply—

* * *

(2) in the case of title V, to estates of decedents dying, gifts made, or generation skipping transfers, after December 31, 2010.

(b) APPLICATION OF CERTAIN LAWS.—The Internal Revenue Code of 1986...shall be applied and administered to...estates, gifts, and transfers described in subsection (a) as if the provisions and amendments described in subsection (a) had never been enacted.

---

[89] IRC § 6716.

EGTRRA's sunset rule was required to comply with an amendment to the Congressional Budget Act of 1974,[90] which would have required a vote of sixty senators to approve as part of the budget reconciliation a bill that would reduce revenues in a fiscal year more than ten years after the present fiscal year.[91] The sunset provision, however, is far from a mere bookkeeping entry.

The precise wording of Section 901(b) of the EGTRRA is important. It states that the repeal is to cause post-2010 estates, gifts, and transfers to be administered as if EGTRRA had never been enacted at all. This could be merely a reinforcement of Section 901(a), but generally every provision of a statute is construed as not being superfluous.[92]

A literal reading of Section 901(b) could cause serious problems because the GST tax is often imposed on trusts years after the actual GST tax-related transfer. In order to repeal EGTRRA as if it had never been enacted, the inclusion ratio for these trusts may need to be recalculated beginning in 2011 to deny the benefits of the post-2003 increases in the GST exemption that were made available solely because of EGTRRA. It is unlikely that Congress anticipated this problem when the sunset rules were drafted, but it is the most reasonable reading of the sunset rules.

For example, the sunset rule could be interpreted to void part of an allocation of GST exemption during the years 2004–2009 to the extent that the GST exemption allocated was higher than it would have been had EGTRRA not been enacted. The exclusion ratio of a generation-skipping trust to which exemption was allocated would be recalculated after 2010, and the numerator of the applicable fraction would be the lesser of the allocated exemption or the maximum GST exemption that would have been available for allocation had EGTRRA not been enacted ($1 million, indexed for inflation after 2001), and the denominator of which would have been the value of the transfer against which the GST exemption is being applied.

> **EXAMPLE 1-36:** Dave creates a $3.5 million generation-skipping trust in 2009, and allocates all of his GST exemption to the trust. At the end of

---

[90] Pub. L. No. 93-344, 93d Cong., 2d Sess. (July 12, 1974), 88 Stat. 297.

[91] Specifically, this repeal was required to comply with a 1986 amendment to the Congressional Budget Act of 1974. Pub. L. No. 99-272, § 20001, 99th Cong., 2d Sess. (Apr. 7, 1986), 100 Stat. 82. The amendment, sponsored by Senator Robert Byrd (D-W. Va.), and known as the "Byrd rule" or the "Byrd amendment," makes it out of order in the Senate to add an extraneous provision to a budget reconciliation. The bill defines a provision as "extraneous" if it reduces receipts beyond the period provided for in the Budget Resolution. The Budget Resolution in question covered a ten-year period, and thus the bill needed to sunset the expenditures after ten years. The Senate would have required sixty votes to defeat the application of the Byrd rule had the bill not included a sunset provision.

[92] Flores-Figueroa v. United States, __ US __, 129 S. Ct. 1886, 173 L. Ed2d 853 (2009).

2009, the trust has an inclusion ratio of 0 (1 − ($3,500,000/$3,500,000)). On January 1, 2011, the trust is now worth $5 million, due to successful investments. The GST inclusion ratio for the trust should arguably be re-calculated by reducing the amount allocated to the trust from $3.5 million to $1.3 million (or whatever the proper figure would have been for the GST exemption adjusted for inflation on that date). This would arguably create an inclusion ratio of 62.857143 percent (1 − ($1,300,000 ÷ $3,500,000)), rather than an inclusion ratio of 0. After 2010, therefore, all taxable distributions and terminations from the trust would be subject to a GST tax at a rate of 34.57142865 percent (0.62857143 × 55%).

The sunset rules could also be interpreted to negate automatic allocations of GST exemption to non-direct skip transfers, which was permitted only by EGTRRA. This would mean that the inclusion ratio for a generation-skipping trust created after EGTRRA would need to be recalculated in 2011 to exclude the effect of automatic allocations of GST exemption.

> **EXAMPLE 1-37:** Don creates a $1 million generation-skipping trust in 2008, and $1 million of his GST exemption is automatically allocated to the transfer under Section 2632(c). After the trust is created (and at the end of 2009), the trust has an inclusion ratio of 0 (1 − ($1 million/$1 million)). On January 1, 2011, the trust is now worth $1.5 million, due to successful investments. The GST inclusion ratio for the trust should arguably be recalculated by ignoring amounts automatically allocated to the transfer. Thus, the inclusion ratio would be 1. Don could make a late allocation of exemption to the trust, but he would need to determine the inclusion ratio based on the value of the trust assets on the date the allocation is made, rather than the value on the date the trust was created. As Don will have only about $1.3 million of GST exemption to allocate to the transfer in 2011, this produces an inclusion ratio of 13.333 percent (1 − ($1.3 million/$1.5 million)). In 2008 and 2009, therefore, there would have been no GST tax imposed on distributions from the trust, because it would have had an inclusion ratio of zero. In 2010, there would have been no GST tax imposed on distributions from the trust because there was no GST tax. In 2011, there would be a 7.33 percent tax on any distributions from the trust (13.3333% × 55%).

See Chapter 4 for a discussion of the other odd possible effect of EGTRRA's sunset rule on generation-skipping transfers in trust.

[2] Taxes, Rates, and Exemptions

If Congress does not act to the contrary, EGTRRA's estate, gift, and GST tax provisions will expire on January 1, 2011. Should that occur, the estate and GST taxes would be resurrected, with a top estate and gift tax rate (and the only GST tax rate) of 55 percent and a 5 percent surtax on certain transfers of over $10 million (but not over $17,184,000). The estate tax applicable exclusion amount and the gift tax exemption will again be reunified at $1 million. The GST exemption would again become disassociated from the estate tax exemption, at $1 million indexed for inflation after 2001 (probably about $1.3 million).

[3] Other Undone EGTRRA Changes

In addition to the general restoration of the estate and GST taxes, as well as the resumption of the pre-2002 rates and exemptions, several other important changes made by EGTRRA would be repealed.

[a] Restored State Death Tax Credit

EGTRRA phased out the state death tax credit over four years, ending with its total repeal in 2005.[93] The state death tax credit was replaced with an unlimited state death tax deduction with respect to estates of decedents dying after December 31, 2004.[94]

This change led many states to eliminate their own estate taxes, which had been set at the maximum amount for which a federal credit was allowed.[95] Approximately one half of the states now have either an inheritance tax or a stand-alone estate tax. The states that decoupled their laws from the federal rules often have exemptions that are lower than the federal exemptions, and some of them expressly do not allow elections on the state estate tax return that differ from those made on the federal estate tax return. These disparities have made estate planning far more complicated than it had been before

---

[93] IRC § 2011(g). See also Arlen & Pratt, "The New York (and Other States) Death Tax Trap," 77 Fla. BJ 55 (Oct. 2003); Steiner, "Coping With the Decoupling of State Estate Taxes After EGTRRA," 30 Est. Plan. 167 (Apr. 2003).

[94] IRC § 2011(g).

[95] One of the more interesting series of events involving the repeal of the state death tax credit occurred in the state of Washington. When EGTRRA was enacted, Washington had an estate tax. A 1981 initiative had expressly limited the Washington estate tax to "an amount equal to the federal credit." Wash. Rev. Code § 83.100.030(1). In 2001, the Washington legislature enacted an amendment that stated that references to the Internal Revenue Code were to "the United States Internal Revenue Code of 1986, as amended or renumbered as of January 1, 2001." Wash. Rev. Code § 83.100.020(15). Several executors sued to contest the validity of this provision, and the Supreme Court of Washington held in *Estate of Hemphill v. Washington*, 153 Wash. 2d 544, 105 P3d 391 (2005), that the repeal of the federal credit for state death taxes automatically repealed the state estate tax, notwithstanding the actions of the legislature. The Washington Legislature then enacted, and the Governor signed into law, an independent Washington estate tax. Wash. Rev. Code §§ 83.100.010 – 83.100.906. See Mumford, "Up and Down and Back Again: Troubled Childhood Notwithstanding, Washington's Stand Alone Estate Tax Deserves to Be Defended," 29 Seattle UL Rev. 687 (Spring 2006).

EGTRRA. In 2011, EGTRRA's sunset rules would reverse the federal rules and restore the state death tax credit,[96] but it would require action in each of the states to reverse the decoupling by the states of their estate tax laws from the federal estate tax laws, which will automatically reinvigorate the estate tax in many states, though in some states specific legislation may be required to readopt their former estate taxes.

[b] Tightened (Slightly) Conservation Easement Rules

EGTRRA liberalized slightly the rules governing the deduction under Section 2031(c) for contributions of certain conservation easements. EGTRRA eliminated the requirement that the easement area fall within twenty-five miles from an urban area, wilderness, or national park, and required only that the easement relate to land that is located within the United States or its possessions. EGTRRA also clarified that the date for determining the easement compliance is the date on which the contribution is made, and not the date of the decedent's death.[97] EGTRRA's sunset rules would reverse these changes, limiting somewhat the utility of these contributions.

[c] Tightened (Significantly) Rules for Allocating GST Exemption

EGTRRA made several very important changes in the GST tax rules relating to allocation of the GST exemption, in addition to increasing the GST exemption significantly after 2003. These changes made it easier to allocate the GST exemption accurately. The sunset rules would repeal these provisions as if EGTRRA had never been enacted. This may cause serious problems because the GST tax is often imposed on trusts years after the GST exemption has been allocated to the transfer. In order to repeal EGTRRA as if it had never been enacted, the inclusion ratio for these trusts may need to be recalculated in 2011 to deny the benefits that were made available solely because of EGTRRA.

[i] Automatic allocation to certain lifetime transfers. EGTRRA extended the automatic allocation of a donor's GST exemption to lifetime transfers that are not direct skips but that are made to generation-skipping trusts.[98] This greatly facilitates the correct (or, sometimes, incorrect) allocation of GST

---

[96] See discussion at ¶ 2.06.

[97] IRC § 2031(c)(8)(A).

[98] IRC § 2632(c); see also Harrington, Plaine & Zaritsky, Generation-Skipping Transfer Tax ¶ 4.04[1][a] (Thomson Reuters/WG&L, 2d ed. 2001); Stephens, Maxfield, Lind & Calfee, Federal Estate and Gift Taxation ¶ 15.03 (Thomson Reuters/WG&L, 8th ed. 2002).

exemption to transfers to trusts that have both skip person and non-skip person beneficiaries.

The sunset rule could, as noted above,[99] be interpreted to negate automatic allocations of GST exemption to non-direct skip transfers, which was permitted only by EGTRRA. This would mean that the inclusion ratio for a generation-skipping trust created after EGTRRA would need to be recalculated in 2011 to exclude the effect of automatic allocations of GST exemption. This would not only force donors to reallocate GST exemption to these transfers, but require that the inclusion ratio be determined based on the fair market value of the trust assets on the date of the later allocation, rather than on the date of the original transfer. If these trusts have grown in value since they were created, this would either increase the inclusion ratio or force the donor to allocate more GST exemption to the transfer.[100]

[ii] Retroactive allocations would no longer be permitted. EGTRRA recognized that a transferor will not usually allocate GST exemption to a trust that he or she expects to benefit only non-skip persons, but sometimes a taxable termination still occurs because, for example, the transferor's child unexpectedly dies and the trust terminates in favor of the transferor's grandchild.[101] EGTRRA did, therefore, permit a transferor to make a retroactive allocation of GST exemption to a transfer in trust if a beneficiary of the trust dies before the transfer (but after the date of enactment), provided that the predeceasing beneficiary was both a non-skip person and a lineal descendant of the transferor's grandparent or a grandparent of the transferor's spouse, assigned to a generation younger than the generation of the transferor.[102] The applicable fraction and inclusion ratio has been determined whenever GST exemption is retroactively allocated under this rule, based on the value of the property on the date that the property was transferred to a trust. EGTRRA's sunset rule would repeal this provision, making it more difficult to determine when to allocate GST exemption as well as to cure situations in which GST exemption has not been allocated.

[iii] Elimination of the rules for qualified severance. EGTRRA greatly liberalized the rules by which a GST trust could be divided into separate trusts, so as to facilitate tax-advantaged investments and administration. This was done through the "qualified severance" rules, which permit a division of a trust into multiple separate trusts if

1. The division were made fractionally;

---

[99] See supra ¶ 1.06[1].

[100] See supra Example 1-37.

[101] See HR Rep. No. 84, 107th Cong., 1st Sess. 199 (2001).

[102] IRC § 2632(d); see also Harrington, Plaine & Zaritsky, Generation-Skipping Transfer Tax ¶ 4.04 (Thomson Reuters/WG&L, 2d ed. 2001).

2. The terms of the new trusts provide, in the aggregate, for the same succession of interests of beneficiaries as in the original trust; and

3. A single undivided trust, with an inclusion ratio of greater than zero (0:1) and less than one (1:0), is divided into two trusts, one of which has an inclusion ratio of one and the other of which has an inclusion ratio of zero.[103]

It is unclear whether the sunset rules would treat trusts that had been the subject of a qualified severance of a single trust as if they were not separate trusts for GST tax purposes after 2011. Such a construction would appear to be consistent with the requirement that the post-2010 law be "applied and administered to...estates, gifts, and transfers...as if the provisions and amendments described in subsection (a) had never been enacted."[104]

[iv] Clouding the determination of the value of property on a timely allocation of GST exemption. EGTRRA provided that the value of property for purposes of determining the GST inclusion ratio (and, thereby, the rate of GST tax imposed on taxable events), in connection with timely and automatic allocations of GST exemption, is the value finally determined for gift or estate tax purposes. The value for purposes of an allocation that was made at the end of an estate tax inclusion period (ETIP) was its estate or gift tax value at the end of the ETIP.[105] This provision was largely designed to clarify the law, and it is not clear what the effect of repealing it would be.

[v] Reducing Treasury's power to extend time to allocate GST exemption. EGTRRA directed the Treasury Secretary to grant extensions of time to allocate GST exemption and to grant exceptions to the time requirement, considering all relevant circumstances including evidence of intent contained in the trust instrument or instrument of transfer and such other factors as the Treasury Secretary deemed relevant.[106] Prior to EGTRRA, the IRS allowed such retroactive allocations under the general authority of Regulations § 301.9100-3.[107]

EGTRRA's sunset rule would remove this direction and leave the Treasury with the authority to allow late allocations based on Regulations § 301.9100-3. The Treasury proposed regulations detailing how it would ad-

---

[103] IRC § 2642(a)(3); see also Harrington, Plaine & Zaritsky, Generation-Skipping Transfer Tax ¶ 4.06[4][i] (Thomson Reuters/WG&L, 2d ed. 2001).

[104] See supra ¶ 1.06[1].

[105] IRC § 2642(b); see also Harrington, Plaine & Zaritsky, Generation-Skipping Transfer Tax ¶ 3.05 (Thomson Reuters/WG&L, 2d ed. 2001).

[106] IRC § 2642(g)(1)(B); see also Harrington, Plaine & Zaritsky, Generation-Skipping Transfer Tax ¶ 4.04[4][a] (Thomson Reuters/WG&L, 2d ed. 2001).

[107] See, e.g., Priv. Ltr. Ruls. 200032015 (Aug. 15, 2000), 199905009 (Feb. 8, 1999).

dress these extension issues in 2008.[108] Repealing this authority would merely force the Treasury to continue granting this relief under the Section 9100 regulations, rather than under the more specific and narrowly designed regulations they have promulgated.

[vi] Eliminate substantial compliance rule for allocations. EGTRRA provided that substantial compliance with the statutory and regulatory requirements for allocating GST tax exemption sufficed to established that GST tax exemption was allocated to a particular transfer or a particular trust. A taxpayer who demonstrated an intent to have an inclusion ratio of zero with respect to a particular transfer or trust was deemed, under this rule, to have allocated to the transfer sufficient GST exemption to produce a zero inclusion ratio, if possible. EGTRRA directed the Treasury to consider all relevant circumstances to determine whether there had been substantial compliance, including evidence of intent contained in the trust instrument or instrument of transfer and such other factors as the Treasury Secretary deems appropriate.[109]

EGTRRA's sunset rule would eliminate the express direction for the Treasury to apply the substantial compliance doctrine after 2010, as if it had never been part of the law. As the IRS had already been applying this doctrine in what it deemed to be appropriate cases before EGTRRA, this revocation might make relatively little difference in the administration of the GST tax laws.[110]

[d] Reinstate the Qualified Family Owned Business Interest Deduction

EGTRRA repealed entirely the rules by which an estate may claim a deduction of up to $675,000 for certain interests in a qualified family owned business interest.[111] The sunset rules would reinstate this complicated deduction for estates of decedents dying after 2010.

---

[108] REG-147775-06, 73 Fed. Reg. 20,870-20,871 (Apr. 17, 2008).

[109] IRC § 2642(g).

[110] See Priv. Ltr. Ruls. 199909034 (Mar. 8, 1999), 199937026 (Sept. 20, 1999), 200017013 (May 1, 2000), 200027009 (July 10, 2000), 200040013 (Oct. 10, 2000); see also Harrington, Plaine & Zaritsky, Generation-Skipping Transfer Tax ¶ 4.04[1][b] (Thomson Reuters/WG&L, 2d ed. 2001).

[111] IRC § 2057(j). On Section 2057 generally, see Bellatti, Estate Planning for Farms and Other Family-Owned Businesses ch. 10 (Thomson Reuters/WG&L 1998); Henkel, Estate Planning and Wealth Preservation: Strategies and Solutions ¶ 5.12 (Thomson Reuters/WG&L 1997); Peschel & Spurgeon, Federal Taxation of Trusts, Grantors and Beneficiaries ¶ 13.09 (Thomson Reuters/WG&L, 3d ed. 1997); Stephens, Maxfield, Lind & Calfee, Federal Estate and Gift Taxation ¶ 5.08 (Thomson Reuters/WG&L, 8th ed. 2002).

[e] Slight Tightening of the Deferred Payment of Estate Taxes Attributable to Closely Held Business Interests

EGTRRA slightly expanded Section 6166 in two ways.[112] First, Section 6166 deferral was allowed for interests in qualifying lending and financing businesses. A "qualifying lending and finance business" was defined for this purpose as a lending and finance business that either

1. Had substantial activity with respect to the lending and finance business on the date of the decedent's death, or
2. During at least three of the five taxable years ending before the date of the decedent's death, had at least one full-time employee substantially all of whose services were the active management of such business, ten full-time, nonowner employees substantially all of whose services were directly related to such business, and $5 million in gross receipts from lending and finance activities.[113]

Unlike most active businesses, deferred estate taxes for a qualifying lending and finance business were required to be paid over five years.[114]

Second, EGTRRA raised from fifteen to forty-five the number of partners that a partnership could have, or shareholders that a corporation could have, and still qualify the estate tax on its business interests for deferral under Section 6166.[115]

EGTRRA's sunset rule would eliminate both of these provisions with respect to estates of decedents dying after December 31, 2010.

---

[112] On the deferral rules generally, see Henkel, Estate Planning and Wealth Preservation: Strategies and Solutions ¶ 46.02 (Thomson Reuters/WG&L 1997); Kasner, Strauss & Strauss, Post Mortem Tax Planning ¶ 9.03 (Thomson Reuters/WG&L, 3d ed. 1998); Westfall & Mair, Estate Planning Law and Taxation ¶ 7.04 (Thomson Reuters/WG&L, 4th ed. 2001).

[113] For this purpose, "lending and financing activities" means the business of (1) making loans; (2) buying or discounting accounts receivable, notes, or installment obligations; (3) engaging in rental and leasing of real and tangible personal property, including entering into leases and buying, servicing, and disposing of leases and leased assets; (4) rendering services or making facilities available in the ordinary course of a lending or finance business; and (5) rendering services or making facilities available in connection with the aforementioned activities carried on by the corporation rendering services or making facilities available or another corporation which is a member of the same affiliated group. A "qualifying lending and finance business" does not include any interest in an entity if the stock or debt of such entity or a controlled group of which such entity was a member was readily tradable on an established securities market or secondary market (as defined by the Secretary) at any time within three years before the date of the decedent's death. IRC § 6166(b)(10)(B).

[114] IRC § 6166(b)(10).

[115] IRC §§ 6166(b)(1)(B)(ii), 6166(b)(1)(C)(ii), 6166(b)(9)(B)(iii)(I).

[f] Reclouding the Waiver of Statute of Limitations on Certain Farm Valuations

EGTRRA resolved a question raised by the Tax Reform Act of 1997 with respect to the special valuation rules of Section 2032A, which permits a reduction in the value of real estate used in certain closely held businesses or family farms. Section 504(c) of the Tax Reform Act of 1997 expanded the class of heirs eligible to lease property for which special-use valuation was claimed without the recapture of the tax benefits previously allowed. The Tax Reform Act of 1997 amendment applied to leases entered into after December 31, 1976, but the IRS later ruled privately that the retroactive effective date in the changes made by the Tax Reform Act of 1997 did not waive of the period of limitations otherwise applicable on a taxpayer's claim.[116] The IRS ruled that a taxpayer's claim for refund of the recapture tax paid on account of the cessation of a qualified use was barred under the generally applicable statute of limitations on refund claims.

EGTRRA provided that a claim for refund or credit would be allowed, though barred by operation of law or rule of law on the date of enactment or within one year thereafter, if the taxpayer filed the claim before the date one year after the date of enactment.

EGTRRA's sunset rule would eliminate this clarifying amendment with respect to estates of decedents dying after December 31, 2010.

¶ 1.07 POSSIBLE RETROACTIVE REINSTATEMENT OF THE ESTATE AND GST TAXES

Several key legislative leaders have expressed a desire to reinstate the estate and GST taxes early in 2010, and to do so retroactively in order to eliminate a period of effective repeal. Retroactive reimposition of these taxes will face legal challenges based on claims of unconstitutionality, but ultimately retroactivity should be permitted.

The U.S. Supreme Court has repeatedly upheld retroactive changes in the tax laws where such retroactivity is "confined to short and limited periods required by the practicalities of producing national legislation."[117] Generally, due

---

[116] Tech. Adv. Mem. 9843001 (Oct. 23, 1998); see discussion in Henkel, Estate Planning and Wealth Preservation: Strategies and Solutions ¶ 48.02[3][c] (Thomson Reuters/WG&L, 1997); Stephens, Maxfield, Lind & Calfee, Federal Estate and Gift Taxation ¶ 4.04[8][b] (Thomson Reuters/WG&L, 8th ed. 2002).

[117] Carlton v. United States, 512 US 24 (1994); see also United States v. Hemme, 476 US 558 (1986); United States v. Darusmont, 449 US 292 (1981); Welch v. Henry, 305 US 134 (1938); United States v. Hudson, 299 US 498 (1937); Milliken v. United

process permits retroactive tax legislation if the retroactivity serves a "rational legislative purpose."[118]

Any discussion of the constitutional limitations on retroactive estate tax legislation must focus on *Carlton v. United States*, in which the Supreme Court rejected a due process challenge to a retroactive elimination of an unintended loophole.[119] On October 22, 1986, the then president signed a statute granting an estate tax deduction for one half the proceeds of "any sale of employer securities by the executor of an estate" to an ESOP. On December 10, 1986, Mr. Carlton, as executor for the estate of Willametta K. Day, bought for the estate 1.5 million shares of MCI Communications Corporation for $11,206,000, and then two days later sold the stock (at a loss of 42 cents per share) to the MCI ESOP, deducting $5,287,000 (one half of the sales price) on the decedent's estate tax return.

On December 22, 1987, Congress retroactively amended the Code to limit the deduction to securities that were "directly owned" by the decedent "immediately before death." The amendment applied retroactively, as if it were incorporated in the original 1986 provision.

Mr. Carlton challenged the amendment on the grounds that its retroactivity violated the Due Process Clause of the Fifth Amendment. The U.S. district court granted summary judgment for the IRS, but a divided Ninth Circuit Court of Appeals reversed, holding that such application was rendered unduly harsh and oppressive, and therefore unconstitutional.[120] The Ninth Circuit stressed Carlton's lack of notice that the rule would be retroactively amended and his reasonable and detrimental reliance on the pre-amendment law.

The Supreme Court reversed and upheld the statute, without dissent (though with two concurring opinions reflecting the views of three justices). The Court stated that a retroactive law is constitutionally valid if (1) the government shows that the statute has a rational legislative purpose and is not arbitrary and irrational and (2) the period of retroactivity is "modest." The Court held that the amendment's retroactive application was rationally related to the legitimate legislative purpose of closing an unintended loophole that would result in revenue losses to the fisc, and that the period of retroactivity (fourteen

---

States, 283 US 15 (1931); and Cooper v. United States, 280 US 409 (1930). See also similar opinions from lower courts in NationsBank of Texas v. United States, 44 Fed. Cl. 661 (1999); Kane v. United States, 942 F. Supp. 233 (ED Pa. 1996), aff'd, 118 F3d 1576 (3d Cir. 1997); Quarty v. United States, 170 F3d 961 (9th Cir. 1999). See also discussions in Stephens, Maxfield, Lind & Calfee, Federal Estate and Gift Taxation ¶ 2.01[3] (Thomson Reuters/WG&L, 8th ed. 2002); Westfall & Mair, Estate Planning Law and Taxation ¶ 9.02 (Thomson Reuters/WG&L, 4th ed. 2001).

[118] Carlton v. United States, 512 US 24, 30–31 (1994).

[119] Carlton v. United States, 512 US 24 (1994).

[120] Carlton v. United States, 972 F2d 1051 (9th Cir. 1992).

months) was modest and consistent with the time requirements inherent in enacting national tax legislation.

Justice Scalia wrote a concurring opinion, with which Justice Thomas joined, agreeing that the statute should be sustained, notwithstanding its retroactivity, but strongly criticizing the analysis that the majority had used. Justice Scalia started strongly, stating

> If I thought that "substantive due process" were a constitutional right rather than an oxymoron, I would think it violated by bait-and-switch taxation. Although there is not much precision in the concept "harsh and oppressive," which is what the Court has adopted as its test of substantive due process unconstitutionality in the field of retroactive tax legislation, see, e.g., United States v. Hemme, 476 U.S. 558, 568–569 (1986), quoting Welch v. Henry, 305 U.S. 134, 147 (1938) surely it would cover a retroactive amendment that cost a taxpayer who relied on the original statute's clear meaning over $600,000. Unlike the tax at issue in Hemme, here the amendment "without notice,…gives a different and more oppressive legal effect to conduct undertaken before enactment of the statute." 476 U.S., at 569.[121]

Justice Scalia was not impressed (at least not favorably) by the majority's characterization of the estate tax amendment as merely "a curative measure," nor was he inclined to accept the "post-legislation legislative history (another oxymoron) to show that, despite the uncontested plain meaning of the statute, Congress never meant it to apply to stock that was not owned by the decedent at the time of death."[122] He believed that, whether Congress had treated a citizen oppressively should not depend on whether the oppression was, after all, only a "curing" of an earlier error.

More importantly, Justice Scalia rejected the majority's distinguishing of the earlier cases on retroactivity based on the fact that they involved the imposition of new taxes, rather than a change in tax rates. He characterized the elimination of a specifically promised tax break that was to have been a reward for costly action, after the action has been taken, as being more harsh and oppressive than merely imposing a new tax on past actions. He then stated that

> The reasoning the Court applies to uphold the statute in this case guarantees that all retroactive tax laws will henceforth be valid. To pass constitutional muster the retroactive aspects of the statute need only be "rationally related to a legitimate legislative purpose." Ante, at 9. Revenue raising is certainly a legitimate legislative purpose, see U.S. Const., Art. I, section 8, cl. 1, and any law that retroactively adds a tax, removes

---

[121] Carlton v. United States, 512 US 24, 39 (1994).
[122] Carlton v. United States, 512 US 24, 39 (1994).

a deduction, or increases a rate rationally furthers that goal. I welcome this recognition that the Due Process Clause does not prevent retroactive taxes, since I believe that the Due Process Clause guarantees no substantive rights, but only (as it says) process, see TXO Production Corp. v. Alliance Resources Corp., 509 U.S.___, ___ (1993) (slip op., at 2) (SCALIA, J., concurring in judgment).[123]

Carlton, even considering Justice Scalia's scathing concurring opinion, strongly suggests that any challenge to a 2010 retroactive reinstatement of the estate and GST taxes would be unsuccessful, but there is one basis on which the reinstatement of the estate and GST taxes differs from the curative provision in *Carlton*. The Ninth Circuit's decision in *Carlton* relied in part on two older Supreme Court decisions, which had rejected retroactive imposition of the first federal gift tax.[124] The Supreme Court rejected the relevance of these cases, stating that they "were decided during an era characterized by exacting review of economic legislation under an approach that 'has long since been discarded.'" More importantly, the Court also stated that

> Blodgett and *Untermyer*, which involved the Nation's first gift tax, essentially have been limited to situations involving "the creation of a wholly new tax," and their "authority is of limited value in assessing the constitutionality of subsequent amendments that bring about certain changes in operation of the tax laws."

As the Ninth Circuit stated in a later case, the law distinguishes between the imposition of a wholly new tax and changes in an extant tax because the Constitution does not approve of the imposition of a new tax when the taxpayer has "no reason to suppose that any transactions of the sort will be taxed at all."[125]

Reasonable minds may differ on whether the re-adoption of the estate and GST taxes constitutes the "creation of a wholly new tax." The government would certainly argue that re-enacting an estate tax that dates to World War I and a GST tax that has been in place for over thirty years should be distinguished from enacting the nation's first tax on lifetime donative transfers. Nonetheless, a reasonable argument can be made that the critical issue is the imposition of a new tax on a closed transaction, and there are few ways to close a transaction more firmly than death.

---

[123] Carlton v. United States, 512 US 24, 40 (1994).

[124] Blodgett v. Holden, 275 US 142 (1927); Untermyer v. Anderson, 276 US 440 (1928).

[125] Quarty v. United States, 170 F3d 961 (9th Cir. 1999), quoting United States v. Darusmont, 449 US at 298, 300 (itself quoting Cohan v. Comm'r, 39 F2d 540, 545 (2d Cir. 1930) (Hand, J.)). See also similar views in Cherne v. United States, 277 F3d 1330 (Fed. Cir.), reh'g denied in part and granted in part, 288 F3d 1355 (Fed. Cir. 2002).

There is certain to be extensive litigation over any retroactive reimposition of the estate and GST taxes, but it seems likely that a U.S. Supreme Court that is generally deferential to Congress on tax issues will sustain any reimposition that occurs in 2010. Even if Justice Scalia finds three more justices to join him and Justice Thomas, they, too, would have sustained the change approved in *Carlton.*

It should also be noted that when Congress plans to retroactively change the tax law, the chairmen of the tax writing committees often issue a statement warning taxpayers not to rely on the current state of the law. Congressional staff members from the House Ways and Means Committee and the Senate Finance Committee confirmed on December 31, 2009, that no joint letter of this nature was forthcoming, because the lawmakers could not agree on how best to proceed with the estate and GST taxes.[126]

Practitioners should caution their clients about the chance of retroactive reimposition of the estate and GST taxes, but they should also consider taking advantage of planning opportunities that may exist during the hiatus, particularly where there would be limited downside risk from doing so.

---

[126] BNA Daily Tax Report (Jan. 5, 2009).

CHAPTER **2**

Formula Bequests in Light of the Repeal of the Estate and GST Taxes and the Imposition of Carryover Basis

¶ 2.01	Introduction	2-2
¶ 2.02	Marital/Nonmarital Formula Clauses During Estate Tax Repeal	2-2
¶ 2.03	Document References to the Absence of an Estate or GST Tax	2-3
¶ 2.04	Credit Shelter/Marital Deduction Formula Clauses in Light of Estate Tax Repeal	2-5
	[1] The Problem With Pre-2010 Formulas	2-5
	[2] Alternate Marital/Nonmarital Formulas in 2010	2-9
	[a] Preserving the Status Quo	2-10
	[b] Basis Driven Divisions	2-10
	[i] Smallest possible nonmarital share.	2-11
	[ii] Largest possible nonmarital share.	2-12
	[iii] "Fairly representative" division.	2-13
	[c] Other Divisions	2-14
¶ 2.05	GST Formula Clauses and GST Tax Repeal	2-16
	[1] The Problems With Present Formulas	2-16
	[2] Alternate Generation-Skipping Transfer Tax Formulas for 2010	2-20
	[a] The Effective Date Problem	2-20
	[b] The Formula Division of the Estate	2-23

		[c]	Granting a Power of Appointment Over a GST-Exempt Trust	2-25
¶ 2.06			State Death Tax Formula Clauses in Light of Estate Tax Repeal	2-29
	[1]		The Problems With Present Formulas	2-29
	[2]		Decoupling	2-29
		[a]	Determining Which State Taxes Apply to Your Client	2-29
			[i] Apportionment.	2-30
			[ii] Nondomiciliary taxation of tangible property.	2-30
			[iii] Multiple domiciles.	2-32
		[b]	Decoupled State Taxes	2-34
	[3]		State Death Tax Formulas	2-36
		[a]	The State-Only QTIP	2-36
		[b]	When There Is No State-Only QTIP	2-38
¶ 2.07			Best Formula Solutions for 2010	2-39
	[1]		One-Trust Arrangement	2-39
	[2]		QTIP Trust Plus Disclaimer	2-42
	[3]		Substantial Sprinkling Nonmarital Trust	2-44

¶ 2.01 INTRODUCTION

The primary feature of virtually all estate plans is testamentary planning. Economic Growth and Tax Relief Act of 2001 (EGTRRA) affects testamentary planning in 2010 more dramatically than it affects any other aspect of estate planning. The practical estate planner must consider how to modify the testamentary plan of most clients in light of EGTRRA and its sunset provisions. In most cases, this will require the inclusion of special provisions that address the treatment of the estate if the client dies while no federal estate tax applies to his or her estate. Some of these changes will be designed to clarify the client's intent, some to take advantage of the now effective carryover basis provisions, and some to take advantage of the few situations in which the repeal of the generation-skipping transfer (GST) tax for 2010 may offer significant planning opportunities.

¶ 2.02 MARITAL/NONMARITAL FORMULA CLAUSES DURING ESTATE TAX REPEAL

An estate planner drafting documents for any tax-planned estate must now consider making alternate dispositions if the client dies in 2010, while the estate tax does not apply. Obviously, estate planners should not abandon estate tax planning due to the anticipated momentary repeal, because most clients will live past 2010. An estate planner should, however, consider whether the efficacy of tax planning for a client expected to die after 2010 would still exist if the client actually dies in 2010, when no estate or GST tax applies.

There is no single 2010 alternate disposition that will be appropriate for all clients. The estate planner and the client must together consider the client's nontax goals, including to whom assets should pass, which family members require or deserve greater shares of the estate, which family members require professional assistance in asset management, and which family members might need additional protection from the claims of future creditors (or a spouse in a divorce). These factors should already be reflected in an estate plan, but many clients spend all of their time in the estate planning process trying to understand the tax planning used in their documents, and they do not focus sufficiently on nontax provision and their goals. The nontax goals become more important in planning for dispositions in 2010, when the estate and GST taxes are not as important.

One tax consideration that must be discussed in evaluating the alternate post-estate tax disposition is the carryover basis in the decedent's assets, including effective use of the $1.3 million aggregate basis increase and $3 million spousal property basis increase. The estate planner should favor a 2010 disposition that takes the fullest possible advantage of both basis adjustments. Unfortunately, as is discussed below, this is not as simple as it might at first glance appear.

¶ 2.03 DOCUMENT REFERENCES TO THE ABSENCE OF AN ESTATE OR GST TAX

Revising a client's documents to include a different disposition in 2010 when the federal estate and GST taxes are not applicable to the client's estate should take into account the possibility that Congress will retroactively re-institute these taxes. Generally, any disposition that is intended to occur if there is a federal estate or GST tax in effect on the date of the decedent's death should also be required if, though there is no such tax in effect on the actual date of death, Congress retroactively reenacts it to be effective as of the date of the decedent's death.

Conditioning a disposition on the existence or application of a tax that may retroactively be imposed with respect to the estate, however, prevents the decedent's personal representative or trustee from dividing the estate or making significant distributions until the status of the estate or GST tax with respect to this estate is settled. This could make it more difficult to administer the estate, and may preclude providing interim distributions to beneficiaries that may require them for necessaries or similar items and services.

The constitutional limitations on retroactive tax legislation provide only the most limited planning assistance for practitioners, and thus cannot be relied upon with any certainty. It is often suggested that the shorter the time between the date of repeal (January 1, 2010, in this case) and the date of reenactment, the less the risk of a successful constitutional challenge to retroactivity, but there is no bright line standard by which to determine that particular legislation is or is not constitutionally retroactive. In *Carlton v. United States*,[1] for example, the U.S. Supreme Court held that an estate tax amendment's retroactive application was constitutional, in part because the period of retroactivity (i.e., fourteen months) was "modest" and "confined to short and limited periods required by the practicalities of producing national legislation."

Carlton involved the elimination of a loophole inadvertently created by Congress in a specifically allowed estate tax deduction; one can only speculate on whether, after their intended repeal, the entire estate and GST taxes can be re-enacted retroactively after fourteen months.[2] Some have argued that the fact that the taxes are, at least presently, due to be reinstated on January 1, 2011, deprives taxpayers of the ability to rely on an ongoing repeal, but others have suggested that having a specific date for the restoration of these taxes makes it easier for taxpayers to justifiably rely on their absence in 2010.

Any congressional action taken after December 31, 2010, it may be noted, would be taken by the 112th Congress, rather than the 111th Congress that presided over the period in which these taxes were to be absent. This could arguably bolster the strength of a constitutional challenge to the retroactivity of the reenactment, though there are no cases expressly stating that one Congress cannot retroactively undo the acts of a prior Congress. It should be further noted that the actual repeal of the estate and GST taxes was passed by the 107th Congress in 2001, and that whether the taxes are reinstated by the 111th Congress or the 112th Congress should be immaterial in the context of a constitutional challenge.

Accordingly, the practical estate planner should strike a balance between leaving an estate or trust administration open indefinitely to await possible retroactive legislation and ignoring entirely the chances of retroactive reinstatement of the estate and GST taxes. It seems most likely that, if retroactive legislation does occur, it will do so before the end of 2010. Thus, one could require that a fiduciary await the possibility of retroactive legislation only until January 1, 2011. One could also require that a fiduciary await retroactive legislation until April 1, 2011, which is two weeks before the executor is required to file the carryover basis tax return for the estate, or pick an arbitrary date that seems reasonable, such as one year from the date of death.

---

[1] Carlton v. United States, 512 US 24 (1994), discussed at ¶ 1.07.

[2] See also United States v. Darusmont, 449 US 292, 296–297 (1981) (per curiam) (noting Congress's practice of confining retroactive application of tax provisions to "short and limited periods").

One must also consider that an estate that contains alternative dispositions, to account for whether there is a federal estate or GST tax applicable
with respect to the decedent's estate, must remain open not only while Congress considers retroactively reinstating these taxes, but also until the final resolution of the litigation that such retroactive legislation will undoubtedly
produce. In *Carlton*, the Supreme Court's opinion was issued nearly seven
years after the legislation that produced the litigation. Thus, even if one limits
the will or trust instrument to consideration of retroactive legislation enacted
before January 1, 2011, the fiduciary may not know the shares of the various
beneficiaries until several years after the date of the decedent's death.

Drafting Tip: The following statement should be included in a will or trust that contains
special provisions applicable only if the decedent dies when there is no federal estate
tax or GST tax applicable. The language can be modified if the special provisions
relate only to the existence of the federal estate tax or only to the existence of the
federal GST tax.

> **Retroactive Legislation.** I include in this instrument certain dispositions
> and direct certain actions, or both, that shall occur only if, on the date of my
> death, no federal estate tax or federal generation-skipping transfer tax applies
> with respect to my estate. These provisions shall not apply if, on the date of my
> death, no federal estate tax or federal generation-skipping transfer tax, as the
> case may be, applies with respect to my estate, but such tax (or taxes) is (or are)
> retroactively reinstated before April 1, 2011, and apply under such retroactive
> legislation with respect to my estate. If such retroactive legislation is finally
> determined to be unconstitutional or otherwise invalid, these references shall
> apply as if such retroactive legislation had never been enacted. My fiduciary shall
> not be liable to any beneficiary for refusing to establish separate shares under
> this instrument or to make distributions where the entitlement of any beneficiary
> to a separate share or distribution cannot be established until the April 1, 2011, or
> until the termination of litigation over such retroactive legislation as referred to in
> this paragraph.

¶ 2.04 CREDIT SHELTER/MARITAL DEDUCTION FORMULA CLAUSES IN LIGHT OF ESTATE TAX REPEAL

[1] The Problem With Pre-2010 Formulas

Most estate plans for married clients include a reduce-to-zero formula that
leaves to the decedent's children or a nonmarital trust for the benefit of the de-

cedent's family an amount (or fractional share) equal to the decedent's applicable exclusion amount. This figure was $3.5 million in 2009, but wills and revocable trusts invariably use a formula clause to describe the amount that will pass to the nonmarital share.

These formula clauses are designed in many ways. One common formula clause leaves to the nonmarital share the largest amount (or fractional share) that can pass without federal estate taxes on the decedent's estate. Such a clause in a 2009 instrument would have produced a $3.5 million nonmarital share and a marital residue. A second approach leaves to the nonmarital share an amount (or fractional share) equal to the decedent's applicable exclusion amount. A third type of clause describes the marital share, rather than the nonmarital share. Such a clause would usually create a marital share equal to the smallest amount (or fractional share) necessary to reduce the federal estate tax on the decedent's estate to zero.

These three approaches all would have produced substantially identical estate divisions before or after 2010, but without an estate tax, they may produce widely disparate results.

> **EXAMPLE 2-1:** Adam, Beth, Charlie, and Dave are siblings. Each is married and has two children. Each has an estate of $10 million. Adam's will leaves to a nonmarital trust for his children the largest amount that can pass without federal estate taxes on his estate, and leaves the residue of his estate to his wife. Beth's will leaves to a nonmarital trust for her children an amount equal to her applicable exclusion amount, and leaves the residue of her estate to her husband. Charlie's will leaves to his wife the smallest amount necessary to reduce the federal estate tax on his estate to zero, and leaves the residue of his estate to a nonmarital trust for his children. Dave's will leaves to a nonmarital trust for his children the largest amount that can pass free of federal estate tax because of his applicable exclusion amount, and leaves the residue of his estate to his wife. In 2009, all four wills created a $3.5 million nonmarital trust and a $6.5 million marital gift.
>
> All four of the siblings die at a family reunion in 2010, after eating insalubrious sausages. All four wills are ambiguous and four suits are brought in state court to construe the instruments. The judges construe each according to the plain language of the instrument, and hold that (a) Adam's will leaves 100 percent of his estate to his nonmarital trust because that is the largest amount that can pass to the nonmarital trust without incurring a federal estate tax, as there is no federal estate tax on the estate of a decedent who dies in 2010; (b) Beth's will leaves everything to her husband because there is no applicable exclusion amount by which to measure the nonmarital trust's share; (c) Charlie's will leaves 100 percent of his estate to his nonmarital trust because no marital gift is required to avoid all federal estate taxes with respect to Charlie's estate; (d) Dave's will leaves 100 percent of his estate to his wife because there is no applicable exclusion amount in 2010 by which to measure the nonmarital trust's share.

The precise meaning of these formula clauses in 2010 may be further complicated by collateral provisions, such as a provision that requires that the marital share be satisfied solely from property qualifying for the marital deduction. There is no marital deduction applicable to estates of decedents dying in 2010, and no assets can qualify for it.

> **EXAMPLE 2-2:** Assume the same facts as in Example 2-1. Beth's will seems to create a 100 percent marital disposition because there is no applicable exclusion amount, but it also provides that Beth's marital gift may be satisfied only with property that qualifies for the federal estate tax marital deduction. As there is no federal estate tax marital deduction with respect to estates of decedents dying in 2010, there is no property that can be used to satisfy the marital gift under Beth's will. It may be argued that Beth's estate cannot be distributed either to the nonmarital trust or the marital share, and that Beth dies intestate.

These formula clauses, unless clarified by codicil or amendment, will certainly produce substantial litigation to construe these wills. The results of a suit to construe such a clause in the absence of a federal estate tax are difficult to discern. Gifts of the maximum that can pass free of federal estate tax, gifts of the minimum marital share that will produce zero tax, and gifts of the applicable exclusion amount are ambiguous in the absence of a federal estate tax.

It is often said that the primary goal of a will or trust construction is to ascertain the testator's or grantor's intention, but the law actually looks for the intention as it is expressed in the governing instrument.[3] Furthermore, a court must determine whether this ambiguity is a patent ambiguity apparent from the face of the instrument or a latent ambiguity that arises only from the extrinsic fact that the federal estate tax has been repealed. Extrinsic evidence may be introduced to construe only latent ambiguities. Patent ambiguities must be construed under the rules of judicial construction.[4]

---

[3] See, e.g., Restatement (Third) of Property (Wills & Don. Trans.) § 11.1 (2003); Unif. Prob. Code § 2-603 ("[T]he intention of a testator as expressed in his will controls."); See, e.g., Diana v. Bentsen, 677 So. 2d 1374 (Fla. App. 1st Dist. 1996); In re Estate of McGahee, 550 So. 2d 83 (Fla. App. 1st Dist. 1989), review denied, 560 So. 2d 232 (Fla. 1990); Matter of Estate of Edgar, 389 NW2d 696 (Mich. 1986); Stack v. United States, 23 F3d 1400 (8th Cir. 1994); In re Estate of Hannan, 513 NW2d 339 (Neb. Ct. App. 1994), rev'd, 523 NW2d 672, 246 Neb. 828 (1995); Matter of Estate of Johnson, 501 NW2d 342 (ND 1993); In re Estate of Stiefel, 24 App. Div. 3d 994, 807 NYS2d 159 (Dep't 2005); Matter of Estate of Campbell, 171 Misc. 2d 892, 655 NYS2d 913 (Sur. Ct. 1997); In re Hyde's Will, 18 NYS2d 243 (Sur. Ct. 1953); Matter of Estate of Klein, 434 NW2d 560 (ND 1989); Matter of Estate of Hamilton, 869 P2d 971 (Utah Ct. App. 1994), cert. denied, 879 P2d 266 (Utah 1994).

[4] Unif. Prob. Code § 603 cmt.; Bob Jones Univ. v. Strandell, 543 SE2d 251, 344 SC 224 (Ct. App. 2001).

These formula clauses would arguably appear to create latent ambiguities because the instrument is not ambiguous until one introduces evidence of the absence of a federal estate tax. Admitting extrinsic evidence, however, may still not clarify the disposition, because such testators or grantors usually only contemplated tax-driven dispositions.

One could argue that the type of formula demonstrates the decedent's choice of priorities. A formula that leaves the children the most that can pass free of federal estate tax, it would be argued, demonstrates that the decedent's highest priority was to provide for the children. A formula that leaves the children the applicable exclusion amount, it would be argued, demonstrates an intent to leave them assets only if there was a tax advantage to doing so.

These arguments are interesting, but the only thing that one can know with any degree of certainty about formula clauses, which divide an estate or trust between marital and nonmarital shares based on federal estate tax rules, is that the cost of litigation will be high. Therefore, it is crucial to modify these clauses at the earliest opportunity to address expressly the disposition of the estate in the absence of a federal estate tax.

The ambiguity in these clauses also raises some potential tax problems even if the courts quickly construe the clauses in a manner that the beneficiaries all view as reasonable. The U.S. Supreme Court's decision in *Commissioner v. Bosch*[5] states that the federal courts and agencies, including the IRS, are bound with respect to state law only by the decisions of the highest court of a state. A federal authority must, where there is no decision by the highest court of a state, apply what it finds to be the state law after giving "proper regard" to relevant rulings of other courts of the state. The IRS and the federal courts are, therefore, free to construe a formula clause in a will or trust differently from the manner in which a state trial court construes the same clause. This could lead to substantial estate and gift tax problems.

> **EXAMPLE 2-3:** Dave dies in 2010. Dave's will creates a nonmarital trust for the benefit of Dave's wife and children, with distributions to be made in the discretion of the trustee. Dave leaves to the nonmarital trust an amount equal to his applicable exclusion amount. The balance of Dave's estate is left outright to Dave's wife. Dave's executor brings an action in state court to construe the will and joins all proper parties, including all of the beneficiaries under the will. The court hears arguments and concludes that the formula clause is ambiguous, and it admits evidence from Dave's drafting attorney as to Dave's goals in using this language. The state court concludes that the nonmarital trust should receive at least as much as it would have received had Dave died on the date he signed the will. In this case, that creates a $3.5 million nonmarital trust. The IRS, however, could dispute this construction and determine that the highest court in the state would have concluded that the entire estate should pass

---

[5] Comm'r v. Bosch, 387 US 456 (1966).

to Dave's widow. The IRS could then deem the widow to have constructively transferred the assets to the nonmarital trust, resulting in a $3.5 million taxable gift by her. Furthermore, because the widow is a beneficiary of the trust and its deemed transferor, her creditors could, under state law, compel the trustee to distribute assets to her to satisfy her obligations. Therefore, the nonmarital trust would be includible in her gross estate.[6]

A few state legislatures are considering legislation that would impose some uniform construction on provisions in a will or trust that refer to the federal estate tax or GST tax rules and terms, and that must be construed with respect to years in which there is no such tax. These provisions should be binding upon the IRS and should eliminate a great deal of uncertainty, but they will often not provide as good a tax result as would be achieved by careful estate planning.[7]

It is understood that at least one other state will consider legislation that would permit the beneficiaries of an estate to agree amongst themselves as to the meaning of such a clause. And, another state is considering legislation that would permit a local court to construe the instrument, and to take testimony from the drafter as to the meaning of the ambiguous provisions. Such approaches may create constructions that appear to produce a more favorable tax result than the division of the estate based on the law in effect on December 31, 2009, but the IRS may well decline to be bound by the decision of the beneficiaries or the construction of a trial court. Practical estate planners should rely on state statutes to resolve these ambiguities only after attempting to convince the client to eliminate the ambiguity by amendment or codicil to the affected instrument.

[2] Alternate Marital/Nonmarital Formulas in 2010

There are several different approaches that one may wish to take in dividing an estate or trust between marital and nonmarital shares when the testator or grantor dies during 2010 and there is no federal estate tax.

---

[6] See Rev. Rul. 84-105, 1984-2 CB 197 (surviving spouse, who acquiesced in underfunding of a testamentary trust for the spouse's benefit by not appealing a local probate court's order, was treated as making a gift to the person or persons who receive the property that would otherwise have comprised the trust). See also Priv. Ltr. Rul. 201004022 (Sept. 15, 2009).

[7] See, e.g., Md. HB 449 (2009); NY A09857 (2009); Tenn. SB 3045 (2009); Va. HB 755 (2009).

[a] Preserving the Status Quo

One of the simplest solutions to dividing an estate between marital and nonmarital shares in 2010 is to preserve the division that would have applied in 2009, with which the client was presumably both cognizant and comfortable. This can be accomplished by adding a clause to the instrument that states that, if there is no federal estate tax applicable with respect to the decedent's estate, the formula clause will be construed as it would have been construed had the decedent died on December 31, 2009.

Drafting Tip: The following provision could be included in a will or trust (or added by codicil or amendment) that contains a formula under which the estate or trust fund is divided between a marital and a nonmarital share based on provisions of federal estate tax law. The language can be modified to refer only to those terms actually used in the instrument.

> **Certain References to Federal Estate Tax.** I direct in this instrument that certain dispositions or divisions be made based on the amount of the federal estate tax "applicable exclusion amount" or the "largest fractional share that can pass free of federal estate taxes" with respect to my estate.[8] If I die when there is no federal estate tax applicable with respect to my estate, these references shall be deemed to refer to the federal estate tax laws as they applied with respect to estates of decedents dying on December 31, 2009.

The potential defect with a clause that preserves the 2009 division of an estate is that it does not necessarily take full advantage of the basis adjustments under the carryover basis rules. The division assures a $3.5 million nonmarital share, which may not leave sufficient marital share assets to take full advantage of the $3 million spousal property basis increase. Also, this division may unnecessarily increase the size of the surviving spouse's taxable estate.

[b] Basis Driven Divisions

Another approach to dividing the estate between marital and nonmarital shares in 2010 is to leave the nonmarital share sufficient assets to take full ad-

---

[8] The various terms that may need to be referred to in such a clause could include the "unified credit," "estate tax exemption," "applicable exemption amount," "applicable credit amount," "applicable exclusion amount," "generation-skipping transfer tax exemption," "GST exemption," "marital deduction," "maximum marital deduction," "unlimited marital deduction," "inclusion ratio," "applicable fraction," or any section number of the federal Internal Revenue Code relating to estate tax or generation skipping transfer tax, or "the largest amount that could pass free of Federal estate tax with respect to my estate."

vantage of the $1.3 million aggregate basis increase, and then leave the marital share the balance of the estate, increasing the likelihood of taking full advantage of the spousal property basis increase. A client whose estate is large enough that more than $4.3 million in appreciation exists against which these basis increases can be allocated, may leave the assets remaining, after fully using both basis increases, to whomever the client chooses, without regard to income tax considerations.

> **EXAMPLE 2-4:** Wilma has an estate of $7 million. Wilma's adjusted basis in her assets is $2 million. Wilma's will creates a nonmarital share equal to that fraction of her estate that will have $1.3 million of net appreciation, considering only assets to which the aggregate basis increase can be allocated. Wilma's will creates a marital share equal to the balance of her residuary estate. This arrangement enables Wilma's executor to allocate her entire $1.3 million aggregate basis increase to the nonmarital share and her entire $3 million spousal property basis increase to the marital share, taking full advantage of both basis increases.

The share of a decedent's estate that can take advantage of the aggregate basis increase or spousal property basis increase is determined by the difference between the decedent's adjusted basis in the various assets and their fair market value. There are several ways in which the assets can be allocated between these two shares, and the manner in which they are allocated determines the size of the shares, as well as the total of the available basis adjustments used effectively by the estate plan.

[i] Smallest possible nonmarital share. One approach is to select assets for the nonmarital share with the smallest total value that reflects $1.3 million in appreciation. This requires that the assets selected have the lowest total adjusted basis and the highest aggregate percentage of appreciation of the assets available to satisfy the two shares. This approach creates the largest possible marital share, but it may also shift a disproportionate share of the total future tax liability on the appreciation in the decedent's property to the nonmarital share.

> **EXAMPLE 2-5:** Wilma has an estate of $7 million. Wilma's basis in her assets is $2 million, as follows:

Asset	Basis	Value
Acme stock	$ 500,000	$2,000,000
Beta stock	$ 500,000	$3,000,000
Gamma stock	$ 500,000	$1,000,000
Delta stock	$ 500,000	$1,000,000
Total	$2,000,000	$7,000,000

Wilma's will creates a nonmarital share and a marital share. Wilma's will directs her personal representative to allocate to the nonmarital share the smallest value of assets (those with lowest basis and the largest percentage of appreciation) that will reflect $1.3 million in appreciation.

Wilma's personal representative will satisfy the nonmarital share with Beta stock worth $1,560,000 and having a basis of $260,000). Wilma's personal representative will allocate Wilma's $1.3 million aggregate basis increase to the assets of the nonmarital share, producing a $1,560,000 nonmarital share with a $1,560,000 adjusted basis. Wilma's marital share will be worth $5,440,000. Wilma's personal representative will allocate all of Wilma's $3 million spousal property basis increase to the marital share, for a total basis in those assets of $4,740,000 ($3 million + $1,740,000).

Drafting Tip: The following language should produce the smallest nonmarital share sufficient to receive a $1.3 million aggregate basis increase:

> **B. Nonmarital Share.** The "Nonmarital Share" shall be a fractional share of my Residuary Estate.
>
> **(1)** The numerator of the fraction shall equal the smallest value of the assets of my Residuary Estate to which my Personal Representative can allocate the entire aggregate basis increase allowed under federal income tax laws for property not acquired by a surviving spouse; and
>
> **(2)** The denominator of the fraction shall equal the value of my Residuary Estate, taking into account only those assets to which my Personal Representative may legally allocate part of my aggregate basis increase.

[ii] Largest possible nonmarital share. The nonmarital share could also be satisfied with assets having the greatest possible value that reflects no more than $1.3 million in net appreciation. This requires that the assets selected have the highest adjusted basis and the smallest aggregate percentage of appreciation of all of the assets available to satisfy the two shares. This approach creates a nonmarital share with the highest possible value, but it may shift a disproportionate share of the total future tax liability on the appreciation in the decedent's property to the marital share.

> **EXAMPLE 2-6:** Assume the same facts as in Example 2-5, except that Wilma's will directs that her personal representative allocate to the nonmarital share the largest value of assets that will reflect $1.3 million in appreciation. This will favor the beneficiaries of the nonmarital share and disadvantage Dave, Wilma's husband. Wilma's personal representative will satisfy the nonmarital share with all of the Gamma and Delta stock (worth $2 million and having a basis of $1 million), and $400,000 of Acme stock (having a basis of $100,000), and will allocate Wilma's entire $1.3 million aggregate basis increase to the nonmarital share, producing a $2.4 million nonmarital share with a $2.4 million adjusted basis. Wilma's marital share will be worth $4.9 million, and will have a basis of

$3.7 million ($700,000, plus all of Wilma's $3 million additional basis adjustment).

Drafting Tip: The following language should produce the largest nonmarital share that will absorb a $1.3 million aggregate basis increase:

> **B. Nonmarital Share.** The "Nonmarital Share" shall be a fractional share of my Residuary Estate.
>
> **(1)** The numerator of the fraction shall equal the largest value of those assets of my Residuary Estate in which the difference between the fair market value on the date of my death and the adjusted basis for federal income tax purposes in which shall be equal to the aggregate basis increase allowed under federal income tax laws for property not acquired by a surviving spouse; and
>
> **(2)** The denominator of the fraction shall equal the value of my Residuary Estate, taking into account only those assets to which my Personal Representative may legally allocate part of my aggregate basis increase.

[iii] "Fairly representative" division. A client who is concerned about avoiding disputes between or among the spouse and the beneficiaries of the nonmarital share may require that the assets allocated to the nonmarital share fairly reflect the appreciation and depreciation in all of the assets available for allocation. This approach will allocate the total available basis adjustments and the total potential capital gains equitably between the two shares.

EXAMPLE 2-7: Assume the same facts as in Example 2-5, except that Wilma's will directs that her personal representative allocate assets between the marital and nonmarital share in a manner that fairly reflects the appreciation and depreciation in the assets available, but that still provides the nonmarital share with $1.3 million of appreciation. The net appreciation in Wilma's estate is 5/7ths of the total fair market value of the assets ($7 million - $2 million = $5 million net appreciation; $5 million/$7million = 5/7 or 71.43%). Therefore, the $1.3 million aggregate basis increase should be satisfied with assets with a total fair market value of $1,820,000 ($1,300,000 x [1/.7143]). Wilma's personal representative will satisfy the nonmarital share with the following assets: (a) 26 percent of the Acme shares ($520,000 value; $130,000 basis); (b) 26 percent of the Beta shares ($780,000 value; $130,000 basis); and (c) 52 percent of the Delta shares ($520,000 value; $260,000 basis). The share will thus have a total value of $1,820,000 value and a basis of $520,000.

Wilma's personal representative will then allocate Wilma's $1.3 million aggregate basis increase to the nonmarital share, producing a $1,820,000 nonmarital share with a $1,820,000 adjusted basis ($130,000 + $130,000 + $260,000 + $1,300,000). Wilma's marital share will be worth $5,180,000 ($7,000,000 - $1,820,000), and will have a basis of

$4,480,000 ($1,480,000, plus Wilma's $3 million spousal property basis increase).

Drafting Tip: The following language should produce a fairly representative selection of assets:

> **B. Nonmarital Share.** The "Nonmarital Share" shall be a fractional share of my Residuary Estate.
>
> **(1)** The numerator of the fraction shall equal the value of the assets of my Residuary Estate to which my Personal Representative can allocate the entire aggregate basis increase allowed under federal income tax laws for property not acquired by a surviving spouse; and
>
> **(2)** The denominator of the fraction shall equal the value of my Residuary Estate.
>
> **(3)** My Personal Representative shall select the assets that shall constitute the Family Share in manner such that the untaxed appreciation income tax purposes of any property allocated to the Family Share shall be fairly representative of the untaxed appreciation of all property available for such allocation (excluding, for this purpose, any property to which my Personal Representative cannot validly allocate any of the aggregate basis increase under federal income tax law). References in this paragraph B to my Residuary Estate shall include only those portions of my Residuary Estate to which my aggregate basis increase may be allocated under federal income tax law.

---

[c] Other Divisions

A client whose nonmarital share has very different beneficiaries from those of the marital share, or who provides very different benefits to the same beneficiaries, should consider creating an alternate formula that assures a fair division of the estate between the nonmarital and marital shares when there is no estate tax. Merely terminating the formula division and leaving the entire estate to the marital share may disinherit family members who have no likely prospect of receiving assets from the surviving spouse. Merely terminating the formula division and leaving the entire estate to a nonmarital share, even if the surviving spouse is one of the beneficiaries, may lead the surviving spouse to renounce the will and claim a statutory share under applicable state law.

> **EXAMPLE 2-8:** Wilma has an estate of $6 million, and her husband, Dave, has a separate estate of $2 million. Wilma's present will creates a nonmarital share for the benefit of Dave and Wilma's three children by a prior marriage. Dave and the two older children are co-trustees, and they have the discretion to distribute income and principal of the nonmarital share unequally among the beneficiaries. The rest of Wilma's estate is left in a marital trust for Dave's exclusive lifetime benefit.

Wilma's will creates a nonmarital share that is equal to the greatest amount that can pass free of estate tax to the nonmarital share trust. This will shift the entire estate to the nonmarital share in 2010 because there is no estate tax. Wilma should amend her will so that, if she dies in 2010, it will create a nonmarital share that would be equal to some specified share of her estate.

The precise percentage division between the marital and nonmarital shares in such estates depends on the nontax goals of the client and the nontax needs of the family, but it should not ignore the $3 million spousal basis adjustment. It is appropriate, in such cases, to leave a marital share large enough to take advantage of the $3 million spousal property basis increase to the maximum extent possible.

Drafting Tip: The following clause creates a 50-percent fractional nonmarital share if there is no federal estate tax applicable on the date of death. The 50-percent figure was arbitrarily chosen.

 B. Estate Tax Exemption Share. The "Estate Tax Exemption Share" shall be a fractional share of my Residuary Estate.

 (1) The numerator of the fraction shall equal the largest value of my Residuary Estate that can pass free of federal estate tax by reason of the unified credit allowable to my estate. This value shall be determined after being reduced by reason of my adjusted taxable gifts, all other dispositions of property included in my gross estate for which no deduction is allowed in computing my federal estate tax, and administration expenses and other charges to principal that are not claimed and allowed as federal estate tax deductions. The numerator of the fraction shall, however, be an amount equal to one half (½) of the value of my Residuary Estate if there is no federal estate tax applicable with respect to my estate on the date of my death.

 (2) The denominator of the fraction shall equal the value of my Residuary Estate.

¶ 2.05 GST FORMULA CLAUSES AND GST TAX REPEAL

[1] The Problems With Present Formulas

Many wills and trusts create GST-exempt and GST-nonexempt shares based on the testator's or grantor's unused GST exemption.[9] Typically, the GST-exempt share is held in a trust in which the beneficial enjoyment is shared by family members assigned to multiple generations below that of the testator or grantor, such as a trust for all of the testator's or grantor's descendants. A trust that continues in this fashion for the longest period permitted by law is often referred to as a "dynasty trust."[10]

The GST nonexempt share is usually held in a trust that continues for the lifetime of the testator's or grantor's then-living children. Often, this share is itself divided into separate shares for each child, and each child is given a testamentary general power of appointment so that, when he or she dies, his or her share of the nonexempt trust is included in his or her gross estate for federal estate tax purposes, rather than being subjected to the GST tax. This permits the use of the child's unexpended applicable exclusion amount to reduce the taxes imposed at his or her death and, if the child exercises the power of

---

[9] The many, many difficult issues relating to the application of the GST tax with respect to decedents dying in 2010, generation-skipping transfers made in 2010, and transfers made in 2010 to generation-skipping trusts, are discussed in greater detail in Chapter 4.

[10] A dynasty trust may continue for the maximum period of the applicable rule against perpetuities, or in states that have repealed the rule against perpetuities, may continue until the class has no more members, typically because there are no more living descendants of the transferor. On planning with dynasty trusts generally, see Harrington, Plaine & Zaritsky, Generation-Skipping Transfer Tax ¶¶ 4.01, 9.04, 9.05 (Thomson Reuters/WG&L, 2d ed. 2001); Esperti, Peterson & Keebler, Irrevocable Trusts: Analysis With Forms ch. 15 (Thomson Reuters/WG&L 1998); Leimberg & Zaritsky, Tax Planning With Life Insurance: Analysis With Forms ¶ 5.03[7][d] (Thomson Reuters/WG&L, 2d ed. 1998); Zaritsky, Tax Planning for Family Wealth Transfers: Analysis With Forms ¶ 4.10 (Thomson Reuters/WG&L, 4th ed. 2002); see also Fox, IV & Huft, "Asset Protection and Dynasty Trusts," 37 Real Prop. Prob. & Tr. J. 287 (2002); Foye, "Using South Dakota Law for Perpetual Trusts," 12 Prob. & Prop. 17 (Jan./Feb. 1998); Oshins & Blattmachr, "Megatrusts and Megainsurancetrusts," 46 J. Am. Soc'y CLU & ChFC 30 (Mar. 1991); Note, Dynasty Trusts and the Rule Against Perpetuities," 116 Harv. L. Rev. 2588 (2003); Slade & Blattmachr, "Skipping Generations With Irrevocable Life Insurance Trusts," 132 Tr. & Est. 10 (Apr. 1993). See also an excellent discussion of the difficult problem of selecting the trustee for a dynasty trust in Mathieu, "How to Choose and Evaluate a Corporate Trustee for Long-Term Trusts," 27 Est. Plan. 80 (Feb. 2000). For a particularly interesting discussion of the continued practical validity of the Rule Against Perpetuities, see Klooster, "Are the Justifications for the Rule Against Perpetuities Still Persuasive?" 30 ACTEC J. 95 (Fall 2004).

appointment in favor of a surviving spouse, permits the use of the marital deduction to defer these taxes further, as well as permitting the use of the surviving spouse's applicable exclusion amount to further reduce or avoid them
altogether.[11]

Unmarried clients will often divide their entire estate between GST exempt and nonexempt shares based solely on the available GST exemption.
Married clients will usually effectuate this division by treating the nonmarital
share as a GST-exempt trust, and sometimes adding to it a special qualified
terminable interest property (QTIP) marital trust for which the reverse QTIP
election under Section 2652(a)(3) is made to treat the decedent as the transferor of the reverse QTIP trust for GST tax purposes.[12] The nonmarital trust
and the reverse QTIP trust will together constitute the GST exempt share of
the estate.

> **EXAMPLE 2-9:** Tom is a widower with an estate of $8 million. Tom's
> will leaves his estate in trust for his three children, his grandchildren, and
> his more remote descendants, including both those now alive and those
> born after Tom's death. Tom's will leaves his estate in two shares. One
> share, the GST exempt share, is equal to Tom's unused GST exemption,
> and will be held in trust for Tom's descendants for the maximum period
> allowed under the applicable rule against perpetuities. The other share, the
> GST nonexempt share, is equal to the rest of Tom's estate and will be
> held in separate trusts for the lifetime benefit of Tom's children. Each of
> Tom's children has a testamentary general power to appoint his or her
> own separate GST nonexempt trust and, in default of appointment, that
> trust fund is distributed to his or her descendants. Therefore, any ambigu-
> ity regarding the relative shares, because of the difficulty interpreting the
> formulas in the absence of estate and GST taxes, could alter the manner
> in which the assets are ultimately disposed.
>
> Tom dies in 2009. Tom's unused GST exemption is $3.5 million,
> and the GST exempt trust is created with a fund of $3.5 million. The rest
> of Tom's estate, $4.5 million ($8 million − $3.5 million), is held as the
> GST nonexempt share. A $1.5 million trust ($4.5 million ÷ 3) is created
> for each of Tom's three children under the GST nonexempt share.
>
> **EXAMPLE 2-10:** Tom and Wanda are a married couple. They each have a
> separate estate of approximately $5 million. Each of them has a will and
> a revocable trust under which, at the first spouse's death, three trusts are
> created. A nonmarital trust is created equal to the first spouse's unused
> applicable exclusion amount. A reverse QTIP trust is created equal to the
> difference, if any, between the first spouse's unused GST exemption and

[11] See Harrington, Plaine & Zaritsky, Generation-Skipping Transfer Tax ¶ 9.05
(Thomson Reuters/WG&L, 2d ed. 2001).

[12] See Harrington, Plaine & Zaritsky, Generation-Skipping Transfer Tax ¶ 4.08
(Thomson Reuters/WG&L, 2d ed. 2001).

his or her unused applicable exclusion amount. (A spouse may have an applicable exclusion amount that is less than his or her GST exemption because he or she has made lifetime or testamentary gifts to children or other non-skip persons.) The residue under both sets of documents is held in a QTIP marital trust for the surviving spouse. When the first spouse dies, the nonmarital trust and any reverse QTIP trust will be the GST-exempt share of the estate, and the residuary QTIP will be the GST nonexempt share of the estate.

The nonmarital trust under each set of instruments is held for the lifetime benefit of the surviving spouse and the couple's descendants. After both spouses have died, the nonmarital trust and the reverse QTIP are held as dynasty trusts for the common benefit of all of the couple's descendants for the maximum period of the applicable rule against perpetuities. The regular QTIP trusts, after the surviving spouse has died, are divided into separate share trusts for each child and his or her descendants, and each child has a general power of appointment over his or her trust fund at his or her later death. Therefore, any ambiguity regarding the relative shares, because of the difficulty interpreting the formulas in the absence of estate and GST taxes, could alter the manner in which the assets are ultimately disposed.

Tom dies in 2009, having made $500,000 of lifetime gifts to his children and other non-skip beneficiaries. Under his instruments, his nonmarital trust is $3 million ($3.5 million − $500,000), his reverse QTIP marital trust is $500,000 ($3.5 million − $3 million), and his residuary QTIP trust is $1.5 million ($5 million − $500,000 − $3 million).

The GST-exempt share for an unmarried testator or grantor can be described either as the largest amount (or fractional share) that can pass without GST tax or as an amount (or fractional share) equal to the transferor's unused GST exemption.[13] Sections 2631(c) and 2010(c) tie the amount of the GST exemption to the amount of estate that can be sheltered from federal estate tax by the unified credit against the estate tax. The absence of a unified credit with respect to estates of decedents dying in 2010 appears to create a 2010 GST exemption of zero.

The amount that can, in 2010, pass to a GST exempt trust funded with the amount of the testator's or grantor's available GST exemption, therefore, appears to be zero. The largest amount that can, in 2010, pass to a GST exempt trust without incurring a GST tax, however, is arguably the entire estate. As with the marital/nonmarital division, two well-drafted clauses that were designed to achieve the same tax and nontax result actually produce opposite re-

---

[13] It may also be described as the largest amount that can be held in this trust with a GST inclusion ratio of zero. For various approaches to drafting this clause, see, generally, Harrington, Plaine & Zaritsky, Generation-Skipping Transfer Tax (Thomson-Reuters/WG&L, 2d ed. 2001).

sults in 2010 because there is no federal estate tax and no GST tax on generation-skipping transfers in 2010.

> **EXAMPLE 2-11:** Adam, Beth, Charlie, and Dave are siblings. None of them is married and each has several children and grandchildren. Each has an estate of $10 million. Adam's will leaves to a GST exempt trust for his grandchildren the largest amount that can pass without federal GST taxes with respect to his estate, and leaves the residue of his estate to a GST nonexempt share for his children. Beth's will leaves to a GST exempt trust for her grandchildren an amount equal to her available GST exemption, and leaves the residue of her estate to a GST nonexempt share for her children. Charlie's will leaves to a GST nonexempt share for his children the smallest amount necessary to reduce the federal GST tax on his estate to zero, and leaves the residue of his estate to a GST exempt trust for his grandchildren. Dave's will leaves to a GST exempt trust for his grandchildren the largest amount that can pass free of federal GST tax because of his available GST exemption, and leaves the residue of his estate to a GST nonexempt share for his children. In 2009, all four wills created a $3.5 million GST-exempt trust for grandchildren, and a $6.5 million GST nonexempt gift for the children.
>
> All four of the siblings die on January 1, 2011, while returning home from a particularly rowdy New Year's Eve party. All four wills are ambiguous and suits are brought in state court to construe all four instruments. The judges construe each according to the plain language of the instrument, and hold that (a) Adam's will leaves 100 percent of his estate to his GST exempt trust for his grandchildren because that is the largest amount that can pass to the GST exempt trust without incurring a federal GST tax, as there is no federal GST tax on generation-skipping transfers in 2010; (b) Beth's will leaves everything to her children because there is no GST exemption by which to measure the GST exempt share; (c) Charlie's will leaves 100 percent of his estate to his GST exempt trust for his grandchildren because no nonexempt gift is required to avoid all federal GST taxes with respect to Charlie's estate; and (d) Dave's will leaves 100 percent of his estate to his children because the GST exemption in 2010 is zero.

The reverse QTIP share of the estate or trust may be described as an amount (or fractional share) equal to the difference between the decedent's available GST exemption and the decedent's available applicable exclusion amount. As both the GST exemption and applicable exclusion amount are zero in 2010, this figure would always be zero.

The reverse QTIP share of the estate or trust can also be described as the largest amount (or fractional share) that can pass free of GST taxes, after taking into account the amount of GST exemption that has been allocated to the nonmarital share. The reverse QTIP marital trust is always a non-skip person because the surviving spouse is always assigned to the grantor's or testator's generation.[14] The GST tax rules continue to apply to the reverse QTIP trust in 2010 because transfers to it are not themselves generation-skipping transfers. The largest amount (or fractional share) that can pass free of GST tax with respect to the reverse QTIP trust, therefore, appears to be zero, because the decedent or grantor has no GST exemption that can be allocated to the trust in 2010.

> **EXAMPLE 2-12:** Tom and Wanda are a married couple. They each have a separate estate of approximately $5 million. Each of them has a will and a revocable trust, under which, at the first spouse's death, three trusts are created. A nonmarital trust is created in an amount equal to the first spouse's unused applicable exclusion amount. In 2010, there is no applicable exclusion amount, and this share would thus arguably be zero. A reverse QTIP trust is created equal to the difference, if any, between the first spouse's unused GST exemption and his or her unused applicable exclusion amount. In 2010, as the GST exemption is zero, this share would arguably be zero. The residue under both sets of documents is held in a QTIP marital trust for the surviving spouse. This would arguably be the entire estate in 2010.

[2] Alternate Generation-Skipping Transfer Tax Formulas for 2010

The revision of an ambiguous formula clause that divides an estate between GST exempt and GST nonexempt shares is more complex than the division between marital and nonmarital shares. The GST tax-based division, like the marital/nonmarital division, involves substantial nontax considerations, and some clients will have definite views about the relative merit of a trust that benefits their children, a trust that benefits their grandchildren, and a trust that benefits all of their descendants.

[a] The Effective Date Problem

One serious problem is that it is very difficult to determine currently the GST taxes that will be later imposed on post-2010 taxable distributions and taxable terminations under generation-skipping trusts created in 2010. Section 2664 states that the GST tax rules (Chapter 13) do not apply to "generation-skipping transfers" after December 31, 2009.[15] Section 901(a) of

---

[14] IRC § 2651(c)(1).

[15] This is not the most artfully drafted of statutes. Chapter 13 must apply to generation-skipping transfers in 2010, at least to the extent required to define "generation-skipping transfer." That definition occurs in Section 2613, which is part of Chapter

EGTRRA, in applicable part, states that the estate tax and GST tax changes made by EGTRRA do not apply "to estates of decedents dying, gifts made, or generation skipping transfers, after December 31, 2010." Section 901(b) provides the greater problem, stating that the tax laws are applied and administered "to ... estates, gifts, and transfers described in subsection (a) [those after December 31, 2009] as if the provisions and amendments described in subsection (a) had never been enacted."

There is much debate and doubt about the meaning of the statement that the estate and GST taxes must be administered after December 31, 2010, as if the EGTRRA "had never been enacted." The best analysis appears to be that total protection from GST taxes is afforded to post-2010 taxable distributions and terminations under trusts created under the will or revocable trust of a decedent who dies in 2010, because there is no federal estate tax in 2010, and thus no transferor.

Section 2612(b) defines a "taxable distribution" as "any distribution from a trust to a skip person (other than a taxable termination or a direct skip)."[16] Section 2612(a) defines a "taxable termination" as "the termination (by death, lapse of time, release of power, or otherwise) of an interest in property held in a trust unless—(A) immediately after such termination, a non-skip person has an interest in such property, or (B) at no time after such termination may a distribution (including distributions on termination) be made from such trust to a skip person."[17] Both of these definitions, therefore, require that there be a skip person; absent a skip person, there can be no taxable distribution or taxable termination.

A "skip person" is defined in Section 2613(a) as either "a natural person assigned to a generation which is 2 or more generations below the generation assignment of the transferor," a trust all of the interests in which are held by skip persons, or a trust in which there is no person holding an interest in the trust and "at no time after such transfer may a distribution (including distributions on termination) be made from such trust to a non-skip person."[18] A

---

13. One cannot seriously argue that the definition of "generation-skipping transfer" is also eliminated by Section 2664 after 2009, because it would create an illogical and unworkable result. See Nixon v. Missouri Mun. League, 541 US 125 (2004) and United States v. American Trucking Ass'ns, Inc., 310 US 534 (1940) (the courts will not construe a statute in a manner that leads to absurd or futile results).

[16] See Harrington, Plaine & Zaritsky, Generation-Skipping Transfer Tax ¶ 2.05[2] (Thomson Reuters/WG&L, 2d ed. 2001).

[17] See Harrington, Plaine & Zaritsky, Generation-Skipping Transfer Tax ¶ 2.05[3] (Thomson Reuters/WG&L, 2d ed. 2001).

[18] See Harrington, Plaine & Zaritsky, Generation-Skipping Transfer Tax ¶ 2.04[1] (Thomson Reuters/WG&L, 2d ed. 2001).

"non-skip person" is defined by Section 2613(b) as "any person who is not a skip person."[19]

The definitions of "taxable termination" and "taxable distribution," therefore, ultimately depend on the definition of "transferor." Identifying the transferor is essential because the generation assignments of the transferees are based on their relationship to the transferor. If there is no transferor, it may be soundly argued that there can be no generation-skipping transfer.[20]

The transferor is the individual with respect to whom property was most recently subject to federal estate or gift tax.[21] A transfer to a GST trust on account of the death of a decedent in 2010 is not subject to either gift or estate tax. The best analysis, therefore, is that there can be no "transferor" for such a trust. There can be no skip person with respect to such a trust, because there is no transferor. There can be no taxable distribution or taxable termination with respect to such a trust, because there can be no skip person.

> **EXAMPLE 2-13:** Harry dies in 2010, leaving his $20 million estate to a single trust for the benefit of his children, grandchildren, and more remote descendants, in perpetuity. Harry was domiciled in a state that has repealed its rule against perpetuities and now permits perpetual trusts. Clearly, no estate tax is imposed with respect to Harry's estate. Also, clearly, no GST tax is imposed on the creation of this trust, because the trust has Harry's children as some of its beneficiaries and so is not itself a skip person. Harry's executor cannot apply any GST exemption to this transfer because the GST exemption in 2010 is zero.
>
> In 2011, the trustee of Harry's trust distributes $50,000 to each of Harry's four grandchildren. This distribution should not be subject to GST tax as a taxable distribution, because the trust was funded in a transfer not subject to estate or gift tax. Therefore, there is no transferor. Absent a transferor, no beneficiary can be a skip person. Without a skip person, no distribution can be a taxable distribution.

---

[19] See Harrington, Plaine & Zaritsky, Generation Skipping Transfer Tax ¶ 2.04[2] (Thomson Reuters/WG&L, 2d ed. 2001).

[20] See Harrington, Plaine & Zaritsky, Generation-Skipping Transfer Tax ¶ 2.02 (Thomson Reuters/WG&L, 2d ed. 2001).

[21] IRC § 2652(a)(1) states

(1) Except as provided in this subsection or section 2653(a) [the reverse QTIP], the term "transferor" means—

  (A) in the case of any property subject to the tax imposed by Chapter 11, the decedent, and
  (B) in the case of any property subject to the tax imposed by Chapter 12, the donor.

An individual shall be treated as transferring any property with respect to which such individual is the transferor.

The IRS could argue that, under EGTRRA's sunset rule, the status of the transferor must be redetermined after 2010 as if EGTRRA had not been enacted, and that, therefore, the transferor of a testamentary transfer should be treated as if he or she had paid a federal estate tax on the transfer. This argument should fail, however, because it ignores the very fundamental absence of an estate tax on transfers in 2010.

[b] The Formula Division of the Estate

Another approach is to divide the estate or trust fund between GST-exempt and GST-nonexempt shares, defining the GST-exempt share as the greatest portion of the estate that can be held in this trust without current or future imposition of the GST tax on distributions or terminations of interest. This would pass the entire estate to the GST-exempt trust if the personal representative or trustee determines that the law would not subject the trust to future GST taxes. This would pass the entire estate to a GST-nonexempt trust if the personal representative or trustee determines that the law would tax future terminations or distributions.

This approach will likely delay funding of the trusts because it could be months or years before a definitive determination can be made with respect to the future application of the GST tax to such trusts. The personal representative or trustee should probably seek a private letter ruling on this issue, and might be able to make a division and funding when the ruling was received. Otherwise, the fiduciary must rely on advice of counsel, and it seems unlikely that counsel would give an unconditional assurance of the future application of the GST taxes to such trusts until the Treasury, IRS, the courts, or Congress clarify the law.

Drafting Tip: The following clause creates either a GST exempt trust, if possible without ultimately being subject to the GST tax, or a GST-nonexempt trust, if avoiding the GST tax on future terminations of interests is not possible.

   The Residue of My Estate. My Personal Representative shall divide my Residuary Estate into a GST Exempt Trust, to be held under Article __, and a GST Nonexempt Trust, to be held under Article __, as provided in this Article.
   A. Gift to GST Exempt Trust. I leave to the GST Exempt Trust a fractional share of my Residuary Estate, which may be all, none, or some portion of my Residuary Estate.
      (1) The numerator of this fraction shall equal the largest value of my Residuary Estate that would, if held as the GST Exempt Trust, be exempt from the federal tax on generation-skipping transfers.
      (2) The denominator of the fraction shall equal the value of my Residuary Estate.
   B. Gift to GST Nonexempt Trust. I leave to the GST Nonexempt Trust the remaining fractional share of my Residuary Estate, after subtracting from my Residuary Estate any portion set aside as the GST Exempt Trust, under paragraph A. of this Article.
   C. Determination of Fractions. My Personal Representative shall determine the largest value of my Residuary Estate that would, if held as the GST Exempt Trust, be exempt from the federal tax on generation-skipping transfers, by applying the rule of this paragraph C.
      (1) A transfer to the GST Exempt Trust shall be deemed to be exempt from the federal tax on generation-skipping transfers if neither distributions from such trust to any beneficiary, nor the termination of the interests of any beneficiary, would not be subject to such a tax.
      (2) My Personal Representative may determine the largest value of my Residuary Estate that would, if held as the GST Exempt Trust, be exempt from the federal tax on generation-skipping transfers, by a private letter ruling obtained from the U.S. Internal Revenue Service, by an unqualified opinion of competent tax counsel, or by any other reasonable method.
      (3) My Personal Representative shall not be liable to anyone for the accuracy of a determination of the largest value of my Residuary Estate that would, if held as the GST Exempt Trust, be exempt from the federal tax on generation-skipping transfers, where such determination is based on a private letter ruling obtained from the U.S. Internal Revenue Service or on an unqualified opinion of competent tax counsel, and shall not be liable to anyone for the accuracy of such a determination, if made by another method, absent gross negligence.
      (4) My Personal Representative shall determine the largest value of my Residuary Estate that would, if held as the GST Exempt Trust, be exempt from the federal tax on generation-skipping transfers, based on the federal tax law in effect on the date of my death. If the federal generation-skipping transfer tax is amended after the date of my death and before January 1, 2011, retroactively, such that it shall apply under such retroactive legislation with respect to my estate, my Personal Representative shall make this determination based on

such retroactively modified tax law. If such retroactive legislation is finally determined to be unconstitutional or otherwise invalid, these references shall apply as if such retroactive legislation had never been enacted. My fiduciaries shall not be liable to any beneficiary for refusing to establish a GST Exempt Trust or a GST Nonexempt Trust under this instrument or to make distributions where the entitlement of any beneficiary to a separate share or distribution cannot be established until the January 1, 2011, or until the termination of litigation over such retroactive legislation as referred to in this paragraph.

[c] Granting a Power of Appointment Over a GST-Exempt Trust

One good approach to revising GST formula divisions in case of a testator's or grantor's death in 2010 is to leave the entire estate or fund to separate share trusts for each child and his or her descendants, and to give an independent trustee the power to grant each child a general power of appointment if needed to avoid the GST tax. No power of appointment would be granted if the Treasury, the courts, or Congress ultimately clarify that such a trust created in 2010 is permanently exempt from the GST tax. The trustee would grant such a power of appointment to the child upon a contrary determination by the Treasury, the courts, or Congress.

Granting a general power of appointment to the child causes the trust assets to be included in the child's gross estate. This renders the trust assets subject to federal estate tax upon the child's death, which makes the child the transferor of the trust for GST tax purposes.[22] The general power of appointment avoids a GST tax at the child's death, imposing instead a federal estate tax that may be reduced or avoided by any unused applicable exclusion amount that the child's estate may possess. Also, the child may appoint the trust assets to a marital trust for his or her surviving spouse, thereby further deferring the estate taxes on those funds.

---

[22] IRC § 2652(a)(1)(A). See also discussion of this technique in Harrington, Plaine & Zaritsky, Generation-Skipping Transfer Tax ¶ 9.05 (Thomson Reuters/WG&L, 2d ed. 2001).

Drafting Tip: The following clause creates separate trusts for each of the testator's children and that child's descendants, and permits the trustee to grant the child a general power of appointment. This language presumes that the trustee will be independent.

My Descendants' Separate Dynasty Trusts. The trustee shall hold the descendants' share as the descendants' dynasty trusts under this Article.

A. Division Among My Descendants. My trustee shall divide the descendants' dynasty trusts' funds among my then-living descendants, per stirpes, and shall hold the separate share for each of my then-living descendants in a separate trust under this Article. Each such descendant assigned to the highest generation to which any beneficiary of his or her separate trust is assigned shall be referred to as the "primary beneficiary" of his or her separate trust under this Article.

B. Terms of the Trust. My trustee shall hold each primary beneficiary's separate trust until the perpetuity date, defined below.

(1) During the Primary Beneficiary's Lifetime. With respect to each primary beneficiary's separate trust, my trustee shall distribute to or expend for the benefit of such primary beneficiary and his or her descendants so much of the net income and principal of such separate trust as my trustee deems appropriate for their health, education, support or maintenance, annually adding to principal any undistributed trust income.

(a) My trustee may distribute income and principal of this trust trust unequally and may make distributions to some beneficiaries and not to others.

(b) My trustee shall make distributions recognizing that my primary concern in establishing this trust is the conservation and management of its principal and accumulated income for as long as shall be practicable. My trustee shall, therefore, lend trust assets to beneficiaries or hold them for the personal use of beneficiaries, rather than making outright distributions, to the greatest extent that my trustee deems it practicable.

(c) My trustee shall determine the amount and timing of all distributions from this trust, taking into account other resources available to each beneficiary from all sources, including all other trusts created by me.

(2) Grant of a Power of Appointment. My trustee may grant to any primary beneficiary of a trust under this Article a testamentary power of appointment exercisable by specific reference to the power in such primary beneficiary's last will.

(a) This power of appointment shall be exercisable in favor of the primary beneficiary's estate, the creditors of the primary beneficiary's estate, and any of the descendants of my parents, and the primary beneficiary may appoint the trust funds to which this power applies either outright or in further trust, and on such terms as the primary beneficiary may designate.

(b) My trustee may require that a primary beneficiary's exercise of a power of appointment granted under this Article shall be valid only if my trustee consents to the primary beneficiary's specific exercise.

(c) My trustee may withdraw any such power of appointment granted under this Article, prior to the death of the primary beneficiary to whom it was granted, by a signed writing delivered to the primary beneficiary. If my trustee withdraws any such power of appointment, any purported exercise thereof by the primary beneficiary's will (whether such will was executed before or after such withdrawal) shall not be valid.

(d) My trustee may grant or withdraw a general power of appointment under this Article repeatedly and from time to time.

(3) **Division Upon Death of Primary Beneficiary.** Upon the death of the primary beneficiary, my trustee shall divide the trust fund not validly appointed by the primary beneficiary among the primary beneficiary's then-living descendants, per stirpes. My trustee shall continue to hold each share for a then-living descendant of the deceased primary beneficiary, with the descendant of such deceased primary beneficiary assigned to the highest generation to which any beneficiary of his or her separate trust is assigned now being the primary beneficiary of that separate trust. All provisions of this Article shall also apply with respect to such new primary beneficiary's separate trust.

C. Upon the Perpetuities Date. Upon the perpetuities date, my trustee shall distribute the remaining fund of each trust under this instrument to my then-living descendants, per stirpes, outright and free of trust, subject to the provisions of the Article entitled "Minor Beneficiaries."

D. "Perpetuities Date." The "perpetuities date" shall be the date twenty (20) years and eleven (11) months after the death of the last survivor of my *husband/wife* and those of the descendants of my grandparents alive on the date of my death.

Some estate planners prefer to grant the transferor's children a general power of appointment that is exercisable only to the extent that the possession of such a power would reduce the total wealth transfer taxes imposed with respect to the trust. Such a power attempts to substitute the child's estate tax for the GST tax on the trust at the child's death, but only if the former would be lower than the latter. The absence of a federal estate and GST tax in 2010 may affect the ability to determine the extent to which such powers can be exercised, though it should probably not distort the tax planning or their design.

EXAMPLE 2-14: Dan's father created a trust for the benefit of Dan, his brother, Dick, and their children and more remote descendants. Dan's father did not allocate any GST exemption to the trust. The trust states that the trustee may distribute income and principal among the descendants of Dan's father (including Dan and his brother) in the trustee's sole discretion. The trust also provides that, at the death of the later to die of Dan or his brother, the later sibling to die will be able to appoint a portion of the trust fund to and among a class that includes the then-living descendants of Dan's grandfather and the creditors of such decedent's estate. The portion of the trust over which this general power of appointment is exercisable is described as that smallest amount which, if included in the decedent's gross estate, would produce a federal estate tax that is $1 less than the federal GST tax that would be imposed with respect to the decedent's death. If Dan survives his brother and dies in 2010, when there is neither a federal estate or GST tax, the best interpretation of this clause is probably that he has no general power of appointment.

Drafting Tip: The following clause creates a power of appointment that is exercisable only to the extent that the estate tax that would be generated by its possession is less than the GST tax that would be created absent its possession.

    B. Special Power of Appointment. Upon the death of a child of mine, the Trustees shall distribute the remaining principal and income of that child's separate trust as that child may direct by specific reference to this power of appointment in that child's will.

    (1) Appointment of the Limited Portion. Each such child may appoint the Limited Portion (defined below) of the principal and income of such child's trust under this Article outright or in further trust, to any person or persons, including such child's estate or the creditors of such child's estate.

    (2) Appointment of the Rest of the Trust. Each such child may appoint the remaining principal and income of such child's trust under this Article (other than the Limited Portion) either outright or in further trust, to or among only my then-living descendants, and such child may not appoint any of the Limited Portion to such child himself or herself, such child's creditors, such child's estate, or the creditors of such child's estate.

    (3) Unappointed Portion. The Trustee shall distribute any unappointed portion of a deceased child's trust under this Article to such child's then-living descendants, per stirpes, or if there are no such descendants then living, to my then-living descendants, per stirpes, except that the assets that would thus be distributed to any then-living child of mine shall be added to such child's trust under this Article.

    (4) "Limited Portion" Defined. The "Limited Portion" of the assets of a child's trust under this Article is the smallest portion of such assets that would, on account of the death of such child possessed of a general power of appointment under this paragraph of this Article, be subject to total federal and state estate, inheritance, and/or generation-skipping transfer taxes, lower in amount than the amount of federal and state estate, inheritance, and/or generation-skipping transfer taxes that would be imposed on such assets were the child to die not possessed of such a general power of appointment.

¶ 2.06 STATE DEATH TAX FORMULA CLAUSES IN LIGHT OF ESTATE TAX REPEAL

[1] The Problems With Present Formulas

EGTRRA repealed the credit against the federal estate tax for state inheritance, estate, and other death taxes, and replaced it with an unlimited state death tax deduction.[23] The top rate for the pre-EGTRRA state death tax credit under was 16 percent, for a decedent's adjusted taxable estate of over $10,040,000.[24] Most states, before EGTRRA was enacted, imposed an estate tax measured by the maximum allowable federal state death tax credit. These state estate taxes resulted in a decedent's estate paying no additional total taxes because of the state death tax; these taxes merely shifted some of their federal estate tax payments to the state.

[2] Decoupling

EGTRRA's repeal of the state death tax credit led some states to abandon their state death taxes, but other states either retained their estate taxes with reference to the federal credit before EGTRRA, retained their inheritance taxes (which do not refer to the federal credit), or enacted stand-alone estate taxes. States that severed the connection between their estate tax and the current federal estate tax law are usually referred to as having "decoupled" from the federal law.

[a] Determining Which State Taxes Apply to Your Client

One of the most difficult problems created by EGTRRA is the wide diversity among the states with respect to their state death taxes and the likelihood that many clients will die owing death taxes to more than one state.[25] State death taxes are usually imposed on the entire estate of a decedent who was domiciled in the state at the time of his or her death, as well as with respect to real property owned by a nonresident decedent and situated within the state. Some states also tax tangible personal property that is physically situated within the state at the time of the decedent's death even if owned by a nonres-

---

[23] IRC § 2011(g). See also discussion at ¶ 1.06[3][a].

[24] IRC § 2011(b)(1).

[25] As noted estate planning attorney Ronald Aucutt is reputed to have quipped, "With respect to death taxes, the states are all over the map."

ident decedent. Intangible personal property is usually deemed to be taxable only by the state in which the deceased owner dies domiciled.[26]

[i] Apportionment. States traditionally apportion the total estate taxes owed by their residents among the various states in which the person holds property taxed at death. The apportionment rules, however, are inconsistent and often conflicting. Accordingly, a decedent who dies with properties subject to estate taxes in more than one state should anticipate paying a larger total state death tax than would have been owed had the individual died with property solely in one state. Though unfair, states can also reach inconsistent conclusions regarding residency and domicile. The U.S. Constitution affords no protection against the same decedent being subjected to estate or inheritance taxes as a domiciliary of more than one state.[27]

[ii] Nondomiciliary taxation of tangible property. A practical estate planner should ascertain whether a client holds real or tangible personal property in any state other than the state in which the client is domiciled (a "nondomiciliary state"). If so, it may be advisable for the client to transfer the real or tangible personal property located in a nondomiciliary state to a family limited partnership or limited liability company (LLC) so as to convert the client's interest into an intangible asset, and thereby avoid the multistate situs issues noted above.[28] This technique will not, of course, be effective in those states that impose their inheritance or estate tax on a nonresident decedent's intangible assets,[29] and it may not be effective if the assets are merely passive investment or personal use assets.

---

[26] See Hellerstein & Hellerstein, State Taxation ¶ 21.03 (Thomson Reuters/WG&L, 3d ed. 1998).

[27] See Dorrance v. Martin, 12 F. Supp. 746 (DNJ 1935), aff'd sub nom. Hill v. Martin, 296 US 393, 56 S. Ct. 278 (1935); Texas v. Florida, 306 US 398 (1938); discussion at Hellerstein & Hellerstein, State Taxation ¶ 21.09 (Thomson Reuters/WG&L, 3d ed. 1998).

[28] See Blodgett v. Silberman, 277 US 1 (1928) (decedent's interest in a New York commercial limited partnership was intangible personal property subject to inheritance tax in Connecticut, the state of the decedent's domicile); Perkins v. Oklahoma Tax Comm'n, 428 P2d 328 (Okla. 1967); Lynch v. Kentucky Tax Comm'n, 333 SW2d 257 (Ky. 1960); Humphrey v. Bullock, 666 SW2d 586 (Tex. 1984).

[29] See, e.g., Ala. Stat. § 43.31.021 (business intangibles); Ala. Stat. § 43.31.031 (all intangibles); Ark. Rev. Code § 26-59-107 (all intangibles); Cal. Rev. & Tax. Code § 13402 (certain business intangibles); DC Code Ann. § 47-3703 (business intangibles); Fla. Stat. Ann. § 198.03 (business intangibles); Ky. Rev. Stat. § 140.010 (business intangibles); Miss. Code Ann. § 27-9-7 (all intangibles); Nev. Rev. Stat. § 375A.100 (all intangibles); NC Gen. Stat. § 1-5-32.2 (all intangibles); Ohio Rev. Code § 5731.19; Okla. Stat. tit. 68, § 807 (business intangibles); Or. Rev. Stat. § 118.010 (all intangibles); SC Code § 12-16-530; Utah Code § 59-11-104 (business intangibles); Va. Code § 58.1-904 (all intangibles); W. Va. Code § 11-11-2 (some business intangibles).

　　See also Fox, Pomeroy, Abbott & O'Donnell, "Ramifications for Estate Planners of the Phase Out of the Federal State Death Tax Credit: Boom, Bust or Unknown?" 16

The New York Department of Taxation and Finance stated, in Opinion TSB-A-08(1)M (October 24, 2008), that a nonresident decedent's interest in either an S corporation or a single-member LLC owning New York real property was subject to New York State estate tax, unless the entity conducted an active business. The opinion concluded that

1. An interest in a S corporation owning New York real property was considered an intangible and not included in a nonresident decedent's New York gross estate, unless the corporation was not entitled to recognition as a valid entity because it did not engage in a business activity,[30] and

2. An interest in a single-member LLC owning New York real property is also considered an intangible and is not included in the nonresident decedent's New York gross estate as long as the LLC is to be treated as a corporation under the "check-the-box" regulations.[31]

The petitioner in the opinion was domiciled outside of New York and contemplated buying a condominium in New York. She asked about the estate tax consequences for the estate of a nonresident decedent of forming a single-member LLC or an S corporation under Florida law, and then having that entity buy the condominium instead. The Office of Counsel stated that an interest in a corporation is considered intangible personal property to which the estate tax does not apply.[32] The Office of Counsel added, however, that this conclusion presumes that the S corporation is entitled to recognition for tax purposes under the test adopted by the U.S. Supreme Court in *Moline Properties, Inc. v. Commissioner.*[33] There, the Court held that a corporation's separate existence must be recognized for tax purposes "so long as [its] purpose is the equivalent of business activity or is followed by the carrying on of business by the corporation." If the S corporation does not qualify for recognition under that standard, the value of the condominium would be included in the nonresident decedent's New York gross estate under state estate tax law.

Similarly, the Office of Counsel noted that the federal income tax law does not define a "single member limited liability company," and that such entities are subject to the "check-the-box" regulations, under which a single-member LLC can elect to be treated as a corporation for federal tax

---

ALI-ABA Sophisticated Est. Plan. Techniques 178, 196 (Sept. 2003), discussing the fact that taxing authorities in Massachusetts might be attempting to subject such interests to estate tax if the partnership lacks a business purpose.

[30] See Moline Props. v. Comm'r, 319 US 436, 438–439 (1943).

[31] Reg. §§ 301.7701-1 through 301.7701-3.

[32] Citing Estate of Fred W. Fuhrmann, 80 Misc. 2d 751 (Sur. Ct., Nassau Co. 1975); Tamagni v. Tax Appeals Tribunal, 91 NY2d 530, 533 (1998) (referring to income from stock dividends as "income from intangible personal property").

[33] Moline Props. v. Comm'r, 319 US 436 (1943).

purposes.[34] If the single-member LLC (SMLLC) does not make that election, it is treated as a "disregarded entity."[35] The Office of Counsel concluded that the check-the-box regulations apply for federal estate tax purposes, and thus for New York estate tax purposes.

An interest in an SMLLC for which there is an election, applicable to the date of death, to be treated as a corporation pursuant to Regulations § 301.7701-3(c) would, therefore, be recognized as an interest in a corporation for purposes of New York Tax Law section 960. As discussed above with regard to the S corporation, that property held by the SMLLC would not be included in a nonresident's New York gross estate under New York Tax Law section 960. By contrast, if there is no election, applicable to the date of death, to treat the SMLLC as if it were a corporation, the SMLLC would be disregarded for New York estate tax purposes, and the value of the condominium would be included in the nonresident decedent's New York gross estate under New York Tax Law section 960.

Therefore, New York, and possibly other states, may view the holding of merely passive assets or personal use assets in a corporation, partnership, or LLC as insufficient to convert the tangible property into intangible property and thereby avoid state estate or inheritance taxes. The practitioner should attempt to include in such entities assets the management of which constitutes an active business. This may be satisfied by renting the assets for an arm's-length rent in a business-like manner, and possibly by the active management of intangible investment assets. The rules of each state must be carefully scrutinized, and there is likely to be a significant variation among these rules.

[iii] Multiple domiciles. A practical estate planner should also be sure that the client has not split his or her time and contacts so as to give more than one state grounds for asserting that the decedent was a legal resident (i.e., domiciliary) of that state. States look at all facts and circumstances to determine residence, which is usually defined as being synonymous with the concept of domicile. The estate planner whose client has a residence in more than one state should attempt to consolidate as many of these factors as possible in one state—preferably, the state with the lowest inheritance or estate taxes.

A survey of the case law concerning an individual's domicile indicates that certain factors are significant. Based on these cases, it is likely that a client's domicile will be—

---

[34] Reg. § 301.7701-3(c).

[35] Reg. § 301.7701-3(b)(1)(ii). "[I]f the entity is disregarded, its activities are treated in the same manner as a sole proprietorship, branch, or division of the owner." Reg. § 301.7701-2(a).

1. Where the client maintains a residence that is larger and that is occupied for the greater part of the year, thus appearing to be the primary residence;
2. Where the client and the client's employer report the client as having earned income;
3. Where the client files state income tax returns as a resident;
4. Where the client reports as his or her residence for federal income tax purposes;
5. Where the client is registered to vote and does, in fact, vote;[36]
6. Where the client holds a state driver's license;
7. Where the client's automobiles are registered and, if relevant, personal property taxes on those automobiles are paid;
8. Where the client's passport states is the location of his or her residence;
9. Where the client's will and revocable trust indicate as the location of his or her residence;
10. Where the client's most important items of tangible personal property, such as artwork, collections, and antiques, are located;
11. Where the client works;
12. Where the client has personal bank and brokerage accounts;
13. Where the client maintains safe deposit boxes;
14. Where prearrangements for the client's funeral have been made;
15. Where the client has membership in social clubs, civic, and religious organizations, especially if those memberships are on a resident basis;
16. Where the charities to which the client contributes are located;
17. Where the client claims homestead exemptions from property taxes, creditor claims, or both;
18. Where the client represented his or her residence to be in any affidavits or other declarations of residency (e.g., notices of residence sent to friends and family, declarations on any census forms or other governmental forms, and hotel registrations and car rentals);
19. Where the client maintains a post office box;
20. Where the client has relationship with a physician, accountant, and lawyer;
21. Where the client's death certificate states as the client's residence;
22. Where designated in the client's listed address in social and professional registries;
23. Where designated in the client's listed address on corporate stock registrations;
24. Where the client has charge accounts;

---

[36] Party affiliation should be irrelevant, but activities in a state political party organization may be very relevant.

25. Where the client notifies corporations and transfer agents to send dividends and interest payments; and

26. Where the client receives magazines to which he or she has subscriptions.[37]

[b] Decoupled State Taxes

States have not been consistent in the manner in which they have decoupled from the federal tax law. Some have tied their estate taxes to the federal state death tax credit as it existed on a fixed date, thus preserving a state estate tax despite the absence of a credit for those taxes. Some of these states have not adopted some or all of the increases in the applicable exclusion amount.[38] Therefore, decedents dying in some states must contend with a state estate tax that has an exemption lower than the federal exemption.

The following states have inheritance or estate taxes that are decoupled from the federal estate tax:[39]

Connecticut	Estate tax with a $2 million exemption and rates ranging from 5 percent to 16 percent[40]
Delaware	Estate tax tied to federal state death tax credit in effect on January 1, 2001, for decedents dying after June 30, 2009, with a $3.5 million exemption[41]
District of Columbia	Estate tax tied to amount of state death tax credit in effect on January 1, 2001, with a $1 million exemption[42]
Indiana	Inheritance tax[43]
Iowa	Inheritance tax[44]
Maine	Estate tax tied to state death tax credit in effect on December 31, 2000, but with a $1 million exemption[45]

---

[37] See Fox, Pomeroy, Abbott & O'Donnell, "Ramifications for Estate Planners of the Phase Out of the Federal State Death Tax Credit: Boom, Bust or Unknown?" 16 ALI-ABA Sophisticated Est. Plan. Techiques 178, 206–210 (Sept. 2003).

[38] For a discussion of decoupling issues, see Zaritsky, Waiting Out EGTRRA's Sunset Period: Practical Planning While Congress Debates Estate Tax Repeal ¶ 3.07 (Thomson Reuters/WG&L 2004).

[39] This chart does not explain all of the details of any of these state death taxes, nor does it address whether the state has a state GST tax designed to absorb the credit for state GST taxes under Section 2604. The reader must consult each individual's state statutes, regulations, and forms for such details.

[40] Conn. Stat. § 12-391(e).

[41] 30 Del. Stat. § 1502(c).

[42] DC Code §§ 47-3701, 47-3702.

[43] Ind. Stat. §§ 6-4.1-11-2, 6-4.1-1-4.

[44] Iowa Code §§ 450.1, 450.2.

[45] 36 Me. Rev. Stat § 4062.

Maryland	Estate tax tied to state death tax credit in effect on December 31, 2000, but with a $1 million exemption[46]
Massachusetts	Estate tax tied to state death tax credit in effect on December 31, 2000, but with a $1 million exemption[47]
Minnesota	Estate tax tied to state death tax credit in effect on December 31, 2000, but with a $1 million exemption[48]
New Jersey	Estate tax tied to state death tax credit in effect on December 31, 2000, but with a $675,000 exemption[49] and inheritance tax[50]
New York	Estate tax tied to state death tax credit in effect on July 22, 1998, but with a $1 million exemption[51]
Ohio	Separate estate tax with rates up to 7 percent and credit equivalent to a $338,333 exemption[52]
Oregon	Estate tax tied to state death tax credit in effect on December 31, 2001, but with a $1 million exemption[53]
Pennsylvania	Inheritance tax[54]
Rhode Island	Estate tax tied to state death tax credit in effect on January 1, 2001, but with an $850,000 exemption, indexed for inflation[55]
Tennessee	Inheritance tax[56]
Vermont	Estate tax tied to state death tax credit in effect on January 1, 2001, but with a $2 million exemption[57]
Washington	Estate tax with a $2 million exemption[58]

---

[46] Md. Tax Code §§ 7-304, 7-309.

[47] 65C Mass. Stat. §§ 2A.

[48] Minn. Stat. §§ 291.005, 291.03.

[49] NJ Rev. Stat. § 54:38-14.

[50] NJ Rev. Stat. §§ 54:33-1 to 54:37-1, and 54:38-1.

[51] NY Tax Law § 951.

[52] Ohio Rev. Stat. § 5731.02.

[53] Ore. Rev. Stat. § 118.100.

[54] 72 Pa. Stat. § 9106.

[55] RI Stat. § 44-22-1.1.

[56] Tenn. Code Ann. § 67-8-303.

[57] 32 Vt. Stat. §§ 7402(8), 7442a, 7475.

[58] Wash. Rev. Code § 83.100.040. The Washington experience was one of the most interesting of the state estate tax experiences. When EGTRRA was enacted, Washington had an estate tax. A 1981 initiative had expressly limited the Washington estate tax to an amount equal to the federal credit. Wash. Rev. Code § 83.100.030(1). In 2001, the legislature enacted an amendment that stated that references to the Internal Revenue Code were to the U.S. Internal Revenue Code of 1986, as amended or renumbered as of January 1, 2001. Wash. Rev. Code § 83.100.020(15). Several executors sued to contest the validity of this provision, and the Supreme Court of Washington held in Estate of Hemphill v. Washington, 153 Wash. 2d 544, 105 P3d 391 (2005), that the repeal of the federal credit for state death taxes automatically repealed the state estate tax, notwithstanding the actions of the legislature. The Washington Legislature then enacted, and its governor signed into law, an independent Washington estate tax. Wash. Rev. Code §§ 83.100.010 – 83.100.906. See "Mumford, Up and Down and Back Again: Troubled Childhood Notwithstanding, Washington's Stand Alone Estate Tax Deserves to Be Defended," 29 Seattle UL Rev. 687 (Spring 2006).

More than thirty additional states are likely to have an estate tax if the state death tax credit is restored in 2011.[59]

[3] State Death Tax Formulas

[a] The State-Only QTIP

The manner in which a state decouples has had a significant effect on the impact of a formula clause dividing a decedent's estate into both marital and nonmarital shares. The practical estate planner should carefully scrutinize the formula clause used in light of the changes in the applicable state death tax rules.

A state that has a stand-alone estate tax, but that did not adopt all of the increases in the federal applicable exemption amount, could cause an estate to owe a substantial state death tax, even though it owes no federal estate tax. The approach often taken in planning the estate of a domiciliary of such a state is to select a formula that either (1) avoids all state and federal estate taxes at the first spouse's death or (2) avoids all federal estate tax, pays some state death tax, and further reduces the state death taxes at the surviving spouse's death.

A formula clause that creates a nonmarital share equal to the largest amount (or fractional share) that can pass free of both federal and state death taxes will postpone all estate taxes until both spouses have died. Such clauses will, in states that have decoupled from both the state death tax credit and the federal applicable exclusion amount, create a nonmarital share that does not take full advantage of the decedent's federal applicable exclusion amount, because to create a larger nonmarital share would generate a state death tax. Failing to take full advantage of the decedent's applicable exclusion amount is likely to be far more costly than the slight state tax savings from avoiding a state estate tax at the first spouse's death.

---

[59] Ala. Stat. § 40-15-12; Alaska 43-31-011; Ark. Stat. §§ 26-59-103, 26-59-106, 26-59-109; Cal. Rev. & Tax. Code §§ 13302, 13411; Colo. Stat. §§ 39-23.5-102, 39-23.5-103; Fla. Stat. § 198.02 and Fla. Const. Art. VII, § 5; Ga. Stat. § 48-12-2; Haw. Stat. §§ 236D-2, 236D-3; Idaho Stat. §§ 14-402, 14-403, 63-3004; 35 Ill. Comp. Stat. §§ 405/2, 405/3; Ind. Stat. §§ 6-4.1-11-2, 6-4.1-1-4; Iowa Stat. §§ 451.2, 451.13; Kan. Stat. § 79-15,203; Ky. Stat. § 140.13D; La. Rev. Stat. §§ 47:2431, 47:2432, 47:2434; Mich. Stat. §§ 205.232, 205.256; Miss. Stat. § 27-905; Mo. Stat. §§ 145.011, 145.091; Mont. Stat. §§ 72-16-904, 72-16-905; Nev. Stat. §§ 375A.025, 375A.100; NH Rev. Stat. §§ 87:1, 87:7; NM Stat. §§ 7-7-2, 7-7-3; ND Cent. Code § 57-37.1-04; 72 Pa. Rev. Stat. § 9102; SC Code §§ 10-40A-1, 10-40A-3; Tn. Code §§ 67-8-202, 67-8-203; Tex. Tax Code §§ 211.001, 211.002, 211.051; Utah Code §§ 59-11-102, 59-11-103; WV Stat. § 11-11-3; Wis. Stat. § 72.01(11m); Wy. Stat. §§ 39-19-103, 39-19-104.

Some estate planners try to avoid all state and federal estate taxes by creating a nonmarital trust equal to the state estate tax exemption and creating a second nonmarital trust equal to the difference between the federal applicable exclusion amount and the state estate tax exemption. This second trust will be held for the lifetime benefit of the surviving spouse, and will be eligible for a QTIP election. The personal representative then elects to deduct the second trust for state purposes, but not for federal purposes, effectively creating full utilization of the federal estate tax exemption while incurring no state estate tax.

Currently, most of the states that have an inheritance or estate tax appear to permit a separate QTIP election,[60] though several states expressly do not,[61] and the law in a few states is unclear. Anecdotal evidence suggests that some tax agencies are routinely approving state-only QTIPs even without express statutory or regulatory authority, while others are not.

The formula by which a separate state QTIP trust is created will usually be based on the difference between the state exemption and the federal applicable exclusion amount. There is no federal applicable exclusion amount in 2010, and thus such formulas should be adjusted with respect to estates of decedents dying in 2010.

> **EXAMPLE 2-15:** Dave's will requires that (a) an amount equal to his state estate tax exemption shall be held in a nonmarital trust for the benefit of his wife and children; (b) an amount equal to the difference between Dave's applicable exclusion amount under federal estate tax law and Dave's state estate tax exemption shall be held in a nonmarital trust for the exclusive benefit of Dave's wife in a form that will qualify as a QTIP for estate tax purposes; and (c) the balance of Dave's estate shall be paid outright to Dave's wife. Dave dies in 2010. There is no problem creating the nonmarital trust equal to Dave's state estate tax exemption, but the provision creating a state-only QTIP is ambiguous. The best interpretation is that, as there is no federal applicable exclusion amount in 2010, there is no state-only QTIP created, and Dave's wife should receive outright everything except the state exemption nonmarital share.

---

[60] See, e.g., Conn. Gen. Stat. § 12-391(f)(1) and Conn. Dep't of Revenue Special Notice SN 2005(10) (Oct. 7, 2005); 45 Ind. Admin. Code r. 4.1-3-5(c); Ky. Rev. Stat. § 140.080(1)(a); 36 Me. Rev. Stat. § 4062(2-B); Md. Code, Tax – Gen., § 7-309(b)(5)(ii); 830 Mass. Admin. Code § 65C.1.1(3)(b)(7); Ohio Stat. § 5731.15(B); Or. Admin. Regs. § 150-118.010(7); RI Tax Div. Rul. Request No. 2003-03; Tenn. Code § 67-8-315(a)(6); Wash. Rev. Code § 11.108.025(4); Wash. Excise Tax Advisory No. 2013.57.015 (May 19, 2003).

[61] See, e.g., Iowa Code § 450.3 and Iowa Admin. Code § 701-86.5(450)(11b); Minn. Rev. Notice 2006-04 (May 8, 2006); NJ Admin. Code §§ 18:26-3A.8, 19; 18:26-11.13 (July 21, 2008). But see Covey & Hastings, Practical Drafting 9464 (Oct. 2008), reporting that New Jersey has repealed this regulation.

The practical estate planner must ascertain the extent to which the client wants to create a nonmarital share larger than that required to shelter the state exemption. Such a larger nonmarital share might usefully remove more assets from the surviving spouse's gross estate if the spouse dies after the federal estate tax has been restored. The easiest solution, in such cases, is to leave the entire residue, above the state nonmarital share, in a QTIP trust for the benefit of the surviving spouse. The executor can then elect to deduct only that part required to avoid estate taxes if the client dies after the estate tax is restored. The executor cannot elect to deduct any part of this trust if the client dies in 2010, as there is no estate tax, and thus no QTIP rules, in 2010.

[b] When There Is No State-Only QTIP

A decedent's domicile in or ownership of tangible property in a state that imposes a state inheritance or estate tax and that does not permit a state-only QTIP may pose significant tax problems in 2010. There will be no federal estate tax with respect to estates of decedents who die in 2010, and there will be no federal estate tax return. There will, therefore, be no possible federal QTIP election, which may preclude the election of QTIP treatment for state estate tax purposes.

This problem can be avoided by converting QTIP trusts into general power of appointment marital trusts, which give the surviving spouse a general testamentary power of appointment, in addition to a lifetime income interest.[62] Such a trust should qualify for the state estate tax marital deduction without election by the executor, and the executor should also be able to allocate the decedent's $3 million spousal property basis increase to such a trust. Such a trust will, however, be included in the surviving spouse's gross estate if the spouse dies after the restoration of the estate tax, and its assets may be subject to the claims of the surviving spouse's creditors.

Not all instruments creating a QTIP trust can be amended to convert the spousal interest into a general power of appointment trust. QTIP trusts are often created in grantor retained annuity trusts and qualified personal residence trusts to be effective if the grantor dies during the reserved annuity or personal use period.[63] Similarly, many irrevocable life insurance trusts create a QTIP trust for the surviving spouse if the insured grantor dies within three years of having assigned the policy to the trust.[64] The practitioner in a state with a state estate tax and no state-only QTIP may want to have these trusts modified (ei-

---

[62] IRC § 2056(b)(5).

[63] See Aucutt & Zaritsky, Structuring Estate Freezes ¶¶ 10.05[3], 11.07[6][a] (Thomson Reuters/WG&L, 2d ed. 1997); Zaritsky, Tax Planning for Family Wealth Transfers: Analysis With Forms ¶ 12.06[3][c] (Thomson Reuters/WG&L, 4th ed. 2002).

[64] See Leimberg & Zaritsky, Tax Planning with Life Insurance: Analysis With Forms ¶ 5.03[5][b] (Thomson Reuters/WG&L, 2d ed. 1998); and Zaritsky, Tax Planning for

ther judicially or, in some states, non-judicially) or to decant the trust assets into a trust that, while otherwise identical, creates a contingent general power of appointment marital trust, rather than a contingent QTIP marital trust.[65]

¶ 2.07 BEST FORMULA SOLUTIONS FOR 2010

[1] One-Trust Arrangement

An estate plan that anticipates that the surviving spouse will be the sole lifetime beneficiary of both the marital and nonmarital shares creates a nonmarital trust that would, if elected by the decedent's personal representative, qualify for the marital deduction as a QTIP trust under Section 2056(b)(7). Such a trust constitutes a suitable nonmarital trust if the personal representative of the decedent's estate makes no election on the decedent's estate tax return to deduct the trust.

This arrangement can be easily drafted as a single trust in which the surviving spouse receives all of the income, payable at least annually. The spouse may also receive one or more of the following interests:

1. The power to withdraw principal for the spouse's health, education, support, and maintenance;

Family Wealth Transfers: Analysis With Forms ¶ 11.04[3][c][ii] (Thomson Reuters/ WG&L, 4th ed. 2002).

[65] Restatement (Third) of Trusts section 65 states that, if all of the beneficiaries of an irrevocable trust consent, they can compel the termination or modification of the trust, unless the termination or modification would be inconsistent with a material purpose of the trust. If the modification or termination would be inconsistent with a material purpose of the trust, the beneficiaries can compel its termination or modification with the consent of the grantor or, after the grantor's death, the authorization of the court, which must find that the reason for termination or modification outweighs the material purpose.

The Uniform Trust Code section 411 permits modification or termination of a noncharitable irrevocable trust by consent of the beneficiaries, in some cases with, and in some cases without, the consent of the grantor. A trust may be modified or terminated with the consent of the grantor and all of the beneficiaries, even if the modification or termination is inconsistent with a material purpose of the trust. In addition, a court may terminate the trust upon the consent of all beneficiaries if the court concludes that the continuance of the trust is not necessary to achieve any material purpose of the trust, and a court may modify the trust if the court concludes that modification is not inconsistent with a material purpose of the trust.

On decanting of trust assets to another trust, see Zeydel & Blattmachr, "Tax Effects of Decanting—Obtaining and Preserving the Benefits," 111 J. Tax'n 288 (Nov. 2009).

2. The power to withdraw the greater of $5,000 or five percent per year of the trust assets;

3. The ability to receive distributions of principal for any purpose what-soever, or for purposes specified in the instrument, in the discretion of the trustee (who may not be the spouse, but may be a related person, provided that the trustee acts independently of the spouse); and

4. A testamentary power to appoint the trust assets among a class that does not include the spouse's estate or its creditors.

The decedent's personal representative should be authorized, if there is a federal estate tax on the date of the decedent's death, to divide the trust as appropriate to create separate trusts in such fashion as to take full advantage of the decedent's applicable exclusion amount, state estate tax exemption, GST exemption, and estate tax marital deduction. The personal representative can then make the requisite elections to take full advantage of these exemptions and deductions.

EXAMPLE 2-16: Harry is married to Wanda and they have three children. Neither has been married before and neither has any other children. Harry's total estate is $7 million, and he wishes to assure that Wanda has the maximum benefit of the total estate after his death and for the rest of her lifetime, consistent with good tax planning. Harry leaves his entire estate in trust and directs that the trustee pay Wanda all of the net income from the trust for her lifetime, in quarterly installments. Harry also directs that the trustee distribute to Wanda as much principal as she requires for her comfort and care or as she requests for her health, education, support, and maintenance. At Wanda's later death, the trust fund will be held in continued trust for their children's lifetime benefit, and then be distributed to their grandchildren. Harry dies in 2009, domiciled in a state that has its own stand-alone estate tax with a $2 million exemption.

Harry's personal representative divides the trust fund into three separate shares, Trust A, Trust B, and Trust C, each of which is held on the same terms. Trust A is equal to Harry's state estate tax exemption of $2 million. Trust B is equal to the difference between Harry's unused $3.5 million applicable exclusion amount and his state estate tax exemption—$1.5 million ($3.5 million − $2 million). This is also equal to the difference between Harry's unused GST exemption and his state estate tax exemption. Harry's personal representative allocates Harry's GST exemption to Trust A and Trust B, so that neither will ever be subject to the GST tax. Neither is subject to the federal estate tax, because of Harry's applicable exclusion amount. Harry's personal representative elects to deduct Trust B on Harry's state estate tax return because the state in which Harry was domiciled permits a "state-only" QTIP election.[66] Trust C is equal to

---

[66] See Gans & Blattmachr, "Quadpartite Will: Decoupling and the Next Generation of Instruments," 32 Est. Plan. 3 (Apr. 2005).

the rest of Harry's estate ($3.5 million). Harry's personal representative elects to deduct this trust as qualifying terminable interest property for both state and federal purposes. Therefore, this arrangement minimizes both state and federal estate taxes to the extent possible while deferring all estate taxes until both Harry and Wanda have died.

EXAMPLE 2-17: Assume the same facts as in Example 2-16, except that Harry dies in 2010. Harry's personal representative divides the trust into two shares, Trust A and Trust B. Trust A is equal to Harry's state estate tax exemption ($2 million). Harry's personal representative elects to deduct Trust A for state estate tax purposes. Harry's personal representative allocates to Trust A assets that have a fair market value of $2 million and an adjusted basis of $1 million, and he allocates $1 million of Harry's aggregate basis increase to Trust A. Harry's personal representative transfers the rest of Harry's estate ($5 million) to Trust B, and allocates to that trust both Harry's unused $300,000 aggregate basis adjustment and his $3 million spousal property basis increase, assuming that the total appreciation in this trust is at least $3.3 million. Therefore, Harry has taken full advantage of the two basis increases.

One advantage of this arrangement is that the personal representative of the decedent's estate has until the filing date for the decedent's last income tax return to make the elections in question with respect to a 2010 estate. This time should be especially valuable in 2010, when every day may bring more information about the likelihood of congressional legislation regarding reimposition of the estate and GST taxes as well as give the Treasury and IRS more time in which to interpret EGTRRA's effective date rules. This additional time may also be useful in states that currently do not permit a state-only QTIP election, to give them time to reconsider the application of this rule in 2010, when no federal QTIP election can be made.

It is also important to note that, in this arrangement, no portion of the property left in trust for the surviving spouse, whether or not it receives an allocation of the $3 million spousal property basis increase, needs to be included in the surviving spouse's gross estate for federal estate tax purposes if the spouse dies after the estate tax is revived in 2011. Therefore, the use of this type of one-trust estate plan may exclude the entire estate of a decedent who dies in 2010 from estate taxation in the estate of his or her surviving spouse.

One consideration in using a one-trust arrangement is that none of the trust assets are distributable to persons other than the surviving spouse during the surviving spouse's lifetime. A surviving spouse may wish to make gifts to various family members, either for estate planning reasons or merely for the pleasure of benefiting them. This can be addressed by giving an independent trustee the ability to make discretionary distributions of principal to the spouse during his or her lifetime. It can also be addressed by giving the surviving spouse the right to withdraw the greater of $5,000 or 5 percent of the trust fund each year, which power does not constitute a general power of appointment.[67]

Another approach to transferring wealth to other family members is for the trustee to partition the trust into a gift portion and a non-gift portion, each of which would be held as a separate trust. The surviving spouse could then buy the remainder interest of the gift portion of the trust from the remainder beneficiaries. This purchase would give the spouse both the income interest and the remainder interest, and thus cause the trust to terminate in outright ownership in the spouse.[68] This would give the surviving spouse assets with which he or she could undertake a program of lifetime giving.

This arrangement could produce serious problems were the trust a QTIP for which the estate or gift tax marital deduction had been claimed. The IRS has stated that, in such cases, the purchase of the remainder interest is itself a constructive gift of the entire principal of the trust.[69] This rule turns, however, on Section 2519, which requires that a marital deduction has been allowed for the creation of the trust, which would not be true for a QTIP created under the will or revocable trust of a decedent who died in 2010.

This arrangement is feasible only if the QTIP does not impose a spendthrift limitation on the remainder beneficiaries' interests in the trust. Such a limitation would prevent the purchase of their interest by the surviving spouse. Such a clause is usually included to provide creditor protection for the remainder beneficiaries, but an all-in-a-QTIP estate plan may wish to exclude, from the spendthrift clause, sales of one's interest to other beneficiaries of the trust. This would permit the transfer of the remainder beneficial interests to the surviving spouse without opening the remainder beneficiaries' interests to the claims of their general creditors.

[2] QTIP Trust Plus Disclaimer

One problem with the one-trust approach is that the nonmarital trust, as finally constituted, will not permit distributions to family members other than the surviving spouse. This may make it difficult to provide needed funds to these family members without taxable gifts by the surviving spouse, and it may force the surviving spouse to pay tax on all of the trust income, possibly at higher rates than would be applicable if income were distributed among several beneficiaries.

A solution to this problem is to provide that any portion of the QTIP trust that the surviving spouse disclaims will be held in a separate trust for the ben-

---

[67] IRC § 2041(b)(2).

[68] See Bogert & Bogert, The Law of Trusts and Trustees § 1003 (rev. 2d ed. 1979).

[69] Rev. Rul. 98-8, 1998-1 CB 541.

efit of other family members or for the benefit of the spouse and other family members.[70] Despite the repeal of the estate tax for 2010, the gift tax remains in effect, including the rules on qualified disclaimers.[71] This gives the surviving spouse nine months after the date of death in which to determine the appropriate amount to disclaim, considering the impact of such disclaimers on the state estate tax liabilities and the likelihood that the estate tax will be retroactively reinstated.[72]

> **EXAMPLE 2-18:** Harry is married to Wanda and they have three children. Neither has been married before and neither has any other children. Harry's total estate is $10 million, and he wishes to assure that Wanda has the benefit of as much of his estate as she may need. Harry leaves his entire estate in trust and directs that the trustee pays Wanda all of the net income from the trust for her lifetime, in quarterly installments. Harry also directs that the trustee distribute to Wanda as much principal as she requires in the trustee's judgement for her comfort and care or as she requests for her health, education, support, and maintenance. Harry further provides that any portion of this trust fund that Wanda disclaims shall be held in another trust for the joint benefit of Wanda and their children, grandchildren, and more remote descendants.
>
> Harry dies on January 10, 2010. Before October 10, 2010, Wanda may disclaim all or some portion of the QTIP trust and have it held as a trust for the entire family. Wanda will make this decision based on her views as to the amount of the trust she can afford to have held for the joint benefit of the other family members and herself, the likelihood that the estate tax will be retroactively reinstated, and the effect of this disclaimer on Wanda's state estate tax liabilities. By October, Wanda hopes to have a better idea whether Congress is likely to reinstate the estate tax retroactively, and she may choose to disclaim a substantial portion of the estate to enable the trustee to use those funds to care for other family members.

---

[70] Generally, the person disclaiming assets may not retain the beneficial enjoyment of the disclaimed property. IRC § 2518(b)(4); Reg. § 25.2518-2(e)(1). This rule does not apply, however, to disclaimers by the surviving spouse. IRC § 2518(b)(4)(A); Reg. § 25.2518-2(e)(2).

[71] IRC § 2518; see discussion of qualified disclaimers in Westfall & Mair, Estate Planning Law and Taxation ¶ 15.08 (Thomson Reuters/WG&L, 4th ed. 2001); Henkel, Estate Planning and Wealth Preservation: Strategies and Solutions ch. 47 (Thomson Reuters/WG&L 1997); Stephens, Maxfield, Lind & Calfee, Federal Estate and Gift Taxation ¶ 10.07 (Thomson Reuters/WG&L, 8th ed. 2002).

[72] A qualified disclaimer must be made within nine months of the date of the transfer that is being disclaimed. IRC § 2518(b)(2). Unlike the estate plan that relies on an executor's election to deduct a transfer as a QTIP trust, no extension is available for the time in which to make a qualified disclaimer.

Of course, this plan depends upon the willingness of the surviving spouse to disclaim part of the trust that is held solely for his or her benefit, and to settle for those assets being held in a trust over which the spouse has a smaller or no benefit. Some spouses seem quite willing to make such disclaimers when the plan is discussed, but become less willing after the testator's or grantor's death, when the actual ownership of the assets or their sole beneficial enjoyment becomes a true option.

A client who does not favor the use of a QTIP marital trust for the surviving spouse may leave the estate outright to the surviving spouse, and then rely on disclaimers to create a QTIP trust or a nonmarital family trust.

> **EXAMPLE 2-19:** Assume the same facts as in Example 2-18, but Harry leaves his entire estate outright to Wanda. Harry's will provides that, any assets that Wanda disclaims from her outright gift will be held in a trust, and that the trustee of this disclaimer trust must pay Wanda all of the net income from the trust for her lifetime, in quarterly installments, together with as much principal as Wanda requires for her comfort and care or as she requests for her health, education, support, and maintenance. Harry further provides that any portion of this disclaimer trust fund that Wanda disclaims shall be held in another trust for the joint benefit of Wanda and their children, grandchildren, and more remote descendants.
>
> Harry dies on January 10, 2010. Before October 10, 2010, Wanda may disclaim all or some portion of the outright gift and have it held as a QTIP trust for her benefit. She may also, by that date, disclaim some or all of the QTIP trust and have it be held in a trust for the entire family. Wanda will make this decision based on her views as to the amount of the trust she can afford to have held for the joint benefit of the other family members and herself, the likelihood that the estate tax will be retroactively reinstated, and the effect of this disclaimer on Wanda's state estate tax liabilities. By October, Wanda hopes to have a better idea whether Congress is likely to reinstate the estate tax retroactively, and she may choose to disclaim a substantial portion of the estate to enable the trustee to use those funds to care for other family members.

[3] Substantial Sprinkling Nonmarital Trust

Some practitioners may argue that the best approach is for all or most of the estate to be held as a nonmarital trust for the joint benefit of the surviving spouse and the other family members. This would make the entire estate excludable from the surviving spouse's gross estate if the estate tax is reimposed before his or her death.

This is not generally a good arrangement for several reasons. First, no portion of the spousal property basis increase can be allocated to this trust. Second, the entire trust would be subject to state estate taxes if the decedent dies domiciled or holding tangible assets in a state with a state estate tax.

Third, if the estate tax is retroactively reinstated, this trust will not qualify for the estate tax marital deduction.

Of course, leaving the marital share outright means that the assets received by the surviving spouse will be included in his or her estate after 2010, when the estate tax is restored. This strongly favors leaving these assets to the spouse in a QTIP trust or even a QTIP trust with a general inter vivos power to appoint the trust assets to the spouse himself or herself. In the latter situation, the spouse could disclaim the power of appointment if it became likely that the estate tax would not be retroactively reinstated in 2010.

CHAPTER **3**

Planning for the Modified Carryover Basis Rules

¶ 3.01	Introduction	3-2
¶ 3.02	The Carryover Basis Rules Apply After 2010	3-3
¶ 3.03	Allocating the Carryover Basis Increases	3-4
	[1] The Tax Return Under Section 6018	3-4
	[a] Small Estates	3-5
	[b] The Meaning of "Cash"	3-6
	[c] Estates of Nonresident Alien Individuals	3-6
	[d] Identifying the Decedent's "Executor"	3-8
	[e] Designing the Executor's Authority to Allocate	
	Basis Increases	3-10
	[2] Spousal Property Basis Increase	3-13
	[a] Specific Gift	3-14
	[i] Form of the spousal gift.	3-14
	[ii] Amount of the gift.	3-16
	[b] Granting the Executor Discretion to Select	
	Assets to Absorb the Spousal Property Basis	
	Increase	3-17
	[3] Property Acquired From a Decedent	3-19
	[a] Property Acquired by the Decedent's Estate	
	From the Decedent	3-19
	[i] Property appointed to the decedent's	
	estate.	3-20
	[ii] Contingent remainder in the decedent's	
	estate.	3-20
	[b] Property Transferred by the Decedent During	
	Life	3-21
	[i] Property in a qualified revocable trust.	3-21
	[ii] Property subject to a reserved right to	
	alter, amend, or terminate.	3-24
	[c] Property Passing Without Consideration	3-26
	[4] Property Owned by the Decedent	3-27

	[a]	Property in a Qualified Revocable Trust	3-28
	[b]	Property Subject to a Power of Appointment	3-28
	[c]	Property Owned Jointly With a Right of Survivorship	3-31
		[i] Property owned jointly with a surviving spouse.	3-32
		[ii] Property owned jointly with someone other than the surviving spouse.	3-32
		[iii] Property acquired jointly by gift, bequest, etc.	3-33
	[d]	Community Property	3-33
	[e]	QTIP Assets	3-34
	[f]	Lifetime Transfers With Retained Beneficial Enjoyment	3-35
	[g]	Property Acquired by the Decedent Within Three Years of Death	3-35
	[h]	Assets Specifically Excluded From Basis Increases	3-36
¶ 3.04		Planning With Negative Basis Assets	3-37
¶ 3.05		The Basis Increase for Built-In Losses and Loss Carryovers	3-40
¶ 3.06		Planning With the $250,000 Personal Residence Exclusion	3-41
¶ 3.07		Gathering Basis Information	3-42
¶ 3.08		Drafting Survivorship Presumptions	3-42
¶ 3.09		Planning With the Holding Period Rules	3-43
¶ 3.10		Passive Losses Under the Carryover Basis Rules	3-45
¶ 3.11		Charitable Remainder Trusts and the Carryover Basis Rules	3-45
¶ 3.12		Carryover Basis and Partnership Interests	3-46
¶ 3.13		Harvesting Losses	3-47

¶ 3.01 INTRODUCTION

EGTRRA's carryover basis rules create one of the most dramatic changes in the tax law for 2010, replacing the traditional estate tax value basis for property received from a decedent with a basis equal to the decedent's adjusted basis (with certain modifications discussed below and, more briefly discussed, in Chapter 1). Without question, substantial and complex planning will be required to make effective use of the carryover basis rules and address the issues raised by them.

Estate planners should anticipate stiff objections from clients to undertaking extensive revisions of their instruments to address a problem that they perceive will only affect estates of decedents who die in 2010 and the beneficiaries of those estates. The practical estate planner should, nevertheless, attempt to convince all clients of the importance of these changes, and if a client insists on not making changes to his or her estate planning documents to address carryover basis issues, the estate planner should assure that the issues are explained to the client in writing and that, after doing so, the client's rejection of the estate planner's advice is well documented.

¶ 3.02 THE CARRYOVER BASIS RULES APPLY AFTER 2010

Some commentators have questioned whether the modified carryover basis in property received from a decedent who dies in 2010 survives the extinguishment of all of the EGTRRA rules in 2011. Section 1014(f) states that the traditional estate tax value basis rules for assets received from a decedent "shall not apply with respect to decedents dying after December 31, 2009." Section 1022(a)(1) states that the new modified carryover basis rules apply to "property acquired from a decedent dying after December 31, 2009." Section 542(f)(1) of EGTRRA also states that the amendments made by that section (including the modified carryover basis rules) "shall apply to estates of decedents dying after December 31, 2009."

It is important to note that all three of these references involve the date of a decedent's death, rather than the date on which basis becomes relevant in calculating the tax liability of the person who received the property from the decedent. This strongly suggests that the application of the carryover basis rules is not tied to the year in which the asset is ultimately sold or exchanged, but rather the year in which the transferor of the assets died.

The EGTRRA sunset provision is contained in Section 901. Section 901 states, in its entirety:

> SEC. 901. SUNSET OF PROVISIONS OF ACT.
>   (a) In General.—All provisions of, and amendments made by, this Act shall not apply—
>   (1) to taxable, plan, or limitation years beginning after December 31, 2010, or
>   (2) in the case of title V, to estates of decedents dying, gifts made, or generation-skipping transfers, after December 31, 2010.
>   (b) Application of Certain Laws.—The Internal Revenue Code of 1986 and the Employee Retirement Income Security Act of 1974 shall be applied and administered to years, estates, gifts, and transfers described in subsection (a) as if the provisions and amendments described in subsection (a) had never been enacted.

Some might suggest that Section 901(b) means that an individual who receives property from the estate of a decedent who dies in 2010 automatically receives a new basis in 2011 equal to the property's estate tax value, because that is what would have occurred had EGTRRA not been enacted. This seems a fatuous argument, and it would allow Section 901(b) to erase the entire EGTRRA carryover basis rule system, contrary to the fundamental rule of statutory construction that one must give meaning to all provisions of a statute.[1] The practical estate planner must therefore presume that property that takes a carryover basis when it is received from a decedent who dies in 2010 will retain that carryover basis when it is sold after 2010.

¶ 3.03 ALLOCATING THE CARRYOVER BASIS INCREASES

EGTRRA permits the executor of a decedent's estate to allocate additional basis to and among a decedent's assets. The two basis adjustments are the $1.3 million "aggregate basis increase"[2] and the $3 million "spousal property basis increase."[3] The executor allocates these increases on a "Large Transfers Return" filed pursuant to Section 6018.[4] This simple delegation of authority to the executor, however, creates several difficult estate planning and administration problems.

[1] The Tax Return Under Section 6018

EGTRRA permits the executor of a decedent's estate to allocate among the decedent's assets a $1.3 million aggregate basis increase and the $3 million spousal property basis increase.[5] This allocation is to be made on "the return required by section 6018," which may be referred to as the "Large Transfers at

---

[1] See, e.g., 2A Sutherland, Statutes and Statutory Construction § 46:5 (Thomson Reuters/West 7th ed. 2002); Gustafson v. Alloyd Co., 513 US 561 (1995); US Nat'l Bank of Oregon v. Independent Ins. Agents of Am., Inc., 508 US 439 (1993); Smith v. United States, 508 US 223 (1993); In re Pub. Nat. Bank of New York, 278 US 555 (1928); see also Nixon v. Missouri Mun. League, 541 US 125 (2004) (the courts should avoid a construction that would lead to an absurd or futile result).

It is also noteworthy that similar language was used to repeal the 1976 carryover basis rules. Pub. L. No. 94-455, § 2005(f)(1), 94th Cong., 2d Sess. (1976), 90 Stat. 1878. These first carryover basis rules were adopted by the Tax Reform Act of 1976, and then repealed retroactively by the Crude Oil Windfall Profit Tax Act of 1980. Pub. L. No. 96-223, § 401(e), 96th Cong., 2d Sess. (1980), 94 Stat. 299. The 1980 law stated that the repeal applied "in respect of decedents dying after December 31, 1976." The IRS and practitioners have long interpreted this language as rendering the original carryover basis rules ineffectual as to all assets, and not merely those disposed of before 1980. This same analysis should extend to the repeal of the modified carryover basis rules by EGTRRA's sunset rules.

[2] IRC § 1022(b).

[3] IRC § 1022(c).

[4] IRC §§ 1022(d)(3)(A), 6018. This return is due with the federal income tax return for the year in which the decedent died. IRC § 6075(a).

[5] IRC § 1022(b)(2)(B).

Death Return."[6] Once made, this allocation can be changed only as provided by the Secretary of the Treasury.[7]

[a] Small Estates

Section 6018's Large Transfers at Death return, on which the decedent's executor allocates the decedent's aggregate and spousal property basis increases, must be filed only if the total fair market value of a decedent's estate, excluding cash, exceeds $1.3 million.[8] The Internal Revenue Code does not explain how an executor is supposed to allocate the decedent's aggregate basis and spousal basis increases where the total value of the estate (excluding cash) is less than $1.3 million. Section 1022 requires that the allocation be made on the Large Transfers at Death return, and Section 6018 requires that such a return be filed only when the fair market value of the decedent's assets (other than cash) exceeds $1.3 million. The most rational interpretation of this apparent bit of questionable legislative drafting is that a decedent's aggregate basis increase is automatically allocated with respect to estates that are not so large as to require that a Large Transfers at Death return be filed. One must assume that the IRS would interpret this statute in such manner, or there would be no way to allocate the basis increases for estates under $1.3 million in value.

> **EXAMPLE 3-1:** Dave dies in 2010, leaving an estate consisting of the following assets:
>
> | Asset | Basis | Fair Market Value |
> |---|---|---|
> | Residence | $100,000 | $ 300,000 |
> | Marketable securities | $400,000 | $1,000,000 |
> | Cash | $500,000 | $ 500,000 |
>
> Technically, Dave's executor cannot file the return under Section 6018, because the total fair market value of Dave's estate, excluding cash, is precisely $1.3 million. Therefore, no Large Transfers at Death return is required to be filed for Dave's estate. Dave's executor could, of course, voluntarily file the Large Transfers at Death return, but the IRS could reject it as not conforming with the statutory requirements. The best analysis is that Dave's executor need not file the return and that the basis in each asset included in Dave's gross estate is increased (but not beyond its fair market value on the date of death) by automatic allocation of Dave's aggregate basis increase.

---

[6] IRC § 1022(d)(3)(A). The title to Section 6018 for 2010 is "Returns Relating to Large Transfers at Death." Thus, the return may be referred to in shorthand as the "Large Transfers at Death Return."

[7] IRC § 1022(d)(3)(B).

[8] IRC § 1022(b)(1).

[b] The Meaning of "Cash"

Section 6018 requires that the Large Transfers at Death return be filed to allocate a decedent's aggregate and spousal property basis increases only if all property (other than cash) acquired from a decedent has a fair market value over $1.3 million. No section of the Code actually defines "cash," though the term appears throughout the Code.

Regulations under several other Code sections adopt various definitions of "cash," generally including coins and currency of the United States or any foreign country, but sometimes also including cashier's checks, traveler's checks, or money orders and other bank drafts.[9] It is not at all clear what "cash" means in the context of Section 6018, though logically, it should be limited to items that can never have a basis other than their face amount, which should exclude from this definition such typical "cash equivalents" as money market funds. One would also assume that "cash" does not include collectible coins or currency with a numismatic or fair market value that is different from its face value.

> **EXAMPLE 3-2:** Assume the same facts as in Example 3-1, except that instead of $500,000 in cash, Dave had $500,000 in a money market fund. Dave's interest in his money market fund is represented by shares, and recent economic upheavals have shown that a money market fund can, in unusual—but not impossible—circumstances, have a value other than the dollar amount of the account deposit. Therefore, Dave's estate should be $1.8 million for purposes of the threshold for filing the Large Transfers at Death return, and Dave's executor should file this return and expressly allocate Dave's aggregate basis increase among Dave's assets.

[c] Estates of Nonresident Alien Individuals

The executor of the estate of a nonresident alien is required to file a Large Transfers at Death return if the sum of the decedent's U.S. source assets, including tangible property situated within the United States, and all other property acquired from a decedent by a U.S. person (excluding "cash") together exceed $60,000.[10]

---

[9] See, e.g., Temp. Reg. § 1.71-1T, A-5; Reg. § 1.6050I-1(c)(1)(ii)(B); Prop. Reg. § 1.42-18(c)(6)(i).

[10] IRC § 6018(b)(3). As with the return requirements for U.S. citizens and resident aliens, the threshold for filing the return is the aggregate basis increase computed without regard to unused built-in losses and loss carryovers. With respect to a nonresident alien's U.S. estate, however, these items are not added to the aggregate basis increase in any event. IRC § 1022(b)(3).

EXAMPLE 3-3: Dominique, a French citizen and resident, dies in 2010, leaving the following assets that have a situs within the United States:

Asset	Basis	Fair Market Value
Apartment	$100,000	$150,000
Stock of U.S. corporations	$100,000	$150,000

Dominique's executor must file a return under Section 6018 because the total of her U.S. situs assets (excluding cash) exceeds $60,000.

Practical estate planners should consider whether a non-citizen who spends some time in the United States each year might be treated as a resident alien, rather than a nonresident alien, for U.S. income tax purposes. An alien who has very few assets situated outside the United States would receive a far more favorable income tax treatment under the carryover basis rules if he or she were deemed to be resident in the United States.

The income tax rules for determining the residency of a non-citizen are complex, but they are worth studying if a non-citizen falls into this situation. Section 7701(b) adopts mechanical tests by which a person is deemed to be a resident of the United States for income tax purposes, and for determining the starting date of that residency. An individual who holds legal permanent residency in the United States (commonly known as holding a green card) is a U.S. resident from the first day of the year in which the residency is granted.[11]

Lack of a green card does not, however, preclude an individual from qualifying as a resident for U.S. income tax purposes. An individual may qualify as a resident if he or she is physically present in the United States for at least thirty-one days in a calendar year and if the sum of one third of the individual's days of physical residence in the United States during the previous year and one sixth of his or her days of physical residence in the United States during the second preceding year equals at least 183. This is known as the "substantial presence" test.[12]

---

[11] IRC § 7701(b)(1)(A)(i); Reg. § 301.7701(b)-1(b)(1).

[12] IRC § 7701(b)(3)(A); Reg. § 301.7701(b)-1(c). For a more detailed discussion of how to determine whether a noncitizen is a U.S. resident under Section 7701(b)(1), see Bittker & Lokken, Federal Taxation of Income, Estates and Gifts ¶ 65.2 (Thomson Reuters/WG&L, 3d ed. 2000); Henkel, Estate Planning and Wealth Preservation: Strategies and Solutions ¶ 52.02 (Thomson Reuters/WG&L 1997); Kuntz & Peroni, U.S. International Taxation ¶ B1.02 (Thomson Reuters/WG&L 1992); Spielman, U.S. International Estate Planning ¶ 4.02 (Thomson Reuters/WG&L 1996).

[d] Identifying the Decedent's "Executor"

The Large Transfers at Death return must be filed by the executor of the decedent's estate.[13] Section 7701(a)(47) states that

> The term "executor" means the executor or administrator of the decedent, or, if there is no executor or administrator appointed, qualified, and acting within the United States, then any person in actual or constructive possession of any property of the decedent.[14]

Regulations under the estate tax provision that contained the same definition of "executor" for estates of decedents dying before January 1, 2010, stated also that

> The term "person in actual or constructive possession of any property of the decedent" includes, among others, the decedent's agents and representatives; safe-deposit companies, warehouse companies, and other custodians of property in this country; brokers holding, as collateral, securities belonging to the decedent; and debtors of the decedent in this country.[15]

It is not uncommon for a decedent's entire estate to be held in forms of title that do not require the probate of a will or the appointment of an executor. The trustee of the decedent's revocable trust and the beneficiaries under life insurance policies and retirement benefit plan beneficiary designations may all be deemed to be executors of the decedent's estate. If there is no executor, all of these people will be required to file Large Transfers at Death returns and to allocate the decedent's aggregate and spousal property basis increases.

Problems will arise (1) when there is an executor appointed by the probate court who lacks information on assets held by other persons or (2) when there is no executor appointed by a probate court and multiple persons are deemed to be executors for tax purposes. In the former situation, the actual executor must file an incomplete return.

If multiple "executors" exist and they cannot or will not file a return together, none of them is likely to have all of the data required to file a complete Large Transfers at Death return. Section 6018(b)(4) states that the executor, in such a situation, must file as complete a return as possible, reporting all of the property known to be passing from the decedent, and including a "description of such property and the name of every person holding a legal or beneficial interest therein." The Treasury will, it appears, then notify the other

---

[13] IRC § 1022(d)(3)(A).

[14] This definition was added by EGTRRA § 542(f)(1), but the same definition was included in Section 2203 for federal estate tax purposes. Section 2203 does not apply with respect to estates of decedents dying in 2010. Section 7701(a)(47) applies only with respect to estates of decedents dying in 2010.

[15] Reg. § 20.2203-1.

persons who qualify as executors because they are receiving property from the decedent, and they will be required to "make a return as to such property."

> **EXAMPLE 3-4:** Denise's estate plan includes a will that names Denise's sister, Edna, as her executor. Denise also has a revocable trust to which she has transferred most of her assets. Denise names her brother, Tom, as trustee of Denise's revocable trust. Denise also owns a vacation house jointly with a right of survivorship with her good friend, Frank. By the time of her death, Denise had transferred all of her assets, other than her vacation house, to her revocable trust, and thus there are no assets passing under her will. Therefore, Denise's will is not submitted for probate and no executor is appointed. Tom and Frank are both "executors" of Denise's estate for purposes of Section 6018. They may, of course, work together and file one return, but if this is not possible, each must file an individual return reporting the property under their control and the other property that they know to have passed to someone else from the decedent.

Litigation is certain to ensue where such multiple "executors" do not freely exchange information or where they disagree on the appropriate allocation of basis increases. Accordingly, the practical estate planner should make every effort to consolidate all of a client's properties under the same person or persons, at least during 2010. This would eliminate some of the disputes that can arise over the proper allocation of a decedent's aggregate and spousal property basis increases, and make it easier to compile and file a complete Large Transfers at Death return.[16]

The practical estate planner should also stress, to the client, the advisability of having as an executor someone who is not a beneficiary and who is not personally affected by the allocation of the decedent's aggregate and spousal property basis increases. The executor who is a beneficiary of other than a cash gift is almost certain to have a conflict of interest in allocating basis increases among the estate assets. Such a conflict of interest will make it difficult for the executor to do his or her job correctly, and will invite lawsuits from other beneficiaries who believe that they have been treated less well than the executor treated himself or herself.

---

[16] This is actually good advice both before and after 2010 because the existence of multiple persons holding property of a decedent who do not share information with the authorized executor, or multiple persons deemed to be executors for estate tax return purposes (under the same rules as apply for the Large Transfers at Death return), can create serious obstacles to the preparation of an accurate and timely estate tax return.

[e] Designing the Executor's Authority to Allocate Basis Increases

A decedent's executor can allocate the decedent's spousal property basis increase only to the property passing to or in trust for the surviving spouse, but the executor can allocate the decedent's aggregate basis increase to almost any appreciated assets that the decedent owned at death and that are acquired from the decedent by any beneficiary, including the surviving spouse.[17] The tax law neither restricts the manner in which the executor may choose the assets to which the basis increases will be allocated nor suggests criteria for such selection—but, state law imposes a fiduciary duty upon an executor to treat all beneficiaries fairly and impartially.[18] This duty will make it difficult for the executor to allocate the basis increases in a manner that both obtains the maximum income tax advantages and treats all beneficiaries fairly.

The allocation of basis increases is certain to produce extensive fiduciary litigation triggered by the perceived lack of fairness and impartiality. The views of beneficiaries tend to be somewhat less than egalitarian in such matters, and almost any decision made by an executor can be subjectively viewed as unfair or partial in the eyes of a beneficiary and his or her attorney.

> **EXAMPLE 3-5:** Dave dies in 2010, leaving his real estate to his son, Adam, and his securities, to his daughter, Davida. The real estate is worth $2 million, as is Dave's portfolio of securities. The real estate, however, has an adjusted basis of $500,000, while the securities have an adjusted basis of $1 million. Dave's executor, Big Bank, can allocate $650,000 of Dave's aggregate basis increase to property passing to each of the two children, on the grounds that they are equal beneficiaries of the estate. Big Bank could, alternatively, allocate Dave's aggregate basis increase based on the net appreciation in the two assets, as follows:
>
> 1. Appreciation in the securities = $1,000,000 ($2,000,000 − $1,000,000)
> 2. Appreciation in the real estate = $1,500,000 ($2,000,000 − $500,000)
> 3. Total estate appreciation = $2,500,000
> 4. Securities % of total appreciation = 40% ($1,000,000/$2,500,000)
> 5. Real estate % of total appreciation = 60% ($1,500,000/$2,500,000)
>
> The executor would then allocate 40 percent of Dave's aggregate basis increase (40% × $1,300,000 = $520,000) to the securities and 60 percent of Dave's aggregate basis increase (60% × $1,300,000 = $780,000) to the real estate.

---

[17] See discussion infra ¶¶ 3.03[3], 3.03[4].

[18] See Scott & Fratcher, The Law of Trusts § 183 (Aspen, 4th ed. 2001); Uniform Trust Code § 803; Mucci v. Stobbs, 666 NE2d 50 (Ill. App. Ct. 1996) ("No Trustee has unrestricted authority. The requirements of loyalty and fair dealing and good faith are at the core of every trust instrument, whether specifically stated or not.").

Both forms of allocation are arguably fair and equitable, but they clearly favor one beneficiary over another. Beneficiaries on the receiving end of the smaller allocation of aggregate basis increase are certain to complain about the perceived inequity.

The fact that the spousal property basis increase can only be allocated to the surviving spouse or a trust for the surviving spouse's benefit does not eliminate questions about the equity and fairness of an executor's allocation of this increase. Other beneficiaries cannot claim that part of the spousal property basis increase should have been allocated to their assets, but they can argue that the spouse should not be entitled to any share of the aggregate basis increase because he or she has already received a much larger basis increase. The spouse, however, may see things differently, and argue that the two increases are independent and that his or her assets should be eligible for a share of the aggregate basis increase.

The problem of fair and equitable allocation becomes even more complicated in many estates because some assets may lack a sufficient holding period to produce long-term capital gain on their sale,[19] or might actually produce ordinary income on their sale by the beneficiary receiving such assets.[20] It is clear that the executor reduces income taxes more substantially by allocating the decedent's aggregate basis increase to these short-term or ordinary income assets. If such assets are not distributed equally among all estate beneficiaries, however, some beneficiaries will often challenge the executor's impartiality and fairness, despite the anticipated increased tax savings.

> **EXAMPLE 3-6:** Assume the same facts as in Example 3-5, except that Adam is a dealer in real estate and on its sale the gain will be taxed to him as ordinary income.[21] Dave's executor would reduce overall taxes due from the beneficiaries by allocating more of Dave's aggregate basis increase to the real estate, but this would be to the disadvantage of Dave's daughter, and might arguably violate the executor's duty of fairness and impartiality.

> **EXAMPLE 3-7:** Assume the same facts as in Example 3-5, except that Dave bought his securities only two months before his death. Dave's estate does not receive an automatic long-term capital gain holding period under Section 1223(9), and thus any securities sold within one year of the

---

[19] The repeal of the estate tax value basis rules for 2010 also eliminate the automatic long-term holding period that is otherwise provided to assets received from a decedent's estate. IRC § 1223(9). A tacked holding period may, however, be available under Section 1223(2). See infra ¶ 3.09.

[20] Assets could produce ordinary income upon their sale if, for example, they constitute inventory in the hands of the recipient or if depreciation claimed with respect to the asset is subject to the recapture rules of Section 1245 or Section 1250.

[21] IRC § 1250.

date of their original purchase (or, in certain cases, within one year of the date of death), will produce a short-term capital gain. Dave's executor would reduce the total income taxes more by allocating Dave's aggregate basis increase to these securities if the estate plans to sell them promptly, but this could also be described as a violation of the executor's duty of fairness and impartiality.

The practical estate planner should, whenever possible, direct in the decedent's governing instruments how the decedent's aggregate basis increase should be allocated, that is, whether the executor should (1) favor an allocation that would reduce income taxes the most; (2) favor an allocation that is proportionate to the value of the interests passing to the different beneficiaries; or (3) favor an allocation that is proportionate to the appreciation in the interests of the different beneficiaries. The executor should also be allowed to take into account the probability that certain assets, such as closely held business interests or family heirlooms, will not be sold in the foreseeable future, and consider any income tax breaks that would eliminate or reduce the tax on the sale of certain assets, such as a principal residence.

A family member serving as an executor should probably be protected from liability for an allocation made in good faith, in the absence of gross negligence. A professional fiduciary may request such protection, but it is the job of a professional fiduciary to make a reasoned judgment of the proper allocations and to consider all material facts, and the practical estate planner should be reluctant to insulate a professional fiduciary from liability for acts of simple negligence in the allocation of the aggregate and spousal property basis increases. A document that delineates the criteria by which the decedent's aggregate and spousal basis increases should be allocated, furthermore, renders it less difficult for the fiduciary to discharge this obligation in a fair and impartial manner.

Drafting Tip: The following clause broadly authorizes a decedent's executor to allocate the decedent's aggregate basis increase in a manner that will minimize taxes, but that is otherwise proportionate based on the net appreciation in the assets received by the various beneficiaries.

> **Allocation of Basis Increase.** My personal representative shall allocate any increases in the adjusted basis of property owned by me at the time of my death, whether passing under my Will or otherwise, to the extent such property is eligible to receive such an allocation, as my personal representative deems to be in the best interests of my estate and its beneficiaries. In making these allocations my personal representative shall:
>
> (a) First, satisfy all charitable bequests with assets to which no aggregate or spousal property basis increases may be allocated;
>
> (b) Second, satisfy all charitable bequests with assets that have an adjusted income tax basis closest to zero of all of my assets available to satisfy these bequests;
>
> (c) Third, generally not allocate basis increases to assets the gain from the sale of which is not subject to federal income tax under present federal income tax laws;
>
> (d) Fourth, allocate basis increases to assets that are reasonably likely to be sold within the three-year period beginning on the date of my death, the sale of which will produce an income tax liability that is taxed at a rate higher than that on long-term capital gains; and
>
> (e) Fifth, allocate the remaining basis increases among assets to which a basis increase may be allocated in proportion to each asset's pro rata share of the total appreciation of all such assets owned by me on the date of my death, without regard to the identity of the recipient of such assets.
>
> Any reference in this paragraph to assets "owned by me on the date of my death" shall apply equally to assets deemed owned by me on the date of my death under the federal income tax rules governing allocation of my aggregate basis increase. My personal representative shall allocate all of my spousal property basis increase to property eligible to receive such an allocation. My *husband/wife* shall be entitled to the benefit of my spousal property basis increase and a proportionate share of my aggregate basis increase, such proportion determined after first allocating my spousal property basis increase. My personal representative shall not be liable to anyone for any allocation of my basis increases made in good faith, in the absence of gross negligence.

---

[2] Spousal Property Basis Increase

The spousal property basis increase permits the executor of a decedent's estate to increase the basis of property acquired from a decedent by the decedent's surviving spouse, or a trust for the spouse's benefit, by up to $3 million.[22] The amount allocated to the property received from a decedent by the surviving spouse cannot increase the basis of any asset above its fair market value on the date of the decedent's death.[23]

[a] Specific Gift

The practical estate planner should consider having a married client who has a substantial estate leave to the surviving spouse or to a trust for the spouse's benefit sufficient appreciated property to take full advantage of the spousal property basis increase. This approach assures that the spousal property basis increase is fully utilized. Unfortunately, this is not as simple a planning technique as it may at first appear.

[i] Form of the spousal gift. The spousal property basis increase is allowed only for property passing to a surviving spouse outright or as qualified terminable interest property (QTIP).[24] No increase can be made to property passing outright to the surviving spouse if the transfer is a "terminable interest," as defined in rules that are substantially similar to the estate tax marital deduction rules regarding nondeductible terminable interests.[25]

A QTIP, for carryover basis purposes, means property that passes from the decedent and in which

1. The surviving spouse is entitled to all the income from the property, payable annually or at more frequent intervals, or has a usufruct interest for life in the property, and
2. No person (including the spouse) has a power to appoint any part of the property to any person other than the surviving spouse.[26]

A marital trust in which the surviving spouse is entitled to all of the trust income payable at least annually and over which the spouse holds a general testamentary power to appoint the trust funds to anyone, including his or her own estate, will qualify as a QTIP for carryover basis purposes, though it would be a general power of appointment trust under Section 2056(b)(5) for estate tax purposes. On the other hand, a marital trust in which the surviving spouse is entitled to all of the income payable at least annually and over which the spouse holds a lifetime power to appoint the trust funds to anyone, including himself or herself, will not qualify as a QTIP for carryover basis purposes,

---

[22] IRC § 1022(c).

[23] IRC § 1022(d)(2).

[24] IRC § 1022(c).

[25] IRC §§ 1022(c)(4)(B), 1022(c)(4)(C).

[26] IRC § 1022(d)(5)(B).

though it would be deductible as a general power of appointment marital trust for federal estate tax purposes.

> **EXAMPLE 3-8:** Dave dies in 2010, leaving his $10 million estate in a trust for the lifetime benefit of his wife, Wilma. At Wilma's death, the trust funds will be distributed to their two children in equal shares. The trust requires that all income be paid to Wilma during her lifetime, not less often than quarter-annually. It also authorizes the trustee (an independent bank) to distribute to Wilma as much principal as the trustee deems appropriate for any reason. The trust does not authorize the trustee or anyone else to distribute principal or income to anyone other than Wilma during Wilma's lifetime. The trust is a QTIP trust for carryover basis purposes, and the executor of Dave's estate may increase the basis of assets passing to the trust by Dave's $3 million spousal property basis increase and by some or all of his $1.3 million aggregate basis increase.[27]

> **EXAMPLE 3-9:** Assume the same facts as in Example 3-8, except that Wilma is given lifetime power to appoint the trust principal to and among Dave's children to the extent needed to meet emergency health needs. Wilma's power of appointment permits her to appoint trust assets to someone other than herself during her lifetime and disqualifies the trust as a QTIP for carryover basis purposes. Dave's executor cannot allocate any of Dave's spousal property basis increase to the trust, but it can allocate to the trust some or all of Dave's $1.3 million aggregate basis increase.

It is clear that the spousal property basis increase cannot be allocated to property passing to the surviving spouse as an estate trust that allows the trustee to accumulate income for ultimate distribution to the surviving spouse's estate.[28] It is also clear that the spousal property basis increase can be allocated to a usufruct,[29] which is similar to a legal life estate but is created under civil law concepts, rather than common law concepts, and thus is found in the United States mostly in Louisiana.

On the other hand, it is less clear whether spousal property basis increase may be allocated to a legal life estate in property, though distinguishing between a legal life estate and a usufruct in this manner would seem to be unreasonable.[30] It is also unclear whether the spousal property basis increase can be

---

[27] If Wilma also dies in 2010, however, the assets of this trust will not be eligible for her aggregate basis increase, because they would not be owned by her at the time of her death. See discussion of the "owned by the decedent" requirement infra ¶ 3.03[4]. If Wilma dies after 2010, however, no portion of the trust funds should be included in her gross estate for federal estate tax purposes, because no election was made to deduct the property passing to this trust as a QTIP for estate tax purposes in 2010.

[28] See Reg. § 20.2056(e)-2(b).

[29] See IRC § 1022(c)(5)(B)(i).

[30] See Berall, Harrison, Blattmachr & Detzel, "Planning for Carryover Basis That Can Be/Should Be/Must Be Done Now," 29 Est. Plan. 99, 101 (Mar. 2002).

allocated to a charitable remainder trust in which the spouse is the sole life-time beneficiary, though the Treasury is directed to promulgate regulations treating an annuity similarly to an income interest, and such regulations might also permit the allocation of the spousal property basis increase to a charitable remainder trust.[31]

Two other typical forms of marital disposition may be suspect under the carryover basis rules. First, the Clayton QTIP, by which any portion of the trust that the decedent's executor does not elect to deduct is held in a form that would not qualify for the marital deduction, should be avoided in 2010. There is no QTIP election in 2010, and such a trust would seemingly be un-workable in 2010.

Second, some marital trusts give the surviving spouse a right to withdraw the trust income currently, rather than compelling that it be distributed. This is permitted under the estate tax marital deduction regulations.[32] These regula-tions do not apply for carryover basis purposes, though it seems likely that the IRS would apply this same analysis to the carryover basis rules. Still, the prac-tical estate planner should be cautious about using income withdrawal rights and should, instead, compel, in a QTIP instrument, all income to be distributed at least annually with respect to trusts created under instruments of a decedent who dies in 2010.[33]

The practical estate planner should recommend that clients convert testa-mentary spousal gifts to outright gifts, QTIP gifts, usufructs, or testamentary general power of appointment trusts. He or she should avoid using estate trusts, inter vivos general power of appointment marital trusts, and, pending further clarification, legal life estates, income withdrawal rights, or charitable remainder trusts.

The carryover basis rules also state that the spousal property basis in-crease cannot be allocated to property passing to a surviving spouse that is a terminable interest.[34] The spousal property basis increase cannot, therefore, be allocated to such assets as patents, copyrights, or terms for years, though it can be allocated to a bond, note, or similar contractual obligation.[35]

[ii] Amount of the gift. The share of a decedent's estate that can take advantage of the spousal property basis increase is, as discussed earlier,[36]

---

[31] IRC § 1022(c)(5)(B).

[32] Reg. § 20.2056(b)-5(f)(8).

[33] See Berall, Harrison, Blattmachr & Detzel, "Planning for Carryover Basis That Can Be/Should Be/Must Be Done Now," 29 Est. Plan. 99, 100 (Mar. 2002).

[34] IRC § 1022(c)(4)(B).

[35] IRC § 1022(c)(4)(B); see Berall, Harrison, Blattmachr & Detzel, "Planning for Carryover Basis That Can Be/Should Be/Must Be Done Now," 29 Est. Plan. 99, 100–101 (Mar. 2002).

[36] See ¶ 2.04[2][b].

based on the net appreciation in assets passing to a spouse, rather than the fair market value of those assets. This creates a problem in describing a gift sufficient to take advantage of this basis increase because the same basis increase can consume relatively large or small portions of the estate.

A practical estate planner must usually select among three techniques for determining the amount of property that will pass to or in trust for a surviving spouse to take full advantage of the spousal property basis increase. One may leave the surviving spouse

1. The largest fair market value of property that reflects $3 million in appreciation;
2. The smallest fair market value of property that reflects $3 million in appreciation; or
3. A share of the fair market value of the total available assets that reflects $3 million in appreciation, selecting assets that are fairly representative of the appreciation and depreciation among assets that qualify for allocation of the spousal property basis increase.

The selection among these choices involves consideration of nontax considerations, such as whether the client wishes to transfer more or less property to the surviving spouse and whether the client anticipates a dispute between the spouse and the nonmarital share beneficiaries over the fairness of the division of the estate. A practical estate planner should draft the instrument in a manner that reflects these nontax considerations, and document the conversation in the attorney's notes and in written communications with the client.

[b] Granting the Executor Discretion to Select Assets to Absorb the Spousal Property Basis Increase

A practical estate planner may choose to direct the client's executor to select which of the estate's assets are to be distributed as the marital share in order to qualify for allocation of the spousal property basis increase. This is an extremely difficult decision for the executor unless the marital and nonmarital shares are held in identical trusts; in all other situations, some beneficiary is very likely to feel slighted. It is usually better for all parties to direct that the spouse receive property fairly representative of the appreciation and depreciation in the assets available for allocation.

A practical estate planner must also pay careful attention to the specific assets that comprise the decedent's estate and the effect of the specific assets on the allocation process. A formula gift to the surviving spouse of an amount equal to that which will absorb the decedent's spousal property basis increase should, however, be satisfiable only from assets to which such basis increase can be allocated under the carryover basis rules.[37] Excluding assets that do not qualify for a basis allocation, such as income in respect of a decedent (IRD), may distort the results if the estate consists largely of such assets.

> **EXAMPLE 3-10:** Hilda's will leaves to her husband, Henry, assets that can absorb her full $3 million spousal property basis increase. Hilda's estate includes $2 million worth of real estate with an adjusted basis of $1 million, $1 million worth of stock with a basis of $500,000, and a $16 million installment sales note. The note was received by Hilda in a sale of closely held stock that had a negligible adjusted basis. The note is an IRD item, and thus no portion of Hilda's spousal property basis increase can be allocated to the note. The only assets that can be transferred to Henry that will absorb Hilda's spousal property basis increase are the real estate and the securities. The $3 million spousal property basis increase will attract only $3 million worth of assets, utilizing only $1.5 million of spousal property basis increase, with $16 million worth of IRD passing to the nonmarital share.

When a practical estate planner identifies a large quantity of estate assets as to which no allocation of spousal property basis increase can be made, he or she should discuss with the client the amount that the surviving spouse should receive. The estate planner should not rely strictly on a formula clause based on the amount of the spousal property basis increase. One alternative is for the formula clause to give the spouse a guaranteed minimum amount of value of assets, to assure that some of the assets not qualifying for the spousal property basis increase will pass to the spouse.

---

[37] See discussion infra ¶ 3.03[4][g].

Drafting Tip: The following is a bequest of the greater of a set dollar amount ($5 million, in this sample provision) or the smallest amount of the estate required to absorb the decedent's entire spousal property basis increase.

> **B. Marital Share.** The "Marital Share" shall be a fractional share of my Residuary Estate.
>
> **(1)** The numerator of the fraction shall equal the greater of:
>
> **(a)** Five million dollars ($5,000,000); and
>
> **(b)** The smallest value of the assets of my Residuary Estate to which my Personal Representative can allocate the entire spousal property basis increase allowed under federal income tax laws for property passing to my surviving spouse; and
>
> **(2)** The denominator of the fraction shall equal the value of my Residuary Estate.
>
> My personal representative shall satisfy this share, to the extent possible, with property to which my spousal property basis increase may be allocated, but in the absence of a sufficient quantity of such assets, shall use other property to satisfy this gift. References in this paragraph B. to my Residuary Estate shall include only those portions of my Residuary Estate to which the spousal property basis increase may be allocated under federal income tax law.

---

[3] Property Acquired From a Decedent

A decedent's executor may allocate the aggregate basis increase and the spousal property basis increase only to property that was both "acquired from a decedent" and "owned by the decedent at the time of death."[38] The phrase "acquired from a decedent" is defined far more broadly than "owned by the decedent at the time of death," but both tests must be met in order for a basis increase to be allocated to an asset.[39]

[a] Property Acquired by the Decedent's Estate From the Decedent

Section 1022(e) states that property acquired from a decedent includes "property acquired by bequest, devise, or inheritance, or by the decedent's estate from the decedent." This phrase should include most forms of transmis-

---

[38] IRC § 1022(d)(1)(A).

[39] See IRC § 1014(b), which lists ten different classes of property deemed to have been acquired from a decedent for purposes of determining the basis of such assets.

sion from a decedent to a beneficiary of the decedent's probate or intestate estate.

[i] Property appointed to the decedent's estate. The reference to "property acquired…by the decedent's estate from the decedent" should include property that the decedent appoints to his or her estate under a general power of appointment. This conclusion may be relatively unimportant because property passing pursuant to the exercise of a power of appointment is not deemed "owned by the decedent." A decedent's executor cannot, therefore, allocate the decedent's aggregate or spousal property basis increases to property over which the decedent only holds a general power of appointment even if the property is appointed to the decedent's estate.[40]

> **EXAMPLE 3-11:** Daniel died in 2005, and his will created a trust for the benefit of his wife, Susan. The trust instrument directs the trustee to pay Susan all of the trust income, at least annually, and gives Susan a testamentary power to appoint the trust fund to anyone she pleases, including her estate. Susan dies in 2010, appointing the trust fund in favor of her estate, but otherwise leaving no separate estate of her own. The best analysis is that while the appointed trust assets may be deemed acquired from Susan at her death, they were not owned by Susan at the time of her death, and, therefore, Susan's executor cannot allocate her aggregate basis increase to and among the appointed assets.

[ii] Contingent remainder in the decedent's estate. Property paid to a decedent's estate from a trust under a contingent remainder interest should be deemed to be "property acquired…by the decedent's estate from the decedent," particularly if the decedent created the trust. This property is not, however, property owned by the decedent at the time of his or her death.

> **EXAMPLE 3-12:** In June 2008, Harry gives his vacation house to a qualified personal residence trust (QPRT), and reserves the right to use it for the next ten years or until his death, whichever first occurs. The trust instrument states that, if Harry dies within ten years, the vacation house will be distributed to his estate. If he lives ten years, the trust will distribute the vacation house to Harry's three children, in equal shares. Harry dies in 2010, and the vacation house is distributed to Harry's estate. The best analysis is that the residence is deemed to have been acquired from Harry for carryover basis purposes.[41]

---

[40] See discussion infra ¶ 3.03[4][b].

[41] Harry's executor cannot allocate his aggregate basis increase and spousal basis increase to this house, however, because it was not owned by Harry at the time of his death. See infra ¶ 3.03[4].

EXAMPLE 3-13: In June, 2008, Harry also created a grantor retained annuity trust (GRAT), to which he transferred $1 million worth of marketable securities. Harry reserved the right to an annual distribution of $274,192.70, payable at the end of each year for four years. Harry provided in the trust instrument that, if he died before the fourth anniversary of the trust, the remaining trust funds would be paid to his estate. Harry died in January 2010, and the entire trust fund is distributed to Harry's estate. The best analysis is that these assets are deemed to have been acquired from Harry for carryover basis purposes.[42]

[b] Property Transferred by the Decedent During Life

Section 1022(e)(2) states that "property acquired from a decedent" includes certain transfers made by the decedent during lifetime even if the decedent does not own the property at the time of death. These transfers include

1. Transfers to a "qualified revocable trust" (as defined in Section 645(b)(1)), and
2. Transfers to any other trust with respect to which the decedent reserved the right to make any change in the enjoyment thereof through the exercise of a power to alter, amend, or terminate the trust.

[i] Property in a qualified revocable trust. Property transferred by the decedent to a "qualified revocable trust" and passing to someone at the decedent's death is deemed to have been acquired from a decedent for purposes of the allocation of the decedent's aggregate and spousal property basis increases.[43] A "qualified revocable trust" is defined in Section 645(b)(1) as a trust or portion of a trust that was, at the decedent's death, treated as owned by the decedent under Section 676 by reason of the deceased grantor's power to revoke the trust. The determination of whether the grantor held the requisite power must be made without regard to Section 672(e), which, for most other grantor trust purposes, imputes to a grantor certain interests and powers held by the grantor's spouse.[44]

The regulations state that a trust can be a qualified revocable trust even if the decedent's power to revoke was exercisable only with the approval or consent of a nonadverse party, but not if the decedent's power to revoke was exercisable only with the approval or consent of an adverse party.[45] A trust that

---

[42] Harry's executor cannot allocate his aggregate basis increase and spousal basis increase to these assets, however, because they were not owned by Harry at the time of his death. See infra ¶ 3.03[4].

[43] IRC § 1022(e)(2)(A).

[44] IRC § 645(b)(1); Reg. § 1.645-1(b)(1).

[45] Reg. § 1.645-1(b)(1).

can be revoked by the decedent's spouse, but not by the decedent, is not a qualified revocable trust, but a trust that can be revoked by the decedent only with the approval or consent of the decedent's spouse may be a qualified revocable trust if the spouse is not an adverse party.[46]

> **EXAMPLE 3-14:** Helen creates a revocable trust and reserves the power, exercisable alone by her at any time, to revoke the trust and revest the trust assets in herself. The trust is a qualified revocable trust, and Helen's executor can allocate to the assets in this trust all or part of her aggregate basis increase (but not enough to raise the adjusted basis of any one asset above its fair market value on the date of her death). The trust is a qualified revocable trust because Helen held at her death the power to revoke the trust and revest the assets in herself, exercisable without the consent of an adverse person, and was taxable as the trust's owner under Section 676.

> **EXAMPLE 3-15:** Henry creates a revocable trust, but he is concerned that his wife, Wanda, must be able to terminate the trust if she deems it necessary to deal with his assets in case of his disability. Henry gives Wanda the power to revoke the trust and revest the assets in Henry at any time. Wanda's power is exercisable during Henry's lifetime. Henry is taxable as the trust's owner under Section 676 because the power granted to Wanda is imputed to Henry under Section 672(e). The trust is not a qualified revocable trust, however, because Henry cannot revoke it, and thus Henry's executor cannot allocate any of his aggregate basis or spousal property basis increases to the assets held by this trust.

> **EXAMPLE 3-16:** Henry creates a revocable trust and reserves the power to revoke the trust and revest the assets in himself, but only with the consent of his daughter, Daphne, who is the trustee of the trust. Daphne has no substantial interest in the trust that would be adversely affected by the exercise of Henry's power to revoke. Henry is taxable as the trust's owner under Section 676(a), and the trust is a qualified revocable trust. Henry's executor can allocate any of his aggregate and spousal property basis increases to the assets held by this trust (but not enough to raise the adjusted basis of those assets beyond their fair market value on the date of death).

As illustrated by the above examples, a practical estate planner must carefully scrutinize a client's revocable trust to assure that the client's power to revoke does not require the consent of an adverse party (that is, an individual who has a substantial interest in the trust that would be adversely affected by the exercise of the power to revoke). A client who wishes to retain such a consent requirement should hold sufficient appreciated assets outside of the trust

---

[46] Reg. § 1.645-1(b)(1).

to take full advantage of the client's aggregate and spousal property basis increases in the event that the client happens to die during 2010.

Some revocable trust documents authorize the trustee to disregard an incapacitated grantor's instruction to revoke the trust. The suspension of the grantor's right to revoke the trust could terminate the status of the trust as a qualified revocable trust. The preamble to the final qualified revocable trust regulations states that a trust will continue to be a qualified revocable trust if an agent or legal representative of the grantor can revoke the trust under state law during the grantor's incapacity even if the grantor remains incapacitated on the date of death.[47]

State law generally treats a grantor's right to revoke a trust as personal, and does not permit a successor in interest, such as a guardian or conservator, to exercise that power, unless the governing instrument or specific state law provides expressly to the contrary.[48] A grantor's right to revoke a trust can, however, be exercised by an attorney-in-fact who has been granted express authority to exercise the power.[49]

The Uniform Trust Code takes a minority approach to the ability of persons other than the grantor to exercise the power to revoke. Section 602 of the Uniform Trust Code states

(E) A settlor's powers with respect to revocation, amendment, or distribution of trust property may be exercised by an agent under a power of attorney only to the extent expressly authorized by the terms of the trust or the power.

(F) A conservator of the settlor or, if no conservator has been appointed, a guardian of the settlor may exercise a settlor's powers with re-

---

[47] 67 Fed. Reg. 78,372.

[48] See, e.g., Barlow v. Loomis, 19 F. Supp. 677 (Cir. Ct. Vt. 1884); United Bldg. & Loan Ass'n v. Garrett, 64 F. Supp. 460 (D. Ark. 1946); Johnson v. Kotyck, 90 Cal. Rep. 2d 99, 76 Cal. App. 4th 83 (1999), review denied (2000); In re Guardianship of Muller, 650 So. 2d 698 (Fla. Dist. Ct. App. 1995); Fleming v. Casady, 202 Iowa 1094, 211 NW 488 (1927); In re Guardianship of Garcia, 262 Neb. 205, 631 NW2d 464 (2001); First Nat'l Bank of Cincinnati v. Oppenheimer, 190 NE2d 70, 92 Ohio Law Abs. 233, 23 Ohio Op. 2d 19 (1963); In re Guardianship of Lombardo, 716 NE2d 189, 86 Ohio St. 3d 600 (1999); In re Guardianship of Lee, 1999 Okla. Civ. App. 90, 982 P2d 539 (1999); Grove v. Payne, 47 Wash. 2d 461, 288 P2d 242, (1955). But cf. In re Rudwick, 2002 WL 3170757 (Va. Cir. Ct. Dec. 5, 2002). See also Annotation, "Guardian's Authority, Without Seeking Court Approval, to Exercise Ward's Right to Revoke Trust," 53 ALR4th 1297 (1987).

[49] In re Guardianship of Muller, 650 So. 2d 698 (Fla. Dist. Ct. App. 1995); In re Estate of Hutta, 20 Fiduc. Rep. 2d 178 (Pa. Com. Pleas. 2000); Kline v. Utah Dep't of Health, 776 P2d 57 (Utah Ct. App. 1989) (not allowing agent under durable power to revoke or amend on behalf of incapacitated settlor); Matter of Mostler, 79 A2d 1067 (Pa. Super. Ct. 1998) (agent allowed to revoke principal's revocable trust under durable power authorizing other actions involving the trust but not expressly authorizing revocation).

spect to revocation, amendment, or distribution of trust property only with the approval of the court supervising the conservator or guardianship.

The final Section 645 regulations deleted from the proposed regulations the requirements that a qualified revocable trust must be a domestic trust and that the Section 645 election must result in the trust being treated as part of a domestic estate.[50] A decedent's executor can, therefore, allocate all or part of the decedent's aggregate and spousal property basis increases to the assets held by a foreign revocable trust if the trust otherwise is a qualified revocable trust.

[ii] Property subject to a reserved right to alter, amend, or terminate. Section 1022(e)(2)(B) states that property is treated as "acquired from a decedent" even though transferred during the decedent's lifetime if the decedent reserved a right to alter, amend, or terminate the transfer. This rule is seemingly designed to cover situations in which the decedent transfers property to an irrevocable trust and, either as a trustee or otherwise, reserves the right to control or alter the beneficial enjoyment of the trust fund without necessarily reserving any personal interest in the trust.

> **EXAMPLE 3-17:** In 2005, Harry transferred $1 million to an irrevocable trust for the benefit of his children, grandchildren, and more remote descendants. Harry is a trustee and, as such, holds the power to distribute income and principal to and among the beneficiaries as he deems appropriate. At Harry's death in 2010, the trust fund has grown to a value of $3 million. The trust assets should be deemed acquired from Harry for carryover basis purposes because he transferred the property to the trust and reserved the right to change its beneficial enjoyment.[51]

A practical estate planner should be careful about assuming that this rule is merely the carryover basis equivalent of the estate tax rule set forth in Section 2038(1). This carryover basis rule differs significantly from the estate tax rule in at least three important respects:

1. The carryover basis rule does not expressly apply to powers exercisable only in conjunction with another, so that a power exercisable only by the unanimous agreement of the decedent and another trustee would not appear to be covered by this rule;
2. The carryover basis rule does not contain an exception for lifetime transfers for bona fide consideration in money or money's worth, so that a power to control the beneficial enjoyment of a trust to which

---

[50] 67 Fed. Reg. 78,372–78,373. Compare Prop. Reg. § 1.645-1(b)(1) (Dec. 18, 2000).

[51] Harry's executor cannot allocate his aggregate basis increase and spousal basis increase to these assets, however, because they were not owned by Harry at the time of his death. See infra ¶ 3.03[4].

the decedent sold assets for full and adequate consideration would appear to be covered by the carryover basis rule; and

3. The carryover basis rule requires that the power to alter the beneficial enjoyment have been reserved by the decedent, whereas the estate tax rule applies also to powers that are created or transferred to the decedent after the transfer, so that a decedent might not be covered by the carryover basis rule if he or she became a trustee after the resignation of an initial trustee of a trust and, in that manner, obtained the power to control beneficial enjoyment.

EXAMPLE 3-18: Assume the same facts as in Example 3-17, except that Harry is one of three co-trustees who must act by majority vote in all matters. Harry appears to lack the actual power to alter, amend, or terminate the trust except with the concurrence of another trustee. Therefore, the trust assets would not appear to be deemed "acquired from a decedent" (i.e., Harry) upon Harry's death, and Harry's executor cannot allocate any of his aggregate basis increase to the trust assets.[52]

EXAMPLE 3-19: Assume the same facts as in Example 3-17, except that Harry is not a trustee of the trust when it is created. One year later, the initial trustee resigns and, without any prior agreement with Harry, the initial trustee nominates Harry to be the successor trustee. Harry dies in 2010, holding the power to alter, amend, or terminate the trust, but this power was not retained by him upon his transfer to the trust in 2005. The trust assets would not, therefore, appear to be deemed "acquired from a decedent" (i.e., Harry) upon Harry's death, and Harry's executor cannot allocate any of his aggregate basis increase to the trust assets.

EXAMPLE 3-20: Assume the same facts as in Example 3-17, except that the trust was created by Harry's father, who funded it with a cash gift of $5,000. Harry was the initial trustee and remains so at his death in 2010. In 2006, however, Harry sold $1 million worth of securities to the trust in exchange for a promissory note in the face amount of $1 million and bearing interest at the applicable federal rate under Section 1274. The trust assets should be deemed to have been acquired from Harry upon his death despite the fact that his only transfer to the trust was a bona fide sale for full and adequate consideration in money or money's worth of property.[53]

---

[52] See, however, the other definitions of "property acquired from a decedent," discussed infra ¶ 3.03[3][c], which may apply in this situation.

[53] Harry's executor cannot allocate his aggregate basis increase and spousal basis increase to these assets, however, because they were not owned by Harry at the time of his death. See infra ¶ 3.03[4].

[c] Property Passing Without Consideration

Section 1022(e)(3) states that property is deemed to have been acquired from a decedent if it passes "from the decedent by reason of death to the extent that such property passed without consideration." This provision is not limited to property transferred during the decedent's lifetime, though it could apply to such property, and such provision appears to be designed as a "catch all" treating virtually all forms of gratuitous transfers at death as property passing from the decedent. Of course, absent clarification from the Congress, the IRS, or the courts, the precise scope of this rule is uncertain. Read literally, however, this rule appears to treat as property passing from a decedent any form of transfer of property from the decedent at his or her death as long as the recipient does not have to provide consideration.

> **EXAMPLE 3-21:** At Harry's death in 2010, his will leaves all of his property to his children, Adam, Beth, and Carl. Harry also owned a joint brokerage account which, under the terms of the account documents, passes at Harry's death to Harry's brother. Harry contributed all of the consideration to buy the securities in the brokerage account, which are worth $250,000 and have a basis of $50,000 at his death. Harry could have terminated the joint ownership in the brokerage account at any time during his lifetime and recovered the assets. The securities in the brokerage account should be deemed to have been acquired by Harry's brother from Harry for carryover basis purposes because they passed by reason of his death and without consideration.

This clause treats property as passing from the decedent "to the extent that such property passed without consideration," but it does not use the more common estate tax term "without adequate and full consideration." This suggests that any type of payment (in money, property, or even services) will remove the passage of property from the scope of this definition, but only to the extent of the value of the consideration.

The statute does not provide any guidance regarding how consideration furnished by the recipient of the property is to be taken into account in determining the extent to which property passes from the decedent. The phrase "to the extent" could require that the value of the property passing from the decedent to the recipient on the date of death be reduced by (1) the value of the consideration actually contributed by the recipient or (2) the proportionate share of the value of the property received on the date of death measured by the relative contribution of the recipient to the contribution of the decedent. This distinction is important because the former approach treats all of the net appreciation in the property as passing from the decedent, and thus renders a larger portion of the total appreciation in the value of the property eligible for allocation of the decedent's aggregate and spousal property basis increases.

EXAMPLE 3-22: Assume the same facts as in Example 3-21, except that Harry's brother contributed $10,000 of the $50,000 invested in the securities held in the brokerage account. The brokerage account passes at Harry's death to his brother for purposes of the carryover basis rules only to the extent it passes without consideration. It is not clear from the statute whether this means that (a) $240,000 (i.e., $250,000 value of securities − $10,000 brother's investment) of the brokerage account is deemed to have passed from the decedent to Harry's brother, or (b) $200,000 of the brokerage account (i.e., $250,000 value of securities × [$10,000 brother's investment/$50,000 total investment]) is deemed to have been acquired by Harry's brother from him for carryover basis purposes.

This rule should not apply, however, to the typical intentional grantor trust created by a decedent during his or her lifetime. Revenue Ruling 85-13,[54] states that, for federal income tax purposes, the grantor of a grantor trust is deemed to own the assets of the trust directly. The basis rules are income tax rules, and thus the ownership of the trust assets of an intentional grantor trust should be treated as ownership of those assets by the grantor. However, while the assets pass to the beneficiaries without consideration in this case, they do not pass from the decedent by reason of death for purposes of the carryover basis rules. Rather, they pass under the inter vivos transfer; the decedent's grantor trust powers rarely constitute a right to control beneficial enjoyment because to do so would frustrate the tax objectives of an intentional grantor trust.

EXAMPLE 3-23: Harry creates an intentional grantor trust. The trust is irrevocable and provides that the trustee may distribute income and principal to the Harry's descendants for the maximum period permitted under state law. Harry retains the nonfiduciary right to reacquire trust assets in exchange for assets of equivalent value, causing the trust to be owned by him for federal income tax purposes.[55] Harry is deemed to own the assets of the trust under the grantor trust rules and that right terminates upon his death. The assets of the trust should not be deemed acquired from Harry by reason of his death even though they pass to the trust beneficiaries without consideration. Accordingly, Harry's executor should not be able to allocate his aggregate basis increases to the trust assets.

[4] Property Owned by the Decedent

The decedent's executor may, as noted above, allocate the decedent's aggregate and spousal property basis increases only to property that was both "ac-

---

[54] Rev. Rul. 85-13, 1985-1 CB 184.
[55] IRC § 675(4)(C).

quired from a decedent" and "owned by the decedent at the time of death."[56] Section 1022 does not, however, define what constitutes property "owned by the decedent," but general rules of statutory construction require that an undefined phrase be given its ordinary or plain meaning.[57] A decedent should, therefore, be deemed to "own" property the legal and equitable title to which is in the decedent's name.

The carryover basis rules treat certain property that might not otherwise be treated as owned by the decedent as being so owned, and also determine the amount of such property deemed owned by the decedent that is eligible for receiving an allocation of the decedent's aggregate or spousal property basis increases. These rules are fundamental to determining how a decedent's executor can allocate the decedent's aggregate and spousal property basis increases.

[a] Property in a Qualified Revocable Trust

Property held in a revocable trust is treated as being owned by the decedent at the time of his or her death if the trust is a "qualified revocable trust."[58] "Qualified revocable trust" is defined with reference to Section 645(b)(1), as discussed above.[59]

[b] Property Subject to a Power of Appointment

A decedent is not treated as owning any property merely because he or she holds a power of appointment over that property.[60] A decedent's executor cannot, therefore, allocate any of the decedent's aggregate or spousal basis increases to assets not owned by the decedent but over which the decedent simply holds a power of appointment. This rule apparently applies even if the power permits the decedent to appoint the assets to the decedent's estate.

> **EXAMPLE 3-24:** Hal is the trustee and primary beneficiary of a trust created under the will of his late mother. The trust gives Hal the right to all of the trust income and so much of its principal as Hal, personally and

---

[56] IRC § 1022(d)(1)(A).

[57] See, e.g., McCreary County, Ky. v. American Civil Liberties Union of Ky., 545 US 844 (2005); Santa Fe Indep. School Dist. v. Doe, 530 US 290 (2000); Edwards v. Aguillard, 482 US 578 (1987) (look to "plain meaning of the statute's words, enlightened by their context and the contemporaneous legislative history [and] the historical context of the statute,…and the specific sequence of events leading to [its] passage").

[58] IRC §§ 1022(d)(1)(B)(ii), 645(b)(1). See discussion of qualified revocable trusts at Danforth, Lane & Zaritsky, Federal Income Taxation of Estates and Trusts ¶ 1.06[4] (Thomson Reuters/WG&L, 3d ed. 2001).

[59] See supra ¶ 3.03[3][b][i].

[60] IRC § 1022(d)(1)(B)(iii).

not in his fiduciary capacity, deems appropriate for any purpose. At Hal's death, the remaining and unappointed trust funds are to be distributed to his three children, in equal shares. Hal dies in 2010. Hal's executor cannot allocate any of Hal's aggregate or spousal property basis increases to any of the trust assets, because Hal did not own them at the time of his death.

A client who holds a general power of appointment over appreciated assets, and whose other appreciated property is insufficient to take full advantage of the client's aggregate and spousal property basis increases, should seek to remove sufficient appreciated assets from the trust and vest them in outright ownership by the client in order to take full advantage of the client's aggregate and spousal property basis increases. This will be easy to do if the client's power of appointment is exercisable during his or her lifetime in favor of the client personally.

> **EXAMPLE 3-25:** Assume the same facts as in Example 3-24, except that Hal exercises his lifetime power and appoints the appreciated trust assets to himself one week before his death in 2010. These assets are now owned by Hal at the time of his death, and thus Hal's executor can allocate all or part of Hal's aggregate and spousal property basis increases to these assets (though not more than enough to bring the adjusted basis of those assets up to their fair market value on the date of death).

A client who holds only a *testamentary* power of appointment cannot, however, exercise it in favor of himself or herself in a manner that will increase the property owned by the client at his or her death. The law should not treat an appointment to one's estate as the equivalent of ownership at the time of death, though some may argue for a contrary interpretation on the grounds that ownership of assets by a decedent's estate has traditionally been treated comparably to ownership by the decedent at the time of death.[61]

Some estate planners may believe that, pending clarification from Congress, the IRS, or the courts, it would be appropriate for a client to exercise a power of appointment in favor of his or her estate. Their argument is that the law is unclear whether an exercise in favor of the decedent's estate creates property that is "owned by the decedent," and that such an exercise may maximize the assets among which the aggregate and spousal property basis increases could be allocated. Unfortunately, appointing property to the decedent's estate subjects it to the claims of the decedent's creditors. Also, if the power of appointment was created before October 22, 1942, appointing it to the estate will cause it to be subject to estate taxes unnecessarily if the de-

---

[61] See Walton v. Comm'r, 115 TC 589 (2000), acq. 2003-2 CB 964.

cedent dies after December 31, 2010.[62] This strategy, therefore, is highly questionable.

A practical estate planner faced with a client who holds only a testamentary general power of appointment over a trust fund that contains appreciated assets, the ownership of which by the client is important to take full advantage of the client's aggregate and spousal property basis increases, should seek other means of shifting the trust assets to the client. The trustee may, for example, be urged to exercise any discretionary powers to distribute trust assets to the client. In order to protect the trustee from claims that such distributions incorrectly favor the client over other trust beneficiaries, the client could agree to leave these assets at death to another trust on similar terms for the same beneficiaries.

> **EXAMPLE 3-26:** Hal is the primary beneficiary of a trust created under the will of his late mother. Large Bank is the trustee of the trust. The trust gives Hal the right to all of the trust income and so much of its principal as the trustee deems appropriate for any purpose. It also gives Hal the right to appoint the trust funds, by provision in Hal's last will, to any person he selects, including his own estate. At Hal's death, the remaining and unappointed trust funds are to be distributed to his three children, in equal shares. On January 1, 2010, Hal, who is aware of his probable inability to survive the year, urges Large Bank to distribute to him sufficient appreciated assets to enable him to take full advantage of his aggregate basis increase. Large Bank explains that it has a fiduciary duty to consider both Hal's interests and those of the remainder beneficiaries. Hal agrees that, if the trustee distributes these assets to him, he will leave the distributed trust funds in continued trust for the benefit of the remainder beneficiaries of the trust created by Hal's mother. The trustee distributes appreciated property to Hal, and these assets are now owned by Hal at the time of his death, and therefore Hal's executor can allocate any of Hal's aggregate basis increase to these assets.

Obviously, the problem is more difficult if the trustee lacks express authority to distribute assets to the client or if the trustee's distribution powers are limited by an ascertainable standard that would not permit such distributions. In such cases, the parties may seek to reform the trust to permit distributions of appreciated assets to a beneficiary likely to die in 2010, in order to take fuller advantage of the beneficiary's aggregate and spousal property basis increases. This might be agreeable to all beneficiaries provided that the remainder disposition of those assets is not changed in fact. Generally, a trust may be reformed to conform the terms to the grantor's intentions, which some

---

[62] IRC § 2041(a).

courts have construed as including the tax goals of the grantor.[63] Section 411 of the Uniform Trust Code, furthermore, permits the grantor and all beneficiaries of a trust to modify or terminate a trust even if the modification or termination is inconsistent with a material purpose of the trust.[64] Therefore, reformation of a trust should be considered as an option in many states.

> **EXAMPLE 3-27:** Hal is the primary beneficiary of a trust created under the will of his late mother. Large Bank is the trustee of the trust. The trust gives Hal the right to all of the trust income, but no power to distribute principal. Hal, the other beneficiaries (including a guardian ad litem for unborn and minor beneficiaries), and the trustee petition a local court to reform the trust to permit Large Bank to distribute appreciated property wherever such distributions will enable the distributee to take full advantage of applicable tax basis increases without unduly prejudicing the interests of the other beneficiaries. The court reforms the trust. Hal agrees that, if the trustee distributes to him sufficient assets to take advantage of his aggregate basis increase, he will leave the distributed assets in continued trust for the benefit of the remainder beneficiaries of the trust created by Hal's mother. The trustee distributes appreciated property to Hal, these assets are now owned by Hal at the time of his death in 2010, and thus Hal's executor can allocate any of Hal's aggregate basis increase to these assets.

[c] Property Owned Jointly With a Right of Survivorship

A decedent is deemed to own at the time of death a portion of the value of property owned jointly by the decedent and another person as joint tenants with a right of survivorship or as tenants by the entirety.[65] The portion of such joint property that is deemed owned by the decedent is based on rules similar

---

[63] See Radford, Bogert & Bogert, The Law of Trusts and Trustees, ch. 47 (Thomson Reuters/West, rev. 2d ed. 1984, supp. 2009); Hodgman & Blickenstaff, "Judicial Reformation of Trusts—The Drafting Tool of Last Resort," 28 Est. Plan. 287 (June 2001).

[64] Court approval would not be required under the Uniform Trust Code generally, but a variation in Alabama, Maine, Nebraska, New Mexico, Ohio, and Virginia requires that the modification agreement be submitted to a court to assure that the grantor and the beneficiaries did all agree to the proposed modification. These versions of the Uniform Trust Code do not, however, require that the court determine the appropriateness or desirability of the proposed modification. See Ala. Code § 19-3B-411; 18-B Me. Rev. Stat. § 411; Neb. Rev. Stat. § 30-3837; NM Stat. Ann. § 46A-4-411; Ohio Rev. Code § 5804-11; Va. Code § 55-544.11.

[65] IRC § 1022(d)(1)(B)(i).

to those currently contained in Section 2040, which applies for estate tax purposes.

[i] Property owned jointly with a surviving spouse. A decedent is deemed to have owned 50 percent of any asset that is owned jointly solely with the decedent's surviving spouse, either as joint tenants with a right of survivorship or as tenants by the entirety. The spouse's actual contributions to the cost of acquiring the asset are irrelevant.[66]

> **EXAMPLE 3-28:** Fred and Wilma are a married couple who, in 2008, buy a vacation house, taking title as tenants by the entirety. Wilma pays the entire purchase price for the property. Fred dies in 2010, survived by Wilma. One half of the value of the vacation house is deemed owned by Fred at the time of his death, and his executor can allocate some or all of Fred's aggregate basis increase to this property (though not more than enough to bring its adjusted basis in 50 percent of the property up to its fair market value on the date of death).

[ii] Property owned jointly with someone other than the surviving spouse. A decedent is deemed to have owned a proportionate share of the value of property owned jointly with a right of survivorship with someone other than the surviving spouse (whether or not the surviving spouse also owns an interest in the same property), in proportion to the consideration furnished by the decedent towards the acquisition of the property.[67]

> **EXAMPLE 3-29:** Able, Baker, and Charlene together buy a vacation house in 2008, taking title as joint tenants with right of survivorship. Each contributed one third of the purchase price and paid one third of the mortgage payments. Able dies in 2010, survived by Baker and Charlene. One third of the value of the vacation house is deemed owned by Able at the time of his death, and his executor can allocate some or all of Able's aggregate basis increase to this property (though not more than enough to bring the adjusted basis of his proportionate share of the property up to its fair market value on the date of death).

> **EXAMPLE 3-30:** Assume the same facts as in Example 3-29, except that Charlene paid the entire purchase price for the property, and allowed her brothers, Able and Baker, to be equal joint tenants with a right of survivorship. Able dies in 2010. No portion of the value of the vacation house is treated as having been owned by Able at the time of his death, and his

---

[66] IRC § 1022(d)(1)(B)(i)(I).

[67] IRC § 1022(d)(1)(B)(i)(II).

executor cannot allocate to the vacation house any of Able's aggregate basis increase.

[iii] Property acquired jointly by gift, bequest, etc. Property acquired by gift, bequest, devise, or inheritance by the decedent and any other person as joint tenants with right of survivorship in interests that are not otherwise specified or fixed by law is treated as if the decedent owned a fractional part, which is determined by dividing the value of the property by the number of joint tenants.[68]

> **EXAMPLE 3-31:** Dave dies in 2010, survived by his daughter, Debbie. At Dave's death, he and Debbie own as joint tenants with a right of survivorship, 1,000 shares of the common stock of Acme Co., which they inherited under the will of Dave's late wife. Dave's executor can allocate some or all of Dave's aggregate basis increase to Dave's 50 percent interest in the Acme shares (though not more than enough to bring the adjusted basis of his proportionate share of the property up to its fair market value on the date of death). The ownership of the Acme shares is determined by dividing the shares by the number of co-owners, without regard to their ages or relationship with the deceased donor (Dave's late wife), because the co-owners are not a married couple and the property was acquired by gift, bequest, devise, or inheritance.

The practical estate planner must carefully evaluate what portion of a client's jointly owned property is likely to be eligible for allocation of the client's aggregate or spousal property basis increases. Records of the parties' individual contributions should be preserved or created where the property is owned jointly with a right of survivorship between someone other than the client and the client's spouse.

[d] Community Property

A decedent who owns at least a one-half interest in community property at the time of his or her death is deemed to own, at that time, the surviving spouse's interest in the same property.[69] This rule applies whether the property is owned by the decedent and the surviving spouse as community property under the laws of a U.S. state, U.S. possession, or foreign country.[70] This rule does not afford the decedent's executor two sets of aggregate and spousal property basis increases, but it does permit the allocation of the decedent's ag-

---

[68] IRC § 1022(d)(1)(B)(i)(III).

[69] IRC § 1022(d)(1)(B)(iv).

[70] IRC § 1022(d)(1)(B)(iv).

gregate and spousal property basis increases to both halves of the community property.

> **EXAMPLE 3-32:** David and his wife, Wendy, live in California, and own an estate that includes a residence, a portfolio of marketable securities, and assorted items of tangible personal property. All of these assets were acquired by David and Wendy after their marriage, and while they lived in California. All of these properties are community property under California law, and are thus deemed owned one-half by each of them. Wendy dies in 2010. Wendy's executor may allocate her aggregate basis increase to and among 100 percent of these assets even though Wendy only owned a one-half interest in the properties at the time of her death. Wendy's executor may also allocate her spousal property basis increase to both Wendy's half and David's half of any property passing to David (or to a QTIP trust for his benefit).

A practical estate planner should try to maximize community property ownership by married clients to the extent that such co-ownership is consistent with the solidity of the clients' marriage, the client's asset protection planning, and applicable state property law. Community property may be brought by a client who resided in a community property state to a common law state, and the practical estate planner must take pains not to allow it to lose its favored community property status.[71]

[e] QTIP Assets

Property held in a QTIP marital trust of which the decedent is the income beneficiary is not "owned by the decedent at the time of death," and thus the decedent's executor should not be able to allocate the decedent's aggregate basis increase to the trust assets.

> **EXAMPLE 3-33:** In 2008, Harriet died, leaving $3 million of her estate in a trust for the benefit of her husband, Harry. The trust directs that Harry will receive all of the income, payable quarter-annually, for the rest of his life, and as much of the principal of the trust as Harry requires for his health, education, support, and maintenance. At Harry's later death, the trust funds will be distributed in equal shares to the couple's three chil-

---

[71] Estate planners should also seriously consider creating community property for common law state residents by holding assets in a trust under the elect-in community property rule of Alaska. See discussion in Zaritsky, Tax Planning for Family Wealth Transfers ¶ 8.07[7] (Thomson Reuters/WG&L, 4th ed. 2002); Ascher, Blattmachr & Zaritsky, "Tax Planning With Consensual Community Property: Alaska's New Community Property Law," 33 Real Prop. Prob. & Tr. J. 615 (Winter 1999); Boxx, "Community Property Across State Lines: Square Pegs and Round Holes," 19 Prob. & Prop. 9 (Jan./Feb. 2005).

dren. Harriet's executor elected to deduct this gift as a QTIP marital trust. Harry dies in 2010. Harry does not own the property held in the QTIP marital trust, and thus his executor cannot allocate any of his aggregate basis increase to that property.

[f] Lifetime Transfers With Retained Beneficial Enjoyment

A decedent does not own at the time of death property that he or she transferred in a trust with a retained beneficial enjoyment, and thus the decedent's executor should not be able to allocate the decedent's aggregate or spousal property basis increases to property held in such trusts.

> **EXAMPLE 3-34:** In June 2008, Harry gives his vacation house to a trust and reserves the right to use it for the next ten years. At the end of the ten years, the vacation house will pass to Harry's three children, in equal shares. Harry dies in 2010. The house would not appear to be eligible to receive a basis adjustment under the aggregate basis increase rules, because Harry did not own it at the time of death.

> **EXAMPLE 3-35:** In June 2008, Harry also created a grantor retained annuity trust to which he transferred $1 million worth of marketable securities. Harry reserved the right to an annual distribution of $274,190.40, payable at the end of each year for four years. After four years, the trust assets would be distributed to Harry's children, in equal shares. Harry died in January 2010. The trust fund at that time was worth $1,500,000. Harry's executor cannot allocate any of his aggregate basis increase to the trust assets, because Harry did not own the trust assets at the time of death.

[g] Property Acquired by the Decedent Within Three Years of Death

A decedent's executor cannot allocate the decedent's aggregate or spousal property basis increases to property acquired by the decedent in a lifetime transfer for less than adequate and full consideration in money or money's worth during the three-year period ending on the date of death.[72] An exception from this disallowance rule is available for property acquired from a decedent's spouse unless the transferor spouse also acquired the property by gift, in whole or in part, or by other lifetime transfer for less than full and adequate consideration in money or money's worth during the three-year period prior to the decedent's death.[73] Only an individual's spouse, therefore, can transfer property to an individual who is dying in order to obtain advantage of the indi-

---

[72] IRC § 1022(d)(1)(C)(i).
[73] IRC § 1022(d)(1)(C)(ii).

vidual's unused aggregate and spousal property basis increases, and one cannot accomplish this indirectly by giving the asset first to the individual's spouse and then having the spouse give it to the individual.

A practical estate planner should urge clients freely to shift appreciated property between spouses to assure that a spouse who is most likely to die in 2010 can take full advantage of his or her aggregate and spousal basis increases. This will require that the estate planner carefully scrutinize both the appreciation in each spouse's assets and the relative health of the spouses.

> **EXAMPLE 3-36:** On January 5, 2010, Harry and Wanda meet with their estate planner to discuss their estate plan. Harry is already in poor health and unlikely to survive the year. Harry and Wanda together have an estate of over $10 million, and their entire estate is divided equally between them, all owned separately. Harry owns as separate assets the following:
>
> | Asset | Basis | Fair Market Value |
> |---|---|---|
> | Vacation house | $ 100,000 | $ 500,000 |
> | Marketable securities | $3,000,000 | $4,500,000 |
>
> Harry's estate plan leaves his entire estate in a trust for Wanda's lifetime benefit, paying her all of the trust income and as much principal as she requires for her health, education, support, and maintenance. Wanda is given a limited testamentary power to appoint the remainder of the trust fund among their descendants and charities she selects. After Wanda's death, the trust fund is held in continued trust for the benefit of the couple's descendants. Wanda's estate plan is reciprocal to Harry's.
>
> Harry lacks sufficient assets to take advantage of his aggregate and spousal property basis increases. Wanda should give Harry assets reflecting another $2,400,000 of appreciation, so that Harry's total assets will have $4,300,000 of total appreciation, thus permitting his executor to take full advantage of Harry's aggregate and spousal property basis increases. These assets will all then be left in trust for the benefit of Wanda, and she will have the advantage of their higher basis. This higher basis will reduce the capital gains taxes paid by the trust on the sale of these assets, and therefore increase the value of Wanda's beneficial interest.

[h] Assets Specifically Excluded From Basis Increases

The executor expressly cannot allocate the aggregate or spousal property basis increases to five types of assets:

1. Items of income in respect of a decedent (as determined under Section 691);[74]
2. Stock of a foreign personal holding company;[75]
3. Stock of a domestic international sales corporation (DISC) or former DISC;[76]
4. Stock of a foreign investment company;[77] or
5. Stock of a passive foreign investment company (unless the company is a qualified electing fund under Section 1295 with respect to the decedent).[78]

These exclusions pose a difficult estate planning problem. Generally, there is little that a client can do to dispose of such assets without recognizing taxable income. The best thing that a practical estate planner can do for a client whose estate is heavily concentrated in these assets, however, is to caution the client about the potential income taxes that will be generated when the assets are disposed of, even after the client's death.

¶ 3.04 PLANNING WITH NEGATIVE BASIS ASSETS

EGTRRA includes several special rules designed to prevent attempts to frustrate the operation of the carryover basis rules and to prevent certain possible adverse consequences of the carryover basis rules. One of these rules provides some relief from the problem of negative basis property held by an estate.

Generally, the amount realized on the transfer of property by a taxpayer includes the amount of any liabilities from which the transferor is discharged or relieved as a result of the sale or disposition. Therefore, the transferor recognizes a gain if the amount of such liabilities, plus any other consideration received, exceeds the transferor's basis in the transferred property.[79] This creates a serious problem for taxpayers who own property that is subject to a debt

---

[74] IRC § 1022(f). On what constitutes "income in respect of a decedent," see Danforth, Lane & Zaritsky, Federal Income Taxation of Estates and Trusts ¶ 15.05 (Thomson Reuters/WG&L, 3d ed. 2001).

[75] IRC § 1022(d)(1)(D)(i).

[76] IRC § 1022(d)(1)(D)(ii).

[77] IRC § 1022(d)(1)(D)(iii).

[78] IRC § 1022(d)(1)(D)(iv).

[79] Reg. § 1.1001-2(a)(1); see also Bittker & Lokken, Federal Taxation of Income, Estates and Gifts ¶ 43.4 (Thomson Reuters/WG&L, 3d ed. 2000); Bittker & McMahon, Federal Income Taxation of Individuals ¶ 29.15 (Thomson Reuters/WG&L, 3d ed. 2002); Zaritsky, Tax Planning for Family Wealth Transfers: Analysis With Forms ¶ 11.02 (Thomson Reuters/WG&L, 4th ed. 2002).

in excess of the taxpayer's basis because the tax liability can, in some cases, exceed the net cash received on the sale of the asset.

> **EXAMPLE 3-37:** Harry owns a shopping center that he bought for $3 million, paying $500,000 in cash and borrowing $2.5 million, secured by a mortgage on the property. Harry is personally liable on the promissory note. Five years later, the value of the shopping center had increased to over $5 million, and Harry refinanced the property, raising the total debt to $4 million. The real estate market then softened, and the present value of the property is $4 million. The debt is still $4 million, but Harry's adjusted basis in the property is only $3 million. If Harry sells the shopping center solely for the buyer's assumption of, or taking the property subject to, the $4 million mortgage debt, Harry will receive no cash. Harry will, however, recognize a gain of $1 million ($4 million debt release − $3 million basis) on the sale. Therefore, Harry's tax on this gain will exceed the cash ($–0–) he receives on the sale.

The carryover basis rules attempt to reduce the amount of gain recognized on the acquisition of negative basis property from the decedent by his or her estate or on the acquisition of negative basis property from the decedent's estate by a beneficiary (other than a tax-exempt beneficiary). The rules do this by disregarding the excess of the amount of the liabilities over the decedent's basis in the property in determining the gain realized.[80]

> **EXAMPLE 3-38:** Dave's estate includes an office building worth $1 million. Dave's basis in the building was $250,000, and Dave's executor allocates all of Dave's aggregate basis increase to other assets. The property is subject to a mortgage in the amount of $600,000. Dave's estate distributes the property to one of Dave's children. Neither the death of Dave nor the distribution of the property to the beneficiary requires recognition of gain to the extent of the $350,000 excess of debt over basis.[81]

This rule does not, however, protect the beneficiary from recognizing gain attributable to such liability on a later disposition.

> **EXAMPLE 3-39:** Assume the same facts as in Example 3-38, except that, after inheriting the building, Dave's son, Adam, sells it for $1 million. The buyer pays Adam $400,000 in cash, and assumes the $600,000 mortgage. Adam recognizes a $650,000 gain on the sale because Adam's ad-

---

[80] IRC § 1022(g)(1).

[81] See HR Rep. No. 84, 107th Cong., 1st Sess. (2001), 147 Cong. Rec. H2774 (May 25, 2001).

justed basis was $350,000, and the amount realized includes both the $400,000 cash and $600,000 mortgage debt assumption.[82]

A practical estate planner must determine when a client holds negative basis assets and evaluate how best to dispose of those assets as part of the client's testamentary estate plan. First, the client must decide whether the beneficiary to whom the negative basis assets will pass should also receive cash or other liquid assets with which to pay the taxes on the negative basis assets when they are ultimately sold.

Second, the client must decide whether to direct specifically that part of the aggregate basis increase be allocated to these negative basis assets to alleviate the burden that receiving them may otherwise cause for the beneficiary. Such an allocation should be addressed specifically by provision in the client's will because an executor's fiduciary obligation to treat all beneficiaries fairly and impartially may preclude an especially favorable allocation of the decedent's aggregate basis increase to negative basis assets.

Third, the estate planner must watch for dispositions of negative basis property to tax-exempt beneficiaries. The nonrecognition rule of Section 1022(g) does not apply if the property passes to a "tax-exempt beneficiary."[83] A tax-exempt beneficiary, for this purpose, includes

1. The United States, any state or political subdivision thereof, any possession of the United States, any Indian tribal government, or any agency or instrumentality of any of the foregoing;
2. An organization (other than a cooperative described in Section 521) that is exempt from income taxes;
3. Any foreign person or entity;[84] and
4. To the extent provided in regulations, any person to whom property is transferred for the principal purpose of tax avoidance.[85]

A disposition by a decedent's estate to such a tax-exempt beneficiary results in the recognition of income by the estate equal to the difference between the amount of the debt from which the estate is relieved or which is assumed

---

[82] The spousal property basis increase could be relevant if the decedent's surviving spouse is a nonresident alien individual, who would be a "tax-exempt beneficiary" under this definition.

[83] IRC § 1022(g)(1)(A).

[84] "Foreign person or entity" is defined by reference to Section 168(h)(2), as

(i) any foreign government, any international organization, or any agency or instrumentality of any of the foregoing, and
(ii) any person who is not a United States person.

Section 168(h)(2)(C) states that a foreign person or entity does not include any foreign partnership or other foreign pass-thru entity.

[85] IRC § 1022(g)(2).

or taken subject to by the beneficiary, and the estate's adjusted carryover basis in the distributed property. A practical estate planner may advise a decedent's executor to consider allocating some of the decedent's aggregate or spousal property basis increases to property that passes to a tax-exempt beneficiary in order to avoid recognition of gain on the distribution of these assets.

¶ 3.05 THE BASIS INCREASE FOR BUILT-IN LOSSES AND LOSS CARRYOVERS

A decedent's $1.3 million basis increase is increased by

1. The sum of the amount of any unused capital loss carryover and any net operating loss carryover which would, but for the decedent's death, have been carried from the decedent's last taxable year to a later taxable year of the decedent, plus
2. The sum of the amount of any losses that would have been allowable under Section 165 (losses incurred in a trade or business, losses incurred in any transaction entered into for profit, though not connected with a trade or business, and other losses arising from fire, storm, shipwreck, or other casualty or theft), had the property acquired from the decedent been sold at fair market value immediately before the decedent's death.[86]

The decedent's executor can allocate this increase along with the rest of the decedent's $1.3 million aggregate basis increase.

The basis increase for carryover net operating losses may arguably produce a double income tax benefit because such losses may be taken as an income tax deduction in the year of death if the decedent is survived by a spouse and the spouse chooses to file a joint income tax return for the year of death.[87] The carryover basis rules do not appear to limit the increase in the aggregate basis increase to losses that are not otherwise deducted.

---

[86] IRC § 1022(b)(2)(C).

[87] See Kelley, Ludtke & Steinmeyer, Jr., 2 Estate Planning for Farmers and Ranchers § 18A:2 (Thomson Reuters/West, 3d ed. 2008).

¶ 3.06 PLANNING WITH THE $250,000 PERSONAL RESIDENCE EXCLUSION

The exclusion of up to $250,000 of the gain on the sale of an individual's principal residence is extended to sales by a decedent's estate or beneficiaries if the property was used by the decedent as a principal residence for two or more years during the five-year period prior to the sale.[88] The legislative history states that the decedent's period of ownership and occupancy will be added to any actual occupancy by the heir in determining whether the heir is entitled to the benefit of the $250,000 exclusion.[89]

This rule allows estates and beneficiaries to preserve this valuable tax benefit despite the decedent's death and the carryover of the decedent's basis in the asset. This rule is limited, however, to property passing to an individual at the decedent's death. A practical estate planner should, therefore, assure that the decedent's principal residence, if otherwise eligible for the $250,000 exclusion, is not left in trust unless an individual beneficiary has an unrestricted right to withdraw the residence from the trust at any time, such as would cause the beneficiary to own the trust assets under Section 678.[90]

There appears to be no time limit on when the estate or beneficiary can take advantage of the decedent's $250,000 exclusion.

> **EXAMPLE 3-40:** Harry owns a house and uses it as his principal residence for five years prior to his death. At Harry's death, the house has an adjusted basis of $200,000 and a fair market value of $350,000. Harry's will makes no specific devise of this property. His executor holds and maintains it for three years, and then sells the house for $450,000. Harry's estate can take advantage of Harry's $250,000 exclusion, and therefore does not pay any income tax on the sale of the house.

> **EXAMPLE 3-41:** Assume the same facts as in Example 3-40, except that Harry only lived in the house for two years before his death, and that Harry's will devised the house specifically to Harry's son, Barry. Barry lives in the house for two more years, and then sells it for $450,000. Barry can combine his two years of residence in the House with his father's two years of residence, and qualify for the $250,000 exclusion from gain on the sale of the residence.

---

[88] IRC § 121(d)(9).

[89] See HR Rep. No. 84, 107th Cong., 1st Sess. (2001), 147 Cong. Rec. H2774 (May 25, 2001).

[90] For more on the operation of Section 678, see Danforth, Lane & Zaritsky, Federal Income Taxation of Estates and Trusts ch. 12 (Thomson Reuters/WG&L, 3d ed. 2001).

¶ 3.07 GATHERING BASIS INFORMATION

One of the most important things that a practical estate planner can do in planning for the carryover basis rules is to begin assembling basis information while the client is alive to alleviate the burden of assembling such information after the client's death. Among the sources of basis information are

1. The decedent's personal records;
2. Federal, state, and local income tax returns;
3. Information retained by the decedent's family members, friends, and business associates;
4. The decedent's brokerage account statements;
5. Records maintained by the decedent's investment advisors;
6. Estate and inheritance tax returns for persons from whom the decedent may have inherited property;
7. Personal property tax returns;
8. Information maintained by guardians and conservators for the decedent or for persons from whom the decedent acquired property;
9. Deeds and other public records; and
10. Records maintained by the decedent's professional advisors, including lawyers and accountants.

The audit of the Section 6018 return is unlikely to be intensive or quick, as no income tax is paid with the return. Therefore, the practical estate planner needs to document the basis calculations as well as possible to create a good record of basis for the persons succeeding to this property from the decedent.[91]

¶ 3.08 DRAFTING SURVIVORSHIP PRESUMPTIONS

Generally, when there is an estate tax law, it is practical to presume in the will and revocable trust of a married person that one spouse will be deemed to have survived the other in case of a common disaster. The spouse deemed to have survived should usually be the spouse with the smaller estate because this provides the best opportunity for the spouses to utilize both sets of applicable exclusion amounts.

In 2010, the presumption should be governed by which spouse has the greater amount of appreciation in his or her estate. The spouse with the lesser

---

[91] See Bekerman & LaPiana, "Carryover Basis—Have We Learned From History?" 19 Prob. & Prop. 38 (Nov./Dec. 2005); Berall, Harrison, Blattmachr & Detzel, "Planning for Carryover Basis That Can Be/Should Be/Must Be Done Now," 29 Est. Plan. 99, 105–106 (Mar. 2002); Dodge, "What's Wrong With Carryover Basis, Especially the Carryover Basis Provisions of H.R. 8," 91 Tax Notes 961 (May 7, 2001).

amount of appreciation should be presumed to have survived in cases of a close order of death.

> **EXAMPLE 3-42:** Henry and Wilma are married. Henry has a separate estate of approximately $8 million and Wilma has a separate estate of approximately $3 million. They each plan to leave an amount equal to their applicable exclusion amount to a trust for the surviving spouse and their descendants, and to leave the balance of their estate outright to the surviving spouse. When the estate tax is in effect, it is usually better to provide that Wilma will be deemed to have survived, in case they die under circumstances in which it is not possible to tell which of them survived. This would permit the full use of Henry's applicable exclusion amount with respect to his estate, and then allow Wilma to use her entire applicable exclusion amount to offset the estate taxes in her estate, because her estate will be increased by the marital gift under Henry's instruments.
>
> If Henry and Wilma die in a common disaster in 2010, however, the person who is deemed to have survived should be the one with the lesser amount of net appreciation in his or her separate assets. If Henry's $8 million separate estate reflects only $1 million of appreciation and Wilma's $3 million separate estate reflects $2.9 million of appreciation, Henry should be deemed to have survived because Wilma's estate can then use her $1.3 million aggregate basis increase and $1.6 million of her spousal property basis increase to give a full basis increase on her entire estate, and Henry can then use his $1.3 million aggregate basis increase to avoid all capital gains taxes with respect to the appreciation in his estate. If Henry were presumed to die first, he would avoid all capital gains on his estate, but Wilma would be left with only a $1.3 million aggregate basis increase to apply in her estate, and she would have $2.9 million of total appreciation.

¶ 3.09 PLANNING WITH THE HOLDING PERIOD RULES

Traditionally, an estate received an automatic holding period sufficient to produce a long-term gain on the sale or exchange of assets received from a decedent.[92] This automatic long-term holding period is eliminated with the advent of carryover basis, but a tacked holding period remains a possibility.

Section 1223(2), however, states:

> In determining the period for which the taxpayer has held property however acquired there shall be included the period for which such property was held by any other person, if under this chapter such property has, for

---

[92] IRC § 1223(9).

the purpose of determining gain or loss from a sale or exchange, the same basis in whole or in part in his hands as it would have in the hands of such other person.

The carryover basis in an estate will give the estate a tacked holding period that includes the period that the decedent held the asset, as well as the period that the estate holds the asset. Section 1223(2) does state, however, that the tacked holding period is available only if the estate's basis is determined "in whole or in part" by the decedent's basis. The allocation of a decedent's aggregate or spousal property basis increases will not eliminate the tacked holding period as long as the allocation does not bring the adjusted basis up to the fair market value of the property on the date of death.

> **EXAMPLE 3-43:** Henry buys some publicly traded stock on November 1, 2009, for $100,000. Henry dies on October 1, 2010, when the stock is worth $150,000. Henry's executor sells the stock immediately after Henry's death to raise funds to pay some of Henry's outstanding debts and his funeral expenses. Henry's executor does not allocate any of Henry's aggregate or spousal property basis increases to this stock. The estate's holding period begins on the date that Henry bought the stock. The estate, therefore, has held the stock for less than one year when it sold the stock, and the $50,000 gain on the sale is a short-term capital gain.

> **EXAMPLE 3-44:** Assume the same facts as in Example 3-43, except that Henry's executor sells the stock on November 2, 2010, and allocates $30,000 of Henry's aggregate basis increase to the stock. The estate recognizes a $20,000 gain on the sale of the stock ($150,000 amount realized − $100,000 carryover basis − $30,000 allocated increase). This gain is a long-term capital gain because the estate can count its holding period from the date Henry bought the stock.

> **EXAMPLE 3-45:** Harriet buys some publicly traded stock on November 1, 2009, for $100,000. Harriet dies on February 1, 2010, when the stock is worth $130,000. Harriet's executor allocates $30,000 of Harriet's aggregate basis increase to the stock, so that its basis is equal to its $130,000 fair market value on the date of Harriet's death. Harriet's executor sells the stock on December 31, 2010, for $160,000. The estate recognizes a $30,000 gain on the sale of the stock ($160,000 amount realized − $100,000 carryover basis − $30,000 allocated basis increase). This gain is a short-term capital gain because the estate takes a new holding period beginning with the date of death and the sale occurred within one year of the date of death.

¶ 3.10 PASSIVE LOSSES UNDER THE CARRYOVER BASIS RULES

Section 469 limits the ability of a taxpayer to deduct from gross income losses incurred in the conduct of a trade or business in which the taxpayer does not "materially participate." Nondeductible losses may be carried over for use in the future as an offset against passive gains.

Section 469(g)(2) states that a taxpayer can deduct suspended passive losses on his or her final income tax return to the extent that they exceed the basis of the property in the hands of the transferee.[93] The traditional estate tax value basis rules significantly limited the amount of suspended passive losses that a decedent could deduct on his or her final income tax return, but the carryover basis rules increase this amount with respect to property that has appreciated in value.

> **EXAMPLE 3-46:** Hilda owns an interest in Acme Business Partnership, in which she does not materially participate. Hilda's share of Acme's losses is $50,000 for taxable years 2005–2009, which Hilda had not been able to deduct because of Section 469's passive loss rules. Hilda dies in 2010. Hilda's basis in her Acme partnership interest is $40,000. The fair market value of Hilda's Acme partnership interest at her death is $100,000. Under the carryover basis rules, Hilda can deduct $40,000 of her passive losses in 2010 on her last income tax return. If Hilda's executor allocates another $10,000 of Hilda's aggregate basis increase to Hilda's carryover basis in the Acme partnership interest, her executor can deduct the additional $10,000 of suspended losses on Hilda's final income tax return.[94]

¶ 3.11 CHARITABLE REMAINDER TRUSTS AND THE CARRYOVER BASIS RULES

Some estate planners may attempt to reduce the impact of the carryover basis rules by leaving low-basis assets to a charitable remainder trust, where the trustee could sell the assets in a tax-exempt environment and then convert the full proceeds into income-producing investments. This appears to be practical if done by the client during his or her lifetime, but inadvisable when done by testamentary disposition.

Regulations § 1.664-1(a)(1)(iii)(*a*) states that

---

[93] IRC § 469(g)(2).

[94] See Berall, Harrison, Blattmachr & Detzel, "Planning for Carryover Basis That Can Be/Should Be/Must Be Done Now," 29 Est. Plan. 99, 101 (Mar. 2002).

The term "charitable remainder trust" means a trust with respect to which a deduction is allowable under section 170, 2055, 2106, or 2522 and which meets the description of a charitable remainder annuity trust (as described in §1.664-2) or a charitable remainder unitrust (as described in §1.664-3).[95]

In the absence of an estate tax, a testamentary charitable remainder trust does not meet this definition, and thus appears to be disqualified.

¶ 3.12 CARRYOVER BASIS AND PARTNERSHIP INTERESTS

Carryover basis may present a special problem for estates that include significant partnership interests. Section 743 adjusts the partnership's basis of its property upon the transfer of a partnership interest by sale or exchange or at the death of a partner if the partnership has a Section 754 in effect.[96] The adjustment under these rules can increase the deductions for depreciation of partnership assets and reduce the gain on the sale of partnership assets by the partnership.

The Section 754 election has traditionally been made where a decedent dies owning a partnership interest that receives a basis adjustment to its fair market value on the date of death,[97] and it will be equally advisable whenever a decedent dies in 2010 and the decedent's executor allocates to the partnership interest part of the decedent's aggregate or spousal property basis increases.

A question may arise about the timing of the Section 754 election under the carryover basis rules. The Section 754 election must be made in a written statement filed with a timely filed partnership return for the taxable year.[98] The executor's allocation of the decedent's aggregate and spousal property basis increases must be made on the "Return Relating to Large Transfers at Death"

---

[95] See also Priv. Ltr. Rul. 9501004 (Jan. 6, 1995).

[96] The Section 743 adjustment is automatic, even without a Section 754 election, if the adjusted basis of the partnership assets exceeds the fair market value of those assets by more than $250,000. This wipes out these losses for purposes of the partners' personal use. IRC § 743(d).

[97] The actual decision whether to make the Section 754 election is made at the partnership level, and often involves detailed accounting by the partnership. Therefore, unless the decedent has a significant partnership interest, the partnership may decline to make the Section 754 election.

[98] Reg. § 1.754-1(b)(1). The statement must (1) include the name and address of the partnership making the election; (2) be signed by any one of the partners; and (3) contain a declaration that the partnership elects under Section 754 to apply the provisions of Sections 734(b) and 743(b). Id.

under Section 6018, which must be filed with the decedent's income tax return for the decedent's last taxable year.[99] A partnership that operates on a fiscal year could be required to file its Section 754 election before the decedent's executor has filed the return allocating basis increases. This would make it very difficult for the partnership to determine whether to make the Section 754 election.

This is complicated by the fact that some partners seek to avoid filing Section 754 elections because they often entail significant increases in accounting costs for the different basis of different partners in the same partnership assets. Therefore, a partnership may decline to file a Section 754 election unless the decedent's executor provides timely assurance of the amount of the basis increase that will be allocated to the decedent's partnership interests.

¶ 3.13 HARVESTING LOSSES

The carryover basis rules do not eliminate gain inherent in a decedent's assets, except to the extent of the allocation of the decedent's aggregate and spousal property basis increases, but they do eliminate any deductible losses in a decedent's assets. Section 1022(a)(2) states that the basis of property received from a decedent is the lesser of the decedent's adjusted basis or the fair market value of the property at the date of the decedent's death.

A practical estate planner must carefully scrutinize a client's assets to sell any loss assets and take advantage of the client's built-in losses. Such losses are, of course, valuable to the extent that the client has offsetting gains against which the losses can be applied. Such losses can also be useful if they create a capital loss carryover, which carryover is added to the decedent's aggregate basis increase.[100]

---

[99] IRC § 6075(a).
[100] IRC § 1022(b)(2)(C)(i).

CHAPTER 4

Generation-Skipping Transfer Tax Planning In 2010

¶ 4.01	Introduction			4-2
¶ 4.02	Retroactive Reimposition of the GST Tax			4-2
¶ 4.03	Section 2664 and EGTRRA's Sunset Rule For the GST Tax			4-3
	[1]	The Scope of Section 2664		4-3
	[2]	The Scope of EGTRRA's Sunset Rule		4-9
		[a]	Section 2653(a) and the Generation Move-Down Rule for Post-2010 Distributions and Terminations for Trusts Created by 2010 Generation-Skipping Transfers	4-10
		[b]	Section 2654(a)(2) and Basis in 2010 Taxable Terminations	4-13
		[c]	Post-2010 Effect of Pre-2010 GST Exemption Allocations	4-13
		[d]	Post-2010 Effect of Pre-2010 Automatic Allocations	4-14
		[e]	Post-2010 Effect of Pre-2010 Qualified Severances	4-16
		[f]	Post-2010 Effect of Certain Pre-2010 Retroactive Allocations	4-17
¶ 4.04	The GST Exemption in 2010			4-18
¶ 4.05	Applying the GST Tax to 2010 Testamentary Transfers			4-20
¶ 4.06	2010 Gifts to Section 2642(c) Annual Exclusion Trusts			4-22
¶ 4.07	2010 Inter Vivos Reverse QTIPs			4-24
¶ 4.08	Estate Tax Inclusion Periods in 2010			4-26
¶ 4.09	GST Tax Planning Suggestions For 2010			4-26
	[1]	Prefer Outright Transfers Over Transfers in Trust		4-26

[2]   Avoid Haste, But Consider the Opportunities of
        Prompt Action   4-27
[3]   Formula Generation-Skipping Transfers   4-28
[4]   Disclaimer-Based Planning   4-35

¶ **4.01 INTRODUCTION**

All estate planning is complicated in 2010, but generation-skipping transfer (GST) tax planning is by far the most difficult because of the inartful, inarticulate, and sometimes incomprehensible way in which Economic Growth and Tax Relief Reconciliation Act of 2001 (EGTRRA) renders this tax inapplicable in 2010 and then restores the pre-EGTRRA rules in 2011. The net result of EGTRRA's machinations is to make the GST tax clearly inapplicable to a few specific transactions in 2010, but to otherwise leave it unclear how other 2010 transactions will affect future GST tax calculations.

¶ **4.02 RETROACTIVE REIMPOSITION OF THE GST TAX**

We cannot know whether Congress will retroactively reinstate the GST tax rules, nor how Congress will treat pre-enactment transfers if the rules are retroactively reinstated.[1] Practitioners should advise clients that certain generation-skipping transfers made in 2010 are not subject to GST tax, but that they are subject to a possible retroactive imposition of this tax. Most clients are unlikely to be willing to engage in GST planning in 2010 in the face of such uncertainty.

The retroactive imposition of the GST tax on a pre-enactment 2010 lifetime transfer could create an extraordinarily expensive transfer, because the gift and estate taxes would both be imposed on the same transaction. Furthermore, the GST tax paid by the donor on a direct skip gift is itself subject to gift tax, further increasing the total tax cost of such transfers.[2]

> **EXAMPLE 4-1:** Tom gives $3 million to his grandson in 2010. Tom has already used up his lifetime gift tax exemption equivalent and his GST tax exemption, as well as having made an annual exclusion gift to this

---

[1] See discussion of possible retroactivity and the constitutional issues it raises at ¶ 1.07.

[2] IRC § 2515. See Harrington, Plaine & Zaritsky, Generation-Skipping Transfer Tax ¶ 3.02 (Thomson Reuters/WG&L, 2d ed. 2001).

grandson in 2010. Tom is prepared to pay a gift tax of $1,050,000 (35% × $3 million), based on the law in place on the date he makes the gift. Tom believes that this is a bargain, as the top gift tax rate in 2009 was 45 percent (which is scheduled to rise to 55 percent in 2011) and there is no GST tax on the transfer.

After Tom makes his gift, however, Congress retroactively reinstates the GST tax and raises the gift and GST tax rates to their 2009 levels. This causes Tom's liability on this transfer to rise from $1,050,000 to $3,307,000, calculated as follows:

GST tax (45% × $3,000,000)	$ 1,350,000
Gift tax (45% × $3,000,000)	$ 1,350,000
Gift tax on GST tax (45% × $1,350,000)	$ 607,500
Total tax cost	$ 3,307,000

Thus, Tom's net effective tax rate for making a direct skip gift at the 2009 rates would be 110.25 percent ($3,307,000 ÷ $3,000,000).

Practitioners should caution clients who contemplate generation-skipping transfers in 2010 about the risk of retroactive reimposition of the GST tax. There is no way to know with any degree of certainty whether such taxes will be reimposed in this manner, and it seems unlikely that any special effective date protection will be granted, under such a reimposition, to lifetime generation-skipping transfers made before the date of enactment.

¶ 4.03 SECTION 2664 AND EGTRRA'S SUNSET RULE FOR THE GST TAX

In addition to the threat of retroactive reimposition of the GST tax, GST tax planning in 2010 is further complicated by the difficulty of determining precisely what GST taxes will be imposed after 2010 on taxable distributions from and taxable terminations of interests in generation-skipping trusts created by transfers in 2010. The precise scope of the GST tax in and after 2010 requires careful examination of both Section 2664 and EGTRRA's sunset rule, neither of which welcomingly invites very close analysis.

[1] The Scope of Section 2664

Section 2664 states that the GST tax rules (Chapter 13) do not apply to "generation-skipping transfers" after December 31, 2009. This simple statement, however, raises several complicated and sometimes unanswerable questions.

First, the basic statement of Section 2664 is internally inconsistent. Chapter 13 cannot be entirely inapplicable to generation-skipping transfers after 2009, because the only definition of "generation-skipping transfer" in the tax law is contained in Chapter 13. Chapter 13 must, therefore, remain applicable in 2010 at least to the extent required to define "generation-skipping transfer."[3]

Second, Section 2664 limits itself to generation-skipping transfers, and so appears to leave Chapter 13 fully operational with respect to 2010 events that are not generation-skipping transfers, but which have a significant impact on the GST tax imposed in later years on trusts and other arrangements created in 2010. Section 2611(a) defines "generation-skipping transfer" as including only (1) a taxable distribution; (2) a taxable termination; and (3) a direct skip transfer.[4]

Section 2612(b) defines a "taxable distribution" as "any distribution from a trust to a skip person (other than a taxable termination or a direct skip)."[5]

Section 2612(a) defines a "taxable termination" as "the termination (by death, lapse of time, release of power, or otherwise) of an interest in property held in a trust unless—(A) immediately after such termination, a non-skip person has an interest in such property, or (B) at no time after such termination

---

[3] To argue that the definition of generation-skipping transfer is also eliminated after 2009 by Section 2664 is unsupportable because it would create an illogical and unworkable result. See Nixon v. Missouri Mun. League, 541 US 125 (2004) and United States v. American Trucking Ass'ns, Inc., 310 US 534 (1940) (the courts will not construe a statute in a manner that leads to absurd or futile results). This same analysis presents itself when one points out that Section 2664 is part of Chapter 13, which Section 2664 renders inapplicable to generation skipping transfers after December 31, 2009. By its own terms, Section 2664 does not apply to generation-skipping transfers, thus seemingly making them fully taxable in 2010.

[4] Section 2611(b) states that a "generation-skipping transfer" expressly does not include

   (1) any transfer which, if made inter vivos by an individual, would not be treated as a taxable gift by reason of section 2503(e) (relating to exclusion of certain transfers for educational or medical expenses), and
   (2) any transfer to the extent—

      (A) the property transferred was subject to a prior tax imposed under this chapter,
      (B) the transferee in the prior transfer was assigned to the same generation as (or a lower generation than) the generation assignment of the transferee in this transfer, and
      (C) such transfers do not have the effect of avoiding tax under this chapter with respect to any transfer.

The various transactions that are not generation-skipping transfers, including those defined in Section 2611(b), will be discussed later in this chapter.

[5] See Harrington, Plaine & Zaritsky, Generation-Skipping Transfer Tax ¶ 2.05[2] (Thomson Reuters/WG&L, 2d ed. 2001).

may a distribution (including distributions on termination) be made from such trust to a skip person."[6]

A "direct skip transfer" is defined in Section 2612(c) as a gift during life or a transfer at death from a transferor directly to a skip person.[7]

All three of these definitions rely on the definition of a "skip person." A skip person is defined in Section 2613(a) as "a natural person assigned to a generation which is 2 or more generations below the generation assignment of the transferor," a trust all of the interests in which are held by skip persons, or a trust in which no person holds an interest in the trust and "at no time after such transfer may a distribution (including distributions on termination) be made from such trust to a non-skip person."[8] A "non-skip person" is defined in Section 2613(b) as "any person who is not a skip person."

Section 2664, therefore, clearly states that no GST tax is imposed on a direct skip transfer, a taxable distribution, or a taxable termination in 2010. Section 2664 appears to have no effect, however, on a transfer to a trust whose beneficiaries include both skip persons and non-skip persons. Such transfers are subject to the traditional GST tax rules, but without a GST exemption to allocate in 2010.[9]

> **EXAMPLE 4-2:** In 2010, Harriet gives $1 million to a trust for the benefit of her grandchildren and more remote descendants, to be held in continued trust for the maximum period of the applicable rule against perpetuities. Harriet does not include her children as beneficiaries, because she believes that she has already made adequate provision for them through other lifetime transfers. Harriet's new trust has only skip persons as beneficiaries, and so it is itself a skip person. Harriet's transfer is, therefore, a direct skip transfer made in 2010. No GST tax is imposed in 2010 on this transfer under Section 2664.

> **EXAMPLE 4-3:** In 2010, Hal gives $1 million to a trust for the benefit of his children, grandchildren, and more remote descendants, to be held in continued trust for the maximum period of the applicable rule against perpetuities. Hal's new trust has both skip persons and non-skip persons as beneficiaries, and so it is not itself a skip person. Hal's transfer is, therefore, not a generation-skipping transfer, and future distributions from the trust to Hal's grandchildren and more remote beneficiaries will be taxable distributions and the death of the last member of each generation of beneficiaries will be a taxable termination. Section 2664 does not apply to this

---

[6] See Harrington, Plaine & Zaritsky, Generation-Skipping Transfer Tax ¶ 2.05[3] (Thomson Reuters/WG&L, 2d ed. 2001).

[7] See Harrington, Plaine & Zaritsky, Generation-Skipping Transfer Tax ¶ 2.05[1] (Thomson Reuters/WG&L, 2d ed. 2001).

[8] See Harrington, Plaine & Zaritsky, Generation-Skipping Transfer Tax ¶ 2.04[1] (Thomson Reuters/WG&L, 2d ed. 2001).

[9] See discussion infra ¶ 4.04.

transfer, and, while no GST tax is imposed on it in 2010, it is not protected by Section 2664 from the imposition of a GST tax on taxable distributions or taxable terminations after 2010.

EXAMPLE 4-4: In 2010, Tom gives $13,000 to a trust for the benefit of his teenaged granddaughter. The trust instrument gives the granddaughter a sixty-day Crummey right to withdraw the gift, but if she does not exercise this withdrawal right, the trust funds remain in trust until she reaches thirty-five years of age. The trustee has discretion to pay income and principal to the granddaughter and, when she reaches thirty-five years of age, the entire trust fund will be distributed to her outright. The granddaughter has a general testamentary power to appoint the trust fund to her estate or any of Tom's descendants if she dies before reaching age 35. This transfer qualifies for the gift tax annual exclusion and if the GST tax applied to direct skip transfers in 2010, would qualify for a zero inclusion ratio under Section 2642(c).[10] Only a skip person (here, the granddaughter) has an interest in the trust, so the trust is itself a skip person. Tom's transfer is, therefore, also a direct skip transfer made in 2010, and thus, by reason of Section 2664, no GST tax is imposed on this transfer. Subject to the application of EGTRRA's sunset provisions, however, because the entitlement to a zero inclusion ratio is an application of Chapter 13 to a 2010 direct skip, the trust should not have a zero inclusion ratio.

Unfortunately, stating that Chapter 13 does not apply to a generation-skipping transfer in 2010 may itself cause problems for generation-skipping transfers in trust. A direct skip gift made in trust in 2010 is not subject to tax, but post-2010 distributions from the trust to a skip person may themselves be subject to the GST tax.

Distributions to a skip person from a trust that is itself a skip person are generally protected from the GST tax by the generation move-down rule of Section 2653(a). Section 2653(a) states that, if immediately after a generation-skipping transfer of property the property is held in trust, then the determination whether any GST tax is imposed on subsequent transfers from the trust is made by treating the trust "as if the transferor of such property were assigned to the first generation above the highest generation of any person who

---

[10] The inclusion ratio is calculated as 1 minus the applicable fraction. The numerator of the applicable fraction is the amount of the GST exemption allocated to the trust or transfer, and the denominator of the applicable fraction is the value of the transferred property (net of federal and state estate or other death taxes actually recovered from the trust attributable to such property, and net of any charitable deduction allowed for the transfer). IRC § 2642(a); see also Harrington, Plaine & Zaritsky, Generation-Skipping Transfer Tax ¶ 4.06 (Thomson Reuters/WG&L, 2d ed. 2001). The author recognizes that the figure produced by Section 2642(a) is not actually a ratio, but a single number. Nonetheless, the Code refers to it as an inclusion ratio and practitioners must get used to this misnomer.

has an interest in such trust immediately after the transfer."[11] Section 2653(a), however, is part of Chapter 13, and Section 2664 states that Chapter 13 does not apply to direct skip transfers made in 2010. Therefore, Section 2664 appears to negate the protection afforded by Section 2653(a) to a generation-skipping transfer in trust when the transfer is made in 2010, unless EGTRRA's sunset rule requires a different result.

EXAMPLE 4-5: In 2010, Harriet gives $1 million to a trust for the benefit of her grandson, providing that the income and principal will be held and administered by the trustee for the benefit of the grandson, and distributed to the grandson in the trustee's discretion. The trust will terminate when the grandson reaches thirty-five years of age or, if earlier, on the date of his death. If the grandson dies before reaching age 35, the trust funds will be distributed to his then-living descendants, per stirpes. The trust is itself a skip person because the only person with an interest in the trust is Harriet's grandson. Harriet's transfer is, therefore, a direct skip transfer made in 2010 and, by reason of Section 2664, no GST tax is imposed in 2010 on this transfer.

In 2011, the trustee distributes $50,000 to Harriet's grandson. This distribution is a payment of income or principal by a trustee to a beneficiary who is assigned to a generation two below that of the transferor and who is, therefore, a skip person. Section 2653(a)'s generation move-down rule arguably does not apply to generation-skipping transfers in 2010, when Harriet made her gift to the trust. Therefore, the 2011 distribution to Harriet's grandson would arguably be a taxable distribution upon which the GST tax would be imposed.[12]

EXAMPLE 4-6: In 2010, Hal gives $1 million to a trust for the benefit of his grandchildren and more remote descendants, providing that the income and principal will be held and administered by the trustee for the benefit of the beneficiaries, and distributed to and among them in the trustee's discretion. The trust will continue for the maximum duration permitted under applicable state law. At termination, the trust fund then remaining will be distributed to Hal's then-living descendants, per stirpes. The trust is itself a skip person because all of the persons who hold interests in the trust are skip persons. The transfer to the trust is a direct skip gift, but because it is made in 2010, no GST tax is imposed on the transfer.

In 2012, all of Hal's grandchildren die in a tragic bowling accident. After their deaths, the trust is held for the benefit of Hal's great-grandchildren and more remote descendants. This succession of a more distant generation to the interests in the trust may be a taxable termination, as defined in Section 2612(a), because the interest of the

---

[11] See Harrington, Plaine & Zaritsky, Generation-Skipping Transfer Tax ¶ 5.05 (Thomson Reuters/WG&L, 2d ed. 2001).

[12] See, however, discussion of the impact of EGTRRA's sunset rule on this transaction infra ¶ 4.03[2].

grandchildren has been terminated by death, no non-skip person has an interest in such property immediately after such termination, and distributions may be made from the trust to skip persons. The generation move-down rule of Section 2653(a) did not apply in 2010, when Hal made his gift to the trust, and arguably it continues not to apply after 2010. Therefore, the 2011 death of Hal's grandchildren would be a taxable termination upon which the GST tax would be imposed.[13]

EXAMPLE 4-7: In 2010, Tom gives $13,000 to a trust for the benefit of his teenaged granddaughter. The trust instrument gives the granddaughter a sixty-day Crummey right to withdraw the gift, but if she does not exercise this withdrawal right, the gift remains in trust until the granddaughter reaches thirty-five years of age.[14] The trustee has discretion to pay income and principal to the granddaughter until she reaches thirty-five years of age, at which time the trust funds will be distributed to her outright. The granddaughter holds a testamentary general power to appoint the trust fund to her estate or to any of Tom's descendants if she dies before reaching age 35. This transfer qualifies for the gift tax annual exclusion and for a zero inclusion ratio under Section 2642(c), but Section 2664 prevents the trust from having a zero inclusion ratio.

In 2011, the trustee distributes $5,000 to Tom's granddaughter. Section 2653(a)'s generation move-down rule did not apply in 2010, when Tom made her gift to the trust, and arguably it continues not to apply after 2010. Therefore, the 2011 distribution to Tom's granddaughter would arguably be a taxable distribution upon which the GST tax could be imposed.

This problem is exacerbated by the fact that, for GST tax purposes, a transfer to a Uniform Transfers (or Gifts) to Minors Act custodial account is treated as a transfer in trust.[15] This makes it extraordinarily difficult to make a significant outright gift to a minor skip person, and increases the likelihood that transfers in 2010 will produce GST tax problems.

On the other hand, one might argue that Section 2664 was meant only to remove the GST tax on certain events that occur in 2010, and, therefore, it was not intended to generate additional taxes on trusts created in 2010. This argument would support the notion that the generation move-down rule of Sec-

---

[13] See, however, discussion of the impact of EGTRRA's sunset rule on this transaction infra ¶ 4.03[2].

[14] On Crummey powers generally, see Henkel, Estate Planning and Wealth Preservation: Strategies and Solutions ¶ 10.03 (Thomson Reuters/WG&L 1997); Westfall & Mair, Estate Planning Law and Taxation ¶ 9.08 (Thomson Reuters/WG&L, 4th ed. 2001); Esperti & Peterson, Irrevocable Trusts: Analysis With Forms ¶ 6.02 (Thomson Reuters/ WG&L, 1998); Zaritsky & Leimberg, Tax Planning With Life Insurance ¶ 5.03[3] (Thomson Reuters/WG&L, 2d ed. 1998); Zaritsky, Tax Planning for Family Wealth Transfers: Analysis With Forms ¶ 4.08 (Thomson Reuters/WG&L, 4th ed. 2002).

[15] Reg. § 26.2652-1(b)(2), Ex. 1.

tion 2653(a) should apply after 2010, despite the fact that no GST was tax imposed on the original creation of the trust. The Code does not preclude this construction; nor does it compel it.

EGTRRA's sunset rule, discussed below, also states that the tax laws, including Chapter 13, apply to transfers after December 31, 2010, as if EGTRRA (including Section 2664) had never been enacted. Arguably, this could make the generation move-down rule apply after 2010 to direct skip transfers made in trust in 2010.

Practical estate planners should give serious consideration to deferring 2010 transfers in trust until the IRS or Congress has provided clarification on the long-range GST tax implications of such transfers.[16] It is likely that clients will simply follow the practitioner's guidance regarding whether to refrain from making these transfers in 2010. Though a practitioner may explain the above-discussed interpretative problem to clients, it is not at all clear that most clients will understand the risks well enough to make an intelligent, informed decision. Furthermore, if Congress only reinstates the GST tax prospectively and if the EGTRRA's sunset rule, as discussed below, is deemed to protect such 2010 transfers from future GST taxes, the estate planner will have lost a valuable planning opportunity. Accordingly, clients must ultimately choose between taking a chance on incurring a tax or passing up a valuable opportunity. Unfortunately, the estate planner can offer little guidance in the making of this choice because we cannot know how these provisions will ultimately be construed or what Congress will ultimately do.

[2] The Scope of EGTRRA's Sunset Rule

EGTRRA's sunset rule is contained in Section 901 of that Act. Section 901(a) of EGTRRA, in applicable part, states that the GST tax changes made by EGTRRA do not apply to "generation skipping transfers, after December 31, 2010." Section 901(b) provides the greater problem, stating that the tax laws are applied and administered "to...transfers described in subsection (a) [those after December 31, 2009] as if the provisions and amendments described in subsection (a) had never been enacted."

There is much debate and uncertainty regarding the meaning of the statement that the GST tax must be administered with respect to transfers after December 31, 2010, as if EGTRRA "had never been enacted." The GST tax, to a far greater extent than the estate and gift taxes, includes many rules by which transactions and elections made in one year affect the tax treatment of events

---

[16] Theoretically, clarification could originate with the courts, but there is little chance that a judicial opinion would be forthcoming within calendar year 2010 on issues as complex as these.

in subsequent years. Thus, the precise application of the sunset rule to the GST tax is often difficult or impossible to divine.

[a] Section 2653(a) and the Generation Move-Down Rule for Post-2010 Distributions and Terminations for Trusts Created by 2010 Generation-Skipping Transfers

The generation move-down rule of Section 2653(a), as discussed above, protects subsequent distributions from, or terminations of interests in, a trust that is itself created by a generation-skipping transfer from being subject to another round of GST tax. Ordinarily, Section 2653(a)'s generation move-down rule would be applied in the year in which the trust was created, but it is reasonable to interpret EGTRRA's sunset rule as requiring, with respect to trusts created by generation-skipping transfers in 2010, that the generation move-down of the transferor be determined when the first post-2010 potentially taxable event occurs.

> **EXAMPLE 4-8:** In 2010, Harriet gives $1 million to a trust for the benefit of her grandchildren, providing that the income and principal will be held and administered by the trustee for the benefit of the grandchildren and distributed to them in the trustee's discretion. Harriet does not make her children beneficiaries of the trust, because they already share interests in other trusts. This trust will terminate when the last of Harriet's grandchildren dies, and the remaining trust funds will be distributed to her then-living descendants, per stirpes. The trust is itself a skip person because all interests in it are held by skip persons. Harriet's transfer is, therefore, a direct skip transfer made in 2010, and by reason of Section 2664, no GST tax is imposed in 2010 on this transfer.
>
> In 2011, the trustee distributes $50,000 to Harriet's grandson. This distribution is a payment of income or principal to a beneficiary assigned to a generation at least two below that of the transferor and who is, therefore, a skip person. The 2011 distribution is arguably not a taxable distribution, because generation-skipping transfers after 2010 must be determined as if EGTRRA had never been enacted. Had EGTRRA not been enacted, Section 2653(a)'s generation move-down rule would have applied to the transfer in 2010, and Harriet would have been deemed to have been assigned to the generation one above that of her grandchildren for purposes of determining the tax on distributions or terminations of interests in this trust. Therefore, distributions from this trust to Harriet's grandchild after 2010 would not be taxable distributions.

> **EXAMPLE 4-9:** In 2010, Hal gives $1 million to a trust for the benefit of his grandchildren and more remote descendants, providing that the income and principal will be held and administered by the trustee for the benefit of the beneficiaries, and distributed to and among them in the trustee's discretion. The trust will continue for the maximum duration permitted under applicable state law. At termination, the trust fund then remaining

will be distributed to Hal's then-living descendants, per stirpes. The trust is itself a skip person because all of its beneficiaries are skip persons. The transfer to the trust is a direct skip gift, but because it is made in 2010, no GST tax is imposed on it.

In 2012, all of Hal's grandchildren die in a tragic shuffleboard accident. After their deaths, the trust is held for the benefit of his great-grandchildren and more remote descendants. This is a taxable termination regardless of whether the generation move-down rule applies.

EXAMPLE 4-10: In 2010, Tom gives $13,000 to a trust for the benefit of his teenage granddaughter. The trust instrument gives the granddaughter a sixty-day Crummey right to withdraw the gift, but if she does not exercise this withdrawal right, the trust funds remain in trust until the granddaughter reaches thirty-five years of age. The trustee is given discretion to pay income and principal to the granddaughter until she reaches thirty-five years of age, at which time the trust funds will be distributed to her outright. The granddaughter holds a testamentary general power to appoint the trust fund to her estate or to any of Tom's descendants if she dies before reaching age 35. This transfer qualifies for the gift tax annual exclusion, but the trust does not get a zero inclusion under Section 2642(c).

In 2011, the trustee distributes $5,000 to Tom's granddaughter. The 2011 distribution is arguably not a taxable distribution, because generation-skipping transfers after 2010 must be determined as if EGTRRA had never been enacted. Had EGTRRA not been enacted, Section 2653(a)'s generation move-down rule would have applied to the transfer in 2010, and Tom would have been deemed to have been assigned to the generation one above that of his granddaughter for purposes of determining the tax on distributions or terminations of interests in this trust. Therefore, distributions from this trust to Tom's granddaughter after 2010 would not be taxable distributions. Also, if EGTRRA's sunset rule treats Section 2664 as not applying after December 31, 2010, the trust in 2011 could be treated as having derived a zero inclusion ratio in 2010.

Although this seems to be the best and most reasonable interpretation of EGTRRA's sunset rule, the IRS and the courts may reject it and view Section 2653(a) as inapplicable to a 2010 transfer to a trust that is a skip person. Practical estate planners should generally prefer outright generation-skipping transfers in 2010 over those made in trust, and should warn clients that generation-skipping transfers in trust made in 2010 may possibly produce GST tax liabilities in later years.

A practitioner who believes that the generation move-down rule will apply after 2010 to a 2010 transfer in trust should make such transfers to trusts for the most remote generation of living descendants, such as great-grandchildren. The GST tax is imposed in the same fashion whether the beneficiaries of the transfer are the transferor's grandchildren or the transferor's great-grandchildren. Section 2653(a) would assign the transferor, who makes a gift to a trust for his or her great-grandchildren, to the generation one above the great-grandchildren's generation. The transferor would, therefore, be assigned to the generation usually occupied by the transferor's grandchildren for purposes of determining the tax on future distributions from and terminations of interests in the great-grandchildren's trust.

A transferor, in such a case, could also grant to a third-party the power to add the grantor's other descendants to the class of beneficiaries. This power would enable the trustee to make distributions to these non-skip person beneficiaries without an additional GST tax because the transferor would still seem to be assigned to the generation of his or her grandchildren, thereby making those other beneficiaries non-skip persons.

The definition of "skip person" under Section 2613 includes a trust if all interests in the trust are held by skip persons. Section 2652(c) states that an "interest" in a trust generally requires a present interest, whether mandatory or discretionary.[17] The generation move-down rule can apply only when there is a transfer to the trust, and so a later addition of beneficiaries ought not cause a redetermination of the transferor's generation assignment.

> **EXAMPLE 4-11:** In 2010, Harriet gives $10 million to a trust for the benefit of her great-grandchildren, providing that the income and principal will be held and administered by the trustee for their benefit and distributed to them in the trustee's discretion. The trust will terminate in ninety years, and the remaining trust funds will be distributed to Harriet's then-living descendants, per stirpes. The transfer to the trust is a direct-skip because all of the interests in the trust are held by beneficiaries assigned to a generation at least two below that of Harriet.
>
> Harriet's attorney advises her that Section 2653(a)'s generation move-down rule applies to this 2010 transfer notwithstanding the language of Section 2664. Harriet is, therefore, assigned to the generation one above that of her great-grandchildren for purposes of determining the tax on future trust distributions or terminations. That is, Harriet is assigned to the same generation as her own grandchildren.
>
> The trust permits Harriet's brother to increase the class of beneficiaries at any time by adding other descendants of Harriet's parents, other

---

[17] IRC § 2653(c)(1) states:

[a] person has an interest in property held in trust if (at the time the determination is made) such person—

   (A) has a right (other than a future right) to receive income or corpus from the trust,
   (B) is a permissible current recipient of income or corpus from the trust and is not described in section 2055(a), or
   (C) is described in section 2055(a) and the trust is—

      (i) a charitable remainder annuity trust,
      (ii) a charitable remainder unitrust within the meaning of section 664, or
      (iii) a pooled income fund within the meaning of section 642(c)(5).

than Harriet herself. In 2014, Harriet's brother adds Harriet's grandchildren as beneficiaries.

It is arguable that the addition of Harriet's grandchildren as beneficiaries does not change the fact that, as transferor, Harriet is assigned to the generation one above her great-grandchildren. Therefore, distributions from this trust to Harriet's grandchildren would not be subject to the GST tax.

[b] Section 2654(a)(2) and Basis in 2010 Taxable Terminations

Section 2654(a)(2) states that the adjusted basis of property that is the subject of a taxable termination on the death of an individual is adjusted to the estate tax value basis of the property. The taxable termination of a beneficiary's interest in a trust occurring in 2010, however, is exempt from the operation of the GST tax rules, which include Section 2654(a)(2). It appears, therefore, that no basis increase occurs with respect to the property that is the subject of a taxable termination at death in 2010.

EGTRRA's sunset rule, however, could be interpreted as readjusting the basis of these assets on January 1, 2011, as if EGTRRA had never been enacted. This would require that the sunset rule ignore both that (1) there was actually no estate tax in 2010 and (2) the carryover basis rules applied in 2010—two very large facts to overlook.

[c] Post-2010 Effect of Pre-2010 GST Exemption Allocations

EGTRRA raised the GST exemption from $1 million (indexed for inflation) to $1.5 million in 2004 and 2005; $2 million for 2006, 2007, and 2008; and $3.5 million for 2009.[18] EGTRRA's sunset rule, Section 901(b), however, states that the GST tax must be applied and administered "to...transfers described in subsection (a) [those after December 31, 2009] as if the provisions and amendments described in subsection (a) had never been enacted."

On January 1, 2011, absent additional legislation, the GST exemption will drop to $1 million, adjusted for inflation, which should produce a GST exemption of between $1,350,000 and $1,400,000.[19] The sunset rule requirement that

---

[18] IRC §§ 2631(c), 2010(c). The $1 million figure was added by the Tax Reform Act of 1986, Pub. L. No. 99-514, § 1431(a), 99th Cong., 2d Sess. (1986), 100 Stat. 2721. The inflation adjustment was added by the Taxpayer Relief Act of 1997, Pub. L. No. 105-34, § 501(d), 105th Cong., 1st Sess. (1997), 111 Stat. 846. On the interesting background of the inflation adjustment, see Schneider & Plaine, "TRA '97 and the Generation-Skipping Transfer Tax," 87 J. Tax'n 341 (Dec. 1997).

[19] See the $1 million figure used in Section 6601(j)(2)(A)(i) to measure the portion of the estate taxes on a closely held business interest that can be deferred at a 2-percent interest rate. This $1 million figure is also adjusted for inflation after 1997, and is

the GST tax be applied after 2010 as if EGTRRA had never been enacted could force the recalculation of post-2010 inclusion ratios. The numerator of the applicable fraction of such redetermined inclusion ratio would arguably be the lesser of the amount of GST exemption that the transferor allocated to the transfer or trust and the GST exemption that would have been available had EGTRRA not been enacted.

> **EXAMPLE 4-12:** In 2009, Harriet died leaving $3.5 million in a genera-tion-skipping trust for the benefit of her children, grandchildren, and more remote descendants. The trust is to continue for the longest period permit-ted by applicable state law. Harriet's executor allocated all of her GST exemption to this trust, producing an inclusion ratio of 0 (1 − [$3,500,000/$3,500,000]). In 2011, the GST exemption drops to $1.4 mil-lion. The law is unclear, but one might interpret EGTRRA's sunset re-quirement, namely, that the GST tax should be administered with respect to transfers after 2010 as if EGTRRA had never been enacted, as forcing a recalculation of the trust's inclusion ratio. The inclusion ratio in such recalculation would be 0.63 (1 − [$1,300,000 ÷ $3,500,000]).

One could argue that this recalculation is not required, because the sunset rule only requires administration of the GST tax as if EGTRRA had not been enacted with respect "to...transfers described in subsection (a) [those after De-cember 31, 2009]...." The transfer to which the higher GST exemption was al-located originally in this situation occurred before January 1, 2010. It is far from clear, however, that this is the answer that the IRS and the courts will adopt, and practical estate planners should be cautious about recommending discretionary taxable distributions from generation-skipping trusts to which the transferor has allocated a higher GST exemption than that which is granted in the restoration of the GST tax in 2011 or before.

[d] Post-2010 Effect of Pre-2010 Automatic Allocations

EGTRRA provided that a donor's GST exemption is automatically allo-cated to lifetime transfers that are not direct skips but that are instead made to generation-skipping trusts. These transfers are referred to as "indirect skips". This rule applies with respect to post-2000 transfers subject to estate or gift tax and to estate tax inclusion periods (ETIPs) ending after December 31, 2000.[20]

$1,340,000 for estates of decedents dying in 2010. Rev. Proc. 2009-50, § 3.36, 2009-45 IRB 617. This same figure will be adjusted for inflation again for estates of decedents dy-ing in 2011, and that figure will be the same as the GST exemption for that year.

[20] EGTRRA § 561(a); IRC § 2632(c); see also Harrington, Plaine & Zaritsky, Gener-ation-Skipping Transfer Tax ¶ 4.04 (Thomson Reuters/WG&L, 2d ed. 2001); Stephens, Maxfield, Lind & Calfee, Federal Estate and Gift Taxation ¶ 15.03 (Thomson Reuters/ WG&L, 8th ed. 2002).

The automatic allocation rule does not apply to a transfer to a trust if

1. The trust provides for distribution or withdrawal of more than 25 percent of the trust corpus by one or more non-skip persons before reaching forty-six years of age or before a specified date that will or may be reasonably expected to occur before the individual (or each individual) reaches forty-six years of age (as determined under Treasury regulations);[21]

2. The trust provides for distribution or withdrawal of more than 25 percent of the trust corpus by one or more non-skip persons who are living on the date of death of another person identified in the instrument (by name or by class) who is more than ten years older than such individuals;[22]

3. The trust provides for mandatory distribution of 25 percent or more of the trust corpus to the estate of, or subjects such corpus to a general power of appointment held by, one or more non-skip persons if they die on or before a date or event that will or may be reasonably expected to occur before the individual (or each individual) reaches forty-six years of age (as determined under Treasury regulations);[23]

4. Any part of the trust would be included in the gross estate of a non-skip person (other than the transferor) if such person died immediately after the transfer;[24]

5. The trust is a charitable lead annuity trust, charitable remainder annuity trust, or a charitable remainder unitrust;[25] or

6. The trust is a charitable lead unitrust the noncharitable beneficiary of which is a non-skip person.[26]

EGTRRA also provided that transferors can elect not to have these automatic allocation rules apply. This "election out" is made on a timely filed gift tax return for the year in which the transfer was made, or deemed to have been made, or on such later date or dates as may be prescribed by the Treasury Secretary.[27]

It is not clear whether the IRS will, after 2010, respect automatic allocations made under EGTRRA's rules between 2001 and 2010 because it must administer the GST tax as if EGTRRA had never been enacted. This might be

---

[21] IRC § 2632(c)(3)(B)(i).

[22] IRC § 2632(c)(3)(B)(ii).

[23] IRC § 2632(c)(3)(B)(iii).

[24] IRC § 2632(c)(3)(B)(iv).

[25] IRC § 2632(c)(3)(B)(v).

[26] IRC § 2632(c)(3)(B)(vi).

[27] IRC § 2632(c)(5)(B). See also Harrington, Plaine & Zaritsky, Generation-Skipping Transfer Tax ¶ 4.04[1][a] (Thomson Reuters/WG&L, 2d ed. 2001).

seen as requiring that transferors make late allocations of GST exemption in 2011 to transfers made between 2001 and 2010. These allocations would, presumably, be based on the values of the transferred assets on the date of the late allocation, which could be substantially different (either higher or lower) than the value on the date of the original transfer.[28] This view, however, appears to be an unreasonable interpretation of the sunset rules, but until there is further clarification, practical estate planners should cautious about recommending voluntary taxable distributions after 2010 from trusts that are exempt from the GST tax because of 2001–2010 automatic allocations.

[e] Post-2010 Effect of Pre-2010 Qualified Severances

EGTRRA created the rules for qualified severances under which the severance of a single trust into multiple trusts is recognized for GST tax purposes, and the resulting separate trusts are treated as independent trusts for GST tax purposes if

1. The division is made fractionally;
2. The terms of the new trusts provide, in the aggregate, for the same succession of interests of beneficiaries as in the original trust; and
3. The undivided trust, if it has an inclusion ratio other than one or zero, is divided into two trusts, one of which has an inclusion ratio of one and the other of which has an inclusion ratio of zero.[29]

The recognition of a severance of a trust into separate trusts for GST tax purposes is important because the transferor may allocate GST exemption to one trust and not to another, as well as administer and invest the exempt trust in a manner quite distinct from that in which the non-exempt trust is administered.[30] The manner in which EGTRRA's sunset rules apply to qualified severances that transpired between 2001 and 2010 is, however, unclear.

It is not clear whether the IRS will, after 2010, respect as separate trusts, for GST tax purposes, trusts that were divided by qualified severances between 2001 and 2010. The IRS must administer the GST taxes after 2010 as if EGTRRA had never been enacted, and, without EGTRRA, no qualified severance could have taken place. This construction of the sunset rule would require trusts that were divided in a qualified severance be treated as a single unit, and

---

[28] IRC § 2642(b)(3).

[29] EGTRRA § 562; IRC § 2642(a)(3).

[30] See Harrington, Plaine & Zaritsky, Generation-Skipping Transfer Tax ¶ 9.03[2][f] (Thomson Reuters/WG&L, 2d ed. 2001). See also Bieber & Hodgman, "Trust Severances and Other Planning Under the New Final and Prop. GST Reg.," 35 Est. Plan. 3 (Jan. 2008); Chorney, "GST Qualified Severance Regulations: Final and Proposed," 33 ACTEC J. 202 (Winter 2008); Zaritsky, "Final and Proposed Regulations on Division of Trusts Facilitate GST Tax Planning," 20 Probate Pract. Rep. 1 (Oct. 2007).

their inclusion ratios be recalculated accordingly. This appears to be an unreasonable requirement, but until there is further clarification, practical estate planners should be cautious about making voluntary post-2010 taxable distributions from trusts that were divided in a qualified severance between 2001 and 2010.

[f] Post-2010 Effect of Certain Pre-2010 Retroactive Allocations

EGTRRA added Section 2632(d), which allows a transferor to make a retroactive allocation of GST exemption to a transfer in trust if a beneficiary of the trust

1. Is a non-skip person;[31]
2. Is a lineal descendant of the transferor's grandparent or of a grandparent of the transferor's spouse;[32]
3. Is assigned to a generation below the generation of the transferor;[33] and
4. Predeceases the transferor.[34]

This retroactive allocation must be made on a timely filed gift tax return for the year of the non-skip person's death, and the amount of the transferor's unused GST exemption is determined immediately before the non-skip person's death. The allocation is effective immediately before death of the non-skip person and uses the gift tax value—as though it had been a timely allocation.[35] Section 2632(d) applies to deaths of non-skip persons after December 31, 2000, and before January 1, 2011, and it is helpful when a child dies during the transferor's lifetime and the trust at issue was not one in which the transferor had anticipated the possible imposition of the GST tax.[36]

It is not clear whether the IRS will, after 2010, respect the inclusion ratio created by such a retroactive allocation that was made under this rule during the years 2001 through 2010. Arguably, the requirement that the IRS administer the GST taxes as if EGTRRA (including this special rule) had never been enacted should require distributions from and terminations of interests in such trusts to be taxed as if no retroactive allocation could ever have been made. This interpretation might compel trusts to recalculate their inclusion ratios after

---

[31] IRC § 2632(d)(1)(A).

[32] IRC § 2632(d)(1)(B)(i).

[33] IRC § 2632(d)(1)(B)(ii).

[34] IRC § 2632(d)(1)(C).

[35] IRC § 2632(d)(2).

[36] See discussion of planning implications of this rule in Harrington, Plaine & Zaritsky, Generation-Skipping Transfer Tax ¶ 4.04[1][b] (Thomson Reuters/WG&L, 2d ed. 2001).

December 31, 2010, to treat such retroactive allocations as having been late allocations, rather than timely allocations. This would increase the inclusion ratio if the trust funds had grown in value between the date of the original transfer and the date of the retroactive allocation, even if the trust assets had dropped in value thereafter.

> **EXAMPLE 4-13:** In 2002, Terry created an irrevocable trust for the benefit of her son and transferred $1 million worth of stock to the trust. The trust provided that income would be paid to Terry's son until he reached thirty-five years of age, when the principal would be distributed outright to the son. The trust also stated that, if the son died before reaching thirty-five years of age, the trust fund would be distributed to his then-living descendants, per stirpes, but it will be held in continued trust until the youngest of such descendants reaches twenty-five years of age. Terry did not allocate GST exemption to the transfer.
>
> Terry's son died in 2008 at the age of thirty, by which time the trust fund had grown to $1.5 million. The trust fund was held in continued trust because the youngest then-living child of Terry's son was only eighteen years of age. Under Section 2632(d), Terry made a retroactive allocation of $1 million of her GST exemption to the trust, giving it a zero inclusion ratio because the allocation was based on the original value of the trust assets. On January 1, 2011, the trust fund is again worth $1 million. It is unclear whether EGTRRA's sunset rule requirement, namely, that the GST tax be administered with respect to transfers after 2010 as if EGTRRA had never been enacted, will cause the trust's inclusion ratio to change from 0 to 0.333 (1 − [$1,000,000/$1,500,000]).

One could certainly argue that this type of retroactive change in inclusion ratio would be unreasonable, but, until there is further clarification, practical estate planners should be cautious about recommending voluntary post-2010 distributions from trusts that were the subject of such retroactive allocations between 2001 and 2010.

¶ 4.04 THE GST EXEMPTION IN 2010

Section 2664 does not render the GST tax rules inapplicable to a 2010 transfer to a generation-skipping trust the interests in which are held by both skip persons and non-skip persons. Such trusts are not themselves skip persons, because an interest in the trust is held by a non-skip person and a transfer to such a trust is not a "generation-skipping transfer." These terms, as discussed infra ¶ 4.05, require that there be a transferor. Therefore, they are applicable to lifetime gifts in 2010 because there is a gift tax in 2010. They may be inapplicable to testamentary transfers in 2010 because there is no estate tax in 2010.

Traditionally, the GST tax on such transfers has been avoided or reduced by allocating to the transfers the donor's GST exemption.[37] Unfortunately, EGTRRA tied the amount of the GST exemption to the amount of the estate tax applicable exclusion amount.[38] The absence of a federal estate tax in 2010 produces an applicable exclusion amount of zero, and, consequently, also produces a GST exemption of zero.[39] A transferor has, therefore, no GST exemption to allocate to 2010 transfers to avoid future imposition of the GST tax on taxable terminations and taxable distributions from such trusts.

> **EXAMPLE 4-14:** Harriet and Henrietta are twin sisters. Each has a family that includes both children and grandchildren. In 2009, Harriet creates a $3.5 million generation-skipping trust for the benefit of her children, grandchildren, and more remote descendants. The trust is to continue for the longest period permitted by applicable state law. Harriet allocates her $3.5 million GST exemption to this transfer, producing an inclusion ratio of zero (1 − [$3,500,000/$3,500,000]). Future distributions to grandchildren and more remote descendants, as well as the termination of the interest of each succeeding generation of beneficiaries, will be protected from the GST tax for the duration of the trust term.
>
> In 2010, Henrietta creates an identical trust for her children, grandchildren, and more remote descendants. Henrietta has no GST exemption to allocate to the trust. Henrietta pays a lower gift tax on her transfer to this trust than her sister paid on the transfer to the trust that her sister created (the top gift tax rate in 2010 is 35 percent, but the top gift tax rate in 2009 was 45 percent). However, future distributions to Henrietta's grandchildren and more remote descendants, as well as the termination of the interest of each succeeding generation of beneficiaries, will be fully subject to the GST tax for the duration of the trust term.

When the GST tax is revived and a new GST exemption granted on January 1, 2011, this new GST exemption can, it appears, be allocated to a transfer that was made in 2010. Normally, a transferor can allocate GST exemption to transfers that he or she has made in prior years, though the inclusion ratio is determined by such late allocations based on the value of the trust assets at the time of the allocation rather than their value on the date that the transfer was made.[40] This rule should extend to an allocation that is granted anew in 2011.

As has been noted, the GST exemption before EGTRRA was $1 million, indexed for inflation. The Joint Committee on Taxation described a 1998 technical correction to Section 2631(c)(2) as clarifying that one can (1) make a late

---

[37] See Harrington, Plaine & Zaritsky, Generation-Skipping Transfer Tax ch. 4 (Thomson Reuters/WG&L, 2d ed. 2001).

[38] IRC § 2631(c).

[39] IRC § 2010(c).

[40] See IRC § 2642(b)(1); see also Harrington, Plaine & Zaritsky, Generation-Skipping Transfer Tax ¶ 4.04[1][b] (Thomson Reuters/WG&L, 2d ed. 2001).

allocation of the inflation-adjustments to trusts created before the year of the adjustment and (2) recalculate the inclusion ratio accordingly based on both the prior and current allocations of exemption and the current value of the trust fund.[41]

On the other hand, the instructions to the federal gift tax return (Form 709) state that one cannot allocate increases in the GST exemption to prior transfers.[42] Also, when granting permission to make a late retroactive allocation of GST exemption, the Treasury states in proposed regulations that the transferor cannot allocate to the prior transfer any increases in the GST exemption that occur after the transfer itself.[43]

None of these authorities are dispositive regarding whether one can allocate a reinstated GST exemption to a transfer made before 2011, but there is ample reason to believe that Congress or the Treasury may not permit such allocations. This may make practical estate planners wary about advising clients to make generation-skipping transfers in 2010 to which they cannot currently allocate GST exemption.

Also, one does not know whether EGTRRA's sunset provisions will, in 2011, treat the transferor as having a $1,340,000 GST exemption in 2010. Such a construction could treat the transferor's attempted timely allocation to a 2010 transfer as being effective.

¶ 4.05 APPLYING THE GST TAX TO 2010 TESTAMENTARY TRANSFERS

The GST tax does not apply to testamentary direct skip transfers, taxable distributions, or taxable terminations occurring in 2010. As discussed above, these transfers, if made in trust, may not benefit from Section 2653(a)'s transferor move-down rule, which could render future distributions from or terminations of interests in such trusts taxable.[44]

Testamentary transfers made in 2010 to a generation-skipping trust, whether or not the trust is itself a skip person, should probably not be subject to the GST tax in later years when distributions are made to skip persons or when interests of non-skip persons terminate, however. This protection from

---

[41] Staff of Joint Comm. on Taxation, "General Explanation of Tax Legislation Enacted in 1998," 105th Cong., 2d Sess. 169–170 (1998) (Comm. Print).

[42] Form 709, 2008 Instructions for Part 2—GST Exemption Reconciliation, Line 1, p. 11.

[43] Prop. Reg. § 26.2642-7(c).

[44] See supra ¶ 4.03[2].

GST tax is based on the absence of an estate tax in 2010, rather than the absence of a GST tax.

The definitions of both "taxable termination" and "taxable distribution," discussed above, require that there be a distribution to a skip person or that, after the termination of interests, one or more skip persons have interests in the trust. There can be no taxable distribution or taxable termination unless an interest in the trust is held by a skip person.

A "skip person" is defined in Section 2613(a) as either "a natural person assigned to a generation which is 2 or more generations below the generation assignment of the transferor," a trust all of the interests in which are held by skip persons, or a trust in which there is no person holding an interest in the trust and "at no time after such transfer may a distribution (including distributions on termination) be made from such trust to a non-skip person."[45] A "non-skip person" is defined by Section 2613(b) as "any person who is not a skip person."[46]

The definitions of "taxable termination" and "taxable distribution," therefore, ultimately depend upon the existence of a "transferor." Identifying the transferor is essential because the generation assignments of the transferees are based on their relationship to the transferor. It is sound to conclude that, if there is no transferor, there can be no generation-skipping transfer.[47]

The transferor is the individual with respect to whom property was most recently subject to federal estate or gift tax.[48] A transfer to a GST trust on account of the death of a decedent in 2010 is not subject to either gift or estate tax. The best analysis is, therefore, that there is no transferor for such a trust, and thus no skip persons, and thus no taxable distributions or taxable terminations.

---

[45] See Harrington, Plaine & Zaritsky, Generation-Skipping Transfer Tax ¶ 2.04[1] (Thomson Reuters/WG&L, 2d ed. 2001).

[46] See Harrington, Plaine & Zaritsky, Generation-Skipping Transfer Tax ¶ 2.04[2] (Thomson Reuters/WG&L, 2d ed. 2001).

[47] See Harrington, Plaine & Zaritsky, Generation-Skipping Transfer Tax ¶ 2.02 (Thomson Reuters/WG&L, 2d ed. 2001).

[48] IRC § 2652(a)(1) states:

  (1) Except as provided in this subsection or section 2653(a) [the reverse QTIP], the term "transferor" means—

   (A) in the case of any property subject to the tax imposed by Chapter 11, the decedent, and
   (B) in the case of any property subject to the tax imposed by Chapter 12, the donor.

An individual shall be treated as transferring any property with respect to which such individual is the transferor.

EXAMPLE 4-15: Harry dies in 2010, leaving his estate to a trust for the benefit of his children, grandchildren, and more remote descendants, for the longest period permitted by applicable state law. No federal estate tax is imposed with respect to Harry's estate, because Harry died in 2010. In 2011, the trustee distributes $250,000 to each of Harry's four grandchildren. This distribution should not be subject to GST tax, because the trust was funded in a transfer not subject to estate or gift tax. Harry's grandchildren are not skip persons, because they are not assigned to a generation more than one below that of the transferor, and there is no "transferor" for the trust. Therefore, the distribution cannot be a taxable distribution.

The IRS could argue that, under EGTRRA's sunset rule, the status of the transferor must be redetermined after 2010 as if EGTRRA had not been enacted, and, therefore, the transferor of a testamentary transfer should be treated as if he or she had paid a federal estate tax on the transfer. This argument, however, ignores the very fundamental absence of an estate tax on transfers in 2010. Still, a practical estate planner should be cautious about recommending discretionary distributions to possible skip persons from testamentary generation-skipping trusts created by estates of decedents who die in 2010 until further clarification is obtained from the IRS or the courts.

¶ 4.06 2010 GIFTS TO SECTION 2642(c) ANNUAL EXCLUSION TRUSTS

Section 2642(c)(1) states that a direct skip transfer that is not a taxable gift, because it qualifies for the gift tax annual exclusion or unlimited exclusion for direct payment of medical or educational expenses, will have an inclusion ratio of zero for GST tax purposes. Section 2642(c)(2) limits this rule, however, by stating that a direct skip transfer in trust will have an inclusion ratio of zero under this rule only if

1. During the life of the individual transferee, no portion of the corpus or income of the trust may be distributed to (or for the benefit of) any person other than such individual, and
2. If the trust does not terminate before the individual dies, the assets of such trust will be includible in the gross estate of such individual.

This creates what is sometimes referred to as the GST annual exclusion, under which a gift to a trust for the benefit of a grandchild or other skip person has an inclusion ratio of zero without allocation of GST exemption if the gift qualifies for the gift tax annual exclusion, no distributions can be made to anyone other than the transferee, and the undistributed trust fund must be included in the transferee's gross estate if he or she dies during the trust term.[49]

A 2010 transfer to a Section 2642(c) trust creates the problem discussed above with respect to other direct skip transfers in trust. The transfer is not itself taxable, because it is a generation-skipping transfer in 2010, but no portion of Chapter 13 arguably applies to protect the trust from future GST taxes. Distributions from the trust after 2010 could, therefore, be taxable distributions because Section 2653(a)'s generation move-down rule arguably does not apply to generation-skipping transfers made in 2010.

It may also be argued that the zero inclusion ratio rule of Section 2642(c) also does not apply to direct skip transfers in 2010. This would further bolster the argument that post-2010 distributions from the trust or terminations of interests in the trust would be subject to GST tax.

This appears to be a particularly harsh interpretation of Section 2664, and it may be countered by noting that the GST tax must be applied to transfers after 2010 as if EGTRRA had never been enacted. Had EGTRRA not been enacted, both the zero inclusion ratio under Section 2642(c) and the transferor move-down rule under Section 2653(a) would have applied, and the distributions from or terminations of interests in this trust would then have been protected from subsequent GST taxes.

> **EXAMPLE 4-16:** In 2010, Theodora gives $13,000 to a trust for the benefit of her great-grandson. The trust instrument gives the great-grandson a thirty-day Crummey right to withdraw the contribution to the trust, but if he does not exercise this withdrawal right, the trust funds remain in trust for the rest of the great-grandson's lifetime. The trustee is given discretion to pay income and principal to the great-grandson as the trustee deems best. When the great-grandson dies, he is given a testamentary general power to appoint the trust fund to his estate or to any of Theodora's descendants. This transfer qualifies for the gift tax annual exclusion and it meets the requirements for a zero inclusion ratio under Section 2642(c). Section 2642(c) is part of Chapter 13 and does not, however, apply with respect to direct skip transfers made in 2010.
>
> In 2011, the trustee distributes $5,000 to the great-grandson. The 2011 distribution is arguably not a taxable distribution, because generation-skipping transfers after 2010 must be determined as if EGTRRA had

---

[49] See Harrington, Plaine & Zaritsky, Generation-Skipping Transfer Tax ¶ 5.02 (Thomson Reuters/WG&L, 2d ed. 2001); Eisen, "Planning to Minimize Generation-Skipping Tax: Tools and Traps," 27 Est. Plan. 73, 75 (Feb. 2000) (referring to the annual exclusion for direct skip gifts to grandchildren and other skip persons as "true freebies"); Melone, "Tax-Favored Strategies for Funding a Child's Higher Education," 27 Est. Plan. 21, 27 (Jan. 2000) (discussing various forms of annual exclusion gifts for education); Slade, "Inter Vivos Generation-Skipping Transfer Tax Planning," 34 U. Miami Est. Plan. Inst. ¶ 501 (2000) (providing a more exhaustive discussion of the application of the GST tax annual exclusion for educational and medical gifts).

never been enacted. Had EGTRRA not been enacted, Section 2653(a)'s generation move-down rule would have applied to the transfer in 2010, and Theodora would have been assigned to the generation one above that of her great-grandson for purposes of determining the tax on distributions or terminations of interests in this trust. Therefore, distributions from this trust to Theodora's great-grandson after 2010 should not be taxable distributions.

Notwithstanding that this is the best analysis, the IRS or the courts could adopt a different one, and thus practical estate planners should, until further clarification is available, be wary about recommending even these modest generation-skipping transfers in trust during 2010.

¶ 4.07 2010 INTER VIVOS REVERSE QTIPs

One form of generation-skipping transfer that a married person can make in 2010 may be a transfer to an inter vivos qualifying terminable interest property (QTIP) marital trust for the lifetime benefit of the transferor's spouse, with the remainder to be held in trust for the transferor's descendants.[50] The transferor can then elect to deduct the transfer for federal gift tax purposes as a QTIP trust.[51] The transferor can elect under the "reverse QTIP" rules to treat himself or herself as the transferor for GST tax purposes even if the spouse dies after 2010.[52] This avoids the imposition of a gift or GST tax on the transfer in 2010.

A reverse QTIP election should be available for a transfer to a QTIP marital trust in 2010 because Section 2664 renders the GST rules inapplicable in 2010 only with respect to generation-skipping transfers. A gift to a QTIP trust, whether or not a reverse QTIP election is made, is not a generation-skipping transfer, because the donor's spouse is always assigned to the same generation as that of the donor, thus preventing the trust from being a skip person.[53]

> **EXAMPLE 4-17:** Harry wants to give $5 million to a trust for his children, grandchildren, and more remote descendants, but he does not want to pay either gift or GST taxes. In 2010, Harry transfers $5 million to a trust and directs that the trustee pay Harry's wife, Wanda, all of the trust income not less often than annually. No distributions may be made from the trust

---

[50] This technique will not work if the transferee spouse is not a U.S. citizen.

[51] IRC § 2523(f).

[52] IRC § 2652. See discussion of the reverse QTIP election in Harrington, Plaine & Zaritsky, Generation-Skipping Transfer Tax ¶ 4.08 (Thomson Reuters/WG&L, 2d ed. 2001).

[53] IRC § 2651(c)(1); see Harrington, Plaine & Zaritsky, Generation-Skipping Transfer Tax ¶ 2.06[1][b] (Thomson Reuters/WG&L, 2d ed. 2001).

to anyone other than Wanda during her lifetime. At Wanda's death, the trustee will hold the trust funds for the benefit of Harry's descendants, paying income and principal to them, in the trustee's discretion, for the longest term permitted by applicable state law. Harry files a timely gift tax return and elects to deduct the transfer to the trust for gift tax purposes (the QTIP election), but to treat himself as the transferor of the trust for GST tax purposes (the reverse QTIP election). The transfer is not subject to GST tax in 2010.

Wanda dies in 2013, survived by Harry as well as their children and grandchildren. The trust is includible in Wanda's gross estate for federal estate tax purposes, but because of the reverse QTIP election, Wanda is not the transferor of the trust and cannot allocate any of her GST exemption to the trust. The trust is still not subject to GST taxes on account of Wanda's death, however, because the couple's children, who are not skip persons, have an interest in the trust. Subsequent distributions from the trust to their grandchildren are taxable distributions, and the death of the last of the couple's children will be a taxable termination with respect to the trust.

One reason for making a gift by QTIP trust in 2010 is that it allows the donor to wait until April 15, 2011, to determine whether to treat himself or herself as the transferor of the trust for GST tax purposes. The donor will not be subject to current gift or GST taxes even if the IRS ultimately rules that the reverse QTIP rule does not apply to transfers made in 2010. Furthermore, if the GST tax is retroactively restored, the donor is likely to be able to make a late allocation of GST exemption, which may restore some of the GST benefits otherwise available to this trust.

Under EGTRRA's changes it is not clear whether a surviving spouse of a pre-2010 QTIP who dies in 2010 becomes the "transferor" of the continuing trusts under that instrument. The QTIP is not included in the surviving spouse's gross estate and no federal estate tax is imposed on the trust, because there is no federal estate tax in 2010. Arguably, therefore, the surviving spouse is not the transferor of the trust, and because the reverse QTIP election was not made when the trust was created, the original transferor is not the "transferor" of the trust.

EGTRRA's sunset rule, however, could be interpreted as treating the surviving spouse as the transferor because that is the result that would have occurred had EGTRRA never been enacted. This interpretation, however, requires that the sunset rule be applied, ignoring the fact that there was actually no estate tax in 2010, which seems a large fact to overlook.

¶ 4.08 ESTATE TAX INCLUSION PERIODS IN 2010

Under Section 2642, special rules apply when the transferred property would be included in the transferor's gross estate for federal estate tax purposes if the transferor were to die immediately after the transfer. Section 2642(f) states that determination of the inclusion ratio is not made until the end of the estate tax inclusion period (ETIP). An allocation of GST exemption can be effective no earlier than the end of the ETIP.[54]

There is no federal estate tax with respect to any decedent who dies in 2010. This should literally cause all ETIPs from all trusts the transferors of which are still alive to end on January 1, 2010. There is, of course, no GST exemption available to allocate to such trusts in 2010, which would make all such trusts fully GST nonexempt. An earlier allocation would arguably be deemed to become effective on January 1, 2010, when the trust fund would also arguably no longer be includible in the gross estate of a deceased transferor.[55]

¶ 4.09 GST TAX PLANNING SUGGESTIONS FOR 2010

The lack of clear rules governing the application of the GST tax in 2010 will have a chilling effect on GST tax planning. Nonetheless, there are several key points of GST tax planning that the practical estate planner should keep in mind in 2010.

[1] Prefer Outright Transfers Over Transfers in Trust

A client who contemplates a generation-skipping transfer in 2010 should generally make it outright, rather than in continued trust, to the extent that such a transfer is practical for nontax reasons. Section 2664 clearly makes the GST tax inapplicable to both outright transfers and transfers in trust in 2010, but the uncertainty surrounding the application of the generation move-down rule of Section 2653(a) makes outright transfers much safer than transfers in trust. Of course, there is also the risk that Congress could retroactively reinstate the GST tax, and render such generation-skipping transfers fully taxable.

---

[54] The ETIP is determined without regard to the special rules of Section 2035, relating to certain transfers made within three years of the transferor's death. IRC § 2642(f)(1)(B). See discussion of the ETIP rules in Harrington, Plaine & Zaritsky, Generation-Skipping Transfer Tax ¶ 4.07 (Thomson Reuters/WG&L, 2d ed. 2001).

[55] See Reg. § 26.2642-1(b)(2), for rules on allocation of GST exemption during an ETIP.

EXAMPLE **4-18:** Harriet and Henrietta are twin sisters. Each has a family that includes both children and grandchildren. Each wishes to make a $3 million gift to her grandchildren in 2010. Harriet creates a $3.5 million generation-skipping trust for the benefit of her grandchildren and more remote descendants. The trust is to continue for the longest period permitted by applicable state law. The trust is a skip person and Harriet's gift is a direct skip transfer. Section 2664, therefore, renders the gift nontaxable (for GST tax purposes) in 2010. Section 2664 and EGTRRA's sunset rule, however, make it uncertain whether distributions and terminations of interests in this trust after 2010 will be subject to GST tax.[56]

Henrietta makes $3.5 million in outright transfers to her adult grandchildren. Henrietta pays gift tax in 2010, at a top rate of 35 percent, but she pays no GST tax on the transfers. Furthermore, these transfers cannot be subject to additional GST tax in later years, because they are not held in trust.

EXAMPLE **4-19:** Large National Bank is the trustee of a $20 million trust created for the descendants of Tessa, who died in 2005. The trustee wishes to make distributions to Tessa's grandchildren in 2010. The trustee can make the distributions outright to the adult grandchildren, without incurring a GST tax, because they are otherwise taxable distributions and protected from the GST tax rules by Section 2664. The trustee can also make distributions to Tessa's younger grandchildren in further trust, creating a separate trust for each distributee. The trustee can make these distributions without incurring a 2010 GST tax because they are otherwise taxable distributions and protected from the GST tax rules by Section 2664. Unfortunately, the trustee cannot be sure that future distributions from those trusts will not themselves be subject to the GST tax.

[2] Avoid Haste, But Consider the Opportunities of Prompt Action

A donor contemplating a 2010 generation-skipping transfer should probably wait until later in the year to make the transfer. This gives the donor more time in which to ascertain whether it is likely that Congress will retroactively reinstate the GST tax, and perhaps even to divine the terms under which it would be reinstated. Of course, there is no guaranty that Congress will not retroactively reinstate the GST tax after 2010, and the U.S. Supreme Court has approved retroactive changes in the estate tax law that occurred as many as fourteen months after the original act that was being changed.[57]

---

[56] See discussion supra ¶ 4.04.

[57] See discussion of *United States v. Carlton* at ¶ 1.07.

[3] Formula Generation-Skipping Transfers

It would be helpful if an individual who is willing to pay a gift tax but not a GST tax could make a gift to skip persons that would become void if either (1) the GST tax were retroactively made applicable to the gift or (2) the gift were determined to leave the transfer subject to future GST tax imposition because of the inapplicability of Section 2653(a)'s generation move-down rule or otherwise. Such a condition could be achieved in a deed of gift that required the donee to return the transferred property to the donor if the transfer were determined to be subject to the GST tax.

This type of conditional transfer must be structured carefully to avoid invalidity under the *Proctor* line of authorities. In *Proctor v. Commissioner,*[58] the taxpayer assigned a remainder interest in two trusts to a third trust subject to a condition that, if a court found the transaction to be a gift, the remainders would be returned to the grantor. The U.S. Court of Appeals for the Fourth Circuit held that the condition was void as against public policy because it tended to discourage the enforcement of the tax laws and it obstructed the administration of justice by requiring a court to pass on a moot point. The court stated that the condition could not become operative, because it required a judgment of a court of last resort and all matters of the agreement would be merged into that final judgment.

The IRS adopted this rationale in Revenue Ruling 86-41,[59] which involved a transfer of an undivided interest in real property with two alternative conditions: one condition would reduce the amount of the transfer if it were determined by the IRS that a taxable gift resulted, and the other required the donee to pay the donor for the difference between the assumed value of the property and the amount the IRS determined to be its value. The IRS ruled that both violated public policy by conditioning the nature of the transaction on the determination of the IRS.

The courts have generally followed the *Proctor* rationale where the transfer is subject to a condition that returns the property to the transferor if a particular tax result is not achieved.[60] The courts have not, however, always followed the *Proctor* line of cases where the transaction was intended to be a sale and no condition subsequent was involved. In *Estate of Dickinson, Jr. v. Commissioner,*[61] the Tax Court upheld the validity of a clause in a buy-sell agreement that required the sale of certain shares of stock at the seller's death and stated that, if the estate tax value of the shares sold was ultimately found to be higher than the agreement price, the agreement would not bind the par-

---

[58] Proctor v. Comm'r, 142 F2d 824 (4th Cir.), cert. denied, 323 US 756 (1944).

[59] Rev. Rul. 86-41, 1986-1 CB 300.

[60] See Ward v. Comm'r, 87 TC 78 (1986); and Harwood v. Comm'r, 82 TC 239 (1984), aff'd, 786 F2d 1174 (9th Cir. 1986).

[61] Estate of Dickinson, Jr. v. Comm'r, 63 TC 771 (1975).

ties to buy and sell at that price, and the sale would be made at the estate tax values. The IRS argued that this provision was invalid as a matter of public policy, relying on *Proctor*, but the Tax Court upheld the revaluation clause.

The Tax Court in *Dickinson* found that the revaluation clause in that case did not attempt to rescind an act already taken by the parties, but merely barred the application of the valuation provisions of the agreement in certain circumstances. The court stated that such provision was not an attempt to negate the government's determination of the value of the stock but rather an attempt to make that determination binding for nontax purposes as well as tax purposes.

In *King v. United States*,[62] a revaluation clause was also sustained in a context similar to that of *Dickinson*. In *King*, a father sold stock to trusts he had created for his children at a price believed to be its fair market value. The trusts paid for the stock with promissory notes. The notes contained a clause stating that if the IRS determined that the market value differed from the price set in the agreement, an adjustment would be made in the face amount of the notes. When the IRS ultimately determined that the stock was worth more than the parties had believed, the corporation had become bankrupt and the stock was worthless.

Again, the IRS, citing *Proctor*, contended that the revaluation clause violated public policy. The Tenth Circuit upheld the clause, finding that it did not seek to alter the nature of the transaction, but merely to make the transaction follow the intent of the parties.

Thus, while revaluation clauses that merely require additional payments by the buyer in case of an undervaluation by the parties have gained some judicial support, the IRS continues to view all revaluation clauses with skepticism. Practitioners using such clauses should anticipate having to litigate the issue in order to obtain satisfactory tax results, and, even then, such results are not assured.[63]

The validity of a conditional transfer would seem to be more permissible in the present environment than it was in *Proctor*. In *Proctor*, the taxpayer imposed the uncertainty himself in an effort to avoid imposition of any federal gift tax. In the current environment, the uncertainty results from the awkward state of the tax law, where the taxability of certain transactions is unclear or unascertainable. This situation suggests that the formula clause is not an at-

---

[62] King v. United States, 545 F2d 700 (10th Cir. 1976).

[63] On "savings clauses" generally, see Handler & Chen, "Formula Disclaimers: Proctor Proofing Gifts Against Revaluations by IRS," 96 J. Tax'n 231 (Apr. 2002); Holbrook, "Valuation Definition Clauses: The Basics (Part 1)," 37 Tenn. B. J. 33 (Mar. 2001); Holbrook, "Value Definition Clauses: Creative Uses (Part 2)," 37 Tenn. B. J. 20 (Apr. 2001); Hood, "Defined Value Gifts: Does IRS Have It All Wrong?" 28 Est. Plan. 582 (Dec. 2001); Strobel & Strobel, "Savings Clauses Can Protect Against Revalued Transfers in Family Transactions," 14 Tax'n for Law. 22 (1985).

tempt to interfere with the tax collection process or the judicial process, and thus should not fall under the *Proctor* line of cases.

This type of formula can also be improved by following a more recent line of cases that have sustained a transfer in which the donor assigns an asset, and then directs that it be divided between two or more transferees according to a formula. Typically, one transferee's interest in an asset is determined by using a ratio the numerator of which is a specific dollar amount and the denominator of which is the asset's assumed value, while the remaining interest in the asset passes to a second transferee. The second transferee, in the cases that have considered such an arrangement, has been a charity.

This arrangement was sustained by the Fifth Circuit in *McCord v. Commissioner*,[64] the Tax Court and the Eighth Circuit in *Estate of Christiansen v. Commissioner*,[65] and the Tax Court again in *Estate of Petter v. Commissioner*.[66] The last of these is perhaps the clearest discussion of the issues raised in this type of formula gift.

Anne Petter was the niece of one of the first investors in what became United Parcel Service (UPS). When her uncle died in 1982, he left Anne his stock. Anne had three adult children and grandchildren, and worked with attorneys to create arrangements that would take care of her heirs and also fund public charities. Anne's estate planning included the creation of an irrevocable life insurance trust, a charitable remainder trust, a family limited liability company (LLC), and some intentional grantor trusts.

Anne was preparing her estate plan when UPS went public, doubling the value of Anne's stock. As part of her estate plan, Anne did a part-gift/part-sale of her interests in the LLC to the intentional grantor trusts, after first giving the trusts seed capital equal to 10 percent of the value of the total LLC units she planned to transfer to the trust. She then simultaneously sold the balance of the units to the trusts and gave some units to two public charities. The document of sale and gift provided that the transferred units would be divided between the charities and the trusts as follows:

> Transferor *** [Section] 1.1.1: assigns to the Trust as a gift the number of Units described in Recital C above that equals one-half the minimum dollar amount that can pass free of federal gift tax by reason of Transferor's applicable exclusion amount allowed by Code Section 2010(c). Transferor currently understands her unused applicable exclusion amount to be $907,820, so that the amount of this gift should be $453,910; and

---

[64] McCord v. Comm'r, 461 F3d 614 (5th Cir. 2006), rev'g and rem'g 120 TC 358 (2003). See also Mulligan, "Formula Transfers: McCord Is Pro-Taxpayer, But Other Developments Are Likely," 34 Est. Plan. 3 (July 2007).

[65] Estate of Christiansen v. Comm'r, 586 F3d 1061 (8th Cir. 2009), aff'g 130 TC 1 (2008).

[66] Estate of Petter v. Comm'r, TC Memo. 2009-280 (2009).

> 1.1.2 assigns to The Seattle Foundation as a gift to the A.Y. Petter Family Advised Fund of The Seattle Foundation the difference between the total number of Units described in Recital C above and the number of Units assigned to the Trust in Section 1.1.1.

The gift documents also provided in Section 1.2:

> The Trust agrees that, if the value of the Units it initially receives is finally determined for federal gift tax purposes to exceed the amount described in Section 1.1.1, Trustee will, on behalf of the Trust and as a condition of the gift to it, transfer the excess Units to The Seattle Foundation as soon as practicable.

Both trusts repaid their promissory notes to Anne. The charities were effectively represented by separate counsel. The transfers were appraised by a qualified appraiser and were fully disclosed with all of the documentation on Anne's federal gift tax return.

On audit of the federal gift tax return, the IRS argued for a higher unit value than that opined by Anne's appraiser. Additionally, the IRS argued that the "defined value" gift clause was unenforceable and violated public policy, and that no additional income tax deduction would be allowed for the additional units of LLC interest allocated to the charities on account of the revaluation.

In the Tax Court (Judge Holmes) held for the taxpayer. The court reviewed the history of defined value gifts and sales, as well as similar transactions, from *Proctor* through *Estate of Christiansen*. The court stated succinctly that "savings clauses are void, but formula clauses are fine." The court then analyzed Anne's transaction documents, and concluded that what she had done was to make "gifts of an ascertainable dollar value of stock; she did not give a specific number of shares or a specific percentage interest in the [LLC]."

The court rejected the IRS public policy arguments, noting that

> the facts in this case show charities sticking up for their interests, and not just passively helping a putative donor reduce her tax bill. The foundations here conducted arm's-length negotiations, retained their own counsel, and won changes to the transfer documents to protect their interests. Perhaps the most important of these was their successful insistence on becoming substituted members in the PFLLC with the same voting rights as all the other members. By ensuring that they became substituted members, rather than mere assignees, the charities made sure that the PFLLC managers owed them fiduciary duties.

Judge Holmes also noted that there are other situations in the Code and regulations where the law expressly approves of formula clauses, such as with respect to charitable remainder trusts and the marital deduction. The court also held that the charitable deduction for the additional allocation of shares to charities was properly taken on the date of the original transfer, even though there were subsequent revaluations and reallocations.

Considering these favorable precedents, one wishing to make a safer form of generation-skipping transfer in 2010 should consider making the gift by a reallocation formula similar to that used in *Estate of Petter*. Ideally, such a transfer should have the following key features:

1. The transfer should be made jointly to a skip person (who may be a trust) and a non-skip person (who may also be an individual, a trust, or a charity, though the case law would be stronger support where the non-skip person is a charity);

2. The transfer to the skip person would be described as the largest fraction of the value of the transferred assets that can pass to this skip person free of the federal GST tax, as in effect on the date of the transfer or retroactively reimposed in a manner that makes it in effect on that date; and

3. The transfer to the non-skip person is the remaining fraction of the gift.

This arrangement should bring the distribution within the scope of the favorable cases on defined value gifts, though it does admittedly involve a slightly different condition than those imposed in the cases. The donor need not use a charity as the non-skip person, but both *Estate of Christiansen* and *Estate of Petter* relied in part for their favorable holdings on the strong public policy favoring charitable gifts. Substituting the transferor's children or another non-skip person for the charity deprives the transaction of this argument and, while the transaction should seem to be supportable, its case will be weaker.

The portion of the transfer that is re-transferred to a non-skip person could pass outright to the transferor's children or to trusts for their benefit. Typically, these trusts would be designed to substitute an estate tax at the child's death for the GST tax, to the extent that such a substitution would reduce overall taxes.[67]

The portion of the transfer that would otherwise be subject to the GST tax should not be allowed to pass back to the donor or to a trust for the donor's benefit. Such a return would bring the transaction closer to the *Proctor* line of precedents than to the defined value gift cases.

---

[67] See discussion of the design of such GST nonexempt trusts in Harrington, Plaine & Zaritsky, Generation-Skipping Transfer Tax ¶ 9.05 (Thomson Reuters/WG&L, 2d ed. 2001).

Drafting Tip: The following is a clause included in a deed of gift to be made outright, to divide the gift between a skip person and a non-skip person. In this instance, the non-skip person is the grantor's private foundation because a charity is always a non-skip person and because the courts in both *Estate of Petter* and *Estate of Christiansen* noted the existence of a public policy favoring gifts to charities. This defined value gift ought still to be sustained if the non-skip person is the grantor's child or a trust that is a non-skip person, but the law is stronger in favor of this transaction when the non-skip person is a charity.

The gift of the accompanying check shall be divided between *SkipPerson* and *Foundation*, in two fractional shares. The fractional shares shall be determined as follows:

A. **Fraction for *SkipPerson*.** The numerator of the fraction passing to *SkipPerson* shall be the largest portion of this gift that can pass to *him/her* without the imposition of a federal tax on generation-skipping transfers, and the denominator of this fraction shall be the fair market value of the total gift.

B. **Fraction for *Foundation*.** The fraction of this gift that shall be made to *Foundation* shall be the remaining fractional share of the transfer under this agreement.

C. **Retroactive Application of the GST Tax.** The determination under paragraph A of the portion of this gift that can pass to *SkipPerson* without the imposition of the federal tax on generation-skipping transfers shall be made taking into account both the law in effect for the date of this gift and any retroactive reimposition of the federal tax on generation skipping transfers that is enacted into law before April 1, 2011.

(1) If the federal tax on generation-skipping transfers is retroactively reinstated before April 1, 2011, the fraction under paragraph A shall be calculated as if that tax were in effect on the earliest date on which it is retroactively reinstated.

(2) If the federal tax on generation-skipping transfers is retroactively reinstated after March 31, 2010, the fraction under paragraph A shall be calculated as if that tax were not in effect on the date of this distribution.

(3) If such retroactive legislation is finally determined to be unconstitutional or otherwise invalid, the fractional share in paragraph A shall be calculated as if such retroactive legislation had never been enacted.

D. **Procedures.** *SkipPerson* and *Foundation* shall take such steps as may be appropriate to assure that this gift is divided according to these fractional shares, which steps may include refunding agreements, opinions of counsel, bonding agreements, or some combination of these.

Drafting Tip: The following is a clause included in a trust agreement that divides a transfer to the trust between a GST-exempt share and a GST-nonexempt share, taking into account the law in effect on the date of the gift, including retroactive changes in the law made within a reasonable time of the date of the transfer (arbitrarily set in this exemplar at March 31, 2010). No charity is involved in this transaction.

The Trustee shall divide any gift made to this Trust in calendar year 2010, between the GST-Exempt Trust and the GST-Nonexempt Trust under this instrument, as directed in the document of gift or, if no direction is made in such document, as follows:

A.   Fraction for GST-Exempt Trust. The numerator of the fraction passing to the GST-Exempt Trust shall be the largest portion of this gift that can pass to the GST-Exempt Trust without causing subsequent distributions from the GST-Exempt Trust to persons assigned to a generation two (2) or more below that of the transferor to be subject to the federal tax on generation-skipping transfers. The denominator of this fraction shall be the full value of the total gift.

B.   Fraction for the GST Non-Exempt Trust. The fraction of this gift that shall be made to the GST Non-Exempt Trust shall be the remaining fractional share of the distribution under this agreement.

C.   Retroactive Application of the GST Tax. The determination under paragraph A of the portion of this gift that can pass to the GST-Exempt Trust without the possible imposition of the federal tax on generation-skipping transfers shall be made taking into account both the law in effect for the date of this gift, and any retroactive reimposition of the federal tax on generation skipping transfers that is enacted into law before April 1, 2011.

(1) If the federal tax on generation-skipping transfers is retroactively reinstated before April 1, 2011, the fraction under paragraph A shall be calculated as if that tax were in effect on the earliest date on which it is retroactively reinstated.

(2) If the federal tax on generation-skipping transfers is retroactively reinstated after March 31, 2010, the fraction under paragraph A shall be calculated as if that tax were not in effect on the date of this distribution.

(3) If such retroactive legislation is finally determined to be unconstitutional or otherwise invalid, the fractional share in paragraph A shall be calculated as if such retroactive legislation had never been enacted.

D.   Procedures. The Trustee shall take such steps as may be appropriate to assure that this gift is divided according to these fractional shares, which steps may include creating reserve accounts or temporary book entries that can be adjusted as the law is clarified or changed, and obtaining opinion of counsel as to the taxability of the GST-Exempt Trust under present law or under the law as later modified, or some combination of these.

[4] Disclaimer-Based Planning

Another option for GST transfers in 2010 is to give property to a skip person (or trust for a skip person), and then rely on the skip person or trustee to decide whether or not to disclaim the gift if the skip person or trustee determines that a GST tax would otherwise be imposed. A donee has nine months in which to decide whether to accept a gift or to disclaim it. A disclaimed gift will, depending on the precise state law and the terms of the deed of gift, be returned to the donor. Such an arrangement gives the donee skip person time to evaluate the potential GST tax consequences and to act accordingly.

The problem with this approach, however, is that a disclaimer must be made within nine months of the gift and before acceptance of the benefits of the transferred property. The donee must not, therefore, accept any of the benefits of the gift and must act, if at all, within nine months of the date of the transfer.[68] Such nine-month period will likely provide some time for more information about the state of the GST tax laws to become available, but it still may not be enough time for reasonable certainty as to the GST tax consequences of the gift.

Another problem with this approach is that a donee may suddenly turn greedy and accept a gift even if a GST tax will be imposed on the transferor. It may be useful to make such gifts in the form of a net gift so that the donee will ignore the tax cost of the transfer when deciding whether to disclaim the transfer.[69]

---

[68] IRC § 2518(b)(2).

[69] On net gifts generally, see Henkel, "Estate Planning and Wealth Preservation: Strategies and Solutions" ¶ 2.02[2][h] (Thomson Reuters/WG&L 1997); Stephens, Maxfield, Lind & Calfee, Federal Estate and Gift Taxation ¶ 10.02[6][d] (Thomson Reuters/WG&L, 8th ed. 2002); Zaritsky, Tax Planning for Family Wealth Transfers ¶ 8.03 (Thomson Reuters/WG&L, 4th ed. 2002); see also Arlein & Frazier, "The Net, Net Gift," Tr. & Est. 25 (Aug. 2008); Boyles, "Net Gifts After Diedrich: When Does the Donor Realize Taxable Income?" 1983-1 Tax Mgmt. Est., Gifts & Tr. J. 23 (1983); Egerton, "Net Gifts Revisited: Are They Still a Viable Option?" 16 U. Miami Est. Plan. Inst. ch. 20 (1982); Grumet & Schnoll-Begun, "Planning for 2000 and Beyond: Net GRATs, GRUTs, CLATs, and CLUTs," 139 Tr. & Est. 30 (May 2000); Handler, "The Net Gift Strategy: Good for a Bear Market," Tr. & Est. 24 (Dec. 2008).

CHAPTER 5

Other Problems in 2010 Estate Planning

¶ 5.01   Introduction 5-2
¶ 5.02   Lifetime Gifts 5-2
         [1]   Locking in the 35 Percent Gift Tax Rate 5-2
         [2]   Incomplete Gifts and Section 2511(c) 5-5
                [a]   Legislative History 5-6
                [b]   Incomplete Gift Trusts That Shift Income 5-7
                [c]   Section 2511(c) and Grantor Trusts 5-11
                [d]   Charitable Remainder Trusts and Section
                     2511(c) 5-11
         [3]   Gift Tax Reporting Requirements 5-13
         [4]   Annual Exclusion Gifts in 2010 5-13
¶ 5.03   Irrevocable Life Insurance Trusts In 2010 5-15
¶ 5.04   Administration of Estates of Decedents Dying in 2010 5-16
         [1]   Return Requirements 5-16
         [2]   Negative Basis Assets 5-18
         [3]   Contesting Constitutionality of Retroactive
              Reinstatement of the Estate Tax 5-19
         [4]   Selling Estate Assets 5-19
¶ 5.05   Administration of Trusts in 2010 5-21
         [1]   Generation-Skipping Trusts 5-21
         [2]   Section 645 Election and Pecuniary Distributions ... 5-23
¶ 5.06   International Aspects of Planning in 2010 5-23
         [1]   Lower Basis Increases 5-23
         [2]   Negative Basis Assets to Foreign Beneficiaries 5-26
         [3]   Section 684: Recognition of Gain on Certain
              Transfers to Foreign Persons 5-27
¶ 5.07   Client Communications 5-28

¶ 5.01 INTRODUCTION

There are several additional estate planning areas in which the state of 2010 law creates special problems. These areas, discussed below, include:

1. Lifetime gifts at 35 percent rate;
2. Incomplete gifts and Section 2511(c);
3. Annual exclusion gifts in 2010;
4. Irrevocable life insurance trusts in 2010;
5. Administration of estates of decedents dying in 2010;
6. Administration of trusts in 2010; and
7. Client communications.

¶ 5.02 LIFETIME GIFTS

[1] Locking in the 35 Percent Gift Tax Rate

A donor should consider making taxable gifts in 2010 because the top gift tax rate is 35 percent, rather than the 45 percent rate that applied in 2009 or the 55 percent rate that is scheduled to apply in 2011. Obviously, a 10 percent or more reduction in the top gift tax rate can represent significant tax savings on a large taxable gift.

> **EXAMPLE 5-1:** Dave gives $1 million to each of his three children, in addition to their annual exclusion gifts. Dave has never before made a taxable gift and he has his entire $1 million lifetime exemption available. Dave's gift taxes will vary depending upon whether the gift is made in 2009, 2010, or 2011 (assuming that the applicable law for 2011 remains unchanged). The tax differences will be as follows:

Year of Gift	Gift Tax on $3 Million Gift
2009	$885,000
2010	$700,000
2011	$945,000

A donor must, however, recognize the possibility that Congress could retroactively reimpose the higher gift tax rate. The constitutional support for a retroactive increase in tax rates is even stronger than that for the retroactive reintroduction of the estate and generation-skipping transfer (GST) taxes because the courts have previously held that a retroactive increase in the gift tax rates was valid under the Constitution.[1]

A donor who wishes to make a gift in 2010 only if the top gift tax rate is 35 percent could make the gift by a formula transfer. In such case, the deed of gift would direct that the donor transfers to the donee the largest fractional share of the specified asset or money that can be transferred at a maximum gift tax rate not exceeding 35 percent. Unless Congress retroactively reinstates a higher gift tax rate, that percentage will be 100 percent. If Congress retroactively reinstates a higher gift tax rate, part of the gift should go, under the deed of gift, to someone the transfer to whom would generate no gift tax, such as a charity or an incomplete gift trust.

An incomplete gift trust is a trust over which the donor retains such powers or interests as to render transfers to the trust incomplete for gift tax purposes. For example, such a trust could name the donor as a discretionary beneficiary and be established in a state that does not recognize as valid self-settled spendthrift trusts. A gift to such a trust is incomplete because the donor's creditors can compel the trustee to exercise the discretion granted under the trust instrument to distribute funds to the donor to satisfy creditor claims.[2] Alternatively, the trust could exclude the grantor as a beneficiary but give the grantor a power to veto distributions to beneficiaries and a special testamentary power to appoint the remainder of the trust fund at the grantor's death.[3]

It should be noted that the IRS may challenge such a formula gift clause as invalid under cases that rejected conditions subsequent tied to determinations by the IRS or the courts.[4] If the gift does not revert to the grantor, however, these cases appear to be inapplicable. Moreover, in the face of an IRS challenge, a strong argument for the validity of this type of formula gift can be found in the decisions that upheld the taxpayer's arguments in the defined value gift cases, discussed in Chapter 4.[5] Finally, while the best chance of success with such a formula gift is where the alternate beneficiary is a charity,

---

[1] See, e.g., NationsBank of Texas, NA v. United States, 269 F3d 1332 (Fed. Cir. 2001); Quarty v. United States, 170 F3d 961 (9th Cir. 1999).

[2] See, e.g., Rev. Rul. 76-103, 1976-1 CB 293; Outwin v. Comm'r, 76 TC 153 (1981), acq. 1982-1 CB 2; Paolozzi v. Comm'r, 23 TC 182 (1954), acq. 1962-1 CB 4.

[3] Reg. § 25.2511-2(b).

[4] See Proctor v. Comm'r, 142 F2d 824 (4th Cir.), cert. denied, 323 US 756 (1944); Ward v. Comm'r, 87 TC 78 (1986); Harwood v. Comm'r, 82 TC 239 (1984), aff'd, 786 F2d 1174 (9th Cir. 1986); Rev. Rul. 86-41, 1986-1 CB 300.

[5] See ¶ 4.09[3], discussing, in part, McCord v. Comm'r, 461 F3d 614 (5th Cir. 2006), rev'g and rem'g 120 TC 358 (2003); Christiansen v. Comm'r, 581 F3d 1061 (8th Cir. 2009), aff'g 130 TC 1 (2008); Estate of Petter v. Comm'r, TC Memo. 2009-280 (2009).

there is still a good chance that a gift to an incomplete gift trust or even a zero-gift grantor retained annuity trust (GRAT) will work, too.[6]

---

[6] For information on the zero-gift GRAT, see Henkel, Estate Planning and Wealth Preservation: Strategies and Solutions ¶ 22.05 (Thomson Reuters/WG&L 1997); Westfall & Mair, Estate Planning Law and Taxation ¶ 2.07 (Thomson Reuters/WG&L, 4th ed. 2001); Esperti & Peterson, Irrevocable Trusts: Analysis With Forms ¶ 7.06 (Thomson Reuters/WG&L, 1998); Zaritsky & Aucutt, Structuring Estate Freezes ¶ 11.07 (Thomson Reuters/WG&L, 2d ed. 1997); Zaritsky, Tax Planning for Family Wealth Transfers: Analysis With Forms ¶ 12.06 (Thomson Reuters/WG&L, 4th ed. 2002).

Drafting Tip: The following is a provision in a deed of gift for a transfer made in 2010 that divides a gift between the grantor's child (or other donee) and the grantor's private foundation.

The accompanying check shall be divided between *Donee* and *Foundation* by fractional shares, which shares shall be determined as follows:

A.   ***Donee*'s Fractional Share.** The numerator of the fraction of the accompanying gift passing to *Donee* shall be the largest portion of the total gift that can pass to *him/her* without the imposition of a federal gift tax at a rate higher than thirty-five percent (35%). The denominator of this fraction shall be the full value of the total gift.

B.   ***Foundation*'s Fractional Share.** The fractional share for *Foundation* shall be the remaining fractional share of the total gift.

C.   **Retroactive Increase in the Gift Tax Rates.** The determination under paragraph A of the portion of this gift that can pass to *Donee* without the imposition of a federal gift tax at a rate higher than thirty-five percent (35%) shall be made taking into account both the law in effect on the date of this gift and any retroactive changes in the federal gift tax rates that may be enacted into law before April 1, 2011.[7]

    (1) If the maximum federal gift tax rate is retroactively increased above thirty-five percent (35%) before April 1, 2011, the fraction under paragraph A shall be calculated as if that higher rate were in effect on the earliest date on which it is retroactively reinstated.

    (2) If the maximum federal gift tax rate is retroactively increased above thirty-five percent (35%) after March 31, 2010, the fraction under paragraph A shall be calculated as if that higher rate did not apply to this gift.

    (3) If such retroactive legislation is finally determined to be unconstitutional or otherwise invalid, the fractional share in paragraph A shall be calculated as if such retroactive legislation had never been enacted.

D.   **Procedures.** *Donee* and *Foundation* shall take such steps as may be appropriate to assure that this gift is divided according to these fractional shares, which steps may include refunding agreements, opinions of counsel, bonding agreements, or some combination of these.

[2] Incomplete Gifts and Section 2511(c)

Section 2511(c), added by Economic Growth and Tax Relief Reconciliation Act of 2001 (EGTRRA) and effective only in 2010, states in its entirety

---

[7] This is an arbitrary date selected for this example. The donor does not want to leave the date open, because it is not clear how long Congress may take to change gift tax rates retroactively.

> Notwithstanding any other provision of this section and except as provided in regulations, a transfer in trust shall be treated as a transfer of property by gift, unless the trust is treated as wholly owned by the donor or the donor's spouse under subpart E of part I of subchapter J of Chapter 1 [the grantor trust rules].

This rule appears to have been intended to reinforce the effectiveness of the gift tax as a backstop to the income tax. There is, however, some debate among practitioners as to the actual scope of this provision.

[a] Legislative History

The actual legislative history of EGTRRA does not discuss Section 2511(c), but the section was amended in 2002, at which time the Joint Committee on Taxation stated, in a report on the technical correction, that the purpose of this section was as follows:

> The provision clarifies that the effect of section 511(e) of the Act (effective for gifts made after 2009) is to treat certain transfers in trust as transfers of property by gift. The result of the clarification is that the gift tax annual exclusion and the marital and charitable deductions may apply to such transfers. Under the provision as clarified, certain amounts transferred in trust will be treated as transfers of property by gift, despite the fact that such transfers would be regarded as incomplete gifts or would not be treated as transferred under the law applicable to gifts made prior to 2010.
>
> For example, if in 2010 an individual transfers property in trust to pay the income to one person for life, remainder to such persons and in such portions as the settlor may decide, then the entire value of the property will be treated as being transferred by gift under the provision, even though the transfer of the remainder interest in the trust would not be treated as a completed gift under current Treas. Reg. sec. 25.2511-2(c). Similarly, if in 2010 an individual transfers property in trust to pay the income to one person for life, and makes no transfer of a remainder interest, the entire value of the property will be treated as being transferred by gift under the provision.[8]

Section 2511(c) appears, therefore, to have been intended primarily to eliminate the use of a specific class of trusts the transfers to which are sufficiently complete for income tax purposes to cause the trusts to be separate taxpayers, but that are not completed gifts for gift tax purposes. Congress apparently was concerned that the widespread use of such trusts to shift taxa-

---

[8] Staff of Joint Comm. on Taxation, 107th Cong., 2d Sess., "General Explanation of Tax Legislation Enacted in the 107th Congress," 249–250 (2003).

ble income to lower-bracket beneficiaries could undercut the integrity of the income tax, particularly in the absence of an estate or GST tax.

[b] Incomplete Gift Trusts That Shift Income

The technique that concerned Congress was sanctioned by the IRS in a series of private letter rulings beginning with Private Letter Ruling 200502014 (September 17, 2004). The taxpayer in this ruling, *X*, proposed to create a trust that would be governed by the law of a state other than that in which *X* resided. The trust would have a corporate trustee situated in the trust law state. The terms of the trust instrument would provide that

1. During *X*'s lifetime, the trustee shall hold and invest the trust assets, and distribute income and principal (including all or none) at such times, to such persons, and in such amounts, as the Distribution Committee by unanimous agreement might designate;

2. Alternatively, the trustee shall, during the taxpayer's lifetime, distribute the trust income and principal (including all or none) at such times and in such amounts, as might be directed by the grantor and one member of the Distribution Committee, to and among a class consisting of the grantor, the grantor's current spouse, the grantor's descendants, the grantor's parent, and the grantor's sibling;

3. The trustee shall accumulate any undistributed income and add it to principal annually;

4. The Distribution Committee shall initially be the grantor's brother and parent;

5. At all times, the Distribution Committee shall consist of at least two persons who are trust beneficiaries (other than the grantor or the grantor's current or then spouse), or who are parents or guardians of such beneficiaries if there are fewer than two adult beneficiaries;

6. If either the grantor's brother or the grantor's parent predeceases the grantor, then the next successor member of the Distribution Committee shall be the grantor's eldest then-living descendant;

7. If any additional member of the Distribution Committee predeceases the grantor, the grantor's eldest then-living descendant who is not already a member of the Distribution Committee shall become the successor member of the Distribution Committee;

8. The members of the Distribution Committee shall exercise their power to appoint the trust assets only in a nonfiduciary capacity, by an acknowledged instrument in writing delivered to the Trustee;

9. At the grantor's death, the remaining trust funds shall be paid over to such person or persons (other than the grantor, the grantor's estate, the grantor's creditors, and the creditors of the grantor's estate), as the grantor may appoint by reference to this power in the grantor's Last Will and Testament;

10. The grantor may release this power of appointment by a writing de-livered to the trustee, or further limit the persons or entities in whose favor or the extent to which this power can be exercised; and

11. At the grantor's death, the trustee shall distribute any unappointed principal to the grantor's brother, if then living, and parent, if then living, in equal shares, or if neither is then living, to the grantor's de-scendants.

The IRS ruled that this trust will not be a grantor trust for federal income tax purposes. The IRS noted that the members of the Distribution Committee will all be "adverse parties," as defined in Section 672(a), because they each will have a substantial beneficial interest in the trust that would be adversely affected by the exercise or nonexercise of the power that the committee held respecting the trust.

Normally, the grantor is treated as the owner of any portion of a trust as to which the beneficial enjoyment of the principal or income is subject to a power of disposition, exercisable by the grantor, by a nonadverse party, or by both together, without the approval or consent of any adverse party.[9] Under the facts of the ruling, the corporate trustee will not be a related or subordinate party, nor will it be an adverse party, under the trust instrument, and the power to be held by the trustee to distribute income and principal among a class of beneficiaries is a power of disposition. The trust will not be a grantor trust, however, because the trustee will not be able to exercise this power without the approval of an adverse party.

Similarly, a trust is usually a grantor trust with respect to any items of in-come that may be applied to or held for future application to the grantor or the grantor's spouse.[10] The trustee's power to distribute trust income and principal to the grantor or the grantor's spouse, however, will not create a grantor trust, because the trustee could exercise this power only with the consent of an ad-verse party.

The IRS noted that the transfers to the trust would not be completed gifts for federal gift tax purposes, because the trustee will not have to distribute an-ything and the grantor will retain the testamentary right to determine the bene-ficiaries of the trust assets remaining at the grantor's death. The IRS stated that the gift tax regulations render a gift incomplete if the donor reserves the power to (1) revest the beneficial title in himself or herself or (2) name new beneficiaries or to change the interests of the beneficiaries as between them-selves, unless the power is a fiduciary power limited by a fixed or ascertaina-

---

[9] IRC § 674(a).
[10] IRC § 677(a).

ble standard.[11] The grantor, in this ruling, will retain that power through the testamentary power of appointment.

The IRS also noted that the members of the Distribution Committee will not have a general power of appointment over the trust fund. The IRS explained that while the exercise or release of a general power of appointment is a taxable gift, a power of appointment is not general if, by its terms, it is exercisable only in favor of one or more designated persons or classes other than the possessor or his creditors, or the possessor's estate or the creditors of the estate.[12] Furthermore, a power of appointment is not a general power of appointment if it is exercisable in conjunction with the creator of the power or with a person who has a substantial interest adverse to the exercise of the power in favor of the holder, the holder's estate, the holder's creditors, or the creditors of the holder's estate.[13]

The IRS discussed the U.S. Supreme Court's decision in *Estate of Sanford v. Commissioner*,[14] in which the taxpayer created a trust, in 1913, for the benefit of named beneficiaries and reserved the power to revoke the trust in whole or in part as well as to designate new beneficiaries other than himself. Six years later, the taxpayer relinquished his power to revoke the trust. The taxpayer continued, however, to retain his right to change the beneficiaries, until such right was later relinquished by the taxpayer in 1924.

The Supreme Court ruled that a donor's gift is not complete for purposes of the gift tax when the donor reserves the power to determine those who would ultimately receive the gifted property. Accordingly, the Court concluded that the taxpayer's gift was finally complete in 1924, when he relinquished his right to change the beneficiaries of the trust.

In Private Letter Ruling 200502014, the IRS concluded that the grantor, by reason of his limited power of appointment, will retain the power to change the beneficiaries of the trust, and therefore the grantor would continue to possess dominion and control over the property transferred to the trust. Accordingly, the contribution of property to the trust by the grantor would not be a completed gift subject to the federal gift tax. Moreover, the members of the Distribution Committee will not have a general power of appointment, because their powers could only be exercised if both trustees consent to a proposed distribution. Any distribution of trust principal or income to the grantor would not trigger a taxable gift, because the members of the Distribution Committee will have a non-general power of appointment.

---

[11] Reg. § 25.2511-2(c). The regulations also state that the relinquishment or termination of a power to change the beneficiaries of transferred property, occurring otherwise than by donor's death, completes the taxable gift. Reg. § 25.2511-2(f).

[12] Reg. § 25.2514-1(c)(1).

[13] IRC § 2514(c)(3)(B); Reg. § 25.2514-3(b)(2).

[14] Estate of Sanford v. Comm'r, 308 US 39 (1939).

Furthermore, the grantor's initial transfer of property to trust will be an incomplete gift because he will retain a testamentary limited power of appointment. Thus, the return of that property to the grantor would not trigger a taxable gift. If the Distribution Committee appoints trust property to a beneficiary other than the grantor, however, or if during the grantor's lifetime, the grantor releases the testamentary power to appoint the trust property, the gifts will become complete.

The IRS did not discuss the likely estate tax treatment of the trust at the grantor's death. However, the trust assets would, presumably, be includible in the grantor's gross estate under Section 2038(a) because the grantor retained the power to alter the beneficial enjoyment of the trust assets.[15]

This arrangement appears to have the potential of shifting taxable income to family members in a lower income tax bracket without actually creating a taxable gift. It should be noted, however, that the IRS seems to be backing away from the position taken in Private Letter Ruling 200502014 and similar private rulings. In Information Release 2007-127 (July 9, 2007), the IRS stated that it was considering the withdrawal of these private letter rulings because of their apparent inability to be reconciled with Revenue Ruling 76-503 and Revenue Ruling 77-158.

In Revenue Ruling 76-503,[16] a trust was created by three siblings, each of whom named an adult child as one of the three trustees who, acting unanimously, had complete discretionary power over the assets of the trust and individually had the right to name a relative as successor. A trustee was replaced by a successor trustee upon the trustee's death or resignation.

The IRS stated that the surviving trustees are in no better position to exercise the power after a decedent-trustee's death than before the death, and so it concluded that the interests of the co-trustees are not adverse to exercise of the power in favor of the decedent-trustee. The IRS stated that one third of the trust fund was includible in a decedent-trustee's estate as property subject to a general power of appointment under Section 2041.

In Revenue Ruling 77-158,[17] a trust was created by three siblings, each of whom named an adult child as one of the three trustees who, through majority vote, had complete discretionary power over the assets of the trust and individually had the right to name a relative as successor. The IRS concluded here, too, that one third of the trust fund was includible in a decedent-trustee's estate as property subject to a general power of appointment under Section 2041.

The analysis applied in these revenue rulings suggests that the distributions of property from the trusts in the private letter rulings would be taxable

---

[15] See also Priv. Ltr. Ruls. 200612002 (Mar. 24, 2006), 200637025 (Sept. 15, 2006), 200647001 (Nov. 24, 2006), 200715005 (Apr. 13, 2007), 200729005 (July 20, 2007), and 200731009 (Aug. 3, 2007).

[16] Rev. Rul. 76-503, 1976-2 CB 275.

[17] Rev. Rul. 77-158, 1977-1 CB 285.

gifts by the trustees. However, the IRS noted, in Information Release 2007-127, that the letter rulings may be distinguishable from the revenue rulings because, in the private letter rulings, the grantor's gift to the trust was incomplete due to the grantor's retention of a testamentary special power of appointment. The IRS nevertheless noted that a contrary conclusion may be suggested by both (1) the power of appointment regulations, which treat a power of appointment created under a revocable trust as having been created on the date the trust is executed even though the trust is revocable[18] and (2) Revenue Ruling 67-370, in which the IRS ruled that a beneficiary's gross estate includes a current interest in a revocable trust created by another.[19]

[c] Section 2511(c) and Grantor Trusts

Although the legislative history shows that Section 2511(c) was intended only to address the treatment of gifts made to non-grantor trusts (rendering them complete), some practitioners have interpreted it to mean that any transfer to a wholly owned grantor trust is not a taxable gift.[20] This is not expressly stated in the statutory language, but some practitioners view it as a reasonable and even necessary inference.

The IRS, however, quickly rejected this view in Notice 2010-19,[21] in which it stated that while further clarification will be issued, Section 2511(c) should not be interpreted as excluding from the gift tax transfers to a trust treated as wholly owned grantor trust. The notice states that Section 2511(c) broadens the types of transfers subject to the gift tax to include certain transfers to trusts that, before 2010, would have been considered incomplete, and thus not subject to the gift tax. It has no bearing on transfers to wholly owned grantor trusts or to transfers that would otherwise have been completed gifts.

[d] Charitable Remainder Trusts and Section 2511(c)

Section 2511(c) may have a significant impact on certain joint and survivor charitable remainder trusts. One may create a charitable remainder trust for the benefit of one or more noncharitable beneficiaries. It is common when the grantor and one other beneficiary (other than the grantor's spouse) are named as noncharitable beneficiaries of the trust to have the grantor reserve the right to revoke the surviving noncharitable beneficiary's interest by provision in the

---

[18] Reg. § 25.2514-1(e), Ex. 1.

[19] Rev. Rul. 67-370, 1967-2 CB 324.

[20] See, for example, similar syntax and constructions in Sections 2032(c) and 2701(c)(3)(C)(i).

[21] Notice 2010-19, 2010-7 IRB 404 (Feb. 16, 2010).

grantor's will. This avoids the grantor making a taxable gift to the other non-charitable beneficiary on formation of the trust.

This technique will not be possible under Section 2511(c), because the interest of the other beneficiary would be an incomplete gift and a charitable remainder trust cannot be a grantor trust.[22] Therefore, practitioners should avoid creating joint and survivor charitable remainder trusts with beneficiaries other than the donor or the donor's spouse during 2010.

> **EXAMPLE 5-2:** Harry creates a charitable remainder trust for himself and his son, Sam. Harry is eighty years of age and Sam is fifty-five years of age. The trust provides for the payment of a five percent unitrust interest to Harry for his lifetime, and then to Sam for his lifetime, with the principal distributed on Sam's death to Old Ivy University. The trust is created on January 10, 2010, with a gift of $5 million. Harry is deemed to make a taxable gift to Sam of the $1,872,200 present value of his interest. Were Harry to retain the power to revoke Sam's interest, there would be no taxable gift on creation of the trust, but all or some portion of the trust fund would be includible in Harry's gross estate at his death, and, if Sam survives Harry, the value of Sam's unitrust interest on the date of Harry's death would not be deductible from Harry's gross estate. Under Section 2511(c), however, Harry cannot reserve such a power over Sam's interest in the trust.

Some practitioners have focused on the last sentence in the Joint Committee on Taxation's report on the technical correction to Section 2511(c), which states

> Similarly, if in 2010 an individual transfers property in trust to pay the income to one person for life, and makes no transfer of a remainder interest, the entire value of the property will be treated as being transferred by gift under the provision.[23]

This sentence poses a significant problem because it is both incorrect and inconsistent with the statute. Section 2511(c) refers to treating transfers in trust as taxable gifts, but the remainder interest in the above example is not transferred. The transfer of the income interest in the example is a completed taxable gift because the trust is not a wholly owned grantor trust, but the grantor did not transfer the remainder interest and thus the remainder interest should not result in a taxable gift.

Were the Joint Committee on Taxation's report to be a correct statement of the operation of Section 2511(c), however, it would render most 2010 charitable remainder trusts impractical. In the typical charitable remainder trust, the

---

[22] Reg. § 1.664-1(a)(4); CCA 200628026 (Mar. 15, 2006).

[23] Staff of Joint Comm. on Taxation, 107th Cong., 2d Sess., "General Explanation of Tax Legislation Enacted in the 107th Congress," 249–250 (2003).

grantor retains the annuity or unitrust amount while the remainder passes to charity. The most reasonable extension of the Joint Committee on Taxation's statement would be that the grantor's entire transfer was a taxable gift, for which only the remainder interest was deductible. The absurdity of this result further supports the view that the last sentence of the Joint Committee's report is simply incorrect.

Nonetheless, the practical estate planner may wish to postpone creating a charitable remainder trust in 2010 until clarification is obtained from the IRS or Congress.

[3] Gift Tax Reporting Requirements

A donor must provide to each recipient of a gift the information included in the gift tax return within thirty days of the date on which the gift tax return is filed. Specifically, the donor must furnish the donee a written statement showing

1. The donor's name, address, and phone number, and
2. The information specified in such return with respect to property received by the person required to receive such statement.[24]

[4] Annual Exclusion Gifts in 2010

The gift tax annual exclusion is not directly affected by the repeal of the estate and GST taxes for 2010, but using it to make gifts to grandchildren or generation-skipping trusts has been very much complicated by these changes. Section 2503 permits a donor to give to each donee up to $13,000 per year, without paying gift tax or using the donor's $1 million lifetime gift tax exemption. Such gifts must be gifts of a present interest.

A practical estate planner will urge his or her clients who have potentially taxable estates to make the maximum possible annual exclusion gifts in order to reduce the client's estate for tax purposes. Even relatively moderate-sized families can shift a substantial amount of wealth to younger generations through annual exclusion gifts.

> **EXAMPLE 5-3:** Harriet is married and she has three children and no grandchildren. Harriet and her husband, Hank, can make up to $78,000 of gifts to their children ($13,000 × 2 donors × 3 children) every year without filing a gift tax return or using any of their lifetime gift tax exemptions.

---

[24] IRC § 6019(b).

EXAMPLE 5-4: Assume the same facts as in Example 5-3, except that Harriet's three children are married and each has two children of his or her own. Harriet and her husband thus have three children and six grandchildren. Harriet and Hank can make $234,000 of gifts to their descendants each year without filing a gift tax return or using any of their lifetime gift tax exemption ($13,000 × 2 donors × [3 children + 6 grandchildren]). This figure can be increased to $312,000 per year if Harriet and Hank also make gifts to their children's spouses ($13,000 × 2 donors × [3 children + 6 grandchildren + 3 children's spouses]).

A practical estate planner will not want his or her clients to curtail annual exclusion gifts, but gifts to grandchildren or more remote descendants pose serious GST tax problems in 2010. As discussed in Chapter 4, outright gifts to skip persons such as grandchildren and more remote descendants are direct skip transfers, and Section 2664 states that the GST tax does not apply to direct skip transfers in 2010.

As a practical matter, nontax considerations usually compel transfers to minors be made in trust or in a trust equivalent, such as a Uniform Transfers to Minors Act (UTMA) custodianship.[25] Transfers to trusts and trust equivalents, however, will qualify for the gift tax annual exclusion if the grandchild has a present interest in the trust, usually provided by a Crummey withdrawal power.[26] Section 2642(c) states beneficially that a gift to a trust for which the gift tax annual exclusion is available will not be subject to GST taxes and will have an inclusion ratio of zero if

1. During the life of the individual transferee, no portion of the corpus or income of the trust may be distributed to (or for the benefit of) any person other than such individual, and
2. If the trust does not terminate before the individual dies, the assets of such trust will be includible in the gross estate of such individual.[27]

Unfortunately, Section 2642(c) is part of the GST tax rules that do not apply to generation-skipping transfers made in 2010. Therefore, it appears that future distributions or expenditures from such a trust for a grandchild made after 2010 may be subject to the GST tax. Of course, EGTRRA's sunset rule

---

[25] See Reg. § 26.2652-1(b)(2) Ex. 1 (custodial account is treated like a trust for GST tax purposes).

[26] On Crummey powers generally, see Henkel, Estate Planning and Wealth Preservation: Strategies and Solutions ¶ 10.03 (Thomson Reuters/WG&L 1997); Westfall & Mair, Estate Planning Law and Taxation ¶ 9.08 (Thomson Reuters/WG&L, 4th ed. 2001); Esperti & Peterson, Irrevocable Trusts: Analysis With Forms ¶ 6.02 (Thomson Reuters/WG&L 1998); Zaritsky & Leimberg, Tax Planning With Life Insurance ¶ 5.03[3] (Thomson Reuters/WG&L, 2d ed. 1998); Zaritsky, Tax Planning for Family Wealth Transfers: Analysis With Forms ¶ 4.08 (Thomson Reuters/WG&L, 4th ed. 2002).

[27] IRC § 2642(c). See discussion at ¶ 4.06.

may cause Section 2642(c) to give such annual exclusion trusts a zero inclusion ratio starting January 1, 2011, but the application of this rule is currently unclear and uncertain.

There are few satisfactory solutions to the question of making annual exclusion gifts to trusts for grandchildren in 2010. A donor could have a legal guardian appointed for the grandchild and make the gift to him or her, but the judicial proceedings required to appoint a guardian for such a purpose may be excessive with respect to annual exclusion gifts made in one year.

A donor could also give the property to a family limited partnership or limited liability company (LLC), and then give the grandchild a partnership or membership interest. This would permit the general partner or managing member to control and manage the funds. State law must be consulted regarding whether the minor can take legal title to a partnership interest or membership interest with sufficient finality to constitute a completed taxable gift, but as acceptance of a gift is generally presumed, a minor may be able to take title to such interests sufficiently to render the gift complete for gift tax purposes. This approach may be particularly suitable for a donor who already has established a family limited partnership or LLC; establishing and maintaining such an entity may, however, be impractical as a vehicle for supporting solely annual exclusion gifts to be made in one year.

The most practical solution in such cases it to make the gift to a Section 2642(c) trust or UTMA custodial account, just as the donor would have done were the law not unclear. It is important that the donor continue to make gifts to utilize all of his or her gift tax annual exclusion, and, although the law creates uncertainty regarding the eventual GST taxation of distributions or expenditures from such a trust for the benefit of a grandchild, it is likely that such trusts will ultimately be construed to be exempt from the GST tax under EGTRRA's sunset provisions, which treat such post-2010 events as if EGTRRA had never been enacted.

¶ 5.03 IRREVOCABLE LIFE INSURANCE TRUSTS IN 2010

Irrevocable life insurance trusts create a special problem in 2010 because such trusts often involve the possibility of future generation-skipping transfers. There is no GST exemption in 2010, and a donor cannot be sure of protecting from future GST tax any 2010 transfers to an irrevocable life insurance trust that will ultimately benefit skip persons.[28]

This problem is particularly complicated for life insurance trusts because premiums often must be paid in 2010. The best solution in 2010 is not to

---

[28] See ¶ 4.04.

make gifts to such trusts, but rather to use policy values to pay premiums and, where policy values are insufficient, to lend money to the trustee to pay premiums.

Where the payment of life insurance premiums is a client's sole means of taking advantage of the gift tax annual exclusion, a slightly more complicated approach may be used to take advantage of the gift tax annual exclusion with respect to insurance premiums by creating a second irrevocable life insurance trust to which the donor makes 2010 annual exclusion gifts. The beneficiaries of the second trust would include the first insurance trust. The trustee of the second trust would lend money to the trustee of the first trust to pay the premiums due on the policies held by the first trust. If the law is ultimately interpreted in a manner that will permit the donor to allocate GST exemption to the 2010 transfers, the donor can do so and the two trusts can be merged without adverse tax consequences. Otherwise, the second trust can be maintained until the first trust has sufficient funds to repay the loan from the second trust.

¶ 5.04 ADMINISTRATION OF ESTATES OF DECEDENTS DYING IN 2010

The repeal (and possible reimposition) of the estate tax and the imposition of carryover basis renders very difficult the proper administration of potentially taxable estates of decedents who die in 2010. Unfortunately, as with many other 2010 planning questions, care and attention to detail are important, but certainty is elusive.

[1] Return Requirements

The executor of an estate of a decedent who dies in 2010 must promptly begin gathering the information required to file a Large Transfers at Death return under Section 6018, including assembling basis information and determining the fair market value of the decedent's assets on the date of death. This means that executors of such estates should proceed promptly to obtain appraisals of any assets that are not publicly traded.

Appraisals always state the purpose for which they are being provided. Appraisals provided to an executors traditionally note that they are provided for estate tax valuation purposes, which alerts the IRS to the fact that the appraiser is probably trying to support the lowest reasonable value for the assets in question. An appraisal prepared for purposes of a lifetime charitable gift, on the other hand, is probably trying to support the highest reasonable value of the assets in question.

Appraisals prepared for estates of decedents dying in 2010 are prepared to determine net appreciation and the allocation of basis, which tends to favor, depending upon the actual situation, either a neutral opinion on the fair market value of the assets or a high valuation of the assets. This suggests that, in general, the IRS should be more willing to accept such appraisals than estate tax valuation appraisals.

The executor and the appraiser know, however, that Congress could reinstate the estate tax retroactively. An executor of the estate of a decedent who dies in 2010, therefore, must also give some thought and effort to collecting the data that will be required to file a traditional estate tax return. It is very likely that Congress would allow executors nine months from the date of any retroactive reinstatement of the estate tax to prepare and file such returns, but one cannot rely with certainty on that assumption. Therefore, an executor should be organizing the valuation and other data simultaneously for use in filing either a Large Transfers at Death return or an estate tax return.

The possibility that the executor may have to file either of two very different returns has at least three interesting effects. First, it increases the time and effort required in administering an estate with respect to decedents dying in 2010, which should, in turn, increase the amounts charged by fiduciaries.

Second, it makes it far more difficult to carry out the job of executor with respect to an estate of a decedent dying in 2010. Added to the difficulty of allocating the decedent's two carryover basis increases, this means that practitioners should strongly encourage clients to employ professional fiduciaries to administer estates of decedents dying in 2010, either as a substitute for a family fiduciary or as an adjunct to a family fiduciary.

Third, this duality of purpose renders appraisals prepared for estates of decedents dying in 2010 especially credible because they are actually being prepared for two somewhat contradictory purposes (1) potential estate tax usage, which favors a low value, and (2) potential carryover basis usage, which favors a high or neutral value. In effect, the appraiser will not know when the appraisal is prepared whether it will more greatly benefit the executor to have a high value or a low value.

EXAMPLE 5-5: Harry dies on January 10, 2010, leaving an estate that includes substantial amounts of artwork, real estate, and closely held business interests. The executor of Harry's estate, Large Bank, must obtain independent professional appraisals of the value of all of these assets. Realistically, they expect that the appraised values will fall within the following ranges:

Asset	Low Market Value	High Market Value
Artwork	$ 100,000	$ 150,000
Real estate	$ 1,000,000	$ 1,500,000
Closely held business interests	$ 2,000,000	$ 4,000,000

If there is no estate tax in effect with respect to this estate and the carryover basis rules apply, the higher values of these assets will help permit the fuller or more complete use of Harry's aggregate and spousal property basis increases. Lower values would preclude the full use of these basis increases, and could result in higher capital gains taxes when assets are later sold.

If the estate tax is applicable to this estate, however, the lower valuations could produce lower estate taxes, permit the placement of a larger share of the estate in a nonmarital trust, and possibly even eliminate the need to file a federal estate tax return altogether (depending upon the value of other estate assets).

[2] Negative Basis Assets

The existence of "negative basis assets" (i.e., assets subject to liabilities in excess of their carryover basis) will make the job of the executor far more complex and raise many potential issues of fiduciary responsibility. As discussed earlier, negative basis property will often have a true value to the recipient far less than its apparent value, and, in some cases, may have a negative value when the potential income tax liability is considered.[29]

> **EXAMPLE 5-6:** Harry's estate includes his interest in Blackacre Shopping Center, which has a fair market value at the time of death of $1 million, and which is subject to an $800,000 mortgage. Harry's basis in Blackacre is $200,000. All of Harry's depreciation of Blackacre has been taken using the straight-line method. Harry leaves his interest in Blackacre Shopping Center to his son, Charlie. Blackacre would have a nominal value of $200,000 ($1,000,000 fair market value − $800,000 mortgage), but its sale would produce an $800,000 long-term capital gain ($1,000,000 sales price − $200,000 basis). The federal capital gains tax rate on this sale is 25 percent, so that Charlie would owe $200,000 in tax on the sale of the property (25% × $800,000). Charlie's interest in Blackacre, therefore, would have no real value.

> **EXAMPLE 5-7:** Assume the same facts as in Example 5-6, except that Harry's basis in Blackacre is $100,000, and his debt secured by the property is $900,000. The nominal value of Blackacre is $100,000 ($1,000,000 fair market value − $900,000 debt), but a sale for that amount would produce a $900,000 capital gain ($1,000,000 sales price − $100,000 basis). Therefore, Charlie's federal capital gains tax on the sale would be $225,000 (25% × $900,000). Charlie's taxes on the sale would exceed the cash produced by the sale by $125,000 ($225,000 − $100,000).

---

[29] See ¶ 3.04.

Obviously, anyone receiving negative basis property that represents a net after-tax economic loss on a sale would disclaim that property within nine months of the date of death to avoid having to pay the tax when the property was sold. An executor should notify a beneficiary that property specifically left to the beneficiary has this rather unique nature. Failure to notify a beneficiary of this fact could lead to a charge that the executor violated the duty of impartiality and fairness in dealing with the beneficiary. An executor should, therefore, make a serious effort to identify such assets and very promptly notify the beneficiary of the problem, as well as urge the beneficiary to meet with an estate planning attorney to consider the possibility of disclaiming the asset.

One solution in such cases is for the executor to allocate a sufficient portion of the decedent's aggregate or spousal property basis increases, or both, to the negative basis property as to reduce or eliminate the amount of gain recognizable on disposition of the property and thus mitigate the tax liability cost inherent in the asset. Unfortunately, a disproportionate allocation of basis increases to one asset that passes to one particular beneficiary or group of beneficiaries may be deemed unfair to the other beneficiaries.

Another solution is for the executor to sell the asset or transfer it to the mortgage holder and allow the estate to sustain the tax liability. This approach makes all beneficiaries share the pain of the tax cost attributable to negative basis assets. This may be a reasonable approach for an independent executor to take, but it could be unacceptable if the executor is also the beneficiary to whom the property was left and who disclaimed his or her interest in the negative basis property.

[3] Contesting Constitutionality of Retroactive Reinstatement of the Estate Tax

An executor of a reasonably large estate should consider whether to contest the constitutionality of any retroactive reinstatement of the estate tax by Congress. Each practitioner must evaluate the precedents personally, but the government is certain to pursue this litigation all the way to the U.S. Supreme Court. Accordingly, the time involved and costs associated with such litigation will be substantial. At a minimum, fiduciaries should pay the estate tax and file a protective claim for refund to preserve their rights in the remote possibility that the Court strikes down the retroactive feature.

[4] Selling Estate Assets

A fiduciary should also be careful about selling assets of the estate of a decedent who dies in 2010. The carryover basis rules mean that all such sales may generate significant capital gains taxes.

On the other hand, a fiduciary has a duty to minimize risk of loss to an estate, and this often includes diversifying the decedent's investments. This will risk the imposition of capital gains taxes, and a fiduciary might instead elect to purchase a "collar" on key investments to minimize the risk of loss without recognizing capital gains.

A collar is the simultaneous purchase and sale of options with respect to the same stock. The estate purchases a protective "put" option, enabling the executor to sell a number of shares of the designated stock for a specified price on a specified date. The estate simultaneously sells a covered "call" option, giving the option buyer a right to buy the same stock on the same date. The price fixed in the put option assures that the estate cannot lose if the stock drops below the strike price for that option. The price in the covered call option assures that the estate cannot profit if the stock rises above the strike price for that option. Together, the estate establishes a limit on its risk of loss in exchange for limiting its chance for gain. The price paid for the covered call usually offsets the cost of the put, and generally allows the estate to establish the collar without actual expenditure.

> **EXAMPLE 5-8:** Hal dies in 2010 leaving an estate that includes 10,000 shares of Acme Corp. common stock. Acme is a publicly traded corporation. Hal's executor decides that it is important to minimize risk of loss with respect to Hal's estate, but it does not wish to sell the Acme stock in order to diversify the estate's portfolio because such a sale would generate a significant capital gains tax liability. Acme stock is selling for $115 per share on the date of Hal's death. The executor sells to an unrelated party a covered call on the Acme stock, empowering the option buyer to buy the Acme stock for $125 per share at the end of six months. The executor simultaneously buys a "put" option permitting it to sell Acme stock for $105 per share at the end of six months. This collar protects the executor from any drop in the value of the Acme stock below $105 per share because the executor can sell the estate's Acme shares for that price. It also forfeits any increase in the value of the Acme shares above $125 per share because, if Acme rises that much, the person who bought the call option will exercise it and the estate will receive only $125 per share. The purchase price for the covered call offsets the cost of the put option, so there is no net cost to the estate of putting this collar on the Acme shares, and the estate recognizes no gain on the transaction.

If the estate tax is retroactively restored and the carryover basis rules repealed, it will be appropriate for the seller of carryover basis property to file a claim for refund for the excess income taxes paid on account of the carryover basis rules.

¶ 5.05 ADMINISTRATION OF TRUSTS IN 2010

[1] Generation-Skipping Trusts

Trustees have some difficult decisions to make in 2010, particularly, but not solely, with respect to generation-skipping distributions. A trustee who makes a distribution to a grandchild or other skip person in 2010 will avoid the GST tax on that distribution, but if the GST tax is retroactively reinstated, the distribution will be taxable and the trustee may be criticized for making such a distribution and incurring the tax. On the other hand, a trustee who declines to make a taxable distribution in 2010, due to the expectation that the GST tax will be retroactively reinstated, may be criticized if the generation-skipping transfer is not retroactively reinstated because the trustee will have missed a one-time opportunity to make a tax-free distribution.

There are several things that a trustee can do to minimize the risk of an adverse result in such circumstances. First, discretionary distributions to skip persons should probably not be made until late in 2010, when the trustee will have the most information available regarding the chance of the GST tax being imposed with respect to 2010 transfers. Congress could, of course, reinstate the GST tax prospectively at any time, and waiting until the end of 2010 gives Congress more time to do so and to render such distributions taxable, but waiting seems to be a prudent course of action.

Second, any distribution of trust income or principal to a skip person may not appear to generate a GST tax in 2010, but the trustee should set aside a reserve for these taxes in case the GST tax is retroactively reinstated. In appropriate situations, a refunding agreement with the beneficiary may be used instead of a reserve, but such an agreement still leaves the trustee responsible for the taxes if the beneficiary spends the distributed funds before the retroactive reinstatement of the taxes and cannot repay the trust.

Third, the trustee should generally favor outright distributions over distributions in further trust. Distributions made in 2010 in further trust could create a problem because the generation move-down rule of Section 2653 may not apply to protect such trusts from GST tax on future distributions or terminations of interest.[30]

Fourth, the trustee should consider making distributions by formula, such that the skip person would receive that portion of the distribution that can pass free of federal GST taxes and a designated non-skip person (a child or charity) receives that portion of the distribution that would be subject to the federal

---

[30] See discussion at ¶ 4.03[2][a].

GST tax. Such a clause ought to be respected for tax purposes under the recent decisions sustaining defined value gifts.[31]

Drafting Tip: The following language can be inserted in a document that accompanies a distribution of money or property from a generation-skipping trust. In this case, the grantor's private foundation is the designated non-skip person.

The accompanying check shall be divided between *SkipPerson* and *Foundation*, in two fractional shares. The fractional shares shall be determined as follows:

A.   **Fractional Share for *SkipPerson*.** The numerator of the fraction determining the share passing to *SkipPerson* shall be the largest portion of this distribution that can pass to *him/her* without the imposition of a federal tax on generation-skipping transfers, and the denominator of this fraction shall be the full value of the total distribution under this agreement; and

B.   **Fractional Share for *Foundation*.** The share of this distribution passing to *Foundation* shall be the remaining fractional share of the distribution under this agreement.

C.   **Retroactive Application of the GST Tax.** The determination under paragraph A of the portion of this distribution that can pass to *SkipPerson* without the imposition of the federal tax on generation-skipping transfers shall be made taking into account the law in effect for the date of this distribution as well as any retroactive reimposition of the federal tax on generation skipping transfers that is enacted into law before April 1, 2011.

(1) If the federal tax on generation-skipping transfers is retroactively reinstated before April 1, 2011, the fraction under paragraph A shall be calculated as if that tax were in effect on the earliest date on which it is retroactively reinstated.

(2) If the federal tax on generation-skipping transfers is retroactively reinstated after March 31, 2010, the fraction under paragraph A shall be calculated as if that tax were not in effect on the date of this distribution.

(3) If such retroactive legislation is finally determined to be unconstitutional or otherwise invalid, the fractional share in paragraph A shall be calculated as if such retroactive legislation had never been enacted.

D.   **Procedures.** *SkipPerson* and *Foundation* shall take such steps as may be appropriate to assure that this distribution is divided according to these fractional shares, which steps may include refunding agreements, opinions of counsel, bonding agreements, or some combination of these.

---

[31] See ¶ 4.09[3], discussing, in part, McCord v. Comm'r, 461 F3d 614 (5th Cir. 2006), rev'g and rem'g 120 TC 358 (2003); Christiansen v. Comm'r, 581 F3d 1061 (8th Cir. 2009), aff'g 130 TC 1 (2008); Estate of Petter v. Comm'r, TC Memo. 2009-280 (2009).

[2] Section 645 Election and Pecuniary Distributions

Distributions of appreciated property in satisfaction of a pecuniary right are generally treated as a sale or exchange of that property.[32] Section 1040(a) limits the gain on the distribution of appreciated carryover basis property in satisfaction of a pecuniary gift to the amount of appreciation occurring after the date of death. This rule, however, applies only to distributions by estates. The Treasury is directed to produce similar rules for distributions by trusts, but it is unclear when, if ever, it will do so.[33] The trustee of a qualified revocable trust[34] should cooperate with the executor to elect to have the trust treated as part of the estate for federal income tax purposes, pending the issuance of such regulations.

¶ 5.06 INTERNATIONAL ASPECTS OF PLANNING IN 2010

EGTRRA's 2010 rules, particularly its carryover basis rules, are especially complex and problematic for estate of decedents who die in 2010 and who are or whose beneficiaries are nonresident alien individuals.

[1] Lower Basis Increases

The estate of a U.S. citizen or U.S. resident receives a $1.3 million aggregate basis increase, increased by the amount of unused built-in losses and loss carryovers. The U.S. estate of a nonresident alien individual, however, receives only a $60,000 aggregate basis increase, with no increase for built-in losses or loss carryovers.[35]

The low limitation on the aggregate basis increase means that many U.S. estates of nonresident foreign individuals who die in 2010 will need to file the Large Transfers at Death return under Section 6018, and allocate the decedent's $60,000 aggregate basis increase. Section 6018(b)(3) specifically requires the executor of the U.S. estate of a foreign decedent to file the Large Transfers at Death return if the U.S. tangible property and the other property acquired from the decedent by a U.S. person exceeds $60,000.

The U.S. estate of a nonresident alien, like the estate of a U.S. citizen, should receive a $3 million spousal property basis increase for property pass-

---

[32] Reg. § 1.661(a)-2(f)(1); Kenan v. Comm'r, 114 F2d 217 (2d Cir. 1940); Rev. Rul. 60-87, 1960-1 CB 286; Rev. Rul. 74-178,. 1974-1 CB 196.

[33] IRC § 1040(b).

[34] See discussion of the meaning of a "qualified revocable trust" at ¶ 3.03[3][b].

[35] IRC § 1022(b)(3).

ing to a U.S. or foreign surviving spouse.[36] Furthermore, this allocation may be undertaken even if the marital trust is not a qualified domestic trust (QDOT), for which there is no election possible in 2010. Therefore, principal distributions from a marital trust created at the death, in 2010, of a U.S. citizen, resident alien, or nonresident alien for the benefit of a non-citizen surviving spouse will not be subject to additional estate taxes even if the distribution is made after 2010.

Of course, if the estate tax is retroactively reinstated, dispositions to a marital trust for a surviving spouse who is not a U.S. citizen will need to conform to the QDOT rules. Therefore, one may wish to condition the additional QDOT provisions, which are added to any other form of marital trust in order to qualify under the QDOT rules, upon the existence of a federal estate tax applicable to the client's estate effective on the date of death, including taxes retroactively imposed on the client's estate.

---

[36] IRC § 1022(b)(4).

Drafting Tip: The following is a sample qualified terminable interest property (QTIP) provision in which the QDOT provisions are effective only if there is a federal estate tax applicable with respect to the decedent's estate, including one retroactively reimposed.

The Trustee shall hold the Marital Share in trust ("the Qualified Terminable Interest Property (QTIP) Marital Trust") as described in this article.

    A.   **During the Life of My *Husband/Wife*.** The Trustee shall distribute the net income quarterly or more frequently to my *husband/wife during *his/her* life.

        (1)   **Ascertainable Standard.** The Trustee shall also distribute to my *husband/wife* as much of the principal as is appropriate for *his/her* health, education, support, or maintenance.

        (2)   **Five or Five Power.** In addition, if and to the extent that my *husband/wife* so directs, the Trustee shall also distribute to my *husband/wife* in December of each calendar year, including the year of my death, the greater of five percent (5%) of the trust principal or five thousand dollars ($5,000.00). This right shall not accumulate from year to year.

        (3)   **Contingent Restrictions.** If there is a federal estate tax that applies with respect to my estate, the following additional provisions shall apply with respect to this QTIP Marital Trust.

            (a) Except as provided in regulations prescribed by the U.S. Secretary of the Treasury, there shall at all times be at least one (1) trustee of this QTIP Marital Trust who is an individual citizen of the United States or a domestic corporation.

            (b) No distribution (other than a distribution of income) may be made from this QTIP Marital Trust unless a trustee who is an individual citizen of the United States or a domestic corporation shall withhold from such distribution the tax imposed on such distribution under applicable federal estate tax law.

        (4)   **Retroactive Reinstatement of the Estate Tax.** The determination under paragraph A.3., as to whether there is a federal estate tax imposed with respect to my estate, shall be made taking into account both the law in effect on the date of my death and any retroactive imposition of the federal estate tax that is enacted into law before April 1, 2011,[37] and that is effective retroactively on the date of my death. If such retroactive legislation is finally determined to be unconstitutional or otherwise invalid, the terms of this QTIP Marital Trust shall be those that would have applied if such retroactive legislation had never been enacted.

---

[37] This is an arbitrary date selected for this example. The donor does not want to leave the date open, because it is not clear how long Congress may take to change gift tax rates retroactively.

[2] Negative Basis Assets to Foreign Beneficiaries

EGTRRA states that the amount realized on the acquisition of negative basis property from the decedent by his or her estate or on the acquisition of negative basis property from the decedent's estate by a beneficiary does not include the excess of the amount of the liabilities over the decedent's basis in the property.[38] This generally reduces the effect of the receipt or distribution of negative basis property by an estate.

This rule does not apply, however, if the estate disposes of the negative basis assets by distributing it to a "tax-exempt beneficiary."[39] A tax-exempt beneficiary, for this purpose, includes any foreign person or entity,[40] which is defined by reference to Section 168(h)(2), as (1) any foreign government, any international organization, or any agency or instrumentality of any of the foregoing, and (2) any person who is not a U.S. person. Section 168(h)(2)(C) states that a foreign person or entity does not include any foreign partnership or other foreign pass-thru entity.

Accordingly, a disposition by a decedent's estate of negative basis property to a foreign person results in the recognition of gain by the estate equal to the difference between the amount of the debt from assumed (or taken "subject to") and the estate's adjusted carryover basis in the distributed property. This will be a serious problem for U.S. estates of foreign persons because they are likely to distribute many of their assets to foreign persons. A practical estate planner may advise a decedent's executor to consider allocating some of the decedent's aggregate or spousal property basis increases to property that passes to a tax-exempt beneficiary in order to avoid recognition of gain on the distribution of these assets.

> **EXAMPLE 5-9:** Aaron dies in 2010. Aaron is a French national who lives outside of the United States. Aaron leaves a U.S. estate that includes a small office building worth $5 million, which is subject to a mortgage of $4.5 million, and in which Aaron had an adjusted basis of $3 million. Aaron's entire estate is left outright to Aaron's brother, Seth, who is also a French national residing outside of the United States. The executor of Aaron's U.S. estate will recognize a $1.5 million taxable gain ($4.5 million debt − $3 million basis) on the distribution of the property to Seth because Seth is a nonresident alien individual (i.e., a tax-exempt beneficiary). Aaron's executor can reduce this gain by $60,000, by allocating Aaron's aggregate basis increase to this property, but the estate will still owe tax on $1,440,000 of gain ($1,500,000 gain − $60,000 basis increase).

---

[38] IRC § 1022(g)(1).

[39] IRC § 1022(g)(1)(B).

[40] IRC § 1022(g)(2).

EXAMPLE 5-10: Assume the same facts as in Example 5-9, except that Aaron's estate is left to his wife, Celeste, who is also a French national and nonresident of the United States. Celeste is a foreign person (i.e., a tax-exempt beneficiary). Aaron's executor, however, can allocate $2 million of Aaron's spousal property basis increase to the U.S. real estate. This will bring the adjusted basis of this property up to its $5 million fair market value ($3 million basis + $2 million spousal property basis increase), and no gain will be recognized on the distribution of the property from the estate to Celeste.

EXAMPLE 5-11: Assume the same facts as in Example 5-9, except that the fair market value of the property on the date of death is $4 million, the estate's adjusted basis is $3 million, and the mortgage is $4.5 million. The mortgage was secured when the value of the property was much higher than it is on the date of Aaron's death. Aaron's executor can only allocate $1 million of Aaron's spousal property basis increase to the property because the allocation cannot increase the property's basis above its fair market value. Therefore, the estate still recognizes a $500,000 gain ($4.5 million debt − $4 million basis) on the distribution of the building to Celeste.

[3] Section 684: Recognition of Gain on Certain Transfers to Foreign Persons

Section 684 currently requires that a U.S. person treat as a sale or exchange the transfer of appreciated property to a foreign trust or estate. The amount of gain that must be recognized by the transferor is the excess of the fair market value of the property transferred over the adjusted basis of such property in the hands of the transferor.[41] EGTRRA extends this rule to post-2009 testamentary transfers to foreign individuals.[42]

EXAMPLE 5-12: Dave died in 2010, and his will directs his executor to distribute all of Dave's stock of Acme Corp. to Dave's niece, Noel, who is a French national living outside of the United States. The Acme shares are worth $250,000 on the date of Dave's death, and his basis in those shares is $50,000. Dave's estate will be required to recognize a $200,000 gain on this distribution ($250,000 value − $50,000 basis) under the special extension of Section 684.

---

[41] See discussion of Section 684 in Bittker & Lokken, Federal Taxation of Income, Estates and Gifts ¶ 71.1 (Thomson Reuters/WG&L, 3d ed. 2000); Danforth, Lane & Zaritsky, Federal Income Taxation of Estates and Trusts ¶¶ 2.17, 6.03 (Thomson Reuters/WG&L, 3d ed. 2001).

[42] IRC § 684.

¶ 5.07　CLIENT COMMUNICATIONS

Estate planners should contact their clients with estate plans that use formula clauses based on estate or GST tax terms to alert them to possible problems that can arise in interpreting the formula provisions in their instruments. There appears to be no ethical or legal duty to notify clients of changes in the law, but an estate planner should do so as a service to clients and to avoid having to explain to beneficiaries why the client's documents produce an unexpected and adverse result.

Many estate planners have since 2001 included basic language in documents dealing with repeal of the estate tax. Unfortunately, almost no one looked closely enough at the many effects and details of the estate and GST repeal and the imposition of carryover basis until it became clear late last year that repeal would actually happen. Some of these documents, therefore, do not produce the optimal result, though they do produce a clear and certain result.

One may want to do triage with respect to client notices and to notify only those clients who are likely to have a problem under their documents. Clearly, one should contact a married client with a taxable estate to assure that the formula language used is appropriate in 2010 and that the form of the marital share will qualify for the spousal property basis increase. Additionally, one should contact any client whose estate plan includes GST tax planning to assure that their formula language still accomplishes the desired objectives. Clients who are not citizens or who have blended families (children of more than one marriage) will require special attention.

The practitioner should write these clients individually addressed letters that strike a delicate balance between informing the client of the special laws in effect in 2010, stressing that in many cases changes to address these laws may be important, and not sounding overly concerned about laws that will only last one year. One does not want to go into great detail about these laws because few clients have any real aptitude for or interest in such information, and the real goal is to convince the client to contact the estate planner to review the client's documents fully.

Drafting Tip: The following is a suggested letter to clients informing them that the estate tax and GST tax are temporarily suspended and that their documents should be reviewed, and, possibly, revised.

Dear _____ :

I am sure that you have read that, due to a surprising failure of Congress to act during the past nine years, the federal estate and the generation-skipping transfer taxes are temporarily repealed in 2010. They are scheduled to revive on January 1, 2011. This one-year repeal, however, may not have any impact on certain state estate taxes.

Your various estate planning documents divide your estate into separate shares in order to minimize federal [and state][43] estate taxes. These divisions are made by formulas that use terms defined by the federal tax laws. The absence of an estate tax and a GST tax may therefore render unclear some of the formula language used in your documents. We believe that these ambiguities should be clarified as soon as practicable, and that other changes may need to be made to your documents to take advantage of certain tax planning opportunities that exist in 2010.

Because of the temporary repeal of these taxes, another important change in the law, which can have effects beyond 2010, is that property received from a decedent's estate will now take a basis for purposes of determining gain on the future sale of the property equal to the decedent's basis. Previously (and again starting next year for decedent's dying after 2010), these assets received an adjusted basis equal to the fair market value of the property on the date of the decedent's death.

This change in the law is quite complex, and each estate has a right to increase the decedent's adjusted basis by up to $1.3 million, which increase can help reduce or eliminate future capital gains taxes payable by the estate or beneficiary. Additionally, where the decedent is survived by a spouse, an additional increase of up to $3 million may be given to property received by such surviving spouse, further reducing future capital gains taxes payable by such spouse. Wills and revocable trusts should include special provisions regarding such allocations.

Please call our office as soon as possible, and we will gladly schedule time to meet with you and review your estate planning documents. In some cases, no changes will be required. In others, we will recommend changes. We cannot know, in advance, whether your documents will require changes to best take advantage of the current state of the estate tax law until we have a chance to review your documents with you.

Even if your documents do require changes, we will attempt to keep them as minimal as possible, in keeping with the limited duration of their usefulness. Nonetheless, we strongly believe that it is important that your estate planning documents should produce the result you would want even if you die in 2010.

---

[43] Insert this language if the client is domiciled in a state that has a separate estate tax.

We look forward to hearing from you in the very near future.

Kindest regards,
[Your name]

A practical estate planner also probably should personally telephone certain clients whose age or health make death within 2010 more than a remote possibility, and whose estates may warrant special attention to take advantage of some of the planning opportunities afforded by the temporary absence of the estate and GST taxes. Once again, an attorney who has clearly concluded the attorney-client relationship in preparing a client's estate plan should not be legally or ethically obligated to contact these clients, but it is both good client relations and good business to do so, and it minimizes the chance that dissatisfied beneficiaries will attempt to hold the attorney accountable for lost taxes or lost tax-saving opportunities.

A number of states are considering adopting rules of construction or other statutes that address the meaning of estate or GST tax references in the instruments of a decedent who dies in 2010.[44] These statutes will produce certainty, though rarely will they produce the optimum tax planning. It is always better to have the instrument reflect the client's actual intent.

The estate planner who meets with a client regarding 2010 updates should review the client's will and revocable trust, of course, but a surprising number of other documents often contain tax sensitive provisions. Premarital agreements often assure a spouse of a right to a specific percentage of the other spouse's "gross estate" or "adjusted gross estate," which terms have no clear meaning in 2010. Buy-sell agreements often include similar tax references. A practitioner should review the client's entire file to determine whether the 2010 law raises significant issues.

An estate planner must also discuss a client's current gift-giving practices. A client's annual or periodic gifts to irrevocable trusts must be reviewed to determine whether those gifts raise GST tax or carryover basis issues when made in 2010.

A practical estate planner must move quickly to assess the degree of each client's problems, and this includes contacting those clients who are most likely to have 2010 problems. This will not be an easy year, and it is one in which the efforts made by an estate planner may produce no real added value for the client. Still, it is a year in which an estate planner can demonstrate an ongoing concern for and ability to protect the interests of his or her clients.

---

[44] See, e.g., Va. HB 755, Md. HB 449, NY A09857, and Tenn. SB 3045.

CHAPTER 6

A Checklist for Planning and Drafting in 2010 or What Do I Do Now?

¶ 6.01	Phase 1: Get In Touch With Your Clients	6-2
¶ 6.02	Phase 2: Fix Formula Problems In Wills and Revocable Trusts	6-2
	[1] Married Clients—Harmonious Family—With an Estate of $3.5 Million to $6 Million	6-2
	[2] Married Client—Non-Harmonious Family—With an Estate of $3.5 Million to $6 Million	6-3
	[3] Married Client—Harmonious Family—With an Estate of $6 Million to $10 Million	6-4
	[4] Married Client—Non-Harmonious Family—With an Estate of $6 Million to $10 Million	6-5
	[5] Married Client—Harmonious or Non-Harmonious Family—With an Estate Over $10 Million	6-6
	[6] Unmarried Surviving Spouse With an Estate of $3.5 Million to $5 Million	6-7
	[7] Unmarried Surviving Spouse With an Estate Over $5 Million	6-7
¶ 6.03	Phase 3: Find Other Formula/Tax Reference Problems	6-8
¶ 6.04	Phase 4: Fix Carryover Basis Problems	6-8
¶ 6.05	Phase 5: Fix Problems With Lifetime Gifts	6-9
¶ 6.06	Phase 6: Advise Trustee of Generation-Skipping Trust	6-10
¶ 6.07	Phase 7: Advise Executor of the Estate of a 2010 Decedent	6-11
¶ 6.08	Phase 8: Advise a Nonresident Alien	6-12

¶ 6.01 PHASE 1: GET IN TOUCH WITH YOUR CLIENTS

1. *Mass communication with clients.* Send a letter to all clients, or at least those who have formula clauses in their instruments, explaining that the law has changed and that, in 2010, their instruments may no longer produce the results they intended. But,

- Do not scare the clients into inaction.
- Do not overwhelm the clients with too much detail concerning these changes or their impact.
- Do not understate the importance of reviewing their documents.

For guidance and information on this topic, see ¶ 5.07.

2. *Individual communication with clients.* Call or write more personal letters to those clients whose health or age makes their death in 2010 a serious possibility. Be sure to—

- Point out there are serious estate planning considerations that need to be evaluated, particularly if GST taxes or substantial amounts of appreciated assets are involved.
- Urge or insist that clients review their documents.

For guidance and information on this topic, see ¶ 5.07.

3. *Individual communication with trustees.* Call or write personal letters to trustees of trusts that have skip persons as beneficiaries to inform them of the importance of careful planning with respect to distributions in 2010. For guidance and information on this topic, see ¶ 5.05.

¶ 6.02 PHASE 2: FIX FORMULA PROBLEMS IN WILLS AND REVOCABLE TRUSTS

[1] Married Clients—Harmonious Family—With an Estate of $3.5 Million to $6 Million

In 2009, the estate plan for this couple would typically include a nonmarital gift equal to the applicable exclusion amount, with the surviving spouse as the sole or primary beneficiary of the nonmarital trust. The nonmarital trust would not likely have significant generation-skipping features, and the trust funds might be distributed to children at stated ages. The marital share would be either given outright or in a qualified terminable interest property (QTIP), although it might be left in a trust that the surviving spouse could revoke. Provision for a state-only QTIP, where permitted, would likely be included, but a provision for a reverse QTIP was unlikely to be included.

Best 2010 adjustment: Leave the entire estate (possibly including the decedent's tangible personal property but excluding the decedent's residence) to a QTIP trust if the decedent dies in 2010. Any disclaimed portion of the QTIP trust should pass to the nonmarital trust (if that trust has different terms than the QTIP trust). This arrangement is good because it

- Is clear and unambiguous;
- Permits the fullest possible utilization of the spousal property basis increase;
- Removes assets from spouse's estate when the federal estate tax is restored after 2010;
- Permits the surviving spouse to fund a nonmarital trust by disclaimer if the estate tax is restored retroactively;
- Permits the trustee to divide the QTIP trust into a reverse QTIP and state-only QTIP (where permitted) if needed; and
- By leaving the residence outright, the Section 121 exclusion on sale of the residence will be preserved.

[2] Married Client—Non-Harmonious Family—With an Estate of $3.5 Million to $6 Million

In 2009, the estate plan for this couple would typically include a nonmarital gift equal to the applicable exclusion amount, with the surviving spouse as a beneficiary of the nonmarital trust, possibly even the primary beneficiary, but not usually the only current beneficiary. The nonmarital share might be divided between a regular nonmarital share (for spouse and descendants) and a spouse-only nonmarital share, based on some arbitrarily set figure. The nonmarital trust would likely not have significant generation-skipping features and might require distributions to or withdrawals by children at stated ages. The marital share would be left in a QTIP trust to assure that it will ultimately pass to the decedent's children. Provision for a reverse QTIP and a state-only QTIP, where permitted, would be included, but a provision for a reverse QTIP was unlikely to be included.

Best 2010 adjustment: Change documents to indicate that the QTIP will receive a specific share equal to the smallest share of the assets that will transfer $3 million of appreciation (i.e., an amount equal to the spousal property basis increase). This gift should be capped at an artificial figure (such as one half of the total estate) to prevent excessive reduction in the nonmarital share. This arrangement is good because it

- Is clear and unambiguous;
- Permits the fullest, if not the full, utilization of the spousal property basis increase;
- Removes the marital and nonmarital share assets from surviving spouse's estate when the estate tax is restored after 2010;
- Assures reasonable funding of the nonmarital trust to protect the interests of the children with whom the spouse does not get along amicably; and
- Permits the trustee to divide the QTIP trust into a reverse QTIP and a state-only QTIP (where permitted) if needed.

[3] Married Client—Harmonious Family—With an Estate of $6 Million to $10 Million

In 2009, the estate plan for this couple would typically include a nonmarital gift equal to the applicable exclusion amount, with a sprinkling nonmarital trust of which the surviving spouse might or might not be a beneficiary. The nonmarital trust would likely have generation-skipping features and automatically divide the trust assets into GST exempt and non-exempt shares, based on the available GST exemption, to minimize GST taxes after surviving spouse's death. The children would have, or the trustee could give them, a general power of appointment over the non-exempt share, possibly limited to the extent that the estate tax would be lower than the GST tax. The marital share would either be given outright or in a QTIP, although it might be left in a trust that the surviving spouse could revoke. Provision for a reverse QTIP and a state-only QTIP, where permitted, would be included in the documents.

Best 2010 adjustment: Change documents to indicate that, if death occurs when there is no estate tax applicable, the marital/nonmarital shares will be specified percentages (marital share of 50 percent, 60 percent, 70 percent, etc.) except that the marital share will receive a specific minimum gift of the smallest share of the assets that will transfer $3 million of appreciation (i.e., the amount of the spousal property basis increase). Tie the determination of GST exempt and nonexempt shares in 2010 to the amount that would pass free of GST taxes on the deaths of each generation of beneficiaries, rather than to the GST exemption. This should create a 100 percent GST exempt share if the ultimate interpretation of EGTRRA's sunset provisions confirms that a decedent dying in 2010 is not a "transferor" for GST tax purposes. If the sunset provisions are construed so that such a decedent is a transferor and that no GST exemption existed in 2010, this formula would treat the trust as a 100-percent nonexempt trust. The trustee should have the power to grant each generation of beneficiaries such general powers of appointment as may be needed to avoid GST taxes. This arrangement is good because it

- Is clear and unambiguous;
- Permits the fullest utilization of the spousal property basis increase;
- Removes assets from surviving spouse's estate when the estate tax is restored after 2010;
- Creates a nonmarital trust from which assets and income can be paid to the children and more remote descendants when not required by the surviving spouse;
- Creates a state-only QTIP (where permitted) to avoid current state estate taxes;
- Divides nonmarital and QTIP trust remainders between the GST exempt and non-exempt shares in a manner that should minimize estate and GST taxes after 2010; and
- Permits the trustee to grant general powers of appointment to the extent needed to take advantage of the applicable exclusion amount or marital deduction of each generation of beneficiaries of the GST nonexempt trust.

[4] Married Client—Non-Harmonious Family—With an Estate of $6 Million to $10 Million

In 2009, the estate plan for this couple would typically include a nonmarital gift equal to the applicable exclusion amount, with a sprinkling nonmarital trust of which the surviving spouse would often not be a beneficiary. The nonmarital trust would likely have generation-skipping features and automatically divide the trust assets into GST exempt and non-exempt shares, based on the available GST exemption, to minimize GST taxes after surviving spouse's death. The children would have, or the trustee could give them, a general power of appointment over the non-exempt share, possibly limited to the extent that the estate tax would be lower than the GST tax. The marital share would either be given outright or in a QTIP to assure that the property ultimately passed to the decedent's children. Provision for a reverse QTIP and a state-only QTIP, where permitted, would be included.

Best 2010 adjustment: Change documents to indicate that, if death occurs when there is no estate tax applicable, the marital/nonmarital shares will be specified percentages (marital share of 50 percent, 60 percent, 70 percent, etc.) except that the marital share will receive a specific minimum gift of a fairly representative share of the assets that will transfer $3 million of appreciation (i.e., an amount equal to the spousal property basis increase). The trustee should have the power to grant each generation of beneficiaries such general powers of appointment as may be needed to avoid GST taxes. This arrangement is good because it

- Is clear and unambiguous;
- Permits the fullest utilization of the spousal property basis increase;
- Removes assets from surviving spouse's estate when estate tax is restored after 2010;
- Creates a nonmarital trust from which assets and income can be paid to the children and more remote descendants when not required by the spouse;
- Creates a state-only QTIP (where permitted) to avoid current state estate taxes; and
- Permits the trustee to grant general powers of appointment to the extent needed to take advantage of the applicable exclusion amount or marital deduction of each generation of beneficiaries of the GST nonexempt trust.

[5] Married Client—Harmonious or Non-Harmonious Family— With an Estate Over $10 Million

In 2009, the estate plan for this couple would typically include a nonmarital gift equal to the applicable exclusion amount. The nonmarital share would be held in a sprinkling nonmarital trust of which the surviving spouse is not a beneficiary. The nonmarital trust would be a generation-skipping trust formed to last for the longest term permitted by law. The nonmarital trust would automatically divide into GST exempt and non-exempt shares, based on the available GST exemption, to minimize GST taxes. The marital share would be in a QTIP. Provisions for a reverse QTIP and a state-only QTIP, where permitted, would be included.

Best 2010 adjustment: Change documents to indicate that, if death occurs when there is no estate tax applicable, the marital/nonmarital shares will be specified percentages (marital share of 50 percent, 60 percent, 70 percent, etc.) except that the marital share will receive a specific minimum gift of the smallest share of the assets that will transfer $3 million of appreciation (i.e., an amount equal to the spousal property basis increase). The trustee should have the power to grant each generation of beneficiaries such general powers of appointment as may be needed to avoid GST taxes. This arrangement is good because it

- Is clear and unambiguous;
- Permits the fullest utilization of the spousal property basis increase;
- Removes assets from surviving spouse's estate when the estate tax is restored after 2010;

- Creates a nonmarital trust from which assets and income can be paid to the children and more remote descendants; and
- Creates a state-only QTIP (where permitted) to avoid current state estate taxes.

[6] Unmarried Surviving Spouse With an Estate of $3.5 Million to $5 Million

In 2009, the estate plan for this client would typically leave all assets to or in trust for the children with little or no GST tax planning.

Best 2010 adjustment: No document changes are required. If there is no GST planning, there is no formula clause and no GST issue.

[7] Unmarried Surviving Spouse With an Estate Over $5 Million

In 2009, the estate plan for this client would typically leave all assets in trust for the children and more remote descendants. The trust would continue for a very long time, often the maximum time permitted by law. The trust would be divided between the GST exempt and nonexempt shares. There might be a power of appointment in the children over the nonexempt share that is tied to the federal estate tax and GST tax differential.

Best 2010 adjustment: Change documents to tie the determination of the GST exempt and nonexempt shares in 2010 to the amount that would pass free of GST taxes, rather than to the GST exemption. This may result in an enlarged GST exempt share which, depending upon the interpretation of EGTRRA's sunset provisions, may not be subject to GST taxes later. If the interpretation of the sunset provisions is that this share would be subject to GST taxes, documents should give the trustee a power to grant each generation of beneficiaries such general powers of appointment as may be needed to avoid GST taxes. This arrangement is good because it

- Is clear and unambiguous, and
- Divides the nonmarital and QTIP trust remainders between the GST exempt and non-exempt shares in a manner that should minimize estate and GST taxes after 2010.

¶ 6.03 PHASE 3: FIND OTHER FORMULA/TAX REFERENCE PROBLEMS

Review premarital/prenuptial agreements and buy-sell agreements for references to estate tax terms, such as "gross estate" or "adjusted gross estate."

¶ 6.04 PHASE 4: FIX CARRYOVER BASIS PROBLEMS

1. Tell the client to start compiling basis information. For guidance and information on this topic, see ¶ 3.07.

- Tell the client to identify sources of basis records.
- Make sure each spouse has the other spouse's computer passwords to access basis data.

2. Add language to the client's will stating what factors to be considered in allocating the carryover basis increases. For guidance and information on this topic, see ¶ 3.03[1][e].

3. Add language to the client's will exonerating a family member who serves as executor from liability for allocations of basis increases made in good faith. For guidance and information on this topic, see ¶ 3.03.

4. Are there any negative basis assets in decedent's estate? For guidance and information on this topic, see ¶ 3.04.

- If so, are they left to specific people? If yes, consider leaving them other property, leaving them cash to pay the taxes, or directing that the executor allocate aggregate basis increase to negative basis assets.
- Are those people "tax-exempt beneficiaries"? If yes, consider leaving them other property or directing that the executor allocate aggregate basis increase to negative basis assets.
- Is the executor one of the people who will receive negative basis assets? If yes, consider changing the executor, leaving the executor other property, or directing that the executor allocate aggregate basis increase to negative basis assets.

5. Is the executor competent and impartial enough to allocate the carryover basis increases? If not, choose someone else. For guidance and information on this topic, see ¶ 3.03[1][e].

6. Is the executor a beneficiary? For guidance and information on this topic, see ¶ 3.03[1][e].

- If so, strongly urge that the client choose a professional fiduciary.
- If the client declines, consider exoneration language.

7. Are different people going to receive different nonprobate assets? For guidance and information on this topic, see ¶ 3.03[1][d].

- Attempt to consolidate all nonprobate assets in the hands of one person, who should also be the executor under the decedent's will. Usually, this involves having the assets transferred to the decedent's revocable trust.

8. Does the client have loss assets? If so, recommend that they be sold and the deductible losses generated. For guidance and information on this topic, see ¶ 3.13.

9. Is the client's residence passing in trust? If so, consider leaving it to an individual instead, to preserve the $250,000 exclusion for the gain on sale of a principal residence. For guidance and information on this topic, see ¶ 3.07.

¶ 6.05 PHASE 5: FIX PROBLEMS WITH LIFETIME GIFTS

1. What gifts will the client make in 2010?

- Are any of these gifts subject to gift tax?
  - If so, is securing the low 2010 35 percent rate important?
  - If so, consider using a formula gift. For guidance and information on this topic, see ¶ 5.02[1].
- Are any of these gifts to grandchildren or other skip persons?
  - If so, can they be made outright, rather than in trust? For guidance and information on this topic, see ¶ 4.03[2].
  - If so, and if they cannot be made outright, can they be made to a family limited partnership or family limited liability company? For guidance and information on this topic, see ¶ 5.02.
- Is avoiding the GST tax important to the client?
  - If so, consider making the gift by formula. For guidance and information on this topic, see ¶ 4.09[3].

2. Will the client pay premium on insurance policies held by an irrevocable life insurance trust (ILIT) or other family members in 2010?

- If so, do the trusts have GST tax potential?
- Has the client been filing gift tax returns to allocate GST exemption to the premium payments to retain a zero inclusion ratio?
- If yes to both of these, consider lending money to the trust or using a feeder trust. For guidance and information on this topic, see ¶ 5.03.

3. Make sure that donor files donee basis information when the donor files his or her gift tax return. For guidance and information on this topic, see ¶ 5.02[3].

¶ 6.06 PHASE 6: ADVISE TRUSTEE OF GENERATION-SKIPPING TRUST

1. Does the trust have any mandatory distributions to skip persons in 2010? If so, consider a refunding agreement and bond to assure that, if the GST tax is retroactively reintroduced, the trustee is protected from personal liability for the taxes.

2. Does the trustee want to make any discretionary distributions to skip persons in 2010?

- If so, discuss relative merits of making them early in the year (in case Congress reinstates the GST tax prospectively) or making them late in the year (to better judge whether Congress will reinstate the GST tax retroactively). For guidance and information on this topic, see ¶ 5.05[1].
- If the trustee still plans to make the distributions, consider making them by formula. For guidance and information on this topic, see ¶ 5.05.
- If the trustee still plans to make the distributions, and if a formula gift is not practical because there is no non-skip person to whom the distribution could be shifted to avoid tax, consider a refunding agreement and bond to assure that the trustee is protected from personal liability for the taxes if the GST tax is retroactively reintroduced.

3. Will there be a taxable termination in 2010?

- If so, does the trust then terminate with an outright distribution to skip persons? If so, consider a refunding agreement and bond to assure that the trustee is protected from personal liability for the taxes if the GST tax is retroactively reintroduced.
- If so and the trust continues, there is nothing special to be done.

¶ 6.07 PHASE 7: ADVISE EXECUTOR OF THE ESTATE OF A 2010 DECEDENT

1. Gather decedent's basis information. For guidance and information on this topic, see ¶ 3.07.

2. Start obtaining fair market value information, including appraisals. Tell appraiser to prepare one appraisal to serve both carryover basis purposes and estate tax purposes. For guidance and information on this topic, see ¶ 5.04[1].

3. Consider election to treat revocable trust as a part of estate under Section 645 if the trust includes pecuniary distributions and the client has appreciated assets. For guidance and information on this topic, see ¶ 5.05[2].

4. Determine whether the decedent has any negative basis assets.

   • If so, determine whether they are left to a specific beneficiary or are part of the general residuary estate.
   • If they pass to specific beneficiaries, notify them immediately of their income tax problems. Be sure to notify all of the beneficiaries of negative basis property on the same day to avoid charges of partiality.
   • If so, and if the executor is to receive negative basis property, consider whether the executor should resign immediately and have an independent professional executor appointed, in order for the new executor to allocate part of the decedent's aggregate or spousal property basis increases to the negative basis property without charges or partiality. For guidance and information on this topic, see ¶¶ 3.04, 5.04[2].

5. Diversify the estate assets, but consider capital gains taxes in deciding what investments to sell and whether it might be better, in lieu of a sale, to place an option "collar" on key publicly traded stocks so as to the reduce risk of loss, pending Congress's decision on whether to repeal the carryover basis rules retroactively.

6. If assets need to be sold to raise liquidity, sell high-basis assets or allocate carryover basis increases to the assets that will be sold.

7. If Congress retroactively reinstates the estate and GST taxes, consider whether to contest the constitutionality of this reinstatement.

¶ 6.08 PHASE 8: ADVISE A NONRESIDENT ALIEN

1. Is either spouse a nonresident alien? Use modified QTIP/QDOT for death in 2010. For guidance and information on this topic, see ¶ 5.06.

2. Are any beneficiaries non-U.S. persons? For guidance and information on this topic, see ¶ 5.06. If so, change documents so that the decedent's will does leave negative basis assets to nonresident alien individuals. For guidance and information on this topic, see ¶ 5.06[2].

3. If the client is a nonresident alien holding U.S. situs assets with substantial appreciation, consider whether adoption of a U.S. residence would be appropriate in order to obtain the higher $1.3 million aggregate basis increase. For guidance and information on this topic, see ¶ 5.06[1].

4. Avoid transferring appreciated property to a foreign person in a transaction that will be treated as a sale or exchange under Section 684. For guidance and information on this topic, see ¶ 5.06[3].

APPENDIX A
Sample Forms

¶ A.01   Form 1: Single Trust Will for Estate of $3.5 Million to $6 Million—QTIP Trust—Executor Divides Trust Into Nonmarital, State-Only QTIP, and Marital Deduction Shares if There is an Estate Tax—Executor Divides Into State-Only Marital and Marital Trusts if There is No Estate Tax—Trustee Can Distribute to Spouse Minimum Amount of Appreciated Assets Sufficient to Enable Spouse to Take Advantage of Aggregate Basis Increase at Surviving Spouse's Death—Remainder Passes Outright to Children and Descendants (No GST Tax Planning) A-3

¶ A.02   Form 2: Single Trust Revocable Trust for Estate of $3.5 Million to $6 Million—QTIP Trust—Trustee Divides Trust Into Nonmarital, State-Only QTIP, and Marital Deduction Shares if There is an Estate Tax—Trustee Divides Into State-Only Marital and Marital Trusts if There is No Estate Tax—Trustee Can Distribute to Spouse Minimum Amount of Appreciated Assets Sufficient to Enable Spouse to Take Advantage of Aggregate Basis Increase at Surviving Spouse's Death—Remainder Passes Outright to Children and Descendants (No GST Tax Planning)—Same Planning as Form 1, But in a Revocable Trust A-19

¶ A.03   Form 3: Will With Disclaimer Based Planning for Estate of $3.5 Million to $6 Million—All Left to QTIP Trust—Disclaimer of QTIP Trust Funds Nonmarital Trust for Spouse and Descendants—QTIP Trust Can Be Divided to Create State-Only QTIP Trust—Trustee Can Distribute to Spouse Minimum Amount of Appreciated Assets Sufficient to Enable Spouse to Take Advantage of Aggregate Basis Increase at Surviving Spouse's Death—Remainder Passes Outright to Children and Descendants (No GST Tax Planning) A-35

¶ A.04   Form 4: Revocable Trust With Disclaimer Based Planning
for Estate of $3.5 Million to $6 Million—All Left to QTIP
Trust—Disclaimer of QTIP Trust Funds Nonmarital Trust
for Spouse and Descendants—QTIP Trust Can Be Divided
to Create State-Only QTIP Trust—Trustee Can Distribute
to Spouse Minimum Amount of Appreciated Assets
Sufficient to Enable Spouse to Take Advantage of
Aggregate Basis Increase at Surviving Spouse's Death—
Remainder Passes Outright to Children and Descendants
(No GST Tax Planning)—Same Planning as Form 3, but in
a Revocable Trust A-49

¶ A.05   Form 5: Will for Estate of $6 Million to $10
Million--Marital Deduction Tax Planning—GST Tax
Planning With Lifetime Trust for Children and Reverse
QTIP—Creates a 40% Nonmarital Share in 2010 to Absorb
Aggregate Property Basis Increase—Trustee Can Distribute
From QTIP Minimum Amount of Principal Sufficient to
Give Spouse Enough Appreciation to Take Advantage of
Aggregate Basis Increase at Surviving Spouse's Death—No
State Estate Tax Planning Because Relevant State Death
Taxes are Repealed or Provide Exemption Equal to Federal
Applicable Exclusion Amount A-63

¶ A.06   Form 6: Revocable Trust for Estate of $6 Million to $10
Million—Marital Deduction Tax Planning—GST Tax
Planning With Lifetime Trust for Children and Reverse
QTIP—Creates a 40% Nonmarital Share in 2010 to Absorb
Aggregate Property Basis Increase—Trustee Can Distribute
From QTIP Minimum Amount of Principal Sufficient to
Give Spouse Enough Appreciation to Take Advantage of
Aggregate Basis Increase at Surviving Spouse's Death—No
State Estate Tax Planning Because Relevant State Death
Taxes are Repealed or Provide Exemption Equal to Federal
Applicable Exclusion Amount—Same Planning as Form 5,
but in a Revocable Trust A-83

¶ A.07   Form 7: Will for Estate of $6 Million to $10 Million—
Marital Deduction Tax Planning—GST Tax Planning With
Lifetime Trust for Children and Reverse QTIP—Creates a
Nonmarital Share Equal to State Estate Tax Exemption—
Trustee Can Distribute From QTIP Minimum Amount of
Principal Sufficient to Give Spouse Enough Appreciation to
Take Advantage of Aggregate Basis Increase at Surviving
Spouse's Death—Creates State-Only QTIP A-104

¶ A.08   Form 8: Revocable Trust for Estate of $6 Million to $10
Million—Marital Deduction Tax Planning—GST Tax
Planning With Lifetime Trust for Children and Reverse
QTIP—Creates a Nonmarital Share Equal to State Estate
Tax Exemption—Trustee Can Distribute From QTIP
Minimum Amount of Principal Sufficient to Give Spouse
Enough Appreciation to Take Advantage of Aggregate
Basis Increase at Surviving Spouse's Death—Creates
State-Only QTIP—Same Planning as Form 7, but in a
Revocable Trust A-126

¶ A.09   Form 9: Will for Estate over $10 Million—Marital Deduction and GST Tax Planning—Dynasty Trust for Children and Descendants—GST Exemption Used Even if it Generates Estate Tax at First Spouse's Death—No State QTIP in Order to Reduce State Estate Taxes at Surviving Spouse's Death—2010 Disposition of 40% of Estate to Nonmarital Share—Trustee Can Distribute From QTIP Minimum Amount of Principal Sufficient to Give Spouse Enough Appreciation to Take Advantage of Aggregate Basis Increase at Surviving Spouse's Death A-149

¶ A.10   Form 10: Revocable Trust for Estate Over $10 Million—Marital Deduction and GST Tax Planning—Dynasty Trust for Children and Descendants—GST Exemption Used Even if it Generates Estate Tax at First Spouse's Death—No State QTIP in Order to Reduce State Estate Taxes at Surviving Spouse's Death—2010 Disposition of 40% of Estate to Nonmarital Share—Trustee Can Distribute From QTIP Minimum Amount of Principal Sufficient to Give Spouse Enough Appreciation to Take Advantage of Aggregate Basis Increase at Surviving Spouse's Death—Same Planning as Form 9, but in a Revocable Trust A-167

¶ A.01 FORM 1: SINGLE TRUST WILL FOR ESTATE OF $3.5 MILLION TO $6 MILLION—QTIP TRUST—EXECUTOR DIVIDES TRUST INTO NONMARITAL, STATE-ONLY QTIP, AND MARITAL DEDUCTION SHARES IF THERE IS AN ESTATE TAX—EXECUTOR DIVIDES INTO STATE-ONLY MARITAL AND MARITAL TRUSTS IF THERE IS NO ESTATE TAX—TRUSTEE CAN DISTRIBUTE TO SPOUSE MINIMUM AMOUNT OF APPRECIATED ASSETS SUFFICIENT TO ENABLE SPOUSE TO TAKE ADVANTAGE OF AGGREGATE BASIS INCREASE AT SURVIVING SPOUSE'S DEATH—REMAINDER PASSES OUTRIGHT TO CHILDREN AND DESCENDANTS (NO GST TAX PLANNING)

Will of *Testator*[1]

I, *Testator*, of [*locality, state*], make this my will. I revoke any other wills and codicils made by me.

Article 1
My Family

I am married to *Spouse* (sometimes referred to as "my *husband/wife*") and I have [*number of children*] children, *Children*.

Article 2
My Personal Effects

A. Disposing of My Personal Effects. I leave my personal effects (defined below) to my *husband/wife*, *Spouse*, if *he/she* survives me, or otherwise to my descendants who survive me, *per stirpes*. If neither my *husband/wife* nor any of my children nor their descendants survive me, these personal effects shall be added to the residue of my estate. An adult person with whom a minor resides may give a binding receipt for any personal effects passing to the minor.

B. Memorandum. I may make a memorandum of how I wish some of my personal effects to be distributed, and I request that my wishes be followed.

Article 3
My Personal Residence

I leave all of my interest in the properties my personal representative (defined below) shall determine to have been used by me or a member of my family as personal residences to my *husband/wife*, *Spouse*, if *he/she* survives me, to the extent that they do not pass to *him/her* by right of survivorship. Personal residences shall also include all adjoining lands and any related casualty insurance policies.

---

[1] **KEY:**

Testator	— full name of the testator
Spouse	— full name of testator's spouse
husband/wife	— "husband" or "wife," as the case may be
Children	— full names of testator's children
he/she	— "he" or "she" (referring to the spouse)
his/her	— "his" or "her" (referring to the spouse)
him/her	— "him" or "her" (referring to the spouse)
BANK	— name of the bank or other corporation that will be the personal representative and trustee

Article 4
My Residuary Estate

A. If My *Husband/Wife* Survives Me. If my *husband/wife*, *Spouse*, survives me, my personal representative shall hold my residuary estate under the Article entitled "The Family Trust."

B. If My *Husband/Wife* Does Not Survive Me. If my *husband/wife* does not survive me, my personal representative shall distribute my residuary estate to my descendants who survive me, *per stirpes*, except that the share for any child or more remote descendant of mine who shall then not yet have reached the age of thirty-five (35) years, shall be held under the Article entitled "Contingent Trust for Certain Beneficiaries."

Article 5
The Family Trust

The family trust shall be held under this Article.

A. Distributing Trust Fund During My *Husband/Wife*'s Life.

1. Distributing Income. The trustee shall distribute the net income of the family trust quarterly or more frequently to my *husband/wife*, *Spouse*, during *his/her* life.

2. Distributing Principal. The trustee shall also distribute to my *husband/wife* as much of the principal of the family trust as is appropriate for any purpose.

3. Distributing Additional Principal if There is No Federal Estate Tax. If the trustee deems it likely that my *husband/wife* will die before January 1, 2011, my trustee shall distribute to my *husband/wife* a fractional share of this trust.

a The numerator of this fraction shall be equal to the smallest value of the assets of this trust fund to which the personal representative of my *husband/wife*'s estate could allocate all of the aggregate basis increase allowed to my *husband/wife* under Federal income tax laws, less the amount of such aggregate basis increase that could be allocated to other assets already owned by my *husband/wife* at the time of this distribution.

b The denominator of this fraction shall equal the value of this entire trust fund.

B. Distributing Trust Fund At My *Husband/Wife*'s Death.

1. Distributing Undistributed Income. At my *husband/wife*'s death, the trustee shall distribute to my *husband/wife*'s estate any undistributed income of the family trust.

2. Appointing Principal. The trustee shall also distribute the principal of the family trust, to the extent it is not used to pay transfer taxes (defined below) as provided below, as my *husband/wife* may direct by specific reference to this special power of appointment in *his/her* last will. My *husband/wife* may appoint the trust fund, either outright or in further trust, but only to or among any one (1) or more of my descendants, and *he/she* may not appoint any portion of the fund of the family trust to my *husband/wife*, *his/her* creditors, *his/her* estate, or the creditors of *his/her* estate.

   3. Distributing Unappointed Trust Fund. The trustee shall distribute the unappointed trust fund to my then-living descendants, *per stirpes*, except that the share for any child or more remote descendant of mine who shall then not yet have reached the age of thirty-five (35) years, shall be held for such descendant under the Article entitled "Contingent Trust for Certain Beneficiaries."

  C. Dividing the Family Trust. The trustee may, but shall not be required to, divide the family trust into two (2) or more separate and independent trusts. Each separate and independent trust shall be identical in terms, conditions, and beneficial interests, but shall each operate as a separate independent trust.

   1. Fractional Shares. My fiduciaries shall divide the family trust on a fractional basis, so that each separate and independent trust shall share proportionately in all increases and decreases in the value of the assets of my estate and of the family trust fund between the date of my death and the date of such division.

   2. Selecting Assets to Fund Separate Shares. My fiduciaries may fractionalize each asset to satisfy these separate and independent trusts. My fiduciaries, if they choose not to fractionalize assets, shall allocate assets as they shall consider to be in the best interests of the beneficiaries, valuing each asset on the date or dates of allocation.

   3. Allocating Income. My fiduciaries shall allocate to each separate and independent trust a ratable portion of all of the income earned by my estate and by the family trust after my death, whether earned before or after the assets are in the possession of the trustee, and income earned on assets used to pay charges according to the same fractional shares.

   4. Effective Date. All divisions of the family trust shall be effective from the date of my death.

Article 6
Contingent Trust for Certain Beneficiaries

  If a beneficiary is entitled to receive any part of my estate or any portion of any trust fund held under this will while the beneficiary is under the age of thirty-five (35) years, the trustee may retain such assets in a separate trust for that beneficiary.

  A. Distributing Trust Fund Before the Contingent Trust Termination Date. Until the contingent trust termination date (defined below), the trustee shall distribute to or for the benefit of the beneficiary as much of the net income and principal as the trustee may consider appropriate for the beneficiary's health, education, support, or maintenance, annually adding to principal any undistributed income.

B. Distributing Trust Fund At the Contingent Trust Termination Date. Upon the contingent trust termination date, the trustee shall distribute the remaining assets to the beneficiary if the beneficiary is then living or otherwise to the beneficiary's estate to be distributed as part of that estate.

C. "Contingent Trust Termination Date" Defined. The "contingent trust termination date" shall be the earlier of (1) the date on which the beneficiary dies or (2) the date on which the beneficiary reaches the age of thirty-five (35) years.

Article 7
Special Limits on Powers of Interested Trustee

The following limitations shall apply, notwithstanding other provisions of this instrument.

A. Limiting Actions by Interested Trustees. No interested trustee (defined below) may participate in the exercise of any discretion to distribute principal to himself or herself, except as is appropriate for his or her health, education, support, and maintenance, or any of them. No interested trustee may participate in the exercise of any discretion to distribute or expend principal or income in a manner that would discharge that trustee's personal obligation to support the beneficiary. No interested trustee may participate in the exercise of any incident of ownership over any policy owned by the trust insuring the life of such trustee.

B. Disinterested Trustees Exercising Certain Powers. A disinterested trustee (defined below) who is serving as a co-trustee with an interested trustee, may exercise those discretions granted under this instrument the exercise of which by an interested trustee are precluded.

1. If Multiple Trustees Include an Interested Trustee Who Cannot Act. The number of trustees who must consent to the exercise of a power granted under this instrument, as determined under the Article entitled "My Fiduciaries" shall be determined by treating the interested trustees who are not entitled, under this Article, to participate in the exercise of the power or discretion, as if they were not then serving.

2. If All Trustees Are Precluded From Acting. If this Article precludes every then-serving trustee from exercising a power otherwise granted to the trustee under this instrument, the then-serving trustee shall appoint a disinterested trustee who may exercise such power (or decline to exercise it) as if that disinterested trustee were the sole then-serving trustee.

Article 8
Debts, Expenses, and Taxes

A. Paying Debts and Expenses. My personal representative shall pay from my residuary estate my debts (but not before their maturity) and funeral and burial expenses, including the cost of a suitable memorial, without court order.

1. Paying Certain Joint Debts. My personal representative shall pay only my proportionate share of any debts for which I am jointly liable with my *husband/wife*.

2. Paying Packing and Shipping Expenses. My personal representative shall pay all packing, shipping, insurance, and other charges relating to the distribution of any of my personal property without seeking reimbursement from the recipient of such personal property.

B. Paying Transfer Taxes. My personal representative shall pay all transfer taxes, other than generation-skipping transfer taxes, payable by reason of my death on assets passing under this will, from my residuary estate.

1. Apportioning Transfer Taxes on Nonprobate Assets. My personal representative shall apportion transfer taxes imposed on any assets not passing under this will to those assets and the transfer taxes on those assets shall be paid from those assets as provided by the laws of the state in which I reside at my death, except as expressly provided elsewhere in this will.

2. Apportioning Generation-Skipping Transfer Taxes. My personal representative shall apportion all generation-skipping transfer taxes for which my estate is legally responsible to those generation-skipping transfers, whether or not under this will.

3. Apportioning Transfer Taxes Away From Deductible Assets. Assets passing to or in trust for the benefit of my *husband/wife* or to any charitable organization, whether under this will or otherwise, shall have the full benefit of any available marital or charitable deduction for Federal and other transfer tax purposes, in determining the share of transfer taxes that should be borne by those assets.

Article 9
My Fiduciaries

A. Naming My Personal Representatives. I name *BANK*, of [*locality, state*], to be my personal representative and the trustee of any trusts under this will, and I give it the right to name one or more persons to serve with it.

B. No Surety or Bond. No personal representative or trustee named by me or by another personal representative or trustee shall be required to provide surety or other security on a bond.

C. Naming Additional Fiduciaries. I authorize my named fiduciaries (defined below) to appoint any person as an additional personal representative or trustee in the same state or another state in which administration may be appropriate to serve at the pleasure of the appointing fiduciaries.

D. Delegating Fiduciary Powers and Authorities. My fiduciaries may delegate to another fiduciary any power or authority granted by me to my fiduciaries, to continue at the pleasure of the delegating fiduciary, unless otherwise agreed. Any person dealing in good faith with a fiduciary may rely upon that fiduciary's representation that a delegation has been made and remains in effect under this paragraph.

E. Fiduciary Resigning. A personal representative or trustee may resign by giving written notice specifying the effective date of the resignation and naming another corporation no substantial portion of the stock of which is owned by beneficiaries of any trust under this will, to be successor personal representative or trustee.

F. Removing a Trustee. A trustee may be removed by the vote of two-thirds (⅔) of the then-living adult beneficiaries to whom trust income may then be distributed.

G. Filling Fiduciary Vacancies.

1. Court Appointing Personal Representative to Fill Vacancy. If no successor personal representative is designated, a court of appropriate jurisdiction shall name a successor personal representative.

2. Beneficiaries Appointing Corporate Trustee to Fill Vacancy. A corporation no substantial portion of the stock of which is owned by beneficiaries of this trust, may be named as successor trustee to fill any vacancy, by majority vote of the adult beneficiaries to whom trust income then may be distributed.

H. No Liability for Acts or Omissions of Predecessors. No fiduciary shall be responsible for or need inquire into any acts or omissions of a prior fiduciary.

I. Compensating Fiduciaries. In addition to reimbursement for expenses, each individual fiduciary is entitled to reasonable compensation for services. Each corporate fiduciary is entitled to compensation based on its written fee schedule in effect at the time its services are rendered or as otherwise agreed, and its compensation may vary from time to time based on that schedule.

J. Management Powers. I authorize my fiduciaries to exercise all powers conferred by applicable state law and to do the following in a fiduciary capacity.

1. Prudent Investor Rule. My fiduciaries may hold and retain as part of my estate or any trust fund any property owned by me, whether or not such investment would be appropriate for a prudent investor. My fiduciaries may also hold and retain as part of my estate or any trust fund any property received from any source, and invest and reinvest my estate or trust fund (or leave it temporarily uninvested) in any type of property and every kind of investment in the same manner as a prudent investor would invest his or her own assets.

2. Holding Assets For Use of Trust Beneficiaries. My trustee may buy and hold in trust, assets that will be used personally by one or more beneficiaries, even if those assets would not otherwise be acquired by a prudent investor investing his or her own assets.

3. Transferring Assets. My fiduciaries may sell or exchange any real or personal property contained in my estate or any trust, for cash or credit, at public or private sale, and with such warranties or indemnifications as my fiduciaries may deem advisable.

4. Borrowing Money. My fiduciaries may borrow money (even from a fiduciary or beneficiary of my estate or any trust) for the benefit of my estate or any trust and secure these debts with assets of my estate or any trust.

5. Granting Security Interests. My fiduciaries may grant security interests and execute all instruments creating such interests upon such terms as my fiduciaries may deem advisable.

6. Compromising Claims. My fiduciaries may compromise and adjust claims against or on behalf of my estate or any trust on such terms as my fiduciaries may deem advisable.

7. Not Disclosing Nominees. My fiduciaries may take title to any securities in the name of any custodian or nominee without disclosing this relationship.

8. Allocating Between Income and Principal. My fiduciaries may determine whether receipts are income or principal and whether disbursements are to be charged against income or principal to the extent not clearly established by state law. A determination made by my fiduciaries in good faith shall not require equitable adjustments.

9. Making Tax Elections. My fiduciaries may make all tax elections and allocations my fiduciaries may consider appropriate; however, this authority is exercisable only in a fiduciary capacity and may not be used to enlarge or shift any beneficial interest except as an incidental consequence of the discharge of fiduciary duties. A tax election or allocation made by my fiduciaries in good faith shall not require equitable adjustments.

10. Distributing to Custodians for Minors. My fiduciaries shall distribute any of my estate or any trust fund to a beneficiary under the age of twenty-one (21) years by distribution to any appropriate person (who may be a fiduciary) chosen by my fiduciaries as custodian under any appropriate Uniform Transfers (or Gifts) to Minors Act, to be held for the maximum period of time allowed by law. My fiduciaries may also sell any asset that cannot be held under this custodianship and invest the sales proceeds in assets that can be so held.

11. Employing Advisors. My fiduciaries may employ such lawyers, accountants, and other advisors as my fiduciaries may deem useful and appropriate for the administration of my estate or any trust. My fiduciaries may employ a professional investment advisor and delegate to this advisor any discretionary investment authorities to manage the investments of my estate or any trust, including any investment in mutual funds, investment trusts, or managed accounts, and may rely on the advisor's investment recommendations without liability to any beneficiary.

12. Buying and Holding Life Insurance. My fiduciaries may buy and hold insurance policies on the life of any beneficiary or any person in whom a beneficiary has an insurable interest and may pay the premiums on such policies from income or principal, as my fiduciaries may deem advisable.

13. Dividing and Distributing Assets. My fiduciaries may divide and distribute the assets of my estate or any trust fund in kind, in money, or partly in each, without regard to the income tax basis of any asset and without the consent of any beneficiary. The decisions of my fiduciaries in dividing any portion of my estate or any trust fund between or among two or more beneficiaries, if made in good faith, shall be binding on all persons.

14. Allocating Basis Increase. My personal representative shall allocate any increases in the adjusted basis of property owned by me at the time of my death, whether passing under my Will or otherwise, to the extent such property is eligible to receive such an allocation, as my personal representative deems to be in the best interests of my estate and its beneficiaries. In making these allocations my personal representative shall:

a. First, satisfy all charitable bequests with assets to which no aggregate or spousal property basis increases may be allocated;

b. Second, satisfy all charitable bequests with assets that have an adjusted income tax basis closest to zero of all of my assets available to satisfy these bequests;

c. Third, generally not allocate basis increase to assets the gain from the sale of which is not subject to federal income tax under present federal income tax laws; and

d. Fourth, allocate basis increases to assets that are reasonably likely to be sold within the three year period beginning on the date of my death, the sale of which will produce an income tax liability that is taxed at a rate higher than that on long-term capital gains.

Any reference in this paragraph to assets "owned by me on the date of my death" shall apply equally to assets deemed owned by me on the date of my death under the federal income tax rules governing allocation of my aggregate basis increase.

Article 10
Trust Administration

A. Spendthrift Limits. No interest in a trust under this will shall be subject to the beneficiary's liabilities or creditor claims or to assignment or anticipation.

B. Protecting Trust Beneficiaries From Creditors. If the trustee shall determine that a beneficiary would not benefit as greatly from any outright distribution of trust income or principal because of the availability of the distribution to the beneficiary's creditors, the trustee shall instead expend those amounts for the benefit of the beneficiary. This direction is intended to enable the trustee to give the beneficiary the fullest possible benefit and enjoyment of all of the trust income and principal to which he or she is entitled.

C. Combining Multiple Trusts. The trustee may invest the assets of multiple trusts in a single fund if the interests of the trusts are accounted for separately.

D. Merging and Consolidating Trust Funds. The trustee may merge or consolidate any trust into any other trust that has the same trustee and substantially the same dispositive provisions.

E. Dividing Trust Funds. The trustee may divide any trust fund into multiple separate trusts.

F. Accountings. The trustee shall not be required to file annual accounts with any court or court official in any jurisdiction.

G. Changing Trust Situs. A disinterested trustee may change the situs of any trust under this will, and to the extent necessary or appropriate, move the trust assets, to a state or country other than the one in which the trust is then administered if the disinterested trustee shall determine it to be in the best interests of the trust or the beneficiaries. The disinterested trustee may elect that the law of such other jurisdiction shall govern the trust to the extent necessary or appropriate under the circumstances.

Article 11
Dividing the Family Trust if a Federal Estate Tax Exists

This Article shall apply if there is, on the date of my death, a Federal estate tax that applies with respect to my estate.

A. My Purposes.

1. Minimizing Federal and *State* Estate Taxes. The division of the family trust into a nonmarital trust, a state-only marital trust and a marital trust, shall minimize the Federal and *State* estate taxes at my *husband/wife*'s death to the extent I can do so while deferring all Federal and *State* estate taxes until both my *husband/wife* and I have died.

2. State-Only Marital Trust. The state-only marital trust shall qualify for the estate tax marital deduction under the laws of *State* and all provisions of this will shall be construed accordingly. My fiduciaries shall, in all matters involving the state-only marital trust, exercise no power in a manner that would infringe upon any legal requirement for the allowance of the estate tax marital deduction under the laws of *State*.

3. Qualifying for Federal Estate Tax Marital Deduction. The marital trust shall qualify for the Federal estate tax marital deduction and all provisions of this will shall be construed accordingly. My fiduciaries shall, in all matters involving the marital trust, exercise no power in a manner that would infringe upon any legal requirement for the allowance of the Federal estate tax marital deduction.

B. Dividing the Family Trust. My personal representative and the trustee shall divide the family trust under this Article in accordance with the rules set forth in the Article entitled "The Family Trust," in the paragraph entitled "Dividing the Family Trust."

C. Defining the Nonmarital Trust. If my *husband/wife* survives me, my fiduciaries shall create by division of the family trust, a nonmarital trust, which shall be a fractional share of the family trust.

    1. Calculating the Numerator. The numerator of the fraction shall equal the smaller of:

        a. the largest value of the family trust that can pass free of *State* estate tax were it to pass to an individual other than my *spouse*. This value shall be determined after being reduced by reason of all other dispositions of property included in my gross estate for which no deduction is allowed in computing my *State* estate tax, and administration expenses and other charges to principal that are not claimed and allowed as *State* estate tax deductions; and

        b. the largest value of the family trust that can pass free of Federal estate tax by reason of the unified credit allowable with respect to my estate. This value shall be determined after being reduced by reason of my adjusted taxable gifts, all other dispositions of property included in my gross estate for which no deduction is allowed in computing my Federal estate tax, and administration expenses and other charges to principal that are not claimed and allowed as Federal estate tax deductions.

    2. Calculating the Denominator. The denominator of the fraction shall equal the value of the family trust.

D. Defining the "State-Only Marital Trust." If my *husband/wife* survives me, and if I die domiciled in *state*, my fiduciaries shall create by division of the family trust, a "state-only marital trust," which shall be a fractional share of the family trust.

    1. Calculating the Numerator. The numerator of the fraction shall be the difference between:

        a. the largest value of the family trust that can pass free of *State* estate tax were it to pass to an individual other than my *husband/wife*. This value shall be determined after being reduced by reason of all other dispositions of property included in my gross estate for which no deduction is allowed in computing my *State* estate tax, and administration expenses and other charges to principal that are not claimed and allowed as *State* estate tax deductions; and

        b. the numerator of the fraction by which the nonmarital trust is calculated under this article.

    2. Calculating the Denominator. The denominator of the fraction shall equal the value of the family trust.

E. Defining the "Marital Trust." If my *husband/wife* survives me, my fiduciaries shall create by division of the family trust, a "marital trust," which shall be the remaining fractional share of the family trust after subtracting the nonmarital trust and the state-only marital trust.

F. Calculating Shares Based on Certain Assumptions. The nonmarital trust and the state-only marital trust shall be computed as if no election were made to qualify any property passing as such share under the Federal estate tax marital deduction, and the maximum possible election were made to qualify all property passing as the marital trust and the marital trust for the Federal estate tax marital deduction.

G. Determining the Effect of Disclaimers.

1. Disclaiming the Marital Trust. My fiduciaries shall add to the nonmarital trust any portion of the marital trust as to which a qualified disclaimer by or for my *husband/wife* is made. The nonmarital trust shall be calculated before any qualified disclaimer by or for my *husband/wife* of any of the marital trust.

2. Apportioning Transfer Taxes to Disclaimed Funds. Transfer taxes imposed on any portion of the marital trust as to which my *husband/wife* has made a qualified disclaimer shall be apportioned to those disclaimed funds.

H. Allocating Assets Between or Among Shares.

1. Making Certain Allocations If My *Husband/Wife* Survives Me. If my *husband/wife* survives me:

a. My personal representative shall allocate to the marital trust and the state-only marital trust only assets that can qualify for the Federal estate tax marital deduction.

b. To the extent possible, my personal representative shall not allocate to the marital trust or the state-only marital trust assets upon which a foreign death tax is payable.

c. The nonmarital trust shall consist solely of assets includable in my gross estate for Federal estate tax purposes.

2. Making Other Allocations. In other respects, my personal representative and the trustee shall allocate assets as my personal representative and the trustee shall consider to be in the best interests of the beneficiaries, valuing each asset on the date or dates of allocation.

Article 12
Dividing the Family Trust if No Federal Estate Tax Exists

This Article shall apply if my *husband/wife* survives me, I die domiciled in *State*, and, on the date of my death, no Federal estate tax applies with respect to my estate.

A. My Purposes. I intend that the division of the family trust into a state-only marital trust, and a marital trust, shall take full advantage of the increases allowed under applicable Federal income tax law to the basis of assets received from me on account of my death, and to minimize the *state* estate tax due at the later death of my *husband/wife*, without incurring any *state* estate tax at my death.

B. Defining the "State-Only Marital Trust." My fiduciaries shall create by division of the family trust, a "state-only marital trust," which shall be a fractional share of the family trust.

    1. Calculating the Numerator. The numerator of the fraction shall be the largest value of the family trust that can pass free of *State* estate tax were it to pass to an individual other than my *husband/wife*. This value shall be determined after being reduced by reason of all other dispositions of property included in my gross estate for which no deduction is allowed in computing my *State* estate tax, and administration expenses and other charges to principal that are not claimed and allowed as *State* estate tax deductions.

    2. Calculating the Denominator. The denominator of this fraction shall equal the value of the family trust.

C. Defining the "Marital Trust." If my *husband/wife* survives me, the "marital trust" shall be the remaining fractional share of the family trust after subtracting the state-only marital trust.

D. Allocating Assets. The trustee shall allocate assets as the trustee shall consider to be in the best interests of the beneficiaries, valuing each asset on the date or dates of allocation.

Article 13
Administering the Marital Trust

A. Making Elections. If, on the date of my death, a Federal estate tax applies with respect to my estate, my personal representative shall elect to qualify the marital trust for the Federal estate tax marital deduction. My personal representative shall elect to qualify the state-only marital trust for the marital deduction under the laws of *State*, but not for Federal estate tax purposes.

B. Assuring Productivity of Assets. My *husband/wife* may direct the trustee to make any unproductive or underproductive assets of the marital trust and the state-only marital trust productive or to convert them to productive assets within a reasonable time.

C. Receiving and Administering Retirement Payments. The trustee shall do the following with respect to all retirement plan or individual retirement arrangement distributions to which the marital trust or the state-only marital trust may be entitled, of which my *husband/wife* is the designated beneficiary for Federal income tax purposes:

    1. Distributing Greater of Income or Required Minimum Distribution. The trustee shall annually withdraw from such retirement plan trust fund or arrangement the greater of all of the income earned by my *husband/wife*'s share of such plan or arrangement, or the required minimum distribution with respect to my *husband/ wife*, as determined for Federal income tax purposes.

2. Distributing Withdrawn Amounts. The trustee shall annually distribute to my *husband/wife* all amounts withdrawn from such plan or arrangement.

D. Paying Transfer Taxes Generally. The trustee shall, unless my *husband/wife* provides otherwise by specific reference to this paragraph in a valid will or other writing, pay or make arrangements for the payment of the incremental transfer taxes imposed on the marital trust upon the death of my *husband/wife*, from the marital trust.

Article 14
Definitions and Miscellaneous

A. Definitions. The following terms shall have the meaning set forth below for all purposes of this will:

1. "Children" and "Descendants" Defined. "Children" and "descendants" include those now living and those later born, subject to the following rules:

a. "Children" and "descendants" include an adopted person and that adopted person's descendants if, that adopted person is adopted before reaching eighteen (18) years of age;

b. "Children" and "descendants" includes those born outside of wedlock, if, during such child's or descendant's lifetime, his or her parent through whom such child or descendant claims hereunder, has acknowledged such person as his or her child in a writing duly signed and notarized during such parent's lifetime; and

c. "Children" and "descendants" include a child produced before the parent's death by donor artificial insemination, in vitro fertilization or other form of surrogate parenthood, whether or not such child was legally adopted by such parent before such parent's death.

2. "Disinterested Trustee" Defined. A "disinterested trustee" means a trustee who is not an interested trustee.

3. "Fiduciary" Defined. "Fiduciary" or "fiduciaries" shall include my personal representative and the trustee, or if they are different persons, either of them.

4. "Interested Trustee" Defined. An "interested trustee" means a trustee who is also (a) a beneficiary of the trust of which he or she is a trustee or the insured under a policy of insurance owned by a trust of which he or she is a trustee; (b) married to and living together with a beneficiary of the trust of which he or she is a trustee; (c) the father, mother, issue, brother or sister, of a beneficiary of the trust of which he or she is a trustee; (d) an employee of a beneficiary of the trust of which he or she is a trustee; (e) a corporation or any employee of a corporation in which the stock holdings of the trustee and the trust are significant from the viewpoint of voting control; or (f) a subordinate employee of a corporation in which the trustee is an executive.

5. "Personal Effects" Defined. My "personal effects" includes all of my jewelry, clothing, furniture, and other items of tangible personal property, but not money (other than collectible money having an inherent value in excess of its face amount) and not assets that my personal representative shall consider primarily to be used in a trade or business or held for investment. My "personal effects" also includes any transferable casualty insurance policies on any items of tangible personal property. Such policies shall pass to the same person who receives the insured property.

6. **"Personal Representative" Defined.** My "personal representative" shall include any executor, ancillary executor, administrator, or ancillary administrator, whether local or foreign and whether of all or part of my estate, multiple personal representatives, and their successors.

7. **"Residuary Estate" Defined.** My "residuary estate"" means my real and personal estate passing under this will, after distribution of my personal effects and my personal residences under Articles 2 and 3 of this will.

8. **"Transfer Taxes" Defined.** "Transfer taxes" means all estate, inheritance, legacy, succession, and other transfer taxes, including any tax on excess retirement accumulations, imposed with respect to my death by any state, the United States, or by any foreign country. "Transfer taxes" also includes all taxes that are reimbursable under Sections 2207 through 2207B of the Internal Revenue Code of 1986, as amended, which right of reimbursement I hereby waive. "Transfer taxes" also includes all interest and penalties on such taxes.

9. **"Trustee" Defined.** The "trustee" or "trustees" shall include each trustee individually, multiple trustees, and their successors.

B. **Retroactive Legislation.** I include in this instrument certain dispositions and direct certain actions that shall occur only if, on the date of my death, no federal estate tax or Federal generation-skipping transfer tax applies with respect to my estate. These provisions shall not apply if, on the date of my death, no federal estate tax or federal generation-skipping transfer tax, as the case may be, applies with respect to my estate, but such tax or taxes is/are retroactively reinstated before April 1, 2011, and apply under such retroactive legislation with respect to my estate. If such retroactive legislation is finally determined to be unconstitutional or otherwise invalid, these references shall apply as if such retroactive legislation had never been enacted.

C. **Absence of Trust Beneficiaries.** If all of the beneficiaries of any trust under this will should die before the trust assets have vested in them, the trustee shall distribute all of the remaining assets of that trust as follows:

1. **One Half to My Heirs and Distributee.** One half (½) (or all, if there are no persons to take under subparagraph C.2. of this Article) to the heirs and distributees who would have inherited my personal estate, and in such shares as they would have inherited it, had I died unmarried and without a valid will, determined on the later of the date of my death or the date of the death of the last of the trust beneficiaries to die; and

2. **One Half to My *Husband/Wife*'s Distributees.** One half (½) (or all, if there are no persons to take under subparagraph C.1. of this Article) to the heirs and distributees who would have inherited my *husband/wife*'s personal estate, and in such shares as they would have inherited it, had he died unmarried and without a valid

will, determined on the later of the date of my death or the date of the death of the last of the trust beneficiaries to die.

D. Applicable Law. My will shall be governed by and construed according to the laws of the *State*.

E. Joint Ownership. I confirm that all assets owned jointly by me and another person with a right of survivorship should pass outright to my joint owner and my estate shall have no interest in those assets.

F. Number. Whenever the context requires, the singular includes the plural and the plural the singular.

G. Survivorship. No person shall be deemed to have survived me for purposes of inheriting under this will unless he or she is living on the date ninety (90) days after the date of my death.

H. Tax-Related Terms. All tax-related terms shall have the same meaning they have in the Internal Revenue Code of 1986, as amended.

[*Add state-specific signature, attesting witness, and self-proving clauses*]

¶ A.02 FORM 2: SINGLE TRUST REVOCABLE TRUST FOR ESTATE OF $3.5 MILLION TO $6 MILLION—QTIP TRUST—TRUSTEE DIVIDES TRUST INTO NONMARITAL, STATE-ONLY QTIP, AND MARITAL DEDUCTION SHARES IF THERE IS AN ESTATE TAX—TRUSTEE DIVIDES INTO STATE-ONLY MARITAL AND MARITAL TRUSTS IF THERE IS NO ESTATE TAX—TRUSTEE CAN DISTRIBUTE TO SPOUSE MINIMUM AMOUNT OF APPRECIATED ASSETS SUFFICIENT TO ENABLE SPOUSE TO TAKE ADVANTAGE OF AGGREGATE BASIS INCREASE AT SURVIVING SPOUSE'S DEATH—REMAINDER PASSES OUTRIGHT TO CHILDREN AND DESCENDANTS (NO GST TAX PLANNING)—SAME PLANNING AS FORM 1, BUT IN A REVOCABLE TRUST

Revocable Trust of *Grantor*[2]

I, *Grantor*, of [*locality, state*] (sometimes in the first person singular, sometimes the "grantor," and sometimes the "trustee"), make this trust (defined below), which may be referred to as *TrustName*.

Article 1
My Family

I am married to *Spouse* (sometimes referred to as "my *husband/wife*") and I have [*number of children*] children, *Children*.

---

[2] **KEY:**

Grantor	— full name of the grantor
TrustName	— what to call the trust in other documents
Spouse	— full name of grantor's spouse
husband/wife	— "husband" or "wife," as the case may be
Children	— full names of grantor's children
he/she	— "he" or "she" (referring to the spouse)
his/her	— "his" or "her" (referring to the spouse)
him/her	— "him" or "her" (referring to the spouse)
BANK	— name of the first alternate trustee, who must be a bank or other corporate trustee

Article 2
Trustee Shall Hold Trust Funds

The trustee (defined below) shall hold certain property, which may be listed in Schedule A, to be administered according to the terms of the trust instrument. I and anyone else may transfer additional property (including life insurance proceeds, where appropriate), to any trustee (which the trustee may refuse to accept if acceptance is not in the best interests of the trust), at any time during my life or after my death, to be held and administered according to the terms of the trust instrument.

Article 3
Revoking the Trust

I may revoke or amend all or any part of the trust fund at any time, without the consent of anyone else, by delivering to the trustee a written instrument specifying the character and date of the intended amendment or revocation, or by specific reference to the trust in my last will. The duties, powers, or liabilities of the trustee (other than me) cannot, however, be changed without such trustee's prior written consent. The trustee shall transfer all of the trust funds to me or to my estate, if the trust is completely revoked.

Article 4
Administering the Trust During My Life

A. Making Payments to Me. During my life, the trustee shall pay any taxes, commissions, or other expenses incurred with respect to the trust, and distribute to me all of the trust's net income at least annually, and so much of its principal and undistributed income (including all or none) as I may request from time to time, or as the trustee shall deem appropriate for my comfort and care.

1. My Absolute Power to Withdraw Trust Funds. My power to withdraw principal and income from the trust is absolute, and exercisable as to all of the trust funds, by me alone and in all events.

2. Assuring Productivity of Trust Assets. I may direct the trustee not to retain any asset or assets that I shall deem not to be sufficiently productive.

B. Qualifying for the Gift Tax Marital Deduction. I intend that any transfers to the trust by my *husband/wife*, *Spouse*, shall qualify for the Federal gift and estate tax marital deduction and all provisions of the trust shall be construed consistent therewith.

Article 5
Disposing of the Residuary Trust Fund

The trustee shall divide and distribute the residuary trust fund (defined below) at my death, under this Article.

A. If My *Husband/Wife* Survives Me. If my *husband/wife*, *Spouse*, survives me, the trustee shall hold the residuary trust fund under the Article entitled "The Family Trust."

B. If My *Husband/Wife* Does Not Survive Me. If my *husband/wife* does not survive me, the trustee shall distribute the residuary trust fund to my descendants who survive me, *per stirpes*, except that the share for any child or more remote descendant of mine who shall then not yet have reached the age of thirty-five (35) years, shall be held under the Article entitled "Contingent Trust for Certain Beneficiaries."

Article 6
The Family Trust

The family trust shall be held under this Article.

A. Distributing Trust Fund During My *Husband/Wife*'s Life.

    1. Distributing Income. The trustee shall distribute the net income of the family trust quarterly or more frequently to my *husband/wife*, *Spouse*, during *his/her* life.

    2. Distributing Principal. The trustee shall also distribute to my *husband/wife* as much of the principal of the family trust as is appropriate for any purpose.

    3. Distributing Additional Principal if There is No Federal Estate Tax. If the trustee deems it likely that my *husband/wife* will die before January 1, 2011, my trustee shall distribute to my *husband/wife* a fractional share of this trust.

        a. The numerator of this fraction shall be equal to the smallest value of the assets of this trust fund to which the personal representative of my *husband/wife*'s estate could allocate all of the aggregate basis increase allowed to my *husband/wife* under Federal income tax laws, less the amount of such aggregate basis increase that could be allocated to other assets already owned by my *husband/wife* at the time of this distribution.

        b. The denominator of this fraction shall equal the value of this entire trust fund.

B. Distributing Trust Fund At My *Husband/Wife*'s Death.

    1. Distributing Undistributed Income. At my *husband/wife*'s death, the trustee shall distribute to my *husband/wife*'s estate any undistributed income of the family trust.

    2. Appointing Principal. The trustee shall also distribute the principal of the family trust, to the extent it is not used to pay transfer taxes (defined below) as provided below, as my *husband/wife* may direct by specific reference to this special power of appointment in *his/her* last will. My *husband/wife* may appoint the trust fund, either outright or in further trust, but only to or among any one (1) or more of my descendants, and *he/she* may not appoint any portion of the fund of the family trust to my *husband/wife*, *his/her* creditors, *his/her* estate, or the creditors of *his/her* estate.

3. Distributing Unappointed Trust Fund. The trustee shall distribute the unappointed trust fund to my then-living descendants, *per stirpes*, except that the share for any child or more remote descendant of mine who shall then not yet have reached the age of thirty-five (35) years, shall be held for such descendant under the Article entitled "Contingent Trust for Certain Beneficiaries."

C. Dividing the Family Trust. The trustee may, but shall not be required to, divide the family trust into two (2) or more separate and independent trusts. Each separate and independent trust shall be identical in terms, conditions, and beneficial interests, but shall each operate as a separate independent trust.

1. Fractional Shares. The trustee shall divide the family trust on a fractional basis, so that each separate and independent trust shall share proportionately in all increases and decreases in the value of the assets of the trust fund between the date of my death and the date of such division.

2. Selecting Assets to Fund Separate Shares. The trustee may fractionalize each asset to satisfy these separate and independent trusts. The trustee, if the trustee chooses not to fractionalize assets, shall allocate assets as the trustee shall consider to be in the best interests of the beneficiaries, valuing each asset on the date or dates of allocation.

3. Allocating Income. The trustee shall allocate to each separate and independent trust a ratable portion of all of the income earned by my estate and by the family trust after my death, whether earned before or after the assets are in the possession of the trustee, and income earned on assets used to pay charges according to the same fractional shares.

4. Effective Date. All divisions of the family trust shall be effective from the date of my death.

Article 7
Contingent Trust for Certain Beneficiaries

If a beneficiary is entitled to receive any portion of any trust fund held under this instrument while the beneficiary is under the age of thirty-five (35) years, the trustee may retain such assets in a separate trust for that beneficiary.

A. Distributing Trust Fund Before the Contingent Trust Termination Date. Until the contingent trust termination date (defined below), the trustee shall distribute to or for the benefit of the beneficiary as much of the net income and principal as the trustee may consider appropriate for the beneficiary's health, education, support, or maintenance, annually adding to principal any undistributed income.

B. Distributing Trust Fund At the Contingent Trust Termination Date. Upon the contingent trust termination date, the trustee shall distribute the remaining assets to the beneficiary if the beneficiary is then living or otherwise to the beneficiary's estate to be distributed as part of that estate.

    C. "Contingent Trust Termination Date" Defined. The "contingent trust termination date" shall be the earlier of (1) the date on which the beneficiary dies or (2) the date on which the beneficiary reaches the age of thirty-five (35) years.

Article 8
Special Limits on Powers of Interested Trustee

    The following limitations shall apply, notwithstanding other provisions of this instrument.

    A. Limiting Actions by Interested Trustees. No interested trustee (defined below) may participate in the exercise of any discretion to distribute principal to himself or herself, except as is appropriate for his or her health, education, support, and maintenance, or any of them. No interested trustee may participate in the exercise of any discretion to distribute or expend principal or income in a manner that would discharge that trustee's personal obligation to support the beneficiary. No interested trustee may participate in the exercise of any incident of ownership over any policy owned by the trust insuring the life of such trustee.

    B. Disinterested Trustees Exercising Certain Powers. A disinterested trustee (defined below) who is serving as a co-trustee with an interested trustee, may exercise those discretions granted under this instrument the exercise of which by an interested trustee are precluded.

    1. If Multiple Trustees Include an Interested Trustee Who Cannot Act. The number of trustees who must consent to the exercise of a power granted under this instrument, as determined under the Article entitled "The Trustees" shall be determined by treating the interested trustees who are not entitled, under this Article, to participate in the exercise of the power or discretion, as if they were not then serving.

    2. If All Trustees Are Precluded From Acting. If this Article precludes every then-serving trustee from exercising a power otherwise granted to the trustee under this instrument, the then-serving trustee shall appoint a disinterested trustee who may exercise such power (or decline to exercise it) as if that disinterested trustee were the sole then-serving trustee.

Article 9
Paying Transfer Taxes

    The trustee shall pay from the residuary trust fund all transfer taxes, other than generation-skipping transfer taxes, payable by reason of my death on assets passing under this trust.

    A. Apportioning Transfer Taxes. The trustee shall pay transfer taxes imposed on any trust assets includible in my gross estate for Federal estate tax purposes, from those assets, as provided by the laws of the state in which I reside at my death, except as expressly provided elsewhere in this instrument.

B. Apportioning Generation-Skipping Transfer Taxes. The trustee shall pay all generation-skipping transfer taxes imposed on transfers under this trust from those transfers.

C. Apportioning Transfer Taxes Away From Deductible Assets. Assets passing to or in trust for the benefit of my *husband/wife* or to any charitable organization, shall have the full benefit of any available marital or charitable deduction for Federal and other transfer tax purposes, in determining the share of transfer taxes that should be borne by those assets.

Article 10
The Trustees

A. Naming The Trustee. I shall be the initial trustee of this trust.

B. Naming Successor Trustees. I name *BANK*, of [*locality, state*], to be the successor trustee, to serve if I am unable or unwilling to serve or to continue serving.

C. No Surety or Bond. No trustee named by me or by another trustee shall be required to provide surety or other security on a bond.

D. Naming Additional Trustees. I authorize the trustee to appoint any person as an additional trustee, to serve at the pleasure of the appointing trustee.

E. Delegating Powers and Authorities. The trustee may delegate to another trustee any power or authority granted by me to the trustee, to continue at the pleasure of the delegating trustee, unless otherwise agreed. Any person dealing in good faith with a trustee may rely upon that trustee's representation that a delegation has been made and remains in effect under this paragraph.

F. Trustee Resigning. Any trustee may resign by giving written notice specifying the effective date of the resignation to me, if I am then-serving as a trustee, or otherwise to each adult beneficiary to whom trust income then may be distributed.

G. Removing a Trustee. A trustee may be removed by the vote of two thirds (⅔) of the then-living adult beneficiaries to whom trust income may then be distributed.

H. Filling Trustee Vacancies. A corporation no substantial portion of the stock of which is owned by beneficiaries of this trust, may be named as successor trustee to fill any vacancy, by majority vote of the adult beneficiaries to whom trust income then may be distributed.

I. No Liability for Acts or Omissions of Predecessors. No trustee shall be responsible for or need inquire into any acts or omissions of a prior trustee.

J. Compensating Trustees. In addition to reimbursement for expenses, each individual trustee is entitled to reasonable compensation for services. Each corporate trustee is entitled to compensation based on its written fee schedule in effect at the time its services are rendered or as otherwise agreed, and its compensation may vary from time to time based on that schedule.

K. Management Powers. I authorize the trustee to exercise all powers conferred by applicable state law and to do the following in a fiduciary capacity.

1. Prudent Investor Rule. The trustee may hold and retain as part of any trust fund any property transferred by me to the trustee, whether or not such investment would be appropriate for a prudent investor. The trustee may also hold and retain as part of any trust fund any property received from any source, and invest and reinvest the trust fund (or leave it temporarily uninvested) in any type of property and every kind of investment in the same manner as a prudent investor would invest his or her own assets.

2. Holding Assets For Use of Trust Beneficiaries. The trustee may buy and hold in trust, assets that will be used personally by one or more beneficiaries, even if those assets would not otherwise be acquired by a prudent investor investing his or her own assets.

3. Transferring Assets. The trustees may sell or exchange any real or personal property contained in any trust, for cash or credit, at public or private sale, and with such warranties or indemnifications as the trustee may deem advisable.

4. Borrowing Money. The trustee may borrow money (even from a trustee, a beneficiary, or any trust) for the benefit of any trust and secure these debts with assets of the trust.

5. Granting Security Interests. The trustee may grant security interests and execute all instruments creating such interests upon such terms as the trustee may deem advisable.

6. Compromising Claims. The trustee may compromise and adjust claims against or on behalf of any trust on such terms as the trustee may deem advisable.

7. Not Disclosing Nominees. The trustee may take title to any securities in the name of any custodian or nominee without disclosing this relationship.

8. Allocating Between Income and Principal. The trustee may determine whether receipts are income or principal and whether disbursements are to be charged against income or principal to the extent not clearly established by state law. A determination made by the trustee in good faith shall not require equitable adjustments.

9. Making Tax Elections. The trustee may make all tax elections and allocations the trustee may consider appropriate; however, this authority is exercisable only in a fiduciary capacity and may not be used to enlarge or shift any beneficial interest except as an incidental consequence of the discharge of fiduciary duties. A tax election or allocation made by the trustee in good faith shall not require equitable adjustments.

10. Distributing to Custodians for Minors. The trustee shall distribute any of any trust fund to a beneficiary under the age of twenty-one (21) years by distribution to any appropriate person (who may be a trustee) chosen by the trustee as custodian under any appropriate Uniform Transfers (or Gifts) to Minors Act, to be held for the maximum period of time allowed by law. The trustee may also sell any asset that cannot be held under this custodianship and invest the sales proceeds in assets that can be so held.

11. Employing Advisors. The trustee may employ such lawyers, accountants, and other advisors as the trustee may deem useful and appropriate for the administration of any trust. The trustee may employ a professional investment advisor and delegate to this advisor any discretionary investment authorities to manage the investments of any trust, including any investment in mutual funds, investment trusts, or managed accounts, and may rely on the advisor's investment recommendations without liability to any beneficiary.

12. Buying and Holding Life Insurance. The trustee may buy and hold insurance policies on the life of any beneficiary or any person in whom a beneficiary has an insurable interest and may pay the premiums on such policies from income or principal, as the trustee may deem advisable.

13. Dividing and Distributing Assets. The trustee may divide and distribute the assets of any trust fund in kind, in money, or partly in each, without regard to the income tax basis of any asset and without the consent of any beneficiary. The decision of the trustee in dividing any portion of any trust fund between or among two or more beneficiaries, if made in good faith, shall be binding on all persons.

14. Allocating Basis Increase. My personal representative shall allocate any increases in the adjusted basis of property owned by me at the time of my death, whether passing under my Will or otherwise, to the extent such property is eligible to receive such an allocation, as my personal representative deems to be in the best interests of my estate and its beneficiaries. The trustee shall cooperate fully with my personal representative in making these allocations. If, however, there is no personal representative appointed for my estate, then the trustee shall allocate any increases in the adjusted basis of property passing under this trust, to the extent such property is eligible to receive such an allocation, as the trustee deems to be in the best interests of my estate and its beneficiaries. In making these allocations the trustee shall:

a. First, satisfy all charitable bequests with assets to which no aggregate or spousal property basis increases may be allocated;

b. Second, satisfy all charitable bequests with assets that have an adjusted income tax basis closest to zero of all of my assets available to satisfy these bequests;

c. Third, generally not allocate basis increase to assets the gain from the sale of which is not subject to federal income tax under present federal income tax laws; and

d. Fourth, allocate basis increases to assets that are reasonably likely to be sold within the three year period beginning on the date of my death, the sale of which will produce an income tax liability that is taxed at a rate higher than that on long-term capital gains.

Any reference in this paragraph to assets "owned by me on the date of my death" shall apply equally to assets deemed owned by me on the date of my death under the federal income tax rules governing allocation of my aggregate basis increase.

L. Disabled Individual Trustee. An individual trustee may not serve during a disability.

1. "Disabled" Defined. An individual trustee is "disabled" or "under a disability" if: (a) he or she is determined to be legally incompetent by a court of competent jurisdiction; (b) a conservator or guardian for such person has been appointed, based upon his or her incapacity; (c) two (2) physicians licensed to practice medicine in the Commonwealth of Virginia certify in writing to another trustee or a person who would become the successor trustee upon such disability, that in the opinion of such physicians, such individual trustee, as a result of illness, age or other cause, no longer has the capacity to act prudently or effectively in financial affairs; or (d) thirty (30) days after any other trustee or a person who would become the successor trustee upon such disability, requests that such individual trustee provide a certificate from a physician licensed to practice medicine that, in the opinion of such physician, such individual trustee has the capacity to act prudently or effectively in financial affairs and such individual trustee fails to provide such certification. The effective date of such incapacity shall be the date of the order or decree adjudicating the incapacity, the date of the order or decree appointing the guardian or conservator, the date of the certificate of incapacity of the two (2) physicians described above, or thirty (30) days after other trustee or any person who would become the successor trustee upon such disability requests a certificate of capacity and one is not provided, whichever first occurs.

2. When I Regain My Capacity. For purposes of this instrument, I shall be deemed to have regained capacity to serve as a trustee if: (a) there is a finding to that effect by a court of competent jurisdiction; (b) when any conservatorship or guardianship for me has been judicially terminated; or (c) upon the written determination by two (2) physicians licensed to practice medicine in the Commonwealth of Virginia (who need not be the same physicians who made the initial determination of my incapacity) that, in their pinion, my capacity is restored, and I shall have the right again to serve as trustee under this instrument, as of the effective date of my restoration of capacity, if I was serving as a trustee at the time I was determined to be incapacitated.

3. No Liability. No person is liable to anyone for actions taken in reliance on these certifications or for dealing with a trustee other than the one removed for disability based on these certifications. This trust shall indemnify any physician for liability for any opinion rendered in good faith as to the existence or recovery from any disability.

Article 11
Trust Administration

A. Spendthrift Limits. No interest in a trust under this instrument shall be subject to the beneficiary's liabilities or creditor claims or to assignment or anticipation.

B. Protecting Trust Beneficiaries From Creditors. If the trustee shall determine that a beneficiary would not benefit as greatly from any outright distribution of trust income or principal because of the availability of the distribution to the beneficiary's creditors, the trustee shall instead expend those amounts for the benefit of the beneficiary. This direction is intended to enable the trustee to give the beneficiary the fullest possible benefit and enjoyment of all of the trust income and principal to which he or she is entitled.

C. Combining Multiple Trusts. The trustee may invest the assets of multiple trusts in a single fund if the interests of the trusts are accounted for separately.

D. Merging and Consolidating Trust Funds. The trustee may merge or consolidate any trust into any other trust that has the same trustee and substantially the same dispositive provisions.

E. Dividing Trust Funds. The trustee may divide any trust fund into multiple separate trusts.

F. Accountings. The trustee shall not be required to file annual accounts with any court or court official in any jurisdiction.

G. Changing Trust Situs. A disinterested trustee may change the situs of any trust, and to the extent necessary or appropriate, move the trust assets, to a state or country other than the one in which the trust is then administered if the disinterested trustee shall determine it to be in the best interests of the trust or the beneficiaries. The disinterested trustee may elect that the law of such other jurisdiction shall govern the trust to the extent necessary or appropriate under the circumstances.

Article 12
Dividing the Family Trust if a Federal Estate Tax Exists

This Article shall apply if there is, on the date of my death, a Federal estate tax that applies with respect to my estate (including this trust fund).

A. My Purposes. I intend that:

1. Minimizing Federal and *State* Estate Taxes. The division of the family trust into a nonmarital trust, a state-only marital trust and a marital trust, shall minimize the Federal and *State* estate taxes at my *husband/wife*'s death to the extent I can do so while deferring all Federal and *State* estate taxes until both my *husband/wife* and I have died.

2. State-Only Marital Trust. The state-only marital trust shall qualify for the estate tax marital deduction under the laws of *State* and all provisions of this will shall be construed accordingly. The trustee shall, in all matters involving the state-only marital trust, exercise no power in a manner that would infringe upon any legal requirement for the allowance of the estate tax marital deduction under the laws of *State*.

3. Qualifying for Federal Estate Tax Marital Deduction. The marital trust shall qualify for the Federal estate tax marital deduction and all provisions of this trust shall be construed accordingly. The trustee shall, in all matters involving the marital trust, exercise no power in a manner that would infringe upon any legal requirement for the allowance of the Federal estate tax marital deduction.

B. Dividing the Family Trust. The trustee shall divide the family trust under this Article in accordance with the rules set forth in the Article entitled "The Family Trust," in the paragraph entitled "Dividing the Family Trust."

C. Defining the "Nonmarital Trust." If my *husband/wife* survives me, the trustee shall create by division of the family trust a "nonmarital trust," which shall be a fractional share of the family trust.

1. Calculating the Numerator. The numerator of the fraction shall be equal to the smaller of:

a. the largest value of the family trust that can pass free of *State* estate tax were it to pass to an individual other than my *spouse*. This value shall be determined after being reduced by reason of all other dispositions of property included in my gross estate for which no deduction is allowed in computing my *State* estate tax, and administration expenses and other charges to principal that are not claimed and allowed as *State* estate tax deductions; and

b. the largest value of the family trust that can pass free of Federal estate tax by reason of the unified credit allowable with respect to my estate. This value shall be determined after being reduced by reason of my adjusted taxable gifts, all other dispositions of property included in my gross estate for which no deduction is allowed in computing my Federal estate tax, and administration expenses and other charges to principal that are not claimed and allowed as Federal estate tax deductions.

2. Calculating the Denominator. The denominator of the fraction shall equal the value of the family trust.

D. Defining the "State-Only Marital Trust." If my *husband/wife* survives me, and if I die domiciled in *state*, the trustee shall create by division of the family trust, a "state-only marital trust," which shall be a fractional share of the family trust.

1. Calculating the Numerator. The numerator of the fraction shall be the difference between:

a. the largest value of the family trust that can pass free of *State* estate tax were it to pass to an individual other than my *husband/wife*. This value shall be determined after being reduced by reason of all other dispositions of property included in my gross estate for which no deduction is allowed in computing my *State* estate tax, and administration expenses and other charges to principal that are not claimed and allowed as *State* estate tax deductions; and

b. the numerator of the fraction that is used to determine the nonmarital trust.

2. Calculating the Denominator. The denominator of this fraction shall equal the value of the family trust.

E. Calculating Shares Based on Certain Assumptions. The nonmarital trust shall be computed as if no election were made to qualify any property passing as such share under the Federal estate tax marital deduction, and the maximum possible election were made to qualify all property passing as the marital trust for the Federal estate tax marital deduction.

F. Determining the Effect of Disclaimers.

1. Disclaiming the Marital Trust. The trustee shall add to the descendants' trust any portion of the marital trust as to which a qualified disclaimer by or for my *husband/wife* is made. The descendants' trust shall be calculated before any qualified disclaimer by or for my *husband/wife* of any of the marital trust.

2. Apportioning Transfer Taxes to Disclaimed Funds. Transfer taxes imposed on any portion of the marital trust as to which my *husband/wife* has made a qualified disclaimer shall be apportioned to those disclaimed funds.

G. Allocating Assets Between or Among Shares.

1. Making Certain Allocations If My *Husband/Wife* Survives Me. If my *husband/wife* survives me:

a. The trustee shall allocate to the marital trust and the state-only marital trust only assets that can qualify for the Federal estate tax marital deduction.

b. To the extent possible, the trustee shall not allocate to the marital trust or the state-only marital trust assets upon which a foreign death tax is payable.

c. The nonmarital trust shall consist solely of assets includable in my gross estate for Federal estate tax purposes.

2. Making Other Allocations. In other respects, the trustee shall allocate assets as the trustee shall consider to be in the best interests of the beneficiaries, valuing each asset on the date or dates of allocation.

Article 13
Dividing the Family Trust if No Federal Estate Tax Exists

This Article shall apply if my *husband/wife* survives me, I die domiciled in *State*, and, on the date of my death, no Federal estate tax applies with respect to my estate.

A. My Purposes. I intend that the division of the family trust into a state-only marital trust, and a marital trust, shall take full advantage of the increases allowed under applicable Federal income tax law to the basis of assets received from me on account of my death, and to minimize the *state* estate tax due at the later death of my *husband/wife*, without incurring any *state* estate tax at my death.

B. Defining the "State-Only Marital Trust." The trustee shall create by division of the family trust, a "state-only marital trust," which shall be a fractional share of the family trust.

1. Calculating the Numerator. The numerator of the fraction shall be the largest value of the family trust that can pass free of *State* estate tax were it to pass to an individual other than my *husband/wife*. This value shall be determined after being reduced by reason of all other dispositions of property included in my gross estate for which no deduction is allowed in computing my *State* estate tax, and administration expenses and other charges to principal that are not claimed and allowed as *State* estate tax deductions.

2. Calculating the Denominator. The denominator of this fraction shall equal the value of the family trust.

C. Defining the "Marital Trust." If my *husband/wife* survives me, the marital trust shall be the remaining fractional share of the family trust after subtracting the state-only marital trust.

D. Allocating Assets. The trustee shall allocate assets as the trustee shall consider to be in the best interests of the beneficiaries, valuing each asset on the date or dates of allocation.

E. Allocating Trust Income. The trustee shall allocate to each share a ratable portion of all of the income earned by my estate or the trust after my death, whether earned before or after the assets are in the possession of the trustee, and income earned on assets used to pay charges according to the same fractional shares.

Article 14
Administering the Marital Trust

A. Making Elections. If, on the date of my death, a Federal estate tax applies with respect to my estate, my personal representative shall elect to qualify the marital trust for the Federal estate tax marital deduction. My trustee shall elect to qualify the state-only marital trust for the marital deduction under the laws of *State*, but not for Federal estate tax purposes.

B. Assuring Productivity of Assets. My *husband/wife* may direct the trustee to make any unproductive or underproductive assets of the marital trust and the state-only marital trust productive or to convert them to productive assets within a reasonable time.

C. Receiving and Administering Retirement Payments. The trustee shall do the following with respect to all retirement plan or individual retirement arrangement distributions to which the marital trust or the state-only marital trust may be entitled, of which my *husband/wife* is the designated beneficiary for Federal income tax purposes:

1. Distributing Greater of Income or Required Minimum Distribution. The trustee shall annually withdraw from such retirement plan trust fund or arrangement the greater of all of the income earned by my *husband/wife*'s share of such plan or arrangement, or the required minimum distribution with respect to my *husband/wife*, as determined for Federal income tax purposes.

2. Distributing Withdrawn Amounts. The trustee shall annually distribute to my *husband/wife* all amounts withdrawn from such plan or arrangement.

D. Paying Transfer Taxes Generally. The trustee shall, unless my *husband/wife* provides otherwise by specific reference to this paragraph in a valid will or other writing, pay or make arrangements for the payment of the incremental transfer taxes imposed on the marital trust upon the death of my *husband/wife*, from the marital trust.

Article 15
Definitions and Miscellaneous

A. Definitions. The following terms shall have the meaning set forth below for all purposes of this trust:

1. "Children" and "Descendants" Defined. "Children" and "descendants" include those now living and those later born, subject to the following rules:

a. "Children" and "descendants" include an adopted person and that adopted person's descendants if, that adopted person is adopted before reaching eighteen (18) years of age;

b. "Children" and "descendants" includes those born outside of wedlock, if, during such child's or descendant's lifetime, his or her parent through whom such child or descendant claims hereunder, has acknowledged such person as his or her child in a writing duly signed and notarized during such parent's lifetime; and

c. "Children" and "descendants" include a child produced before the parent's death by donor artificial insemination, in vitro fertilization or other form of surrogate parenthood, whether or not such child was legally adopted by such parent before such parent's death.

2. "Disinterested Trustee" Defined. A "disinterested trustee" means a trustee who is not an interested trustee.

3. "Interested Trustee" Defined. An "interested trustee" means a trustee who is also (a) a beneficiary of the trust of which he or she is a trustee or the insured under a policy of insurance owned by a trust of which he or she is a trustee; (b) married to and living together with a beneficiary of the trust of which he or she is a trustee; (c) the father, mother, issue, brother or sister, of a beneficiary of the trust of which he or she is a trustee; (d) an employee of a beneficiary of the trust of which he or she is a trustee; (e) a corporation or any employee of a corporation in which the stock holdings of the trustee and the trust are significant from the viewpoint of voting control; or (f) a subordinate employee of a corporation in which the trustee is an executive.

4. "Personal Representative" Defined. A "personal representative" means the legal representative of a decedent's estate. The "personal representative" shall include any executor, ancillary executor, administrator, or ancillary administrator, whether local or foreign and whether of all or part of my estate, multiple personal representatives, and their successors.

5. "Residuary Trust Fund" Defined. The residuary trust fund means the real and personal property passing under this instrument, after paying any amounts certified by the personal representative of my estate as needed to settle my debts and expenses of estate administration.

6. "Transfer Taxes" Defined. "Transfer taxes" means all estate, inheritance, legacy, succession, and other transfer taxes, including any tax on excess retirement accumulations, imposed with respect to my death by any state, the United States, or by any foreign country. "Transfer taxes" also includes all taxes that are reimbursable under Sections 2207 through 2207B of the Internal Revenue Code of 1986, as amended, which right of reimbursement I hereby waive. "Transfer taxes" also includes all interest and penalties on such taxes.

7. "Trustee" Defined. The "trustee" or "trustees" shall include each trustee individually, multiple trustees, and their successors.

B. Retroactive Legislation. I include in this instrument certain dispositions and direct certain actions that shall occur only if, on the date of my death, no federal estate tax or Federal generation-skipping transfer tax applies with respect to my estate. These provisions shall not apply if, on the date of my death, no federal estate tax or federal generation-skipping transfer tax, as the case may be, applies with respect to my estate, but such tax or taxes is/are retroactively reinstated before April 1, 2011, and apply under such retroactive legislation with respect to my estate. If such retroactive legislation is finally determined to be unconstitutional or otherwise invalid, these references shall apply as if such retroactive legislation had never been enacted.

C. Absence of Trust Beneficiaries. If all of the beneficiaries of any trust under this instrument should die before the trust assets have vested in them, the trustee shall distribute all of the remaining assets of that trust as follows:

1. One Half to My Heirs and Distributee. One half (½) (or all, if there are no persons to take under subparagraph B.2. of this Article) to the heirs and distributees who would have inherited my personal estate, and in such shares as they would have inherited it, had I died unmarried and without a valid will, determined on the later of the date of my death or the date of the death of the last of the trust beneficiaries to die; and

2. One Half to My *Husband/Wife*'s Distributees. One half (½) (or all, if there are no persons to take under subparagraph B.1. of this Article) to the heirs and distributees who would have inherited my *husband/wife*'s personal estate, and in such shares as they would have inherited it, had he died unmarried and without a valid will, determined on the later of the date of my death or the date of the death of the last of the trust beneficiaries to die.

D. Applicable Law. This instrument shall be governed by and construed according to the laws of the *State*.

E. Number. Whenever the context requires, the singular includes the plural and the plural the singular.

F. Survivorship. No person shall be deemed to have survived me for purposes of this instrument, unless he or she is living on the date ninety (90) days after the date of my death.

G. Tax-Related Terms. All tax-related terms shall have the same meaning they have in the Internal Revenue Code of 1986, as amended.

[Add state-specific signature and notary clauses, schedule of assets, and where required, attesting witness clause]

¶ A.03 FORM 3: WILL WITH DISCLAIMER BASED PLANNING FOR ESTATE OF $3.5 MILLION TO $6 MILLION—ALL LEFT TO QTIP TRUST—DISCLAIMER OF QTIP TRUST FUNDS NONMARITAL TRUST FOR SPOUSE AND DESCENDANTS—QTIP TRUST CAN BE DIVIDED TO CREATE STATE-ONLY QTIP TRUST—TRUSTEE CAN DISTRIBUTE TO SPOUSE MINIMUM AMOUNT OF APPRECIATED ASSETS SUFFICIENT TO ENABLE SPOUSE TO TAKE ADVANTAGE OF AGGREGATE BASIS INCREASE AT SURVIVING SPOUSE'S DEATH—REMAINDER PASSES OUTRIGHT TO CHILDREN AND DESCENDANTS (NO GST TAX PLANNING)

Will of *Testator*[3]

I, *Testator*, of [*locality, state*], make this my will. I revoke any other wills and codicils made by me.

Article 1
My Family

I am married to *Spouse* (sometimes referred to as "my *husband/wife*") and I have [*number of children*] children, *Children*.

Article 2
My Personal Effects

A. Disposing of My Personal Effects. I leave my personal effects (defined below) to my *husband/wife*, *Spouse*, if *he/she* survives me, or otherwise to my descendants who survive me, *per stirpes*. If neither my *husband/wife* nor any of my

---

[3] **KEY:**

Testator	— full name of the testator
Spouse	— full name of testator's spouse
husband/wife	— "husband" or "wife," as the case may be
Children	— full names of testator's children
he/she	— "he" or "she" (referring to the spouse)
his/her	— "his" or "her" (referring to the spouse)
him/her	— "him" or "her" (referring to the spouse)
AlternatePR	— name of the alternate personal representative (after spouse)
FirstTrustee	— name of the first trustee
SecondTrustee	— name of the alternate trustee

children nor their descendants survive me, these personal effects shall be added to the residue of my estate. An adult person with whom a minor resides may give a binding receipt for any personal effects passing to the minor.

B. Memorandum. I may make a memorandum of how I wish some of my personal effects to be distributed, and I request that my wishes be followed.

Article 3
My Personal Residence

I leave all of my interest in the properties my personal representative (defined below) shall determine to have been used by me or a member of my family as personal residences to my *husband/wife*, *Spouse*, if *he/she* survives me, to the extent that they do not pass to *him/her* by right of survivorship. Personal residences shall also include all adjoining lands and any related casualty insurance policies.

Article 4
My Residuary Estate

I leave my residuary estate (defined below), as follows:

A. If My *Husband/Wife* Survives Me. I leave my residuary estate, if my *husband/wife*, *Spouse*, survives, me, to the trustee to be held under the article entitled "The "Spouse" Trust". I leave any portion of the *Spouse* trust that my *husband/wife* shall disclaim to the trustee, to be held under the Article entitled "The Family Trust."

B. If My *Husband/Wife* Does Not Survive Me. If my *husband/wife* does not survive me, my personal representative shall distribute my residuary estate to my descendants who survive me, *per stirpes*, except that the share for any child or more remote descendant of mine who shall then not yet have reached the age of thirty-five (35) years, shall be held under the Article entitled "Contingent Trust for Certain Beneficiaries."

Article 5
The *Spouse* Trust

The *Spouse* trust shall be held under this Article.

A. Distributing Trust Fund During My *Husband/Wife*'s Life.

1. Distributing Net Income. The trustee shall distribute the net income of the *Spouse* trust quarterly or more frequently to my *husband/wife*, *Spouse*, during *his/her* life.

2. Distributing Principal. The trustee shall also distribute to my *husband/wife* as much of the principal of the *Spouse* trust as is appropriate for any purpose.

3. Distributing Additional Principal if There is No Federal Estate Tax. If the trustee deems it likely that my *husband/wife* will die before January 1, 2011, my trustee shall distribute to my *husband/wife* a fractional share of this trust.

a. The numerator of this fraction shall be equal to the smallest value of the assets of this trust fund to which the personal representative of my *husband/wife*'s estate could allocate all of the aggregate basis increase allowed to my *husband/wife* under Federal income tax laws, less the amount of such aggregate basis increase that could be allocated to other assets already owned by my *husband/wife* at the time of this distribution.

b. The denominator of this fraction shall equal the value of this entire trust fund.

B. Distributing Trust Fund At My *Husband/Wife*'s Death. At my *husband/wife*'s death, the trustee shall distribute to my *husband/wife*'s estate any undistributed income of the *Spouse* trust. The trustee shall also distribute my residuary estate to my descendants who survive me, *per stirpes*, except that the share for any child or more remote descendant of mine who shall then not yet have reached the age of thirty-five (35) years, shall be held under the Article entitled "Contingent Trust for Certain Beneficiaries."

Article 6.
The Family Trust

The trustee shall hold any portion of the *Spouse* trust that my *husband/wife* disclaims under this article.

A. Trust for My *Husband/Wife* and Descendants. For the rest of the life of my *husband/wife*, the trustee shall distribute to my *husband/wife*, my children, and my more remote descendants, as much of the trust's net income and principal (including all or none) as is appropriate for their health, education, support, or maintenance, annually adding to principal any undistributed trust income. In making these distributions, the trustee shall take into account all other readily available income and assets, including the income and assets of the *Spouse* trust.

B. Distributing Trust Fund at My *Husband/Wife*'s Death. At my *husband/wife*'s death, the trustee shall distribute the remaining assets of the family trust to my descendants who survive me, per stirpes, except that the share for any child or more remote descendant of mine who shall then not yet have reached the age of thirty-five (35) years, shall be held under the Article entitled "Contingent Trust for Certain Beneficiaries."

Article 7
Contingent Trust for Certain Beneficiaries

If a beneficiary is entitled to receive any part of my estate or any portion of any trust fund held under this will while the beneficiary is under the age of thirty-five (35) years, the trustee may retain such assets in a separate trust for that beneficiary.

A. Distributing Trust Fund Before the Contingent Trust Termination Date. Until the contingent trust termination date (defined below), the trustee shall distribute to or for the benefit of the beneficiary as much of the net income and principal as the trustee may consider appropriate for the beneficiary's health, education, support, or maintenance, annually adding to principal any undistributed income.

B. Distributing Trust Fund At the Contingent Trust Termination Date. Upon the contingent trust termination date, the trustee shall distribute the remaining assets to the beneficiary if the beneficiary is then living or otherwise to the beneficiary's estate to be distributed as part of that estate.

C. "Contingent Trust Termination Date" Defined. The "contingent trust termination date" shall be the earlier of (1) the date on which the beneficiary dies or (2) the date on which the beneficiary reaches the age of thirty-five (35) years.

Article 8
Special Limits on Powers of Interested Trustee

The following limitations shall apply, notwithstanding other provisions of this instrument.

A. Limiting Actions by Interested Trustees. No interested trustee (defined below) may participate in the exercise of any discretion to distribute principal to himself or herself, except as is appropriate for his or her health, education, support, and maintenance, or any of them. No interested trustee may participate in the exercise of any discretion to distribute or expend principal or income in a manner that would discharge that trustee's personal obligation to support the beneficiary. No interested trustee may participate in the exercise of any incident of ownership over any policy owned by the trust insuring the life of such trustee.

B. Disinterested Trustees Exercising Certain Powers. A disinterested trustee (defined below) who is serving as a co-trustee with an interested trustee, may exercise those discretions granted under this instrument the exercise of which by an interested trustee are precluded.

1. If Multiple Trustees Include an Interested Trustee Who Cannot Act. The number of trustees who must consent to the exercise of a power granted under this instrument, as determined under the Article entitled "My Fiduciaries" shall be determined by treating the interested trustees who are not entitled, under this Article, to participate in the exercise of the power or discretion, as if they were not then serving.

2. If All Trustees Are Precluded From Acting. If this Article precludes every then-serving trustee from exercising a power otherwise granted to the trustee

under this instrument, the then-serving trustee shall appoint a disinterested trustee who may exercise such power (or decline to exercise it) as if that disinterested trustee were the sole then-serving trustee.

Article 9
Debts, Expenses, and Taxes

A. Paying Debts and Expenses. My personal representative shall pay from my residuary estate my debts (but not before their maturity) and funeral and burial expenses, including the cost of a suitable memorial, without court order.

    1. Paying Certain Joint Debts. My personal representative shall pay only my proportionate share of any debts for which I am jointly liable with my *husband/wife*.

    2. Paying Packing and Shipping Expenses. My personal representative shall pay all packing, shipping, insurance, and other charges relating to the distribution of any of my personal property without seeking reimbursement from the recipient of such personal property.

B. Paying Transfer Taxes. My personal representative shall pay all transfer taxes, other than generation-skipping transfer taxes, payable by reason of my death on assets passing under this will, from my residuary estate.

    1. Apportioning Transfer Taxes on Nonprobate Assets. My personal representative shall apportion transfer taxes imposed on any assets not passing under this will to those assets and the transfer taxes on those assets shall be paid from those assets as provided by the laws of the state in which I reside at my death, except as expressly provided elsewhere in this will.

    2. Apportioning Generation-Skipping Transfer Taxes. My personal representative shall apportion all generation-skipping transfer taxes for which my estate is legally responsible to those generation-skipping transfers, whether or not under this will.

    3. Apportioning Transfer Taxes Away From Deductible Assets. Assets passing to my *husband/wife*, whether under this will or otherwise, or to the *Spouse* trust shall have the full benefit of any marital deduction allowed with respect to such assets, in determining the share of transfer taxes that should be borne by those assets. Assets passing to any charitable organization, whether under this will or otherwise, shall have the full benefit of any available charitable deduction, in determining the share of transfer taxes that should be borne by those assets.

Article 10
My Fiduciaries

A. Naming My Personal Representatives. I name my *husband/wife*, *Spouse*, to be my personal representative, and I give *him/her* the right to name one or more persons to serve with *him/her* or in *his/her* place. If my *husband/wife* fails or ceases to serve and there is no other person serving or named to serve, I name the *AlternatePR*, of [*locality, state*], to be my personal representative.

B. Naming My Trustees. I name *FirstTrustee*, of [*locality, state*], to be the trustee of any trust under this will. If *FirstTrustee* shall be unable or unwilling to serve or to continue serving, I name *SecondTrustee*, of [*locality, state*] to be the trustee of any trust under this will.

C. No Surety or Bond. No personal representative or trustee named by me or by another personal representative or trustee shall be required to provide surety or other security on a bond.

D. Naming Additional Fiduciaries. I authorize my named fiduciaries (defined below) to appoint any person as an additional personal representative or trustee in the same state or another state in which administration may be appropriate to serve at the pleasure of the appointing fiduciaries.

E. Delegating Fiduciary Powers and Authorities. My fiduciaries may delegate to another fiduciary any power or authority granted by me to my fiduciaries, to continue at the pleasure of the delegating fiduciary, unless otherwise agreed. Any person dealing in good faith with a fiduciary may rely upon that fiduciary's representation that a delegation has been made and remains in effect under this paragraph.

F. Fiduciary Resigning.

1. Personal Representative May Resign. A personal representative may resign by giving written notice specifying the effective date of the resignation to the designated successor.

2. Trustee May Resign. Any trustee may resign by giving written notice specifying the effective date of the resignation to the designated successor. If no successor is designated, the resigning trustee shall give notice to each adult beneficiary to whom trust income then may be distributed.

G. Removing a Trustee. A trustee may be removed by the vote of two-thirds (⅔) of the then-living adult beneficiaries to whom trust income may then be distributed.

H. Filling Fiduciary Vacancies.

1. Court Appointing Personal Representative to Fill Vacancy. If no successor personal representative is designated, a court of appropriate jurisdiction shall name a successor personal representative.

2. Beneficiaries Appointing Corporate Trustee to Fill Vacancy. A corporation no substantial portion of the stock of which is owned by beneficiaries of this

trust, may be named as successor trustee to fill any vacancy, by majority vote of the adult beneficiaries to whom trust income then may be distributed.

I. No Liability for Acts or Omissions of Predecessors. No fiduciary shall be responsible for or need inquire into any acts or omissions of a prior fiduciary.

J. Compensating Fiduciaries. In addition to reimbursement for expenses, each individual fiduciary is entitled to reasonable compensation for services. Each corporate fiduciary is entitled to compensation based on its written fee schedule in effect at the time its services are rendered or as otherwise agreed, and its compensation may vary from time to time based on that schedule.

K. Management Powers. I authorize my fiduciaries to exercise all powers conferred by applicable state law and to do the following in a fiduciary capacity.

1. Prudent Investor Rule. My fiduciaries may hold and retain as part of my estate or any trust fund any property owned by me, whether or not such investment would be appropriate for a prudent investor. My fiduciaries may also hold and retain as part of my estate or any trust fund any property received from any source, and invest and reinvest my estate or trust fund (or leave it temporarily uninvested) in any type of property and every kind of investment in the same manner as a prudent investor would invest his or her own assets.

2. Holding Assets For Use of Trust Beneficiaries. My trustee may buy and hold in trust, assets that will be used personally by one or more beneficiaries, even if those assets would not otherwise be acquired by a prudent investor investing his or her own assets.

3. Transferring Assets. My fiduciaries may sell or exchange any real or personal property contained in my estate or any trust, for cash or credit, at public or private sale, and with such warranties or indemnifications as my fiduciaries may deem advisable.

4. Borrowing Money. My fiduciaries may borrow money (even from a fiduciary or beneficiary of my estate or any trust) for the benefit of my estate or any trust and secure these debts with assets of my estate or any trust.

5. Granting Security Interests. My fiduciaries may grant security interests and execute all instruments creating such interests upon such terms as my fiduciaries may deem advisable.

6. Compromising Claims. My fiduciaries may compromise and adjust claims against or on behalf of my estate or any trust on such terms as my fiduciaries may deem advisable.

7. Not Disclosing Nominees. My fiduciaries may take title to any securities in the name of any custodian or nominee without disclosing this relationship.

8. Allocating Between Income and Principal. My fiduciaries may determine whether receipts are income or principal and whether disbursements are to be charged against income or principal to the extent not clearly established by state law.

A determination made by my fiduciaries in good faith shall not require equitable adjustments.

9. Making Tax Elections. My fiduciaries may make all tax elections and allocations my fiduciaries may consider appropriate; however, this authority is exercisable only in a fiduciary capacity and may not be used to enlarge or shift any beneficial interest except as an incidental consequence of the discharge of fiduciary duties. A tax election or allocation made by my fiduciaries in good faith shall not require equitable adjustments.

10. Distributing to Custodians for Minors. My fiduciaries shall distribute any of my estate or any trust fund to a beneficiary under the age of twenty-one (21) years by distribution to any appropriate person (who may be a fiduciary) chosen by my fiduciaries as custodian under any appropriate Uniform Transfers (or Gifts) to Minors Act, to be held for the maximum period of time allowed by law. My fiduciaries may also sell any asset that cannot be held under this custodianship and invest the sales proceeds in assets that can be so held.

11. Employing Advisors. My fiduciaries may employ such lawyers, accountants, and other advisors as my fiduciaries may deem useful and appropriate for the administration of my estate or any trust. My fiduciaries may employ a professional investment advisor and delegate to this advisor any discretionary investment authorities to manage the investments of my estate or any trust, including any investment in mutual funds, investment trusts, or managed accounts, and may rely on the advisor's investment recommendations without liability to any beneficiary.

12. Buying and Holding Life Insurance. My fiduciaries may buy and hold insurance policies on the life of any beneficiary or any person in whom a beneficiary has an insurable interest and may pay the premiums on such policies from income or principal, as my fiduciaries may deem advisable.

13. Dividing and Distributing Assets. My fiduciaries may divide and distribute the assets of my estate or any trust fund in kind, in money, or partly in each, without regard to the income tax basis of any asset and without the consent of any beneficiary. The decision of my fiduciaries in dividing any portion of my estate or any trust fund between or among two or more beneficiaries, if made in good faith, shall be binding on all persons.

14. Allocation of Basis Increase. My personal representative shall allocate any increases in the adjusted basis of property owned by me at the time of my death, whether passing under my Will or otherwise, to the extent such property is eligible to receive such an allocation, as my personal representative deems to be in the best interests of my estate and its beneficiaries. In making these allocations my personal representative shall:

a. First, satisfy all charitable bequests with assets to which no aggregate or spousal property basis increases may be allocated;

b. Second, satisfy all charitable bequests with assets that have an adjusted income tax basis closest to zero of all of my assets available to satisfy these bequests;

c. Third, generally not allocate basis increase to assets the gain from the sale of which is not subject to federal income tax under present federal income tax laws;

d. Fourth, allocate basis increases to assets that are reasonably likely to be sold within the three year period beginning on the date of my death, the sale of which will produce an income tax liability that is taxed at a rate higher than that on long-term capital gains; and

e. Fifth, allocate the remaining basis increase among assets in proportion to each asset's pro rata share of the total appreciation of all such assets owned by this trust on the date of my death.

Any reference in this paragraph to assets "owned by me on the date of my death" shall apply equally to assets deemed owned by me on the date of my death under the federal income tax rules governing allocation of my aggregate basis increase. My personal representative shall not be liable to anyone for any allocation of my basis increases made in good faith, in the absence of gross negligence.

Article 11
Trust Administration

A. Spendthrift Limits. No interest in a trust under this will shall be subject to the beneficiary's liabilities or creditor claims or to assignment or anticipation.

B. Protecting Trust Beneficiaries From Creditors. If the trustee shall determine that a beneficiary would not benefit as greatly from any outright distribution of trust income or principal because of the availability of the distribution to the beneficiary's creditors, the trustee shall instead expend those amounts for the benefit of the beneficiary. This direction is intended to enable the trustee to give the beneficiary the fullest possible benefit and enjoyment of all of the trust income and principal to which he or she is entitled.

C. Combining Multiple Trusts. The trustee may invest the assets of multiple trusts in a single fund if the interests of the trusts are accounted for separately.

D. Merging and Consolidating Trust Funds. The trustee may merge or consolidate any trust into any other trust that has the same trustee and substantially the same dispositive provisions.

E. Dividing Trust Funds. The trustee may divide any trust fund into multiple separate trusts.

F. Accountings. The trustee shall not be required to file annual accounts with any court or court official in any jurisdiction.

G. Changing Trust Situs. A disinterested trustee may change the situs of any trust under this will, and to the extent necessary or appropriate, move the trust assets, to a state or country other than the one in which the trust is then administered if the disinterested trustee shall determine it to be in the best interests of the trust or the

beneficiaries. The disinterested trustee may elect that the law of such other jurisdiction shall govern the trust to the extent necessary or appropriate under the circumstances.

Article 12
Marital Deduction Rules

A. My Purposes. I intend that the *Spouse* trust shall be eligible for qualification for the Federal estate tax marital deduction as qualifying terminable interest property in trust, if my fiduciaries make an appropriate election. My fiduciaries shall, in all matters involving the *Spouse* trust, exercise no power in a manner that would infringe upon any legal requirement for the allowance of the Federal estate tax marital deduction.

B. Making Elections. My personal representative may elect to qualify all or any portion of the *Spouse* trust for the Federal estate tax marital deduction.

C. Partial Elections.

1. Authority. My personal representative may elect to qualify less than all of the *Spouse* trust for the Federal estate tax marital deduction. My personal representative shall, if my personal representative makes such a partial election, divide the trust fund as to which such partial election was made into two (2) separate trusts and make all principal payments first from the trust fund that qualifies for the Federal estate tax marital deduction.

2. Division in Case of Partial Election. The following additional rules shall apply in allocating assets between deducted and nondeducted portions of the *Spouse* trust:

a. My personal representative shall allocate to the deducted share only assets that can qualify for the Federal estate tax marital deduction.

b. My personal representative shall not, to the extent possible, allocate to the deductible share assets upon which a foreign death tax is payable.

c. My personal representative shall allocate to the deductible share solely assets includable in my gross estate for Federal estate tax purposes.

d. My personal representative shall, in other respects, allocate assets between these shares as my personal representative shall consider to be in the best interests of the beneficiaries, valuing each asset on the date of allocation.

D. Assuring Productivity of Assets. My *husband/wife* may direct the trustee to make any unproductive or underproductive assets of the *Spouse* trust productive or to convert them to productive assets within a reasonable time.

E. Receiving and Administering Retirement Payments. If the *Spouse* trust is entitled to receive distributions under any retirement plan or individual retirement arrangement, of which my *husband/wife* is the designated beneficiary for Federal income tax purposes, then the trustee shall do the following:

1. Distributing Greater of Income or Required Minimum Distribution. The trustee shall annually withdraw from such retirement plan trust fund or arrangement the greater of all of the income earned by my *husband/wife*'s share of such plan or arrangement, or the required minimum distribution with respect to my *husband/wife*, as determined for Federal income tax purposes.

2. Distributing Withdrawn Amounts. The trustee shall annually distribute to my *husband/wife* all amounts withdrawn from such plan or arrangement.

F. Paying Transfer Taxes.

1. Paying Transfer Taxes Generally. The trustee shall, unless my *husband/wife* provides otherwise by specific reference to this paragraph in a valid will or other writing, pay or make arrangements for the payment of the incremental transfer taxes imposed on the *Spouse* trust upon the death of my *husband/wife*, from the *Spouse* trust.

2. Paying Transfer Taxes In Case of a Partial QTIP Election. If my personal representative shall elect to qualify only part of the *Spouse* trust for the Federal estate tax marital deduction and shall create two (2) trusts as required by this Article, the transfer taxes imposed on both trusts at my *husband/wife*'s death shall be paid from the deductible trust fund to the extent possible.

G. The "State-Only Marital Trust." If my *husband/wife* survives me, and if I die domiciled in *state*, my fiduciaries shall create by division of the *spouse* trust, a "state-only marital trust," on terms that are otherwise identical with those of the *spouse* trust.

1. The Fractional Share. The share of the *spouse* trust which shall be the state-only marital trust shall be a fractional share of the *spouse* trust.

a. The numerator of the fraction shall be the difference between:

i. The largest value of the family trust that can pass free of *State* estate tax were it to pass to an individual other than my *husband/wife*. This value shall be determined after being reduced by reason of all other dispositions of property included in my gross estate for which no deduction is allowed in computing my *State* estate tax, and administration expenses and other charges to principal that are not claimed and allowed as *State* estate tax deductions; and

ii. The value of any portion of the *spouse* trust that has been disclaimed by my *husband/wife*.

b. The denominator of this fraction shall equal the value of this entire trust fund.

2. Separate Trusts. The state-only marital trust shall be a separate trust from the *spouse* trust, but shall be administered on terms identical to those of the *spouse* trust.

3. Selecting Assets to Fund Separate Trusts. My fiduciaries may fractionalize each asset to divide the *spouse* trust and create the state-only marital trust, but if they choose not to fractionalize assets, they shall allocate assets between these two shares as they shall consider to be in the best interests of the beneficiaries, valuing each asset on the date or dates of allocation.

4. Allocating Income. My fiduciaries shall allocate to the *spouse* trust and the state-only marital trust a ratable portion of all of the income earned by my estate and by the *spouse* trust after my death, whether earned before or after the assets are in the possession of the trustee, and income earned on assets used to pay charges according to the same fractional shares.

5. Effective Date of Division. All divisions of the *spouse* trust shall be effective from the date of my death.

6. State and Federal Elections. My personal representative shall elect to qualify the state-only marital trust for the marital deduction under the laws of *State*, but not for Federal estate tax purposes.

7. Other Provisions. The provisions of this article regarding "Assuring Productivity of Assets," "Receiving and Administering Retirement Payments," and "Paying Transfer Taxes" shall apply equally to the state-only marital trust and the *spouse* trust.

Article 13
Definitions and Miscellaneous

A. Definitions. The following terms shall have the meaning set forth below for all purposes of this will:

1. "Children" and "Descendants" Defined. "Children" and "descendants" include those now living and those later born, subject to the following rules:

a. "Children" and "descendants" include an adopted person and that adopted person's descendants if, that adopted person is adopted before reaching eighteen (18) years of age;

b. "Children" and "descendants" includes those born outside of wedlock, if, during such child's or descendant's lifetime, his or her parent through whom such child or descendant claims hereunder, has acknowledged such person as his or her child in a writing duly signed and notarized during such parent's lifetime; and

c. "Children" and "descendants" include a child produced before the parent's death by donor artificial insemination, in vitro fertilization or other form of surrogate parenthood, whether or not such child was legally adopted by such parent before such parent's death.

2. "Disinterested Trustee" Defined. A "disinterested trustee" means a trustee who is not an interested trustee.

3. "Fiduciary" Defined. "Fiduciary" or "fiduciaries" shall include my personal representative and the trustee, or if they are different persons, either of them.

4. "Interested Trustee" Defined. An "interested trustee" means a trustee who is also (a) a beneficiary of the trust of which he or she is a trustee or the insured under a policy of insurance owned by a trust of which he or she is a trustee; (b) married to and living together with a beneficiary of the trust of which he or she is a trustee; (c) the father, mother, issue, brother or sister, of a beneficiary of the trust of which he or she is a trustee; (d) an employee of a beneficiary of the trust of which he or she is a trustee; (e) a corporation or any employee of a corporation in which the stock holdings of the trustee and the trust are significant from the viewpoint of voting control; or (f) a subordinate employee of a corporation in which the trustee is an executive.

5. "Personal Effects" Defined. My "personal effects" includes all of my jewelry, clothing, furniture, and other items of tangible personal property, but not money (other than collectible money having an inherent value in excess of its face amount) and not assets that my personal representative shall consider primarily to be used in a trade or business or held for investment. My "personal effects" also includes any transferable casualty insurance policies on any items of tangible personal property. Such policies shall pass to the same person who receives the insured property.

6. "Personal Representative" Defined. My "personal representative" or shall include any executor, ancillary executor, administrator, or ancillary administrator, whether local or foreign and whether of all or part of my estate, multiple personal representatives, and their successors.

7. "Residuary Estate" Defined. My "residuary estate" means my real and personal estate passing under this will, after distribution of my personal effects and my personal residences under Articles 2 and 3 of this will.

8. "Transfer Taxes" Defined. "Transfer taxes" means all estate, inheritance, legacy, succession, and other transfer taxes, including any tax on excess retirement accumulations, imposed with respect to my death by any state, the United States, or by any foreign country. "Transfer taxes" also includes all taxes that are reimbursable under Sections 2207 through 2207B of the Internal Revenue Code of 1986, as amended, which right of reimbursement I hereby waive. "Transfer taxes" also includes all interest and penalties on such taxes.

9. "Trustee" Defined. The "trustee" or "trustees" shall include each trustee individually, multiple trustees, and their successors.

B. Retroactive Legislation. I include in this instrument certain dispositions and direct certain actions that shall occur only if, on the date of my death, no federal estate tax or Federal generation-skipping transfer tax applies with respect to my estate. These provisions shall not apply if, on the date of my death, no federal estate tax or federal generation-skipping transfer tax, as the case may be, applies with respect to my estate, but such tax or taxes is/are retroactively reinstated before April 1, 2011, and apply under such retroactive legislation with respect to my estate. If such retroactive legislation is finally determined to be unconstitutional or otherwise invalid, these references shall apply as if such retroactive legislation had never been enacted.

C. Absence of Trust Beneficiaries. If all of the beneficiaries of any trust under this will should die before the trust assets have vested in them, the trustee shall distribute all of the remaining assets of that trust as follows:

1. One Half to My Heirs and Distributee. One half (½) (or all, if there are no persons to take under subparagraph C.2. of this Article) to the heirs and distributees who would have inherited my personal estate, and in such shares as they would have inherited it, had I died unmarried and without a valid will, determined on the later of the date of my death or the date of the death of the last of the trust beneficiaries to die; and

2. One Half to My *Husband/Wife*'s Distributees. One half (½) (or all, if there are no persons to take under subparagraph C.1. of this Article) to the heirs and distributees who would have inherited my *husband/wife*'s personal estate, and in such shares as they would have inherited it, had he died unmarried and without a valid will, determined on the later of the date of my death or the date of the death of the last of the trust beneficiaries to die.

D. Applicable Law. My will shall be governed by and construed according to the laws of the *State*.

E. Joint Ownership. I confirm that all assets owned jointly by me and another person with a right of survivorship should pass outright to my joint owner and my estate shall have no interest in those assets.

F. Number. Whenever the context requires, the singular includes the plural and the plural the singular.

G. Survivorship. No person shall be deemed to have survived me for purposes of inheriting under this will unless he or she is living on the date ninety (90) days after the date of my death.

H. Tax-Related Terms. All tax-related terms shall have the same meaning they have in the Internal Revenue Code of 1986, as amended.

[*Add state-specific signature, attesting witness, and self-proving clauses*]

¶ A.04 FORM 4: REVOCABLE TRUST WITH DISCLAIMER BASED PLANNING FOR ESTATE OF $3.5 MILLION TO $6 MILLION—ALL LEFT TO QTIP TRUST— DISCLAIMER OF QTIP TRUST FUNDS NONMARITAL TRUST FOR SPOUSE AND DESCENDANTS—QTIP TRUST CAN BE DIVIDED TO CREATE STATE-ONLY QTIP TRUST—TRUSTEE CAN DISTRIBUTE TO SPOUSE MINIMUM AMOUNT OF APPRECIATED ASSETS SUFFICIENT TO ENABLE SPOUSE TO TAKE ADVANTAGE OF AGGREGATE BASIS INCREASE AT SURVIVING SPOUSE'S DEATH—REMAINDER PASSES OUTRIGHT TO CHILDREN AND DESCENDANTS (NO GST TAX PLANNING)—SAME PLANNING AS FORM 3, BUT IN A REVOCABLE TRUST

Revocable Trust of *Grantor*[4]

I, *Grantor*, of [*locality, state*] (sometimes in the first person singular, sometimes the "grantor", and sometimes the "trustee"), make this trust (defined below), which may be referred to as *TrustName*.

Article 1
My Family

I am married to *Spouse* (sometimes referred to as "my *husband/wife*") and I have [*number of children*] children, *Children*.

Article 2
Trustee Shall Hold Trust Funds

The trustee (defined below) shall hold certain property, which may be listed in Schedule A, to be administered according to the terms of the trust instrument. I and

---

[4] **KEY:**

Grantor	— full name of the grantor
TrustName	— what to call the trust in other documents
Spouse	— full name of grantor's spouse
husband/wife	— "husband" or "wife", as the case may be
Children	— full names of grantor's children
he/she	— "he" or "she" (referring to the spouse)
his/her	— "his" or "her" (referring to the spouse)
him/her	— "him" or "her" (referring to the spouse)
BANK	— name of the first alternate trustee, who must be a bank or other corporate trustee

anyone else may transfer additional property (including life insurance proceeds, where appropriate), to any trustee (which the trustee may refuse to accept if acceptance is not in the best interests of the trust), at any time during my life or after my death, to be held and administered according to the terms of the trust instrument.

Article 3
Revoking the Trust

I may revoke or amend all or any part of the trust fund at any time, without the consent of anyone else, by delivering to the trustee a written instrument specifying the character and date of the intended amendment or revocation, or by specific reference to the trust in my last will. The duties, powers, or liabilities of the trustee (other than me) cannot, however, be changed without such trustee's prior written consent. The trustee shall transfer all of the trust funds to me or to my estate, if the trust is completely revoked.

Article 4
Administering the Trust During My Life

A. Making Payments to Me. During my life, the trustee shall pay any taxes, commissions, or other expenses incurred with respect to the trust, and distribute to me all of the trust's net income at least annually, and so much of its principal and undistributed income (including all or none) as I may request from time to time, or as the trustee shall deem appropriate for my comfort and care.

1. My Absolute Power to Withdraw Trust Funds. My power to withdraw principal and income from the trust is absolute, and exercisable as to all of the trust funds, by me alone and in all events.

2. Assuring Productivity of Trust Assets. I may direct the trustee not to retain any asset or assets that I shall deem not to be sufficiently productive.

B. Qualifying for the Gift Tax Marital Deduction. I intend that any transfers to the trust by my *husband/wife*, *Spouse*, shall qualify for the Federal gift and estate tax marital deduction and all provisions of the trust shall be construed consistent therewith.

Article 5
Disposing of the Residuary Trust Fund

The trustee shall divide and distribute the residuary trust fund (defined below) at my death, under this Article:

A. If My *Husband/Wife* Survives Me. If my *husband/wife*, *Spouse*, survives, me, the trustee shall hold the residuary trust fund under the article entitled "The *Spouse* Trust". The trustee shall hold any portion of the *Spouse* trust that my *husband/wife* shall disclaim under the Article entitled "The Family Trust."

B. If My *Husband/Wife* Does Not Survive Me. If my *husband/wife* does not survive me, the trustee shall distribute the residuary trust fund to my descendants who survive me, *per stirpes*, except that the share for any child or more remote descendant of mine who shall then not yet have reached the age of thirty-five (35) years, shall be held under the Article entitled "Contingent Trust for Certain Beneficiaries."

Article 6
The *Spouse* Trust

The *Spouse* trust shall be held under this Article.

A. Distributing Trust Fund During My *Husband/Wife*'s Life.

1. Distributing Income. The trustee shall distribute the net income of the *Spouse* trust quarterly or more frequently to my *husband/wife*, *Spouse*, during *his/her* life.

2. Distributing Principal. The trustee shall also distribute to my *husband/wife* as much of the principal of the *Spouse* trust as is appropriate for any purpose.

3. Distributing Additional Principal if There is No Federal Estate Tax. If the trustee deems it likely that my *husband/wife* will die before January 1, 2011, the trustee shall distribute to my *husband/wife* a fractional share of this trust.

a. The numerator of this fraction shall be equal to the smallest value of the assets of this trust fund to which the personal representative of my *husband/wife*'s estate could allocate all of the aggregate basis increase allowed to my *husband/wife* under Federal income tax laws, less the amount of such aggregate basis increase that could be allocated to other assets already owned by my *husband/wife* at the time of this distribution.

b. The denominator of this fraction shall equal the value of the *spouse* trust fund.

B. Distributing Trust Fund At My *Husband/Wife*'s Death.

1. Distributing Undistributed Income. At my *husband/wife*'s death, the trustee shall distribute to my *husband/wife*'s estate any undistributed income of the *Spouse* trust.

2. Distributing Principal. At my *husband/wife*'s death, the trustee shall also distribute my residuary estate to my descendants who survive me, *per stirpes*, except that the share for any child or more remote descendant of mine who shall then not yet have reached the age of thirty-five (35) years, shall be held under the Article entitled "Contingent Trust for Certain Beneficiaries."

Article 7
The Family Trust

The trustee shall hold any portion of the *Spouse* trust that my *husband/wife* disclaims under this article.

A. Trust for My *Husband/Wife* and Descendants. For the rest of the life of my *husband/wife*, the trustee shall distribute to my *husband/wife*, my children, and my more remote descendants, as much of the trust's net income and principal (including all or none) as is appropriate for their health, education, support, or maintenance, annually adding to principal any undistributed trust income. In making these distributions, the trustee shall take into account all other readily available income and assets, including the income and assets of the *Spouse* trust.

B. Distributing Trust Fund at My *Husband/Wife*'s Death. At my *husband/wife*'s death, the trustee shall distribute the remaining assets of the family trust to my descendants who survive me, per stirpes, except that the share for any child or more remote descendant of mine who shall then not yet have reached the age of thirty-five (35) years, shall be held under the Article entitled "Contingent Trust for Certain Beneficiaries."

Article 8
Contingent Trust for Certain Beneficiaries

If a beneficiary is entitled to receive any portion of any trust fund held under this instrument while the beneficiary is under the age of thirty-five (35) years, the trustee may retain such assets in a separate trust for that beneficiary.

A. Distributing Trust Fund Before the Contingent Trust Termination Date. Until the contingent trust termination date (defined below), the trustee shall distribute to or for the benefit of the beneficiary as much of the net income and principal as the trustee may consider appropriate for the beneficiary's health, education, support, or maintenance, annually adding to principal any undistributed income.

B. Distributing Trust Fund At the Contingent Trust Termination Date. Upon the contingent trust termination date, the trustee shall distribute the remaining assets to the beneficiary if the beneficiary is then living or otherwise to the beneficiary's estate to be distributed as part of that estate.

C. "Contingent Trust Termination Date" Defined. The "contingent trust termination date" shall be the earlier of (1) the date on which the beneficiary dies or (2) the date on which the beneficiary reaches the age of thirty-five (35) years.

Article 9
Special Limits on Powers of Interested Trustee

The following limitations shall apply, notwithstanding other provisions of this instrument.

A. Limiting Actions by Interested Trustees. No interested trustee (defined below) may participate in the exercise of any discretion to distribute principal to himself or herself, except as is appropriate for his or her health, education, support, and maintenance, or any of them. No interested trustee may participate in the exercise of any discretion to distribute or expend principal or income in a manner that would discharge that trustee's personal obligation to support the beneficiary. No interested trustee may participate in the exercise of any incident of ownership over any policy owned by the trust insuring the life of such trustee.

B. Disinterested Trustees Exercising Certain Powers. A disinterested trustee (defined below) who is serving as a co-trustee with an interested trustee, may exercise those discretions granted under this instrument the exercise of which by an interested trustee are precluded.

1. If Multiple Trustees Include an Interested Trustee Who Cannot Act. The number of trustees who must consent to the exercise of a power granted under this instrument, as determined under the Article entitled "The Trustees" shall be determined by treating the interested trustees who are not entitled, under this Article, to participate in the exercise of the power or discretion, as if they were not then serving.

2. If All Trustees Are Precluded From Acting. If this Article precludes every then-serving trustee from exercising a power otherwise granted to the trustee under this instrument, the then-serving trustee shall appoint a disinterested trustee who may exercise such power (or decline to exercise it) as if that disinterested trustee were the sole then-serving trustee.

Article 10
Paying Transfer Taxes

The trustee shall pay from the residuary trust fund all transfer taxes, other than generation-skipping transfer taxes, payable by reason of my death on assets passing under this trust.

A. Apportioning Transfer Taxes. The trustee shall pay transfer taxes imposed on any trust assets includible in my gross estate for Federal estate tax purposes, from those assets, as provided by the laws of the state in which I reside at my death, except as expressly provided elsewhere in this instrument.

B. Apportioning Generation-Skipping Transfer Taxes. The trustee shall pay all generation-skipping transfer taxes imposed on transfers under this trust from those transfers.

C. Apportioning Transfer Taxes Away From Deductible Assets. Assets passing to or in trust for the benefit of my *husband/wife* or to any charitable organization, shall have the full benefit of any available marital or charitable deduction for Federal and other transfer tax purposes, in determining the share of transfer taxes that should be borne by those assets.

Article 11
The Trustees

A. Naming The Trustee. I shall be the initial trustee of this trust.

B. Naming Successor Trustees. I name *BANK*, of [*locality, state*], to be the successor trustee, to serve if I am unable or unwilling to serve or to continue serving.

C. No Surety or Bond. No trustee named by me or by another trustee shall be required to provide surety or other security on a bond.

D. Naming Additional Trustees. I authorize the trustee to appoint any person as an additional trustee, to serve at the pleasure of the appointing trustee.

E. Delegating Powers and Authorities. The trustee may delegate to another trustee any power or authority granted by me to the trustee, to continue at the pleasure of the delegating trustee, unless otherwise agreed. Any person dealing in good faith with a trustee may rely upon that trustee's representation that a delegation has been made and remains in effect under this paragraph.

F. Trustee Resigning. Any trustee may resign by giving written notice specifying the effective date of the resignation to me, if I am then-serving as a trustee, or otherwise to each adult beneficiary to whom trust income then may be distributed.

G. Removing a Trustee. A trustee may be removed by the vote of two thirds (⅔) of the then-living adult beneficiaries to whom trust income may then be distributed.

H. Filling Trustee Vacancies. A corporation no substantial portion of the stock of which is owned by beneficiaries of this trust, may be named as successor trustee to fill any vacancy, by majority vote of the adult beneficiaries to whom trust income then may be distributed.

I. No Liability for Acts or Omissions of Predecessors. No trustee shall be responsible for or need inquire into any acts or omissions of a prior trustee.

J. Compensating Trustees. In addition to reimbursement for expenses, each individual trustee is entitled to reasonable compensation for services. Each corporate trustee is entitled to compensation based on its written fee schedule in effect at the time its services are rendered or as otherwise agreed, and its compensation may vary from time to time based on that schedule.

K. Management Powers. I authorize the trustee to exercise all powers conferred by applicable state law and to do the following in a fiduciary capacity.

    1. Prudent Investor Rule. The trustee may hold and retain as part of any trust fund any property transferred by me to the trustee, whether or not such investment would be appropriate for a prudent investor. The trustee may also hold and retain as part of any trust fund any property received from any source, and invest and reinvest the trust fund (or leave it temporarily uninvested) in any type of property and every kind of investment in the same manner as a prudent investor would invest his or her own assets.

2. Holding Assets For Use of Trust Beneficiaries. The trustee may buy and hold in trust, assets that will be used personally by one or more beneficiaries, even if those assets would not otherwise be acquired by a prudent investor investing his or her own assets.

3. Transferring Assets. The trustees may sell or exchange any real or personal property contained in any trust, for cash or credit, at public or private sale, and with such warranties or indemnifications as the trustee may deem advisable.

4. Borrowing Money. The trustee may borrow money (even from a trustee, a beneficiary, or any trust) for the benefit of any trust and secure these debts with assets of the trust.

5. Granting Security Interests. The trustee may grant security interests and execute all instruments creating such interests upon such terms as the trustee may deem advisable.

6. Compromising Claims. The trustee may compromise and adjust claims against or on behalf of any trust on such terms as the trustee may deem advisable.

7. Not Disclosing Nominees. The trustee may take title to any securities in the name of any custodian or nominee without disclosing this relationship.

8. Allocating Between Income and Principal. The trustee may determine whether receipts are income or principal and whether disbursements are to be charged against income or principal to the extent not clearly established by state law. A determination made by the trustee in good faith shall not require equitable adjustments.

9. Making Tax Elections. The trustee may make all tax elections and allocations the trustee may consider appropriate; however, this authority is exercisable only in a fiduciary capacity and may not be used to enlarge or shift any beneficial interest except as an incidental consequence of the discharge of fiduciary duties. A tax election or allocation made by the trustee in good faith shall not require equitable adjustments.

10. Distributing to Custodians for Minors. The trustee shall distribute any of any trust fund to a beneficiary under the age of twenty-one (21) years by distribution to any appropriate person (who may be a trustee) chosen by the trustee as custodian under any appropriate Uniform Transfers (or Gifts) to Minors Act, to be held for the maximum period of time allowed by law. The trustee may also sell any asset that cannot be held under this custodianship and invest the sales proceeds in assets that can be so held.

11. Employing Advisors. The trustee may employ such lawyers, accountants, and other advisors as the trustee may deem useful and appropriate for the administration of any trust. The trustee may employ a professional investment advisor and delegate to this advisor any discretionary investment authorities to manage the investments of any trust, including any investment in mutual funds, investment trusts, or managed accounts, and may rely on the advisor's investment recommendations without liability to any beneficiary.

12. Buying and Holding Life Insurance. The trustee may buy and hold insurance policies on the life of any beneficiary or any person in whom a beneficiary has an insurable interest and may pay the premiums on such policies from income or principal, as the trustee may deem advisable.

13. Dividing and Distributing Assets. The trustee may divide and distribute the assets of any trust fund in kind, in money, or partly in each, without regard to the income tax basis of any asset and without the consent of any beneficiary. The decision of the trustee in dividing any portion of any trust fund between or among two or more beneficiaries, if made in good faith, shall be binding on all persons.

14. Allocation of Basis Increase. My personal representative shall allocate any increases in the adjusted basis of property owned by me at the time of my death, whether passing under my Will or otherwise, to the extent such property is eligible to receive such an allocation, as my personal representative deems to be in the best interests of my estate and its beneficiaries. The trustee shall cooperate fully with my personal representative in making these allocations. If, however, there is no personal representative appointed for my estate, then the trustee shall allocate any increases in the adjusted basis of property passing under this trust, to the extent such property is eligible to receive such an allocation, as the trustee deems to be in the best interests of my estate and its beneficiaries. In making these allocations the trustee shall:

a. First, satisfy all charitable bequests with assets to which no aggregate or spousal property basis increases may be allocated;

b. Second, satisfy all charitable bequests with assets that have an adjusted income tax basis closest to zero of all of my assets available to satisfy these bequests;

c. Third, generally not allocate basis increase to assets the gain from the sale of which is not subject to federal income tax under present federal income tax laws;

d. Fourth, allocate basis increases to assets that are reasonably likely to be sold within the three year period beginning on the date of my death, the sale of which will produce an income tax liability that is taxed at a rate higher than that on long-term capital gains; and

e. Fifth, allocate the remaining basis increase among assets in proportion to each asset's pro rata share of the total appreciation of all such assets owned by this trust on the date of my death.

Any reference in this paragraph to assets "owned by me on the date of my death" shall apply equally to assets deemed owned by me on the date of my death under the federal income tax rules governing allocation of my aggregate basis increase. The trustee shall not be liable to anyone for any allocation of my basis increases made in good faith, in the absence of gross negligence.

L. Disabled Individual Trustee. An individual trustee may not serve during a disability.

1. "Disabled" Defined. An individual trustee is "disabled" or "under a disability" if: (a) he or she is determined to be legally incompetent by a court of competent jurisdiction; (b) a conservator or guardian for such person has been appointed, based upon his or her incapacity; (c) two (2) physicians licensed to practice medicine in the Commonwealth of Virginia certify in writing to another trustee or a person who would become the successor trustee upon such disability, that in the opinion of such physicians, such individual trustee, as a result of illness, age or other cause, no longer has the capacity to act prudently or effectively in financial affairs; or (d) thirty (30) days after any other trustee or a person who would become the successor trustee upon such disability, requests that such individual trustee provide a certificate from a physician licensed to practice medicine that, in the opinion of such physician, such individual trustee has the capacity to act prudently or effectively in financial affairs and such individual trustee fails to provide such certification. The effective date of such incapacity shall be the date of the order or decree adjudicating the incapacity, the date of the order or decree appointing the guardian or conservator, the date of the certificate of incapacity of the two (2) physicians described above, or thirty (30) days after other trustee or any person who would become the successor trustee upon such disability requests a certificate of capacity and one is not provided, whichever first occurs.

2. When I Regain My Capacity. For purposes of this instrument, I shall be deemed to have regained capacity to serve as a trustee if: (a) there is a finding to that effect by a court of competent jurisdiction; (b) when any conservatorship or guardianship for me has been judicially terminated; or (c) upon the written determination by two (2) physicians licensed to practice medicine in the Commonwealth of Virginia (who need not be the same physicians who made the initial determination of my incapacity) that, in their pinion, my capacity is restored, and I shall have the right again to serve as trustee under this instrument, as of the effective date of my restoration of capacity, if I was serving as a trustee at the time I was determined to be incapacitated.

3. No Liability. No person is liable to anyone for actions taken in reliance on these certifications or for dealing with a trustee other than the one removed for disability based on these certifications. This trust shall indemnify any physician for liability for any opinion rendered in good faith as to the existence or recovery from any disability.

Article 12
Trust Administration

A. Spendthrift Limits. No interest in a trust under this instrument shall be subject to the beneficiary's liabilities or creditor claims or to assignment or anticipation.

B. Protecting Trust Beneficiaries From Creditors. If the trustee shall determine that a beneficiary would not benefit as greatly from any outright distribution of trust income or principal because of the availability of the distribution to the beneficiary's creditors, the trustee shall instead expend those amounts for the benefit of the beneficiary. This direction is intended to enable the trustee to give the beneficiary the fullest possible benefit and enjoyment of all of the trust income and principal to which he or she is entitled.

C. Combining Multiple Trusts. The trustee may invest the assets of multiple trusts in a single fund if the interests of the trusts are accounted for separately.

D. Merging and Consolidating Trust Funds. The trustee may merge or consolidate any trust into any other trust that has the same trustee and substantially the same dispositive provisions.

E. Dividing Trust Funds. The trustee may divide any trust fund into multiple separate trusts.

F. Accountings. The trustee shall not be required to file annual accounts with any court or court official in any jurisdiction.

G. Changing Trust Situs. A disinterested trustee may change the situs of any trust, and to the extent necessary or appropriate, move the trust assets, to a state or country other than the one in which the trust is then administered if the disinterested trustee shall determine it to be in the best interests of the trust or the beneficiaries. The disinterested trustee may elect that the law of such other jurisdiction shall govern the trust to the extent necessary or appropriate under the circumstances.

Article 13
Marital Deduction Rules

A. My Purposes. I intend that the *Spouse* trust shall be eligible for qualification for the Federal estate tax marital deduction as qualifying terminable interest property in trust, if my personal representative or the trustee makes an appropriate election. The trustee shall, in all matters involving the *Spouse* trust, exercise no power in a manner that would infringe upon any legal requirement for the allowance of the Federal estate tax marital deduction.

B. Making Elections. My personal representative or the trustee may elect to qualify all or any portion of the *Spouse* trust for the Federal estate tax marital deduction.

C. Partial Elections.

1. Authority. My personal representative or the trustee may elect to qualify less than all of the *Spouse* trust for the Federal estate tax marital deduction. The trustee shall, if my personal representative or the trustee makes such a partial election, divide the trust fund as to which such partial election was made into two (2) separate trusts and make all principal payments first from the trust fund that qualifies for the Federal estate tax marital deduction.

2. Division in Case of Partial Election. The following additional rules shall apply in allocating assets between deducted and nondeducted portions of the *Spouse* trust:

a. The trustee shall allocate to the deducted share only assets that can qualify for the Federal estate tax marital deduction.

b. The trustee shall not, to the extent possible, allocate to the deductible share assets upon which a foreign death tax is payable.

c. The trustee shall allocate to the deductible share solely assets includable in my gross estate for Federal estate tax purposes.

d. The trustee shall, in other respects, allocate assets between these shares as my personal representative shall consider to be in the best interests of the beneficiaries, valuing each asset on the date of allocation.

D. Assuring Productivity of Assets. My *husband/wife* may direct the trustee to make any unproductive or underproductive assets of the *Spouse* trust productive or to convert them to productive assets within a reasonable time.

E. Receiving and Administering Retirement Payments. If the *Spouse* trust is entitled to receive distributions under any retirement plan or individual retirement arrangement, of which my *husband/wife* is the designated beneficiary for Federal income tax purposes, then the trustee shall do the following:

1. Distributing Greater of Income or Required Minimum Distribution. The trustee shall annually withdraw from such retirement plan trust fund or arrangement the greater of all of the income earned by my *husband/wife*'s share of such plan or arrangement, or the required minimum distribution with respect to my *husband/wife*, as determined for Federal income tax purposes.

2. Distributing Withdrawn Amounts. The trustee shall annually distribute to my *husband/wife* all amounts withdrawn from such plan or arrangement.

F. Paying Transfer Taxes.

1. Paying Transfer Taxes Generally. The trustee shall, unless my *husband/wife* provides otherwise by specific reference to this paragraph in a valid will or other writing, pay or make arrangements for the payment of the incremental transfer taxes imposed on the *Spouse* trust upon the death of my *husband/wife*, from the *Spouse* trust.

2. Paying Transfer Taxes In Case of a Partial QTIP Election. If my personal representative or the trustee shall elect to qualify only part of the *Spouse* trust for the Federal estate tax marital deduction and shall create two (2) trusts as required by this Article, the transfer taxes imposed on both trusts at my *husband/wife*'s death shall be paid from the deductible trust fund to the extent possible.

G. The "State-Only Marital Trust." If my *husband/wife* survives me, and if I die domiciled in *state*, my fiduciaries shall create by division of the *spouse* trust, a "state-only marital trust," on terms that are otherwise identical with those of the *spouse* trust.

1. The Fractional Share. The share of the *spouse* trust which shall be the state-only marital trust shall be a fractional share of the *spouse* trust.

a. The numerator of the fraction shall be the difference between:

i. The largest value of the family trust that can pass free of *State* estate tax were it to pass to an individual other than my *husband/wife*. This value shall be determined after being reduced by reason of all other dispositions of property included in my gross estate for which no deduction is allowed in computing my *State* estate tax, and administration expenses and other charges to principal that are not claimed and allowed as *State* estate tax deductions; and

ii. The value of any portion of the *spouse* trust that has been disclaimed by my *husband/wife*.

b. The denominator of this fraction shall equal the value of the residuary trust fund.

2. Separate Trusts. The state-only marital trust shall be a separate trust from the *spouse* trust, but shall be administered on terms identical to those of the *spouse* trust.

3. Selecting Assets to Fund Separate Trusts. My fiduciaries may fractionalize each asset to divide the *spouse* trust and create the state-only marital trust, but if they choose not to fractionalize assets, they shall allocate assets between these two shares as they shall consider to be in the best interests of the beneficiaries, valuing each asset on the date or dates of allocation.

4. Allocating Income. My fiduciaries shall allocate to the *spouse* trust and the state-only marital trust a ratable portion of all of the income earned by my estate and by the *spouse* trust after my death, whether earned before or after the assets are in the possession of the trustee, and income earned on assets used to pay charges according to the same fractional shares.

5. Effective Date of Division. All divisions of the *spouse* trust shall be effective from the date of my death.

6. State and Federal Elections. My personal representative shall elect to qualify the state-only marital trust for the marital deduction under the laws of *State*, but not for Federal estate tax purposes.

7. Other Provisions. The provisions of this article regarding "Assuring Productivity of Assets," "Receiving and Administering Retirement Payments," and "Paying Transfer Taxes" shall apply equally to the state-only marital trust and the *spouse* trust.

Article 14
Definitions and Miscellaneous

A. Definitions. The following terms shall have the meaning set forth below for all purposes of this trust:

1. "Children" and "Descendants" Defined. "Children" and "descendants" include those now living and those later born, subject to the following rules:

a. "Children" and "descendants" include an adopted person and that adopted person's descendants if, that adopted person is adopted before reaching eighteen (18) years of age;

b. "Children" and "descendants" includes those born outside of wedlock, if, during such child's or descendant's lifetime, his or her parent through whom such child or descendant claims hereunder, has acknowledged such person as his or her child in a writing duly signed and notarized during such parent's lifetime; and

c. "Children" and "descendants" include a child produced before the parent's death by donor artificial insemination, in vitro fertilization or other form of surrogate parenthood, whether or not such child was legally adopted by such parent before such parent's death.

2. "Disinterested Trustee" Defined. A "disinterested trustee" means a trustee who is not an interested trustee.

3. "Interested Trustee" Defined. An "interested trustee" means a trustee who is also (a) a beneficiary of the trust of which he or she is a trustee or the insured under a policy of insurance owned by a trust of which he or she is a trustee; (b) married to and living together with a beneficiary of the trust of which he or she is a trustee; (c) the father, mother, issue, brother or sister, of a beneficiary of the trust of which he or she is a trustee; (d) an employee of a beneficiary of the trust of which he or she is a trustee; (e) a corporation or any employee of a corporation in which the stock holdings of the trustee and the trust are significant from the viewpoint of voting control; or (f) a subordinate employee of a corporation in which the trustee is an executive.

4. "Personal Representative" Defined. A "personal representative" means the legal representative of a decedent's estate. The "personal representative" shall include any executor, ancillary executor, administrator, or ancillary administrator, whether local or foreign and whether of all or part of my estate, multiple personal representatives, and their successors.

5. "Residuary Trust Fund" Defined. The residuary trust fund means the real and personal property passing under this instrument, after paying any amounts certified by the personal representative of my estate as needed to settle my debts and expenses of estate administration.

6. "Transfer Taxes" Defined. "Transfer taxes" means all estate, inheritance, legacy, succession, and other transfer taxes, including any tax on excess retirement accumulations, imposed with respect to my death by any state, the United States, or by any foreign country. "Transfer taxes" also includes all taxes that are reimbursable under Sections 2207 through 2207B of the Internal Revenue Code of 1986, as amended, which right of reimbursement I hereby waive. "Transfer taxes" also includes all interest and penalties on such taxes.

7. "Trustee" Defined. The "trustee" or "trustees" shall include each trustee individually, multiple trustees, and their successors.

B. Retroactive Legislation. I include in this instrument certain dispositions and direct certain actions that shall occur only if, on the date of my death, no federal estate tax or Federal generation-skipping transfer tax applies with respect to my estate. These provisions shall not apply if, on the date of my death, no federal estate tax or federal generation-skipping transfer tax, as the case may be, applies with respect to my estate, but such tax or taxes is/are retroactively reinstated before April 1, 2011, and apply under such retroactive legislation with respect to my estate. If such retroactive legislation is finally determined to be unconstitutional or otherwise invalid, these references shall apply as if such retroactive legislation had never been enacted.

C. Absence of Trust Beneficiaries. If all of the beneficiaries of any trust under this instrument should die before the trust assets have vested in them, the trustee shall distribute all of the remaining assets of that trust as follows:

1. One Half to My Heirs and Distributee. One half (½) (or all, if there are no persons to take under subparagraph C.2. of this Article) to the heirs and distributees who would have inherited my personal estate, and in such shares as they would have inherited it, had I died unmarried and without a valid will, determined on the later of the date of my death or the date of the death of the last of the trust beneficiaries to die; and

2. One Half to My *Husband/Wife*'s Distributees. One half (½) (or all, if there are no persons to take under subparagraph C.1. of this Article) to the heirs and distributees who would have inherited my *husband/wife*'s personal estate, and in such shares as they would have inherited it, had he died unmarried and without a valid will, determined on the later of the date of my death or the date of the death of the last of the trust beneficiaries to die.

D. Applicable Law. This instrument shall be governed by and construed according to the laws of the *State*.

E. Number. Whenever the context requires, the singular includes the plural and the plural the singular.

F. Survivorship. No person shall be deemed to have survived me for purposes of this instrument, unless he or she is living on the date ninety (90) days after the date of my death.

G. Tax-Related Terms. All tax-related terms shall have the same meaning they have in the Internal Revenue Code of 1986, as amended.

[Add state-specific signature and notary clauses, schedule of assets, and where required, attesting witness clause]

¶ A.05 FORM 5: WILL FOR ESTATE OF $6 MILLION TO $10 MILLION--MARITAL DEDUCTION TAX PLANNING— GST TAX PLANNING WITH LIFETIME TRUST FOR CHILDREN AND REVERSE QTIP—CREATES A 40% NONMARITAL SHARE IN 2010 TO ABSORB AGGREGATE PROPERTY BASIS INCREASE— TRUSTEE CAN DISTRIBUTE FROM QTIP MINIMUM AMOUNT OF PRINCIPAL SUFFICIENT TO GIVE SPOUSE ENOUGH APPRECIATION TO TAKE ADVANTAGE OF AGGREGATE BASIS INCREASE AT SURVIVING SPOUSE'S DEATH—NO STATE ESTATE TAX PLANNING BECAUSE RELEVANT STATE DEATH TAXES ARE REPEALED OR PROVIDE EXEMPTION EQUAL TO FEDERAL APPLICABLE EXCLUSION AMOUNT

Will of *Testator*[5]

I, *Testator*, of [*locality, state*], make this my will. I revoke any other wills and codicils made by me.

Article 1
My Family

I am married to *Spouse* (sometimes referred to as "my *husband/wife*") and I have [*number of children*] children, *Children*.

---

[5] **KEY:**

Testator	— full name of the testator
Spouse	— full name of testator's spouse
husband/wife	— "husband" or "wife", as the case may be
Children	— full names of testator's children
he/she	— "he" or "she" (referring to the spouse)
his/her	— "his" or "her" (referring to the spouse)
him/her	— "him" or "her" (referring to the spouse)
AlternatePR	— name of the alternate personal representative (after spouse)
FirstTrustee	— name of the first trustee
SecondTrustee	— name of the alternate trustee

Article 2
My Personal Effects

A. Disposing of My Personal Effects. I leave my personal effects (defined below) to my *husband/wife*, *Spouse*, if *he/she* survives me, or otherwise to my descendants who survive me, *per stirpes*. If neither my *husband/wife* nor any of my children nor their descendants survive me, these personal effects shall be added to the residue of my estate. An adult person with whom a minor resides may give a binding receipt for any personal effects passing to the minor.

B. Memorandum. I may make a memorandum of how I wish some of my personal effects to be distributed, and I request that my wishes be followed.

Article 3
My Personal Residence

I leave all of my interest in the properties my personal representative (defined below) shall determine to have been used by me or a member of my family as personal residences to my *husband/wife*, *Spouse*, if *he/she* survives me, to the extent that they do not pass to *him/her* by right of survivorship. Personal residences shall also include all adjoining lands and any related casualty insurance policies.

Article 4
My Residuary Estate

A. If a Federal Estate Tax Exists. If there is, on the date of my death, a Federal estate tax and/or a Federal generation-skipping transfer tax, as the case may be, that applies with respect to my estate, I leave my residuary estate (defined below), as follows:

1. If My *Husband/Wife* Survives Me. If my *husband/wife*, *Spouse*, survives me, my personal representative shall divide my residuary estate into a nonmarital share, a GST exempt marital share, and a marital share (all defined below).

a. The nonmarital share shall be held under the Article entitled "The Family Trust."

b. The GST exempt marital share shall be held under the Article entitled "The Reverse QTIP Marital Trust."

c. The marital share shall be held under the Article entitled "The QTIP Marital Trust."

2. If My *Husband/Wife* Does Not Survive Me. If my *husband/wife* does not survive me, my personal representative shall divide my residuary estate into a descendants' GST exempt share and a descendants' power of appointment share (both defined below).

a. The descendants' GST exempt share shall be held under the Article entitled "The Descendants' Trust."

b. My personal representative shall distribute the descendants' power of appointment share to my descendants who survive me, *per stirpes*, except that the share for any child of mine shall be added to the trust fund for such child under the Article entitled "Child's Power of Appointment Trust," for that child, and the share for any more remote descendant of mine who shall then not yet have reached the age of thirty-five (35) years, shall be held under the Article entitled "Contingent Trust for Certain Beneficiaries."

B. If No Federal Estate Tax Exists. If there is, on the date of my death, no Federal estate tax or Federal generation-skipping transfer tax that apply with respect to my estate, I leave my residuary estate, as follows:

1. If My *Husband/Wife* Survives Me. If my *husband/wife* survives me, my personal representative shall divide my residuary estate into a descendants' nonmarital share and a marital share.

a. The nonmarital share shall be held under the Article entitled "The Family Trust."

b. The marital share shall be held under the Article entitled "The QTIP Marital Trust."

2. If My *Husband/Wife* Does Not Survive Me. If my *husband/wife* does not survive me, my personal representative shall hold my residuary estate under the Article entitled "The Descendants' Trust."

Article 5
The Family Trust

A. Until the Family Trust Termination Date. Until the family trust termination date (defined below), the trustee (defined below) shall distribute to or for the benefit of my *husband/wife*, my then-living children and my then-living more remote descendants, as much of the net income and principal of the family trust as the trustee may deem appropriate for their health, education, support, or maintenance, annually adding to principal any undistributed income, annually adding to principal any undistributed income.

1. Distributions May be Unequal. The Trustee may distribute income and principal of the family trust unequally and may make distributions to some beneficiaries and not to others.

2. Other Assets. The trustee shall consider other income and assets readily available to each beneficiary, including assets available from other trusts created under my will, in making distributions.

3. Priority Purposes. In making these distributions, my primary purpose is to provide for the support in reasonable comfort of my *husband/wife* for the rest of *his/her* life and the education and support of my children until they have completed their education.

B. Upon the Family Trust Termination Date. Upon the family trust termination date, the trustee shall distribute the remaining trust funds to my then-living descendants, per stirpes, subject to the provisions of the Article entitled Contingent Trust for Certain Beneficiaries.

C. "Family Trust Termination Date" Defined. The family trust termination date shall be the date of the death of the last to die of my *husband/wife* and my children alive on the date of my death.

Article 6
The Reverse QTIP Marital Trust

The reverse QTIP marital trust shall be held under this Article.

A. Distributing Trust Fund During My *Husband/Wife*'s Life. The trustee shall distribute the net income of the reverse QTIP marital trust quarterly or more frequently to my *husband/wife* during *his/her* life. The trustee shall also distribute to my *husband/wife* as much of the principal of the reverse QTIP marital trust as is appropriate for any purpose.

B. Distributing Trust Fund At My *Husband/Wife*'s Death.

1. Distributing Income. At my *husband/wife*'s death, the trustee shall distribute to my *husband/wife*'s estate any undistributed income of the reverse QTIP marital trust.

2. Appointing Trust Principal. At my *husband/wife*'s death, the trustee shall distribute the principal of the reverse QTIP marital trust, to the extent it is not used to pay transfer taxes (defined below) as provided below, as my *husband/wife* may direct by specific reference to this special power of appointment in *his/her* last will.

a. My *husband/wife* may appoint the reverse QTIP marital trust fund, either outright or in further trust, but only to or among any one (1) or more of my descendants.

b. My *husband/wife* may not appoint any portion of the reverse QTIP marital trust fund to my *husband/wife*, *his/her* creditors, *his/her* estate, or the creditors of *his/her* estate.

3. Distributing Unappointed Assets. The trustee shall add the unappointed principal of the reverse QTIP marital trust to the trust held under the Article entitled "The Descendants' Trust."

Article 7
The QTIP Marital Trust

The QTIP marital trust shall be held under this Article.

A. Distributing Trust Fund During My *Husband/Wife*'s Life. The trustee shall distribute the net income of the QTIP marital trust quarterly or more frequently to my *husband/wife*, *Spouse*, during *his/her* life.

  1. Principal Distributions. The trustee shall also distribute to my *husband/wife* as much of the principal of the QTIP marital trust as is appropriate for any purpose.

  2. Distributing Additional Principal if There is No Federal Estate Tax. If the trustee deems it likely that my *husband/wife* will die before January 1, 2011, the trustee shall distribute to my *husband/wife* a fractional share of this trust.

    a. The numerator of this fraction shall be equal to the smallest value of the assets of this trust fund to which the personal representative of my *husband/wife*'s estate could allocate all of the aggregate basis increase allowed to my *husband/wife* under Federal income tax laws, less the amount of such aggregate basis increase that could be allocated to other assets already owned by my *husband/wife* at the time of this distribution.

    b. The denominator of this fraction shall equal the value of the *spouse* trust fund.

B. Distributing Trust Fund At My *Husband/Wife*'s Death.

  1. Distributing Income. At my *husband/wife*'s death, the trustee shall distribute to my *husband/wife*'s estate any undistributed income of the QTIP marital trust.

  2. Appointing Trust Principal. At my *husband/wife*'s death, the trustee shall distribute the principal of the QTIP marital trust, to the extent it is not used to pay transfer taxes as provided below, as my *husband/wife* may direct by specific reference to this special power of appointment in *his/her* last will.

    a. My *husband/wife* may appoint the QTIP marital trust fund, either outright or in further trust, but only to or among any one (1) or more of my descendants.

    b. My *husband/wife* may not appoint any portion of the QTIP marital trust fund to my *husband/wife*, *his/her* creditors, *his/her* estate, or the creditors of *his/her* estate.

  3. Distributing Unappointed Trust Fund. The trustee shall distribute the unappointed QTIP marital trust fund to my then-living descendants, *per stirpes*, except that the share for any child of mine shall be added to the child's power of appointment trust for that child, and the share for any more remote descendant of mine who shall then not yet have reached the age of thirty-five (35) years, shall be held for such descendant under the Article entitled "Contingent Trust for Certain Beneficiaries."

Article 8
Child's Power of Appointment Trust

The child's power of appointment trust for each child of mine shall be held as a separate trust under this Article.

A. Distributing Trust Fund During the Child's Life. The trustee shall distribute to or for the benefit of each child for whom a trust is created under this Article, as much of the net income and principal as the child shall request at any time or as the trustee may consider appropriate for any purpose, annually adding to principal any undistributed income.

B. Distributing Trust Fund At the Child's Death. Upon the death of a child of mine who survives me, the trustee shall distribute the remaining principal and income of such child's trust under this Article as that child may direct by specific reference to this power of appointment in that child's last will.

1. Appointing Everything But Limited Portion. Each such child may appoint the remaining principal and income of such child's trust under this Article (other than the limited portion (defined below)) of such trust fund, either outright or in further trust, to or among any persons, including such child's estate.

2. Appointing Limited Portion. Each such child may appoint the limited portion of the principal and income of such child's trust under this Article outright or in further trust, but only to or among my then-living descendants, and such child may not appoint any of the limited portion to such child himself or herself, such child's creditors, such child's estate, or the creditors of such child's estate.

3. Distributing Unappointed Trust Fund. The trustee shall distribute any unappointed portion of the fund of a deceased child's trust under this Article to such child's then-living descendants, *per stirpes*, or if there are no such descendants then living, to my then-living descendants, *per stirpes*, except that the fund that would thus be distributed to any then-living child of mine shall be added to such child's trust under this Article.

4. "Limited Portion" Defined. The "limited portion" of the fund of a child's trust under this Article is that portion which would pass to one or more persons assigned to the same or a higher generation as the deceased child for Federal generation-skipping transfer tax purposes, were such child to die without a valid will. If such child dies in a year in which there is no Federal generation-skipping transfer tax applicable with respect to such child's estate, the "limited portion" shall be the entire fund of the child's trust.

Article 9
The Descendants' Trust

A. Until the Descendants' Trust Termination Date. Until the descendants' trust termination date (defined below), the trustee (defined below) shall distribute to or for the benefit of my then-living children and my then-living more remote descendants, as much of the net income and principal of the family trust as the trustee may deem appropriate for their health, education, support, or maintenance, annually adding to principal any undistributed income, annually adding to principal any undistributed income.

1. Distributions May be Unequal. The Trustee may distribute income and principal of the family trust unequally and may make distributions to some beneficiaries and not to others.

2. Other Assets. The trustee shall consider other income and assets readily available to each beneficiary, including assets available from other trusts created under my will, in making distributions.

3. Priority Purpose. In making these distributions, my primary purpose is to provide for the education and support of my children until they have completed their education.

B. Upon the Descendants' Trust Termination Date. Upon the descendants' trust termination date, the trustee shall distribute the remaining trust funds to my then-living descendants, per stirpes, subject to the provisions of the Article entitled Contingent Trust for Certain Beneficiaries.

C. "Descendants' Trust Termination Date" Defined. The descendants' trust termination date shall be the date of the death of the last to die of my children alive on the date of my death.

Article 10
Contingent Trust for Certain Beneficiaries

If a beneficiary (other than a child of mine) is entitled to receive any part of my estate or any portion of any trust fund held under this will while the beneficiary is under the age of thirty-five (35) years, the trustee may retain such assets in a separate trust for that beneficiary.

A. Distributing Trust Fund Before the Contingent Trust Termination Date. Until the contingent trust termination date (defined below), the trustee shall distribute to or for the benefit of the beneficiary as much of the net income and principal as the trustee may consider appropriate for the beneficiary's health, education, support, or maintenance, annually adding to principal any undistributed income.

B. Distributing Trust Fund At the Contingent Trust Termination Date. Upon the contingent trust termination date, the trustee shall distribute the remaining assets to the beneficiary if the beneficiary is then living or otherwise to the beneficiary's estate to be distributed as part of that estate.

C. "Contingent Trust Termination Date" Defined. The "contingent trust termination date" shall be the earlier of (1) the date on which the beneficiary dies or (2) the date on which the beneficiary reaches the age of thirty-five (35) years.

Article 11
Special Limits on Powers of Interested Trustee

The following limitations shall apply, notwithstanding other provisions of this instrument.

A. Limiting Actions by Interested Trustees. No interested trustee (defined below) may participate in the exercise of any discretion to distribute principal to himself or herself, except as is appropriate for his or her health, education, support, and maintenance, or any of them. No interested trustee may participate in the exercise of any discretion to distribute or expend principal or income in a manner that would discharge that trustee's personal obligation to support the beneficiary. No interested trustee may participate in the exercise of any incident of ownership over any policy owned by the trust insuring the life of such trustee.

B. Disinterested Trustees Exercising Certain Powers. A disinterested trustee (defined below) who is serving as a co-trustee with an interested trustee, may exercise those discretions granted under this instrument the exercise of which by an interested trustee are precluded.

1. If Multiple Trustees Include an Interested Trustee Who Cannot Act. The number of trustees who must consent to the exercise of a power granted under this instrument, as determined under the Article entitled "My Fiduciaries" shall be determined by treating the interested trustees who are not entitled, under this Article, to participate in the exercise of the power or discretion, as if they were not then serving.

2. If All Trustees Are Precluded From Acting. If this Article precludes every then-serving trustee from exercising a power otherwise granted to the trustee under this instrument, the then-serving trustee shall appoint a disinterested trustee who may exercise such power (or decline to exercise it) as if that disinterested trustee were the sole then-serving trustee.

Article 12
Debts, Expenses, and Taxes

A. Paying Debts and Expenses. My personal representative shall pay from my residuary estate my debts (but not before their maturity) and funeral and burial expenses, including the cost of a suitable memorial, without court order.

1. Paying Certain Joint Debts. My personal representative shall pay only my proportionate share of any debts for which I am jointly liable with my *husband/ wife*.

2. Paying Packing and Shipping Expenses. My personal representative shall pay all packing, shipping, insurance, and other charges relating to the distribution of any of my personal property without seeking reimbursement from the recipient of such personal property.

B. Paying Transfer Taxes. My personal representative shall pay all transfer taxes, other than generation-skipping transfer taxes, payable by reason of my death on assets passing under this will, from my residuary estate.

1. Apportioning Transfer Taxes on Nonprobate Assets. My personal representative shall apportion transfer taxes imposed on any assets not passing under this will to those assets and the transfer taxes on those assets shall be paid from those assets as provided by the laws of the state in which I reside at my death, except as expressly provided elsewhere in this will.

2. Apportioning Generation-Skipping Transfer Taxes. My personal representative shall apportion all generation-skipping transfer taxes for which my estate is legally responsible to those generation-skipping transfers, whether or not under this will.

3. Apportioning Transfer Taxes Away From Deductible Assets. Assets passing as the GST exempt marital share or as the marital share shall have the full benefit of the Federal estate tax marital deduction allowed with respect to any transfer taxes, and shall not bear any transfer taxes. Other assets passing to my *husband/ wife* or to any charitable organization, whether under this will or otherwise, shall have the full benefit of any available marital or charitable deduction for Federal and other transfer tax purposes, in determining the share of transfer taxes that should be borne by those assets.

Article 13
My Fiduciaries

A. Naming My Personal Representatives. I name my *husband/wife*, *Spouse*, to be my personal representative, and I give *him/her* the right to name one or more persons to serve with *him/her* or in *his/her* place. If my *husband/wife* fails or ceases to serve and there is no other person serving or named to serve, I name the *AlternatePR*, of [locality, state], to be my personal representative.

B. Naming My Trustees. I name *FirstTrustee*, of [locality, state], to be the trustee of any trust under this will. If *FirstTrustee* shall be unable or unwilling to serve or to continue serving, I name *SecondTrustee*, of [locality, state] to be the trustee of any trust under this will.

C. No Surety or Bond. No personal representative or trustee named by me or by another personal representative or trustee shall be required to provide surety or other security on a bond.

D. Naming Additional Fiduciaries. I authorize my named fiduciaries (defined below) to appoint any person as an additional personal representative or trustee in the same state or another state in which administration may be appropriate to serve at the pleasure of the appointing fiduciaries.

E. Delegating Fiduciary Powers and Authorities. My fiduciaries may delegate to another fiduciary any power or authority granted by me to my fiduciaries, to continue at the pleasure of the delegating fiduciary, unless otherwise agreed. Any person dealing in good faith with a fiduciary may rely upon that fiduciary's representation that a delegation has been made and remains in effect under this paragraph.

F. Fiduciary Resigning.

1. Personal Representative May Resign. A personal representative may resign by giving written notice specifying the effective date of the resignation to the designated successor.

2. Trustee May Resign. Any trustee may resign by giving written notice specifying the effective date of the resignation to the designated successor. If no successor is designated, the resigning trustee shall give notice to each adult beneficiary to whom trust income then may be distributed.

G. Removing a Trustee.
A trustee may be removed by the vote of two-thirds (⅔) of the then-living adult beneficiaries to whom trust income may then be distributed.

H. Filling Fiduciary Vacancies.

1. Court Appointing Personal Representative to Fill Vacancy. If no successor personal representative is designated, a court of appropriate jurisdiction shall name a successor personal representative.

2. Beneficiaries Appointing Corporate Trustee to Fill Vacancy. A corporation no substantial portion of the stock of which is owned by beneficiaries of this trust, may be named as successor trustee to fill any vacancy, by majority vote of the adult beneficiaries to whom trust income then may be distributed.

I. No Liability for Acts or Omissions of Predecessors.
No fiduciary shall be responsible for or need inquire into any acts or omissions of a prior fiduciary.

J. Compensating Fiduciaries.
In addition to reimbursement for expenses, each individual fiduciary is entitled to reasonable compensation for services. Each corporate fiduciary is entitled to compensation based on its written fee schedule in effect at the time its services are rendered or as otherwise agreed, and its compensation may vary from time to time based on that schedule.

K. Management Powers.
I authorize my fiduciaries to exercise all powers conferred by applicable state law and to do the following in a fiduciary capacity.

1. Prudent Investor Rule. My fiduciaries may hold and retain as part of my estate or any trust fund any property owned by me, whether or not such investment would be appropriate for a prudent investor. My fiduciaries may also hold and retain as part of my estate or any trust fund any property received from any source, and invest and reinvest my estate or trust fund (or leave it temporarily uninvested) in any type of property and every kind of investment in the same manner as a prudent investor would invest his or her own assets.

2. Holding Assets For Use of Trust Beneficiaries. My trustee may buy and hold in trust, assets that will be used personally by one or more beneficiaries, even if those assets would not otherwise be acquired by a prudent investor investing his or her own assets.

3. Transferring Assets. My fiduciaries may sell or exchange any real or personal property contained in my estate or any trust, for cash or credit, at public or private sale, and with such warranties or indemnifications as my fiduciaries may deem advisable.

4. Borrowing Money. My fiduciaries may borrow money (even from a fiduciary or beneficiary of my estate or any trust) for the benefit of my estate or any trust and secure these debts with assets of my estate or any trust.

5. Granting Security Interests. My fiduciaries may grant security interests and execute all instruments creating such interests upon such terms as my fiduciaries may deem advisable.

6. Compromising Claims. My fiduciaries may compromise and adjust claims against or on behalf of my estate or any trust on such terms as my fiduciaries may deem advisable.

7. Not Disclosing Nominees. My fiduciaries may take title to any securities in the name of any custodian or nominee without disclosing this relationship.

8. Allocating Between Income and Principal. My fiduciaries may determine whether receipts are income or principal and whether disbursements are to be charged against income or principal to the extent not clearly established by state law. A determination made by my fiduciaries in good faith shall not require equitable adjustments.

9. Making Tax Elections. My fiduciaries may make all tax elections and allocations my fiduciaries may consider appropriate; however, this authority is exercisable only in a fiduciary capacity and may not be used to enlarge or shift any beneficial interest except as an incidental consequence of the discharge of fiduciary duties. A tax election or allocation made by my fiduciaries in good faith shall not require equitable adjustments.

10. Distributing to Custodians for Minors. My fiduciaries shall distribute any of my estate or any trust fund to a beneficiary under the age of twenty-one (21) years by distribution to any appropriate person (who may be a fiduciary) chosen by my fiduciaries as custodian under any appropriate Uniform Transfers (or Gifts) to Minors Act, to be held for the maximum period of time allowed by law. My fiduciaries may also sell any asset that cannot be held under this custodianship and invest the sales proceeds in assets that can be so held.

11. Employing Advisors. My fiduciaries may employ such lawyers, accountants, and other advisors as my fiduciaries may deem useful and appropriate for the administration of my estate or any trust. My fiduciaries may employ a professional investment advisor and delegate to this advisor any discretionary investment authorities to manage the investments of my estate or any trust, including any investment in mutual funds, investment trusts, or managed accounts, and may rely on the advisor's investment recommendations without liability to any beneficiary.

12. Buying and Holding Life Insurance. My fiduciaries may buy and hold insurance policies on the life of any beneficiary or any person in whom a beneficiary has an insurable interest and may pay the premiums on such policies from income or principal, as my fiduciaries may deem advisable.

13. Dividing and Distributing Assets. My fiduciaries may divide and distribute the assets of my estate or any trust fund in kind, in money, or partly in each, without regard to the income tax basis of any asset and without the consent of any beneficiary. The decision of my fiduciaries in dividing any portion of my estate or any trust fund between or among two or more beneficiaries, if made in good faith, shall be binding on all persons.

14. Allocation of Basis Increase. My personal representative shall allocate any increases in the adjusted basis of property owned by me at the time of my death, whether passing under my Will or otherwise, to the extent such property is eligible to receive such an allocation, as my personal representative deems to be in the best interests of my estate and its beneficiaries. In making these allocations my personal representative shall:

a. First, satisfy all charitable bequests with assets to which no aggregate or spousal property basis increases may be allocated;

b. Second, satisfy all charitable bequests with assets that have an adjusted income tax basis closest to zero of all of my assets available to satisfy these bequests;

c. Third, generally not allocate basis increase to assets the gain from the sale of which is not subject to federal income tax under present federal income tax laws;

d. Fourth, allocate basis increases to assets that are reasonably likely to be sold within the three year period beginning on the date of my death, the sale of which will produce an income tax liability that is taxed at a rate higher than that on long-term capital gains; and

e. Fifth, allocate the remaining basis increase among assets in proportion to each asset's pro rata share of the total appreciation of all such assets owned by me on the date of my death.

Any reference in this paragraph to assets "owned by me on the date of my death" shall apply equally to assets deemed owned by me on the date of my death under the federal income tax rules governing allocation of my aggregate basis increase. My personal representative shall not be liable to anyone for any allocation of my basis increases made in good faith, in the absence of gross negligence.

**Article 14
Trust Administration**

A. Spendthrift Limits. No interest in a trust under this will shall be subject to the beneficiary's liabilities or creditor claims or to assignment or anticipation.

B. Protecting Trust Beneficiaries From Creditors. If the trustee shall determine that a beneficiary would not benefit as greatly from any outright distribution of trust income or principal because of the availability of the distribution to the beneficiary's creditors, the trustee shall instead expend those amounts for the benefit of the beneficiary. This direction is intended to enable the trustee to give the beneficiary the fullest possible benefit and enjoyment of all of the trust income and principal to which he or she is entitled.

C. Combining Multiple Trusts. The trustee may invest the assets of multiple trusts in a single fund if the interests of the trusts are accounted for separately.

D. Merging and Consolidating Trust Funds. The trustee may merge or consolidate any trust into any other trust that has the same trustee and substantially the same dispositive provisions.

E. Dividing Trust Funds. The trustee may divide any trust fund into multiple separate trusts.

F. Accountings. The trustee shall not be required to file annual accounts with any court or court official in any jurisdiction.

G. Changing Trust Situs. A disinterested trustee may change the situs of any trust under this will, and to the extent necessary or appropriate, move the trust assets, to a state or country other than the one in which the trust is then administered if the disinterested trustee shall determine it to be in the best interests of the trust or the beneficiaries. The disinterested trustee may elect that the law of such other jurisdiction shall govern the trust to the extent necessary or appropriate under the circumstances.

H. Rule Against Perpetuities. All assets of every trust created under this instrument (including every trust created by the exercise of a power of appointment created under this instrument, unless the exercise of such power of appointment starts a new period for the rule against perpetuities or similar rule that limits the time that property may remain in trust) that does not by its own terms do so earlier, shall vest in and be distributed to the persons then entitled to the income from such property at the expiration of the date twenty (20) years and eleven (11) months after the death of the last survivor of my *husband/wife* and those of the descendants of my grandparents alive on the date of this instrument. Upon termination of a trust under this provision, the accumulated trust income and principal shall be distributed to those beneficiaries then entitled to receive or have benefit of the income from such trust in the proportion in which they are so entitled. If the proportion of the income interests of the beneficiaries of such trust cannot be determined with reasonable certainty, the accumulated trust income and principal shall be distributed equally to such beneficiaries.

Article 15
Calculating Shares of the Residuary Estate if a Federal Estate Tax Exists

This Article shall apply if there is, on the date of my death, a Federal estate tax and/or a Federal generation-skipping transfer tax, as the case may be, that applies with respect to my estate.

A. My Purposes. I intend that:

1. Minimizing Federal Estate Taxes. The division of my residuary estate into a nonmarital share, a GST exempt marital share and a marital share, shall minimize the Federal estate taxes at my *husband/wife*'s death to the extent I can do so while deferring all Federal estate taxes until both my *husband/wife* and I have died.

2. Taking Advantage of My GST Exemption. The creation of a nonmarital share, a GST exempt marital share, and, if my *husband/wife* does not survive me, the descendants' GST exempt share, shall take advantage of my available GST exemption (defined below).

3. Qualifying for Federal Estate Tax Marital Deduction. The GST exempt marital share and the marital share shall qualify for the Federal estate tax marital deduction and all provisions of this will shall be construed accordingly. My fiduciaries shall, in all matters involving the GST exempt marital share and the marital share, exercise no power in a manner that would infringe upon any legal requirement for the allowance of the Federal estate tax marital deduction.

B. Defining the "Descendants' Nonmarital Share." If my *husband/wife* survives me, the "descendants' nonmarital share" shall be a fractional share of my residuary estate.

1. Calculating the Numerator. The numerator of the fraction shall equal the largest value of my residuary estate that can pass free of Federal estate tax by reason of the unified credit allowable with respect to my estate. This value shall be determined after being reduced by reason of my adjusted taxable gifts, all other dispositions of property included in my gross estate for which no deduction is allowed in computing my Federal estate tax, and administration expenses and other charges to principal that are not claimed and allowed as Federal estate tax deductions.

2. Calculating the Denominator. The denominator of the fraction shall equal the value of my residuary estate.

C. Defining the "GST Exempt Marital Share." If my *husband/wife* survives me, the "GST exempt marital share" shall be a fractional share of my residuary estate.

1. Calculating the Numerator. The numerator of the fraction shall be the amount of my available GST exemption (to the extent not allocated to the nonmarital share.)

2. Calculating the Denominator. The denominator of the fraction shall equal the value of my residuary estate.

D. Defining the "Marital Share." If my *husband/wife* survives me, the "marital share" shall be the remaining fractional share of my residuary estate after subtracting the nonmarital share and the GST exempt marital share.

E. Defining the "Descendants' GST Exempt Share." If my *husband/wife* does not survive me, the "descendants' GST exempt share" shall be a fractional share of my residuary estate.

1. Calculating the Numerator. The numerator of the fraction shall be equal to the amount of my available GST exemption.

2. Calculating the Denominator. The denominator of the fraction shall equal the value of my residuary estate.

F. Defining the "Descendants' Power of Appointment Share." If my *husband/wife* does not survive me, the "descendants' power of appointment share" shall be the remaining fractional share of my residuary estate after subtracting the descendants' GST exempt share.

G. Calculating Shares Based on Certain Assumptions. The spouse's nonmarital share shall be computed as if no election were made to qualify any property passing as such share under the Federal estate tax marital deduction, and the maximum possible election were made to qualify all property passing as the GST exempt marital share and the marital share for the Federal estate tax marital deduction.

H. Determining the Effect of Disclaimers.

1. Disclaiming the GST Exempt Marital Share or Marital Share. My fiduciaries shall add to the nonmarital share any portion of the GST exempt marital share or the marital share as to which a qualified disclaimer by or for my *husband/wife* is made. The spouse's nonmarital share shall be calculated before any qualified disclaimer by or for my *husband/wife* of any of the GST exempt marital share or of the marital share.

2. Apportioning Transfer Taxes to Disclaimed Funds. Transfer taxes imposed on assets as to which my *husband/wife* has made a qualified disclaimer shall be apportioned to those disclaimed funds.

I. Allocating Assets Between or Among Shares.

1. Making Certain Allocations If My *Husband/Wife* Survives Me. If my *husband/wife* survives me:

a. My personal representative shall allocate to the marital share and the GST exempt marital share only assets that can qualify for the Federal estate tax marital deduction.

b. My personal representative shall not, to the extent possible, allocate to the marital share or the GST exempt marital share assets upon which a foreign death tax is payable.

c. My personal representative shall allocate to the nonmarital share, the GST exempt marital share and, if my *husband/wife* does not survive me, the descendants' GST exempt share, solely of assets includable in my gross estate for Federal estate tax purposes.

2. Making Other Allocations. My personal representative shall, in other respects, allocate assets as my personal representative shall consider to be in the best interests of the beneficiaries, valuing each asset on the date or dates of allocation.

J. Allocating Income. My personal representative and trustee shall allocate to each share a ratable portion of all of the income earned by my estate after my death, whether earned before or after the assets are in the possession of the trustee, and income earned on assets used to pay charges according to the same fractional shares.

K. My "Available GST Exemption" Defined. For the purposes of this Article, my "available GST exemption" means an amount equal to (1) my GST exemption, determined for Federal tax purposes, minus (2) all allocations of my GST exemption made or deemed made to transfers other than those to transfers under this will.

Article 16
Calculating Shares of the Residuary Estate if No Federal Estate Tax Exists

This Article shall apply if there is, on the date of my death, no Federal estate tax that applies with respect to my estate.

A. My Purposes. I intend that the division of the my residuary estate into a nonmarital share and a marital share to take full advantage of the increases allowed under applicable Federal income tax law to the basis of assets received from me on account of my death, to the extent that it can be so done without unfairly affecting the amount of the various shares of my estate.

B. Defining the "Nonmarital Share." The "nonmarital share" shall be a fractional share of my residuary estate.

1. Calculating the Numerator. The numerator of the fraction shall equal the lesser of:

a. The smallest value of the assets of my residuary estate to which my personal representative can allocate the entire aggregate basis increase allowed under Federal income tax laws with respect to my estate for property not acquired from a spouse; and

b. Forty percent (40%) of the value of my residuary estate.

2. Calculating the Denominator. The denominator of the fraction shall equal the value of my residuary estate. References in this paragraph B to my residuary estate shall include only those portions of my residuary estate to which my aggregate basis increase may be allocated under federal income tax law.

C. Defining the "Marital Share." If my *husband/wife* survives me, the marital share shall be the remaining fractional share of my residuary estate after subtracting the nonmarital share.

D. Allocating Assets. If my *husband/wife* survives me:

1. Allocating Basis in a Fairly Representative Manner. My personal representative shall allocate to the nonmarital share only assets to which my personal representative can allocate my aggregate basis increase. Otherwise, my personal representative shall select the assets that shall constitute the nonmarital share in manner such that the net appreciation of any property allocated to the nonmarital share shall be fairly representative of the net appreciation of all property available for such allocation (excluding any property to which my personal representative cannot, under Federal income tax law, validly allocate any of the aggregate basis increase or the spousal property basis increase).

2. Allocating Assets Otherwise. In other respects, my personal representative shall allocate assets as my personal representative shall consider to be in the best interests of the beneficiaries, valuing each asset on the date or dates of allocation.

E. Allocating Trust Income. My personal representative and trustee shall allocate to each share a ratable portion of all of the income earned by my estate after my death, whether earned before or after the assets are in the possession of the trustee, and income earned on assets used to pay charges according to the same fractional shares.

Article 17
Administering the QTIP and Reverse QTIP Marital Trusts

A. Making Elections. If there is, on the date of my death, a Federal estate tax that applies with respect to my estate, my personal representative may elect to qualify all or any portion of the QTIP marital trust and the reverse QTIP marital trust for the Federal estate tax marital deduction, and to treat me as the transferor of the reverse QTIP marital trust for Federal generation-skipping transfer tax purposes.

1. Making Partial Elections. If my personal representative shall elect to qualify less than all of the QTIP marital trust or the reverse QTIP marital trust for the Federal estate tax marital deduction, my personal representative shall divide the trust fund as to which such partial election was made into two (2) separate trusts and make all principal payments first from the trust fund that qualifies for the Federal estate tax marital deduction.

2. Allocating Assets Between or Among Shares. My personal representative shall allocate assets between these shares as my personal representative shall consider to be in the best interests of the beneficiaries, valuing each asset on the date of allocation.

B. Assuring Productivity of Assets. My *husband/wife* may direct the trustee to make any unproductive or underproductive assets of the QTIP marital trust and the reverse QTIP marital trust productive or to convert them to productive assets within a reasonable time.

C. Receiving and Administering Retirement Payments. If the QTIP marital trust or the reverse QTIP marital trust is entitled to receive distributions under any retirement plan or individual retirement arrangement, of which my *husband/wife* is the designated beneficiary for Federal income tax purposes, then the trustee shall do the following:

1. Distributing Greater of Income or Required Minimum Distribution. The trustee shall annually withdraw from such retirement plan trust fund or arrangement the greater of all of the income earned by my *husband/wife*'s share of such plan or arrangement, or the required minimum distribution with respect to my *husband/wife*, as determined for Federal income tax purposes.

2. Distributing Withdrawn Amounts. The trustee shall annually distribute to my *husband/wife* all amounts withdrawn from such plan or arrangement.

D. Paying Transfer Taxes.

1. Paying Transfer Taxes Generally. The trustee shall, unless my *husband/wife* provides otherwise by specific reference to this paragraph in a valid will or other writing, pay or make arrangements for the payment of the incremental transfer taxes imposed on the reverse QTIP marital trust and on the QTIP marital trust upon the death of my *husband/wife*, from the QTIP marital trust and not from the reverse QTIP marital trust.

2. Paying Transfer Taxes In Case of a Partial QTIP Election. If my personal representative shall elect to qualify only part of the QTIP marital trust, the reverse QTIP marital trust, or both, and shall create two trusts as required by this Article, the transfer taxes imposed on both trusts at my *husband/wife*'s death shall be paid from the qualified trust fund to the extent possible.

Article 18
Definitions and Miscellaneous

A. Definitions. The following terms shall have the meaning set forth below for all purposes of this will:

1. "Children" and "Descendants" Defined. "Children" and "descendants" include those now living and those later born, subject to the following rules:

a. "Children" and "descendants" include an adopted person and that adopted person's descendants if, that adopted person is adopted before reaching eighteen (18) years of age;

b. "Children" and "descendants" includes those born outside of wedlock, if, during such child's or descendant's lifetime, his or her parent through whom such child or descendant claims hereunder, has acknowledged such person as his or her child in a writing duly signed and notarized during such parent's lifetime; and

c. "Children" and "descendants" include a child produced before the parent's death by donor artificial insemination, in vitro fertilization or other form of surrogate parenthood, whether or not such child was legally adopted by such parent before such parent's death.

2. **"Disinterested Trustee" Defined.** A "disinterested trustee" means a trustee who is not an interested trustee.

3. **"Fiduciary" Defined.** "Fiduciary" or "fiduciaries" shall include my personal representative and the trustee, or if they are different persons, either of them.

4. **"Interested Trustee" Defined.** An "interested trustee" means a trustee who is also (a) a beneficiary of the trust of which he or she is a trustee or the insured under a policy of insurance owned by a trust of which he or she is a trustee; (b) married to and living together with a beneficiary of the trust of which he or she is a trustee; (c) the father, mother, issue, brother or sister, of a beneficiary of the trust of which he or she is a trustee; (d) an employee of a beneficiary of the trust of which he or she is a trustee; (e) a corporation or any employee of a corporation in which the stock holdings of the trustee and the trust are significant from the viewpoint of voting control; or (f) a subordinate employee of a corporation in which the trustee is an executive.

5. **"Personal Effects" Defined.** My "personal effects" includes all of my jewelry, clothing, furniture, and other items of tangible personal property, but not money (other than collectible money having an inherent value in excess of its face amount) and not assets that my personal representative shall consider primarily to be used in a trade or business or held for investment. My "personal effects" also includes any transferable casualty insurance policies on any items of tangible personal property. Such policies shall pass to the same person who receives the insured property.

6. **"Personal Representative" Defined.** My "personal representative" shall include any executor, ancillary executor, administrator, or ancillary administrator, whether local or foreign and whether of all or part of my estate, multiple personal representatives, and their successors.

7. **"Residuary Estate" Defined.** My "residuary estate" means my real and personal estate passing under this will, after distribution of my personal effects and my personal residences under Articles 2 and 3 of this will.

8. **"Transfer Taxes" Defined.** "Transfer taxes" means all estate, inheritance, legacy, succession, and other transfer taxes, including any tax on excess retirement accumulations, imposed with respect to my death by any state, the United States, or by any foreign country. "Transfer taxes" also includes all taxes that are reimbursable under Sections 2207 through 2207B of the Internal Revenue Code of 1986, as amended, which right of reimbursement I hereby waive. "Transfer taxes" also includes all interest and penalties on such taxes.

9. **"Trustee" Defined.** The "trustee" or "trustees" shall include each trustee individually, multiple trustees, and their successors.

B. Retroactive Legislation. I include in this instrument certain dispositions and direct certain actions that shall occur only if, on the date of my death, no federal estate tax or Federal generation-skipping transfer tax applies with respect to my estate. These provisions shall not apply if, on the date of my death, no federal estate tax or federal generation-skipping transfer tax, as the case may be, applies with respect to my estate, but such tax or taxes is/are retroactively reinstated before April 1, 2011, and apply under such retroactive legislation with respect to my estate. If such retroactive legislation is finally determined to be unconstitutional or otherwise invalid, these references shall apply as if such retroactive legislation had never been enacted.

C. Absence of Trust Beneficiaries. If all of the beneficiaries of any trust under this will should die before the trust assets have vested in them, the trustee shall distribute all of the remaining assets of that trust as follows:

1. One Half to My Heirs and Distributee. One half (½) (or all, if there are no persons to take under subparagraph C.2. of this Article) to the heirs and distributees who would have inherited my personal estate, and in such shares as they would have inherited it, had I died unmarried and without a valid will, determined on the later of the date of my death or the date of the death of the last of the trust beneficiaries to die; and

2. One Half to My *Husband/Wife*'s Distributees. One half (½) (or all, if there are no persons to take under subparagraph C.1. of this Article) to the heirs and distributees who would have inherited my *husband/wife*'s personal estate, and in such shares as they would have inherited it, had he died unmarried and without a valid will, determined on the later of the date of my death or the date of the death of the last of the trust beneficiaries to die.

D. Applicable Law. My will shall be governed by and construed according to the laws of the *State*.

E. Joint Ownership. I confirm that all assets owned jointly by me and another person with a right of survivorship should pass outright to my joint owner and my estate shall have no interest in those assets.

F. Number. Whenever the context requires, the singular includes the plural and the plural the singular.

G. Survivorship. No person shall be deemed to have survived me for purposes of inheriting under this will unless he or she is living on the date ninety (90) days after the date of my death.

H. Tax-Related Terms. All tax-related terms shall have the same meaning they have in the Internal Revenue Code of 1986, as amended.

[*Add state-specific signature, attesting witness, and self-proving clauses*]

¶ A.06 FORM 6: REVOCABLE TRUST FOR ESTATE OF $6 MILLION TO $10 MILLION—MARITAL DEDUCTION TAX PLANNING—GST TAX PLANNING WITH LIFETIME TRUST FOR CHILDREN AND REVERSE QTIP—CREATES A 40% NONMARITAL SHARE IN 2010 TO ABSORB AGGREGATE PROPERTY BASIS INCREASE—TRUSTEE CAN DISTRIBUTE FROM QTIP MINIMUM AMOUNT OF PRINCIPAL SUFFICIENT TO GIVE SPOUSE ENOUGH APPRECIATION TO TAKE ADVANTAGE OF AGGREGATE BASIS INCREASE AT SURVIVING SPOUSE'S DEATH—NO STATE ESTATE TAX PLANNING BECAUSE RELEVANT STATE DEATH TAXES ARE REPEALED OR PROVIDE EXEMPTION EQUAL TO FEDERAL APPLICABLE EXCLUSION AMOUNT—SAME PLANNING AS FORM 5, BUT IN A REVOCABLE TRUST

Revocable Trust of *Grantor*[6]

I, *Grantor*, of [*locality, state*] (sometimes in the first person singular, sometimes the "grantor," and sometimes the "trustee"), make this trust (defined below), which may be referred to as *TrustName*.

Article 1
My Family

I am married to *Spouse* (sometimes referred to as "my *husband/wife*") and I have [*number of children*] children, *Children*.

---

[6] **KEY:**

Grantor	— full name of the grantor
TrustName	— what to call the trust in other documents
Spouse	— full name of grantor's spouse
husband/wife	— "husband" or "wife," as the case may be
Children	— full names of grantor's children
he/she	— "he" or "she" (referring to the spouse)
his/her	— "his" or "her" (referring to the spouse)
him/her	— "him" or "her" (referring to the spouse)
FirstTrustee	— name of the first alternate trustee
SecondTrustee	— name of the second alternate trustee

Article 2
Trustee Shall Hold Trust Funds

The trustee (defined below) shall hold certain property, which may be listed in Schedule A, to be administered according to the terms of the trust instrument. I and anyone else may transfer additional property (including life insurance proceeds, where appropriate), to any trustee (which the trustee may refuse to accept if acceptance is not in the best interests of the trust), at any time during my life or after my death, to be held and administered according to the terms of the trust instrument.

Article 3
Revoking the Trust

I may revoke or amend all or any part of the trust fund at any time, without the consent of anyone else, by delivering to the trustee a written instrument specifying the character and date of the intended amendment or revocation, or by specific reference to the trust in my last will. The duties, powers, or liabilities of the trustee (other than me) cannot, however, be changed without such trustee's prior written consent. The trustee shall transfer all of the trust funds to me or to my estate, if the trust is completely revoked.

Article 4
Administering the Trust During My Life

A. Making Payments to Me. During my life, the trustee shall pay any taxes, commissions, or other expenses incurred with respect to the trust, and distribute to me all of the trust's net income at least annually, and so much of its principal and undistributed income (including all or none) as I may request from time to time, or as the trustee shall deem appropriate for my comfort and care.

1. My Absolute Power to Withdraw Trust Funds. My power to withdraw principal and income from the trust is absolute, and exercisable as to all of the trust funds, by me alone and in all events.

2. Assuring Productivity of Trust Assets. I may direct the trustee not to retain any asset or assets that I shall deem not to be sufficiently productive.

B. Qualifying for the Gift Tax Marital Deduction. I intend that any transfers to the trust by my *husband/wife*, *Spouse*, shall qualify for the Federal gift and estate tax marital deduction and all provisions of the trust shall be construed consistent therewith.

Article 5
Disposing of the Residuary Trust Fund

The trustee shall divide and distribute the residuary trust fund (defined below) at my death, under this Article.

A. If a Federal Estate Tax Exists. If there is, on the date of my death, a Federal estate tax and/or a Federal generation-skipping transfer tax, as the case may be, that applies with respect to my estate (including this trust fund), the trustee shall divide and distribute the residuary trust fund, as follows:

1. If My *Husband/Wife* Survives Me. If my *husband/wife*, *Spouse*, survives me, the trustee shall divide the residuary trust fund into a descendants' nonmarital share, a spouse's nonmarital share, a GST exempt marital share, and a marital share (all defined below).

a. The nonmarital share shall be held under the Article entitled "The Family Trust."

b. The GST exempt marital share shall be held under the Article entitled "The Reverse QTIP Marital Trust."

c. The marital share shall be held under the Article entitled "The QTIP Marital Trust."

2. If My *Husband/Wife* Does Not Survive Me. If my *husband/wife* does not survive me, the trustee shall divide the residuary trust fund into a descendants' GST exempt share and a descendants' power of appointment share (both defined below).

a. The descendants' GST exempt share shall be held under the Article entitled "The Descendants' Trust."

b. The trustee shall distribute the descendants' power of appointment share to my descendants who survive me, *per stirpes*, except that the share for any child of mine shall be added to the trust fund for such child under the Article entitled "Child's Power of Appointment Trust," for that child, and the share for any more remote descendant of mine who shall then not yet have reached the age of thirty-five (35) years, shall be held under the Article entitled "Contingent Trust for Certain Beneficiaries."

B. If No Federal Estate Tax Exists. If there is, on the date of my death, no Federal estate tax or Federal generation-skipping transfer tax that applies with respect to my estate (including this trust fund), the trustee shall divide the residuary trust fund as follows:

1. If My *Husband/Wife* Survives Me. If my *husband/wife* survives me, the trustee shall divide the residuary trust fund into a nonmarital share and a marital share.

a. The nonmarital share shall be held under the Article entitled "The Family Trust."

b. The marital share shall be held under the Article entitled "The QTIP Marital Trust."

2. If My *Husband/Wife* Does Not Survive Me. If my *husband/wife* does not survive me, the trustee shall hold the residuary trust fund under the Article entitled "The Descendants' Trust."

C. Debts and Expenses of Administration. The trustee shall pay to the personal representative of my estate such amounts as the personal representative of my estate shall certify as needed for the payment of my debts and expenses of estate administration.

Article 6
The Family Trust

A. Until the Family Trust Termination Date. Until the family trust termination date (defined below), the trustee shall distribute to or for the benefit of my *husband/wife*, my then-living children and my then-living more remote descendants, as much of the net income and principal of the family trust as the trustee may deem appropriate for their health, education, support, or maintenance, annually adding to principal any undistributed income, annually adding to principal any undistributed income.

1. Distributions May be Unequal. The Trustee may distribute income and principal of the family trust unequally and may make distributions to some beneficiaries and not to others.

2. Other Assets. The trustee shall consider other income and assets readily available to each beneficiary, including assets available from other trusts created under my will, in making distributions.

3. Priority Purposes. In making these distributions, my primary purpose is to provide for the support in reasonable comfort of my *husband/wife* for the rest of *his/her* life and the education and support of my children until they have completed their education.

B. Upon the Family Trust Termination Date. Upon the family trust termination date, the trustee shall distribute the remaining trust funds to my then-living descendants, per stirpes, subject to the provisions of the Article entitled Contingent Trust for Certain Beneficiaries.

C. "Family Trust Termination Date" Defined. The family trust termination date shall be the date of the death of the last to die of my *husband/wife* and my children alive on the date of my death.

Article 7
The Reverse QTIP Marital Trust

The reverse QTIP marital trust shall be held under this Article.

A. Distributing Trust Fund During My *Husband/Wife*'s Life. The trustee shall distribute the net income of the reverse QTIP marital trust quarterly or more frequently to my *husband/wife* during *his/her* life. The trustee shall also distribute to my *husband/wife* as much of the principal of the reverse QTIP marital trust as is appropriate for any purpose.

B. Distributing Trust Fund At My *Husband/Wife*'s Death.

1. Distributing Income. At my *husband/wife*'s death, the trustee shall distribute to my *husband/wife*'s estate any undistributed income of the reverse QTIP marital trust.

2. Appointing Trust Principal. At my *husband/wife*'s death, the trustee shall distribute the principal of the reverse QTIP marital trust, to the extent it is not used to pay transfer taxes (defined below) as provided below, as my *husband/wife* may direct by specific reference to this special power of appointment in *his/her* last will.

a. My *husband/wife* may appoint the reverse QTIP marital trust fund, either outright or in further trust, but only to or among any one (1) or more of my descendants.

b. My *husband/wife* may not appoint any portion of the reverse QTIP marital trust fund to my *husband/wife*, *his/her* creditors, *his/her* estate, or the creditors of *his/her* estate.

3. Distributing Unappointed Assets. The trustee shall add the unappointed principal of the reverse QTIP marital trust to the trust held under the Article entitled "The Descendants' Trust."

Article 8
The QTIP Marital Trust

The QTIP marital trust shall be held under this Article.

A. Distributing Trust Fund During My *Husband/Wife*'s Life. The trustee shall distribute the net income of the QTIP marital trust quarterly or more frequently to my *husband/wife*, *Spouse*, during *his/her* life.

1. Principal Distributions. The trustee shall also distribute to my *husband/wife* as much of the principal of the QTIP marital trust as is appropriate for any purpose.

2. Distributing Additional Principal if There is No Federal Estate Tax. If the trustee deems it likely that my *husband/wife* will die before January 1, 2011, the trustee shall distribute to my *husband/wife* a fractional share of this trust.

a. The numerator of this fraction shall be equal to the smallest value of the assets of this trust fund to which the personal representative of my *husband/wife*'s estate could allocate all of the aggregate basis increase allowed to my *husband/wife* under Federal income tax laws, less the amount of such aggregate basis increase that could be allocated to other assets already owned by my *husband/wife* at the time of this distribution.

b. The denominator of this fraction shall equal the value of the *spouse* trust fund.

B. Distributing Trust Fund At My *Husband/Wife*'s Death.

1. Distributing Income. At my *husband/wife*'s death, the trustee shall distribute to my *husband/wife*'s estate any undistributed income of the QTIP marital trust.

2. Appointing Trust Principal. At my *husband/wife*'s death, the trustee shall distribute the principal of the QTIP marital trust, to the extent it is not used to pay transfer taxes as provided below, as my *husband/wife* may direct by specific reference to this special power of appointment in *his/her* last will.

a. My *husband/wife* may appoint the QTIP marital trust fund, either outright or in further trust, but only to or among any one (1) or more of my descendants.

b. My *husband/wife* may not appoint any portion of the QTIP marital trust fund to my *husband/wife*, *his/her* creditors, *his/her* estate, or the creditors of *his/her* estate.

3. Distributing Unappointed Trust Fund. The trustee shall distribute the unappointed QTIP marital trust fund to my then-living descendants, *per stirpes*, except that the share for any child of mine shall be added to the child's power of appointment trust for that child, and the share for any more remote descendant of mine who shall then not yet have reached the age of thirty-five (35) years, shall be held for such descendant under the Article entitled "Contingent Trust for Certain Beneficiaries."

Article 9
Child's Power of Appointment Trust

The child's power of appointment trust for each child of mine shall be held as a separate trust under this Article.

A. Distributing Trust Fund During the Child's Life. The trustee shall distribute to or for the benefit of each child for whom a trust is created under this Article, as much of the net income and principal as the child shall request at any time or as the trustee may consider appropriate for any purpose, annually adding to principal any undistributed income.

B. Distributing Trust Fund At the Child's Death. Upon the death of a child of mine who survives me, the trustee shall distribute the remaining principal and income of such child's trust under this Article as that child may direct by specific reference to this power of appointment in that child's last will.

1. Appointing Everything But Limited Portion. Each such child may appoint the remaining principal and income of such child's trust under this Article (other than the limited portion (defined below)) of such trust fund, either outright or in further trust, to or among any persons, including such child's estate.

2. Appointing Limited Portion. Each such child may appoint the limited portion of the principal and income of such child's trust under this Article outright or in further trust, but only to or among my then-living descendants, and such child may not appoint any of the limited portion to such child himself or herself, such child's creditors, such child's estate, or the creditors of such child's estate.

3. Distributing Unappointed Trust Fund. The trustee shall distribute any unappointed portion of the fund of a deceased child's trust under this Article to such child's then-living descendants, *per stirpes*, or if there are no such descendants then living, to my then-living descendants, *per stirpes*, except that the fund that would thus be distributed to any then-living child of mine shall be added to such child's trust under this Article.

4. "Limited Portion" Defined. The "limited portion" of the fund of a child's trust under this Article is that portion which would pass to one or more persons assigned to the same or a higher generation as the deceased child for Federal generation-skipping transfer tax purposes, were such child to die without a valid will. If such child dies in a year in which there is no Federal generation-skipping transfer tax applicable with respect to such child's estate, the "limited portion" shall be the entire fund of the child's trust.

Article 10
The Descendants' Trust

A. Until the Descendants' Trust Termination Date. Until the descendants' trust termination date (defined below), the trustee (defined below) shall distribute to or for the benefit of my then-living children and my then-living more remote descendants, as much of the net income and principal of the family trust as the trustee may deem appropriate for their health, education, support, or maintenance, annually adding to principal any undistributed income, annually adding to principal any undistributed income.

1. Distributions May be Unequal. The Trustee may distribute income and principal of the family trust unequally and may make distributions to some beneficiaries and not to others.

2. Other Assets. The trustee shall consider other income and assets readily available to each beneficiary, including assets available from other trusts created under my will, in making distributions.

3. Priority Purpose. In making these distributions, my primary purpose is to provide for the education and support of my children until they have completed their education.

B. Upon the Descendants' Trust Termination Date. Upon the descendants' trust termination date, the trustee shall distribute the remaining trust funds to my then-living descendants, per stirpes, subject to the provisions of the Article entitled Contingent Trust for Certain Beneficiaries.

C. "Descendants' Trust Termination Date" Defined. The descendants' trust termination date shall be the date of the death of the last to die of my children alive on the date of my death.

Article 11
Contingent Trust for Certain Beneficiaries

If a beneficiary (other than a child of mine) is entitled to receive any portion of any trust fund held under this instrument while the beneficiary is under the age of thirty-five (35) years, the trustee may retain such assets in a separate trust for that beneficiary.

A. Distributing Trust Fund Before the Contingent Trust Termination Date. Until the contingent trust termination date (defined below), the trustee shall distribute to or for the benefit of the beneficiary as much of the net income and principal as the trustee may consider appropriate for the beneficiary's health, education, support, or maintenance, annually adding to principal any undistributed income.

B. Distributing Trust Fund At the Contingent Trust Termination Date. Upon the contingent trust termination date, the trustee shall distribute the remaining assets to the beneficiary if the beneficiary is then living or otherwise to the beneficiary's estate to be distributed as part of that estate.

C. "Contingent Trust Termination Date" Defined. The "contingent trust termination date" shall be the earlier of (1) the date on which the beneficiary dies or (2) the date on which the beneficiary reaches the age of thirty-five (35) years.

Article 12
Special Limits on Powers of Interested Trustee

The following limitations shall apply, notwithstanding other provisions of this instrument.

A. Limiting Actions by Interested Trustees. No interested trustee (defined below) may participate in the exercise of any discretion to distribute principal to himself or herself, except as is appropriate for his or her health, education, support, and maintenance, or any of them. No interested trustee may participate in the exercise of any discretion to distribute or expend principal or income in a manner that would discharge that trustee's personal obligation to support the beneficiary. No interested trustee may participate in the exercise of any incident of ownership over any policy owned by the trust insuring the life of such trustee.

B. Disinterested Trustees Exercising Certain Powers. A disinterested trustee (defined below) who is serving as a co-trustee with an interested trustee, may exercise those discretions granted under this instrument the exercise of which by an interested trustee are precluded.

1. If Multiple Trustees Include an Interested Trustee Who Cannot Act. The number of trustees who must consent to the exercise of a power granted under this instrument, as determined under the Article entitled "The Trustees" shall be determined by treating the interested trustees who are not entitled, under this Article, to participate in the exercise of the power or discretion, as if they were not then serving.

2. If All Trustees Are Precluded From Acting. If this Article precludes every then-serving trustee from exercising a power otherwise granted to the trustee

under this instrument, the then-serving trustee shall appoint a disinterested trustee who may exercise such power (or decline to exercise it) as if that disinterested trustee were the sole then-serving trustee.

Article 13
Paying Transfer Taxes

The trustee shall pay from the residuary trust fund all transfer taxes, other than generation-skipping transfer taxes, payable by reason of my death on assets passing under this trust.

A. Apportioning Transfer Taxes. The trustee shall pay transfer taxes imposed on any trust assets includible in my gross estate for Federal estate tax purposes, from those assets, as provided by the laws of the state in which I reside at my death, except as expressly provided elsewhere in this instrument.

B. Apportioning Generation-Skipping Transfer Taxes. The trustee shall pay all generation-skipping transfer taxes imposed on transfers under this trust from those transfers.

C. Apportioning Transfer Taxes Away From Deductible Assets. Assets passing as the GST exempt marital share or as the marital share shall have the full benefit of the Federal estate tax marital deduction allowed with respect to any transfer taxes, and shall not bear any transfer taxes. Other assets passing to my *husband/ wife* or to any charitable organization, whether under this trust or otherwise, shall have the full benefit of any available marital or charitable deduction for Federal and other transfer tax purposes, in determining the share of transfer taxes that should be borne by those assets.

Article 14
The Trustees

A. Naming The Trustee. I shall be the initial trustee of this trust.

B. Naming Successor Trustees. I name *FirstTrustee*, of [*locality, state*], to be the successor trustee, to serve if I am unable or unwilling to serve or to continue serving. I name *SecondTrustee*, of [*locality, state*] to be the successor trustee, to serve if both *FirstTrustee* and I are unable or unwilling to serve or to continue serving.

C. No Surety or Bond. No trustee named by me or by another trustee shall be required to provide surety or other security on a bond.

D. Naming Additional Trustees. I authorize the trustee to appoint any person as an additional trustee, to serve at the pleasure of the appointing trustee.

E. Delegating Powers and Authorities. The trustee may delegate to another trustee any power or authority granted by me to the trustee, to continue at the pleasure of the delegating trustee, unless otherwise agreed. Any person dealing in good faith with a trustee may rely upon that trustee's representation that a delegation has been made and remains in effect under this paragraph.

F. Trustee Resigning. Any trustee may resign by giving written notice specifying the effective date of the resignation to me, if I am then-serving as a trustee, or otherwise to the designated successor. If I am not alive or am not then-serving as a trustee, and if no successor is designated, the resigning trustee shall give notice to each adult beneficiary to whom trust income then may be distributed.

G. Removing a Trustee. A trustee may be removed by the vote of two thirds (⅔) of the then-living adult beneficiaries to whom trust income may then be distributed.

H. Filling Trustee Vacancies. A corporation no substantial portion of the stock of which is owned by beneficiaries of this trust, may be named as successor trustee to fill any vacancy, by majority vote of the adult beneficiaries to whom trust income then may be distributed.

I. No Liability for Acts or Omissions of Predecessors. No trustee shall be responsible for or need inquire into any acts or omissions of a prior trustee.

J. Compensating Trustees. In addition to reimbursement for expenses, each individual trustee is entitled to reasonable compensation for services. Each corporate trustee is entitled to compensation based on its written fee schedule in effect at the time its services are rendered or as otherwise agreed, and its compensation may vary from time to time based on that schedule.

K. Management Powers. I authorize the trustee to exercise all powers conferred by applicable state law and to do the following in a fiduciary capacity.

1. Prudent Investor Rule. The trustee may hold and retain as part of any trust fund any property transferred by me to the trustee, whether or not such investment would be appropriate for a prudent investor. The trustee may also hold and retain as part of any trust fund any property received from any source, and invest and reinvest the trust fund (or leave it temporarily uninvested) in any type of property and every kind of investment in the same manner as a prudent investor would invest his or her own assets.

2. Holding Assets For Use of Trust Beneficiaries. The trustee may buy and hold in trust, assets that will be used personally by one or more beneficiaries, even if those assets would not otherwise be acquired by a prudent investor investing his or her own assets.

3. Transferring Assets. The trustees may sell or exchange any real or personal property contained in any trust, for cash or credit, at public or private sale, and with such warranties or indemnifications as the trustee may deem advisable.

4. Borrowing Money. The trustee may borrow money (even from a trustee, a beneficiary, or any trust) for the benefit of any trust and secure these debts with assets of the trust.

5. Granting Security Interests. The trustee may grant security interests and execute all instruments creating such interests upon such terms as the trustee may deem advisable.

6. Compromising Claims. The trustee may compromise and adjust claims against or on behalf of any trust on such terms as the trustee may deem advisable.

7. Not Disclosing Nominees. The trustee may take title to any securities in the name of any custodian or nominee without disclosing this relationship.

8. Allocating Between Income and Principal. The trustee may determine whether receipts are income or principal and whether disbursements are to be charged against income or principal to the extent not clearly established by state law. A determination made by the trustee in good faith shall not require equitable adjustments.

9. Making Tax Elections. The trustee may make all tax elections and allocations the trustee may consider appropriate; however, this authority is exercisable only in a fiduciary capacity and may not be used to enlarge or shift any beneficial interest except as an incidental consequence of the discharge of fiduciary duties. A tax election or allocation made by the trustee in good faith shall not require equitable adjustments.

10. Distributing to Custodians for Minors. The trustee shall distribute any of any trust fund to a beneficiary under the age of twenty-one (21) years by distribution to any appropriate person (who may be a trustee) chosen by the trustee as custodian under any appropriate Uniform Transfers (or Gifts) to Minors Act, to be held for the maximum period of time allowed by law. The trustee may also sell any asset that cannot be held under this custodianship and invest the sales proceeds in assets that can be so held.

11. Employing Advisors. The trustee may employ such lawyers, accountants, and other advisors as the trustee may deem useful and appropriate for the administration of any trust. The trustee may employ a professional investment advisor and delegate to this advisor any discretionary investment authorities to manage the investments of any trust, including any investment in mutual funds, investment trusts, or managed accounts, and may rely on the advisor's investment recommendations without liability to any beneficiary.

12. Buying and Holding Life Insurance. The trustee may buy and hold insurance policies on the life of any beneficiary or any person in whom a beneficiary has an insurable interest and may pay the premiums on such policies from income or principal, as the trustee may deem advisable.

13. Dividing and Distributing Assets. The trustee may divide and distribute the assets of any trust fund in kind, in money, or partly in each, without regard to the income tax basis of any asset and without the consent of any beneficiary. The decision of the trustee in dividing any portion of any trust fund between or among two or more beneficiaries, if made in good faith, shall be binding on all persons.

14. Allocation of Basis Increase. My personal representative shall allocate any increases in the adjusted basis of property owned by me at the time of my death, whether passing under my Will or otherwise, to the extent such property is eligible to receive such an allocation, as my personal representative deems to be in the best interests of my estate and its beneficiaries. The trustee shall cooperate fully with my personal representative in making these allocations. If, however, there is no personal representative appointed for my estate, then the trustee shall allocate any increases in the adjusted basis of property passing under this trust, to the extent such property is eligible to receive such an allocation, as the trustee deems to be in the best interests of my estate and its beneficiaries. In making these allocations the trustee shall:

a. First, satisfy all charitable bequests with assets to which no aggregate or spousal property basis increases may be allocated;

b. Second, satisfy all charitable bequests with assets that have an adjusted income tax basis closest to zero of all of my assets available to satisfy these bequests;

c. Third, generally not allocate basis increase to assets the gain from the sale of which is not subject to federal income tax under present federal income tax laws;

d. Fourth, allocate basis increases to assets that are reasonably likely to be sold within the three year period beginning on the date of my death, the sale of which will produce an income tax liability that is taxed at a rate higher than that on long-term capital gains; and

e. Fifth, allocate the remaining basis increase among assets in proportion to each asset's pro rata share of the total appreciation of all such assets owned by this trust on the date of my death.

Any reference in this paragraph to assets "owned by me on the date of my death" shall apply equally to assets deemed owned by me on the date of my death under the federal income tax rules governing allocation of my aggregate basis increase. The trustee shall not be liable to anyone for any allocation of my basis increases made in good faith, in the absence of gross negligence.

L. Disabled Individual Trustee. An individual trustee may not serve during a disability.

1. "Disabled" Defined. An individual trustee is "disabled" or "under a disability" if: (a) he or she is determined to be legally incompetent by a court of competent jurisdiction; (b) a conservator or guardian for such person has been appointed, based upon his or her incapacity; (c) two (2) physicians licensed to practice medicine in the Commonwealth of Virginia certify in writing to another trustee or a person who would become the successor trustee upon such disability, that in the opinion of such physicians, such individual trustee, as a result of illness, age or other cause, no longer has the capacity to act prudently or effectively in financial affairs; or (d) thirty (30) days after any other trustee or a person who would become the successor trustee upon such disability, requests that such individual trustee provide a certificate from a physician licensed to practice medicine that, in the opinion of such physician, such individual trustee has the capacity to act prudently or effectively in financial affairs and such individual trustee fails to provide such certification. The effective date of such incapacity shall be the date of the order or decree adjudicating the incapacity, the date of the order or decree appointing the guardian or conservator, the date of the certificate of incapacity of the two (2) physicians described above, or thirty (30) days after other trustee or any person who would become the successor trustee upon such disability requests a certificate of capacity and one is not provided, whichever first occurs.

2. **When I Regain My Capacity.** For purposes of this instrument, I shall be deemed to have regained capacity to serve as a trustee if: (a) there is a finding to that effect by a court of competent jurisdiction; (b) when any conservatorship or guardianship for me has been judicially terminated; or (c) upon the written determination by two (2) physicians licensed to practice medicine in the Commonwealth of Virginia (who need not be the same physicians who made the initial determination of my incapacity) that, in their pinion, my capacity is restored, and I shall have the right again to serve as trustee under this instrument, as of the effective date of my restoration of capacity, if I was serving as a trustee at the time I was determined to be incapacitated.

3. **No Liability.** No person is liable to anyone for actions taken in reliance on these certifications or for dealing with a trustee other than the one removed for disability based on these certifications. This trust shall indemnify any physician for liability for any opinion rendered in good faith as to the existence or recovery from any disability.

Article 15
Trust Administration

A. **Spendthrift Limits.** No interest in a trust under this instrument shall be subject to the beneficiary's liabilities or creditor claims or to assignment or anticipation.

B. **Protecting Trust Beneficiaries From Creditors.** If the trustee shall determine that a beneficiary would not benefit as greatly from any outright distribution of trust income or principal because of the availability of the distribution to the beneficiary's creditors, the trustee shall instead expend those amounts for the benefit of the beneficiary. This direction is intended to enable the trustee to give the beneficiary the fullest possible benefit and enjoyment of all of the trust income and principal to which he or she is entitled.

C. **Combining Multiple Trusts.** The trustee may invest the assets of multiple trusts in a single fund if the interests of the trusts are accounted for separately.

D. **Merging and Consolidating Trust Funds.** The trustee may merge or consolidate any trust into any other trust that has the same trustee and substantially the same dispositive provisions.

E. **Dividing Trust Funds.** The trustee may divide any trust fund into multiple separate trusts.

F. **Accountings.** The trustee shall not be required to file annual accounts with any court or court official in any jurisdiction.

G. **Changing Trust Situs.** A disinterested trustee may change the situs of any trust, and to the extent necessary or appropriate, move the trust assets, to a state or country other than the one in which the trust is then administered if the disinterested trustee shall determine it to be in the best interests of the trust or the beneficiaries. The disinterested trustee may elect that the law of such other jurisdiction shall govern the trust to the extent necessary or appropriate under the circumstances.

H. Rule Against Perpetuities. All assets of every trust created under this instrument (including every trust created by the exercise of a power of appointment created under this instrument, unless the exercise of such power of appointment starts a new period for the rule against perpetuities or similar rule that limits the time that property may remain in trust) that does not by its own terms do so earlier, shall vest in and be distributed to the persons then entitled to the income from such property at the expiration of the date twenty (20) years and eleven (11) months after the death of the last survivor of my *husband/wife* and those of the descendants of my grandparents alive on the date of this instrument. Upon termination of a trust under this provision, the accumulated trust income and principal shall be distributed to those beneficiaries then entitled to receive or have benefit of the income from such trust in the proportion in which they are so entitled. If the proportion of the income interests of the beneficiaries of such trust cannot be determined with reasonable certainty, the accumulated trust income and principal shall be distributed equally to such beneficiaries.

Article 16
Calculating Shares of the Residuary Trust Fund if a Federal Estate Tax Exists

This Article shall apply if there is, on the date of my death, a Federal estate tax and/or a Federal generation-skipping transfer tax, as the case may be, that applies with respect to my estate (including this trust fund).

A. My Purposes. I intend that:

1. Minimizing Federal Estate Taxes. The division of the residuary trust fund into a nonmarital share, a GST exempt marital share and a marital share, shall minimize the Federal estate taxes at my *husband/wife*'s death to the extent I can do so while deferring all Federal estate taxes until both my *husband/wife* and I have died.

2. Taking Advantage of My GST Exemption. The creation of a nonmarital share, a GST exempt marital share, and, if my *husband/wife* does not survive me, the descendants' GST exempt share, shall take advantage of my available GST exemption (defined below).

3. Qualifying for Federal Estate Tax Marital Deduction. The GST exempt marital share and the marital share shall qualify for the Federal estate tax marital deduction and all provisions of this trust shall be construed accordingly. The trustee shall, in all matters involving the GST exempt marital share and the marital share, exercise no power in a manner that would infringe upon any legal requirement for the allowance of the Federal estate tax marital deduction.

B. Defining the "Descendants' Nonmarital Share." If my *husband/wife* survives me, the "descendants' nonmarital share" shall be a fractional share of the residuary trust fund.

1. Calculating the Numerator. The numerator of the fraction shall equal the largest value of the residuary trust fund that can pass free of Federal estate tax by reason of the unified credit and the credit for state death taxes allowable with respect to my estate, to the extent the use of such credit does not increase the state death taxes with respect to my estate. This value shall be determined after being reduced by reason of my adjusted taxable gifts, all other dispositions of property included in my gross estate for which no deduction is allowed in computing my Federal estate tax, and administration expenses and other charges to principal that are not claimed and allowed as Federal estate tax deductions.

2. Calculating the Denominator. The denominator of the fraction shall equal the value of the residuary trust fund.

C. Defining the "GST Exempt Marital Share." If my *husband/wife* survives me, the "GST exempt marital share" shall be a fractional share of the residuary trust fund.

1. Calculating the Numerator. The numerator of the fraction shall be the amount of my available GST exemption (to the extent not allocated to the nonmarital share.)

2. Calculating the Denominator. The denominator of the fraction shall equal the value of the residuary trust fund.

D. Defining the "Marital Share." If my *husband/wife* survives me, the "marital share" shall be the remaining fractional share of the residuary trust fund after subtracting the nonmarital share and the GST exempt marital share.

E. Defining the "Descendants' GST Exempt Share." If my *husband/wife* does not survive me, the "descendants' GST exempt share" shall be a fractional share of the residuary trust fund.

1. Calculating the Numerator. The numerator of the fraction shall be equal to the amount of my available GST exemption.

2. Calculating the Denominator. The denominator of the fraction shall equal the value of the residuary trust fund.

F. Defining the "Descendants' Power of Appointment Share." If my *husband/wife* does not survive me, the "descendants' power of appointment share" shall be the remaining fractional share of the residuary trust fund after subtracting the descendants' GST exempt share.

G. Calculating Shares Based on Certain Assumptions. The spouse's nonmarital share shall be computed as if no election is made to qualify any property passing as such share under the Federal estate tax marital deduction, and the maximum possible election is made to qualify all property passing as the GST exempt marital share and the marital share for the Federal estate tax marital deduction.

H. Determining the Effect of Disclaimers.

1. Disclaiming the GST Exempt Marital Share or Marital Share. The trustee shall add to the nonmarital share any portion of the GST exempt marital share or the marital share as to which a qualified disclaimer by or for my *husband/wife* is made. The nonmarital share shall be calculated before any qualified disclaimer by or for my *husband/wife* of any of the GST exempt marital share or of the marital share.

2. Apportioning Transfer Taxes to Disclaimed Funds. Transfer taxes imposed on assets as to which my *husband/wife* has made a qualified disclaimer shall be apportioned to those disclaimed funds.

I. Allocating Assets Between or Among Shares.

1. Making Certain Allocations If My *Husband/Wife* Survives Me. If my *husband/wife* survives me:

a. The trustee shall allocate to the marital share and the GST exempt marital share only assets that can qualify for the Federal estate tax marital deduction.

b. The trustee shall not, to the extent possible, allocate to the marital share or the GST exempt marital share assets upon which a foreign death tax is payable.

c. The trustee shall allocate to the nonmarital share, the GST exempt marital share and, if my *husband/wife* does not survive me, the descendants' GST exempt share, solely of assets includable in my gross estate for Federal estate tax purposes.

2. Making Other Allocations. The trustee shall, in other respects, allocate assets as the trustee shall consider to be in the best interests of the beneficiaries, valuing each asset on the date or dates of allocation.

J. Allocating Income. The trustee shall allocate to each share a ratable portion of all of the income earned by my estate or the trust after my death, whether earned before or after the assets are in the possession of the trustee, and income earned on assets used to pay charges according to the same fractional shares.

K. My "Available GST Exemption" Defined. For the purposes of this Article, my "available GST exemption" means an amount equal to (1) my GST exemption, determined for Federal tax purposes, minus (2) all allocations of my GST exemption made or deemed made to transfers other than those to transfers under this trust instrument.

Article 17
Calculating Shares of the Residuary Trust Fund if No Federal Estate Tax Exists

This Article shall apply if there is, on the date of my death, no Federal estate tax that applies with respect to my estate (including this trust fund).

A. My Purposes. I intend that the division of the residuary trust fund into a descendants' nonmarital share and a marital share to take full advantage of the increases allowed under applicable Federal income tax law to the basis of assets received from me on account of my death, to the extent that it can be so done without unfairly affecting the amount of the various shares of my estate.

B. Defining the "Nonmarital Share." The "nonmarital share" shall be a fractional share of the residuary trust fund.

1. Calculating the Numerator. The numerator of the fraction shall equal the lesser of:

a. the smallest value of the assets of the residuary trust fund to which the personal representative of my estate can allocate the entire aggregate basis increase allowed under Federal income tax laws with respect to my estate for property not acquired from a spouse; and

b. forty percent (40%) of the value of the residuary trust fund.

2. Calculating the Denominator. The denominator of the fraction shall equal the value of the residuary trust fund. References in this paragraph B to my residuary trust fund shall include only those portions of my residuary trust fund to which my aggregate basis increase may be allocated under federal income tax law.

C. Defining the "Marital Share." If my *husband/wife* survives me, the marital share shall be the remaining fractional share of the residuary trust fund after subtracting the nonmarital share.

D. Allocating Assets. If my *husband/wife* survives me:

1. Allocating Basis in a Fairly Representative Manner. The trustee shall allocate to the nonmarital share only assets to which my personal representative can allocate my aggregate basis increase. Otherwise, the trustee shall select the assets that shall constitute the nonmarital share in manner such that the net appreciation of any property allocated to the nonmarital share shall be fairly representative of the net appreciation of all property available for such allocation (excluding any property to which the trustee cannot, under Federal income tax law, validly allocate any of the aggregate basis increase or the spousal property basis increase).

2. Allocating Assets Otherwise. In other respects, the trustee shall allocate assets as the trustee shall consider to be in the best interests of the beneficiaries, valuing each asset on the date or dates of allocation.

E. Allocating Trust Income. The trustee shall allocate to each share a ratable portion of all of the income earned by my estate or the trust after my death, whether earned before or after the assets are in the possession of the trustee, and income earned on assets used to pay charges according to the same fractional shares.

Article 18
Administering the QTIP and Reverse QTIP Marital Trusts

A. Making QTIP and Reverse QTIP Elections. If there is, on the date of my death, a Federal estate tax that applies with respect to my estate, the trustee may elect to qualify all or any portion of the QTIP marital trust and the reverse QTIP marital trust for the Federal estate tax marital deduction, and to treat me as the transferor of the reverse QTIP marital trust for Federal generation-skipping transfer tax purposes.

1. Making Partial Elections. If the trustee shall elect to qualify less than all of the QTIP marital trust or the reverse QTIP marital trust for the Federal estate tax marital deduction, the trustee shall divide the trust fund as to which such partial election was made into two (2) separate trusts and make all principal payments first from the trust fund that qualifies for the Federal estate tax marital deduction.

2. Allocating Assets Between or Among Shares. The trustee shall allocate assets between these shares as the trustee shall consider to be in the best interests of the beneficiaries, valuing each asset on the date of allocation.

B. Assuring Productivity of Assets. My *husband/wife* may direct the trustee to make any unproductive or underproductive assets of the QTIP marital trust and the reverse QTIP marital trust productive or to convert them to productive assets within a reasonable time.

C. Receiving and Administering Retirement Payments. If the QTIP marital trust or the reverse QTIP marital trust is entitled to receive distributions under any retirement plan or individual retirement arrangement, of which my *husband/wife* is the designated beneficiary for Federal income tax purposes, then the trustee shall do the following:

1. Distributing Greater of Income or Required Minimum Distribution. The trustee shall annually withdraw from such retirement plan trust fund or arrangement the greater of all of the income earned by my *husband/wife*'s share of such plan or arrangement, or the required minimum distribution with respect to my *husband/wife*, as determined for Federal income tax purposes.

2. Distributing Withdrawn Amounts. The trustee shall annually distribute to my *husband/wife* all amounts withdrawn from such plan or arrangement.

D. Paying Transfer Taxes.

1. Paying Transfer Taxes Generally. The trustee shall, unless my *husband/wife* provides otherwise by specific reference to this paragraph in a valid will or other writing, pay or make arrangements for the payment of the incremental transfer taxes imposed on the reverse QTIP marital trust and on the QTIP marital trust upon the death of my *husband/wife*, from the QTIP marital trust and not from the reverse QTIP marital trust.

2. Paying Transfer Taxes In Case of a Partial QTIP Election. If the trustee shall elect to qualify only part of the QTIP marital trust, the reverse QTIP marital trust, or both, and shall create two trusts as required by this Article, the transfer taxes imposed on both trusts at my *husband/wife*'s death shall be paid from the qualified trust fund to the extent possible.

Article 19
Definitions and Miscellaneous

A. Definitions. The following terms shall have the meaning set forth below for all purposes of this trust:

1. "Children" and "Descendants" Defined. "Children" and "descendants" include those now living and those later born, subject to the following rules:

a. "Children" and "descendants" include an adopted person and that adopted person's descendants if, that adopted person is adopted before reaching eighteen (18) years of age;

b. "Children" and "descendants" includes those born outside of wedlock, if, during such child's or descendant's lifetime, his or her parent through whom such child or descendant claims hereunder, has acknowledged such person as his or her child in a writing duly signed and notarized during such parent's lifetime; and

c. "Children" and "descendants" include a child produced before the parent's death by donor artificial insemination, in vitro fertilization or other form of surrogate parenthood, whether or not such child was legally adopted by such parent before such parent's death.

2. "Disinterested Trustee" Defined. A "disinterested trustee" means a trustee who is not an interested trustee.

3. "Interested Trustee" Defined. An "interested trustee" means a trustee who is also (a) a beneficiary of the trust of which he or she is a trustee or the insured under a policy of insurance owned by a trust of which he or she is a trustee; (b) married to and living together with a beneficiary of the trust of which he or she is a trustee; (c) the father, mother, issue, brother or sister, of a beneficiary of the trust of which he or she is a trustee; (d) an employee of a beneficiary of the trust of which he or she is a trustee; (e) a corporation or any employee of a corporation in which the stock holdings of the trustee and the trust are significant from the viewpoint of voting control; or (f) a subordinate employee of a corporation in which the trustee is an executive.

4. "Personal Representative" Defined. A "personal representative" means the legal representative of a decedent's estate. The "personal representative" shall include any executor, ancillary executor, administrator, or ancillary administrator, whether local or foreign and whether of all or part of my estate, multiple personal representatives, and their successors.

5. "Residuary Trust Fund" Defined. The "residuary trust fund" means the real and personal property passing under this instrument, after paying any amounts certified by the personal representative of my estate as needed to settle my debts and expenses of estate administration.

6. "Transfer Taxes" Defined. "Transfer taxes" means all estate, inheritance, legacy, succession, and other transfer taxes, including any tax on excess retirement accumulations, imposed with respect to my death by any state, the United States, or by any foreign country. "Transfer taxes" also includes all taxes that are reimbursable under Sections 2207 through 2207B of the Internal Revenue Code of 1986, as amended, which right of reimbursement I hereby waive. "Transfer taxes" also includes all interest and penalties on such taxes.

7. "Trustee" Defined. The "trustee" or "trustees" shall include each trustee individually, multiple trustees, and their successors.

B. Retroactive Legislation. I include in this instrument certain dispositions and direct certain actions that shall occur only if, on the date of my death, no federal estate tax or Federal generation-skipping transfer tax applies with respect to my estate. These provisions shall not apply if, on the date of my death, no federal estate tax or federal generation-skipping transfer tax, as the case may be, applies with respect to my estate, but such tax or taxes is/are retroactively reinstated before April 1, 2011, and apply under such retroactive legislation with respect to my estate. If such retroactive legislation is finally determined to be unconstitutional or otherwise invalid, these references shall apply as if such retroactive legislation had never been enacted.

C. Absence of Trust Beneficiaries. If all of the beneficiaries of any trust under this instrument should die before the trust assets have vested in them, the trustee shall distribute all of the remaining assets of that trust as follows:

1. One Half to My Heirs and Distributee. One half (½) (or all, if there are no persons to take under subparagraph C.2. of this Article) to the heirs and distributees who would have inherited my personal estate, and in such shares as they would have inherited it, had I died unmarried and without a valid will, determined on the later of the date of my death or the date of the death of the last of the trust beneficiaries to die; and

2. One Half to My *Husband/Wife*'s Distributees. One half (½) (or all, if there are no persons to take under subparagraph C.1. of this Article) to the heirs and distributees who would have inherited my *husband/wife*'s personal estate, and in such shares as they would have inherited it, had he died unmarried and without a valid will, determined on the later of the date of my death or the date of the death of the last of the trust beneficiaries to die.

D. Applicable Law. This instrument shall be governed by and construed according to the laws of the *State*.

E. Number. Whenever the context requires, the singular includes the plural and the plural the singular.

F. Survivorship. No person shall be deemed to have survived me for purposes of this instrument, unless he or she is living on the date ninety (90) days after the date of my death.

G. Tax-Related Terms. All tax-related terms shall have the same meaning they have in the Internal Revenue Code of 1986, as amended.

[Add state-specific signature and notary clauses, schedule of assets, and where required, attesting witness clause]

¶ A.07 FORM 7: WILL FOR ESTATE OF $6 MILLION TO $10 MILLION—MARITAL DEDUCTION TAX PLANNING— GST TAX PLANNING WITH LIFETIME TRUST FOR CHILDREN AND REVERSE QTIP—CREATES A NONMARITAL SHARE EQUAL TO STATE ESTATE TAX EXEMPTION—TRUSTEE CAN DISTRIBUTE FROM QTIP MINIMUM AMOUNT OF PRINCIPAL SUFFICIENT TO GIVE SPOUSE ENOUGH APPRECIATION TO TAKE ADVANTAGE OF AGGREGATE BASIS INCREASE AT SURVIVING SPOUSE'S DEATH—CREATES STATE-ONLY QTIP

Will of *Testator*[7]

I, *Testator*, of [*locality, state*], make this my will. I revoke any other wills and codicils made by me.

Article 1
My Family

I am married to *Spouse* (sometimes referred to as "my *husband/wife*") and I have [*number of children*] children, *Children*.

Article 2
My Personal Effects

A. Disposing of My Personal Effects. I leave my personal effects (defined below) to my *husband/wife*, *Spouse*, if *he/she* survives me, or otherwise to my descendants who survive me, *per stirpes*. If neither my *husband/wife* nor any of my children nor their descendants survive me, these personal effects shall be added to

---

[7] **KEY:**

Testator	— full name of the testator
Spouse	— full name of testator's spouse
husband/wife	— "husband" or "wife," as the case may be
Children	— full names of testator's children
he/she	— "he" or "she" (referring to the spouse)
his/her	— "his" or "her" (referring to the spouse)
him/her	— "him" or "her" (referring to the spouse)
AlternatePR	— name of the alternate personal representative (after spouse)
FirstTrustee	— name of the first trustee
SecondTrustee	— name of the alternate trustee

the residue of my estate. An adult person with whom a minor resides may give a binding receipt for any personal effects passing to the minor.

B. Memorandum. I may make a memorandum of how I wish some of my personal effects to be distributed, and I request that my wishes be followed.

Article 3
My Personal Residence

I leave all of my interest in the properties my personal representative (defined below) shall determine to have been used by me or a member of my family as personal residences to my *husband/wife*, *Spouse*, if *he/she* survives me, to the extent that they do not pass to *him/her* by right of survivorship. Personal residences shall also include all adjoining lands and any related casualty insurance policies.

Article 4
My Residuary Estate

A. If a Federal Estate Tax Exists. If there is, on the date of my death, a Federal estate tax and/or a Federal generation-skipping transfer tax, as the case may be, that applies with respect to my estate, I leave my residuary estate (defined below), as follows:

1. If My *Husband/Wife* Survives Me. If my *husband/wife*, *Spouse*, survives me, my personal representative shall divide my residuary estate into a nonmarital share, a state-only marital share, a GST exempt marital share, and a marital share (all defined below).

a. The nonmarital share shall be held under the Article entitled "The Family Trust."

b. The state-only marital share shall be held under the Article entitled "The State-Only Trust."

c. The GST exempt marital share shall be held under the Article entitled "The Reverse QTIP Marital Trust."

d. The marital share shall be held under the Article entitled "The QTIP Marital Trust."

2. If My *Husband/Wife* Does Not Survive Me. If my *husband/wife* does not survive me, my personal representative shall divide my residuary estate into a descendants' GST exempt share and a descendants' power of appointment share (both defined below).

a. The descendants' GST exempt share shall be held under the Article entitled "The Descendants' Trust."

b. My personal representative shall distribute the descendants' power of appointment share to my descendants who survive me, *per stirpes*, except that the share for any child of mine shall be added to the trust fund for such child under the

Article entitled "Child's Power of Appointment Trust," for that child, and the share for any more remote descendant of mine who shall then not yet have reached the age of thirty-five (35) years, shall be held under the Article entitled "Contingent Trust for Certain Beneficiaries."

B. If No Federal Estate Tax Exists. If there is, on the date of my death, no Federal estate tax or Federal generation-skipping transfer tax that applies with respect to my estate, I leave my residuary estate, as follows:

1. If My *Husband/Wife* Survives Me. If my *husband/wife* survives me, my personal representative shall divide my residuary estate into a nonmarital share, a state-only marital share and a marital share.

a. The nonmarital share shall be held under the Article entitled "The Decendants' Trust."

b. The state-only marital share shall be held under the Article entitled "The State-Only Marital Trust."

c. The marital share shall be held under the Article entitled "The QTIP Marital Trust."

2. If My *Husband/Wife* Does Not Survive Me. If my *husband/wife* does not survive me, my personal representative shall hold my residuary estate under the Article entitled "The Descendants' Trust."

Article 5
The Family Trust

A. Until the Family Trust Termination Date. Until the family trust termination date (defined below), the trustee (defined below) shall distribute to or for the benefit of my *husband/wife*, my then-living children and my then-living more remote descendants, as much of the net income and principal of the family trust as the trustee may deem appropriate for their health, education, support, or maintenance, annually adding to principal any undistributed income, annually adding to principal any undistributed income.

1. Distributions May be Unequal. The Trustee may distribute income and principal of the family trust unequally and may make distributions to some beneficiaries and not to others.

2. Other Assets. The trustee shall consider other income and assets readily available to each beneficiary, including assets available from other trusts created under my will, in making distributions.

3. Priority Purposes. In making these distributions, my primary purpose is to provide for the support in reasonable comfort of my *husband/wife* for the rest of *his/her* life and the education and support of my children until they have completed their education.

B. Upon the Family Trust Termination Date. Upon the family trust termination date, the trustee shall distribute the remaining trust funds to my then-living descendants, per stirpes, subject to the provisions of the Article entitled Contingent Trust for Certain Beneficiaries.

C. "Family Trust Termination Date" Defined. The family trust termination date shall be the date of the death of the last to die of my *husband/wife* and my children alive on the date of my death.

Article 6
The State-Only Marital Trust

The state-only marital trust shall be held under this Article.

A. Distributing Trust Fund During My *Husband/Wife*'s Life. The trustee shall distribute the net income of the state-only marital trust quarterly or more frequently to my *husband/wife* during *his/her* life. The trustee shall also distribute to my *husband/wife* as much of the principal of the state-only marital trust as is appropriate for any purpose.

B. Distributing Trust Fund At My *Husband/Wife*'s Death.

1. Distributing Income. At my *husband/wife*'s death, my trustee shall distribute to my *husband/wife*'s estate any undistributed income of the state-only marital trust.

2. Distribution of Principal. At my *husband/wife*'s death, my trustee shall distribute the principal of the state-only marital trust, to the extent it is not used to pay death taxes (defined below), as my *husband/wife* may direct by specific reference to this special power of appointment in *his/her* last will.

a. My *husband/wife* may appoint the state-only marital trust fund, either outright or in further trust, but only to or among any one (1) or more of my descendants.

b. My *husband/wife* may not appoint any portion of the state-only marital trust to my *husband/wife*, *his/her* creditors, *his/her* estate, or the creditors of *his/her* estate.

3. Distributing Unappointed Assets. The trustee shall add the unappointed principal of the state-only marital trust to the trust held under the Article entitled "The Descendants' Trust."

Article 7
The Reverse QTIP Marital Trust

The reverse QTIP marital trust shall be held under this Article.

A. Distributing Trust Fund During My *Husband/Wife*'s Life. The trustee shall distribute the net income of the reverse QTIP marital trust quarterly or more frequently to my *husband/wife* during *his/her* life. The trustee shall also distribute to my *husband/wife* as much of the principal of the reverse QTIP marital trust as is appropriate for any purpose.

B. Distributing Trust Fund At My *Husband/Wife*'s Death.

1. Distributing Income. At my *husband/wife*'s death, the trustee shall distribute to my *husband/wife*'s estate any undistributed income of the reverse QTIP marital trust.

2. Appointing Trust Principal. At my *husband/wife*'s death, the trustee shall distribute the principal of the reverse QTIP marital trust, to the extent it is not used to pay transfer taxes (defined below) as provided below, as my *husband/wife* may direct by specific reference to this special power of appointment in *his/her* last will.

a. My *husband/wife* may appoint the reverse QTIP marital trust fund, either outright or in further trust, but only to or among any one (1) or more of my descendants.

b. My *husband/wife* may not appoint any portion of the reverse QTIP marital trust fund to my *husband/wife*, *his/her* creditors, *his/her* estate, or the creditors of *his/her* estate.

3. Distributing Unappointed Assets. The trustee shall add the unappointed principal of the reverse QTIP marital trust to the trust held under the Article entitled "The Descendants' Trust."

Article 8
The QTIP Marital Trust

The QTIP marital trust shall be held under this Article.

A. Distributing Trust Fund During My *Husband/Wife*'s Life. The trustee shall distribute the net income of the QTIP marital trust quarterly or more frequently to my *husband/wife*, *Spouse*, during *his/her* life.

1. Principal Distributions. The trustee shall also distribute to my *husband/wife* as much of the principal of the QTIP marital trust as is appropriate for any purpose.

2. Distributing Additional Principal if There is No Federal Estate Tax. If the trustee deems it likely that my *husband/wife* will die before January 1, 2011, the trustee shall distribute to my *husband/wife* a fractional share of this trust.

a. The numerator of this fraction shall be equal to the smallest value of the assets of this trust fund to which the personal representative of my *husband/wife*'s estate could allocate all of the aggregate basis increase allowed to my *husband/wife* under Federal income tax laws, less the amount of such aggregate basis increase that could be allocated to other assets already owned by my *husband/wife* at the time of this distribution.

b. The denominator of this fraction shall equal the value of the *spouse* trust fund.

B. Distributing Trust Fund At My *Husband/Wife*'s Death.

1. Distributing Income. At my *husband/wife*'s death, the trustee shall distribute to my *husband/wife*'s estate any undistributed income of the QTIP marital trust.

2. Appointing Trust Principal. At my *husband/wife*'s death, the trustee shall distribute the principal of the QTIP marital trust, to the extent it is not used to pay transfer taxes as provided below, as my *husband/wife* may direct by specific reference to this special power of appointment in *his/her* last will.

a. My *husband/wife* may appoint the QTIP marital trust fund, either outright or in further trust, but only to or among any one (1) or more of my descendants.

b. My *husband/wife* may not appoint any portion of the QTIP marital trust fund to my *husband/wife*, *his/her* creditors, *his/her* estate, or the creditors of *his/her* estate.

3. Distributing Unappointed Trust Fund. The trustee shall distribute the unappointed QTIP marital trust fund to my then-living descendants, *per stirpes*, except that the share for any child of mine shall be added to the child's power of appointment trust for that child, and the share for any more remote descendant of mine who shall then not yet have reached the age of thirty-five (35) years, shall be held for such descendant under the Article entitled "Contingent Trust for Certain Beneficiaries."

Article 9
Child's Power of Appointment Trust

The child's power of appointment trust for each child of mine shall be held as a separate trust under this Article.

A. Distributing Trust Fund During the Child's Life. The trustee shall distribute to or for the benefit of each child for whom a trust is created under this Article, as much of the net income and principal as the child shall request at any time or as the trustee may consider appropriate for any purpose, annually adding to principal any undistributed income.

B. Distributing Trust Fund At the Child's Death. Upon the death of a child of mine who survives me, the trustee shall distribute the remaining principal and income of such child's trust under this Article as that child may direct by specific reference to this power of appointment in that child's last will.

1. Appointing Everything But Limited Portion. Each such child may appoint the remaining principal and income of such child's trust under this Article (other than the limited portion (defined below)) of such trust fund, either outright or in further trust, to or among any persons, including such child's estate.

2. Appointing Limited Portion. Each such child may appoint the limited portion of the principal and income of such child's trust under this Article outright or in further trust, but only to or among my then-living descendants, and such child may not appoint any of the limited portion to such child himself or herself, such child's creditors, such child's estate, or the creditors of such child's estate.

3. Distributing Unappointed Trust Fund. The trustee shall distribute any unappointed portion of the fund of a deceased child's trust under this Article to such child's then-living descendants, *per stirpes*, or if there are no such descendants then living, to my then-living descendants, *per stirpes*, except that the fund that would thus be distributed to any then-living child of mine shall be added to such child's trust under this Article.

4. "Limited Portion" Defined. The "limited portion" of the fund of a child's trust under this Article is that portion which would pass to one or more persons assigned to the same or a higher generation as the deceased child for Federal generation-skipping transfer tax purposes, were such child to die without a valid will. If such child dies in a year in which there is no Federal generation-skipping transfer tax applicable with respect to such child's estate, the "limited portion" shall be the entire fund of the child's trust.

Article 10
The Descendants' Trust

A. Until the Descendants' Trust Termination Date. Until the descendants' trust termination date (defined below), the trustee (defined below) shall distribute to or for the benefit of my then-living children and my then-living more remote descendants, as much of the net income and principal of the family trust as the trustee may deem appropriate for their health, education, support, or maintenance, annually adding to principal any undistributed income, annually adding to principal any undistributed income.

1. Distributions May be Unequal. The Trustee may distribute income and principal of the family trust unequally and may make distributions to some beneficiaries and not to others.

2. Other Assets. The trustee shall consider other income and assets readily available to each beneficiary, including assets available from other trusts created under my will, in making distributions.

3. Priority Purpose. In making these distributions, my primary purpose is to provide for the education and support of my children until they have completed their education.

B. Upon the Descendants' Trust Termination Date. Upon the descendants' trust termination date, the trustee shall distribute the remaining trust funds to my then-living descendants, per stirpes, subject to the provisions of the Article entitled Contingent Trust for Certain Beneficiaries.

C. "Descendants' Trust Termination Date" Defined. The descendants' trust termination date shall be the date of the death of the last to die of my children alive on the date of my death.

Article 11
Contingent Trust for Certain Beneficiaries

If a beneficiary (other than a child of mine) is entitled to receive any part of my estate or any portion of any trust fund held under this will while the beneficiary is under the age of thirty-five (35) years, the trustee may retain such assets in a separate trust for that beneficiary.

A. Distributing Trust Fund Before the Contingent Trust Termination Date. Until the contingent trust termination date (defined below), the trustee shall distribute to or for the benefit of the beneficiary as much of the net income and principal as the trustee may consider appropriate for the beneficiary's health, education, support, or maintenance, annually adding to principal any undistributed income.

B. Distributing Trust Fund At the Contingent Trust Termination Date. Upon the contingent trust termination date, the trustee shall distribute the remaining assets to the beneficiary if the beneficiary is then living or otherwise to the beneficiary's estate to be distributed as part of that estate.

C. "Contingent Trust Termination Date" Defined. The "contingent trust termination date" shall be the earlier of (1) the date on which the beneficiary dies or (2) the date on which the beneficiary reaches the age of thirty-five (35) years.

Article 12
Special Limits on Powers of Interested Trustee

The following limitations shall apply, notwithstanding other provisions of this instrument.

A. Limiting Actions by Interested Trustees. No interested trustee (defined below) may participate in the exercise of any discretion to distribute principal to himself or herself, except as is appropriate for his or her health, education, support, and maintenance, or any of them. No interested trustee may participate in the exercise of any discretion to distribute or expend principal or income in a manner that would discharge that trustee's personal obligation to support the beneficiary. No interested trustee may participate in the exercise of any incident of ownership over any policy owned by the trust insuring the life of such trustee.

B. Disinterested Trustees Exercising Certain Powers. A disinterested trustee (defined below) who is serving as a co-trustee with an interested trustee, may exercise those discretions granted under this instrument the exercise of which by an interested trustee are precluded.

1. If Multiple Trustees Include an Interested Trustee Who Cannot Act. The number of trustees who must consent to the exercise of a power granted under this instrument, as determined under the Article entitled "My Fiduciaries" shall be determined by treating the interested trustees who are not entitled, under this Article, to participate in the exercise of the power or discretion, as if they were not then serving.

2. If All Trustees Are Precluded From Acting. If this Article precludes every then-serving trustee from exercising a power otherwise granted to the trustee under this instrument, the then-serving trustee shall appoint a disinterested trustee who may exercise such power (or decline to exercise it) as if that disinterested trustee were the sole then-serving trustee.

Article 13
Debts, Expenses, and Taxes

A. Paying Debts and Expenses. My personal representative shall pay from my residuary estate my debts (but not before their maturity) and funeral and burial expenses, including the cost of a suitable memorial, without court order.

1. Paying Certain Joint Debts. My personal representative shall pay only my proportionate share of any debts for which I am jointly liable with my *husband/ wife*.

2. Paying Packing and Shipping Expenses. My personal representative shall pay all packing, shipping, insurance, and other charges relating to the distribution of any of my personal property without seeking reimbursement from the recipient of such personal property.

B. Paying Transfer Taxes. My personal representative shall pay all transfer taxes, other than generation-skipping transfer taxes, payable by reason of my death on assets passing under this will, from my residuary estate.

1. Apportioning Transfer Taxes on Nonprobate Assets. My personal representative shall apportion transfer taxes imposed on any assets not passing under this will to those assets and the transfer taxes on those assets shall be paid from those assets as provided by the laws of the state in which I reside at my death, except as expressly provided elsewhere in this will.

2. Apportioning Generation-Skipping Transfer Taxes. My personal representative shall apportion all generation-skipping transfer taxes for which my estate is legally responsible to those generation-skipping transfers, whether or not under this will.

3. Apportioning Transfer Taxes Away From Deductible Assets. Assets passing as the GST exempt marital share or as the marital share shall have the full benefit of the Federal estate tax marital deduction allowed with respect to any transfer taxes, and shall not bear any transfer taxes. Other assets passing to my *husband/ wife* or to any charitable organization, whether under this will or otherwise, shall have the full benefit of any available marital or charitable deduction for Federal and other transfer tax purposes, in determining the share of transfer taxes that should be borne by those assets.

Article 14
My Fiduciaries

A. Naming My Personal Representatives. I name my *husband/wife*, *Spouse*, to be my personal representative, and I give *him/her* the right to name one or more persons to serve with *him/her* or in *his/her* place. If my *husband/wife* fails or ceases to serve and there is no other person serving or named to serve, I name the *AlternatePR*, of [locality, state], to be my personal representative.

B. Naming My Trustees. I name *FirstTrustee*, of [locality, state], to be the trustee of any trust under this will. If *FirstTrustee* shall be unable or unwilling to serve or to continue serving, I name *SecondTrustee*, of [locality, state] to be the trustee of any trust under this will.

C. No Surety or Bond. No personal representative or trustee named by me or by another personal representative or trustee shall be required to provide surety or other security on a bond.

D. Naming Additional Fiduciaries. I authorize my named fiduciaries (defined below) to appoint any person as an additional personal representative or trustee in the same state or another state in which administration may be appropriate to serve at the pleasure of the appointing fiduciaries.

E. Delegating Fiduciary Powers and Authorities. My fiduciaries may delegate to another fiduciary any power or authority granted by me to my fiduciaries, to continue at the pleasure of the delegating fiduciary, unless otherwise agreed. Any person dealing in good faith with a fiduciary may rely upon that fiduciary's representation that a delegation has been made and remains in effect under this paragraph.

F. Fiduciary Resigning.

 1. Personal Representative May Resign. A personal representative may resign by giving written notice specifying the effective date of the resignation to the designated successor.

 2. Trustee May Resign. Any trustee may resign by giving written notice specifying the effective date of the resignation to the designated successor. If no successor is designated, the resigning trustee shall give notice to each adult beneficiary to whom trust income then may be distributed.

G. Removing a Trustee. A trustee may be removed by the vote of two-thirds (⅔) of the then-living adult beneficiaries to whom trust income may then be distributed.

H. Filling Fiduciary Vacancies.

 1. Court Appointing Personal Representative to Fill Vacancy. If no successor personal representative is designated, a court of appropriate jurisdiction shall name a successor personal representative.

 2. Beneficiaries Appointing Corporate Trustee to Fill Vacancy. A corporation no substantial portion of the stock of which is owned by beneficiaries of this

trust, may be named as successor trustee to fill any vacancy, by majority vote of the adult beneficiaries to whom trust income then may be distributed.

I. No Liability for Acts or Omissions of Predecessors. No fiduciary shall be responsible for or need inquire into any acts or omissions of a prior fiduciary.

J. Compensating Fiduciaries. In addition to reimbursement for expenses, each individual fiduciary is entitled to reasonable compensation for services. Each corporate fiduciary is entitled to compensation based on its written fee schedule in effect at the time its services are rendered or as otherwise agreed, and its compensation may vary from time to time based on that schedule.

K. Management Powers. I authorize my fiduciaries to exercise all powers conferred by applicable state law and to do the following in a fiduciary capacity.

1. Prudent Investor Rule. My fiduciaries may hold and retain as part of my estate or any trust fund any property owned by me, whether or not such investment would be appropriate for a prudent investor. My fiduciaries may also hold and retain as part of my estate or any trust fund any property received from any source, and invest and reinvest my estate or trust fund (or leave it temporarily uninvested) in any type of property and every kind of investment in the same manner as a prudent investor would invest his or her own assets.

2. Holding Assets For Use of Trust Beneficiaries. My trustee may buy and hold in trust, assets that will be used personally by one or more beneficiaries, even if those assets would not otherwise be acquired by a prudent investor investing his or her own assets.

3. Transferring Assets. My fiduciaries may sell or exchange any real or personal property contained in my estate or any trust, for cash or credit, at public or private sale, and with such warranties or indemnifications as my fiduciaries may deem advisable.

4. Borrowing Money. My fiduciaries may borrow money (even from a fiduciary or beneficiary of my estate or any trust) for the benefit of my estate or any trust and secure these debts with assets of my estate or any trust.

5. Granting Security Interests. My fiduciaries may grant security interests and execute all instruments creating such interests upon such terms as my fiduciaries may deem advisable.

6. Compromising Claims. My fiduciaries may compromise and adjust claims against or on behalf of my estate or any trust on such terms as my fiduciaries may deem advisable.

7. Not Disclosing Nominees. My fiduciaries may take title to any securities in the name of any custodian or nominee without disclosing this relationship.

8. Allocating Between Income and Principal. My fiduciaries may determine whether receipts are income or principal and whether disbursements are to be charged against income or principal to the extent not clearly established by state law.

A determination made by my fiduciaries in good faith shall not require equitable adjustments.

9. Making Tax Elections. My fiduciaries may make all tax elections and allocations my fiduciaries may consider appropriate; however, this authority is exercisable only in a fiduciary capacity and may not be used to enlarge or shift any beneficial interest except as an incidental consequence of the discharge of fiduciary duties. A tax election or allocation made by my fiduciaries in good faith shall not require equitable adjustments.

10. Distributing to Custodians for Minors. My fiduciaries shall distribute any of my estate or any trust fund to a beneficiary under the age of twenty-one (21) years by distribution to any appropriate person (who may be a fiduciary) chosen by my fiduciaries as custodian under any appropriate Uniform Transfers (or Gifts) to Minors Act, to be held for the maximum period of time allowed by law. My fiduciaries may also sell any asset that cannot be held under this custodianship and invest the sales proceeds in assets that can be so held.

11. Employing Advisors. My fiduciaries may employ such lawyers, accountants, and other advisors as my fiduciaries may deem useful and appropriate for the administration of my estate or any trust. My fiduciaries may employ a professional investment advisor and delegate to this advisor any discretionary investment authorities to manage the investments of my estate or any trust, including any investment in mutual funds, investment trusts, or managed accounts, and may rely on the advisor's investment recommendations without liability to any beneficiary.

12. Buying and Holding Life Insurance. My fiduciaries may buy and hold insurance policies on the life of any beneficiary or any person in whom a beneficiary has an insurable interest and may pay the premiums on such policies from income or principal, as my fiduciaries may deem advisable.

13. Dividing and Distributing Assets. My fiduciaries may divide and distribute the assets of my estate or any trust fund in kind, in money, or partly in each, without regard to the income tax basis of any asset and without the consent of any beneficiary. The decision of my fiduciaries in dividing any portion of my estate or any trust fund between or among two or more beneficiaries, if made in good faith, shall be binding on all persons.

14. Allocation of Basis Increase. My personal representative shall allocate any increases in the adjusted basis of property owned by me at the time of my death, whether passing under my Will or otherwise, to the extent such property is eligible to receive such an allocation, as my personal representative deems to be in the best interests of my estate and its beneficiaries. In making these allocations my personal representative shall:

a. First, satisfy all charitable bequests with assets to which no aggregate or spousal property basis increases may be allocated;

b. Second, satisfy all charitable bequests with assets that have an adjusted income tax basis closest to zero of all of my assets available to satisfy these bequests;

c. Third, generally not allocate basis increase to assets the gain from the sale of which is not subject to federal income tax under present federal income tax laws;

d. Fourth, allocate basis increases to assets that are reasonably likely to be sold within the three year period beginning on the date of my death, the sale of which will produce an income tax liability that is taxed at a rate higher than that on long-term capital gains; and

e. Fifth, allocate the remaining basis increase among assets in proportion to each asset's pro rata share of the total appreciation of all such assets owned by me on the date of my death.

Any reference in this paragraph to assets "owned by me on the date of my death" shall apply equally to assets deemed owned by me on the date of my death under the federal income tax rules governing allocation of my aggregate basis increase. My personal representative shall not be liable to anyone for any allocation of my basis increases made in good faith, in the absence of gross negligence.

Article 15
Trust Administration

A. Spendthrift Limits. No interest in a trust under this will shall be subject to the beneficiary's liabilities or creditor claims or to assignment or anticipation.

B. Protecting Trust Beneficiaries From Creditors. If the trustee shall determine that a beneficiary would not benefit as greatly from any outright distribution of trust income or principal because of the availability of the distribution to the beneficiary's creditors, the trustee shall instead expend those amounts for the benefit of the beneficiary. This direction is intended to enable the trustee to give the beneficiary the fullest possible benefit and enjoyment of all of the trust income and principal to which he or she is entitled.

C. Combining Multiple Trusts. The trustee may invest the assets of multiple trusts in a single fund if the interests of the trusts are accounted for separately.

D. Merging and Consolidating Trust Funds. The trustee may merge or consolidate any trust into any other trust that has the same trustee and substantially the same dispositive provisions.

E. Dividing Trust Funds. The trustee may divide any trust fund into multiple separate trusts.

F. Accountings. The trustee shall not be required to file annual accounts with any court or court official in any jurisdiction.

G. Changing Trust Situs. A disinterested trustee may change the situs of any trust under this will, and to the extent necessary or appropriate, move the trust assets, to a state or country other than the one in which the trust is then administered if the disinterested trustee shall determine it to be in the best interests of the trust or the

beneficiaries. The disinterested trustee may elect that the law of such other jurisdiction shall govern the trust to the extent necessary or appropriate under the circumstances.

H. Rule Against Perpetuities. All assets of every trust created under this instrument (including every trust created by the exercise of a power of appointment created under this instrument, unless the exercise of such power of appointment starts a new period for the rule against perpetuities or similar rule that limits the time that property may remain in trust) that does not by its own terms do so earlier, shall vest in and be distributed to the persons then entitled to the income from such property at the expiration of the date twenty (20) years and eleven (11) months after the death of the last survivor of my *husband/wife* and those of the descendants of my grandparents alive on the date of this instrument. Upon termination of a trust under this provision, the accumulated trust income and principal shall be distributed to those beneficiaries then entitled to receive or have benefit of the income from such trust in the proportion in which they are so entitled. If the proportion of the income interests of the beneficiaries of such trust cannot be determined with reasonable certainty, the accumulated trust income and principal shall be distributed equally to such beneficiaries.

Article 16
Calculating Shares of the Residuary Estate if a Federal Estate Tax Exists

This Article shall apply if there is, on the date of my death, a Federal estate tax and/or a Federal generation-skipping transfer tax, as the case may be, that applies with respect to my estate.

A. My Purposes. I intend that:

1. Minimizing Federal and *State* Estate Taxes. The division of my residuary estate into a nonmarital share, a state-only marital share, a GST exempt marital share and a marital share, shall minimize the Federal and *State* estate taxes at my *husband/wife*'s death to the extent I can do so while deferring all Federal and *State* estate taxes until both my *husband/wife* and I have died.

2. Taking Advantage of My GST Exemption. The creation of a nonmarital share, a GST exempt marital share, and, if my *husband/wife* does not survive me, the descendants' GST exempt share, shall take advantage of my available GST exemption (defined below).

3. Qualifying for Federal Estate Tax Marital Deduction. The GST exempt marital share and the marital share shall qualify for the Federal estate tax marital deduction and all provisions of this will shall be construed accordingly. My fiduciaries shall, in all matters involving the GST exempt marital share and the marital share, exercise no power in a manner that would infringe upon any legal requirement for the allowance of the Federal estate tax marital deduction.

4. Qualifying for *State* Estate Tax Marital Deduction. The state-only marital share shall qualify for the estate tax marital deduction under the laws of *State* and all provisions of this will shall be construed accordingly. My fiduciaries shall, in all matters involving the state-only marital share, exercise no power in a manner that would infringe upon any legal requirement for the allowance of the estate tax marital deduction under the laws of *State*.

B. Defining the "Nonmarital Share." If my *husband/wife* survives me, the "nonmarital share" shall be a fractional share of my residuary estate.

1. Calculating the Numerator. The numerator of the fraction shall equal the smaller of:

a. the largest value of my residuary estate that can pass free of *State* estate tax were it to pass to an individual other than my *spouse*. This value shall be determined after being reduced by reason of all other dispositions of property included in my gross estate for which no deduction is allowed in computing my *State* estate tax, and administration expenses and other charges to principal that are not claimed and allowed as *State* estate tax deductions; and

b. the largest value of my residuary estate that can pass free of Federal estate tax by reason of the unified credit and the credit for state death taxes allowable with respect to my estate, to the extent the use of such credit does not increase the state death taxes with respect to my estate. This value shall be determined after being reduced by reason of my adjusted taxable gifts, all other dispositions of property included in my gross estate for which no deduction is allowed in computing my Federal estate tax, and administration expenses and other charges to principal that are not claimed and allowed as Federal estate tax deductions.

2. Calculating the Denominator. The denominator of the fraction shall equal the value of my residuary estate.

C. Defining the "State-Only Marital Trust." If my *husband/wife* survives me, and if I die domiciled in *state*, my fiduciaries shall create a "state-only marital share," which shall be a fractional share of my residuary estate.

1. Calculating the Numerator. The numerator of the fraction shall be the difference between:

a. The largest value of the family trust that can pass free of *State* estate tax were it to pass to an individual other than my *husband/wife*. This value shall be determined after being reduced by reason of all other dispositions of property included in my gross estate for which no deduction is allowed in computing my *State* estate tax, and administration expenses and other charges to principal that are not claimed and allowed as *State* estate tax deductions; and

b. The numerator of the fraction by which the nonmarital trust is calculated under this article.

2. Calculating the Denominator. The denominator of the fraction shall equal the value of my residuary estate.

D. Defining the "GST Exempt Marital Share." If my *husband/wife* survives me, the "GST exempt marital share" shall be a fractional share of my residuary estate.

1. Calculating the Numerator. The numerator of the fraction shall be the amount of my available GST exemption (to the extent not allocated to the nonmarital share.)

2. Calculating the Denominator. The denominator of the fraction shall equal the value of my residuary estate.

E. Defining the "Marital Share." If my *husband/wife* survives me, the "marital share" shall be the remaining fractional share of my residuary estate after subtracting the nonmarital share, the state-only marital share, and the GST exempt marital share.

F. Defining the "Descendants' GST Exempt Share." If my *husband/wife* does not survive me, the "descendants' GST exempt share" shall be a fractional share of my residuary estate.

1. Calculating the Numerator. The numerator of the fraction shall be equal to the amount of my available GST exemption.

2. Calculating the Denominator. The denominator of the fraction shall equal the value of my residuary estate.

G. Defining the "Descendants' Power of Appointment Share." If my *husband/wife* does not survive me, the "descendants' power of appointment share" shall be the remaining fractional share of my residuary estate after subtracting the descendants' GST exempt share.

H. Calculating Shares Based on Certain Assumptions. The spouse's nonmarital share shall be computed as if no election were made to qualify any property passing as such share under the Federal estate tax marital deduction, and the maximum possible election were made to qualify all property passing as the GST exempt marital share and the marital share for the Federal estate tax marital deduction.

I. Determining the Effect of Disclaimers.

1. Disclaiming the GST Exempt Marital Share or Marital Share. My fiduciaries shall add to the nonmarital share any portion of the GST exempt marital share or the marital share as to which a qualified disclaimer by or for my *husband/wife* is made. The nonmarital share shall be calculated before any qualified disclaimer by or for my *husband/wife* of any of the GST exempt marital share or of the marital share.

2. Apportioning Transfer Taxes to Disclaimed Funds. Transfer taxes imposed on assets as to which my *husband/wife* has made a qualified disclaimer shall be apportioned to those disclaimed funds.

J. Allocating Assets Between or Among Shares.

1. Making Certain Allocations If My *Husband/Wife* Survives Me. If my *husband/wife* survives me:

a. My personal representative shall allocate to the marital share, the state-only marital share and the GST exempt marital share only assets that can qualify for the Federal estate tax marital deduction.

b. My personal representative shall not, to the extent possible, allocate to the marital share, the state-only marital share or the GST exempt marital share assets upon which a foreign death tax is payable.

c. My personal representative shall allocate to the nonmarital share, the GST exempt marital share and, if my *husband/wife* does not survive me, the descendants' GST exempt share, solely of assets includable in my gross estate for Federal estate tax purposes.

2. Making Other Allocations. My personal representative shall, in other respects, allocate assets as my personal representative shall consider to be in the best interests of the beneficiaries, valuing each asset on the date or dates of allocation.

K. Allocating Income. My personal representative and trustee shall allocate to each share a ratable portion of all of the income earned by my estate after my death, whether earned before or after the assets are in the possession of the trustee, and income earned on assets used to pay charges according to the same fractional shares.

L. My "Available GST Exemption" Defined. For the purposes of this Article, my "available GST exemption" means an amount equal to (1) my GST exemption, determined for Federal tax purposes, minus (2) all allocations of my GST exemption made or deemed made to transfers other than those to transfers under this will.

Article 17
Calculating Shares of the Residuary Estate if No Federal Estate Tax Exists

This Article shall apply if there is, on the date of my death, no Federal estate tax and/or Federal generation-skipping transfer tax that applies with respect to my estate.

A. My Purposes. I intend that the division of my residuary estate into a nonmarital share, a state-only marital share, and a marital share, shall take advantage of the increases allowed under applicable Federal income tax law to the basis of assets received from me on account of my death, to the extent possible while minimizing the *state* estate tax due at the later death of my *husband/wife*, without incurring any *state* estate tax at my death.

B. Defining the "Descendants' Nonmarital Share." The "descendants' nonmarital share" shall be a fractional share of my residuary estate.

1. Calculating the Numerator. The numerator of the fraction shall equal the lesser of:

a. the largest value of my residuary estate that can pass free of *State* estate tax by reason of the exemptions allowable to my estate under the law of *State*. This value shall be determined after being reduced by reason of all other dispositions of property included in my gross estate for which no deduction is allowed in computing my *State* estate tax, and administration expenses and other charges to principal that are not claimed and allowed as *State* estate tax deductions; and

      b. the smallest value of the assets of my residuary estate to which my personal representative can allocate the entire aggregate basis increase allowed under Federal income tax laws for property not acquired by a surviving spouse.

      2. Calculating the Denominator. The denominator of the fraction shall equal the value of my residuary estate. References in this paragraph B to my residuary estate shall include only those portions of my residuary estate to which my aggregate basis increase may be allocated under federal income tax law.

    C. Defining the "State-Only Marital Share." The "state-only marital share" shall be a fractional share of my residuary estate.

      1. Calculating the Numerator. The numerator of the fraction shall be the difference between:

      a. the largest value that can pass free of *State* estate tax by reason of the exemptions allowable to my estate under the law of *State*. This value shall be determined after being reduced by reason of all other dispositions of property included in my gross estate for which no deduction is allowed in computing my *State* estate tax, and administration expenses and other charges to principal that are not claimed and allowed as *State* estate tax deductions; and

      b. the numerator of the nonmarital share under this article.

      2. Calculating the Denominator. The denominator of this fraction shall equal the value of my residuary estate.

    D. Defining the "Marital Share." If my *husband/wife* survives me, the "marital share" shall be the remaining fractional share of my residuary estate after subtracting the nonmarital share and state-only marital share.

    E. Allocating Assets. If my *husband/wife* survives me:

      1. Allocating Basis in a Fairly Representative Manner. My personal representative shall allocate to the nonmarital share only assets to which my personal representative can allocate my aggregate basis increase. Otherwise, my personal representative shall select the assets that shall constitute the nonmarital share in manner such that the net appreciation for Federal income tax purposes of any property allocated to the nonmarital share shall be fairly representative of the net appreciation of all property available for such allocation (excluding any property to which my personal representative cannot, under Federal income tax law, validly allocate any of the aggregate basis increase or the spousal property basis increase).

      2. Allocating Assets Otherwise. In other respects, my personal representative shall allocate assets as my personal representative shall consider to be in the best interests of the beneficiaries, valuing each asset on the date or dates of allocation.

E. Allocating Trust Income. My personal representative and trustee shall allocate to each share a ratable portion of all of the income earned by my estate after my death, whether earned before or after the assets are in the possession of the trustee, and income earned on assets used to pay charges according to the same fractional shares.

Article 18
Administering the QTIP, and Reverse QTIP and State-Only Marital Trusts

A. Making Elections. If there is, on the date of my death, a Federal estate tax that may be imposed with respect to my estate, my personal representative may elect to qualify all or any portion of the QTIP marital trust and the reverse QTIP marital trust for the Federal estate tax marital deduction, and to treat me as the transferor of the reverse QTIP marital trust for Federal generation-skipping transfer tax purposes.

1. Making Partial Elections. If my personal representative shall elect to qualify less than all of the QTIP marital trust or the reverse QTIP marital trust for the Federal estate tax marital deduction, my personal representative shall divide the trust fund as to which such partial election was made into two (2) separate trusts and make all principal payments first from the trust fund that qualifies for the Federal estate tax marital deduction.

2. Allocating Assets Between or Among Shares. My personal representative shall allocate assets between these shares as my personal representative shall consider to be in the best interests of the beneficiaries, valuing each asset on the date of allocation.

B. Assuring Productivity of Assets. My *husband/wife* may direct the trustee to make any unproductive or underproductive assets of the QTIP marital trust and the reverse QTIP marital trust productive or to convert them to productive assets within a reasonable time.

C. Receiving and Administering Retirement Payments. If the QTIP marital trust or the reverse QTIP marital trust is entitled to receive distributions under any retirement plan or individual retirement arrangement, of which my *husband/wife* is the designated beneficiary for Federal income tax purposes, then the trustee shall do the following:

1. Distributing Greater of Income or Required Minimum Distribution. The trustee shall annually withdraw from such retirement plan trust fund or arrangement the greater of all of the income earned by my *husband/wife*'s share of such plan or arrangement, or the required minimum distribution with respect to my *husband/wife*, as determined for Federal income tax purposes.

2. Distributing Withdrawn Amounts. The trustee shall annually distribute to my *husband/wife* all amounts withdrawn from such plan or arrangement.

D. Paying Transfer Taxes.

1. Paying Transfer Taxes Generally. The trustee shall, unless my *husband/wife* provides otherwise by specific reference to this paragraph in a valid will or other writing, pay or make arrangements for the payment of the incremental transfer taxes imposed on the reverse QTIP marital trust and on the QTIP marital trust upon the death of my *husband/wife*, from the QTIP marital trust and not from the reverse QTIP marital trust.

2. Paying Transfer Taxes In Case of a Partial QTIP Election. If my personal representative shall elect to qualify only part of the QTIP marital trust, the reverse QTIP marital trust, or both, and shall create two trusts as required by this Article, the transfer taxes imposed on both trusts at my *husband/wife*'s death shall be paid from the qualified trust fund to the extent possible.

E. The "State-Only Marital Trust."

1. Selecting Assets to Fund the State-Only Marital Trusts. My fiduciaries may fractionalize each asset of my residuary estate to create the state-only marital share, but if they choose not to fractionalize assets, they shall allocate assets to this share as they shall consider to be in the best interests of the beneficiaries, valuing each asset on the date or dates of allocation.

2. Allocating Income. My fiduciaries shall allocate to the state-only marital share a ratable portion of all of the income earned by my estate after my death, whether earned before or after the assets are in the possession of the trustee, and income earned on assets used to pay charges according to the same fractional shares.

3. State and Federal Elections. My personal representative shall elect to qualify the state-only marital trust for the marital deduction under the laws of *State*, but not for Federal estate tax purposes.

4. Other Provisions. The provisions of this article regarding "Assuring Productivity of Assets," "Receiving and Administering Retirement Payments," and "Paying Transfer Taxes" shall apply equally to the state-only marital trust and the QTIP marital trust.

Article 19
Definitions and Miscellaneous

A. Definitions. The following terms shall have the meaning set forth below for all purposes of this will:

1. "Children" and "Descendants" Defined. "Children" and "descendants" include those now living and those later born, subject to the following rules:

a. "Children" and "descendants" include an adopted person and that adopted person's descendants if, that adopted person is adopted before reaching eighteen (18) years of age;

b. "Children" and "descendants" includes those born outside of wedlock, if, during such child's or descendant's lifetime, his or her parent through whom such child or descendant claims hereunder, has acknowledged such person as his or her child in a writing duly signed and notarized during such parent's lifetime; and

c. "Children" and "descendants" include a child produced before the parent's death by donor artificial insemination, in vitro fertilization or other form of surrogate parenthood, whether or not such child was legally adopted by such parent before such parent's death.

2. "Disinterested Trustee" Defined. A "disinterested trustee" means a trustee who is not an interested trustee.

3. "Fiduciary" Defined. "Fiduciary" or "fiduciaries" shall include my personal representative and the trustee, or if they are different persons, either of them.

4. "Interested Trustee" Defined. An "interested trustee" means a trustee who is also (a) a beneficiary of the trust of which he or she is a trustee or the insured under a policy of insurance owned by a trust of which he or she is a trustee; (b) married to and living together with a beneficiary of the trust of which he or she is a trustee; (c) the father, mother, issue, brother or sister, of a beneficiary of the trust of which he or she is a trustee; (d) an employee of a beneficiary of the trust of which he or she is a trustee; (e) a corporation or any employee of a corporation in which the stock holdings of the trustee and the trust are significant from the viewpoint of voting control; or (f) a subordinate employee of a corporation in which the trustee is an executive.

5. "Personal Effects" Defined. My "personal effects" includes all of my jewelry, clothing, furniture, and other items of tangible personal property, but not money (other than collectible money having an inherent value in excess of its face amount) and not assets that my personal representative shall consider primarily to be used in a trade or business or held for investment. My "personal effects" also includes any transferable casualty insurance policies on any items of tangible personal property. Such policies shall pass to the same person who receives the insured property.

6. "Personal Representative" Defined. My "personal representative" shall include any executor, ancillary executor, administrator, or ancillary administrator, whether local or foreign and whether of all or part of my estate, multiple personal representatives, and their successors.

7. "Residuary Estate" Defined. My "residuary estate" means my real and personal estate passing under this will, after distribution of my personal effects and my personal residences under Articles 2 and 3 of this will.

8. "Transfer Taxes" Defined. "Transfer taxes" means all estate, inheritance, legacy, succession, and other transfer taxes, including any tax on excess retirement accumulations, imposed with respect to my death by any state, the United States, or by any foreign country. "Transfer taxes" also includes all taxes that are reimbursable under Sections 2207 through 2207B of the Internal Revenue Code of 1986, as amended, which right of reimbursement I hereby waive. "Transfer taxes" also includes all interest and penalties on such taxes.

9. "Trustee" Defined. The "trustee" or "trustees" shall include each trustee individually, multiple trustees, and their successors.

B. Retroactive Legislation. I include in this instrument certain dispositions and direct certain actions that shall occur only if, on the date of my death, no federal estate tax or Federal generation-skipping transfer tax applies with respect to my estate. These provisions shall not apply if, on the date of my death, no federal estate tax or federal generation-skipping transfer tax, as the case may be, applies with respect to my estate, but such tax or taxes is/are retroactively reinstated before April 1, 2011, and apply under such retroactive legislation with respect to my estate. If such retroactive legislation is finally determined to be unconstitutional or otherwise invalid, these references shall apply as if such retroactive legislation had never been enacted.

C. Absence of Trust Beneficiaries. If all of the beneficiaries of any trust under this will should die before the trust assets have vested in them, the trustee shall distribute all of the remaining assets of that trust as follows:

1. One Half to My Heirs and Distributee. One half (½) (or all, if there are no persons to take under subparagraph C.2. of this Article) to the heirs and distributees who would have inherited my personal estate, and in such shares as they would have inherited it, had I died unmarried and without a valid will, determined on the later of the date of my death or the date of the death of the last of the trust beneficiaries to die; and

2. One Half to My *Husband/Wife*'s Distributees. One half (½) (or all, if there are no persons to take under subparagraph C.1. of this Article) to the heirs and distributees who would have inherited my *husband/wife*'s personal estate, and in such shares as they would have inherited it, had he died unmarried and without a valid will, determined on the later of the date of my death or the date of the death of the last of the trust beneficiaries to die.

D. Applicable Law. My will shall be governed by and construed according to the laws of the *State*.

E. Joint Ownership. I confirm that all assets owned jointly by me and another person with a right of survivorship should pass outright to my joint owner and my estate shall have no interest in those assets.

F. Number. Whenever the context requires, the singular includes the plural and the plural the singular.

G. Survivorship. No person shall be deemed to have survived me for purposes of inheriting under this will unless he or she is living on the date ninety (90) days after the date of my death.

H. Tax-Related Terms. All tax-related terms shall have the same meaning they have in the Internal Revenue Code of 1986, as amended.

[Add state-specific signature, attesting witness, and self-proving clauses]

¶ A.08 FORM 8: REVOCABLE TRUST FOR ESTATE OF $6 MILLION TO $10 MILLION—MARITAL DEDUCTION TAX PLANNING—GST TAX PLANNING WITH LIFETIME TRUST FOR CHILDREN AND REVERSE QTIP—CREATES A NONMARITAL SHARE EQUAL TO STATE ESTATE TAX EXEMPTION—TRUSTEE CAN DISTRIBUTE FROM QTIP MINIMUM AMOUNT OF PRINCIPAL SUFFICIENT TO GIVE SPOUSE ENOUGH APPRECIATION TO TAKE ADVANTAGE OF AGGREGATE BASIS INCREASE AT SURVIVING SPOUSE'S DEATH—CREATES STATE-ONLY QTIP— SAME PLANNING AS FORM 7, BUT IN A REVOCABLE TRUST

Revocable Trust of *Grantor*[8]

I, *Grantor*, of [locality, state] (sometimes in the first person singular, sometimes the "grantor," and sometimes the "trustee"), make this trust (defined below), which may be referred to as *TrustName*.

Article 1
My Family

I am married to *Spouse* (sometimes referred to as "my *husband/wife*") and I have [number of children] children, *Children*.

Article 2
Trustee Shall Hold Trust Funds

The trustee (defined below) shall hold certain property, which may be listed in Schedule A, to be administered according to the terms of the trust instrument. I and anyone else may transfer additional property (including life insurance proceeds,

---

[8] **KEY**:

Grantor	— full name of the grantor
TrustName	— what to call the trust in other documents
Spouse	— full name of grantor's spouse
husband/wife	— "husband" or "wife", as the case may be
Children	— full names of grantor's children
he/she	— "he" or "she" (referring to the spouse)
his/her	— "his" or "her" (referring to the spouse)
him/her	— "him" or "her" (referring to the spouse)
FirstTrustee	— name of the first alternate trustee
SecondTrustee	— name of the second alternate trustee

where appropriate), to any trustee (which the trustee may refuse to accept if accept-ance is not in the best interests of the trust), at any time during my life or after my death, to be held and administered according to the terms of the trust instrument.

Article 3
Revoking the Trust

I may revoke or amend all or any part of the trust fund at any time, without the consent of anyone else, by delivering to the trustee a written instrument specifying the character and date of the intended amendment or revocation, or by specific reference to the trust in my last will. The duties, powers, or liabilities of the trustee (other than me) cannot, however, be changed without such trustee's prior written consent. The trustee shall transfer all of the trust funds to me or to my estate, if the trust is completely revoked.

Article 4
Administering the Trust During My Life

A. Making Payments to Me. During my life, the trustee shall pay any taxes, commissions, or other expenses incurred with respect to the trust, and distribute to me all of the trust's net income at least annually, and so much of its principal and undistributed income (including all or none) as I may request from time to time, or as the trustee shall deem appropriate for my comfort and care.

1. My Absolute Power to Withdraw Trust Funds. My power to withdraw principal and income from the trust is absolute, and exercisable as to all of the trust funds, by me alone and in all events.

2. Assuring Productivity of Trust Assets. I may direct the trustee not to retain any asset or assets that I shall deem not to be sufficiently productive.

B. Qualifying for the Gift Tax Marital Deduction. I intend that any transfers to the trust by my *husband/wife*, *Spouse*, shall qualify for the Federal gift and estate tax marital deduction and all provisions of the trust shall be construed consistent therewith.

Article 5
Disposing of the Residuary Trust Fund

The trustee shall divide and distribute the residuary trust fund (defined below) at my death, under this Article:

A. If a Federal Estate Tax Exists. If there is, on the date of my death, a Federal estate tax and/or a Federal generation-skipping transfer tax, as the case may be, that applies with respect to my estate (including this trust fund), the trustee shall divide and distribute the residuary trust fund, as follows:

1. If My *Husband/Wife* Survives Me. If my *husband/wife*, *Spouse*, survives me, the trustee shall divide the residuary trust fund into a nonmarital share, a state-only marital share, a GST exempt marital share, and a marital share (all defined below).

a. The nonmarital share shall be held under the Article entitled "The Family Trust."

b. The spouse's nonmarital share shall be held under the Article entitled "The State-Only Marital Trust."

c. The GST exempt marital share shall be held under the Article entitled "The Reverse QTIP Marital Trust."

d. The marital share shall be held under the Article entitled "The QTIP Marital Trust."

2. If My *Husband/Wife* Does Not Survive Me. If my *husband/wife* does not survive me, the trustee shall divide the residuary trust fund into a descendants' GST exempt share and a descendants' power of appointment share (both defined below).

a. The descendants' GST exempt share shall be held under the Article entitled "The Descendants' Trust."

b. The trustee shall distribute the descendants' power of appointment share to my descendants who survive me, *per stirpes*, except that the share for any child of mine shall be added to the trust fund for such child under the Article entitled "Child's Power of Appointment Trust," for that child, and the share for any more remote descendant of mine who shall then not yet have reached the age of thirty-five (35) years, shall be held under the Article entitled "Contingent Trust for Certain Beneficiaries."

B. If No Federal Estate Tax Exists. If there is, on the date of my death, no Federal estate tax or Federal generation-skipping transfer tax that applies with respect to my estate (including this trust fund), the trustee shall divide the residuary trust fund as follows:

1. If My *Husband/Wife* Survives Me. If my *husband/wife* survives me, the trustee shall divide the residuary trust fund into a nonmarital share, a state-only marital share and a marital share.

a. The nonmarital share shall be held under the Article entitled "The Family Trust."

b. The state-only marital share shall be held under the Article entitled "The State-Only Marital Trust."

c. The marital share shall be held under the Article entitled "The QTIP Marital Trust."

2. If My *Husband/Wife* Does Not Survive Me. If my *husband/wife* does not survive me, the trustee shall hold the residuary trust fund under the Article entitled "The Descendants' Trust."

C. Debts and Expenses of Administration. The trustee shall pay to the personal representative of my estate such amounts as the personal representative of my estate shall certify as needed for the payment of my debts and expenses of estate administration.

Article 6
The Family Trust

A. Until the Family Trust Termination Date. Until the family trust termination date (defined below), the trustee (defined below) shall distribute to or for the benefit of my *husband/wife*, my then-living children and my then-living more remote descendants, as much of the net income and principal of the family trust as the trustee may deem appropriate for their health, education, support, or maintenance, annually adding to principal any undistributed income, annually adding to principal any undistributed income.

1. Distributions May be Unequal. The Trustee may distribute income and principal of the family trust unequally and may make distributions to some beneficiaries and not to others.

2. Other Assets. The trustee shall consider other income and assets readily available to each beneficiary, including assets available from other trusts created under my will, in making distributions.

3. Priority Purposes. In making these distributions, my primary purpose is to provide for the support in reasonable comfort of my *husband/wife* for the rest of *his/her* life and the education and support of my children until they have completed their education.

B. Upon the Family Trust Termination Date. Upon the family trust termination date, the trustee shall distribute the remaining trust funds to my then-living descendants, per stirpes, subject to the provisions of the Article entitled Contingent Trust for Certain Beneficiaries.

C. "Family Trust Termination Date" Defined. The family trust termination date shall be the date of the death of the last to die of my *husband/wife* and my children alive on the date of my death.

Article 7
The State-Only Marital Trust

The state-only marital trust shall be held under this Article.

A. Distributing Trust Fund During My *Husband/Wife*'s Life. The trustee shall distribute the net income of the state-only marital trust quarterly or more frequently to my *husband/wife* during *his/her* life. The trustee shall also distribute to my *husband/wife* as much of the principal of the state-only marital trust as is appropriate for any purpose.

B. Distributing Trust Fund At My *Husband/Wife*'s Death.

1. Distributing Income. At my *husband/wife*'s death, my trustee shall distribute to my *husband/wife*'s estate any undistributed income of the state-only marital trust.

2. Distribution of Principal. At my *husband/wife*'s death, my trustee shall distribute the principal of the state-only marital trust, to the extent it is not used to pay death taxes (defined below), as my *husband/wife* may direct by specific reference to this special power of appointment in *his/her* last will.

a. My *husband/wife* may appoint the state-only marital trust fund, either outright or in further trust, but only to or among any one (1) or more of my descendants.

b. My *husband/wife* may not appoint any portion of the state-only marital trust to my *husband/wife*, *his/her* creditors, *his/her* estate, or the creditors of *his/her* estate.

3. Distributing Unappointed Assets. The trustee shall add the unappointed principal of the state-only marital trust to the trust held under the Article entitled "The Descendants' Trust."

Article 8
The Reverse QTIP Marital Trust

The reverse QTIP marital trust shall be held under this Article.

A. Distributing Trust Fund During My *Husband/Wife*'s Life. The trustee shall distribute the net income of the QTIP marital trust quarterly or more frequently to my *husband/wife*, *Spouse*, during *his/her* life.

1. Principal Distributions. The trustee shall also distribute to my *husband/wife* as much of the principal of the QTIP marital trust as is appropriate for any purpose.

2. Distributing Additional Principal if There is No Federal Estate Tax. If the trustee deems it likely that my *husband/wife* will die before January 1, 2011, the trustee shall distribute to my *husband/wife* a fractional share of this trust.

a. The numerator of this fraction shall be equal to the smallest value of the assets of this trust fund to which the personal representative of my *husband/wife*'s estate could allocate all of the aggregate basis increase allowed to my *husband/wife* under Federal income tax laws, less the amount of such aggregate basis increase that could be allocated to other assets already owned by my *husband/wife* at the time of this distribution.

b. The denominator of this fraction shall equal the value of the *spouse* trust fund.

B. Distributing Trust Fund At My *Husband/Wife*'s Death.

1. Distributing Income. At my *husband/wife*'s death, the trustee shall distribute to my *husband/wife*'s estate any undistributed income of the reverse QTIP marital trust.

2. Appointing Trust Principal. At my *husband/wife*'s death, the trustee shall distribute the principal of the reverse QTIP marital trust, to the extent it is not used to pay transfer taxes (defined below) as provided below, as my *husband/wife* may direct by specific reference to this special power of appointment in *his/her* last will.

a. My *husband/wife* may appoint the reverse QTIP marital trust fund, either outright or in further trust, but only to or among any one (1) or more of my descendants.

b. My *husband/wife* may not appoint any portion of the reverse QTIP marital trust fund to my *husband/wife*, *his/her* creditors, *his/her* estate, or the creditors of *his/her* estate.

3. Distributing Unappointed Assets. The trustee shall add the unappointed principal of the reverse QTIP marital trust to the trust held under the Article entitled "The Descendants' Trust."

Article 9
The QTIP Marital Trust

The QTIP marital trust shall be held under this Article.

A. Distributing Trust Fund During My *Husband/Wife*'s Life. The trustee shall distribute the net income of the QTIP marital trust quarterly or more frequently to my *husband/wife*, *Spouse*, during *his/her* life.

1. Principal Distributions. The trustee shall also distribute to my *husband/wife* as much of the principal of the QTIP marital trust as is appropriate for any purpose.

2. Distributing Additional Principal if There is No Federal Estate Tax. If the trustee deems it likely that my *husband/wife* will die before January 1, 2011, the trustee shall distribute to my *husband/wife* a fractional share of this trust.

a. The numerator of this fraction shall be equal to the smallest value of the assets of this trust fund to which the personal representative of my *husband/wife*'s estate could allocate all of the aggregate basis increase allowed to my *husband/wife* under Federal income tax laws, less the amount of such aggregate basis increase that could be allocated to other assets already owned by my *husband/wife* at the time of this distribution.

b. The denominator of this fraction shall equal the value of the *spouse* trust fund.

B. Distributing Trust Fund At My *Husband/Wife*'s Death.

1. Distributing Income. At my *husband/wife*'s death, the trustee shall distribute to my *husband/wife*'s estate any undistributed income of the QTIP marital trust.

2. Appointing Trust Principal. At my *husband/wife*'s death, the trustee shall distribute the principal of the QTIP marital trust, to the extent it is not used to pay transfer taxes as provided below, as my *husband/wife* may direct by specific reference to this special power of appointment in *his/her* last will.

a. My *husband/wife* may appoint the QTIP marital trust fund, either outright or in further trust, but only to or among any one (1) or more of my descendants.

b. My *husband/wife* may not appoint any portion of the QTIP marital trust fund to my *husband/wife*, *his/her* creditors, *his/her* estate, or the creditors of *his/her* estate.

3. Distributing Unappointed Trust Fund. The trustee shall distribute the unappointed QTIP marital trust fund to my then-living descendants, *per stirpes*, except that the share for any child of mine shall be added to the child's power of appointment trust for that child, and the share for any more remote descendant of mine who shall then not yet have reached the age of thirty-five (35) years, shall be held for such descendant under the Article entitled "Contingent Trust for Certain Beneficiaries."

Article 10
Child's Power of Appointment Trust

The child's power of appointment trust for each child of mine shall be held as a separate trust under this Article.

A. Distributing Trust Fund During the Child's Life. The trustee shall distribute to or for the benefit of each child for whom a trust is created under this Article, as much of the net income and principal as the child shall request at any time or as the trustee may consider appropriate for any purpose, annually adding to principal any undistributed income.

B. Distributing Trust Fund At the Child's Death. Upon the death of a child of mine who survives me, the trustee shall distribute the remaining principal and income of such child's trust under this Article as that child may direct by specific reference to this power of appointment in that child's last will.

1. Appointing Everything But Limited Portion. Each such child may appoint the remaining principal and income of such child's trust under this Article (other than the limited portion (defined below)) of such trust fund, either outright or in further trust, to or among any persons, including such child's estate.

2. Appointing Limited Portion. Each such child may appoint the limited portion of the principal and income of such child's trust under this Article outright or in further trust, but only to or among my then-living descendants, and such child may not appoint any of the limited portion to such child himself or herself, such child's creditors, such child's estate, or the creditors of such child's estate.

3. Distributing Unappointed Trust Fund. The trustee shall distribute any unappointed portion of the fund of a deceased child's trust under this Article to such child's then-living descendants, *per stirpes*, or if there are no such descendants then living, to my then-living descendants, *per stirpes*, except that the fund that would thus be distributed to any then-living child of mine shall be added to such child's trust under this Article.

4. "Limited Portion" Defined. The "limited portion" of the fund of a child's trust under this Article is that portion which would pass to one or more persons assigned to the same or a higher generation as the deceased child for Federal generation-skipping transfer tax purposes, were such child to die without a valid will. If such child dies in a year in which there is no Federal generation-skipping transfer tax applicable with respect to such child's estate, the "limited portion" shall be the entire fund of the child's trust.

Article 11
The Descendants' Trust

A. Until the Descendants' Trust Termination Date. Until the descendants' trust termination date (defined below), the trustee (defined below) shall distribute to or for the benefit of my then-living children and my then-living more remote descendants, as much of the net income and principal of the family trust as the trustee may deem appropriate for their health, education, support, or maintenance, annually adding to principal any undistributed income, annually adding to principal any undistributed income.

1. Distributions May be Unequal. The Trustee may distribute income and principal of the family trust unequally and may make distributions to some beneficiaries and not to others.

2. Other Assets. The trustee shall consider other income and assets readily available to each beneficiary, including assets available from other trusts created under my will, in making distributions.

3. Priority Purpose. In making these distributions, my primary purpose is to provide for the education and support of my children until they have completed their education.

B. Upon the Descendants' Trust Termination Date. Upon the descendants' trust termination date, the trustee shall distribute the remaining trust funds to my then-living descendants, per stirpes, subject to the provisions of the Article entitled Contingent Trust for Certain Beneficiaries.

C. "Descendants' Trust Termination Date" Defined. The descendants' trust termination date shall be the date of the death of the last to die of my children alive on the date of my death.

Article 12
Contingent Trust for Certain Beneficiaries

If a beneficiary (other than a child of mine) is entitled to receive any portion of any trust fund held under this instrument while the beneficiary is under the age of thirty-five (35) years, the trustee may retain such assets in a separate trust for that beneficiary.

A. Distributing Trust Fund Before the Contingent Trust Termination Date. Until the contingent trust termination date (defined below), the trustee shall distribute to or for the benefit of the beneficiary as much of the net income and principal as the trustee may consider appropriate for the beneficiary's health, education, support, or maintenance, annually adding to principal any undistributed income.

B. Distributing Trust Fund At the Contingent Trust Termination Date. Upon the contingent trust termination date, the trustee shall distribute the remaining assets to the beneficiary if the beneficiary is then living or otherwise to the beneficiary's estate to be distributed as part of that estate.

C. "Contingent Trust Termination Date" Defined. The "contingent trust termination date" shall be the earlier of (1) the date on which the beneficiary dies or (2) the date on which the beneficiary reaches the age of thirty-five (35) years.

Article 13
Special Limits on Powers of Interested Trustee

The following limitations shall apply, notwithstanding other provisions of this instrument.

A. Limiting Actions by Interested Trustees. No interested trustee (defined below) may participate in the exercise of any discretion to distribute principal to himself or herself, except as is appropriate for his or her health, education, support, and maintenance, or any of them. No interested trustee may participate in the exercise of any discretion to distribute or expend principal or income in a manner that would discharge that trustee's personal obligation to support the beneficiary. No interested trustee may participate in the exercise of any incident of ownership over any policy owned by the trust insuring the life of such trustee.

B. Disinterested Trustees Exercising Certain Powers. A disinterested trustee (defined below) who is serving as a co-trustee with an interested trustee, may exercise those discretions granted under this instrument the exercise of which by an interested trustee are precluded.

1. If Multiple Trustees Include an Interested Trustee Who Cannot Act. The number of trustees who must consent to the exercise of a power granted under this instrument, as determined under the Article entitled "The Trustees" shall be determined by treating the interested trustees who are not entitled, under this Article, to participate in the exercise of the power or discretion, as if they were not then serving.

2. If All Trustees Are Precluded From Acting. If this Article precludes every then-serving trustee from exercising a power otherwise granted to the trustee

under this instrument, the then-serving trustee shall appoint a disinterested trustee who may exercise such power (or decline to exercise it) as if that disinterested trustee were the sole then-serving trustee.

Article 14
Paying Transfer Taxes

The trustee shall pay from the residuary trust fund all transfer taxes, other than generation-skipping transfer taxes, payable by reason of my death on assets passing under this trust.

A. Apportioning Transfer Taxes. The trustee shall pay transfer taxes imposed on any trust assets includible in my gross estate for Federal estate tax purposes, from those assets, as provided by the laws of the state in which I reside at my death, except as expressly provided elsewhere in this instrument.

B. Apportioning Generation-Skipping Transfer Taxes. The trustee shall pay all generation-skipping transfer taxes imposed on transfers under this trust from those transfers.

C. Apportioning Transfer Taxes Away From Deductible Assets. Assets passing as the GST exempt marital share or as the marital share shall have the full benefit of the Federal estate tax marital deduction allowed with respect to any transfer taxes, and shall not bear any transfer taxes. Other assets passing to my *husband/ wife* or to any charitable organization, whether under this trust or otherwise, shall have the full benefit of any available marital or charitable deduction for Federal and other transfer tax purposes, in determining the share of transfer taxes that should be borne by those assets.

Article 15
The Trustees

A. Naming The Trustee. I shall be the initial trustee of this trust.

B. Naming Successor Trustees. I name *FirstTrustee*, of [*locality, state*], to be the successor trustee, to serve if I am unable or unwilling to serve or to continue serving. I name *SecondTrustee*, of [*locality, state*] to be the successor trustee, to serve if both *FirstTrustee* and I are unable or unwilling to serve or to continue serving.

C. No Surety or Bond. No trustee named by me or by another trustee shall be required to provide surety or other security on a bond.

D. Naming Additional Trustees. I authorize the trustee to appoint any person as an additional trustee, to serve at the pleasure of the appointing trustee.

E. Delegating Powers and Authorities. The trustee may delegate to another trustee any power or authority granted by me to the trustee, to continue at the pleasure of the delegating trustee, unless otherwise agreed. Any person dealing in good faith with a trustee may rely upon that trustee's representation that a delegation has been made and remains in effect under this paragraph.

F. Trustee Resigning. Any trustee may resign by giving written notice specifying the effective date of the resignation to me, if I am then-serving as a trustee, or otherwise to the designated successor. If I am not alive or am not then-serving as a trustee, and if no successor is designated, the resigning trustee shall give notice to each adult beneficiary to whom trust income then may be distributed.

G. Removing a Trustee. A trustee may be removed by the vote of two-thirds (⅔) of the then-living adult beneficiaries to whom trust income may then be distributed.

H. Filling Trustee Vacancies. A corporation no substantial portion of the stock of which is owned by beneficiaries of this trust, may be named as successor trustee to fill any vacancy, by majority vote of the adult beneficiaries to whom trust income then may be distributed.

I. No Liability for Acts or Omissions of Predecessors. No trustee shall be responsible for or need inquire into any acts or omissions of a prior trustee.

J. Compensating Trustees. In addition to reimbursement for expenses, each individual trustee is entitled to reasonable compensation for services. Each corporate trustee is entitled to compensation based on its written fee schedule in effect at the time its services are rendered or as otherwise agreed, and its compensation may vary from time to time based on that schedule.

K. Management Powers. I authorize the trustee to exercise all powers conferred by applicable state law and to do the following in a fiduciary capacity.

1. Prudent Investor Rule. The trustee may hold and retain as part of any trust fund any property transferred by me to the trustee, whether or not such investment would be appropriate for a prudent investor. The trustee may also hold and retain as part of any trust fund any property received from any source, and invest and reinvest the trust fund (or leave it temporarily uninvested) in any type of property and every kind of investment in the same manner as a prudent investor would invest his or her own assets.

2. Holding Assets For Use of Trust Beneficiaries. The trustee may buy and hold in trust, assets that will be used personally by one or more beneficiaries, even if those assets would not otherwise be acquired by a prudent investor investing his or her own assets.

3. Transferring Assets. The trustees may sell or exchange any real or personal property contained in any trust, for cash or credit, at public or private sale, and with such warranties or indemnifications as the trustee may deem advisable.

4. Borrowing Money. The trustee may borrow money (even from a trustee, a beneficiary, or any trust) for the benefit of any trust and secure these debts with assets of the trust.

5. Granting Security Interests. The trustee may grant security interests and execute all instruments creating such interests upon such terms as the trustee may deem advisable.

6. Compromising Claims. The trustee may compromise and adjust claims against or on behalf of any trust on such terms as the trustee may deem advisable.

7. Not Disclosing Nominees. The trustee may take title to any securities in the name of any custodian or nominee without disclosing this relationship.

8. Allocating Between Income and Principal. The trustee may determine whether receipts are income or principal and whether disbursements are to be charged against income or principal to the extent not clearly established by state law. A determination made by the trustee in good faith shall not require equitable adjustments.

9. Making Tax Elections. The trustee may make all tax elections and allocations the trustee may consider appropriate; however, this authority is exercisable only in a fiduciary capacity and may not be used to enlarge or shift any beneficial interest except as an incidental consequence of the discharge of fiduciary duties. A tax election or allocation made by the trustee in good faith shall not require equitable adjustments.

10. Distributing to Custodians for Minors. The trustee shall distribute any of any trust fund to a beneficiary under the age of twenty-one (21) years by distribution to any appropriate person (who may be a trustee) chosen by the trustee as custodian under any appropriate Uniform Transfers (or Gifts) to Minors Act, to be held for the maximum period of time allowed by law. The trustee may also sell any asset that cannot be held under this custodianship and invest the sales proceeds in assets that can be so held.

11. Employing Advisors. The trustee may employ such lawyers, accountants, and other advisors as the trustee may deem useful and appropriate for the administration of any trust. The trustee may employ a professional investment advisor and delegate to this advisor any discretionary investment authorities to manage the investments of any trust, including any investment in mutual funds, investment trusts, or managed accounts, and may rely on the advisor's investment recommendations without liability to any beneficiary.

12. Buying and Holding Life Insurance. The trustee may buy and hold insurance policies on the life of any beneficiary or any person in whom a beneficiary has an insurable interest and may pay the premiums on such policies from income or principal, as the trustee may deem advisable.

13. Dividing and Distributing Assets. The trustee may divide and distribute the assets of any trust fund in kind, in money, or partly in each, without regard to the income tax basis of any asset and without the consent of any beneficiary. The decision of the trustee in dividing any portion of any trust fund between or among two or more beneficiaries, if made in good faith, shall be binding on all persons.

14. Allocation of Basis Increase. My personal representative shall allocate any increases in the adjusted basis of property owned by me at the time of my death, whether passing under my Will or otherwise, to the extent such property is eligible to receive such an allocation, as my personal representative deems to be in the best interests of my estate and its beneficiaries. The trustee shall cooperate fully with my personal representative in making these allocations. If, however, there is no personal representative appointed for my estate, then the trustee shall allocate any increases in the adjusted basis of property passing under this trust, to the extent such property is eligible to receive such an allocation, as the trustee deems to be in the best interests of my estate and its beneficiaries. In making these allocations the trustee shall:

a. First, satisfy all charitable bequests with assets to which no aggregate or spousal property basis increases may be allocated;

b. Second, satisfy all charitable bequests with assets that have an adjusted income tax basis closest to zero of all of my assets available to satisfy these bequests;

c. Third, generally not allocate basis increase to assets the gain from the sale of which is not subject to federal income tax under present federal income tax laws;

d. Fourth, allocate basis increases to assets that are reasonably likely to be sold within the three year period beginning on the date of my death, the sale of which will produce an income tax liability that is taxed at a rate higher than that on long-term capital gains; and

e. Fifth, allocate the remaining basis increase among assets in proportion to each asset's pro rata share of the total appreciation of all such assets owned by this trust on the date of my death.

The trustee shall not be liable to anyone for any allocation of my basis increases made in good faith, in the absence of gross negligence.

L. Disabled Individual Trustee. An individual trustee may not serve during a disability.

1. "Disabled" Defined. An individual trustee is "disabled" or "under a disability" if: (a) he or she is determined to be legally incompetent by a court of competent jurisdiction; (b) a conservator or guardian for such person has been appointed, based upon his or her incapacity; (c) two (2) physicians licensed to practice medicine in the Commonwealth of Virginia certify in writing to another trustee or a person who would become the successor trustee upon such disability, that in the opinion of such physicians, such individual trustee, as a result of illness, age or other cause, no longer has the capacity to act prudently or effectively in financial affairs; or (d) thirty (30) days after any other trustee or a person who would become the successor trustee upon such disability, requests that such individual trustee provide a certificate from a physician licensed to practice medicine that, in the opinion of such physician, such individual trustee has the capacity to act prudently or effectively in financial affairs and such individual trustee fails to provide such certification. The effective date of such incapacity shall be the date of the order or decree adjudicating the incapacity, the date of the order or decree appointing the guardian or conservator, the date of the certificate of incapacity of the two (2) physicians described above, or thirty (30) days after other trustee or any person who would become the successor trustee upon such disability requests a certificate of capacity and one is not provided, whichever first occurs.

2. When I Regain My Capacity. For purposes of this instrument, I shall be deemed to have regained capacity to serve as a trustee if: (a) there is a finding to that effect by a court of competent jurisdiction; (b) when any conservatorship or guardianship for me has been judicially terminated; or (c) upon the written determination by two (2) physicians licensed to practice medicine in the Commonwealth of Virginia (who need not be the same physicians who made the initial determination of my incapacity) that, in their pinion, my capacity is restored, and I shall have the right again to serve as trustee under this instrument, as of the effective date of my restoration of capacity, if I was serving as a trustee at the time I was determined to be incapacitated.

3. No Liability. No person is liable to anyone for actions taken in reliance on these certifications or for dealing with a trustee other than the one removed for disability based on these certifications. This trust shall indemnify any physician for liability for any opinion rendered in good faith as to the existence or recovery from any disability.

Article 16
Trust Administration

A. Spendthrift Limits. No interest in a trust under this instrument shall be subject to the beneficiary's liabilities or creditor claims or to assignment or anticipation.

B. Protecting Trust Beneficiaries From Creditors. If the trustee shall determine that a beneficiary would not benefit as greatly from any outright distribution of trust income or principal because of the availability of the distribution to the beneficiary's creditors, the trustee shall instead expend those amounts for the benefit of the beneficiary. This direction is intended to enable the trustee to give the beneficiary the fullest possible benefit and enjoyment of all of the trust income and principal to which he or she is entitled.

C. Combining Multiple Trusts. The trustee may invest the assets of multiple trusts in a single fund if the interests of the trusts are accounted for separately.

D. Merging and Consolidating Trust Funds. The trustee may merge or consolidate any trust into any other trust that has the same trustee and substantially the same dispositive provisions.

E. Dividing Trust Funds. The trustee may divide any trust fund into multiple separate trusts.

F. Accountings. The trustee shall not be required to file annual accounts with any court or court official in any jurisdiction.

G. Changing Trust Situs. A disinterested trustee may change the situs of any trust, and to the extent necessary or appropriate, move the trust assets, to a state or country other than the one in which the trust is then administered if the disinterested trustee shall determine it to be in the best interests of the trust or the beneficiaries. The disinterested trustee may elect that the law of such other jurisdiction shall govern the trust to the extent necessary or appropriate under the circumstances.

H. Rule Against Perpetuities. All assets of every trust created under this instrument (including every trust created by the exercise of a power of appointment created under this instrument, unless the exercise of such power of appointment starts a new period for the rule against perpetuities or similar rule that limits the time that property may remain in trust) that does not by its own terms do so earlier, shall vest in and be distributed to the persons then entitled to the income from such property at the expiration of the date twenty (20) years and eleven (11) months after the death of the last survivor of my *husband/wife* and those of the descendants of my grandparents alive on the date of this instrument. Upon termination of a trust under this provision, the accumulated trust income and principal shall be distributed to those beneficiaries then entitled to receive or have benefit of the income from such trust in the proportion in which they are so entitled. If the proportion of the income interests of the beneficiaries of such trust cannot be determined with reasonable certainty, the accumulated trust income and principal shall be distributed equally to such beneficiaries.

Article 17
Calculating Shares of the Residuary Trust Fund if a Federal Estate Tax Exists

This Article shall apply if there is, on the date of my death, a Federal estate tax and/or a Federal generation-skipping transfer tax, as the case may be, that applies with respect to my estate (including this trust fund).

A. My Purposes. I intend that:

1. Minimizing Federal and *State* Estate Taxes. The division of the residuary trust fund into a nonmarital share, a state-only marital share, a GST exempt marital share and a marital share, shall minimize the Federal and *State* estate taxes at my *husband/wife*'s death to the extent I can do so while deferring all Federal and *State* estate taxes until both my *husband/wife* and I have died.

2. Taking Advantage of My GST Exemption. The creation of a nonmarital share, a GST exempt marital share, and, if my *husband/wife* does not survive me, the descendants' GST exempt share, shall take advantage of my available GST exemption (defined below).

3. Qualifying for Federal Estate Tax Marital Deduction. The GST exempt marital share and the marital share shall qualify for the Federal estate tax marital deduction and all provisions of this trust shall be construed accordingly. The trustee shall, in all matters involving the GST exempt marital share and the marital share, exercise no power in a manner that would infringe upon any legal requirement for the allowance of the Federal estate tax marital deduction.

4. Qualifying for *State* Estate Tax Marital Deduction. The state-only marital share shall qualify for the estate tax marital deduction under the laws of *State* and all provisions of this trust shall be construed accordingly. The trustee shall, in all matters involving the state-only marital share, exercise no power in a manner that would infringe upon any legal requirement for the allowance of the estate tax marital deduction under the laws of *State*.

B. Defining the "Nonmarital Share." If my *husband/wife* survives me, the "descendants' nonmarital share" shall be a fractional share of the residuary trust fund.

1. Calculating the Numerator. The numerator of the fraction shall equal the smaller of:

a. the largest value of the residuary trust fund that can pass free of *State* estate tax were it to pass to an individual other than my *spouse*. This value shall be determined after being reduced by reason of all other dispositions of property included in my gross estate for which no deduction is allowed in computing my *State* estate tax, and administration expenses and other charges to principal that are not claimed and allowed as *State* estate tax deductions; and

b. the largest value of the residuary trust fund that can pass free of Federal estate tax by reason of the unified credit and the credit for state death taxes allowable with respect to my estate, to the extent the use of such credit does not increase the state death taxes with respect to my estate. This value shall be determined after being reduced by reason of my adjusted taxable gifts, all other dispositions of property included in my gross estate for which no deduction is allowed in computing my Federal estate tax, and administration expenses and other charges to principal that are not claimed and allowed as Federal estate tax deductions.

2. Calculating the Denominator. The denominator of the fraction shall equal the value of the residuary trust fund.

C. Defining the "State-Only Marital Trust." If my *husband/wife* survives me, and if I die domiciled in *state*, the trustee shall a "state-only marital trust," which shall be a fractional share of the residuary trust fund.

1. Calculating the Numerator. The numerator of the fraction shall be the difference between:

a. The largest value of the family trust that can pass free of *State* estate tax were it to pass to an individual other than my *husband/wife*. This value shall be determined after being reduced by reason of all other dispositions of property included in my gross estate for which no deduction is allowed in computing my *State* estate tax, and administration expenses and other charges to principal that are not claimed and allowed as *State* estate tax deductions; and

b. The numerator of the fraction by which the nonmarital trust is calculated under this article.

D. Defining the "GST Exempt Marital Share." If my *husband/wife* survives me, the "GST exempt marital share" shall be a fractional share of the residuary trust fund.

1. Calculating the Numerator. The numerator of the fraction shall be the amount of my available GST exemption (to the extent not allocated to the nonmarital share).

2. Calculating the Denominator. The denominator of the fraction shall equal the value of the residuary trust fund.

E. Defining the "Marital Share." If my *husband/wife* survives me, the "marital share" shall be the remaining fractional share of the residuary trust fund after subtracting the nonmarital share, the state-only marital share, and the GST exempt marital share.

F. Defining the "Descendants' GST Exempt Share." If my *husband/wife* does not survive me, the "descendants' GST exempt share" shall be a fractional share of the residuary trust fund.

1. Calculating the Numerator. The numerator of the fraction shall be equal to the amount of my available GST exemption.

2. Calculating the Denominator. The denominator of the fraction shall equal the value of the residuary trust fund.

G. Defining the "Descendants' Power of Appointment Share." If my *husband/wife* does not survive me, the "descendants' power of appointment share' shall be the remaining fractional share of the residuary trust fund after subtracting the descendants' GST exempt share.

H. Calculating Shares Based on Certain Assumptions. The spouse's nonmarital share shall be computed as if no election is made to qualify any property passing as such share under the Federal estate tax marital deduction, and the maximum possible election is made to qualify all property passing as the GST exempt marital share and the marital share for the Federal estate tax marital deduction.

I. Determining the Effect of Disclaimers.

1. Disclaiming the GST Exempt Marital Share or Marital Share. The trustee shall add to the nonmarital share any portion of the GST exempt marital share or the marital share as to which a qualified disclaimer by or for my *husband/wife* is made. The nonmarital share shall be calculated before any qualified disclaimer by or for my *husband/wife* of any of the GST exempt marital share or of the marital share.

2. Apportioning Transfer Taxes to Disclaimed Funds. Transfer taxes imposed on assets as to which my *husband/wife* has made a qualified disclaimer shall be apportioned to those disclaimed funds.

J. Allocating Assets Between or Among Shares.

1. Making Certain Allocations If My *Husband/Wife* Survives Me. If my *husband/wife* survives me:

a. The trustee shall allocate to the marital share, the state-only marital share and the GST exempt marital share only assets that can qualify for the Federal estate tax marital deduction.

b. The trustee shall not, to the extent possible, allocate to the marital share, the state-only marital share or the GST exempt marital share assets upon which a foreign death tax is payable.

c. The trustee shall allocate to the nonmarital share, the GST exempt marital share and, if my *husband/wife* does not survive me, the descendants' GST exempt share, solely of assets includable in my gross estate for Federal estate tax purposes.

2. Making Other Allocations. The trustee shall, in other respects, allocate assets as the trustee shall consider to be in the best interests of the beneficiaries, valuing each asset on the date or dates of allocation.

K. Allocating Income. The trustee shall allocate to each share a ratable portion of all of the income earned by my estate or the trust after my death, whether earned before or after the assets are in the possession of the trustee, and income earned on assets used to pay charges according to the same fractional shares.

L. My "Available GST Exemption" Defined. For the purposes of this Article, my "available GST exemption" means an amount equal to (1) my GST exemption, determined for Federal tax purposes, minus (2) all allocations of my GST exemption made or deemed made to transfers other than those to transfers under this trust instrument.

Article 18
Calculating the Residuary Trust Fund if No Federal Estate Tax Exists

This Article shall apply if there is, on the date of my death, no Federal estate tax or Federal generation-skipping transfer tax that applies with respect to my estate (including this trust fund).

A. My Purposes. I intend that the division of the residuary trust fund into a nonmarital share, a state-only marital share, and a marital share, shall take advantage of the increases allowed under applicable Federal income tax law to the basis of assets received from me on account of my death, to the extent possible while minimizing the *state* estate tax due at the later death of my *husband/wife*, without incurring any *state* estate tax at my death.

B. Defining the "Descendants' Nonmarital Share." The "descendants' nonmarital share" shall be a fractional share of the residuary trust fund.

1. Calculating the Numerator. The numerator of the fraction shall equal the greater of:

a. the largest value of the residuary trust fund that can pass free of *State* estate tax by reason of the exemptions allowable to my estate under the law of *State*. This value shall be determined after being reduced by reason of all other dispositions of property included in my gross estate for which no deduction is allowed in computing my *State* estate tax, and administration expenses and other charges to principal that are not claimed and allowed as *State* estate tax deductions; and

b. the smallest value of the assets of the residuary trust fund to which the personal representative of my estate can allocate the entire aggregate basis increase allowed under Federal income tax laws for property not acquired by a surviving spouse.

2. Calculating the Denominator. The denominator of the fraction shall equal the value of the residuary trust fund. References in this paragraph B to my residuary trust fund shall include only those portions of my residuary trust fund to which my aggregate basis increase may be allocated under federal income tax law.

C. Defining the "State-Only Marital Share." The "state-only marital share" shall be a fractional share of the residuary trust fund.

1. Calculating the Numerator. The numerator of the fraction shall be the difference between:

a. the largest value that can pass free of *State* estate tax by reason of the exemptions allowable to my estate under the law of *State*. This value shall be determined after being reduced by reason of all other dispositions of property included in my gross estate for which no deduction is allowed in computing my *State* estate tax, and administration expenses and other charges to principal that are not claimed and allowed as *State* estate tax deductions; and

b. the numerator of the nonmarital share under this Article.

2. Calculating the Denominator. The denominator of this fraction shall equal the value of the residuary trust fund.

D. Defining the "Marital Share." If my *husband/wife* survives me, the marital share shall be the remaining fractional share of the residuary trust fund after subtracting the nonmarital share and the state-only marital share.

E. Allocating Assets. If my *husband/wife* survives me:

1. Allocating Basis in a Fairly Representative Manner. The trustee shall allocate to the nonmarital share only assets to which my personal representative can allocate my aggregate basis increase. Otherwise, the trustee shall select the assets that shall constitute the nonmarital share in manner such that the net appreciation of any property allocated to the nonmarital share shall be fairly representative of the net appreciation of all property available for such allocation (excluding any property to which the trustee cannot, under Federal income tax law, validly allocate any of the aggregate basis increase or the spousal property basis increase).

2. Allocating Assets Otherwise. In other respects, the trustee shall allocate assets as the trustee shall consider to be in the best interests of the beneficiaries, valuing each asset on the date or dates of allocation.

F. Allocating Trust Income. The trustee shall allocate to each share a ratable portion of all of the income earned by my estate or the trust after my death, whether earned before or after the assets are in the possession of the trustee, and income earned on assets used to pay charges according to the same fractional shares.

Article 19
Administering the QTIP, Reverse QTIP and State-Only Marital Trusts

A. Making QTIP and Reverse QTIP Elections. If there is, on the date of my death, a Federal estate tax that may be imposed with respect to my estate, the trustee may elect to qualify all or any portion of the QTIP marital trust and the reverse QTIP marital trust for the Federal estate tax marital deduction, and to treat me as the transferor of the reverse QTIP marital trust for Federal generation-skipping transfer tax purposes.

1. Making Partial Elections. If the trustee shall elect to qualify less than all of the QTIP marital trust or the reverse QTIP marital trust for the Federal estate tax marital deduction, the trustee shall divide the trust fund as to which such partial election was made into two (2) separate trusts and make all principal payments first from the trust fund that qualifies for the Federal estate tax marital deduction.

2. Allocating Assets Between or Among Shares. The trustee shall allocate assets between these shares as the trustee shall consider to be in the best interests of the beneficiaries, valuing each asset on the date of allocation.

B. Assuring Productivity of Assets. My *husband/wife* may direct the trustee to make any unproductive or underproductive assets of the QTIP marital trust and the reverse QTIP marital trust productive or to convert them to productive assets within a reasonable time.

C. Receiving and Administering Retirement Payments. If the QTIP marital trust or the reverse QTIP marital trust is entitled to receive distributions under any retirement plan or individual retirement arrangement, of which my *husband/wife* is the designated beneficiary for Federal income tax purposes, then the trustee shall do the following:

1. Distributing Greater of Income or Required Minimum Distribution. The trustee shall annually withdraw from such retirement plan trust fund or arrangement the greater of all of the income earned by my *husband/wife*'s share of such plan or arrangement, or the required minimum distribution with respect to my *husband/wife*, as determined for Federal income tax purposes.

2. Distributing Withdrawn Amounts. The trustee shall annually distribute to my *husband/wife* all amounts withdrawn from such plan or arrangement.

D. Paying Transfer Taxes.

1. Paying Transfer Taxes Generally. The trustee shall, unless my *husband/wife* provides otherwise by specific reference to this paragraph in a valid will or other writing, pay or make arrangements for the payment of the incremental transfer taxes imposed on the reverse QTIP marital trust and on the QTIP marital trust upon the death of my *husband/wife*, from the QTIP marital trust and not from the reverse QTIP marital trust.

2. Paying Transfer Taxes In Case of a Partial QTIP Election. If the trustee shall elect to qualify only part of the QTIP marital trust, the reverse QTIP marital trust, or both, and shall create two trusts as required by this Article, the transfer taxes imposed on both trusts at my *husband/wife*'s death shall be paid from the qualified trust fund to the extent possible.

E. The "State-Only Marital Trust."

1. Selecting Assets to Fund the State-Only Marital Trusts. The trustee may fractionalize each asset of the residuary trust fund to create the state-only marital share, but if the trustee chooses not to fractionalize assets, the trustee shall allocate assets to this share as the trustee shall consider to be in the best interests of the beneficiaries, valuing each asset on the date or dates of allocation.

2. Allocating Income. The trustee shall allocate to the state-only marital share a ratable portion of all of the income earned by my estate and the trust after my death, whether earned before or after the assets are in the possession of the trustee, and income earned on assets used to pay charges according to the same fractional shares.

3. State and Federal Elections. The trustee and the personal representative of my estate shall elect to qualify the state-only marital trust for the marital deduction under the laws of *State*, but not for Federal estate tax purposes.

4. Other Provisions. The provisions of this article regarding "Assuring Productivity of Assets," "Receiving and Administering Retirement Payments," and "Paying Transfer Taxes" shall apply equally to the state-only marital trust and the QTIP marital trust.

Article 20
Definitions and Miscellaneous

A. Definitions. The following terms shall have the meaning set forth below for all purposes of this trust:

1. "Children" and "Descendants" Defined. "Children" and "descendants" include those now living and those later born, subject to the following rules:

a. "Children" and "descendants" include an adopted person and that adopted person's descendants if, that adopted person is adopted before reaching eighteen (18) years of age;

b. "Children" and "descendants" includes those born outside of wedlock, if, during such child's or descendant's lifetime, his or her parent through whom such child or descendant claims hereunder, has acknowledged such person as his or her child in a writing duly signed and notarized during such parent's lifetime; and

c. "Children" and "descendants" include a child produced before the parent's death by donor artificial insemination, in vitro fertilization or other form of surrogate parenthood, whether or not such child was legally adopted by such parent before such parent's death.

2. "Disinterested Trustee" Defined. A "disinterested trustee" means a trustee who is not an interested trustee.

3. "Interested Trustee" Defined. An "interested trustee" means a trustee who is also (a) a beneficiary of the trust of which he or she is a trustee or the insured under a policy of insurance owned by a trust of which he or she is a trustee; (b) married to and living together with a beneficiary of the trust of which he or she is a trustee; (c) the father, mother, issue, brother or sister, of a beneficiary of the trust of which he or she is a trustee; (d) an employee of a beneficiary of the trust of which he or she is a trustee; (e) a corporation or any employee of a corporation in which the stock holdings of the trustee and the trust are significant from the viewpoint of voting control; or (f) a subordinate employee of a corporation in which the trustee is an executive.

4. "Personal Representative" Defined. A "personal representative" means the legal representative of a decedent's estate. The "personal representative" shall include any executor, ancillary executor, administrator, or ancillary administrator, whether local or foreign and whether of all or part of my estate, multiple personal representatives, and their successors.

5. "Residuary Trust Fund" Defined. The "residuary trust fund" means the real and personal property passing under this instrument, after paying any amounts certified by the personal representative of my estate as needed to settle my debts and expenses of estate administration.

6. "Transfer Taxes" Defined. "Transfer taxes" means all estate, inheritance, legacy, succession, and other transfer taxes, including any tax on excess retirement accumulations, imposed with respect to my death by any state, the United States, or by any foreign country. "Transfer taxes" also includes all taxes that are reimbursable under Sections 2207 through 2207B of the Internal Revenue Code of 1986, as amended, which right of reimbursement I hereby waive. "Transfer taxes" also includes all interest and penalties on such taxes.

7. "Trustee" Defined. The "trustee" or "trustees" shall include each trustee individually, multiple trustees, and their successors.

B. Retroactive Legislation. I include in this instrument certain dispositions and direct certain actions that shall occur only if, on the date of my death, no federal estate tax or Federal generation-skipping transfer tax applies with respect to my estate. These provisions shall not apply if, on the date of my death, no federal estate tax or federal generation-skipping transfer tax, as the case may be, applies with respect to my estate, but such tax or taxes is/are retroactively reinstated before April 1, 2011, and apply under such retroactive legislation with respect to my estate. If such retroactive legislation is finally determined to be unconstitutional or otherwise invalid, these references shall apply as if such retroactive legislation had never been enacted.

C. Absence of Trust Beneficiaries. If all of the beneficiaries of any trust under this instrument should die before the trust assets have vested in them, the trustee shall distribute all of the remaining assets of that trust as follows:

1. One Half to My Heirs and Distributee. One half (½) (or all, if there are no persons to take under subparagraph C.2. of this Article) to the heirs and distributees who would have inherited my personal estate, and in such shares as they would have inherited it, had I died unmarried and without a valid will, determined on the later of the date of my death or the date of the death of the last of the trust beneficiaries to die; and

    2. One Half to My *Husband/Wife*'s Distributees. One half (½) (or all, if there are no persons to take under subparagraph C.1. of this Article) to the heirs and distributees who would have inherited my *husband/wife*'s personal estate, and in such shares as they would have inherited it, had he died unmarried and without a valid will, determined on the later of the date of my death or the date of the death of the last of the trust beneficiaries to die.

    D. Applicable Law. This instrument shall be governed by and construed according to the laws of the *State*.

    E. Number. Whenever the context requires, the singular includes the plural and the plural the singular.

    F. Survivorship. No person shall be deemed to have survived me for purposes of this instrument, unless he or she is living on the date ninety (90) days after the date of my death.

    G. Tax-Related Terms. All tax-related terms shall have the same meaning they have in the Internal Revenue Code of 1986, as amended.

[Add state-specific signature and notary clauses, schedule of assets, and where required, attesting witness clause]

¶ A.09 FORM 9: WILL FOR ESTATE OVER $10 MILLION— MARITAL DEDUCTION AND GST TAX PLANNING— DYNASTY TRUST FOR CHILDREN AND DESCENDANTS—GST EXEMPTION USED EVEN IF IT GENERATES ESTATE TAX AT FIRST SPOUSE'S DEATH—NO STATE QTIP IN ORDER TO REDUCE STATE ESTATE TAXES AT SURVIVING SPOUSE'S DEATH—2010 DISPOSITION OF 40% OF ESTATE TO NONMARITAL SHARE—TRUSTEE CAN DISTRIBUTE FROM QTIP MINIMUM AMOUNT OF PRINCIPAL SUFFICIENT TO GIVE SPOUSE ENOUGH APPRECIATION TO TAKE ADVANTAGE OF AGGREGATE BASIS INCREASE AT SURVIVING SPOUSE'S DEATH

Will of *Testator*[9]

I, *Testator*, of [locality, state], make this my will. I revoke any other wills and codicils made by me.

Article 1
My Family

I am married to *Spouse* (sometimes referred to as "my *husband/wife*") and I have [number of children] children, *Children*.

---

[9] **KEY:**

Testator	— full name of the testator
Spouse	— full name of testator's spouse
husband/wife	— "husband" or "wife," as the case may be
Children	— full names of testator's children
he/she	— "he" or "she" (referring to the spouse)
his/her	— "his" or "her" (referring to the spouse)
him/her	— "him" or "her" (referring to the spouse)
AlternatePR	— name of the alternate personal representative (after spouse)
FirstTrustee	— name of the first trustee
SecondTrustee	— name of the alternate trustee

Article 2
My Personal Effects

A. Disposing of My Personal Effects. I leave my personal effects (defined below) to my *husband/wife*, *Spouse*, if *he/she* survives me, or otherwise to my descendants who survive me, *per stirpes*. If neither my *husband/wife* nor any of my children nor their descendants survive me, these personal effects shall be added to the residue of my estate. An adult person with whom a minor resides may give a binding receipt for any personal effects passing to the minor.

B. Memorandum. I may make a memorandum of how I wish some of my personal effects to be distributed, and I request that my wishes be followed.

Article 3
My Personal Residence

I leave all of my interest in the properties my personal representative (defined below) shall determine to have been used by me or a member of my family as personal residences to my *husband/wife*, *Spouse*, if *he/she* survives me, to the extent that they do not pass to *him/her* by right of survivorship. Personal residences shall also include all adjoining lands and any related casualty insurance policies.

Article 4
My Residuary Estate

A. If a Federal Estate Tax Exists. If there is, on the date of my death, a Federal estate tax and/or a Federal generation-skipping transfer tax, as the case may be, that applies with respect to my estate, I leave my residuary estate (defined below), as follows:

1. If My *Husband/Wife* Survives Me. If my *husband/wife*, *Spouse*, survives me, my personal representative shall divide my residuary estate into a descendants' share, a GST exempt marital share, and a marital share (all defined below).

a. The descendants' share shall be held under the Article entitled "The Dynasty Trust."

b. The marital share shall be held under the Article entitled "The QTIP Marital Trust."

2. If My *Husband/Wife* Does Not Survive Me. If my *husband/wife* does not survive me, my personal representative shall divide my residuary estate into a descendants' GST exempt share and a descendants' power of appointment share (both defined below).

a. The descendants' GST exempt share shall be held under the Article entitled "The Dynasty Trust."

b. My personal representative shall distribute the descendants' power of appointment share to my descendants who survive me, *per stirpes*, except that the share for any child of mine shall be added to the trust fund for such child under the Article entitled "Child's Power of Appointment Trust," for that child, and the share for any more remote descendant of mine who shall then not yet have reached the age of thirty-five (35) years, shall be held under the Article entitled "Contingent Trust for Certain Beneficiaries."

B. If No Federal Estate Tax Exists. If there is, on the date of my death, no Federal estate or generation-skipping transfer tax that applies with respect to my estate, I leave my residuary estate, as follows:

1. If My *Husband/Wife* Survives Me. If my *husband/wife* survives me, my personal representative shall divide my residuary estate into a descendants' share and a marital share.

a. The descendants' share shall be held under the Article entitled "The Dynasty Trust."

b. The marital share shall be held under the Article entitled "The QTIP Marital Trust."

2. If My *Husband/Wife* Does Not Survive Me. If my *husband/wife* does not survive me, my personal representative shall hold my residuary estate under the Article entitled "The Dynasty Trust."

Article 5
The Dynasty Trust

The Dynasty Trust shall be held under this Article.

A. Distributing Trust Fund Before Perpetuities Date. Until the perpetuities date (defined below), the trustee shall distribute to or expend for the benefit of my then-living children and my then-living more remote descendants, as much of the net income and principal of the dynasty trust as the trustee may deem appropriate for any purpose, annually adding to principal any undistributed income.

1. Making Unequal Distributions. The trustee may distribute income and principal of the dynasty trust unequally and may make distributions to some beneficiaries and not to others.

2. Preserving Corpus. The trustee shall administer the dynasty trust in a manner designed to conserve its principal as long as possible. The trustee shall, therefore, lend income and principal of the dynasty trust to beneficiaries or buy assets for their use, rather than distributing income or principal outright to beneficiaries, unless the trustee determines that outright distributions are more appropriate.

B. Distributing Trust Fund At Perpetuities Date. Upon the perpetuities date, the trustee shall distribute the remaining trust fund to my then-living descendants, *per stirpes.*

C. "Perpetuities Date" Defined. The "perpetuities date" shall be the date twenty-one years after the death of the last to die of my children and more remote descendants living on the date of my death.

Article 6
The QTIP Marital Trust

The QTIP marital trust shall be held under this Article.

A. Distributing Trust Fund During My *Husband/Wife*'s Life. The trustee shall distribute the net income of the QTIP marital trust quarterly or more frequently to my *husband/wife*, *Spouse*, during *his/her* life.

1. Principal Distributions. The trustee shall also distribute to my *husband/wife* as much of the principal of the QTIP marital trust as is appropriate for any purpose.

2. Distributing Additional Principal if There is No Federal Estate Tax. If the trustee deems it likely that my *husband/wife* will die before January 1, 2011, the trustee shall distribute to my *husband/wife* a fractional share of this trust.

a. The numerator of this fraction shall be equal to the smallest value of the assets of this trust fund to which the personal representative of my *husband/wife*'s estate could allocate all of the aggregate basis increase allowed to my *husband/wife* under Federal income tax laws, less the amount of such aggregate basis increase that could be allocated to other assets already owned by my *husband/wife* at the time of this distribution.

b. The denominator of this fraction shall equal the value of the QTIP marital trust fund.

B. Distributing Trust Fund At My *Husband/Wife*'s Death.

1. Distributing Income. At my *husband/wife*'s death, the trustee shall distribute to my *husband/wife*'s estate any undistributed income of the QTIP marital trust.

2. Appointing Trust Principal. At my *husband/wife*'s death, the trustee shall distribute the principal of the QTIP marital trust, to the extent it is not used to pay transfer taxes as provided below, as my *husband/wife* may direct by specific reference to this special power of appointment in *his/her* last will.

a. My *husband/wife* may appoint the QTIP marital trust fund, either outright or in further trust, but only to or among any one (1) or more of my descendants.

b. My *husband/wife* may not appoint any portion of the QTIP marital trust fund to my *husband/wife*, *his/her* creditors, *his/her* estate, or the creditors of *his/her* estate.

3. Distributing Unappointed Trust Fund. The trustee shall distribute the unappointed QTIP marital trust fund to my then-living descendants, *per stirpes*, except that the share for any child of mine shall be added to the child's power of appointment trust for that child, and the share for any more remote descendant of mine who shall then not yet have reached the age of thirty-five (35) years, shall be held for such descendant under the Article entitled "Contingent Trust for Certain Beneficiaries."

Article 7
Child's Power of Appointment Trust

The child's power of appointment trust for each child of mine shall be held as a separate trust under this Article.

A. Distributing Trust Fund During the Child's Life. The trustee shall distribute to or for the benefit of each child for whom a trust is created under this Article, as much of the net income and principal as the child shall request at any time or as the trustee may consider appropriate for any purpose, annually adding to principal any undistributed income.

B. Distributing Trust Fund At the Child's Death. Upon the death of a child of mine who survives me, the trustee shall distribute the remaining principal and income of such child's trust under this Article as that child may direct by specific reference to this power of appointment in that child's last will.

1. Appointing Everything But Limited Portion. Each such child may appoint the remaining principal and income of such child's trust under this Article (other than the limited portion (defined below)) of such trust fund, either outright or in further trust, to or among any persons, including such child's estate.

2. Appointing Limited Portion. Each such child may appoint the limited portion of the principal and income of such child's trust under this Article outright or in further trust, but only to or among my then-living descendants, and such child may not appoint any of the limited portion to such child himself or herself, such child's creditors, such child's estate, or the creditors of such child's estate.

3. Distributing Unappointed Trust Fund. The trustee shall distribute any unappointed portion of the fund of a deceased child's trust under this Article to such child's then-living descendants, *per stirpes*, or if there are no such descendants then living, to my then-living descendants, *per stirpes*, except that the fund that would thus be distributed to any then-living child of mine shall be added to such child's trust under this Article.

4. "Limited Portion" Defined. The "limited portion" of the fund of a child's trust under this Article is that portion which would pass to one or more persons assigned to the same or a higher generation as the deceased child for Federal generation-skipping transfer tax purposes, were such child to die without a valid will. If such child dies in a year in which there is no Federal generation-skipping transfer tax applicable with respect to such child's estate, the "limited portion" shall be the entire fund of the child's trust.

Article 8
Contingent Trust for Certain Beneficiaries

If a beneficiary (other than a child of mine) is entitled to receive any part of my estate or any portion of any trust fund held under this will while the beneficiary is under the age of thirty-five (35) years, the trustee may retain such assets in a separate trust for that beneficiary.

A. Distributing Trust Fund Before the Contingent Trust Termination Date. Until the contingent trust termination date (defined below), the trustee shall distribute to or for the benefit of the beneficiary as much of the net income and principal as the trustee may consider appropriate for the beneficiary's health, education, support, or maintenance, annually adding to principal any undistributed income.

B. Distributing Trust Fund At the Contingent Trust Termination Date. Upon the contingent trust termination date, the trustee shall distribute the remaining assets to the beneficiary if the beneficiary is then living or otherwise to the beneficiary's estate to be distributed as part of that estate.

C. "Contingent Trust Termination Date" Defined. The "contingent trust termination date" shall be the earlier of (1) the date on which the beneficiary dies or (2) the date on which the beneficiary reaches the age of thirty-five (35) years.

Article 9
Special Limits on Powers of Interested Trustee

The following limitations shall apply, notwithstanding other provisions of this instrument.

A. Limiting Actions by Interested Trustees. No interested trustee (defined below) may participate in the exercise of any discretion to distribute principal to himself or herself, except as is appropriate for his or her health, education, support, and maintenance, or any of them. No interested trustee may participate in the exercise of any discretion to distribute or expend principal or income in a manner that would discharge that trustee's personal obligation to support the beneficiary. No interested trustee may participate in the exercise of any incident of ownership over any policy owned by the trust insuring the life of such trustee.

B. Disinterested Trustees Exercising Certain Powers. A disinterested trustee (defined below) who is serving as a co-trustee with an interested trustee, may exercise those discretions granted under this instrument the exercise of which by an interested trustee are precluded.

1. If Multiple Trustees Include an Interested Trustee Who Cannot Act. The number of trustees who must consent to the exercise of a power granted under this instrument, as determined under the Article entitled "My Fiduciaries" shall be determined by treating the interested trustees who are not entitled, under this Article, to participate in the exercise of the power or discretion, as if they were not then serving.

2. If All Trustees Are Precluded From Acting. If this Article precludes every then-serving trustee from exercising a power otherwise granted to the trustee under this instrument, the then-serving trustee shall appoint a disinterested trustee who may exercise such power (or decline to exercise it) as if that disinterested trustee were the sole then-serving trustee.

Article 10
Debts, Expenses, and Taxes

A. Paying Debts and Expenses. My personal representative shall pay from my residuary estate my debts (but not before their maturity) and funeral and burial expenses, including the cost of a suitable memorial, without court order.

1. Paying Certain Joint Debts. My personal representative shall pay only my proportionate share of any debts for which I am jointly liable with my *husband/wife*.

2. Paying Packing and Shipping Expenses. My personal representative shall pay all packing, shipping, insurance, and other charges relating to the distribution of any of my personal property without seeking reimbursement from the recipient of such personal property.

B. Paying Transfer Taxes. My personal representative shall pay all transfer taxes, other than generation-skipping transfer taxes, payable by reason of my death on assets passing under this will, from my residuary estate.

1. Apportioning Transfer Taxes on Nonprobate Assets. My personal representative shall apportion transfer taxes imposed on any assets not passing under this will to those assets and the transfer taxes on those assets shall be paid from those assets as provided by the laws of the state in which I reside at my death, except as expressly provided elsewhere in this will.

2. Apportioning Generation-Skipping Transfer Taxes. My personal representative shall apportion all generation-skipping transfer taxes for which my estate is legally responsible to those generation-skipping transfers, whether or not under this will.

3. Apportioning Transfer Taxes Away From Deductible Assets. Assets passing as the marital share shall have the full benefit of the Federal estate tax marital deduction allowed with respect to any transfer taxes, and shall not bear any transfer taxes. Other assets passing to my *husband/wife* or to any charitable organization, whether under this will or otherwise, shall have the full benefit of any available marital or charitable deduction for Federal and other transfer tax purposes, in determining the share of transfer taxes that should be borne by those assets.

Article 11
My Fiduciaries

A. Naming My Personal Representatives. I name my *husband/wife*, *Spouse*, to be my personal representative, and I give *him/her* the right to name one or more persons to serve with *him/her* or in *his/her* place. If my *husband/wife* fails or ceases to serve and there is no other person serving or named to serve, I name the *AlternatePR*, of [*locality, state*], to be my personal representative.

B. Naming My Trustees. I name *FirstTrustee*, of [*locality, state*], to be the trustee of any trust under this will. If *FirstTrustee* shall be unable or unwilling to serve or to continue serving, I name *SecondTrustee*, of [*locality, state*] to be the trustee of any trust under this will.

C. No Surety or Bond. No personal representative or trustee named by me or by another personal representative or trustee shall be required to provide surety or other security on a bond.

D. Naming Additional Fiduciaries. I authorize my named fiduciaries (defined below) to appoint any person as an additional personal representative or trustee in the same state or another state in which administration may be appropriate to serve at the pleasure of the appointing fiduciaries.

E. Delegating Fiduciary Powers and Authorities. My fiduciaries may delegate to another fiduciary any power or authority granted by me to my fiduciaries, to continue at the pleasure of the delegating fiduciary, unless otherwise agreed. Any person dealing in good faith with a fiduciary may rely upon that fiduciary's representation that a delegation has been made and remains in effect under this paragraph.

F. Fiduciary Resigning.

1. Personal Representative May Resign. A personal representative may resign by giving written notice specifying the effective date of the resignation to the designated successor.

2. Trustee May Resign. Any trustee may resign by giving written notice specifying the effective date of the resignation to the designated successor. If no successor is designated, the resigning trustee shall give notice to each adult beneficiary to whom trust income then may be distributed.

G. Removing a Trustee. A trustee may be removed by the vote of two-thirds (⅔) of the then-living adult beneficiaries to whom trust income may then be distributed.

H. Filling Fiduciary Vacancies.

1. Court Appointing Personal Representative to Fill Vacancy. If no successor personal representative is designated, a court of appropriate jurisdiction shall name a successor personal representative.

2. Beneficiaries Appointing Corporate Trustee to Fill Vacancy. A corporation no substantial portion of the stock of which is owned by beneficiaries of this

trust, may be named as successor trustee to fill any vacancy, by majority vote of the adult beneficiaries to whom trust income then may be distributed.

I. No Liability for Acts or Omissions of Predecessors. No fiduciary shall be responsible for or need inquire into any acts or omissions of a prior fiduciary.

J. Compensating Fiduciaries. In addition to reimbursement for expenses, each individual fiduciary is entitled to reasonable compensation for services. Each corporate fiduciary is entitled to compensation based on its written fee schedule in effect at the time its services are rendered or as otherwise agreed, and its compensation may vary from time to time based on that schedule.

K. Management Powers. I authorize my fiduciaries to exercise all powers conferred by applicable state law and to do the following in a fiduciary capacity.

1. Prudent Investor Rule. My fiduciaries may hold and retain as part of my estate or any trust fund any property owned by me, whether or not such investment would be appropriate for a prudent investor. My fiduciaries may also hold and retain as part of my estate or any trust fund any property received from any source, and invest and reinvest my estate or trust fund (or leave it temporarily uninvested) in any type of property and every kind of investment in the same manner as a prudent investor would invest his or her own assets.

2. Holding Assets For Use of Trust Beneficiaries. My trustee may buy and hold in trust, assets that will be used personally by one or more beneficiaries, even if those assets would not otherwise be acquired by a prudent investor investing his or her own assets.

3. Transferring Assets. My fiduciaries may sell or exchange any real or personal property contained in my estate or any trust, for cash or credit, at public or private sale, and with such warranties or indemnifications as my fiduciaries may deem advisable.

4. Borrowing Money. My fiduciaries may borrow money (even from a fiduciary or beneficiary of my estate or any trust) for the benefit of my estate or any trust and secure these debts with assets of my estate or any trust.

5. Granting Security Interests. My fiduciaries may grant security interests and execute all instruments creating such interests upon such terms as my fiduciaries may deem advisable.

6. Compromising Claims. My fiduciaries may compromise and adjust claims against or on behalf of my estate or any trust on such terms as my fiduciaries may deem advisable.

7. Not Disclosing Nominees. My fiduciaries may take title to any securities in the name of any custodian or nominee without disclosing this relationship.

8. Allocating Between Income and Principal. My fiduciaries may determine whether receipts are income or principal and whether disbursements are to be charged against income or principal to the extent not clearly established by state law.

A determination made by my fiduciaries in good faith shall not require equitable adjustments.

9. Making Tax Elections. My fiduciaries may make all tax elections and allocations my fiduciaries may consider appropriate; however, this authority is exercisable only in a fiduciary capacity and may not be used to enlarge or shift any beneficial interest except as an incidental consequence of the discharge of fiduciary duties. A tax election or allocation made by my fiduciaries in good faith shall not require equitable adjustments.

10. Distributing to Custodians for Minors. My fiduciaries shall distribute any of my estate or any trust fund to a beneficiary under the age of twenty-one (21) years by distribution to any appropriate person (who may be a fiduciary) chosen by my fiduciaries as custodian under any appropriate Uniform Transfers (or Gifts) to Minors Act, to be held for the maximum period of time allowed by law. My fiduciaries may also sell any asset that cannot be held under this custodianship and invest the sales proceeds in assets that can be so held.

11. Employing Advisors. My fiduciaries may employ such lawyers, accountants, and other advisors as my fiduciaries may deem useful and appropriate for the administration of my estate or any trust. My fiduciaries may employ a professional investment advisor and delegate to this advisor any discretionary investment authorities to manage the investments of my estate or any trust, including any investment in mutual funds, investment trusts, or managed accounts, and may rely on the advisor's investment recommendations without liability to any beneficiary.

12. Buying and Holding Life Insurance. My fiduciaries may buy and hold insurance policies on the life of any beneficiary or any person in whom a beneficiary has an insurable interest and may pay the premiums on such policies from income or principal, as my fiduciaries may deem advisable.

13. Dividing and Distributing Assets. My fiduciaries may divide and distribute the assets of my estate or any trust fund in kind, in money, or partly in each, without regard to the income tax basis of any asset and without the consent of any beneficiary. The decision of my fiduciaries in dividing any portion of my estate or any trust fund between or among two or more beneficiaries, if made in good faith, shall be binding on all persons.

14. Allocation of Basis Increase. My personal representative shall allocate any increases in the adjusted basis of property owned by me at the time of my death, whether passing under my Will or otherwise, to the extent such property is eligible to receive such an allocation, as my personal representative deems to be in the best interests of my estate and its beneficiaries. In making these allocations my personal representative shall:

a. First, satisfy all charitable bequests with assets to which no aggregate or spousal property basis increases may be allocated;

b. Second, satisfy all charitable bequests with assets that have an adjusted income tax basis closest to zero of all of my assets available to satisfy these bequests;

      c. Third, generally not allocate basis increase to assets the gain from the sale of which is not subject to federal income tax under present federal income tax laws;

      d. Fourth, allocate basis increases to assets that are reasonably likely to be sold within the three year period beginning on the date of my death, the sale of which will produce an income tax liability that is taxed at a rate higher than that on long-term capital gains; and

      e. Fifth, allocate the remaining basis increase among assets in proportion to each asset's pro rata share of the total appreciation of all such assets owned by me on the date of my death.

      Any reference in this paragraph to assets "owned by me on the date of my death" shall apply equally to assets deemed owned by me on the date of my death under the federal income tax rules governing allocation of my aggregate basis increase. My personal representative shall not be liable to anyone for any allocation of my basis increases made in good faith, in the absence of gross negligence.

Article 12
Trust Administration

      A. Spendthrift Limits. No interest in a trust under this will shall be subject to the beneficiary's liabilities or creditor claims or to assignment or anticipation.

      B. Protecting Trust Beneficiaries From Creditors. If the trustee shall determine that a beneficiary would not benefit as greatly from any outright distribution of trust income or principal because of the availability of the distribution to the beneficiary's creditors, the trustee shall instead expend those amounts for the benefit of the beneficiary. This direction is intended to enable the trustee to give the beneficiary the fullest possible benefit and enjoyment of all of the trust income and principal to which he or she is entitled.

      C. Combining Multiple Trusts. The trustee may invest the assets of multiple trusts in a single fund if the interests of the trusts are accounted for separately.

      D. Merging and Consolidating Trust Funds. The trustee may merge or consolidate any trust into any other trust that has the same trustee and substantially the same dispositive provisions.

      E. Dividing Trust Funds. The trustee may divide any trust fund into multiple separate trusts.

      F. Accountings. The trustee shall not be required to file annual accounts with any court or court official in any jurisdiction.

      G. Changing Trust Situs. A disinterested trustee may change the situs of any trust under this will, and to the extent necessary or appropriate, move the trust assets, to a state or country other than the one in which the trust is then administered if the disinterested trustee shall determine it to be in the best interests of the trust or the

beneficiaries. The disinterested trustee may elect that the law of such other jurisdiction shall govern the trust to the extent necessary or appropriate under the circumstances.

Article 13
Calculating Shares of Residuary Estate if a Federal Estate Tax Exists

This Article shall apply if there is, on the date of my death, a Federal estate tax and/or a Federal generation-skipping transfer tax, as the case may be, that applies with respect to my estate.

A. My Purposes. I intend that:

1. Minimizing Federal and *State* Estate Taxes. The division of my residuary estate into a descendants' share and a marital share, shall minimize the Federal and *State* estate taxes at my *husband/wife*'s death to the extent I can do so while deferring a substantial portion of the Federal estate taxes until both my *husband/wife* and I have died. I realize that, by creating a descendant's share that takes full advantage of my available GST exemption, I may cause an estate tax to be due at my death that could otherwise have been deferred until the later death of my *husband/wife*, but I have done so in order to take the fullest advantage of my GST exemption. I also realize that by creating a descendant's share that takes full advantage of my available GST exemption I may incur a state estate tax at my death, but by doing so it is my expectation and intent to reduce to a greater degree the state estate taxes incurred at my *husband/wife*'s later death.

2. Taking Advantage of My GST Exemption. The creation of a descendants' share and, if my *husband/wife* does not survive me, the descendants' GST exempt share, shall take advantage of my available GST exemption (defined below).

3. Qualifying for Federal Estate Tax Marital Deduction. The marital share shall qualify for the Federal estate tax marital deduction and all provisions of this will shall be construed accordingly. My fiduciaries shall, in all matters involving the marital share, exercise no power in a manner that would infringe upon any legal requirement for the allowance of the Federal estate tax marital deduction.

B. Defining the "Descendants' Share." If my *husband/wife* survives me, the "descendants' share" shall be a fractional share of my residuary estate.

1. Calculating the Numerator. The numerator of the fraction shall be the amount of my available GST exemption.

2. Calculating the Denominator. The denominator of the fraction shall equal the value of my residuary estate.

C. Defining the "Marital Share." If my *husband/wife* survives me, the "marital share" shall be the remaining fractional share of my residuary estate after subtracting the descendants' share.

D. Defining the "Descendants' GST Exempt Share." If my *husband/wife* does not survive me, the descendants' GST exempt share shall be a fractional share of my residuary estate.

1. Calculating the Numerator. The numerator of the fraction shall be equal to the amount of my available GST exemption.

2. Calculating the Denominator. The denominator of the fraction shall equal the value of my residuary estate.

E. Defining the "Descendants' Power of Appointment Share." If my *husband/wife* does not survive me, the descendants' power of appointment share, shall be the remaining fractional share of my residuary estate after subtracting the descendants' GST exempt share.

F. Determining the Effect of Disclaimers.

1. Disclaiming the Marital Share. My fiduciaries shall add to the descendants' share any portion of the marital share as to which a qualified disclaimer by or for my *husband/wife* is made. The descendants' share shall be calculated before any qualified disclaimer by or for my *husband/wife* of any of the marital share.

2. Apportioning Transfer Taxes to Disclaimed Funds. Transfer taxes imposed on assets as to which my *husband/wife* has made a qualified disclaimer shall be apportioned to those disclaimed funds.

G. Allocating Assets Between or Among Shares.

1. Making Certain Allocations If My *Husband/Wife* Survives Me. If my *husband/wife* survives me:

a. My personal representative shall allocate to the marital share only assets that can qualify for the Federal estate tax marital deduction.

b. My personal representative shall not, to the extent possible, allocate to the marital share assets upon which a foreign death tax is payable.

c. My personal representative shall allocate to the descendants' share and, if my *husband/wife* does not survive me, the descendants' GST exempt share, solely of assets includable in my gross estate for Federal estate tax purposes.

2. Making Other Allocations. My personal representative shall, in other respects, allocate assets as my personal representative shall consider to be in the best interests of the beneficiaries, valuing each asset on the date or dates of allocation.

H. Allocating Income. My personal representative and trustee shall allocate to each share a ratable portion of all of the income earned by my estate after my death, whether earned before or after the assets are in the possession of the trustee, and income earned on assets used to pay charges according to the same fractional shares.

I. My "Available GST Exemption" Defined. For the purposes of this Article, my "available GST exemption" means an amount equal to (1) my GST exemption, determined for Federal tax purposes, minus (2) all allocations of my GST exemption made or deemed made to transfers other than those to transfers under this will.

Article 14
Calculating Shares of the Residuary Estate if No Federal Estate Tax Exists

This Article shall apply if there is, on the date of my death, no Federal estate or generation-skipping transfer tax that applies with respect to my estate.

A. My Purposes. I intend that the division of the my residuary estate into a descendants' share and a marital share to take full advantage of the increases allowed under applicable Federal income tax law to the basis of assets received from me on account of my death, to the extent that it can be so done without unfairly affecting the amount of the various shares of my estate.

B. Defining the "Descendants' Share." The "descendants' share" shall be a fractional share of my residuary estate.

1. Calculating the Numerator. The numerator of the fraction shall equal the greater of the following two figures:

a. the smallest value of the assets of my residuary estate to which my personal representative can allocate the entire aggregate basis increase allowed under Federal income tax laws for property not acquired by a surviving spouse; and

b. forty percent (40%) of the value of my residuary estate.

2. Calculating the Denominator. The denominator of the fraction shall equal the value of my residuary estate.

C. Defining the "Marital Share." If my *husband/wife* survives me, the "marital share" shall be the remaining fractional share of my residuary estate after subtracting the descendants' share.

D. Allocating Assets. If my *husband/wife* survives me:

1. Allocating Basis in a Fairly Representative Manner. My personal representative shall allocate to the descendants' share only assets to which my personal representative can allocate my aggregate basis increase. Otherwise, my personal representative shall select the assets that shall constitute the descendants' share in manner such that the net appreciation of any property allocated to the descendants' share shall be fairly representative of the net appreciation of all property available for such allocation (excluding any property to which my personal representative cannot, under Federal income tax law, validly allocate any of the aggregate basis increase or the spousal property basis increase).

2. Allocating Assets Otherwise. In other respects, my personal representative shall allocate assets as my personal representative shall consider to be in the best interests of the beneficiaries, valuing each asset on the date or dates of allocation.

E. Allocating Trust Income. My personal representative and trustee shall allocate to each share a ratable portion of all of the income earned by my estate after my death, whether earned before or after the assets are in the possession of the trustee, and income earned on assets used to pay charges according to the same fractional shares.

Article 15
Administering the QTIP Marital Trust

A. Making Elections. If there is, on the date of my death, a Federal estate tax that may be imposed with respect to my estate, my personal representative may elect to qualify all or any portion of the QTIP marital trust for the Federal estate tax marital deduction.

1. Making Partial Elections. If my personal representative shall elect to qualify less than all of the QTIP marital trust for the Federal estate tax marital deduction, my personal representative shall divide the trust fund as to which such partial election was made into two (2) separate trusts and make all principal payments first from the trust fund that qualifies for the Federal estate tax marital deduction.

2. Allocating Assets Between or Among Shares. My personal representative shall allocate assets between these shares as my personal representative shall consider to be in the best interests of the beneficiaries, valuing each asset on the date of allocation.

B. Assuring Productivity of Assets. My *husband/wife* may direct the trustee to make any unproductive or underproductive assets of the QTIP marital trust productive or to convert them to productive assets within a reasonable time.

C. Receiving and Administering Retirement Payments. If the QTIP marital trust is entitled to receive distributions under any retirement plan or individual retirement arrangement, of which my *husband/wife* is the designated beneficiary for Federal income tax purposes, then the trustee shall do the following:

1. Distributing Greater of Income or Required Minimum Distribution. The trustee shall annually withdraw from such retirement plan trust fund or arrangement the greater of all of the income earned by my *husband/wife*'s share of such plan or arrangement, or the required minimum distribution with respect to my *husband/wife*, as determined for Federal income tax purposes.

2. Distributing Withdrawn Amounts. The trustee shall annually distribute to my *husband/wife* all amounts withdrawn from such plan or arrangement.

D. Paying Transfer Taxes.

1. Paying Transfer Taxes Generally. The trustee shall, unless my *husband/wife* provides otherwise by specific reference to this paragraph in a valid will or other writing, pay or make arrangements for the payment of the incremental transfer taxes imposed on the QTIP marital trust upon the death of my *husband/wife*, from the QTIP marital trust.

2. Paying Transfer Taxes In Case of a Partial QTIP Election. If my personal representative shall elect to qualify only part of the QTIP marital trust, and shall create two trusts as required by this Article, the transfer taxes imposed on both trusts at my *husband/wife*'s death shall be paid from the qualified trust fund to the extent possible.

Article 16
Definitions and Miscellaneous

A. Definitions. The following terms shall have the meaning set forth below for all purposes of this will:

1. "Children" and "Descendants" Defined. "Children" and "descendants" include those now living and those later born, subject to the following rules:

a. "Children" and "descendants" include an adopted person and that adopted person's descendants if, that adopted person is adopted before reaching eighteen (18) years of age;

b. "Children" and "descendants" includes those born outside of wedlock, if, during such child's or descendant's lifetime, his or her parent through whom such child or descendant claims hereunder, has acknowledged such person as his or her child in a writing duly signed and notarized during such parent's lifetime; and

c. "Children" and "descendants" include a child produced before the parent's death by donor artificial insemination, in vitro fertilization or other form of surrogate parenthood, whether or not such child was legally adopted by such parent before such parent's death.

2. "Disinterested Trustee" Defined. A "disinterested trustee" means a trustee who is not an interested trustee.

3. "Fiduciary" Defined. "Fiduciary" or "fiduciaries" shall include my personal representative and the trustee, or if they are different persons, either of them.

4. "Interested Trustee" Defined. An "interested trustee" means a trustee who is also (a) a beneficiary of the trust of which he or she is a trustee or the insured under a policy of insurance owned by a trust of which he or she is a trustee; (b) married to and living together with a beneficiary of the trust of which he or she is a trustee; (c) the father, mother, issue, brother or sister, of a beneficiary of the trust of which he or she is a trustee; (d) an employee of a beneficiary of the trust of which he or she is a trustee; (e) a corporation or any employee of a corporation in which the stock holdings of the trustee and the trust are significant from the viewpoint of voting control; or (f) a subordinate employee of a corporation in which the trustee is an executive.

5. "Personal Effects" Defined. My "personal effects" includes all of my jewelry, clothing, furniture, and other items of tangible personal property, but not money (other than collectible money having an inherent value in excess of its face amount) and not assets that my personal representative shall consider primarily to be used in a trade or business or held for investment. My "personal effects" also includes any transferable casualty insurance policies on any items of tangible personal property. Such policies shall pass to the same person who receives the insured property.

6. "Personal Representative" Defined. My "personal representative" shall include any executor, ancillary executor, administrator, or ancillary administrator, whether local or foreign and whether of all or part of my estate, multiple personal representatives, and their successors.

7. "Residuary Estate" Defined. My "residuary estate"" means my real and personal estate passing under this will, after distribution of my personal effects and my personal residences under Articles 2 and 3 of this will.

8. "Transfer Taxes" Defined. "Transfer taxes" means all estate, inheritance, legacy, succession, and other transfer taxes, including any tax on excess retirement accumulations, imposed with respect to my death by any state, the United States, or by any foreign country. "Transfer taxes" also includes all taxes that are reimbursable under Sections 2207 through 2207B of the Internal Revenue Code of 1986, as amended, which right of reimbursement I hereby waive. "Transfer taxes" also includes all interest and penalties on such taxes.

9. "Trustee" Defined. The "trustee" or "trustees" shall include each trustee individually, multiple trustees, and their successors.

B. Retroactive Legislation. I include in this instrument certain dispositions and direct certain actions that shall occur only if, on the date of my death, no federal estate tax or Federal generation-skipping transfer tax applies with respect to my estate. These provisions shall not apply if, on the date of my death, no federal estate tax or federal generation-skipping transfer tax, as the case may be, applies with respect to my estate, but such tax or taxes is/are retroactively reinstated before April 1, 2011, and apply under such retroactive legislation with respect to my estate. If such retroactive legislation is finally determined to be unconstitutional or otherwise invalid, these references shall apply as if such retroactive legislation had never been enacted.

C. Absence of Trust Beneficiaries. If all of the beneficiaries of any trust under this will should die before the trust assets have vested in them, the trustee shall distribute all of the remaining assets of that trust as follows:

1. One Half to My Heirs and Distributee. One half (½) (or all, if there are no persons to take under subparagraph C.2. of this Article) to the heirs and distributees who would have inherited my personal estate, and in such shares as they would have inherited it, had I died unmarried and without a valid will, determined on the later of the date of my death or the date of the death of the last of the trust beneficiaries to die; and

2. One Half to My *Husband/Wife*'s Distributees. One half (½) (or all, if there are no persons to take under subparagraph C.1. of this Article) to the heirs and distributees who would have inherited my *husband/wife*'s personal estate, and in such shares as they would have inherited it, had he died unmarried and without a valid will, determined on the later of the date of my death or the date of the death of the last of the trust beneficiaries to die.

D. Applicable Law. My will shall be governed by and construed according to the laws of the *State*.

E. Joint Ownership. I confirm that all assets owned jointly by me and another person with a right of survivorship should pass outright to my joint owner and my estate shall have no interest in those assets.

F. Number. Whenever the context requires, the singular includes the plural and the plural the singular.

G. Survivorship. No person shall be deemed to have survived me for purposes of inheriting under this will unless he or she is living on the date ninety (90) days after the date of my death.

H. Tax-Related Terms. All tax-related terms shall have the same meaning they have in the Internal Revenue Code of 1986, as amended.

[*Add state-specific signature, attesting witness, and self-proving clauses*]

¶ A.10 FORM 10: REVOCABLE TRUST FOR ESTATE OVER $10 MILLION—MARITAL DEDUCTION AND GST TAX PLANNING—DYNASTY TRUST FOR CHILDREN AND DESCENDANTS—GST EXEMPTION USED EVEN IF IT GENERATES ESTATE TAX AT FIRST SPOUSE'S DEATH—NO STATE QTIP IN ORDER TO REDUCE STATE ESTATE TAXES AT SURVIVING SPOUSE'S DEATH—2010 DISPOSITION OF 40% OF ESTATE TO NONMARITAL SHARE—TRUSTEE CAN DISTRIBUTE FROM QTIP MINIMUM AMOUNT OF PRINCIPAL SUFFICIENT TO GIVE SPOUSE ENOUGH APPRECIATION TO TAKE ADVANTAGE OF AGGREGATE BASIS INCREASE AT SURVIVING SPOUSE'S DEATH—SAME PLANNING AS FORM 9, BUT IN A REVOCABLE TRUST

Revocable Trust of *Grantor*[10]

I, *Grantor*, of [*locality, state*] (sometimes in the first person singular, sometimes the "grantor," and sometimes the "trustee"), make this trust (defined below), which may be referred to as *TrustName*.

Article 1
My Family

I am married to *Spouse* (sometimes referred to as "my *husband/wife*") and I have [*number of children*] children, *Children*.

---

[10] **KEY**:

Grantor	— full name of the grantor
TrustName	— what to call the trust in other documents
Spouse	— full name of grantor's spouse
husband/wife	— "husband" or "wife," as the case may be
Children	— full names of grantor's children
he/she	— "he" or "she" (referring to the spouse)
his/her	— "his" or "her" (referring to the spouse)
him/her	— "him" or "her" (referring to the spouse)
FirstTrustee	— name of the first alternate trustee
SecondTrustee	— name of the second alternate trustee

Article 2
Trustee Shall Hold Trust Funds

The trustee (defined below) shall hold certain property, which may be listed in Schedule A, to be administered according to the terms of the trust instrument. I and anyone else may transfer additional property (including life insurance proceeds, where appropriate), to any trustee (which the trustee may refuse to accept if acceptance is not in the best interests of the trust), at any time during my life or after my death, to be held and administered according to the terms of the trust instrument.

Article 3
Revoking the Trust

I may revoke or amend all or any part of the trust fund at any time, without the consent of anyone else, by delivering to the trustee a written instrument specifying the character and date of the intended amendment or revocation, or by specific reference to the trust in my last will. The duties, powers, or liabilities of the trustee (other than me) cannot, however, be changed without such trustee's prior written consent. The trustee shall transfer all of the trust funds to me or to my estate, if the trust is completely revoked.

Article 4
Administering the Trust During My Life

A. Making Payments to Me. During my life, the trustee shall pay any taxes, commissions, or other expenses incurred with respect to the trust, and distribute to me all of the trust's net income at least annually, and so much of its principal and undistributed income (including all or none) as I may request from time to time, or as the trustee shall deem appropriate for my comfort and care.

1. My Absolute Power to Withdraw Trust Funds. My power to withdraw principal and income from the trust is absolute, and exercisable as to all of the trust funds, by me alone and in all events.

2. Assuring Productivity of Trust Assets. I may direct the trustee not to retain any asset or assets that I shall deem not to be sufficiently productive.

B. Qualifying for the Gift Tax Marital Deduction. I intend that any transfers to the trust by my *husband/wife*, *Spouse*, shall qualify for the Federal gift and estate tax marital deduction and all provisions of the trust shall be construed consistent therewith.

Article 5
Disposing of the Residuary Trust Fund

The trustee shall divide and distribute the residuary trust fund (defined below) at my death, under this Article:

A. If a Federal Estate Tax Exists. If there is, on the date of my death, a Federal estate tax and/or a Federal generation-skipping transfer tax, as the case may be, that applies with respect to my estate (including this trust fund), the trustee shall divide and distribute the residuary trust fund, as follows:

1. If My *Husband/Wife* Survives Me. If my *husband/wife*, *Spouse*, survives me, the trustee shall divide the residuary trust fund into a descendants' share, a GST exempt marital share, and a marital share (all defined below).

a. The descendants' share shall be held under the Article entitled "The Dynasty Trust."

b. The marital share shall be held under the Article entitled "The QTIP Marital Trust."

2. If My *Husband/Wife* Does Not Survive Me. If my *husband/wife* does not survive me, the trustee shall divide the residuary trust fund into a descendants' GST exempt share and a descendants' power of appointment share (both defined below).

a. The descendants' GST exempt share shall be held under the Article entitled "The Dynasty Trust."

b. The trustee shall distribute the descendants' power of appointment share to my descendants who survive me, *per stirpes*, except that the share for any child of mine shall be added to the trust fund for such child under the Article entitled "Child's Power of Appointment Trust," for that child, and the share for any more remote descendant of mine who shall then not yet have reached the age of thirty-five (35) years, shall be held under the Article entitled "Contingent Trust for Certain Beneficiaries."

B. If No Federal Estate Tax Exists. If there is, on the date of my death, no Federal estate or generation-skipping transfer tax that applies with respect to my estate (including this trust fund), the trustee shall divide the residuary trust fund into a descendants' share and a marital share.

1. If My *Husband/Wife* Survives Me. If my *husband/wife*, *Spouse*, survives me, the trustee shall divide the residuary trust fund into a descendants' nonmarital share and a marital share.

a. The descendants' share shall be held under the Article entitled "The Dynasty Trust."

b. The marital share shall be held under the Article entitled "The QTIP Marital Trust."

2. If My *Husband/Wife* Does Not Survive Me. If my *husband/wife* does not survive me, the trustee shall hold the residuary trust fund under the Article entitled "The Dynasty Trust."

C. Debts and Expenses of Administration. The trustee shall pay to the personal representative of my estate such amounts as the personal representative of my estate shall certify as needed for the payment of my debts and expenses of estate administration.

Article 6
The Dynasty Trust

The dynasty trust shall be held under this Article.

A. Distributing Trust Fund Before Perpetuities Date. Until the perpetuities date (defined below), the trustee shall distribute to or expend for the benefit of my then-living children and my then-living more remote descendants, as much of the net income and principal of the dynasty trust as the trustee may deem appropriate for any purpose, annually adding to principal any undistributed income.

1. Making Unequal Distributions. The trustee may distribute income and principal of the dynasty trust unequally and may make distributions to some beneficiaries and not to others.

2. Preserving Corpus. The trustee shall administer the dynasty trust in a manner designed to conserve its principal as long as possible. The trustee shall, therefore, lend income and principal of the dynasty trust to beneficiaries or buy assets for their use, rather than distributing income or principal outright to beneficiaries, unless the trustee determines that outright distributions are more appropriate.

B. Distributing Trust Fund At Perpetuities Date. Upon the perpetuities date, the trustee shall distribute the remaining trust fund to my then-living descendants, *per stirpes*.

C. "Perpetuities Date" Defined. The "perpetuities date" shall be the date twenty-one years after the death of the last to die of my children and more remote descendants living on the date of my death.

Article 7
The QTIP Marital Trust

The QTIP marital trust shall be held under this Article.

A. Distributing Trust Fund During My *Husband/Wife*'s Life. The trustee shall distribute the net income of the QTIP marital trust quarterly or more frequently to my *husband/wife*, *Spouse*, during *his/her* life.

1. Principal Distributions. The trustee shall also distribute to my *husband/wife* as much of the principal of the QTIP marital trust as is appropriate for any purpose.

2. Distributing Additional Principal if There is No Federal Estate Tax. If the trustee deems it likely that my *husband/wife* will die before January 1, 2011, the trustee shall distribute to my *husband/wife* a fractional share of this trust.

a. The numerator of this fraction shall be equal to the smallest value of the assets of this trust fund to which the personal representative of my *husband/wife*'s estate could allocate all of the aggregate basis increase allowed to my *husband/wife* under Federal income tax laws, less the amount of such aggregate basis increase that could be allocated to other assets already owned by my *husband/wife* at the time of this distribution.

b. The denominator of this fraction shall equal the value of the QTIP marital trust fund.

B. Distributing Trust Fund At My *Husband/Wife*'s Death.

1. Distributing Income. At my *husband/wife*'s death, the trustee shall distribute to my *husband/wife*'s estate any undistributed income of the QTIP marital trust.

2. Appointing Trust Principal. At my *husband/wife*'s death, the trustee shall distribute the principal of the QTIP marital trust, to the extent it is not used to pay transfer taxes as provided below, as my *husband/wife* may direct by specific reference to this special power of appointment in *his/her* last will.

a. My *husband/wife* may appoint the QTIP marital trust fund, either outright or in further trust, but only to or among any one (1) or more of my descendants.

b. My *husband/wife* may not appoint any portion of the QTIP marital trust fund to my *husband/wife*, *his/her* creditors, *his/her* estate, or the creditors of *his/her* estate.

3. Distributing Unappointed Trust Fund. The trustee shall distribute the unappointed QTIP marital trust fund to my then-living descendants, *per stirpes*, except that the share for any child of mine shall be added to the child's power of appointment trust for that child, and the share for any more remote descendant of mine who shall then not yet have reached the age of thirty-five (35) years, shall be held for such descendant under the Article entitled "Contingent Trust for Certain Beneficiaries."

Article 8
Child's Power of Appointment Trust

The child's power of appointment trust for each child of mine shall be held as a separate trust under this Article.

A. Distributing Trust Fund During the Child's Life. The trustee shall distribute to or for the benefit of each child for whom a trust is created under this Article, as much of the net income and principal as the child shall request at any time or as the trustee may consider appropriate for any purpose, annually adding to principal any undistributed income.

B. Distributing Trust Fund At the Child's Death. Upon the death of a child of mine who survives me, the trustee shall distribute the remaining principal and income of such child's trust under this Article as that child may direct by specific reference to this power of appointment in that child's last will.

1. Appointing Everything But Limited Portion. Each such child may appoint the remaining principal and income of such child's trust under this Article (other than the limited portion (defined below)) of such trust fund, either outright or in further trust, to or among any persons, including such child's estate.

2. Appointing Limited Portion. Each such child may appoint the limited portion of the principal and income of such child's trust under this Article outright or in further trust, but only to or among my then-living descendants, and such child may not appoint any of the limited portion to such child himself or herself, such child's creditors, such child's estate, or the creditors of such child's estate.

3. Distributing Unappointed Trust Fund. The trustee shall distribute any unappointed portion of the fund of a deceased child's trust under this Article to such child's then-living descendants, *per stirpes*, or if there are no such descendants then living, to my then-living descendants, *per stirpes*, except that the fund that would thus be distributed to any then-living child of mine shall be added to such child's trust under this Article.

4. "Limited Portion" Defined. The "limited portion" of the fund of a child's trust under this Article is that portion which would pass to one or more persons assigned to the same or a higher generation as the deceased child for Federal generation-skipping transfer tax purposes, were such child to die without a valid will. If such child dies in a year in which there is no Federal generation-skipping transfer tax applicable with respect to such child's estate, the "limited portion" shall be the entire fund of the child's trust.

Article 9
Contingent Trust for Certain Beneficiaries

If a beneficiary (other than a child of mine) is entitled to receive any portion of any trust fund held under this instrument while the beneficiary is under the age of thirty-five (35) years, the trustee may retain such assets in a separate trust for that beneficiary.

A. Distributing Trust Fund Before the Contingent Trust Termination Date. Until the contingent trust termination date (defined below), the trustee shall distribute to or for the benefit of the beneficiary as much of the net income and principal as the trustee may consider appropriate for the beneficiary's health, education, support, or maintenance, annually adding to principal any undistributed income.

B. Distributing Trust Fund At the Contingent Trust Termination Date. Upon the contingent trust termination date, the trustee shall distribute the remaining assets to the beneficiary if the beneficiary is then living or otherwise to the beneficiary's estate to be distributed as part of that estate.

C. "Contingent Trust Termination Date" Defined. The "contingent trust termination date" shall be the earlier of (1) the date on which the beneficiary dies or (2) the date on which the beneficiary reaches the age of thirty-five (35) years.

Article 10
Special Limits on Powers of Interested Trustee

The following limitations shall apply, notwithstanding other provisions of this instrument.

A. Limiting Actions by Interested Trustees. No interested trustee (defined below) may participate in the exercise of any discretion to distribute principal to himself or herself, except as is appropriate for his or her health, education, support, and maintenance, or any of them. No interested trustee may participate in the exercise of any discretion to distribute or expend principal or income in a manner that would discharge that trustee's personal obligation to support the beneficiary. No interested trustee may participate in the exercise of any incident of ownership over any policy owned by the trust insuring the life of such trustee.

B. Disinterested Trustees Exercising Certain Powers. A disinterested trustee (defined below) who is serving as a co-trustee with an interested trustee, may exercise those discretions granted under this instrument the exercise of which by an interested trustee are precluded.

1. If Multiple Trustees Include an Interested Trustee Who Cannot Act. The number of trustees who must consent to the exercise of a power granted under this instrument, as determined under the Article entitled "The Trustees" shall be determined by treating the interested trustees who are not entitled, under this Article, to participate in the exercise of the power or discretion, as if they were not then serving.

2. If All Trustees Are Precluded From Acting. If this Article precludes every then-serving trustee from exercising a power otherwise granted to the trustee under this instrument, the then-serving trustee shall appoint a disinterested trustee who may exercise such power (or decline to exercise it) as if that disinterested trustee were the sole then-serving trustee.

Article 11
Paying Transfer Taxes

The trustee shall pay from the residuary trust fund all transfer taxes, other than generation-skipping transfer taxes, payable by reason of my death on assets passing under this trust.

A. Apportioning Transfer Taxes. The trustee shall pay transfer taxes imposed on any trust assets includible in my gross estate for Federal estate tax purposes, from those assets, as provided by the laws of the state in which I reside at my death, except as expressly provided elsewhere in this instrument.

B. Apportioning Generation-Skipping Transfer Taxes. The trustee shall pay all generation-skipping transfer taxes imposed on transfers under this trust from those transfers.

C. Apportioning Transfer Taxes Away From Deductible Assets. Assets passing as the marital share shall have the full benefit of the Federal estate tax marital deduction allowed with respect to any transfer taxes, and shall not bear any transfer taxes. Other assets passing to my *husband/wife* or to any charitable organization, whether under this trust or otherwise, shall have the full benefit of any available marital or charitable deduction for Federal and other transfer tax purposes, in determining the share of transfer taxes that should be borne by those assets.

Article 12
The Trustees

A. Naming The Trustee. I shall be the initial trustee of this trust.

B. Naming Successor Trustees. I name *FirstTrustee*, of [*locality, state*], to be the successor trustee, to serve if I am unable or unwilling to serve or to continue serving. I name *SecondTrustee*, of [*locality, state*] to be the successor trustee, to serve if both *FirstTrustee* and I are both unable or unwilling to serve or to continue serving.

C. No Surety or Bond. No trustee named by me or by another trustee shall be required to provide surety or other security on a bond.

D. Naming Additional Trustees. I authorize the trustee to appoint any person as an additional trustee, to serve at the pleasure of the appointing trustee.

E. Delegating Powers and Authorities. The trustee may delegate to another trustee any power or authority granted by me to the trustee, to continue at the pleasure of the delegating trustee, unless otherwise agreed. Any person dealing in good faith with a trustee may rely upon that trustee's representation that a delegation has been made and remains in effect under this paragraph.

F. Trustee Resigning. Any trustee may resign by giving written notice specifying the effective date of the resignation to me, if I am then-serving as a trustee, or otherwise to the designated successor. If I am not alive or am not then-serving as a trustee, and if no successor is designated, the resigning trustee shall give notice to each adult beneficiary to whom trust income then may be distributed.

G. Removing a Trustee. A trustee may be removed by the vote of two thirds (⅔) of the then-living adult beneficiaries to whom trust income may then be distributed.

H. Filling Trustee Vacancies. A corporation no substantial portion of the stock of which is owned by beneficiaries of this trust, may be named as successor trustee to fill any vacancy, by majority vote of the adult beneficiaries to whom trust income then may be distributed.

I. No Liability for Acts or Omissions of Predecessors. No trustee shall be responsible for or need inquire into any acts or omissions of a prior trustee.

J. Compensating Trustees. In addition to reimbursement for expenses, each individual trustee is entitled to reasonable compensation for services. Each corporate trustee is entitled to compensation based on its written fee schedule in effect at the time its services are rendered or as otherwise agreed, and its compensation may vary from time to time based on that schedule.

K. Management Powers. I authorize the trustee to exercise all powers conferred by applicable state law and to do the following in a fiduciary capacity.

1. Prudent Investor Rule. The trustee may hold and retain as part of any trust fund any property transferred by me to the trustee, whether or not such investment would be appropriate for a prudent investor. The trustee may also hold and retain as part of any trust fund any property received from any source, and invest and reinvest the trust fund (or leave it temporarily uninvested) in any type of property and every kind of investment in the same manner as a prudent investor would invest his or her own assets.

2. Holding Assets For Use of Trust Beneficiaries. The trustee may buy and hold in trust, assets that will be used personally by one or more beneficiaries, even if those assets would not otherwise be acquired by a prudent investor investing his or her own assets.

3. Transferring Assets. The trustees may sell or exchange any real or personal property contained in any trust, for cash or credit, at public or private sale, and with such warranties or indemnifications as the trustee may deem advisable.

4. Borrowing Money. The trustee may borrow money (even from a trustee, a beneficiary, or any trust) for the benefit of any trust and secure these debts with assets of the trust.

5. Granting Security Interests. The trustee may grant security interests and execute all instruments creating such interests upon such terms as the trustee may deem advisable.

6. Compromising Claims. The trustee may compromise and adjust claims against or on behalf of any trust on such terms as the trustee may deem advisable.

7. Not Disclosing Nominees. The trustee may take title to any securities in the name of any custodian or nominee without disclosing this relationship.

8. Allocating Between Income and Principal. The trustee may determine whether receipts are income or principal and whether disbursements are to be charged against income or principal to the extent not clearly established by state law. A determination made by the trustee in good faith shall not require equitable adjustments.

9. Making Tax Elections. The trustee may make all tax elections and allocations the trustee may consider appropriate; however, this authority is exercisable only in a fiduciary capacity and may not be used to enlarge or shift any beneficial interest except as an incidental consequence of the discharge of fiduciary duties. A tax election or allocation made by the trustee in good faith shall not require equitable adjustments.

10. Distributing to Custodians for Minors. The trustee shall distribute any of any trust fund to a beneficiary under the age of twenty-one (21) years by distribution to any appropriate person (who may be a trustee) chosen by the trustee as custodian under any appropriate Uniform Transfers (or Gifts) to Minors Act, to be held for the maximum period of time allowed by law. The trustee may also sell any asset that cannot be held under this custodianship and invest the sales proceeds in assets that can be so held.

11. Employing Advisors. The trustee may employ such lawyers, account- ants, and other advisors as the trustee may deem useful and appropriate for the administration of any trust. The trustee may employ a professional investment advisor and delegate to this advisor any discretionary investment authorities to manage the investments of any trust, including any investment in mutual funds, investment trusts, or managed accounts, and may rely on the advisor's investment recommendations without liability to any beneficiary.

12. Buying and Holding Life Insurance. The trustee may buy and hold insurance policies on the life of any beneficiary or any person in whom a beneficiary has an insurable interest and may pay the premiums on such policies from income or principal, as the trustee may deem advisable.

13. Dividing and Distributing Assets. The trustee may divide and dis- tribute the assets of any trust fund in kind, in money, or partly in each, without regard to the income tax basis of any asset and without the consent of any beneficiary. The decision of the trustee in dividing any portion of any trust fund between or among two or more beneficiaries, if made in good faith, shall be binding on all persons.

14. Allocation of Basis Increase. My personal representative shall allocate any increases in the adjusted basis of property owned by me at the time of my death, whether passing under my Will or otherwise, to the extent such property is eligible to receive such an allocation, as my personal representative deems to be in the best interests of my estate and its beneficiaries. The trustee shall cooperate fully with my personal representative in making these allocations. If, however, there is no personal representative appointed for my estate, then the trustee shall allocate any increases in the adjusted basis of property passing under this trust, to the extent such property is eligible to receive such an allocation, as the trustee deems to be in the best interests of my estate and its beneficiaries. In making these allocations the trustee shall:

a. First, satisfy all charitable bequests with assets to which no aggre- gate or spousal property basis increases may be allocated;

b. Second, satisfy all charitable bequests with assets that have an adjusted income tax basis closest to zero of all of my assets available to satisfy these bequests;

c. Third, generally not allocate basis increase to assets the gain from the sale of which is not subject to federal income tax under present federal income tax laws;

d. Fourth, allocate basis increases to assets that are reasonably likely to be sold within the three year period beginning on the date of my death, the sale of which will produce an income tax liability that is taxed at a rate higher than that on long-term capital gains; and

e. Fifth, allocate the remaining basis increase among assets in proportion to each asset's pro rata share of the total appreciation of all such assets owned by this trust on the date of my death.

Any reference in this paragraph to assets "owned by me on the date of my death" shall apply equally to assets deemed owned by me on the date of my death under the federal income tax rules governing allocation of my aggregate basis increase. The trustee shall not be liable to anyone for any allocation of my basis increases made in good faith, in the absence of gross negligence.

L. Disabled Individual Trustee. An individual trustee may not serve during a disability.

1. "Disabled" Defined. An individual trustee is "disabled" or "under a disability" if: (a) he or she is determined to be legally incompetent by a court of competent jurisdiction; (b) a conservator or guardian for such person has been appointed, based upon his or her incapacity; (c) two (2) physicians licensed to practice medicine in the Commonwealth of Virginia certify in writing to another trustee or a person who would become the successor trustee upon such disability, that in the opinion of such physicians, such individual trustee, as a result of illness, age or other cause, no longer has the capacity to act prudently or effectively in financial affairs; or (d) thirty (30) days after any other trustee or a person who would become the successor trustee upon such disability, requests that such individual trustee provide a certificate from a physician licensed to practice medicine that, in the opinion of such physician, such individual trustee has the capacity to act prudently or effectively in financial affairs and such individual trustee fails to provide such certification. The effective date of such incapacity shall be the date of the order or decree adjudicating the incapacity, the date of the order or decree appointing the guardian or conservator, the date of the certificate of incapacity of the two (2) physicians described above, or thirty (30) days after other trustee or any person who would become the successor trustee upon such disability requests a certificate of capacity and one is not provided, whichever first occurs.

2. When I Regain My Capacity. For purposes of this instrument, I shall be deemed to have regained capacity to serve as a trustee if: (a) there is a finding to that effect by a court of competent jurisdiction; (b) when any conservatorship or guardianship for me has been judicially terminated; or (c) upon the written determination by two (2) physicians licensed to practice medicine in the Commonwealth of Virginia (who need not be the same physicians who made the initial determination of my incapacity) that, in their pinion, my capacity is restored, and I shall have the right again to serve as trustee under this instrument, as of the effective date of my restoration of capacity, if I was serving as a trustee at the time I was determined to be incapacitated.

3. No Liability. No person is liable to anyone for actions taken in reliance on these certifications or for dealing with a trustee other than the one removed for disability based on these certifications. This trust shall indemnify any physician for liability for any opinion rendered in good faith as to the existence or recovery from any disability.

Article 13
Trust Administration

A. Spendthrift Limits. No interest in a trust under this instrument shall be subject to the beneficiary's liabilities or creditor claims or to assignment or anticipation.

B. Protecting Trust Beneficiaries From Creditors. If the trustee shall determine that a beneficiary would not benefit as greatly from any outright distribution of trust income or principal because of the availability of the distribution to the beneficiary's creditors, the trustee shall instead expend those amounts for the benefit of the beneficiary. This direction is intended to enable the trustee to give the beneficiary the fullest possible benefit and enjoyment of all of the trust income and principal to which he or she is entitled.

C. Combining Multiple Trusts. The trustee may invest the assets of multiple trusts in a single fund if the interests of the trusts are accounted for separately.

D. Merging and Consolidating Trust Funds. The trustee may merge or consolidate any trust into any other trust that has the same trustee and substantially the same dispositive provisions.

E. Dividing Trust Funds. The trustee may divide any trust fund into multiple separate trusts.

F. Accountings. The trustee shall not be required to file annual accounts with any court or court official in any jurisdiction.

G. Changing Trust Situs. A disinterested trustee may change the situs of any trust, and to the extent necessary or appropriate, move the trust assets, to a state or country other than the one in which the trust is then administered if the disinterested trustee shall determine it to be in the best interests of the trust or the beneficiaries. The disinterested trustee may elect that the law of such other jurisdiction shall govern the trust to the extent necessary or appropriate under the circumstances.

Article 14
Calculating Shares of the Residuary Trust Fund if a Federal Estate Tax Exists

This Article shall apply if there is, on the date of my death, a Federal estate tax and/or a Federal generation-skipping transfer tax, as the case may be, that applies with respect to my estate (including this trust fund).

A. My Purposes. I intend that:

1. Minimizing Federal and *State* Estate Taxes. The division of the residuary trust fund into a descendants' share and a marital share, shall minimize the Federal and *State* estate taxes at my *husband/wife*'s death to the extent I can do so while deferring a substantial portion of the Federal estate taxes until both my *husband/wife* and I have died. I realize that, by creating a descendant's share that takes full advantage of my available GST exemption, I may cause an estate tax to be due at my death that could otherwise have been deferred until the later death of my *husband/wife*, but I have done so in order to take the fullest advantage of my GST exemption. I also realize that by creating a descendant's share that takes full advantage of my available GST exemption I may incur a state estate tax at my death, but by doing so it is my expectation and intent to reduce to a greater degree the state estate taxes incurred at my *husband/wife*'s later death.

2. Taking Advantage of My GST Exemption. The creation of a descendants' share and, if my *husband/wife* does not survive me, the descendants' GST exempt share, shall take advantage of my available GST exemption (defined below).

3. Qualifying for Federal Estate Tax Marital Deduction. The marital share shall qualify for the Federal estate tax marital deduction and all provisions of this trust shall be construed accordingly. In all matters involving the marital share, the trustee shall exercise no power in a manner that would infringe upon any legal requirement for the allowance of the Federal estate tax marital deduction.

B. Defining the "Descendants' Share." If my *husband/wife* survives me, the "descendants' share" shall be a fractional share of the residuary trust fund.

1. Calculating the Numerator. The numerator of the fraction shall be the amount of my available GST exemption (to the extent not allocated to the descendants' share and any spouse's nonmarital share.)

2. Calculating the Denominator. The denominator of the fraction shall equal the value of the residuary trust fund.

C. Defining the "Marital Share." If my *husband/wife* survives me, the "marital share" shall be the remaining fractional share of the residuary trust fund after subtracting the descendants' share.

D. Defining the "Descendants' GST Exempt Share." If my *husband/wife* does not survive me, the "descendants' GST exempt share" shall be a fractional share of the residuary trust fund.

1. Calculating the Numerator. The numerator of the fraction shall be equal to the amount of my available GST exemption.

2. Calculating the Denominator. The denominator of the fraction shall equal the value of the residuary trust fund.

E. Defining the "Descendants' Power of Appointment Share." If my *husband/wife* does not survive me, the "descendants' power of appointment share' shall be the remaining fractional share of the residuary trust fund after subtracting the descendants' GST exempt share.

F. Determining the Effect of Disclaimers.

1. Disclaiming the Marital Share. Any portion of the marital share as to which a qualified disclaimer by or for my *husband/wife* is made shall be added to the descendant's share. The descendants' share shall be calculated before any qualified disclaimer by or for my *husband/wife* of any of the marital share.

2. Apportioning Transfer Taxes to Disclaimed Funds. Transfer taxes imposed on assets as to which my *husband/wife* has made a qualified disclaimer shall be apportioned to those disclaimed funds.

G. Allocating Assets Between or Among Shares.

1. Making Certain Allocations If My *Husband/Wife* Survives Me. If my *husband/wife* survives me:

a. The trustee shall allocate to the marital share only assets that can qualify for the Federal estate tax marital deduction.

b. The trustee shall not, to the extent possible, allocate to the marital share assets upon which a foreign death tax is payable.

c. The trustee shall allocate to the descendants' share and, if my *husband/wife* does not survive me, the descendants' GST exempt share, solely of assets includable in my gross estate for Federal estate tax purposes.

2. Making Other Allocations. The trustee shall, in other respects, allocate assets as the trustee shall consider to be in the best interests of the beneficiaries, valuing each asset on the date or dates of allocation.

H. Allocating Income. The trustee shall allocate to each share a ratable portion of all of the income earned by my estate or the trust after my death, whether earned before or after the assets are in the possession of the trustee, and income earned on assets used to pay charges according to the same fractional shares.

I. My "Available GST Exemption" Defined. For the purposes of this Article, my "available GST exemption" means an amount equal to (1) my GST exemption, determined for Federal tax purposes, minus (2) all allocations of my GST exemption made or deemed made to transfers other than those to transfers under this trust instrument.

Article 15
Calculating Shares of the Residuary Trust Fund if No Federal Estate Tax Exists

This Article shall apply if there is, on the date of my death, no Federal estate or generation-skipping transfer tax that applies with respect to my estate (including this trust fund).

A. My Purposes. I intend that the division of the residuary trust fund into a descendants' share and a marital share to take full advantage of the increases allowed under applicable Federal income tax law to the basis of assets received from me on account of my death, to the extent that it can be so done without unfairly affecting the amount of the various shares of my estate.

B. Defining the "Descendants' Share." The "descendants' share" shall be a fractional share of the residuary trust fund.

1. Calculating the Numerator. The numerator of the fraction shall equal the greater of the following two figures:

a. the smallest value of the assets of the residuary trust fund to which the trustee or my personal representative can allocate the entire aggregate basis increase allowed under Federal income tax laws for property not acquired by a surviving spouse; and

b. forty percent (40%) of the value of the residuary trust fund.

2. Calculating the Denominator. The denominator of the fraction shall equal the value of the residuary trust fund.

C. Defining the "Marital Share." If my *husband/wife* survives me, the marital share shall be the remaining fractional share of the residuary trust fund after subtracting the descendants' share.

D. Allocating Assets. If my *husband/wife* survives me:

1. Allocating Basis in a Fairly Representative Manner. The trustee shall allocate to the descendants' share only assets to which my personal representative can allocate my aggregate basis increase. Otherwise, the trustee shall select the assets that shall constitute the descendants' share in manner such that the net appreciation of any property allocated to the descendants' share shall be fairly representative of the net appreciation of all property available for such allocation (excluding any property to which the trustee cannot, under Federal income tax law, validly allocate any of the aggregate basis increase or the spousal property basis increase).

2. Allocating Assets Otherwise. In other respects, the trustee shall allocate assets as the trustee shall consider to be in the best interests of the beneficiaries, valuing each asset on the date or dates of allocation.

E. Allocating Trust Income. The trustee shall allocate to each share a ratable portion of all of the income earned by my estate or the trust after my death, whether earned before or after the assets are in the possession of the trustee, and income earned on assets used to pay charges according to the same fractional shares.

Article 16
Administering the QTIP Marital Trust

A. Making QTIP and Reverse QTIP Elections. If there is, on the date of my death, a Federal estate tax that may be imposed with respect to my estate, the trustee may elect to qualify all or any portion of the QTIP marital trust for the Federal estate tax marital deduction.

1. Making Partial Elections. If the trustee shall elect to qualify less than all of the QTIP marital trust for the Federal estate tax marital deduction, the trustee shall divide the trust fund as to which such partial election was made into two (2) separate trusts and make all principal payments first from the trust fund that qualifies for the Federal estate tax marital deduction.

2. Allocating Assets Between or Among Shares. The trustee shall allocate assets between these shares as the trustee shall consider to be in the best interests of the beneficiaries, valuing each asset on the date of allocation.

B. Assuring Productivity of Assets. My *husband/wife* may direct the trustee to make any unproductive or underproductive assets of the QTIP marital trust productive or to convert them to productive assets within a reasonable time.

C. Receiving and Administering Retirement Payments. If the QTIP marital trust is entitled to receive distributions under any retirement plan or individual retirement arrangement, of which my *husband/wife* is the designated beneficiary for Federal income tax purposes, then the trustee shall do the following:

1. Distributing Greater of Income or Required Minimum Distribution. The trustee shall annually withdraw from such retirement plan trust fund or arrangement the greater of all of the income earned by my *husband/wife*'s share of such plan or arrangement, or the required minimum distribution with respect to my *husband/wife*, as determined for Federal income tax purposes.

2. Distributing Withdrawn Amounts. The trustee shall annually distribute to my *husband/wife* all amounts withdrawn from such plan or arrangement.

D. Paying Transfer Taxes.

1. Paying Transfer Taxes Generally. The trustee shall, unless my *husband/wife* provides otherwise by specific reference to this paragraph in a valid will or other writing, pay or make arrangements for the payment of the incremental transfer taxes imposed on the QTIP marital trust upon the death of my *husband/wife*, from the QTIP marital trust.

2. Paying Transfer Taxes In Case of a Partial QTIP Election. If the trustee shall elect to qualify only part of the QTIP marital trust and shall create two trusts as required by this Article, the transfer taxes imposed on both trusts at my *husband/wife*'s death shall be paid from the qualified trust fund to the extent possible.

Article 17
Definitions and Miscellaneous

A. Definitions. The following terms shall have the meaning set forth below for all purposes of this trust:

1. "Children" and "Descendants" Defined. "Children" and "descendants" include those now living and those later born, subject to the following rules:

a. "Children" and "descendants" include an adopted person and that adopted person's descendants if, that adopted person is adopted before reaching eighteen (18) years of age;

b. "Children" and "descendants" includes those born outside of wedlock, if, during such child's or descendant's lifetime, his or her parent through whom such child or descendant claims hereunder, has acknowledged such person as his or her child in a writing duly signed and notarized during such parent's lifetime; and

c. "Children" and "descendants" include a child produced before the parent's death by donor artificial insemination, in vitro fertilization or other form of surrogate parenthood, whether or not such child was legally adopted by such parent before such parent's death.

2. "Disinterested Trustee" Defined. A "disinterested trustee" means a trustee who is not an interested trustee.

3. "Interested Trustee" Defined. An "interested trustee" means a trustee who is also (a) a beneficiary of the trust of which he or she is a trustee or the insured under a policy of insurance owned by a trust of which he or she is a trustee; (b) married to and living together with a beneficiary of the trust of which he or she is a trustee; (c) the father, mother, issue, brother or sister, of a beneficiary of the trust of which he or she is a trustee; (d) an employee of a beneficiary of the trust of which he or she is a trustee; (e) a corporation or any employee of a corporation in which the stock holdings of the trustee and the trust are significant from the viewpoint of voting control; or (f) a subordinate employee of a corporation in which the trustee is an executive.

4. "Personal Representative" Defined. A "personal representative" means the legal representative of a decedent's estate. The "personal representative" shall include any executor, ancillary executor, administrator, or ancillary administrator, whether local or foreign and whether of all or part of my estate, multiple personal representatives, and their successors.

5. "Residuary Trust Fund" Defined. The "residuary trust fund" means the real and personal property passing under this instrument, after paying any amounts certified by the personal representative of my estate as needed to settle my debts and expenses of estate administration.

6. "Transfer Taxes" Defined. "Transfer taxes" means all estate, inheritance, legacy, succession, and other transfer taxes, including any tax on excess retirement accumulations, imposed with respect to my death by any state, the United States, or by any foreign country. "Transfer taxes" also includes all taxes that are reimbursable under Sections 2207 through 2207B of the Internal Revenue Code of 1986, as amended, which right of reimbursement I hereby waive. "Transfer taxes" also includes all interest and penalties on such taxes.

7. "Trustee" Defined. The "trustee" or "trustees" shall include each trustee individually, multiple trustees, and their successors.

B. Retroactive Legislation. I include in this instrument certain dispositions and direct certain actions that shall occur only if, on the date of my death, no federal estate tax or Federal generation-skipping transfer tax applies with respect to my estate. These provisions shall not apply if, on the date of my death, no federal estate tax or federal generation-skipping transfer tax, as the case may be, applies with respect to my estate, but such tax or taxes is/are retroactively reinstated before April 1, 2011, and apply under such retroactive legislation with respect to my estate. If such retroactive legislation is finally determined to be unconstitutional or otherwise invalid, these references shall apply as if such retroactive legislation had never been enacted.

C. Absence of Trust Beneficiaries. If all of the beneficiaries of any trust under this instrument should die before the trust assets have vested in them, the trustee shall distribute all of the remaining assets of that trust as follows:

1. One Half to My Heirs and Distributee. One half (½) (or all, if there are no persons to take under subparagraph C.2. of this Article) to the heirs and distributees who would have inherited my personal estate, and in such shares as they would have inherited it, had I died unmarried and without a valid will, determined on the later of the date of my death or the date of the death of the last of the trust beneficiaries to die; and

2. One Half to My *Husband/Wife*'s Distributees. One half (½) (or all, if there are no persons to take under subparagraph C.1. of this Article) to the heirs and distributees who would have inherited my *husband/wife*'s personal estate, and in such shares as they would have inherited it, had he died unmarried and without a valid will, determined on the later of the date of my death or the date of the death of the last of the trust beneficiaries to die.

D. Applicable Law. This instrument shall be governed by and construed according to the laws of the *State*.

E. Number. Whenever the context requires, the singular includes the plural and the plural the singular.

F. Survivorship. No person shall be deemed to have survived me for purposes of this instrument, unless he or she is living on the date ninety (90) days after the date of my death.

G. Tax-Related Terms. All tax-related terms shall have the same meaning they have in the Internal Revenue Code of 1986, as amended.

[*Add state-specific signature and notary clauses, schedule of assets, and where required, attesting witness clause*]

APPENDIX **B**

Select EGTRRA Provisions

¶ B.01   The Estate, Gift, and Generation-Skipping Transfer Tax
Provisions of the Economic Growth and Tax Relief
Reconciliation Act of 2001. . . . .   B-1

¶ B.02   EGTRRA's Sunset Provision B-28

¶ B.03   2002 Technical Changes to the Estate, Gift, and
Generation-Skipping Transfer Tax Provisions of the
Economic Growth and Tax Reform Reconciliation Act of
2001. . . . .   B-29

¶ B.01 THE ESTATE, GIFT, AND GENERATION-SKIPPING TRANSFER TAX PROVISIONS OF THE ECONOMIC GROWTH AND TAX RELIEF RECONCILIATION ACT OF 2001.

The following are the original provisions of EGTRRA relating to estates, gifts, and generation-skipping transfers. These identify the changes made by EGTRRA in the law that existed in 2001, including the provisions applicable in 2010.

TITLE V—ESTATE, GIFT, AND GENERATION-SKIPPING TRANSFER TAX PROVISIONS

Subtitle A—Repeal of Estate and Generation-Skipping Transfer Taxes

SEC. 501. REPEAL OF ESTATE AND GENERATION-SKIPPING TRANSFER TAXES.

(a) ESTATE TAX REPEAL.—Subchapter C of chapter 11 of subtitle B (relating to miscellaneous) is amended by adding at the end the following new section:

"SEC. 2210. TERMINATION.

"(a) IN GENERAL.—Except as provided in subsection (b), this chapter shall not apply to the estates of decedents dying after December 31, 2009.

"(b) CERTAIN DISTRIBUTIONS FROM QUALIFIED DOMESTIC TRUSTS.—In applying section 2056A with respect to the surviving spouse of a decedent dying before January 1, 2010—

"(1) section 2056A(b)(1)(A) shall not apply to distributions made after December 31, 2020, and

"(2) section 2056A(b)(1)(B) shall not apply after December 31, 2009.".

(b) GENERATION-SKIPPING TRANSFER TAX REPEAL.—Subchapter G of chapter 13 of subtitle B (relating to administration) is amended by adding at the end the following new section:

"SEC. 2664. TERMINATION.

"This chapter shall not apply to generation-skipping transfers after December 31, 2009.".

(c) CONFORMING AMENDMENTS.—

(1) The table of sections for subchapter C of chapter 11 is amended by adding at the end the following new item:

"Sec. 2210. Termination.".

(2) The table of sections for subchapter G of chapter 13 is amended by adding at the end the following new item:

"Sec. 2664. Termination.".

(d) EFFECTIVE DATE.—The amendments made by this section shall apply to the estates of decedents dying, and generation-skipping transfers, after December 31, 2009.

Applicability.
26 USC 2210
note.

115 STAT. 70   PUBLIC LAW 107–16—JUNE 7, 2001

Subtitle B—Reductions of Estate and Gift Tax Rates

SEC. 511. ADDITIONAL REDUCTIONS OF ESTATE AND GIFT TAX RATES.

(a) MAXIMUM RATE OF TAX REDUCED TO 50 PERCENT.—The table contained in section 2001(c)(1) is amended by striking the two highest brackets and inserting the following:

> "Over $2,500,000 .... $1,025,800, plus 50% of the excess over $2,500,000.".

26 USC 2001.

(b) REPEAL OF PHASEOUT OF GRADUATED RATES.—Subsection (c) of section 2001 is amended by striking paragraph (2).

(c) ADDITIONAL REDUCTIONS OF MAXIMUM RATE OF TAX.—Subsection (c) of section 2001, as amended by subsection (b), is amended by adding at the end the following new paragraph:—

"(2) PHASEDOWN OF MAXIMUM RATE OF TAX.—

Regulations.

"(A) IN GENERAL.—In the case of estates of decedents dying, and gifts made, in calendar years after 2002 and before 2010, the tentative tax under this subsection shall be determined by using a table prescribed by the Secretary (in lieu of using the table contained in paragraph (1)) which is the same as such table; except that—

"(i) the maximum rate of tax for any calendar year shall be determined in the table under subparagraph (B), and

"(ii) the brackets and the amounts setting forth the tax shall be adjusted to the extent necessary to reflect the adjustments under subparagraph (A).

"(B) MAXIMUM RATE.—

"In calendar year:	The maximum rate is:
2003	49 percent
2004	48 percent
2005	47 percent
2006	46 percent
2007, 2008, and 2009	45 percent.".

(d) MAXIMUM GIFT TAX RATE REDUCED TO MAXIMUM INDIVIDUAL RATE AFTER 2009.—Subsection (a) of section 2502 (relating to rate of tax) is amended to read as follows:

"(a) COMPUTATION OF TAX.—

"(1) IN GENERAL.—The tax imposed by section 2501 for each calendar year shall be an amount equal to the excess of—

"(A) a tentative tax, computed under paragraph (2), on the aggregate sum of the taxable gifts for such calendar year and for each of the preceding calendar periods, over

"(B) a tentative tax, computed under paragraph (2), on the aggregate sum of the taxable gifts for each of the preceding calendar periods.

"(2) RATE SCHEDULE.—

"If the amount with respect to which the tentative tax to be computed is:	The tentative tax is:
Not over $10,000	18% of such amount.
Over $10,000 but not over $20,000 ...	$1,800, plus 20% of the excess over $10,000.
Over $20,000 but not over $40,000 ...	$3,800, plus 22% of the excess over $20,000.

"If the amount with respect to which the tentative tax to be computed is:	The tentative tax is:
Over $40,000 but not over $60,000 ...	$8,200, plus 24% of the excess over $40,000.
Over $60,000 but not over $80,000 ...	$13,000, plus 26% of the excess over $60,000.
Over $80,000 but not over $100,000	$18,200, plus 28% of the excess over $80,000.
Over $100,000 but not over $150,000	$23,800, plus 30% of the excess over $100,000.
Over $150,000 but not over $250,000	$38,800, plus 32% of the excess over $150,000.
Over $250,000 but not over $500,000	$70,800, plus 34% of the excess over $250,000.
Over $500,000	$155,800, plus 35% of the excess over $500,000.".

(e) TREATMENT OF CERTAIN TRANSFERS IN TRUST.—Section 2511 (relating to transfers in general) is amended by adding at the end the following new subsection:

    26 USC 2511.

    "(c) TREATMENT OF CERTAIN TRANSFERS IN TRUST.—Notwithstanding any other provision of this section and except as provided in regulations, a transfer in trust shall be treated as a taxable gift under section 2503, unless the trust is treated as wholly owned by the donor or the donor's spouse under subpart E of part I of subchapter J of chapter 1.".

    (f) EFFECTIVE DATES.—

        (1) SUBSECTIONS (a) AND (b).—The amendments made by subsections (a) and (b) shall apply to estates of decedents dying, and gifts made, after December 31, 2001.

        (2) SUBSECTION (c).—The amendment made by subsection (c) shall apply to estates of decedents dying, and gifts made, after December 31, 2002.

        (3) SUBSECTIONS (d) AND (e).—The amendments made by subsections (d) and (e) shall apply to gifts made after December 31, 2009.

    Applicability.
    26 USC 2001 note.

    26 USC 2001 note.

    26 USC 2502 note.

Subtitle C—Increase in Exemption Amounts

SEC. 521. INCREASE IN EXEMPTION EQUIVALENT OF UNIFIED CREDIT, LIFETIME GIFTS EXEMPTION, AND GST EXEMPTION AMOUNTS.

    (a) IN GENERAL.—Subsection (c) of section 2010 (relating to applicable credit amount) is amended by striking the table and inserting the following new table:

"In the case of estates of decedents dying during:	The applicable exclusion amount is:
2002 and 2003	$1,000,000
2004 and 2005	$1,500,000
2006, 2007, and 2008	$2,000,000
2009	$3,500,000.".

    (b) LIFETIME GIFT EXEMPTION INCREASED TO $1,000,000.—

        (1) FOR PERIODS BEFORE ESTATE TAX REPEAL.—Paragraph (1) of section 2505(a) (relating to unified credit against gift tax) is amended by inserting "(determined as if the applicable exclusion amount were $1,000,000)" after "calendar year".

        (2) FOR PERIODS AFTER ESTATE TAX REPEAL.—Paragraph (1) of section 2505(a) (relating to unified credit against gift

115 STAT. 72   PUBLIC LAW 107–16—JUNE 7, 2001

tax), as amended by paragraph (1), is amended to read as follows:

"(1) the amount of the tentative tax which would be determined under the rate schedule set forth in section 2502(a)(2) if the amount with respect to which such tentative tax is to be computed were $1,000,000, reduced by".

(c) GST EXEMPTION.—

26 USC 2631.

(1) IN GENERAL.—Subsection (a) of 2631 (relating to GST exemption) is amended by striking "of $1,000,000" and inserting "amount".

(2) EXEMPTION AMOUNT.—Subsection (c) of section 2631 is amended to read as follows:

"(c) GST EXEMPTION AMOUNT.—For purposes of subsection (a), the GST exemption amount for any calendar year shall be equal to the applicable exclusion amount under section 2010(c) for such calendar year.".

(d) REPEAL OF SPECIAL BENEFIT FOR FAMILY-OWNED BUSINESS INTERESTS.—Section 2057 (relating to family-owned business interests) is amended by adding at the end the following new subsection:

"(j) TERMINATION.—This section shall not apply to the estates of decedents dying after December 31, 2003.".

Applicability.
26 USC 2010 note.

(e) EFFECTIVE DATES.—

(1) IN GENERAL.—Except as provided in paragraphs (2) and (3), the amendments made by this section shall apply to estates of decedents dying, and gifts made, after December 31, 2001.

(2) SUBSECTION (b)(2).—The amendments made by subsection (b)(2) shall apply to gifts made after December 31, 2009.

(3) SUBSECTIONS (c) AND (d).—The amendments made by subsections (c) and (d) shall apply to estates of decedents dying, and generation-skipping transfers, after December 31, 2003.

Subtitle D—Credit for State Death Taxes

SEC. 531. REDUCTION OF CREDIT FOR STATE DEATH TAXES.

(a) IN GENERAL.—Section 2011(b) (relating to amount of credit) is amended—

(1) by striking "CREDIT.—The credit allowed" and inserting "CREDIT.—

"(1) IN GENERAL.—Except as provided in paragraph (2), the credit allowed",

(2) by striking "For purposes" and inserting the following: "(3) ADJUSTED TAXABLE ESTATE.—For purposes", and

(3) by inserting after paragraph (1) the following new paragraph:

"(2) REDUCTION OF MAXIMUM CREDIT.—

"(A) IN GENERAL.—In the case of estates of decedents dying after December 31, 2001, the credit allowed by this section shall not exceed the applicable percentage of the credit otherwise determined under paragraph (1).

"(B) APPLICABLE PERCENTAGE.—

"In the case of estates of decedents dying during:	The applicable percentage is:
2002	75 percent

PUBLIC LAW 107–16—JUNE 7, 2001   115 STAT. 73

2003	50 percent
2004	25 percent.".

(b) EFFECTIVE DATE.—The amendments made by this subsection shall apply to estates of decedents dying after December 31, 2001.

Applicability.
26 USC 2011
note.

SEC. 532. CREDIT FOR STATE DEATH TAXES REPLACED WITH DEDUCTION FOR SUCH TAXES.

(a) REPEAL OF CREDIT.—Section 2011 (relating to credit for State death taxes) is amended by adding at the end the following new subsection:

26 USC 2011.

"(g) TERMINATION.—This section shall not apply to the estates of decedents dying after December 31, 2004.".

(b) DEDUCTION FOR STATE DEATH TAXES.—Part IV of subchapter A of chapter 11 is amended by adding at the end the following new section:

"SEC. 2058. STATE DEATH TAXES.

"(a) ALLOWANCE OF DEDUCTION.—For purposes of the tax imposed by section 2001, the value of the taxable estate shall be determined by deducting from the value of the gross estate the amount of any estate, inheritance, legacy, or succession taxes actually paid to any State or the District of Columbia, in respect of any property included in the gross estate (not including any such taxes paid with respect to the estate of a person other than the decedent).

"(b) PERIOD OF LIMITATIONS.—The deduction allowed by this section shall include only such taxes as were actually paid and deduction therefor claimed before the later of—

"(1) 4 years after the filing of the return required by section 6018, or

"(2) if—

"(A) a petition for redetermination of a deficiency has been filed with the Tax Court within the time prescribed in section 6213(a), the expiration of 60 days after the decision of the Tax Court becomes final,

"(B) an extension of time has been granted under section 6161 or 6166 for payment of the tax shown on the return, or of a deficiency, the date of the expiration of the period of the extension, or

"(C) a claim for refund or credit of an overpayment of tax imposed by this chapter has been filed within the time prescribed in section 6511, the latest of the expiration of—

"(i) 60 days from the date of mailing by certified mail or registered mail by the Secretary to the taxpayer of a notice of the disallowance of any part of such claim,

"(ii) 60 days after a decision by any court of competent jurisdiction becomes final with respect to a timely suit instituted upon such claim, or

"(iii) 2 years after a notice of the waiver of disallowance is filed under section 6532(a)(3).

Notwithstanding sections 6511 and 6512, refund based on the deduction may be made if the claim for refund is filed within the period provided in the preceding sentence. Any such refund shall be made without interest.".

(c) CONFORMING AMENDMENTS.—

115 STAT. 74 PUBLIC LAW 107–16—JUNE 7, 2001

26 USC 2012.

(1) Subsection (a) of section 2012 is amended by striking "the credit for State death taxes provided by section 2011 and".

(2) Subparagraph (A) of section 2013(c)(1) is amended by striking "2011,".

(3) Paragraph (2) of section 2014(b) is amended by striking ", 2011,".

(4) Sections 2015 and 2016 are each amended by striking "2011 or".

(5) Subsection (d) of section 2053 is amended to read as follows:

"(d) CERTAIN FOREIGN DEATH TAXES.—

Regulations.

"(1) IN GENERAL.—Notwithstanding the provisions of subsection (c)(1)(B), for purposes of the tax imposed by section 2001, the value of the taxable estate may be determined, if the executor so elects before the expiration of the period of limitation for assessment provided in section 6501, by deducting from the value of the gross estate the amount (as determined in accordance with regulations prescribed by the Secretary) of any estate, succession, legacy, or inheritance tax imposed by and actually paid to any foreign country, in respect of any property situated within such foreign country and included in the gross estate of a citizen or resident of the United States, upon a transfer by the decedent for public, charitable, or religious uses described in section 2055. The determination under this paragraph of the country within which property is situated shall be made in accordance with the rules applicable under subchapter B (sec. 2101 and following) in determining whether property is situated within or without the United States. Any election under this paragraph shall be exercised in accordance with regulations prescribed by the Secretary.

"(2) CONDITION FOR ALLOWANCE OF DEDUCTION.—No deduction shall be allowed under paragraph (1) for a foreign death tax specified therein unless the decrease in the tax imposed by section 2001 which results from the deduction provided in paragraph (1) will inure solely for the benefit of the public, charitable, or religious transferees described in section 2055 or section 2106(a)(2). In any case where the tax imposed by section 2001 is equitably apportioned among all the transferees of property included in the gross estate, including those described in sections 2055 and 2106(a)(2) (taking into account any exemptions, credits, or deductions allowed by this chapter), in determining such decrease, there shall be disregarded any decrease in the Federal estate tax which any transferees other than those described in sections 2055 and 2106(a)(2) are required to pay.

"(3) EFFECT ON CREDIT FOR FOREIGN DEATH TAXES OF DEDUCTION UNDER THIS SUBSECTION.—

"(A) ELECTION.—An election under this subsection shall be deemed a waiver of the right to claim a credit, against the Federal estate tax, under a death tax convention with any foreign country for any tax or portion thereof in respect of which a deduction is taken under this subsection.

"(B) CROSS REFERENCE.—

"See section 2014(f) for the effect of a deduction taken under this paragraph on the credit for foreign death taxes.".

(6) Subparagraph (A) of section 2056A(b)(10) is amended—

PUBLIC LAW 107–16—JUNE 7, 2001   115 STAT. 75

(A) by striking "2011,", and

(B) by inserting "2058," after "2056,".

(7)(A) Subsection (a) of section 2102 is amended to read as follows: 26 USC 2102.

"(a) IN GENERAL.—The tax imposed by section 2101 shall be credited with the amounts determined in accordance with sections 2012 and 2013 (relating to gift tax and tax on prior transfers).".

(B) Section 2102 is amended by striking subsection (b) and by redesignating subsection (c) as subsection (b).

(C) Section 2102(b)(5) (as redesignated by subparagraph (B)) and section 2107(c)(3) are each amended by striking "2011 to 2013, inclusive," and inserting "2012 and 2013".

(8) Subsection (a) of section 2106 is amended by adding at the end the following new paragraph:

"(4) STATE DEATH TAXES.—The amount which bears the same ratio to the State death taxes as the value of the property, as determined for purposes of this chapter, upon which State death taxes were paid and which is included in the gross estate under section 2103 bears to the value of the total gross estate under section 2103. For purposes of this paragraph, the term 'State death taxes' means the taxes described in section 2011(a).".

(9) Section 2201 is amended—

(A) by striking "as defined in section 2011(d)", and

(B) by adding at the end the following new flush sentence:

"For purposes of this section, the additional estate tax is the difference between the tax imposed by section 2001 or 2101 and the amount equal to 125 percent of the maximum credit provided by section 2011(b), as in effect before its repeal by the Economic Growth and Tax Relief Reconciliation Act of 2001.".

(10) Section 2604 (relating to credit for certain State taxes) is amended by adding at the end the following new subsection:

"(c) TERMINATION.—This section shall not apply to the generation-skipping transfers after December 31, 2004.".

(11) Paragraph (2) of section 6511(i) is amended by striking "2011(c), 2014(b)," and inserting "2014(b)".

(12) Subsection (c) of section 6612 is amended by striking "section 2011(c) (relating to refunds due to credit for State taxes),".

(13) The table of sections for part II of subchapter A of chapter 11 is amended by striking the item relating to section 2011.

(14) The table of sections for part IV of subchapter A of chapter 11 is amended by adding at the end the following new item:

"Sec. 2058. State death taxes.".

(15) The table of sections for subchapter A of chapter 13 is amended by striking the item relating to section 2604.

(d) EFFECTIVE DATE.—The amendments made by this section shall apply to estates of decedents dying, and generation-skipping transfers, after December 31, 2004.   Applicability.
26 USC 2011
note.

115 STAT. 76　　　　PUBLIC LAW 107–16—JUNE 7, 2001

Subtitle E—Carryover Basis at Death; Other Changes Taking Effect With Repeal

SEC. 541. TERMINATION OF STEP-UP IN BASIS AT DEATH.

26 USC 1014.

Section 1014 (relating to basis of property acquired from a decedent) is amended by adding at the end the following new subsection:

"(f) TERMINATION.—This section shall not apply with respect to decedents dying after December 31, 2009.".

SEC. 542. TREATMENT OF PROPERTY ACQUIRED FROM A DECEDENT DYING AFTER DECEMBER 31, 2009.

(a) GENERAL RULE.—Part II of subchapter O of chapter 1 (relating to basis rules of general application) is amended by inserting after section 1021 the following new section:

"SEC. 1022. TREATMENT OF PROPERTY ACQUIRED FROM A DECEDENT DYING AFTER DECEMBER 31, 2009.

"(a) IN GENERAL.—Except as otherwise provided in this section—

"(1) property acquired from a decedent dying after December 31, 2009, shall be treated for purposes of this subtitle as transferred by gift, and

"(2) the basis of the person acquiring property from such a decedent shall be the lesser of—

"(A) the adjusted basis of the decedent, or

"(B) the fair market value of the property at the date of the decedent's death.

"(b) BASIS INCREASE FOR CERTAIN PROPERTY.—

"(1) IN GENERAL.—In the case of property to which this subsection applies, the basis of such property under subsection (a) shall be increased by its basis increase under this subsection.

"(2) BASIS INCREASE.—For purposes of this subsection—

"(A) IN GENERAL.—The basis increase under this subsection for any property is the portion of the aggregate basis increase which is allocated to the property pursuant to this section.

"(B) AGGREGATE BASIS INCREASE.—In the case of any estate, the aggregate basis increase under this subsection is $1,300,000.

"(C) LIMIT INCREASED BY UNUSED BUILT-IN LOSSES AND LOSS CARRYOVERS.—The limitation under subparagraph (B) shall be increased by—

"(i) the sum of the amount of any capital loss carryover under section 1212(b), and the amount of any net operating loss carryover under section 172, which would (but for the decedent's death) be carried from the decedent's last taxable year to a later taxable year of the decedent, plus

"(ii) the sum of the amount of any losses that would have been allowable under section 165 if the property acquired from the decedent had been sold at fair market value immediately before the decedent's death.

"(3) DECEDENT NONRESIDENTS WHO ARE NOT CITIZENS OF THE UNITED STATES.—In the case of a decedent nonresident not a citizen of the United States—

"(A) paragraph (2)(B) shall be applied by substituting '$60,000' for '$1,300,000', and

"(B) paragraph (2)(C) shall not apply.

"(c) ADDITIONAL BASIS INCREASE FOR PROPERTY ACQUIRED BY SURVIVING SPOUSE.—

"(1) IN GENERAL.—In the case of property to which this subsection applies and which is qualified spousal property, the basis of such property under subsection (a) (as increased under subsection (b)) shall be increased by its spousal property basis increase.

"(2) SPOUSAL PROPERTY BASIS INCREASE.—For purposes of this subsection—

"(A) IN GENERAL.—The spousal property basis increase for property referred to in paragraph (1) is the portion of the aggregate spousal property basis increase which is allocated to the property pursuant to this section.

"(B) AGGREGATE SPOUSAL PROPERTY BASIS INCREASE.— In the case of any estate, the aggregate spousal property basis increase is $3,000,000.

"(3) QUALIFIED SPOUSAL PROPERTY.—For purposes of this subsection, the term 'qualified spousal property' means—

"(A) outright transfer property, and

"(B) qualified terminable interest property.

"(4) OUTRIGHT TRANSFER PROPERTY.—For purposes of this subsection—

"(A) IN GENERAL.—The term 'outright transfer property' means any interest in property acquired from the decedent by the decedent's surviving spouse.

"(B) EXCEPTION.—Subparagraph (A) shall not apply where, on the lapse of time, on the occurrence of an event or contingency, or on the failure of an event or contingency to occur, an interest passing to the surviving spouse will terminate or fail—

"(i)(I) if an interest in such property passes or has passed (for less than an adequate and full consideration in money or money's worth) from the decedent to any person other than such surviving spouse (or the estate of such spouse), and

"(II) if by reason of such passing such person (or his heirs or assigns) may possess or enjoy any part of such property after such termination or failure of the interest so passing to the surviving spouse, or

"(ii) if such interest is to be acquired for the surviving spouse, pursuant to directions of the decedent, by his executor or by the trustee of a trust.

For purposes of this subparagraph, an interest shall not be considered as an interest which will terminate or fail merely because it is the ownership of a bond, note, or similar contractual obligation, the discharge of which would not have the effect of an annuity for life or for a term.

"(C) INTEREST OF SPOUSE CONDITIONAL ON SURVIVAL FOR LIMITED PERIOD.—For purposes of this paragraph, an interest passing to the surviving spouse shall not be considered as an interest which will terminate or fail on the death of such spouse if—

"(i) such death will cause a termination or failure of such interest only if it occurs within a period not exceeding 6 months after the decedent's death, or only if it occurs as a result of a common disaster resulting in the death of the decedent and the surviving spouse, or only if it occurs in the case of either such event, and

"(ii) such termination or failure does not in fact occur.

"(5) QUALIFIED TERMINABLE INTEREST PROPERTY.—For purposes of this subsection—

"(A) IN GENERAL.—The term 'qualified terminable interest property' means property—

"(i) which passes from the decedent, and

"(ii) in which the surviving spouse has a qualifying income interest for life.

"(B) QUALIFYING INCOME INTEREST FOR LIFE.—The surviving spouse has a qualifying income interest for life if—

"(i) the surviving spouse is entitled to all the income from the property, payable annually or at more frequent intervals, or has a usufruct interest for life in the property, and

"(ii) no person has a power to appoint any part of the property to any person other than the surviving spouse.

Clause (ii) shall not apply to a power exercisable only at or after the death of the surviving spouse. To the extent provided in regulations, an annuity shall be treated in a manner similar to an income interest in property (regardless of whether the property from which the annuity is payable can be separately identified).

"(C) PROPERTY INCLUDES INTEREST THEREIN.—The term 'property' includes an interest in property.

"(D) SPECIFIC PORTION TREATED AS SEPARATE PROPERTY.—A specific portion of property shall be treated as separate property. For purposes of the preceding sentence, the term 'specific portion' only includes a portion determined on a fractional or percentage basis.

"(d) DEFINITIONS AND SPECIAL RULES FOR APPLICATION OF SUBSECTIONS (b) AND (c).—

"(1) PROPERTY TO WHICH SUBSECTIONS (b) AND (c) APPLY.—

"(A) IN GENERAL.—The basis of property acquired from a decedent may be increased under subsection (b) or (c) only if the property was owned by the decedent at the time of death.

"(B) RULES RELATING TO OWNERSHIP.—

"(i) JOINTLY HELD PROPERTY.—In the case of property which was owned by the decedent and another person as joint tenants with right of survivorship or tenants by the entirety—

"(I) if the only such other person is the surviving spouse, the decedent shall be treated as the owner of only 50 percent of the property,

PUBLIC LAW 107–16—JUNE 7, 2001   115 STAT. 79

"(II) in any case (to which subclause (I) does not apply) in which the decedent furnished consideration for the acquisition of the property, the decedent shall be treated as the owner to the extent of the portion of the property which is proportionate to such consideration, and

"(III) in any case (to which subclause (I) does not apply) in which the property has been acquired by gift, bequest, devise, or inheritance by the decedent and any other person as joint tenants with right of survivorship and their interests are not otherwise specified or fixed by law, the decedent shall be treated as the owner to the extent of the value of a fractional part to be determined by dividing the value of the property by the number of joint tenants with right of survivorship.

"(ii) REVOCABLE TRUSTS.—The decedent shall be treated as owning property transferred by the decedent during life to a qualified revocable trust (as defined in section 645(b)(1)).

"(iii) POWERS OF APPOINTMENT.—The decedent shall not be treated as owning any property by reason of holding a power of appointment with respect to such property.

"(iv) COMMUNITY PROPERTY.—Property which represents the surviving spouse's one-half share of community property held by the decedent and the surviving spouse under the community property laws of any State or possession of the United States or any foreign country shall be treated for purposes of this section as owned by, and acquired from, the decedent if at least one-half of the whole of the community interest in such property is treated as owned by, and acquired from, the decedent without regard to this clause.

"(C) PROPERTY ACQUIRED BY DECEDENT BY GIFT WITHIN 3 YEARS OF DEATH.—

"(i) IN GENERAL.—Subsections (b) and (c) shall not apply to property acquired by the decedent by gift or by inter vivos transfer for less than adequate and full consideration in money or money's worth during the 3-year period ending on the date of the decedent's death.

"(ii) EXCEPTION FOR CERTAIN GIFTS FROM SPOUSE.— Clause (i) shall not apply to property acquired by the decedent from the decedent's spouse unless, during such 3-year period, such spouse acquired the property in whole or in part by gift or by inter vivos transfer for less than adequate and full consideration in money or money's worth.

"(D) STOCK OF CERTAIN ENTITIES.—Subsections (b) and (c) shall not apply to—

"(i) stock or securities of a foreign personal holding company,

"(ii) stock of a DISC or former DISC,

"(iii) stock of a foreign investment company, or

"(iv) stock of a passive foreign investment company unless such company is a qualified electing fund (as defined in section 1295) with respect to the decedent.

"(2) FAIR MARKET VALUE LIMITATION.—The adjustments under subsections (b) and (c) shall not increase the basis of any interest in property acquired from the decedent above its fair market value in the hands of the decedent as of the date of the decedent's death.

"(3) ALLOCATION RULES.—

"(A) IN GENERAL.—The executor shall allocate the adjustments under subsections (b) and (c) on the return required by section 6018.

"(B) CHANGES IN ALLOCATION.—Any allocation made pursuant to subparagraph (A) may be changed only as provided by the Secretary.

"(4) INFLATION ADJUSTMENT OF BASIS ADJUSTMENT AMOUNTS.—

"(A) IN GENERAL.—In the case of decedents dying in a calendar year after 2010, the $1,300,000, $60,000, and $3,000,000 dollar amounts in subsections (b) and (c)(2)(B) shall each be increased by an amount equal to the product of—

"(i) such dollar amount, and

"(ii) the cost-of-living adjustment determined under section 1(f)(3) for such calendar year, determined by substituting '2009' for '1992' in subparagraph (B) thereof.

"(B) ROUNDING.—If any increase determined under subparagraph (A) is not a multiple of—

"(i) $100,000 in the case of the $1,300,000 amount,

"(ii) $5,000 in the case of the $60,000 amount, and

"(iii) $250,000 in the case of the $3,000,000 amount,

such increase shall be rounded to the next lowest multiple thereof.

"(e) PROPERTY ACQUIRED FROM THE DECEDENT.—For purposes of this section, the following property shall be considered to have been acquired from the decedent:

"(1) Property acquired by bequest, devise, or inheritance, or by the decedent's estate from the decedent.

"(2) Property transferred by the decedent during his lifetime—

"(A) to a qualified revocable trust (as defined in section 645(b)(1)), or

"(B) to any other trust with respect to which the decedent reserved the right to make any change in the enjoyment thereof through the exercise of a power to alter, amend, or terminate the trust.

"(3) Any other property passing from the decedent by reason of death to the extent that such property passed without consideration.

"(f) COORDINATION WITH SECTION 691.—This section shall not apply to property which constitutes a right to receive an item of income in respect of a decedent under section 691.

"(g) CERTAIN LIABILITIES DISREGARDED.—

PUBLIC LAW 107–16—JUNE 7, 2001   115 STAT. 81

"(1) IN GENERAL.—In determining whether gain is recognized on the acquisition of property—

"(A) from a decedent by a decedent's estate or any beneficiary other than a tax-exempt beneficiary, and

"(B) from the decedent's estate by any beneficiary other than a tax-exempt beneficiary,

and in determining the adjusted basis of such property, liabilities in excess of basis shall be disregarded.

"(2) TAX-EXEMPT BENEFICIARY.—For purposes of paragraph (1), the term 'tax-exempt beneficiary' means—

"(A) the United States, any State or political subdivision thereof, any possession of the United States, any Indian tribal government (within the meaning of section 7871), or any agency or instrumentality of any of the foregoing,

"(B) an organization (other than a cooperative described in section 521) which is exempt from tax imposed by chapter 1,

"(C) any foreign person or entity (within the meaning of section 168(h)(2)), and

"(D) to the extent provided in regulations, any person to whom property is transferred for the principal purpose of tax avoidance.

"(h) REGULATIONS.—The Secretary shall prescribe such regulations as may be necessary to carry out the purposes of this section.".

(b) INFORMATION RETURNS, ETC.—

(1) LARGE TRANSFERS AT DEATH.—So much of subpart C of part II of subchapter A of chapter 61 as precedes section 6019 is amended to read as follows:

"Subpart C—Returns Relating to Transfers During Life or at Death

"Sec. 6018. Returns relating to large transfers at death.
"Sec. 6019. Gift tax returns.

"SEC. 6018. RETURNS RELATING TO LARGE TRANSFERS AT DEATH.

"(a) IN GENERAL.—If this section applies to property acquired from a decedent, the executor of the estate of such decedent shall make a return containing the information specified in subsection (c) with respect to such property.

"(b) PROPERTY TO WHICH SECTION APPLIES.—

"(1) LARGE TRANSFERS.—This section shall apply to all property (other than cash) acquired from a decedent if the fair market value of such property acquired from the decedent exceeds the dollar amount applicable under section 1022(b)(2)(B) (without regard to section 1022(b)(2)(C)).

"(2) TRANSFERS OF CERTAIN GIFTS RECEIVED BY DECEDENT WITHIN 3 YEARS OF DEATH.—This section shall apply to any appreciated property acquired from the decedent if—

"(A) subsections (b) and (c) of section 1022 do not apply to such property by reason of section 1022(d)(1)(C), and

"(B) such property was required to be included on a return required to be filed under section 6019.

"(3) NONRESIDENTS NOT CITIZENS OF THE UNITED STATES.—In the case of a decedent who is a nonresident not a citizen of the United States, paragraphs (1) and (2) shall be applied—

115 STAT. 82　　　　PUBLIC LAW 107–16—JUNE 7, 2001

"(A) by taking into account only—
　　　"(i) tangible property situated in the United States, and
　　　"(ii) other property acquired from the decedent by a United States person, and
"(B) by substituting the dollar amount applicable under section 1022(b)(3) for the dollar amount referred to in paragraph (1).

"(4) Returns by Trustees or Beneficiaries.—If the executor is unable to make a complete return as to any property acquired from or passing from the decedent, the executor shall include in the return a description of such property and the name of every person holding a legal or beneficial interest therein. Upon notice from the Secretary, such person shall in like manner make a return as to such property.

"(c) Information Required To Be Furnished.—The information specified in this subsection with respect to any property acquired from the decedent is—
　　　"(1) the name and TIN of the recipient of such property,
　　　"(2) an accurate description of such property,
　　　"(3) the adjusted basis of such property in the hands of the decedent and its fair market value at the time of death,
　　　"(4) the decedent's holding period for such property,
　　　"(5) sufficient information to determine whether any gain on the sale of the property would be treated as ordinary income,
　　　"(6) the amount of basis increase allocated to the property under subsection (b) or (c) of section 1022, and
　　　"(7) such other information as the Secretary may by regulations prescribe.

Applicability.
"(d) Property Acquired From Decedent.—For purposes of this section, section 1022 shall apply for purposes of determining the property acquired from a decedent.

"(e) Statements To Be Furnished To Certain Persons.—Every person required to make a return under subsection (a) shall furnish to each person whose name is required to be set forth in such return (other than the person required to make such return) a written statement showing—
　　　"(1) the name, address, and phone number of the person required to make such return, and
　　　"(2) the information specified in subsection (c) with respect to property acquired from, or passing from, the decedent to the person required to receive such statement.

Deadline.
The written statement required under the preceding sentence shall be furnished not later than 30 days after the date that the return required by subsection (a) is filed.".

26 USC 6019.
　　　(2) Gifts.—Section 6019 (relating to gift tax returns) is amended—
　　　　　(A) by striking "Any individual" and inserting "(a) In General.—Any individual", and
　　　　　(B) by adding at the end the following new subsection:
"(b) Statements To Be Furnished To Certain Persons.—Every person required to make a return under subsection (a) shall furnish to each person whose name is required to be set forth in such return (other than the person required to make such return) a written statement showing—
　　　"(1) the name, address, and phone number of the person required to make such return, and

PUBLIC LAW 107–16—JUNE 7, 2001   115 STAT. 83

"(2) the information specified in such return with respect to property received by the person required to receive such statement.

The written statement required under the preceding sentence shall be furnished not later than 30 days after the date that the return required by subsection (a) is filed.". Deadline.

(3) TIME FOR FILING SECTION 6018 RETURNS.—

(A) RETURNS RELATING TO LARGE TRANSFERS AT DEATH.—Subsection (a) of section 6075 is amended to read as follows: 26 USC 6075.

"(a) RETURNS RELATING TO LARGE TRANSFERS AT DEATH.— The return required by section 6018 with respect to a decedent shall be filed with the return of the tax imposed by chapter 1 for the decedent's last taxable year or such later date specified in regulations prescribed by the Secretary.".

(B) CONFORMING AMENDMENTS.—Paragraph (3) of section 6075(b) is amended—

(i) by striking "ESTATE TAX RETURN" in the heading and inserting "SECTION 6018 RETURN", and

(ii) by striking "(relating to estate tax returns)" and inserting "(relating to returns relating to large transfers at death)".

(4) PENALTIES.—Part I of subchapter B of chapter 68 (relating to assessable penalties) is amended by adding at the end the following new section:

"SEC. 6716. FAILURE TO FILE INFORMATION WITH RESPECT TO CERTAIN TRANSFERS AT DEATH AND GIFTS.

"(a) INFORMATION REQUIRED TO BE FURNISHED TO THE SECRETARY.—Any person required to furnish any information under section 6018 who fails to furnish such information on the date prescribed therefor (determined with regard to any extension of time for filing) shall pay a penalty of $10,000 ($500 in the case of information required to be furnished under section 6018(b)(2)) for each such failure.

"(b) INFORMATION REQUIRED TO BE FURNISHED TO BENEFICIARIES.—Any person required to furnish in writing to each person described in section 6018(e) or 6019(b) the information required under such section who fails to furnish such information shall pay a penalty of $50 for each such failure.

"(c) REASONABLE CAUSE EXCEPTION.—No penalty shall be imposed under subsection (a) or (b) with respect to any failure if it is shown that such failure is due to reasonable cause.

"(d) INTENTIONAL DISREGARD.—If any failure under subsection (a) or (b) is due to intentional disregard of the requirements under sections 6018 and 6019(b), the penalty under such subsection shall be 5 percent of the fair market value (as of the date of death or, in the case of section 6019(b), the date of the gift) of the property with respect to which the information is required.

"(e) DEFICIENCY PROCEDURES NOT TO APPLY.—Subchapter B of chapter 63 (relating to deficiency procedures for income, estate, gift, and certain excise taxes) shall not apply in respect of the assessment or collection of any penalty imposed by this section.".

(5) CLERICAL AMENDMENTS.—

(A) The table of sections for part I of subchapter B of chapter 68 is amended by adding at the end the following new item:

"Sec. 6716. Failure to file information with respect to certain transfers at death and gifts.".

(B) The item relating to subpart C in the table of subparts for part II of subchapter A of chapter 61 is amended to read as follows:

"Subpart C. Returns relating to transfers during life or at death.".

(c) EXCLUSION OF GAIN ON SALE OF PRINCIPAL RESIDENCE MADE AVAILABLE TO HEIR OF DECEDENT IN CERTAIN CASES.—Subsection (d) of section 121 (relating to exclusion of gain from sale of principal residence) is amended by adding at the end the following new paragraph:

26 USC 121.

"(9) PROPERTY ACQUIRED FROM A DECEDENT.—The exclusion under this section shall apply to property sold by—

"(A) the estate of a decedent,

"(B) any individual who acquired such property from the decedent (within the meaning of section 1022), and

"(C) a trust which, immediately before the death of the decedent, was a qualified revocable trust (as defined in section 645(b)(1)) established by the decedent,

determined by taking into account the ownership and use by the decedent.".

(d) TRANSFERS OF APPRECIATED CARRYOVER BASIS PROPERTY TO SATISFY PECUNIARY BEQUEST.—

(1) IN GENERAL.—Section 1040 (relating to transfer of certain farm, etc., real property) is amended to read as follows:

"SEC. 1040. USE OF APPRECIATED CARRYOVER BASIS PROPERTY TO SATISFY PECUNIARY BEQUEST.

"(a) IN GENERAL.—If the executor of the estate of any decedent satisfies the right of any person to receive a pecuniary bequest with appreciated property, then gain on such exchange shall be recognized to the estate only to the extent that, on the date of such exchange, the fair market value of such property exceeds such value on the date of death.

Regulations.

"(b) SIMILAR RULE FOR CERTAIN TRUSTS.—To the extent provided in regulations prescribed by the Secretary, a rule similar to the rule provided in subsection (a) shall apply where—

"(1) by reason of the death of the decedent, a person has a right to receive from a trust a specific dollar amount which is the equivalent of a pecuniary bequest, and

"(2) the trustee of a trust satisfies such right with property.

"(c) BASIS OF PROPERTY ACQUIRED IN EXCHANGE DESCRIBED IN SUBSECTION (a) OR (b).—The basis of property acquired in an exchange with respect to which gain realized is not recognized by reason of subsection (a) or (b) shall be the basis of such property immediately before the exchange increased by the amount of the gain recognized to the estate or trust on the exchange.".

(2) The item relating to section 1040 in the table of sections for part III of subchapter O of chapter 1 is amended to read as follows:

"Sec. 1040. Use of appreciated carryover basis property to satisfy pecuniary bequest.".

(e) AMENDMENTS RELATED TO CARRYOVER BASIS.—

PUBLIC LAW 107–16—JUNE 7, 2001   115 STAT. 85

(1) RECOGNITION OF GAIN ON TRANSFERS TO NON-RESIDENTS.—

(A) Subsection (a) of section 684 is amended by inserting "or to a nonresident alien" after "or trust".   26 USC 684.

(B) Subsection (b) of section 684 is amended to read as follows:

"(b) EXCEPTIONS.—

"(1) TRANSFERS TO CERTAIN TRUSTS.—Subsection (a) shall not apply to a transfer to a trust by a United States person to the extent that any United States person is treated as the owner of such trust under section 671.

"(2) LIFETIME TRANSFERS TO NONRESIDENT ALIENS.—Subsection (a) shall not apply to a lifetime transfer to a nonresident alien.".

(C) The section heading for section 684 is amended by inserting "**AND NONRESIDENT ALIENS**" after "**ESTATES**".

(D) The item relating to section 684 in the table of sections for subpart F of part I of subchapter J of chapter 1 is amended by inserting "and nonresident aliens" after "estates".

(2) CAPITAL GAIN TREATMENT FOR INHERITED ART WORK OR SIMILAR PROPERTY.—

(A) IN GENERAL.—Subparagraph (C) of section 1221(a)(3) (defining capital asset) is amended by inserting "(other than by reason of section 1022)" after "is determined".

(B) COORDINATION WITH SECTION 170.—Paragraph (1) of section 170(e) (relating to certain contributions of ordinary income and capital gain property) is amended by adding at the end the following: "For purposes of this paragraph, the determination of whether property is a capital asset shall be made without regard to the exception contained in section 1221(a)(3)(C) for basis determined under section 1022.".

(3) DEFINITION OF EXECUTOR.—Section 7701(a) (relating to definitions) is amended by adding at the end the following:

"(47) EXECUTOR.—The term 'executor' means the executor or administrator of the decedent, or, if there is no executor or administrator appointed, qualified, and acting within the United States, then any person in actual or constructive possession of any property of the decedent.".

(4) CERTAIN TRUSTS.—Subparagraph (A) of section 4947(a)(2) is amended by inserting "642(c)," after "170(f)(2)(B),".

(5) OTHER AMENDMENTS.—

(A) Section 1246 is amended by striking subsection (e).

(B) Subsection (e) of section 1291 is amended—

(i) by striking "(e),"; and

(ii) by striking "; except that" and all that follows and inserting a period.

(C) Section 1296 is amended by striking subsection (i).

115 STAT. 86   PUBLIC LAW 107–16—JUNE 7, 2001

(6) CLERICAL AMENDMENT.—The table of sections for part II of subchapter O of chapter 1 is amended by inserting after the item relating to section 1021 the following new item:

"Sec. 1022. Treatment of property acquired from a decedent dying after December 31, 2009.".

Applicability.
26 USC 121 note.

(f) EFFECTIVE DATE.—
(1) IN GENERAL.—Except as provided in paragraph (2), the amendments made by this section shall apply to estates of decedents dying after December 31, 2009.
(2) TRANSFERS TO NONRESIDENTS.—The amendments made by subsection (e)(1) shall apply to transfers after December 31, 2009.
(3) SECTION 4947.—The amendment made by subsection (e)(4) shall apply to deductions for taxable years beginning after December 31, 2009.

Subtitle F—Conservation Easements

SEC. 551. EXPANSION OF ESTATE TAX RULE FOR CONSERVATION EASEMENTS.

26 USC 2031.

(a) REPEAL OF CERTAIN RESTRICTIONS ON WHERE LAND IS LOCATED.—Clause (i) of section 2031(c)(8)(A) (defining land subject to a qualified conservation easement) is amended to read as follows:
"(i) which is located in the United States or any possession of the United States,".
(b) CLARIFICATION OF DATE FOR DETERMINING VALUE OF LAND AND EASEMENT.—Section 2031(c)(2) (defining applicable percentage) is amended by adding at the end the following new sentence: "The values taken into account under the preceding sentence shall be such values as of the date of the contribution referred to in paragraph (8)(B).".

Applicability.
26 USC 2031 note.

(c) EFFECTIVE DATE.—The amendments made by this section shall apply to estates of decedents dying after December 31, 2000.

Subtitle G—Modifications of Generation-Skipping Transfer Tax

SEC. 561. DEEMED ALLOCATION OF GST EXEMPTION TO LIFETIME TRANSFERS TO TRUSTS; RETROACTIVE ALLOCATIONS.

(a) IN GENERAL.—Section 2632 (relating to special rules for allocation of GST exemption) is amended by redesignating subsection (c) as subsection (e) and by inserting after subsection (b) the following new subsections:
"(c) DEEMED ALLOCATION TO CERTAIN LIFETIME TRANSFERS TO GST TRUSTS.—
"(1) IN GENERAL.—If any individual makes an indirect skip during such individual's lifetime, any unused portion of such individual's GST exemption shall be allocated to the property transferred to the extent necessary to make the inclusion ratio for such property zero. If the amount of the indirect skip exceeds such unused portion, the entire unused portion shall be allocated to the property transferred.

"(2) UNUSED PORTION.—For purposes of paragraph (1), the unused portion of an individual's GST exemption is that portion of such exemption which has not previously been—

"(A) allocated by such individual,

"(B) treated as allocated under subsection (b) with respect to a direct skip occurring during or before the calendar year in which the indirect skip is made, or

"(C) treated as allocated under paragraph (1) with respect to a prior indirect skip.

"(3) DEFINITIONS.—

"(A) INDIRECT SKIP.—For purposes of this subsection, the term 'indirect skip' means any transfer of property (other than a direct skip) subject to the tax imposed by chapter 12 made to a GST trust.

"(B) GST TRUST.—The term 'GST trust' means a trust that could have a generation-skipping transfer with respect to the transferor unless—

"(i) the trust instrument provides that more than 25 percent of the trust corpus must be distributed to or may be withdrawn by one or more individuals who are non-skip persons—

"(I) before the date that the individual attains age 46,

"(II) on or before one or more dates specified in the trust instrument that will occur before the date that such individual attains age 46, or

"(III) upon the occurrence of an event that, in accordance with regulations prescribed by the Secretary, may reasonably be expected to occur before the date that such individual attains age 46,

"(ii) the trust instrument provides that more than 25 percent of the trust corpus must be distributed to or may be withdrawn by one or more individuals who are non-skip persons and who are living on the date of death of another person identified in the instrument (by name or by class) who is more than 10 years older than such individuals,

"(iii) the trust instrument provides that, if one or more individuals who are non-skip persons die on or before a date or event described in clause (i) or (ii), more than 25 percent of the trust corpus either must be distributed to the estate or estates of one or more of such individuals or is subject to a general power of appointment exercisable by one or more of such individuals,

"(iv) the trust is a trust any portion of which would be included in the gross estate of a non-skip person (other than the transferor) if such person died immediately after the transfer,

"(v) the trust is a charitable lead annuity trust (within the meaning of section 2642(e)(3)(A)) or a charitable remainder annuity trust or a charitable remainder unitrust (within the meaning of section 664(d)), or

"(vi) the trust is a trust with respect to which a deduction was allowed under section 2522 for the amount of an interest in the form of the right to receive annual payments of a fixed percentage of the net fair market value of the trust property (determined yearly) and which is required to pay principal to a non-skip person if such person is alive when the yearly payments for which the deduction was allowed terminate.

For purposes of this subparagraph, the value of transferred property shall not be considered to be includible in the gross estate of a non-skip person or subject to a right of withdrawal by reason of such person holding a right to withdraw so much of such property as does not exceed the amount referred to in section 2503(b) with respect to any transferor, and it shall be assumed that powers of appointment held by non-skip persons will not be exercised.

"(4) AUTOMATIC ALLOCATIONS TO CERTAIN GST TRUSTS.— For purposes of this subsection, an indirect skip to which section 2642(f) applies shall be deemed to have been made only at the close of the estate tax inclusion period. The fair market value of such transfer shall be the fair market value of the trust property at the close of the estate tax inclusion period.

"(5) APPLICABILITY AND EFFECT.—

"(A) IN GENERAL.—An individual—

"(i) may elect to have this subsection not apply to—

"(I) an indirect skip, or

"(II) any or all transfers made by such individual to a particular trust, and

"(ii) may elect to treat any trust as a GST trust for purposes of this subsection with respect to any or all transfers made by such individual to such trust.

"(B) ELECTIONS.—

"(i) ELECTIONS WITH RESPECT TO INDIRECT SKIPS.— An election under subparagraph (A)(i)(I) shall be deemed to be timely if filed on a timely filed gift tax return for the calendar year in which the transfer was made or deemed to have been made pursuant to paragraph (4) or on such later date or dates as may be prescribed by the Secretary.

"(ii) OTHER ELECTIONS.—An election under clause (i)(II) or (ii) of subparagraph (A) may be made on a timely filed gift tax return for the calendar year for which the election is to become effective.

"(d) RETROACTIVE ALLOCATIONS.—

"(1) IN GENERAL.—If—

"(A) a non-skip person has an interest or a future interest in a trust to which any transfer has been made,

"(B) such person—

"(i) is a lineal descendant of a grandparent of the transferor or of a grandparent of the transferor's spouse or former spouse, and

"(ii) is assigned to a generation below the generation assignment of the transferor, and

"(C) such person predeceases the transferor,

then the transferor may make an allocation of any of such transferor's unused GST exemption to any previous transfer or transfers to the trust on a chronological basis.

"(2) SPECIAL RULES.—If the allocation under paragraph (1) by the transferor is made on a gift tax return filed on or before the date prescribed by section 6075(b) for gifts made within the calendar year within which the non-skip person's death occurred—

"(A) the value of such transfer or transfers for purposes of section 2642(a) shall be determined as if such allocation had been made on a timely filed gift tax return for each calendar year within which each transfer was made,

"(B) such allocation shall be effective immediately before such death, and

"(C) the amount of the transferor's unused GST exemption available to be allocated shall be determined immediately before such death.

"(3) FUTURE INTEREST.—For purposes of this subsection, a person has a future interest in a trust if the trust may permit income or corpus to be paid to such person on a date or dates in the future.".

(b) CONFORMING AMENDMENT.—Paragraph (2) of section 2632(b) is amended by striking "with respect to a prior direct skip" and inserting "or subsection (c)(1)". 26 USC 2632.

(c) EFFECTIVE DATES.—

(1) DEEMED ALLOCATION.—Section 2632(c) of the Internal Revenue Code of 1986 (as added by subsection (a)), and the amendment made by subsection (b), shall apply to transfers subject to chapter 11 or 12 made after December 31, 2000, and to estate tax inclusion periods ending after December 31, 2000.

Applicability.
26 USC 2632 note.

(2) RETROACTIVE ALLOCATIONS.—Section 2632(d) of the Internal Revenue Code of 1986 (as added by subsection (a)) shall apply to deaths of non-skip persons occurring after December 31, 2000.

SEC. 562. SEVERING OF TRUSTS.

(a) IN GENERAL.—Subsection (a) of section 2642 (relating to inclusion ratio) is amended by adding at the end the following new paragraph:

"(3) SEVERING OF TRUSTS.—

"(A) IN GENERAL.—If a trust is severed in a qualified severance, the trusts resulting from such severance shall be treated as separate trusts thereafter for purposes of this chapter.

"(B) QUALIFIED SEVERANCE.—For purposes of subparagraph (A)—

"(i) IN GENERAL.—The term 'qualified severance' means the division of a single trust and the creation (by any means available under the governing instrument or under local law) of two or more trusts if—

"(I) the single trust was divided on a fractional basis, and

"(II) the terms of the new trusts, in the aggregate, provide for the same succession of interests of beneficiaries as are provided in the original trust.

"(ii) TRUSTS WITH INCLUSION RATIO GREATER THAN ZERO.—If a trust has an inclusion ratio of greater than zero and less than 1, a severance is a qualified severance only if the single trust is divided into two trusts, one of which receives a fractional share of the total value of all trust assets equal to the applicable fraction of the single trust immediately before the severance. In such case, the trust receiving such fractional share shall have an inclusion ratio of zero and the other trust shall have an inclusion ratio of 1.

"(iii) REGULATIONS.—The term 'qualified severance' includes any other severance permitted under regulations prescribed by the Secretary.

"(C) TIMING AND MANNER OF SEVERANCES.—A severance pursuant to this paragraph may be made at any time. The Secretary shall prescribe by forms or regulations the manner in which the qualified severance shall be reported to the Secretary.".

Regulations.

(b) EFFECTIVE DATE.—The amendment made by this section shall apply to severances after December 31, 2000.

Applicability.
26 USC 2642 note.

SEC. 563. MODIFICATION OF CERTAIN VALUATION RULES.

(a) GIFTS FOR WHICH GIFT TAX RETURN FILED OR DEEMED ALLOCATION MADE.—Paragraph (1) of section 2642(b) (relating to valuation rules, etc.) is amended to read as follows:

26 USC 2642.

"(1) GIFTS FOR WHICH GIFT TAX RETURN FILED OR DEEMED ALLOCATION MADE.—If the allocation of the GST exemption to any transfers of property is made on a gift tax return filed on or before the date prescribed by section 6075(b) for such transfer or is deemed to be made under section 2632 (b)(1) or (c)(1)—

"(A) the value of such property for purposes of subsection (a) shall be its value as finally determined for purposes of chapter 12 (within the meaning of section 2001(f)(2)), or, in the case of an allocation deemed to have been made at the close of an estate tax inclusion period, its value at the time of the close of the estate tax inclusion period, and

"(B) such allocation shall be effective on and after the date of such transfer, or, in the case of an allocation deemed to have been made at the close of an estate tax inclusion period, on and after the close of such estate tax inclusion period.".

(b) TRANSFERS AT DEATH.—Subparagraph (A) of section 2642(b)(2) is amended to read as follows:

"(A) TRANSFERS AT DEATH.—If property is transferred as a result of the death of the transferor, the value of such property for purposes of subsection (a) shall be its value as finally determined for purposes of chapter 11; except that, if the requirements prescribed by the Secretary respecting allocation of post-death changes in value are not met, the value of such property shall be determined as of the time of the distribution concerned.".

PUBLIC LAW 107–16—JUNE 7, 2001   115 STAT. 91

(c) EFFECTIVE DATE.—The amendments made by this section shall apply to transfers subject to chapter 11 or 12 of the Internal Revenue Code of 1986 made after December 31, 2000.

Applicability.
26 USC 2642
note.

SEC. 564. RELIEF PROVISIONS.

(a) IN GENERAL.—Section 2642 is amended by adding at the end the following new subsection:

26 USC 2642.

"(g) RELIEF PROVISIONS.—

"(1) RELIEF FROM LATE ELECTIONS.—

"(A) IN GENERAL.—The Secretary shall by regulation prescribe such circumstances and procedures under which extensions of time will be granted to make—

Regulations.

"(i) an allocation of GST exemption described in paragraph (1) or (2) of subsection (b), and

"(ii) an election under subsection (b)(3) or (c)(5) of section 2632.

Such regulations shall include procedures for requesting comparable relief with respect to transfers made before the date of the enactment of this paragraph.

"(B) BASIS FOR DETERMINATIONS.—In determining whether to grant relief under this paragraph, the Secretary shall take into account all relevant circumstances, including evidence of intent contained in the trust instrument or instrument of transfer and such other factors as the Secretary deems relevant. For purposes of determining whether to grant relief under this paragraph, the time for making the allocation (or election) shall be treated as if not expressly prescribed by statute.

"(2) SUBSTANTIAL COMPLIANCE.—An allocation of GST exemption under section 2632 that demonstrates an intent to have the lowest possible inclusion ratio with respect to a transfer or a trust shall be deemed to be an allocation of so much of the transferor's unused GST exemption as produces the lowest possible inclusion ratio. In determining whether there has been substantial compliance, all relevant circumstances shall be taken into account, including evidence of intent contained in the trust instrument or instrument of transfer and such other factors as the Secretary deems relevant.".

(b) EFFECTIVE DATES.—

(1) RELIEF FROM LATE ELECTIONS.—Section 2642(g)(1) of the Internal Revenue Code of 1986 (as added by subsection (a)) shall apply to requests pending on, or filed after, December 31, 2000.

Applicability.
26 USC 2642
note.

(2) SUBSTANTIAL COMPLIANCE.—Section 2642(g)(2) of such Code (as so added) shall apply to transfers subject to chapter 11 or 12 of the Internal Revenue Code of 1986 made after December 31, 2000. No implication is intended with respect to the availability of relief from late elections or the application of a rule of substantial compliance on or before such date.

115 STAT. 92   PUBLIC LAW 107–16—JUNE 7, 2001

Subtitle H—Extension of Time for Payment of Estate Tax

SEC. 571. INCREASE IN NUMBER OF ALLOWABLE PARTNERS AND SHAREHOLDERS IN CLOSELY HELD BUSINESSES.

(a) IN GENERAL.—Paragraphs (1)(B)(ii), (1)(C)(ii), and (9)(B)(iii)(I) of section 6166(b) (relating to definitions and special rules) are each amended by striking "15" and inserting "45".

(b) EFFECTIVE DATE.—The amendments made by this section shall apply to estates of decedents dying after December 31, 2001.

26 USC 6166.

Applicability.
26 USC 6166
note.

SEC. 572. EXPANSION OF AVAILABILITY OF INSTALLMENT PAYMENT FOR ESTATES WITH INTERESTS QUALIFYING LENDING AND FINANCE BUSINESSES.

(a) IN GENERAL.—Section 6166(b) (relating to definitions and special rules) is amended by adding at the end the following new paragraph:

"(10) STOCK IN QUALIFYING LENDING AND FINANCE BUSINESS TREATED AS STOCK IN AN ACTIVE TRADE OR BUSINESS COMPANY.—

"(A) IN GENERAL.—If the executor elects the benefits of this paragraph, then—

"(i) STOCK IN QUALIFYING LENDING AND FINANCE BUSINESS TREATED AS STOCK IN AN ACTIVE TRADE OR BUSINESS COMPANY.—For purposes of this section, any asset used in a qualifying lending and finance business shall be treated as an asset which is used in carrying on a trade or business.

"(ii) 5-YEAR DEFERRAL FOR PRINCIPAL NOT TO APPLY.—The executor shall be treated as having selected under subsection (a)(3) the date prescribed by section 6151(a).

"(iii) 5 EQUAL INSTALLMENTS ALLOWED.—For purposes of applying subsection (a)(1), '5' shall be substituted for '10'.

"(B) DEFINITIONS.—For purposes of this paragraph—

"(i) QUALIFYING LENDING AND FINANCE BUSINESS.—The term 'qualifying lending and finance business' means a lending and finance business, if—

"(I) based on all the facts and circumstances immediately before the date of the decedent's death, there was substantial activity with respect to the lending and finance business, or

"(II) during at least 3 of the 5 taxable years ending before the date of the decedent's death, such business had at least 1 full-time employee substantially all of whose services were the active management of such business, 10 full-time, non-owner employees substantially all of whose services were directly related to such business, and $5,000,000 in gross receipts from activities described in clause (ii).

"(ii) LENDING AND FINANCE BUSINESS.—The term 'lending and finance business' means a trade or business of—

"(I) making loans,

PUBLIC LAW 107–16—JUNE 7, 2001   115 STAT. 93

"(II) purchasing or discounting accounts receivable, notes, or installment obligations,

"(III) engaging in rental and leasing of real and tangible personal property, including entering into leases and purchasing, servicing, and disposing of leases and leased assets,

"(IV) rendering services or making facilities available in the ordinary course of a lending or finance business, and

"(V) rendering services or making facilities available in connection with activities described in subclauses (I) through (IV) carried on by the corporation rendering services or making facilities available, or another corporation which is a member of the same affiliated group (as defined in section 1504 without regard to section 1504(b)(3)).

"(iii) LIMITATION.—The term 'qualifying lending and finance business' shall not include any interest in an entity, if the stock or debt of such entity or a controlled group (as defined in section 267(f)(1)) of which such entity was a member was readily tradable on an established securities market or secondary market (as defined by the Secretary) at any time within 3 years before the date of the decedent's death.".

(b) EFFECTIVE DATE.—The amendment made by this section shall apply to estates of decedents dying after December 31, 2001.

Applicability.
26 USC 6166
note.

SEC. 573. CLARIFICATION OF AVAILABILITY OF INSTALLMENT PAYMENT.

(a) IN GENERAL.—Subparagraph (B) of section 6166(b)(8) (relating to all stock must be non-readily-tradable stock) is amended to read as follows:

26 USC 6166.

"(B) ALL STOCK MUST BE NON-READILY-TRADABLE STOCK.—

"(i) IN GENERAL.—No stock shall be taken into account for purposes of applying this paragraph unless it is non-readily-tradable stock (within the meaning of paragraph (7)(B)).

"(ii) SPECIAL APPLICATION WHERE ONLY HOLDING COMPANY STOCK IS NON-READILY-TRADABLE STOCK.—If the requirements of clause (i) are not met, but all of the stock of each holding company taken into account is non-readily-tradable, then this paragraph shall apply, but subsection (a)(1) shall be applied by substituting '5' for '10'.".

(b) EFFECTIVE DATE.—The amendment made by this section shall apply to estates of decedents dying after December 31, 2001.

Applicability.
26 USC 6166
note.

Subtitle I—Other Provisions

SEC. 581. WAIVER OF STATUTE OF LIMITATION FOR TAXES ON CERTAIN FARM VALUATIONS.

26 USC 2032A
note.

If on the date of the enactment of this Act (or at any time within 1 year after the date of the enactment) a refund or credit of any overpayment of tax resulting from the application of section

115 STAT. 94   PUBLIC LAW 107–16—JUNE 7, 2001

2032A(c)(7)(E) of the Internal Revenue Code of 1986 is barred by any law or rule of law, the refund or credit of such overpayment shall, nevertheless, be made or allowed if claim therefor is filed before the date 1 year after the date of the enactment of this Act.

¶ B.02 EGTRRA'S SUNSET PROVISION

This is the entirety of EGTRRA's sunset provision, which causes the estate, gift, and generation-skipping transfer tax provisions of that law to terminate on December 31, 2010, and restores the pre-EGTRRA rules on January 1, 2011.

TITLE IX—COMPLIANCE WITH CONGRESSIONAL BUDGET ACT

26 USC 1 note.   **SEC. 901. SUNSET OF PROVISIONS OF ACT.**

(a) IN GENERAL.—All provisions of, and amendments made by, this Act shall not apply—

(1) to taxable, plan, or limitation years beginning after December 31, 2010, or

(2) in the case of title V, to estates of decedents dying, gifts made, or generation skipping transfers, after December 31, 2010.

(b) APPLICATION OF CERTAIN LAWS.—The Internal Revenue Code of 1986 and the Employee Retirement Income Security Act of 1974 shall be applied and administered to years, estates, gifts, and transfers described in subsection (a) as if the provisions and amendments described in subsection (a) had never been enacted.

¶ B.03 2002 TECHNICAL CHANGES TO THE ESTATE, GIFT, AND GENERATION-SKIPPING TRANSFER TAX PROVISIONS OF THE ECONOMIC GROWTH AND TAX REFORM RECONCILIATION ACT OF 2001.

The following are the technical corrections made, in 2002, by the Job Creation and Worker Assistance Act of 2002, which changed EGTRRA's provisions relating to estates, gifts, and generation-skipping transfers. These are particularly important in their rewriting of Section 2511(c).

TITLE IV—MISCELLANEOUS AND TECHNICAL PROVISIONS

***

Subtitle B—Technical Corrections

SEC. 411. AMENDMENTS RELATED TO ECONOMIC GROWTH AND TAX RELIEF RECONCILIATION ACT OF 2001.

***

(g) AMENDMENTS RELATED TO SECTION 511 OF THE ACT.—

(1) Section 2511(c) is amended by striking "taxable gift under section 2503," and inserting "transfer of property by gift,".

(2) Section 2101(b) is amended by striking the last sentence.

(h) AMENDMENT RELATED TO SECTION 532 OF THE ACT.—Section 2016 is amended by striking "any State, any possession of the United States, or the District of Columbia,".

Table of
IRC Sections

[Text references are to paragraphs; note references are to chapters (boldface numbers) and notes ("n.").]

IRC §

121	1.05[3][b]; **1** n.77; 6.02[1]
121(d)(9)	**1** n.76; **3** n.88
165	1.05[2][a][i]; 3.05
168(h)(2)	**1** n.72; **3** n.84; 5.06[2]
168(h)(2)(C)	**3** n.84; 5.06[2]
170	3.11
172	1.05[2][a][i]
469	3.10
469(g)(2)	3.10; **3** n.93
501(a)	1.02[1]
504(c)	1.06[3][f]
511(e)	1.04
521	**1** n.72; 3.04
642(c)(5)	**4** n.17
645	1.05[2][a][iii]; 3.03[3][b][i]; 5.05[2]; 6.07
645(b)(1)	**1** n.57; 3.03[3][b]; 3.03[3][b][i]; 3.03[4][a]; **3** ns. 44, 58
664	**4** n.17
672(a)	5.02[2][b]
674(a)	**5** n.9
675(4)(C)	**3** n.55
672(e)	3.03[3][b][i]
676	1.05[2][a][iii]; 3.03[3][b][i]
676(a)	3.03[3][b][i]
677(a)	**5** n.10
678	3.06; **3** n.90
684	1.05[3][d]; **1** ns. 81, 82; 5.06[3]; **5** n.42; 6.08
691	1.05[2][a][iv]; 3.03[4][h]
734(b)	**3** n.98
743	3.12; **3** n.96
743(b)	**3** n.98
743(d)	**3** n.96
754	3.12; **3** ns. 96–98
1001	**1** n.71
1014	**1** n.16
1014(b)	**3** n.39
1014(b)(2)	**1** n.53
1014(b)(3)	**1** n.53
1014(f)	**1** n.19; 3.02
1015(c)	**1** n.17
1015(d)	**1** n.18

1015(d)(6)	**1** n.17
1022	1.05[2][a][ii]; 1.05[4]; 3.03[1][a]; 3.03[4]
1022(a)	**1** n.19
1022(a)(1)	3.02
1022(a)(2)	3.13
1022(b)	**3** n.2
1022(b)(1)	**3** n.8
1022(b)(1)(A)	**1** n.83
1022(b)(2)(B)	**1** n.21; **3** n.5
1022(b)(2)(C)	**1** n.24; **3** n.86
1022(b)(2)(C)(i)	**3** n.100
1022(b)(3)	**1** ns. 25, 26; **3** n.10; **5** n.35
1022(b)(3)(B)	**1** n.23
1022(b)(4)	**5** n.36
1022(c)	**1** ns. 28, 32; **3** ns. 3, 22, 24
1022(c)(4)(B)	**1** ns. 33, 34, 38; **3** ns. 25, 34, 35
1022(c)(4)(B)(i)(I)	**1** n.35
1022(c)(4)(B)(i)(II)	**1** n.36
1022(c)(4)(B)(ii)	**1** n.37
1022(c)(4)(C)	**1** n.33; **3** n.25
1022(c)(5)	**1** n.42
1022(c)(5)(A)(i)	**1** n.43
1022(c)(5)(B)	**1** ns. 45, 46; **3** n.31
1022(c)(5)(B)(i)	**1** ns. 44, 48; **3** n.29
1022(c)(5)(B)(ii)	**1** n.45
1022(d)(1)	**1** n.66
1022(d)(1)(A)	**1** ns. 62, 64; **3** ns. 38, 56
1022(d)(1)(B)(i)	**3** n.65
1022(d)(1)(B)(i)(I)	**1** n.54; **3** n.66
1022(d)(1)(B)(i)(II)	**1** ns. 55, 56; **3** n.67
1022(d)(1)(B)(i)(III)	**3** n.68
1022(d)(1)(B)(ii)	**1** n.57; **3** n.58
1022(d)(1)(B)(iii)	**1** n.58; **3** n.60
1022(d)(1)(B)(iv)	**1** n.60; **3** ns. 69, 70
1022(d)(1)(C)(i)	**3** n.72
1022(d)(1)(C)(ii)	**3** n.73
1022(d)(1)(D)	**1** n.67
1022(d)(1)(D)(i)	**3** n.75
1022(d)(1)(D)(ii)	**3** n.76
1022(d)(1)(D)(iii)	**3** n.77
1022(d)(1)(D)(iv)	**3** n.78

*[Text references are to paragraphs; note references are to chapters
(boldface numbers) and notes ("n.").]*

IRC §

1022(d)(2) . . . . **1** ns. 22, 30; **3** n.23
1022(d)(3)(A) . . . .**3** ns. 4, 6, 13
1022(d)(3)(B) **3** n.7
1022(d)(4) . . . .**1** ns. 27, 51
1022(d)(5)(B) **3** n.26
1022(e) . . . . **1** n.53; 3.03[3][a]
1022(e)(2) . . . . 3.03[3][b]
1022(e)(2)(A) **3** n.43
1022(e)(2)(B) . . . . 3.03[3][b][ii]
1022(e)(3) . . . . 3.03[3][c]
1022(f) **1** n.65; **3** n.74
1022(g) **1** n.74; 3.04
1022(g)(1) **1** n.72; **3** n.80; **5** n.38
1022(g)(1)(A) **3** n.83
1022(g)(1)(B) **5** n.39
1022(g)(2) **1** n.72; **3** n.85; **5** n.40
1040 . . . . **1** n.80
1040(a) . . . . 5.05[2]
1040(b) **1** n.79; **5** n.33
1212(b) . . . . 1.05[2][a][i]
1223(2) 3.09; **3** n.19
1223(9) . . . . 3.03[1][e]; **3** ns. 19, 92
1245 . . . . **3** n.20
1250 . . . .**3** ns. 20, 21
1274 . . . . 3.03[3][b][ii]
1295 . . . . 1.05[2][a][iv]; 3.03[4][h]
2010(c) . . . 1.03; 2.05[1]; 4.09[3]; **4** ns. 18, 39
2011(b)(1) **2** n.24
2011(g) . . . . **1** ns. 93, 94; **2** n.23
2031(c) . . . . 1.06[3][b]
2031(c)(8)(A) **1** n.97
2032 . . . . **1** n.16
2032(c) **5** n.20
2032A . . . . .1.02[2]; 1.06[3][f]
2035 . . . . **4** n.54
2036(a)(1) **1** n.63
2038(1) . . . . 3.03[3][b][ii]
2040 . . . . 1.05[2][a][iii]; 3.03[4][c]
2041 . . . . **1** n.14; 5.02[2][b]
2041(a) **3** n.62
2041(b)(2) **2** n.67
2044 . . . . **1** n.61
2055 . . . . 3.11
2055(a) **4** n.17
2056(b)(5) . . . . **2** n.62; 3.03[2][a][i]
2056(b)(7) . . . . 1.05[2][a][iii]; 2.07[1]
2056A . . . . 1.02[3]
2056A(b)(2) . . . . 1.02[3]; **1** n.8
2057 . . . . 1.02[2]; **1** n.111
2057(j) **1** n.111
2106 . . . . 3.11
2203 . . . . **3** n.14
2210(a) **1** n.3
2210(b) **1** n.7
2503 . . . . 5.02[4]
2503(e) **4** n.4
2511(c) . . . . 1.04; **1** n.12; 5.01; 5.02[2];
    5.02[2][a]; 5.02[2][c]; 5.02[2][d]; B.03
2514(c)(3)(B) **5** n.13
2515 . . . . **4** n.2

IRC §

2518 . . . . **2** n.71
2518(b)(2) . . . . **2** n.72; **4** n .68
2518(b)(4) **2** n.70
2518(b)(4)(A) **2** n.70
2519 . . . . 2.07[1]
2522 . . . . 3.11
2523(f) **4** n.51
2604 . . . . **2** n.39
2611(a) . . . . **1** n.9; 4.03[1]
2611(b) 1.03; **4** n.4
2612(a) . . . . **1** n.9; 2.05[2][a]; 4.03[1]
2612(b) . . . . **1** n.9; 2.05[2][a]; 4.03[1]
2612(c) . . . . **1** n.9; 4.03[1]
2613 . . . . **2** n.15; 4.03[2][a]
2613(a) . . . . .2.05[2][a]; 4.03[1]; 4.05
2613(b) . . . . .2.05[2][a]; 4.03[1]; 4.05
2631(c) . . . . 1.03; 2.05[1]; **4** ns. 18, 38
2631(c)(2) 4.04
2632(c) . . . . 1.06[1]; **1** n.98; **4** n.20
2632(c)(3)(B)(i) **4** n.21
2632(c)(3)(B)(ii) **4** n.22
2632(c)(3)(B)(iii) **4** n.23
2632(c)(3)(B)(iv) **4** n.24
2632(c)(3)(B)(v) **4** n.25
2632(c)(3)(B)(vi) **4** n.26
2632(c)(5)(B) **4** n.27
2632(d) . . . . **1** n.102; 4.03[2][f]
2632(d)(1)(A) **4** n.31
2632(d)(1)(B)(i) **4** n.32
2632(d)(1)(B)(ii) **4** n.33
2632(d)(1)(C) **4** n.34
2632(d)(2) **4** n.35
2642 . . . . 4.08
2642(a) **4** n.10
2642(a)(3) **1** n.103; **4** n.29
2642(b) **1** n.105
2642(b)(1) **4** n.40
2642(b)(3) **4** n.28
2642(c) . . . 4.03[1]; 4.03[2][a]; 4.06; 5.02[4]; **5**
                                                    n.27
2642(c)(1) 4.06
2642(c)(2) 4.06
2642(f) 4.08
2642(f)(1)(B) **4** n.54
2642(g) **1** n.109
2642(g)(1)(B) **1** n.106
2651(c)(1) **2** n.14; **4** n.53
2652 . . . . **4** n.52
2652(a)(1) **2** n.21; **4** n.48
2652(a)(1)(A) **2** n.22
2652(a)(3) . . . . 2.05[1]
2652(c) . . . . 4.03[2][a]
2653 . . . . 5.05[1]
2653(a) . . . . . 1.03; **2** n.21; 4.03[1]; 4.03[2][a];
    4.05; 4.06; 4.09[1]; 4.09[3]; **4** n.48
2653(c)(1) **4** n.17
2654(a)(2) . . . . 4.03[2][b]
2664 . . . 1.03; **2** n.15; 4.03; 4.03[1]; 4.03[2][a];
    4.06; 4.07; 4.09[1]; **4** n.3; 5.02[4]
2701(c)(3)(C)(i) **5** n.20

[Text references are to paragraphs; note references are to chapters (boldface numbers) and notes ("n.").]

IRC §

6018 . . . . 1.05[4]; **1** n.85; 3.03; 3.03[1];
3.03[1][a]; 3.03[1][b]; 3.03[1][c];
3.03[1][d]; 3.07; 3.12; **3** ns. 4, 6;
5.04[1]; 5.06[1]
6018(b) **1** n.87
6018(b)(1) . . . . **1** ns. 84, 86
6018(b)(3) . . . . **1** n.88; **3** n.10; 5.06[1]
6018(b)(4) . . . . 3.03[1][d]
6019 . . . . **1** n.85
6019(b) **5** n.24
6075(a) . . . . **3** ns. 4, 99
6166 . . . . 1.02[2]; 1.06[3][e]
6166(b)(1)(B)(ii) **1** n.115

IRC §

6166(b)(1)(C)(ii) **1** n.115
6166(b)(9)(B)(iii)(I) **1** n.115
6166(b)(10) . . . . **1** ns. 113, 114
6601(j)(2)(A)(i) **4** n.19
6716 . . . . **1** ns. 85, 89
7701(a)(4) . . . . 1.05[4]
7701(a)(47) . . . . 3.03[1][d]; **3** n.14
7701(b) . . . . 3.03[1][c]
7701(b)(1) **3** n.13
7701(b)(1)(A)(i) **3** n.11
7701(b)(3)(A) **3** n.12
7871 . . . . **1** n.72
9100 . . . . 1.06[3][c][v]

Table of
Treasury Regulations

[Text references are to paragraphs; note references are to chapters (boldface numbers) and notes ("n.").]

Reg. §

1.645-1(b)(1) . . . . **3** ns. 44–46
1.661(a)-2(f)(1) **1** n.78; **5** n.32
1.664-1(a)(1)(iii)(*a*) 3.11
1.664-1(a)(4) **5** n.22
1.664-2 . . . . 3.11
1.664-3 . . . . **3** n.98
1.754-1(b)(1) **3** n.98
1.1001-2 . . . . **1** n.71
1.1001-2(a)(1) **3** n.79
1.1015-1(a)(3) **1** n.18
1.6050I-1(c)(1)(ii)(B) **3** n.9
20.2056(b)-3(b) **1** n.40
20.2056(b)-3(d), Ex. 4 . . . . **1** n.41
20.2056(b)-5(f)(8) **3** n.32
20.2056(b)-7(h), Ex. 11 . . . . **1** n.47
20.2056(b)-7(h), Ex. 12 . . . . **1** n.47
20.2056(e)-2(b) **1** n.50; **3** n.28
20.2203-1 . . . . **3** n.15
25.2511-2(b) **5** n.3
25.2511-2(c) . . . . **1.04; 5.02[2][a]; 5** n.11
25.2511-2(f) **5** n.11
25.2514-1(c)(1) **5** n.12
25.2514-1(e), Ex. 1 . . . . **5** n.18
25.2514-3(b)(2) **5** n.13
25.2518-2(e)(1) **2** n.70
25.2518-2(e)(2) **2** n.70
26.2642-1(b)(2) **4** n.55

Reg. §

26.2652-1(b)(2), Ex. 1 . . . . . . **4** n.15; **5** n.25
301.7701-1 – 301.7701-3 . . . . **2** n.31
301.7701-2(a) **2** n.35
301.7701-3(b)(1)(ii) **2** n.35
301.7701-3(c) . . . . **2.06[2][a][ii]; 2** n.34
301.7701(b)-1(b)(1) **3** n.11
301.7701(b)-1(c) **3** n.12
301.9100-3 . . . . **1.06[3][c][v]**

TEMPORARY
REGULATIONS

Temp. Reg. §

1.71-1T, A-5 . . . . **3** n.9

PROPOSED
REGULATIONS

Prop. Reg. §

1.42-18(c)(6)(i) **3** n.9
1.645-1(b)(1) **3** n.50
26.2642-7(c) **4** n.43

Table of Revenue Rulings, Revenue Procedures, and Other IRS Releases

[Text references are to paragraphs; note references are to chapters (boldface numbers) and notes ("n.").]

REVENUE RULINGS

Rev. Rul.

60-87	**5** n.32
66-85	**1** n.5
67-370	5.02[2][b]; **5** n.19
74-178	**5** n.32
74-424	**1** n.5
76-103	**5** n.2
76-503	**1** n.14; 5.02[2][b]; **5** n.16
77-158	**1** n.14; 5.02[2][b]; **5** n.17
84-105	**2** n.6
85-13	3.03[3][c]; **3** n.54
86-41	4.09[3]; **4** n.59; **5** n.4
98-8	**2** n.69

REVENUE PROCEDURES

Rev. Proc.

2009-50	**4** n.19

PRIVATE LETTER RULINGS (Including TECHNICAL ADVICE MEMORANDA)

Priv. Ltr. Rul.

9308002	**1** n.59
9501004	**3** n.95
9843001	**1** n.116
199905009	**1** n.107

Priv. Ltr. Rul.

199909034	**1** n.110
199937026	**1** n.110
200017013	**1** n.110
200027009	**1** n.110
200032015	**1** n.107
200040013	**1** n.110
200101021	**1** n.59
200403094	**1** n.59
200502014	**1** n.14; 5.02[2][b]
200604028	**1** n.59
200612002	**1** n.14; **5** n.15
200637025	**1** n.14; **5** n.15
200647001	**1** n.14; **5** n.15
200715005	**1** n.14; **5** n.15
200729005	**1** n.14; **5** n.15
200731009	**1** n.14; **5** n.15
201004022	**2** n.6

CHIEF COUNSEL ADVISORY

CCA

200628026	**5** n.22

IRS INFORMATION RELEASES

IRS Info. Rel.

2007-123	**1** n.14
2007-127	5.02[2][b]

[Text references are to paragraphs; note references are to chapters (boldface numbers) and notes ("n.").]

NOTICES

Notice

2010-19 . . . . 5.02[2][c]; **5** n.21

Table of Public Laws

[Text references are to paragraphs; note references are to chapters (boldface numbers) and notes ("n.").]

ECONOMIC GROWTH AND TAX RELIEF RECONCILIATION ACT OF 2001, Pub. L. No. 107-16

EGTRRA §

Generally	**1** n.1
511(e)	5.02[2][a]
542(f)(1)	3.02; **3** n.14
561(a)	**4** n.20
562	**4** n.29
901	1.06[1]; 3.02; 4.03[2]
901(a)	1.06[1]; 2.05[2][a]; 4.03[2]; 4.03[2][c]
901(b)	1.06[1]; 2.05[2][a]; 3.02; 4.03[2]; 4.03[2][c]

HOLOCAUST RESTITUTION TAX FAIRNESS ACT OF 2002, Pub. L. No. 107-358, § 2

1 n.12

TAXPAYER RELIEF ACT OF 1997, Pub. L. No. 105-34, § 501(d)

4 n.18

TAX REFORM ACT OF 1986, Pub. L. No. 99-514, § 1431(a)

4 n.18

CONGRESSIONAL BUDGET ACT OF 1974, Pub. L. No. 99-272, § 20001 ("Byrd rule") (1986)

1 n.91

CRUDE OIL WINDFALL PROFIT TAX ACT, Pub. L. No. 96-223, § 401(e)

3 n.1

TAX REFORM ACT OF 1976, Pub. L. No. 94-455, § 2005(f)(1)

3 n.1

CONGRESSIONAL BUDGET ACT OF 1974, Pub. L. No. 93-344

1 n.90

[Text references are to paragraphs; note references are to chapters (boldface numbers) and notes ("n.").]

UNIFORM ACTS

Unif. Probate Code §

603 . . . . **2** n.4
2-603 . . . . **2** n.3

Unif. Trust Code §

411 . . . . **2** n.411; 3.03[4][b]
602 . . . . 3.03[3][b][i]
803 . . . . **3** n.18

Table
of Cases

[Text references are to paragraphs; note references are to chapters (boldface numbers) and notes ("n.").]

A

Aguillard, Edwards v. **3** n.57
Alliance Res. Corp., TXO Production Corp.
v. 1.07
Alloyd Co., Gustafson v. **3** n.1
American Civil Liberties Union of Ky., Mc-
Creary County, Ky. v. **3** n.57
American Trucking Ass'ns, United States v.
. . . . **2** n.15; **4** n.3
Anderson, Untermyer v. 1.07; **1** n.124

B

Barlow v. Loomis **3** n.48
Bentsen, Diana v. **2** n.3
Blodgett v. Holden 1.07; **1** n.124
Blodgett v. Silberman **2** n.28
Bob Jones Univ. v. Strandell **2** n.4
Bosch, Comm'r v. . . . . 2.04[1]; **2** n.5
Bullock, Humphrey v. **2** n.28

C

Campbell, Estate of, Matter of **2** n.3
Carlton v. United States (US) . . . 1.07; **1** ns.
117–119, 121–123; 2.03; **2** n.1; **4** n.57
Carlton v. United States (9th Cir.) . . . **1** n.120
Casady, Fleming v. **3** n.48
Cherne v. United States **1** n.125
Christiansen, Estate of v. Comm'r   4.09[3];
4 n.65; **5** ns. 5, 31
Cohan v. Comm'r **1** n.125
Cooper v. United States **1** n.117

D

Darusmont, United States v. . . . . . **1** ns. 117,
125; **2** n.2
Diana v. Bentsen **2** n.3

D (continued)

Dickinson, Jr., Estate of v. Comm'r . . . .
. . . . 4.09[3]; **4** n.61
Doe, Santa Fe Indep. Sch. Dist. v. **3** n.57
Dorrance v. Martin **2** n.27

E

Edgar, Estate of, Matter of **2** n.3
Edwards v. Aguillard **3** n.57

F

First Nat'l Bank of Cincinnati v. Oppen-
heimer **3** n.48
Fleming v. Casady **3** n.48
Flores-Figueroa v. United States **1** n.92
Florida, Texas v. **2** n.27
Fuhrmann, Fred W., Estate of **2** n.32

G

Garcia, Guardianship of, In re **3** n.48
Grove v. Payne **3** n.48
Gustafson v. Alloyd Co. **3** n.1

H

Hamilton, Estate of, Matter of **2** n.3
Hannan, Estate of, In re **2** n.3
Harwood v. Comm'r **4** n.60; **5** n.4
Hemme, United States v. 1.07; **1** n.117
Hemphill, Estate of v. Washington . . . **1** n.96;
2 n.58
Henry, Welch v. 1.07; **1** n.117
Hill v. Martin **2** n.27
Holden, Blodgett v. 1.07; **1** n.124
Hudson, United States v. **1** n.117
Humphrey v. Bullock **2** n.28
Hutta, Estate of, In re **3** n.49

*[Text references are to paragraphs; note references are to chapters
(boldface numbers) and notes ("n.").]*

Hyde's Will, In re 2 n.3

I

Independent Ins. Agents of Am., Inc., U.S.
  Nat'l Bank of Ore. v. 3 n.1

J

Johnson v. Kotyck 3 n.48
Johnson, Estate of, In re 2 n.3

K

Kane v. United States 1 n.117
Kenan v. Comm'r 5 n.32
Kentucky Tax Comm'n, Lynch v. . . . 2 n.28
King v. United States . . . . . . 4.09[3]; 4 n.62
Klein, Estate of, Matter of 2 n.3
Kline v. Utah Dep't of Health 3 n.49
Kotyck, Johnson v. 3 n.48
Kotyck, United Bldg. & Loan Ass'n v. 3 n.48

L

Lee, Guardianship of, In re 3 n.48
Lombardo, Guardianship of, In re . . . 3 n.48
Loomis, Barlow v. 3 n.48
Lynch v. Kentucky Tax Comm'n 2 n.28

M

Martin, Dorrance v. 2 n.27
Martin, Hill v. 2 n.27
McCord v. Comm'r . . . 4.09[3]; 4 n.64; 5 ns. 5, 31
McCreary County, Ky. v. American Civil
  Liberties Union of Ky. 3 n.57
McGahee, Estate of, In re 2 n.3
Milliken v. United States 1 n.117
Missouri Mun. League, Nixon v. 2 n.15; 3 n.1; 4 n.3
Moline Props., Inc. v. Comm'r . . . .
  . . . . 2.06[2][a][ii]; 2 ns. 30, 33
Mostler, Matter of 3 n.49
Muller, Guardianship of, In re . . . . 3 ns. 48, 49

N

NationsBank of Tex. v. United States (Fed.
  Cir.) 5 n.1

NationsBank of Tex. v. United States (Fed.
  Cl.) 1 n.117
Nixon v. Missouri Mun. League . . . 2 n.15; 3 n.1; 4 n.3

O

Oklahoma Tax Comm'n, Perkins v. . . . .
  . . . . 2 n.28
Opppenheimer, First Nat'l Bank of Cincinnati v. 3 n.48
Outwin v. Comm'r 5 n.2

P

Paolozzi v. Comm'r 5 n.2
Payne, Grove v. 3 n.48
Perkins v. Oklahoma Tax Comm'n . . . .
  . . . . 2 n.28
Petter, Estate of v. Comm'r . . . . . 4.09[3]; 4 n.66; 5 ns. 5, 31
Proctor v. Comm'r . . . 4.09[3]; 4 n.58; 5 n.4
Public Nat'l Bank of NY, In re 3 n.1

Q

Quarty v. United States . . . 1 ns. 117, 125; 5 n.1

R

Rudwick, In re 3 n.48

S

Sanford, Estate of v. Comm'r   5.02[2][b]; 5 n.14
Santa Fe Indep. Sch. Dist. v. Doe . . . 3 n.57
Silberman, Blodgett v. 2 n.28
Smith v. United States 3 n.1
Stack v. United States 2 n.3
Stiefel, Estate of, In re 2 n.3
Strandell, Bob Jones Univ. v. 2 n.4

T

Tamagni v. Tax Appeals Tribunal . . . 2 n.32
Tax Appeals Tribunal, Tamagni v. . . . .
  . . . . 2 n.32
Texas v. Florida 2 n.27
TXO Production Corp. v. Alliance Res. Corp.
  . . . . 1.07

[Text references are to paragraphs; note references are to chapters (boldface numbers) and notes ("n.").]

U

United Bldg. & Loan Ass'n v. Kotyck 3 n.48

Untermyer v. Anderson 1.07; **1** n.124

U.S. Nat'l Bank of Ore. v. Independent Ins. Agents of Am., Inc. **3** n.1

Utah Dep't of Health, Kline v. **3** n.49

W

Walton v. Comm'r **3** n.61

Ward v. Comm'r **4** n.60; **5** n.4

Washington, Hemphill, Estate of v. **1** n.96; **2** n.58

Welch v. Henry 1.07; **1** n.117

Index

[References are to paragraphs.]

A

Administration of estates of decedents dying in 2010 . . . . 5.04[1]–5.04[4]
. appraisals . . . . 5.04[1]
. collar, defined . . . . 5.04[4]
. constitutionality of retroactive reinstatement of estate tax . . . . 5.04[3]
. difficulty of proper administration of potentially taxable estates 5.04
. Large Transfers at Death return, requirements
. . . . 5.04[1]
. negative basis assets . . . . 5.04[2]
. return requirements . . . . 5.04[1]
. selling estate assets . . . . 5.04[4]
Administration of trusts 5.05
. client communication 6.01
. executor of estate of 2010 decedent, advising
. . . . 6.07
. generation-skipping trusts . . . . 5.05[1]
. . formula distributions . . . . 5.05[1]
. . planning and drafting checklist, advising trustee of GST 6.06
. . trustee options regarding distributions
. . . . 5.05[1]
. individual communication with trustees . 5.07, 6.01
. planning and drafting checklist, advising executor 6.07
. Sec. 645 election and pecuniary distributions
. . . . 5.05[2]
Aggregate basis increase
. modified carryover basis rule . 1.05[2][a][iii], 1.05[2][a][iv]
. $1.3 million increase . . . . 1.05[2][a][i], 3.03
Amendments
See Technical corrections to EGTRRA (2002)

Analysis of law
See Technical analysis of 2010 and 2011 law
Annual exclusion gifts . . . . 5.02[4]
Annual exclusion trusts 4.06

B

Basis driven divisions, credit shelter/marital deduction formula clauses . . . . . 2.04[2][b]
Built-in losses
. modified carryover basis rule 3.05
Buy-sell agreements agreements, review of
. . . . 5.07, 6.03

C

Carlton v. U.S.
. due process challenge to retroactive reinstatement 1.07
. formula bequests 2.03
Carryover basis
See Carryover basis for property received from a decedent; Modified carryover basis rule, generally; Modified carryover basis rule, planning
Carryover basis for property received from a decedent 1.05
See also Modified carryover basis rule, generally; Modified carryover basis rule, planning
. bequests to foreign persons . . . . . 1.05[3][d]
. limit on gain recognized on pecuniary bequests . . . . 1.05[3][c]
. modified carryover basis rule . . . . . . 1.05[2]
See Modified carryover basis rule, generally, for more specific subheadings
. no gain based on liability in excess of basis
. . . . 1.05[3][a]

Carryover basis for property received from a decedent — Cont'd

. reporting requirements under Sec. 6018
. . . . 1.05[4]
. special recognition and nonrecognition rules
. . . . 1.05[3][a] – 1.05[3][d]
. traditional basis rules . . . . 1.05[1]
. $250,000 exclusion of gain on sale of principal residence . . . . 1.05[3][b]

Charitable remainder trusts

. incomplete gifts and Sec. 2511(c) . 5.02[2][d]
. modified carryover basis rule 3.11

Checklist

See Planning and drafting checklist

Clayton QTIP . . . . 3.03[2][a][i]

Client communications 5.07, 6.01

. sample letter to client 5.07

Client rejection of estate planner's advice, documentation of 3.01

Communication with clients

See Client communications

Communication with trustees

See Trustee communications

Congressional Budget Act of 1974 . . 1.06[1]

Congressional future actions uncertain

. Technical analysis of 2010 and 2011 law
. . . . 1.01

Conservation easement rules

. EGTRRA sunset rules . . . . 1.06[3][b]

Constitutionality of retroactive reinstatement of estate and GST taxes . . . . 1.07, 5.04[3]

. formal bequests, limitations 2.03

Corrections

See Technical corrections to EGTRRA (2002)

Credit shelter/marital deduction formula clauses 2.04

D

Date of death, application of rules tied to modified carryover basis rule 3.02

Decedents dying in 2010

See Administration of estates of decedents dying in 2010

Decedent's property

See Property acquired from a decedent, allocating carryover basis increases; Property owned by the decedent, allocation of carryover basis increases

Decoupling, state death tax formula clauses
. . . . 2.06[2], 2.06[2][b]

Drafting

See Planning and drafting checklist

Due process, possible retroactive reinstatement of estate taxes and GST taxes . . 1.07

Dynasty trusts

. formula bequests . . . . 2.05[1]
. . alternate GST tax formulas for 2010
. . . . 2.05[2][c]
. will for estate of over $10 million, trust for children and decedents; sample form . App. A.09

E

Economic Growth and Tax Relief Reconciliation Act of 2001 (EGTRRA)

. estate, gift, and generation-skipping transfer tax, original provisions . . . . . . App. B.01
. sunset provisions . . . . 1.06, App. B.02
. technical corrections, 2002 . 1.03, 1.04, App. B.03

EGTRRA

See Economic Growth and Tax Relief Reconciliation Act of 2001 (EGTRRA)

Estate, gift, and generation-skipping transfer tax provisions

See Economic Growth and Tax Relief Reconciliation Act of 2001 (EGTRRA)

Estate tax inclusion periods (ETIP) 4.08

Estate tax repeal, formula bequests

. credit shelter/marital deduction formula clauses 2.04
. . alternate marital/nonmarital formulas in 2010 . . . . 2.04[2]
. . basis driven divisions . . . . 2.04[2][b]
. . collateral provisions . . . . 2.04[1]
. . differing marital and nonmarital beneficiaries or percentage divisions
. . . . 2.04[2][c]
. . fairly representative division . 2.04[2][b][iii]
. . largest possible nonmarital share
. . . . 2.04[2][b][ii]
. . other divisions . . . . 2.04[2][c]
. . pre-2010 formula problems . . . . . . 2.04[1]
. . preserving the status quo . . . . . 2.04[2][a]
. . smallest possible nonmarital share
. . . . 2.04[2][b][i]
. document references to the absence of an estate or GST tax 2.03
. marital/nonmarital formula clauses during estate tax repeal 2.02
. state death tax formula clauses 2.06

ETIP

See Estate tax inclusion periods (ETIP)

Executor, modified carryover basis rule
. . . . 3.03[1][d], 3.03[1][e]

Executor of estate of 2010 decedent, advising
. . . . 6.07

F

Fairly representative division, credit shelter/ marital deduction formula clauses
. . . . 2.04[2][b][iii]

Family member serving as executor, modified carryover basis rule . . . . . . 3.03[1][e]

Foreign beneficiary
See also International aspects of planning
. negative basis assets to foreign beneficiaries
. . . . 5.06[2]

Foreign persons
See also International aspects of planning
. carryover basis for property received from a decedent, bequests to foreign persons
. . . . 1.05[3][d]
. Sec. 684, recognition of gain on certain transfers to foreign persons . . . . 5.06[3]

Forms
See Sample forms, wills and revocable trusts

Formula bequests 2.01-2.07
See also Formula problems
. best formula solutions for 2010 estate plans
. . . . 2.07
. . QTIP trust plus disclaimer . . . . . . 2.07[2]
. . substantial sprinkling nonmarital trust
. . . . 2.07[3]
. Carlton v. U.S. 2.03
. congressional action after Dec. 31, 2010 2.03
. constitutional limitations, retroactive tax legislation 2.03
. document references to the absence of an estate or GST tax 2.03
. estate tax repeal
. . credit shelter/marital deduction formula clauses 2.04
. . . alternate marital/nonmarital formulas in 2010 . . . . 2.04[2]
. . . basis driven divisions . . . . . . 2.04[2][b]
. . . collateral provisions . . . . 2.04[1]
. . . differing marital and nonmarital beneficiaries or percentage divisions
. . . . 2.04[2][c]
. . . fairly representative division
. . . . 2.04[2][b][iii]
. . . largest possible nonmarital share
. . . . 2.04[2][b][ii]
. . . other divisions . . . . 2.04[2][c]
. . . pre-2010 formula problems . . . . . 2.04[1]
. . . preserving the status quo . . . . 2.04[2][a]

Formula bequests—Cont'd
. *estate tax repeal* —Cont'd
. . *credit shelter/marital deduction formula clauses*—Cont'd
. . . smallest possible nonmarital share
. . . . 2.04[2][b][i]
. . document references to the absence of an estate or GST tax 2.03
. . marital/nonmarital formula clauses during estate tax repeal 2.02
. . state death tax formula clauses 2.06
. GST formula clauses and GST tax repeal 2.05
See Generation-skipping transfers (GST), formula clauses and tax repeal, for more specific subheadings
. one trust arrangement, formula solutions
. . . . 2.07[1]
. . advantages . . . . 2.07[1]
. . problems . . . . 2.07[2]
. state death tax formula clauses 2.06
. . apportionment . . . . 2.06[2][a][i]
. . check-the-box regulations . . . 2.06[2][a][ii]
. . decoupled state taxes . . . . 2.06[2][b]
. . decoupling . . . . 2.06[2]
. . multiple domiciles . . . . 2.06[2][a][iii]
. . nondomiciliary taxation of tangible property
. . . . 2.06[2][a][ii]
. . no state-only QTIP . . . . 2.06[3][b]
. . problems with present formulas . . . 2.06[1]
. . QTIP . . . . 2.06[3][a], 2.06[3][b]
. . single member limited liability company
. . . . 2.06[2][a][ii]
. . state death tax formulas . . . . 2.06[3]
. . state-only QTIP . . . . 2.06[3][a]
. . state taxes applicable to client, determination . . . . 2.06[2]

Formula generation-skipping transfers
. . . . 4.09[3], 6.05

Formula problems 6.02, 6.03
See also Formula bequests
. reference to estate tax terms in agreements
. . . . 5.07, 6.03
. wills and revocable trusts . . 6.02[1]–6.02[7]

G

Generation-skipping transfer (GST) exemption, EGTRRA sunset rules
See also Generation-skipping transfer (GST) tax, generally
. exemption allocation
. . . . 1.06[3][c][i]-1.06[3][c][vi]
. . automatic allocation of certain lifetime transfers . . . . 1.06[3][c][i]

Generation-skipping transfer (GST) exemption, EGTRRA sunset rules — Cont'd
. *exemption allocation—Cont'd*
. . determination of the value of property on a timely allocation of GST exemption . . . . 1.06[3][c][iv]
. . eliminate substantial compliance rule for allocations . . . . 1.06[3][c][vi]
. . elimination of the rules for qualified severance . . . . 1.06[3][c][iii]
. . reducing Treasury's power to extend time to allocate GST exemption . . 1.06[3][c][v]
. . retroactive allocations would not longer be permitted . . . . 1.06[3][c][ii]
. GST exemptions, interpretations of sunset rules . . . . 1.06[1]

Generation-skipping transfer (GST) tax, generally
See also Generation-skipping transfer (GST) tax planning; Generation-skipping transfers (GST), formula clauses and tax repeal
. constitutionality of retroactive reinstatement of estate taxes and GST taxes 1.07
. due process, possible retroactive reinstatement of estate taxes and GST taxes 1.07
. legislative history regarding repeal of estate and GST taxes 1.01
. possible retroactive reinstatement of estate taxes and GST taxes 1.07
. repeal, technical amendment to Sec. 2511(c) . . . . 1.03, App. B.03

Generation-skipping transfer (GST) tax planning 4.01–4.09
See also Generation-skipping transfer (GST) tax, generally
. annual exclusion trusts 4.06
. estate tax inclusion periods (ETIP) 4.08
. exemption 4.04
. generally 4.01
. gifts to Sec. 2642(c) annual exclusion trusts 4.06
. inter vivos reverse QTIPS 4.07
. . married persons 4.07
. planning suggestions . . . . . . 4.09[1]–4.09[4]
. . avoidance of invalidity, Proctor v. Com. authorities . . . . 4.09[3]
. . avoiding haste, consider opportunities of prompt action . . . . 4.09[2]
. . conditional transfers . . . . 4.09[3]
. . disclaimer based planning . . . . 4.09[4]
. . formula generation-skipping transfers . . . . 4.09[3], 6.05
. . prefer outright transfers over transfers in trust . . . . 4.09[1]
. . retroactive reinstatement possibility, timing of 2010 transfers . . . . 4.09[2]
. retroactive reimposition tax 4.02

Generation-skipping transfer (GST) tax planning—Cont'd
. Sec. 2664 and EGTRRA's sunset rules . 4.03
. . basis in taxable terminations, Sec. 2654(a)(2) . . . . 4.03[2][b]
. . definitions . . . . 4.03[1]
. . difficulties of GST planning . . . . . 4.03[1]
. . direct skip transfer, defined . . . . . 4.03[1]
. . generation move down rule . . . . . . 4.03[1]
. . . Sec. 2653(a) and the generation move-down rule for post-2010 distributions and terminations for trusts created by 2010 generation-skipping transfers . . . . 4.03[2][a]
. . GST tax rules (Chapter 13), applicability to post Dec. 31, 2009 transfers . . . 4.03[1]
. . . internal inconsistency of Sec. 2664 . . . . 4.03[1]
. . non-skip person, defined . . . . 4.03[1]
. . original provisions of EGTRRA . App. B.01
. . post-2010 effect of pre-2010 GST exemption allocations . . . 4.03[2][c]–4.03[2][f]
. . . automatic allocations . . . . 4.03[2][d]
. . . generally . . . . 4.03[2][c]
. . . qualified severances . . . . 4.03[2][e]
. . . retroactive allocations . . . . . . 4.03[2][f]
. . Sec. 2653(a) and the generation move-down rule for post-2010 distributions and terminations, trusts created by 2010 GST . . . . 4.03[2][a]
. . Sec. 2654(a)(2), basis in taxable terminations . . . . 4.03[2][b]
. . Sec. 2664, scope . . . . 4.03[1]
. . skip person, defined . . . . 4.03[1], 4.03[2][a]
. . sunset rules . . . . App. B.02
. . . interpretation of rule . . . . 4.03[2][a]
. . . scope . . . . 4.03[2]
. . taxable distribution, defined . . . . . 4.03[1]
. . taxable termination, defined . . . . . 4.03[1]
. . Uniform Transfers (or gifts) to Minors Act custodial account, transfers to . . 4.03[1]
. testamentary transfers, applying GST tax to 2010 . . . . 4.05

Generation-skipping transfers (GST), formula clauses and tax repeal
See also Generation-skipping transfer (GST) tax, generally
. formula bequests 2.05
. . alternate generation-skipping transfer tax formulas for 2010 . . . . 2.05[2]
. . . children, granting a power of appointment over a GST-exempt trust . . . 2.05[2][c]
. . . determination of later imposed GST taxes on post-2010 taxable distributions and taxable terminations under trusts created in 2010 . . . . 2.05[2][a]

Generation-skipping transfers (GST), formula clauses and tax repeal —Cont'd
. *formula bequests*—*Cont'd*
. . *alternate generation*—*Cont'd*
. . . dynasty trusts . . . . 2.05[2][c]
. . . effective date problem . . . . . 2.05[2][a]
. . . formula division of the estate . 2.05[2][b], 2.05[2][c]
. . . granting a power of appointment over a GST-exempt trust, clause . . . 2.05[2][c]
. . . GST exempt or nonexempt trust creation clause . . . . 2.05[2][b]
. . . skip-person, defined . . . . 2.05[2][a]
. . . special power of appointment, clause . . . . 2.05[2][c]
. . . taxable distribution, defined . . 2.05[2][a]
. . . taxable termination, defined . . 2.05[2][a]
. . . transferor, defined . . . . 2.05[2][a]
. . document references to the absence of an estate or GST tax 2.03
. . dynasty trust . . . . 2.05[1]
. . exempt and non-exempt shares . . 2.05[1]
. . problems with present formulas . . 2.05[1]
. . reverse QTIP . . . . 2.05[1]
. . unmarried clients, exempt and non-exempt shares . . . . 2.05[1]

Gifts
See Lifetime gifts

Gifts to Sec. 2642(c) annual exclusion trusts
. generation-skipping transfer (GST) tax planning 4.06

Gifts to spouse, modified carryover basis rule . . . . 1.05[2][a][iv]

Gift tax 1.03, 1.04
See also Lifetime gifts
. Economic Growth and Tax Relief Reconciliation Act of 2001 (EGTRRA), original provisions . . . . App. B.01
. technical amendment to Sec. 2511(c) . . . 1.04, App. B.03

Grantor trusts, incomplete gifts and Sec. 2511(c) . . . . 5.02[2][c]

GST
See headings under Generation-skipping transfer (GST)

H

Harvesting losses, modified carryover basis rule 3.13

Holding period rules, modified carryover basis rule 3.09

I

Income in respect of decedent, modified carryover basis rule . . . . 1.05[2][a][iv]

Incomplete gifts and Sec. 2511(c) . . . 5.02[2]
. charitable remainder trusts . . . . . . 5.02[2][d]
. gift trusts that shift income . . . . . 5.02[2][b]
. grantor trusts . . . . 5.02[2][c]
. legislative history . . . . 5.02[2][a]

Individual client communications . 5.07, 6.01

International aspects of planning 5.06
. lower basis increases . . . . 5.06[1]
. negative basis assets to foreign beneficiaries . . . . 5.06[2]
. planning and drafting checklist, advising nonresident alien 6.08
. Sec. 684, recognition of gain on certain transfers to foreign persons . . . . . 5.06[3]
. tax-exempt beneficiary, exemption for distribution to . . . . 5.06[2]

Inter vivos reverse QTIPS 4.07

Irrevocable life insurance trusts 5.03
. planning and drafting checklist, fixing problems 6.05

J

Jobs Creation And Worker Assistance Act of 2002, EGTRRA technical corrections . 1.03, 1.04, App. B.03

Jointly owned property with a right of survivorship, allocation of carryover basis increases . . . . 3.03[4][c][i] – 3.03[4][c][iii]

L

Large Transfers at Death return
. administration of estates of decedents dying in 2010, requirements . . . . 5.04[1]
. modified carryover basis rule . . . . . . 3.03[1]
. . cash, defined . . . . 3.03[1][b]
. . executor, identification of decedent's . . . . 3.03[1][d]
. . executor's authority to allocate basis increases . . . . 3.03[1][e]
. . family member serving as executor . . . . 3.03[1][e]
. . multiple executors . . . . 3.03[1][d]
. . nonresident alien individual estates . . . . 3.03[1][c]
. . person in actual or constructive possession of any property of decedent . 3.03[1][d]
. . small estates . . . . 3.03[1][a]

Life insurance proceeds, modified carryover basis rule . . . . 1.05[2][a][iv]

Lifetime gifts 5.02
. annual exclusion gifts in 2010 . . . . . 5.02[4]
. gift tax reporting requirements . . . . . 5.02[3]
. incomplete gifts and Sec. 2511(c) . . . 5.02[2]
. . charitable remainder trusts . . . . . 5.02[2][d]
. . gift trusts that shift income . . . . 5.02[2][b]
. . grantor trusts . . . . 5.02[2][c]
. . legislative history . . . . 5.02[2][a]
. planning and drafting checklist, fixing
   problems 6.05
. 35% gift tax rate, locking in . . . . . . 5.02[1]
Lifetime transfers
. EGTRRA sunset rules, GST exemption allocation . . . . 1.06[3][c][i]
. property owned by the decedent, allocation of
   carryover basis increases . . . . . 3.03[4][f]
Limited liability company (LLC), single
   member . . . . 2.06[2][a][ii]
Loss carryovers 3.05

M

Marital deduction
. credit shelter/marital deduction formula
   clauses 2.04
. unlimited estate tax marital deduction
   . . . . 1.05[2][b]
Married clients
   See Wills and revocable trusts
Married persons, inter vivos reverse QTIPS
   . . . . 4.07
Mass client communications 5.07, 6.01
Modified carryover basis rule, generally 1.05
   See also Modified carryover basis rule, plan-
   ning
. aggregate basis increase . . . . 1.05[2][a][iii],
   1.05[2][a][iv]
. assets to which basis increase may not be allocated . . . . 1.05[2][a][iv]
. assets to which basis increases may be allocated . . . . 1.05[2][a][iii]
. basis adjustments . . . . 1.05[2][a]
. carryover basis more favorable than estate tax
   . . . . 1.05[2][b]
. items of income in respect of decedent,
   nonallocable assets . . . . . . 1.05[2][a][iv]
. life insurance proceeds, nonallocable assets
   . . . . 1.05[2][a][iv]
. $1.3 million aggregate basis increase
   . . . . 1.05[2][a][i]
. spousal property basis increase . 1.05[2][a][ii],
   1.05[2][a][iii], 1.05[2][a][iv]
. technical analysis of law, basis for property
   received from a decedent 1.05

Modified carryover basis rule, generally —
   Cont'd
. 3-year rule exception, gifts to spouse
   . . . . 1.05[2][a][iv]
. unlimited estate tax marital deduction
   . . . . 1.05[2][b]
Modified carryover basis rule, planning
   . . . . 3.01-3.13
   See also Carryover basis for property re-
   ceived from a decedent; Modified carry-
   over basis rule, generally
. allocating carryover basis increases 3.03
. . Large Transfers at Death return, Sec. 6018
   . . . . 3.03[1]
. . $1.3 million aggregate basis increase . 3.03
. . property acquired from a decedent . 3.03[3]
. . property owned by the decedent . . . 3.03[4]
. . spousal property basis increase . . . 3.03[2]
. basis increase for built-in losses and loss carryovers 3.05
. basis information gathering, sources . . . 3.07
. charitable remainder trusts 3.11
. client objections 3.01
. client rejection of estate planner's advice,
   documentation of 3.01
. complexity of planning required 3.01
. date of death, application of rules tied to 3.02
. drafting survivorship presumptions 3.08
. EGTRRA sunset provisions, Sec. 901 . . 3.02,
   App. B.02
. harvesting losses 3.13
. Large Transfers at Death return, Sec. 6018
   . . . . 3.03[1]
. . cash, defined . . . . 3.03[1][b]
. . executor, identification of decedent's
   . . . . 3.03[1][d]
. . executor's authority to allocate basis increases . . . . 3.03[1][e]
. . family member serving as executor
   . . . . 3.03[1][e]
. . multiple executors . . . . 3.03[1][d]
. . nonresident alien individual estates
   . . . . 3.03[1][c]
. . person in actual or constructive possession
   of any property of decedent . 3.03[1][d]
. . small estates . . . . 3.03[1][a]
. negative basis assets, planning 3.04
. partnership interests 3.12
. passive losses under carryover basis rules
   . . . . 3.10
. planning and drafting checklist, fixing
   problems 6.04
. planning with holding period rules 3.09
. planning with the $250,000 personal resi-
   dence exclusion 3.06

**Modified carryover basis rule, planning —
Cont'd**

. property acquired from a decedent, allocating
carryover basis increases . . . . 3.03[3]

  *See also Modified carryover basis rule,
  generally*

. . by bequest, devise, or inheritance, or by the
decedent's estate from the decedent
. . . . 3.03[3][a]

. . by the decedent's estate from the decedent
. . . . 3.03[3][a]

. . . contingent remainder in the decedent's estate . . . . 3.03[3][a][ii]

. . . property appointed to the decedent's estate
. . . . 3.03[3][a][i]

. . passing without consideration . . 3.03[3][c]

. . transferred by the decedent during life
. . . . 3.03[3][b]

. . . acquired from a decedent . . . . 3.03[3][b]

. . . in a qualified revocable trust . 3.03[3][b][i]

. . . state law, grantor's rights . . . 3.03[3][b][i]

. . . subject to a reserved right to alter, amend,
or terminate . . . . 3.03[3][b][ii]

. . . Uniform Trust Code . . . . . 3.03[3][b][i]

. property owned by the decedent, allocation of
carryover basis increases . . . . 3.03[4]

. . acquired by the decedent within three years
of death . . . . 3.03[4][g]

. . assets specifically excluded from basis increases . . . . 3.03[4][h]

. . clients holding testamentary power
. . . . 3.03[4][b]

. . community property . . . . 3.03[4][d]

. . lifetime transfers with retained beneficial
enjoyment . . . . 3.03[4][f]

. . property in a qualified revocable trust
. . . . 3.03[4][a]

. . property owned jointly with a right of survivorship . . . 3.03[4][c][i] – 3.03[4][c][iii]

. . . by gift, bequest, etc. . . . . . 3.03[4][c][iii]

. . . with someone other than the surviving
spouse . . . . 3.03[4][c][ii]

. . . with a surviving spouse . . . . 3.03[4][c][i]

. . property subject to a power of appointment
. . . . 3.03[4][b]

. . QTIP assets . . . . 3.03[4][e]

. . shifting appreciated property between
spouses . . . . 3.03[4][g]

. . Uniform Trust Code . . . . 3.03[4][b]

. rules applicable after 2010 . . . . 3.02

. Sec. 469 limitations on nondeductible losses
. . . . 3.10

. Sec. 754 election, partnership interests . . 3.12

. spousal property basis increase, allocation of
. . . . 3.03[2]

**Modified carryover basis rule, planning —
Cont'd**

. *spousal property basis increase, allocation
of — Cont'd*

. . amount of gift, determination techniques
. . . . 3.03[2][a][ii]

. . Clayton QTIP . . . . 3.03[2][a][i]

. . form of the spousal gift . . . . . 3.03[2][a][i]

. . granting the executor discretion to select assets to absorb . . . . 3.03[2][b]

. . marital trust . . . . 3.03[2][a][i]

. . QTIP . . . . 3.03[2][a][i]

. . specific gift . . . . 3.03[2][a]

. tax return, Sec. 6018 . . . . 3.03[1]

**Multiple domiciles, state death tax formula
clauses** . . . . 2.06[2][a][iii]

**Multiple executors, modified carryover basis
rule** . . . . 3.03[1][d]

N

Negative basis assets

. administration of estates of decedents dying
in 2010 . . . . 5.04[2]

. foreign beneficiaries . . . . 5.06[2]

. modified carryover basis rule 3.04

Nonrecognition rules

  *See Special recognition and nonrecognition
  rules, carryover basis for property received
  from a decedent*

Nonresident alien

. modified carryover basis rule, estates, Large
Transfers at Death return . . . . . 3.03[1][c]

. planning and drafting checklist 6.08

. . beneficiaries, nonresident aliens 6.08

. . spouse, nonresident alien 6.08

. . U.S. situs assets, nonresident alien holding
. . . . 6.08

Non-skip person, defined . . . . 4.03[1]

O

One trust arrangement, formula bequests
. . . . 2.07

P

**Partnership interests, modified carryover ba-
sis rule** 3.12

Passive losses under carryover basis rules
. . . . 3.10

Personal residence, $250,000 exclusion
. . . . 1.05[3][b], 3.06

Planning and drafting checklist . . . 6.01-6.08
  See also Generation-skipping transfer (GST)
  tax planning; Modified carryover basis
  rule, planning
. client communications 5.07, 6.01
. executor of estate of 2010 decedent, advising
   . . . . 6.07
. formula generation-skipping transfers . 4.09[3],
                         6.05
. formula problems 6.02, 6.03
  See also Formula bequests
. . reference to estate tax terms in agreements
   . . . . 5.07, 6.03
. . wills and revocable trusts . 6.02[1]–6.02[7]
. individual client communication . . 5.07, 6.01
. lifetime gifts, fixing problems 6.05
. mass client communications 5.07, 6.01
. nonresident aliens 6.08
. . beneficiaries, nonresident aliens 6.08
. . spouse, nonresident alien 6.08
. . U.S. situs assets, nonresident alien holding
   . . . . 6.08
. survivorship presumptions, drafting 3.08
. tax reference problems, review for reference
     to estate tax terms 5.07, 6.03
. . buy-sell agreements agreements, review of
   . . . . 5.07, 6.03
. . premarital agreements, review of   5.07, 6.03
. . prenuptial agreements, review of   5.07, 6.03
. trustee communications 5.07, 6.01
. trustee of generation-skipping trust, advising
   . . . . 6.06
. wills and revocable trusts, fixing formula
     problems . . . . 6.02[1]–6.02[7]
. . married clients, harmonious family
. . . estate of $3.5 million to $6 million
   . . . . 6.02[1]
. . . estate of $6 million to $10 million
   . . . . 6.02[3]
. . married clients, harmonious or
     non-harmonious family
. . . estate of over $10 million . . . . . . 6.02[5]
. . married clients, non-harmonious family
. . . estate of $3.5 million to $6 million
   . . . . 6.02[2]
. . . estate of $6 million to $10 million
   . . . . 6.02[4]
. . QTIP provisions 6.02
. . reverse QTIP provision 6.02
. . state-only QTIP provision 6.02
. . unmarried surviving spouse
. . . estate of $3.5 million to $5 million
   . . . . 6.02[6]
. . . estate over $5 million . . . . 6.02[7]
Premarital agreements, review of . 5.07, 6.03

Prenuptial agreements, review of . 5.07, 6.03
**Property acquired from a decedent, allocat-
ing carryover basis increases** . . . . 3.03[3]
  See also Property owned by the decedent, al-
  location of carryover basis increases
. by bequest, devise, or inheritance, or by the
     decedent's estate from the decedent
   . . . . 3.03[3][a]
. by the decedent's estate from the decedent
   . . . . 3.03[3][a]
. . contingent remainder in the decedent's es-
     tate . . . . 3.03[3][a][ii]
. . property appointed to the decedent's estate
   . . . . 3.03[3][a][i]
. passing without consideration . . . . 3.03[3][c]
. transferred by the decedent during life
   . . . . 3.03[3][b]
. . acquired from a decedent . . . . . 3.03[3][b]
. . in a qualified revocable trust . 3.03[3][b][i]
. . state law, grantor's rights . . . 3.03[3][b][i]
. . subject to a reserved right to alter, amend,
     or terminate . . . . 3.03[3][b][ii]
. . Uniform Trust Code . . . . 3.03[3][b][i]
**Property owned by the decedent, allocation
of carryover basis increases** . . . . . 3.03[4]
  See also Property acquired from a decedent,
  allocating carryover basis increases
. acquired by the decedent within three years
     of death . . . . 3.03[4][g]
. assets specifically excluded from basis in-
     creases . . . . 3.03[4][h]
. community property . . . . 3.03[4][d]
. lifetime transfers with retained beneficial en-
     joyment . . . . 3.03[4][f]
. property in a qualified revocable trust
   . . . . 3.03[4][a]
. property owned jointly with a right of survi-
     vorship . . . . . 3.03[4][c][i]–3.03[4][c][iii]
. . by gift, bequest, etc. . . . . . . 3.03[4][c][iii]
. . with someone other than the surviving
     spouse . . . . 3.03[4][c][ii]
. . with a surviving spouse . . . . . 3.03[4][c][i]
. property subject to a power of appointment
   . . . . 3.03[4][b]
. . clients holding testamentary power
   . . . . 3.03[4][b]
. QTIP assets . . . . 3.03[4][e]
. shifting appreciated property between spouses
   . . . . 3.03[4][g]

Q

QTIP
  See Qualified terminable interest property
  (QTIP)

Qualified severance
. EGTRRA sunset rules . . . . . . 1.06[3][c][iii]
. post-2010 effect of pre-2010 GST exemption
    allocations . . . . 4.03[2][e]

Qualified terminable interest property (QTIP)
. Clayton QTIP . . . . 3.03[2][a][i]
. formula bequests
. . QTIP trust plus disclaimer . . . . . . 2.07[2]
. . reverse QTIP . . . . 2.05[1]
. inter vivos reverse QTIPS 4.07
. married persons, inter vivos reverse QTIPS
    . . . . 4.07
. property owned by the decedent, allocation of
    carryover basis increases
. . QTIP assets . . . . 3.03[4][e]
. reverse QTIP
. . formula bequests . . . . 2.05[1]
. . inter vivos reverse QTIPS 4.07
. . wills and revocable trusts, provision . . 6.02
. spousal property basis increase, allocation of
    . . . . 3.03[2][a][i]
. state death tax formula clauses, estate tax re-
    peal . . . . 2.06[3][a], 2.06[3][b]
. wills and revocable trusts, fixing formula
    problems, provisions 6.02
. . reverse QTIP provision 6.02
. . state-only QTIP provision 6.02

R

Recognition rules
    *See Special recognition and nonrecognition
    rules, carryover basis for property received
    from a decedent*

**Repeal and restoration of estate tax, techni-
cal analysis of 2010 and 2011 law** . . . 1.02
. estate tax preserved for certain qualified do-
    mestic trusts (QDOTs) . . . . 1.02[3]
. general repeal of estate tax . . . . 1.02[1]
. legislative history . . . . 1.02[2]
. recapture estate taxes preserved . . . . 1.02[2]

Reporting requirements
. lifetime gifts . . . . 5.02[3]
. Sec. 6018, carryover basis . . 1.05[4], 3.03[1]

**Residence, $250,000 personal residence exclu-
sion** . . . . 1.05[3][b], 3.06

**Retroactive allocations, GST exemption allo-
cation, EGTRRA sunset rules** 1.06[3][c][ii]
. post-2010 effect of pre-2010 allocations
    . . . . 4.03[2][f]

**Retroactive reimposition of tax, genera-
tion-skipping transfer (GST) tax planning**
    . . . . 4.02

**Retroactive reinstatement of estate and GST
tax**
. constitutionality of reinstatement 1.07, 5.04[3]
. . formal bequests, limitations 2.03
. GST planning suggestions, timing of 2010
    transfers . . . . 4.09[2]

Returns
    See Large Transfers at Death return

Reverse QTIP
. formula bequests . . . . 2.05[1]
. inter vivos reverse QTIPS 4.07
. wills and revocable trusts, provision . . . 6.02

Revocable trusts
    See Wills and revocable trusts

S

Sample forms, wills and revocable trusts
    . . . . App. A.01 – A.10
. revocable trust for estate of $3.5 million to
    $6 million
. . single trust . . . . App. A.02
. . trust with disclaimer based planning . . App.
    A.04
. revocable trust for estate of $6 million to $10
    million . . . . App. A.06, App. A.08
. revocable trust for estate of over $10 million
    . . . . App. A.10
. will for estate of $3.5 million to $6 million
. . single trust will . . . . App. A.01
. . will with disclaimer based planning . . App.
    A.03
. will for estate of $6 million to $10 million
    . . . . App. A.05, App. A.07
. will for estate of over $10 million App. A.09
. . dynasty trust for children and decedents
    . . . . App. A.09

**Sec. 469 limitations on nondeductible losses,
modified carryover basis rule** 3.10

**Sec. 645 election and pecuniary distributions,
administration of trusts** . . . . 5.05[2]

**Sec. 754 election, partnership interests, modi-
fied carryover basis rule** 3.12

Sec. 2664 and EGTRRA's sunset rules
    *See also Generation-skipping transfer (GST)
    tax planning*
. Generation-skipping transfer (GST) tax plan-
    ning
. . original provisions of EGTRRA . App. B.01
. . sunset rules . . . . App. B.02

**Selling estate assets, administration of estates
of decedents dying in 2010** . . . . . . 5.04[4]

**Single member limited liability company
(LLC)** . . . . 2.06[2][a][ii]

Skip person, defined . . . . . 4.03[1], 4.03[2][a]

**Small estates, Large Transfers at Death re-
turn** . . . . 3.03[1][a]

**Special recognition and nonrecognition rules,
carryover basis for property received from
a decedent** . . . . 1.05[3][a] – 1.05[3][d]
. bequests to foreign persons . . . . . 1.05[3][d]
. limit on gain recognized on pecuniary bequests . . . . 1.05[3][c]
. no gain based on liability in excess of basis
. . . . 1.05[3][a]
. $250,000 exclusion of gain on sale of princi-
pal residence . . . . 1.05[3][b]

Spousal property basis increase
. modified carryover basis rule, allocation of
. . . . 3.03[2]
. . amount of gift, determination techniques
. . . . 3.03[2][a][ii]
. . Clayton QTIP . . . . 3.03[2][a][i]
. . form of the spousal gift . . . . . 3.03[2][a][i]
. . granting the executor discretion to select assets to absorb . . . . 3.03[2][b]
. . marital trust . . . . 3.03[2][a][i]
. . QTIP . . . . 3.03[2][a][i]
. . specific gift . . . . 3.03[2][a]
. modified carryover basis rule, generally
. 1.05[2][a][ii], 1.05[2][a][iii], 1.05[2][a][iv]

Spouse, nonresident alien 6.08

State death tax
. formula clauses 2.06
. . apportionment . . . . 2.06[2][a][i]
. . check-the-box regulations . . . 2.06[2][a][ii]
. . decoupled state taxes . . . . 2.06[2][b]
. . decoupling . . . . 2.06[2]
. . multiple domiciles . . . . 2.06[2][a][iii]
. . nondomiciliary taxation of tangible property
. . . . 2.06[2][a][ii]
. . no state-only QTIP . . . . 2.06[3][b]
. . problems with present formulas . . . 2.06[1]
. . QTIP . . . . 2.06[3][a], 2.06[3][b]
. . single member limited liability company
. . . . 2.06[2][a][ii]
. . state death tax formulas . . . . 2.06[3]
. . state-only QTIP . . . . 2.06[3][a]
. . state taxes applicable to client, determination . . . . 2.06[2]
. sunset provisions of EGTRRA . . . 1.06[3][a]

Sunset provisions of EGTRRA . . . 1.06, App.
B.02
. Congressional Budget Act of 1974 . . 1.06[1]
. conservation easement rules . . . . . 1.06[3][b]
. deferred payment of estate taxes attributable
to closely-held business interests
. . . . 1.06[3][e]
. GST exemption allocation
. . . . 1.06[3][c][i]-1.06[3][c][vi]

Sunset provisions of EGTRRA — Cont'd
. *GST exemption allocation — Cont'd*
. . automatic allocation of certain lifetime
transfers . . . . 1.06[3][c][i]
. . determination of the value of property on a
timely allocation of GST exemption
. . . . 1.06[3][c][iv]
. . eliminate substantial compliance rule for allocations . . . . 1.06[3][c][vi]
. . elimination of the rules for qualified severance . . . . 1.06[3][c][iii]
. . reducing Treasury's power to extend time to
allocate GST exemption . . 1.06[3][c][v]
. . retroactive allocations would not longer be
permitted . . . . 1.06[3][c][ii]
. GST exemptions, interpretations of sunset
rules . . . . 1.06[1]
. GST tax planning
*See Generation-skipping transfer (GST) tax
planning*
. interpretations of sunset rules . . . . . . 1.06[1]
. other undone EGTRRA changes, EGTRRA
changes repealed . . . . 1.06[3]
. reinstatement of qualified family owned business interest deduction . . . . . . 1.06[3][d]
. restored state death tax credit . . . . 1.06[3][a]
. Sec. 901 of EGTRRA . . . 1.06[1], App. B.02
. Sec. 2664 and sunset rules
*See Generation-skipping transfer (GST) tax
planning*
. taxes, rates, and exemptions . . . . . . 1.06[2]
. Tax Reform Act of 1997 . . . . 1.06[3][f]
. technical examination of the sunset rule
. . . . 1.06[1]
. waiver of statute of limitations on certain
farm valuations . . . . 1.06[3][f]

Surviving spouse
. property owned jointly with a right of survivorship . . . . 3.03[4][c][i]
. . with someone other than the surviving
spouse . . . . 3.03[4][c][ii]
. wills and revocable trusts, unmarried surviving spouse
. . estate of $3.5 million to $5 million 6.02[6]
. . estate over $5 million . . . . 6.02[7]

Survivorship presumptions, drafting . . . 3.08
. modified carryover basis rule 3.08
. planning and drafting checklist 3.08

T

Taxable gifts 1.04

**Tax reference problems, review for reference
to estate tax terms** 5.07, 6.03

Tax Reform Act of 1997 . . . . 1.06[3][f]

Technical amendments

  *See Technical corrections to EGTRRA
    (2002)*

Technical analysis of 2010 and 2011 law
  . . . . 1.01-1.07

. alteration of practices regarding lifetime trans-
    fers for transactions occurring in 2010
  . . . . 1.01

. Carlton v. U.S., due process challenge . . 1.07

. carryover basis for property received from a
    decedent 1.05

    *See Carryover basis for property received
      from a decedent, for more specific sub-
      headings*

. Congressional future actions uncertain . . 1.01

. constitutionality of retroactive reinstatement
    of estate taxes and GST taxes 1.07

. due process, possible retroactive reinstatement
    of estate taxes and GST taxes 1.07

. EGTRRA sunset rules 1.06

. . Congressional Budget Act of 1974 . 1.06[1]

. . conservation easement rules . . . . 1.06[3][b]

. . deferred payment of estate taxes attributable
    to closely-held business interests
  . . . . 1.06[3][e]

. . GST exemption allocation
  . . . . 1.06[3][c][i]-1.06[3][c][vi]

. . . automatic allocation of certain lifetime
    transfers . . . . 1.06[3][c][i]

. . . determination of the value of property on
    a timely allocation of GST exemption
  . . . . 1.06[3][c][iv]

. . . eliminate substantial compliance rule for
    allocations . . . . 1.06[3][c][vi]

. . . elimination of the rules for qualified sev-
    erance . . . . 1.06[3][c][iii]

. . . reducing Treasury's power to extend time
    to allocate GST exemption 1.06[3][c][v]

. . . retroactive allocations would not longer be
    permitted . . . . 1.06[3][c][ii]

. . GST exemptions, interpretations of sunset
    rules . . . . 1.06[1]

. . interpretations of sunset rules . . . . 1.06[1]

. . other undone EGTRRA changes, EGTRRA
    changes repealed . . . . 1.06[3]

. . reinstatement of qualified family owned
    business interest deduction . . 1.06[3][d]

. . Sec. 901 of EGTRRA . 1.06[1], App. B.02

. . state death tax credit, restored . . 1.06[3][a]

. . taxes, rates, and exemptions . . . . . 1.06[2]

. . Tax Reform Act of 1997 . . . . . 1.06[3][f]

. . technical examination of the sunset rule
  . . . . 1.06[1]

. . waiver of statute of limitations on certain
    farm valuations . . . . 1.06[3][f]

. estate tax, constitutional limitations on retro-
    active reinstatement 1.07

**Technical analysis of 2010 and 2011 law —
  Cont'd**

. generation-skipping transfer tax rules, repeal

. . technical amendment to Sec. 2511(c) . App.
    B.03

. GST tax rules, repeal 1.03

. . technical amendment to Sec. 2511(c) . 1.03

. legislative history regarding repeal of estate
    and GST taxes 1.01

. overview 1.01

. possible retroactive reinstatement of estate
    taxes and GST taxes 1.07

. reevaluation of estate plans 1.01

. repeal and restoration of estate tax 1.02

. . estate tax preserved for certain qualified do-
    mestic trusts (QDOTs) . . . . 1.02[3]

. . general repeal of estate tax . . . . . . 1.02[1]

. . legislative history . . . . 1.02[2]

. . recapture estate taxes preserved . . . 1.02[2]

. taxable gifts 1.03, 1.04

. . technical amendment to Sec. 2511(c) . 1.04,
    App. B.03

Technical corrections to EGTRRA (2002)
  . . . . 1.03, 1.04, App. B.03

Testamentary planning
  See Formula bequests

**Testamentary transfers, applying GST tax to
  2010**

. generation-skipping transfer (GST) tax plan-
    ning 4.05

35% gift tax rate, lifetime gifts . . . . 5.02[1]

Trustee communications

. advising trustees of generation-skipping trust
  . . . . 6.06

. planning and drafting checklist . . . 5.07, 6.01

Trusts

  *See Administration of trusts; Wills and revo-
    cable trusts*

$250,000 personal residence exclusion
  . . . . 1.05[3][b], 3.06

2002 Technical corrections

  *See Technical corrections to EGTRRA
    (2002)*

U

Uniform Transfers (or gifts) to Minors Act
  . . . . 4.03[1]

Uniform Trust Code . . . . 3.03[4][b]

Unlimited estate tax marital deduction
  . . . . 1.05[2][b]

Unmarried clients, formula bequests . 2.05[1]

W

Wills and revocable trusts
. planning and drafting checklist, fixing
   formula problems . . . . . . 6.02[1]–6.02[7]
. . married clients, harmonious family
. . . estate of $3.5 million to $6 million
   . . . . 6.02[1]
. . . estate of $6 million to $10 million
   . . . . 6.02[3]
. . married clients, harmonious or
   non-harmonious family
. . . estate of over $10 million . . . . . . 6.02[5]
. . married clients, non-harmonious family
. . . estate of $3.5 million to $6 million
   . . . . 6.02[2]
. . . estate of $6 million to $10 million
   . . . . 6.02[4]
. . QTIP provisions 6.02
. . reverse QTIP provision 6.02
. . state-only QTIP provision 6.02
. . unmarried surviving spouse
. . . estate of $3.5 million to $5 million
   . . . . 6.02[6]
. . . estate over $5 million . . . . 6.02[7]

Wills and revocable trusts —Cont'd
. sample forms . . . . App. A.01–A.10
. . revocable trust for estate of $3.5 million to
   $6 million
. . . single trust . . . . App. A.02
. . . trust with disclaimer based planning . App.
   A.04
. . revocable trust for estate of $6 million to
   $10 million . . . . App. A.06, App. A.08
. . revocable trust for estate of over $10 mil-
   lion . . . . App. A.10
. . will for estate of $3.5 million to $6 million
. . . single trust will . . . . App. A.01
. . . will with disclaimer based planning . App.
   A.03
. . will for estate of $6 million to $10 million
   . . . . App. A.05, App. A.07
. . will for estate of over $10 million . . . App.
   A.09
. . . dynasty trust for children and decedents
   . . . . App. A.09